SCULPTURE IN STONE

Camí
Santamera

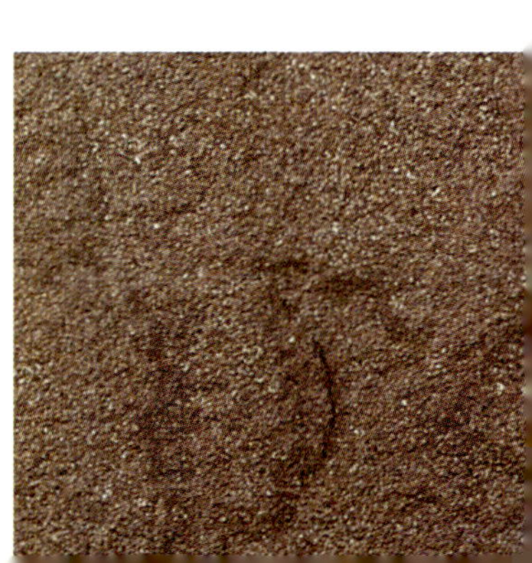

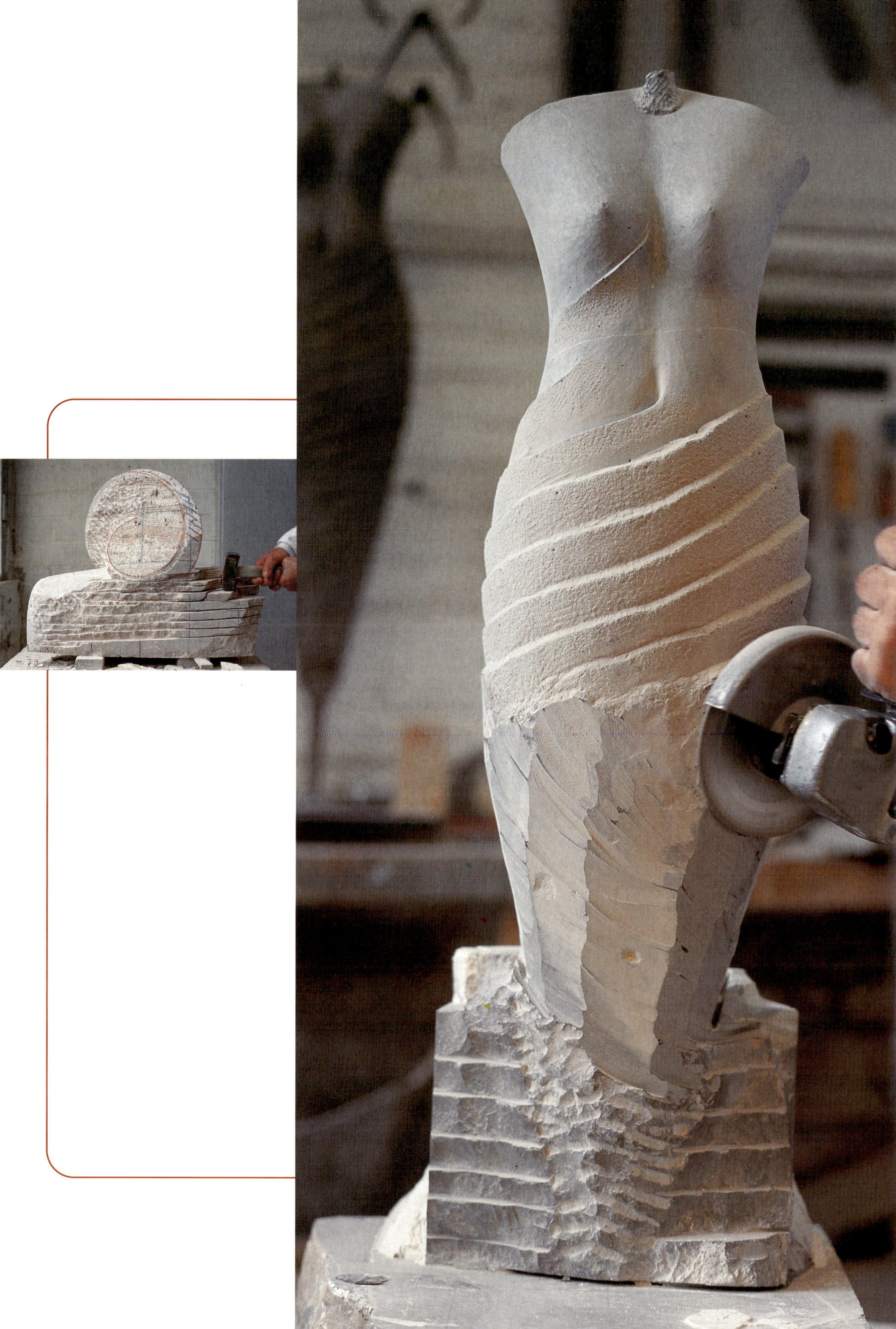

SCULPTURE IN STONE

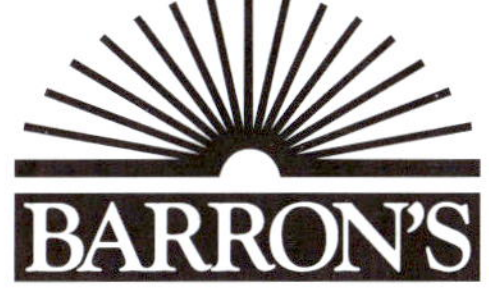

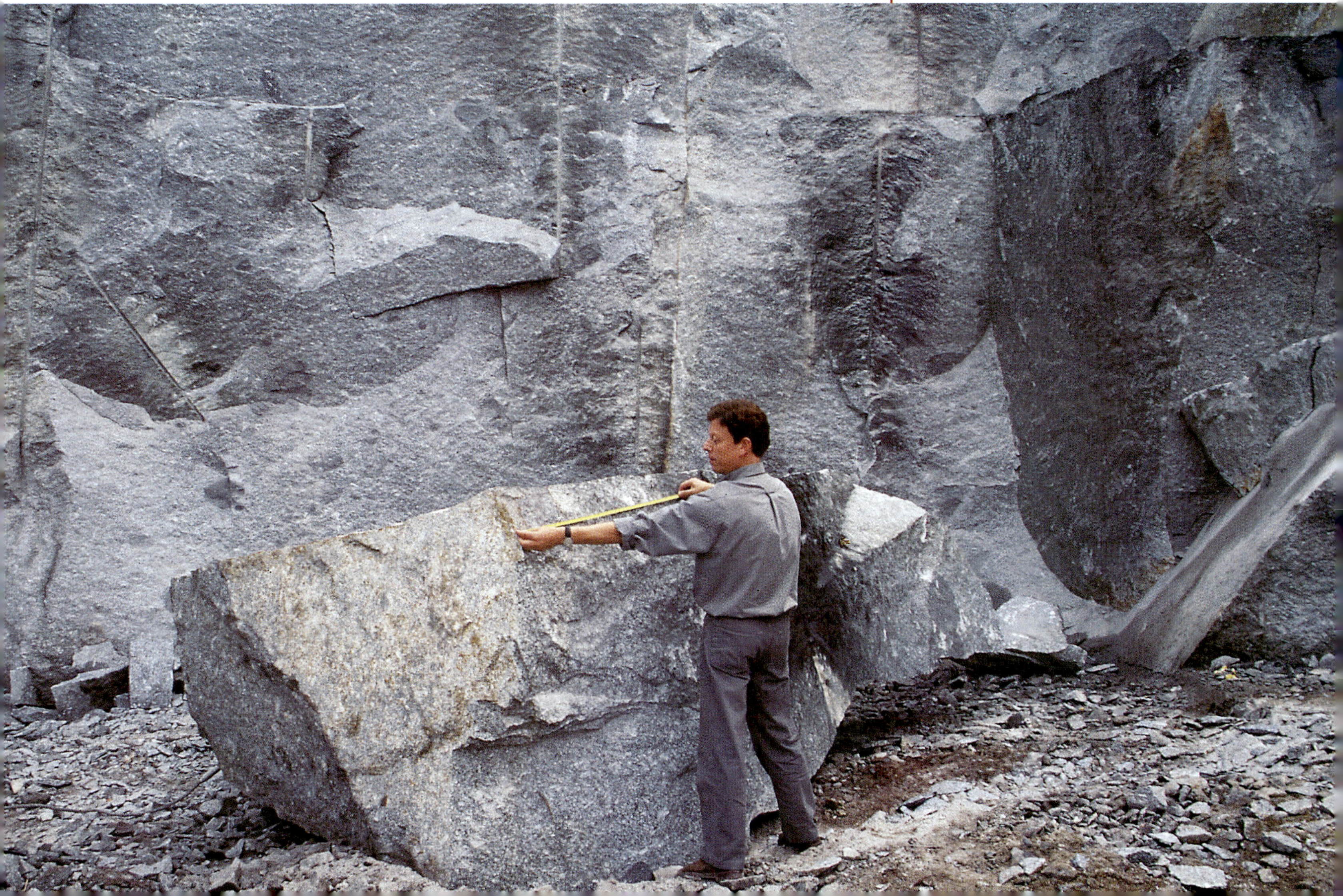

Sculpture in Stone

Editorial Director:
Maria Fernanda Canal

Texts:
Josepmaria Teixido i **Camí**
Jacinto Chicharro **Santamera**

Execution of the exercises proposed by Camí and Santamera:
Feliu Martín
Mariano Andrés Vilella
Lee Hyun-chan
Camí

Collection Design:
Josep Guasch

Design and Layout:
Josep Guasch

Photographs:
Norbert Foto
Santamera
Camí
Contributors:
Scala Photo
Zardoya
Boreal
Prisma
©MNAC (Calveras/Merida/Sagristà)
Chang, Woo
Robert K. Murase

Illustrations:
Toni Vidal

Illustration Archive:
Maria Carmen Ramos

First edition for the United States, its territories and possessions, and Canada published by Barron's Educational Series, Inc., 2001.

Original title of the book in Spanish: *Escultura en Piedra*

All inquiries should be addressed to:
Barron's Educational Series, Inc.
250 Wireless Boulevard
Hauppauge, New York 11788
http://www.barronseduc.com

International Standard Book No. 0-7641-5424-9

Library of Congress Catalog Card No. 2001086790

Printed in Spain

9 8 7 6 5 4 3 2 1

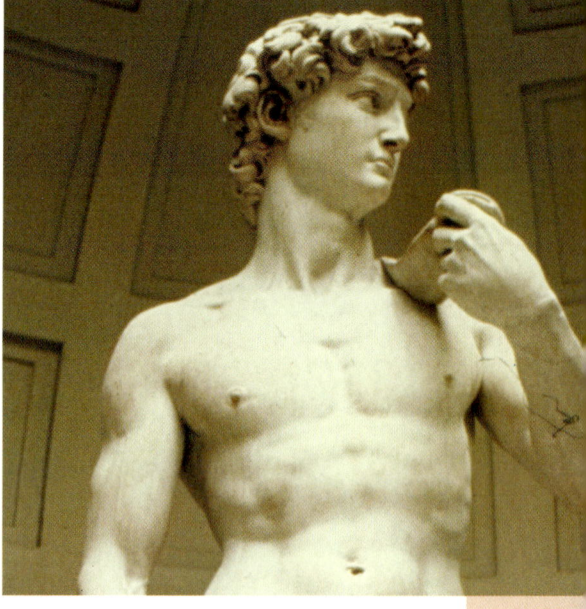

Cont

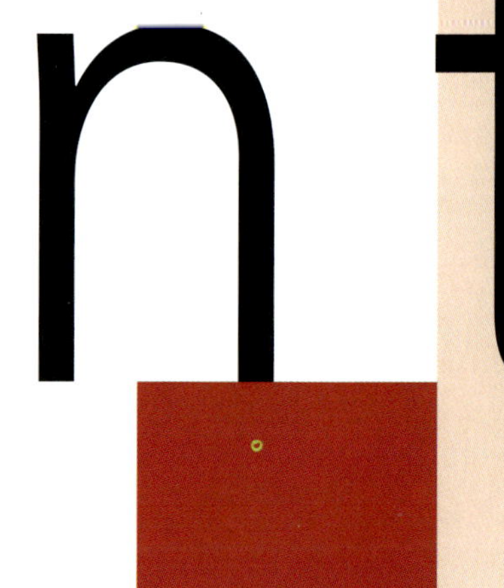

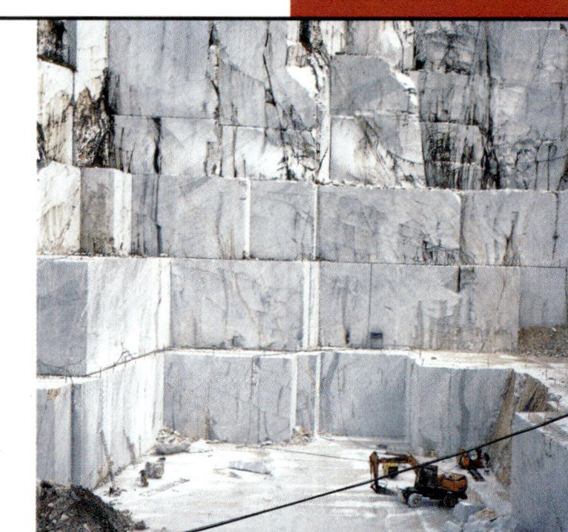

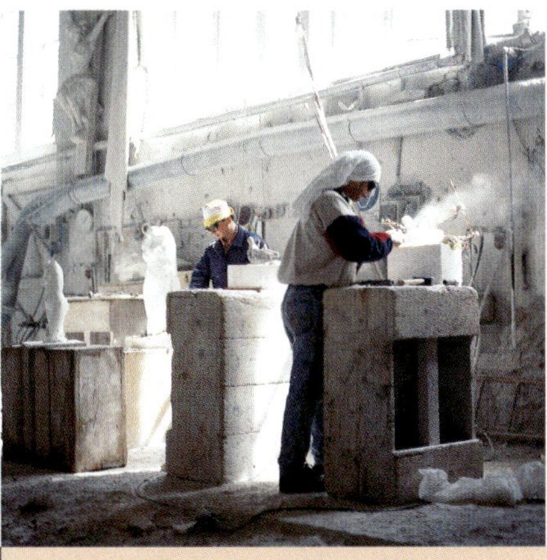

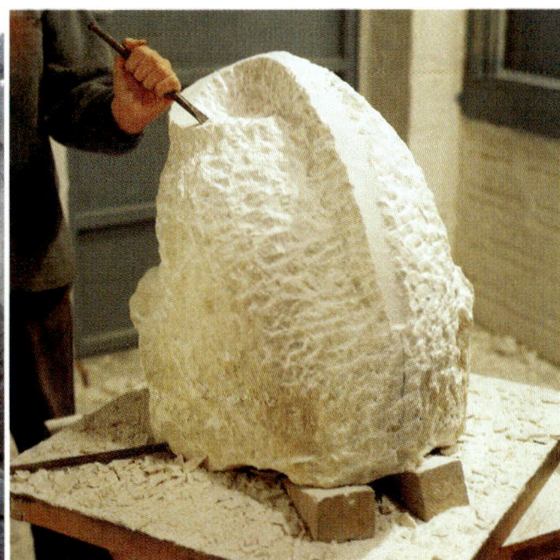

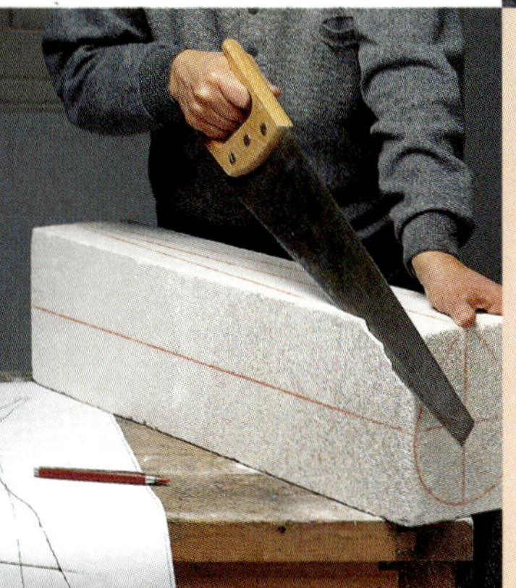

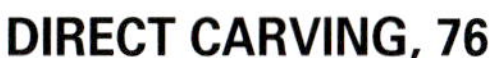

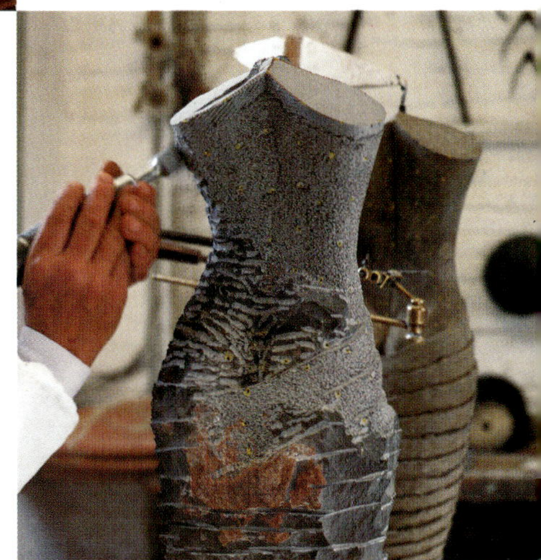

ents

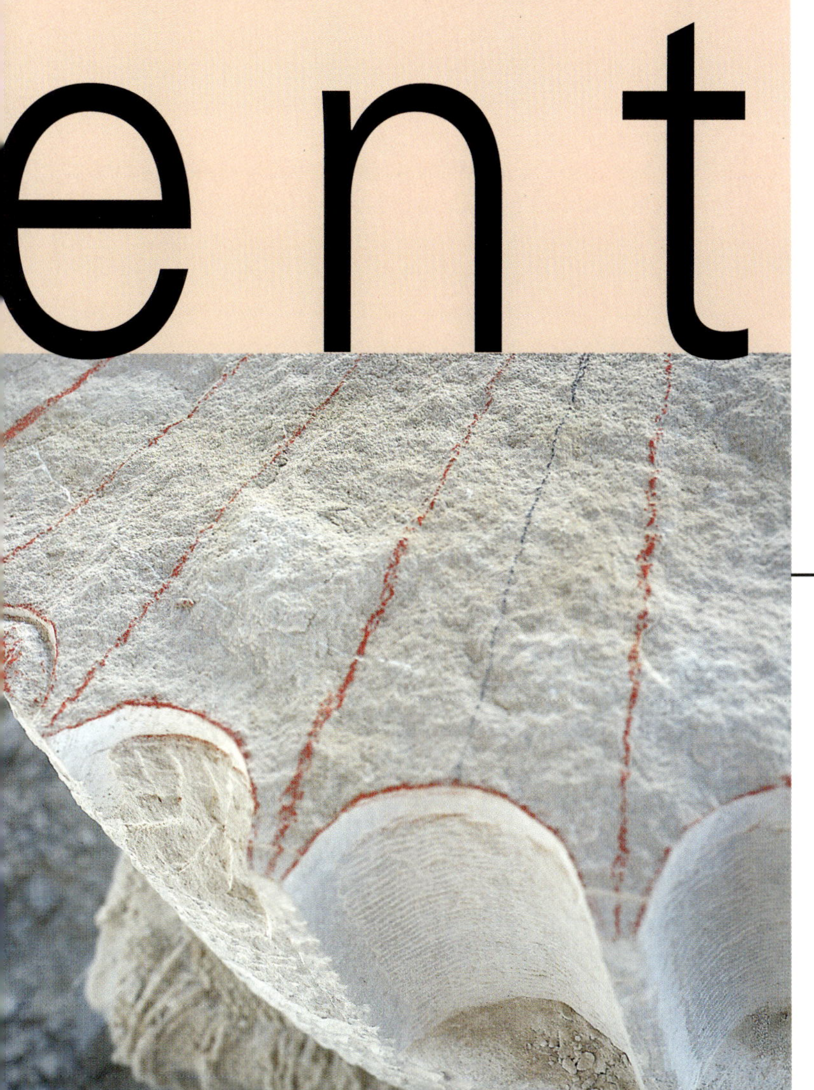

In Praise of Stone

Interest in sculpture increased considerably over the course of the twentieth century. However, despite its profusion, although discreet, in public places and its eloquent treatment in biennial exhibitions, museums, cultural centers, symposia, and some galleries, sculpture at the dawn of the twenty-first century, like much of contemporary art, continues to draw a reluctant public.

Starting in the 1950s, the proliferation of styles and movements, the development of new technologies and the use of new materials, formalistic problems, and the marriage of painting and sculpture have destabilized the terminology and expanded the concept of sculpture. However, there are still artists who remain faithful to noble subjects and direct carving. For them, the process of removing something to create something else remains unchanged. And even for those who feel art ceased to imitate quite some time ago, stone continues to occupy a privileged place. This is primarily because it allows us to rediscover the true roots of the third dimension through physical confrontation with rebellious matter. In addition, stone establishes the link with architecture, lending itself to monumental art and buildings.

From organic sculpture to an awareness of pure form, from closed or porous volume to the appropriation of space and its adaptation, stone sculpture joins the spiritual and the material, and we come to realize that it is less an art form for the select few than we had thought. Whether it's a solid block or broken into various parts, striated or polished, convex or concave, truncated or packed with an excess of reality, flattened or sealed by pressure, worked from the inside out or vice versa, stone brings emotion to life from a curved mass, from a simple arris, from a fold, a crack, or an apparent slip. In the studied articulation of the stone's proportions, numerous factors create the tensions necessary to make the structure viable.

Nonetheless, whether it is realistic, allegorical, or nonfigurative, whether it has sensual curves or geometric lines, stone sculpture is usually in tune with the order and harmony of the Universe, whether in marble, travertine, or granite, and may even adopt a false neutrality.

Stone, the subject of this work, moves us in principle because it is a familiar material and we find its resistance stimulating. Examined by the authors, with all its revolutions and an inventory of the tools to master it, illustrated by an iconography that traces the historical process, particularly in recent decades, stone seems immutable and even to laugh at passing trends. From Bourdelle to Maillot, from Laurens to Zadkine, from Arp to Brancusi, to cite just as few, stone affirms its presence and asserts its influence on the second half of the twentieth century.

"It is by carving stone," Brancusi tells us, "that we discover the spirit of matter. The hand thinks and follows the thought of matter." As we can well understand, stone is an inseparable part of the history of sculpture and, even more, it is the world's memory. It is this memory that the two authors, who are also artists in the truest sense of the word, have been able to keep alive, evoking it and delving into it in the various chapters without lapsing into overly didactic commentary, with language that is concise and detailed, fluid and precise. Each study is considered in depth with the broadest range of concepts, and in summary as well. Nothing unnecessary is included and nothing is missing. Everything is balanced and falls smoothly together.

Enhanced by the efficiency of their observations and the subtlety of their analyses, enlivened with color reproductions, this epic of stone is neither a catalog nor a sketch. It is a document, or better yet, a panorama overflowing with information, technical references, and milestones representing the important works in the development of sculpture. The result is that this rigorous work can be recommended to all, to amateurs or the initiated, to beginning or experienced artists, who will find in these refreshing pages something that will clarify, refine, or complete their knowledge, regardless of their aesthetic choices.

Gérard Xuriguera

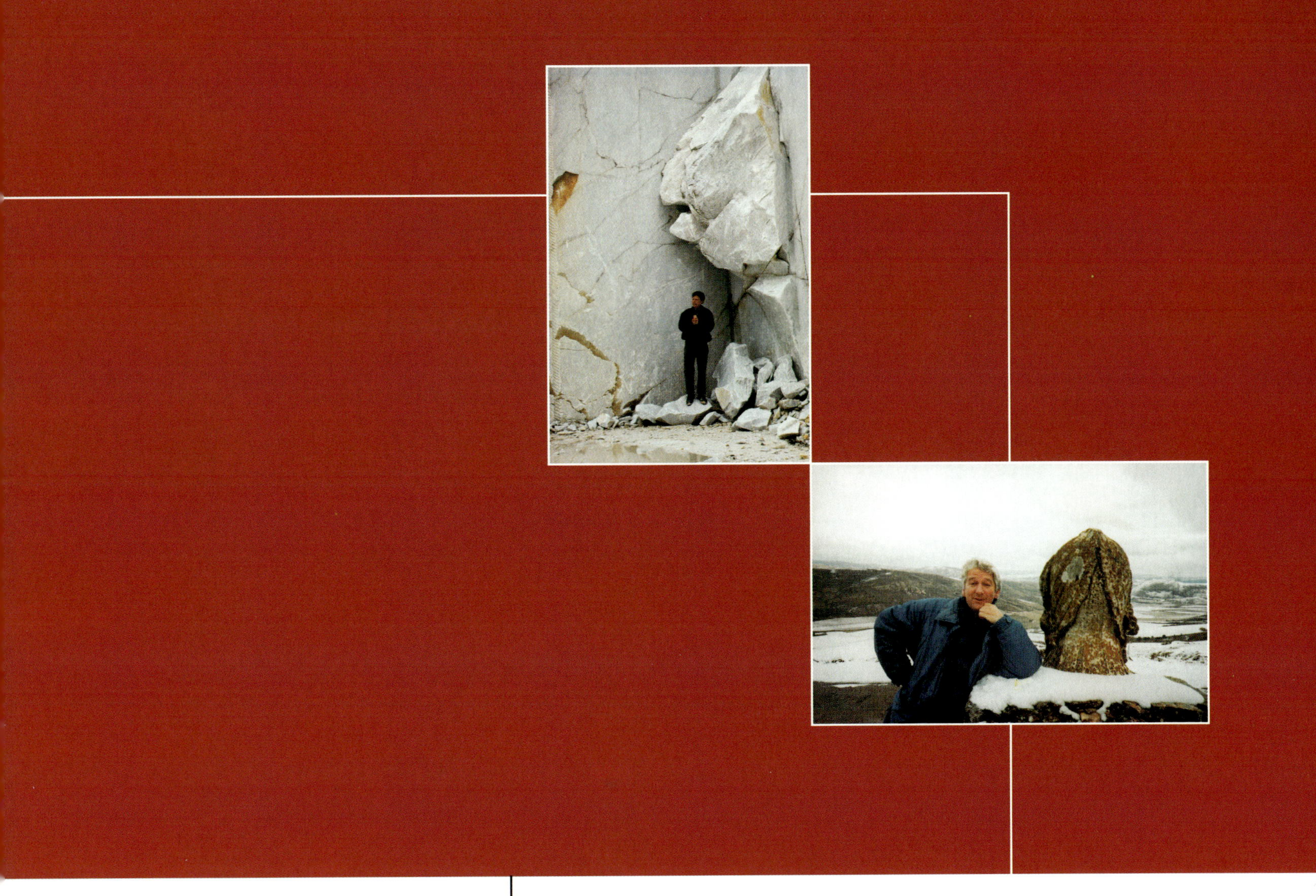

Camí has been an active sculptor since 1975. He has a degree in Sculpture and is a graduate in Sculpture and Interior Design from the Massana School in Barcelona where he teaches Sculpture. He has had 20 individual shows and some 100 group shows. He works in stone, wood, and especially iron. His monumental sculptures can be seen in Badalona and Soller (Spain), Santo Tirso and Cantanhede (Portugal), Quito (Ecuador), and Puyo (South Korea).

Santamera has degrees in Art History, Cinematography, and Religious Sciences. He thinks of himself as a sculptor of people. His workshop is the classroom; his tools are history, philosophy, psychology, anthropology, methodology, and common sense. He does not consider himself an expert in anything, but is interested in everything about humans and their expression in the arts.

Camí and Santamera have collaborated on several projects over 20 years. Their projects include sculpture and photography shows, videos, publications, and more.

The specialization of one and the panoramic view of the other come together in this book as it did earlier in another book, *Carving: Wood Sculpture*, which has had three editions and has been translated into five languages. This is their contribution to closing the distance between books on art history and literature on one hand and technical manuals on the other.

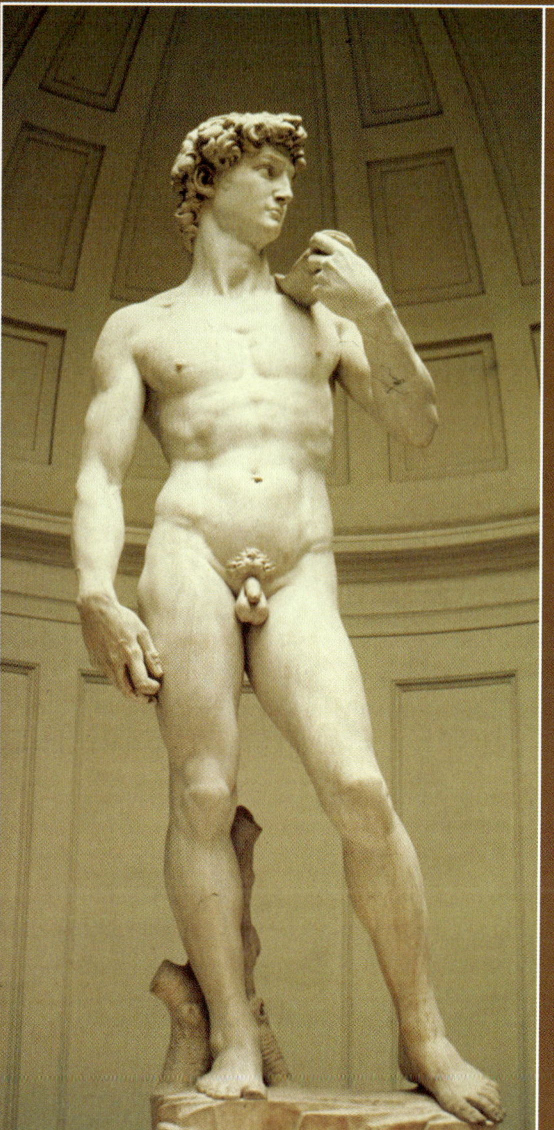

Michelangelo. *David*. 1504.
Carrara Marble.
Accademia, Florence (Italy).

Some sculptures, and Michelangelo's *David* is a prime example, have played a role in history that goes beyond aesthetics. It was a commissioned work that was originally meant to adorn the upper section of the cathedral in Florence but never reached its intended location, something that had happened a century earlier with Donatello's *David*.

A popular uprising changed its purpose and meaning. The citizens of Florence made it a symbol of their victory over the Medici banking family. The marble body of an adolescent shepherd, designed with disproportionate fist and face that when seen from a distance would seem to be in proportion, became the body of an adult Goliath with no need to hide his stone when the statue was placed at ground level to guard the Town Hall and threaten the bankers.

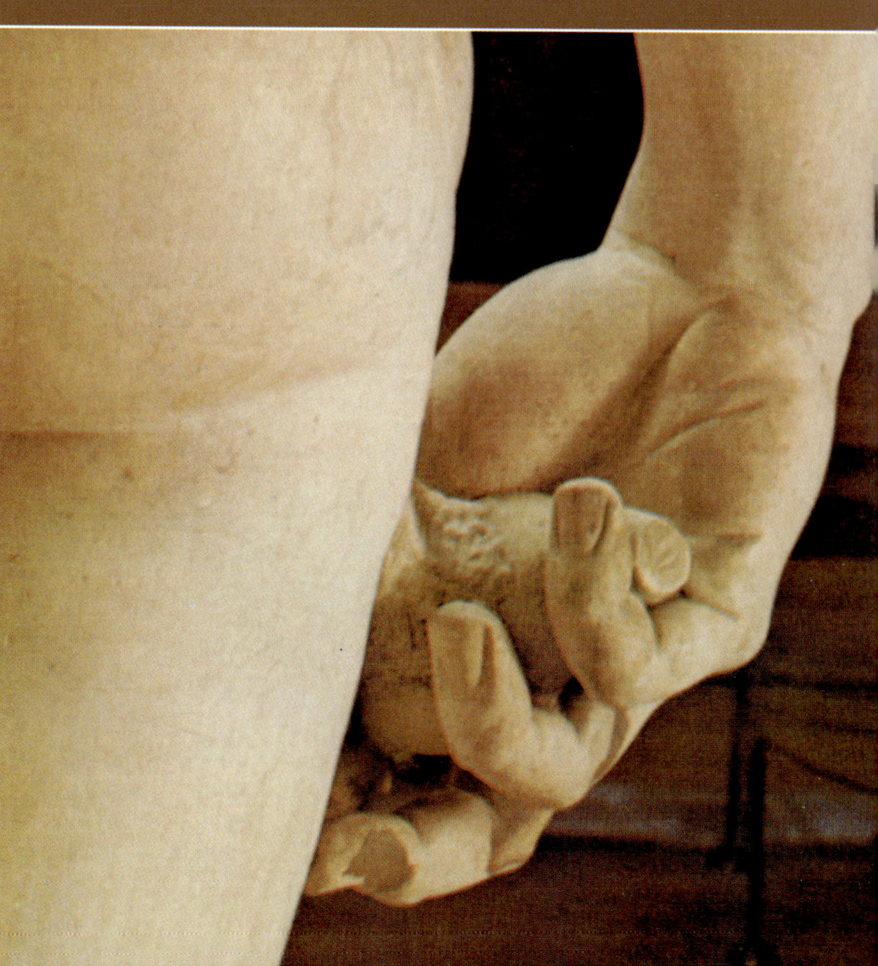

History

Let us begin this book, written for those who want to begin to carve in stone, with a partial look at what stone carving has meant throughout history and around the world. Our look is partial because this is a field that is impossible to encompass in its entirety as it often becomes confused with the history of sculpture in general. We will be satisfied if your reading of this book leads you to a desire for more detailed knowledge about the broad range of subjects covered here.

In the first section, we mix eras and places to better discern their outlines: sculpture in caverns, amulets, historical documents, symbols of power, portraits, and funeral art. Later we briefly describe their evolution in the European context: Classicism, the Roman World, the Gothic, Renaissance, and Baroque periods, and the nineteenth and twentieth centuries.

Stone sculpture, like the other arts, has allowed the expression of thoughts, feelings, and intuited ideas that, because they are human, become universal. Thus, we believe that anyone can be drawn to it and has the skill to interpret it freely and without complication.

First and foremost, we invite our readers, with our subjective opinions and without relinquishing metaphor, to set up a personal dialogue with sculptures that come to us from other ages, allowing themselves to follow their intuition, sensing in their own bodies the aesthetic feelings the works produce.

Only later, when we want to gain further knowledge about works that already speak to us, will we consult historians for help in placing the works in context so that we can better understand their objective importance.

We also believe that knowledge of other eras would be enriched if historians would listen to the theories, as absurd as they might seem, that are proposed when any museum visitor begins a unmediated dialogue with a piece of sculpture. For example, anyone who saw *Athena Mourning*, with her helmet and spear, would ask, "Can it be that women in ancient Athens held such a secondary place in society as the history books would indicate?"

As for us, sometimes in this book we look at history to help us understand sculpture, and sometimes we look at sculpture to help us understand history.

So let's allow ourselves to be captivated by form. Let's feel the serene power of basalt or the warmth of sandstone and, if we have time left, let's jump to the chapters on technique.

In the Shelter of Rock

"And then we will go on
to the high caverns in the rock,
which are so well concealed;
there we shall enter
and taste the fresh juice of the pomegranates."
Saint John of the Cross.

Nature, forming caverns, wanted to open up its heart to reveal moments of living intimacy. Using wind and water, she carved evocative shapes or sober reliefs on cave walls that humans in Altamira enlivened with color. Humans, living in the shadow of superb sculptures adorning the landscape of Cappadocia, learned to work the fields, but they awaited the harvest in the rock shelters they had carved with their own hands.

Years later in the same spot, a hermit planted crosses on the "high caverns" that, as Saint John of the Cross himself would later observe, "are the exalted high mysteries and depths of the wisdom of God." And so the cave, a place of refuge, became a place for private reflection and even intimacy. The silence spoke of mysteries taking shape until the rock was transformed, not just into caves but also into temples found from Malinalco in Mexico to Ethiopia.

This ancestral practice of carving rock until it becomes a temple, fusing sculpture with architecture, is a constant that is repeated throughout history and all over the world.

In the third century before Christ, Buddhists in India expanded the use of cave sculpture, a practice that flourished in China. In the Longmen caves alone, there are nearly 100,000 sculptures, and twelfth-century Sri Lanka left us an immense reclining Buddha enlivened by streaks in the sandstone.

Also in India, Buddhists in the second century before Christ carved cave walls, digging into the rock until it was transformed into temples called *Chailyas*.

In the seventh century, Hindus carved in stone the incarnations of Vishnu in the rock shelters of Mahabalipuran (Madras) and, for the glory of Shiva, carved on site great granite rocks using energetic and *nonfinito* strokes, until transforming them into an elephant, bulls, or small temples. They even incorporated a spring to give life to some reliefs that depict the descent of the Ganges, something that to this day remains the best representation of Hindu society.

In the tenth century, the cave brought its secrets to light when, near Mysore, it transformed the peak of a granite mountain into the colossal human figure of Gomateswara. It is 60 feet (17.5 m) tall and the Jainists impregnate it every 11 years with milk, saffron, gold dust, and so on.

Zen Buddhism leaped ahead in this cult of beauty that reveres stone in its natural state. We refer to the design of "stone" flowers formed by rocks and vegetation that blended opposites harmoniously: high/low, close/far, light/shadow, and so on. However, what we particularly like are the dry gardens made of pebbles and rocks. In the eleventh century, there were already theories about this "religious practice" that required only one thing: that one should not place a stone poorly. Soami, in about 1500 in Kyoto, does this masterfully.

What were humans looking for inside the stone? And what did they find? What did the monk contemplate when looking at the perfectly proportioned garden? Did he perhaps discern the mystery of his own interior life? It may be that the Sumerian sculptors were trying to depict this precise moment in their small votive statues with their dazzling eyes.

▼ *Reclining Buddha*. Twelfth century.
Sandstone.
Polannaruma (Sri Lanka).
The mystery took shape until it transformed the rock.

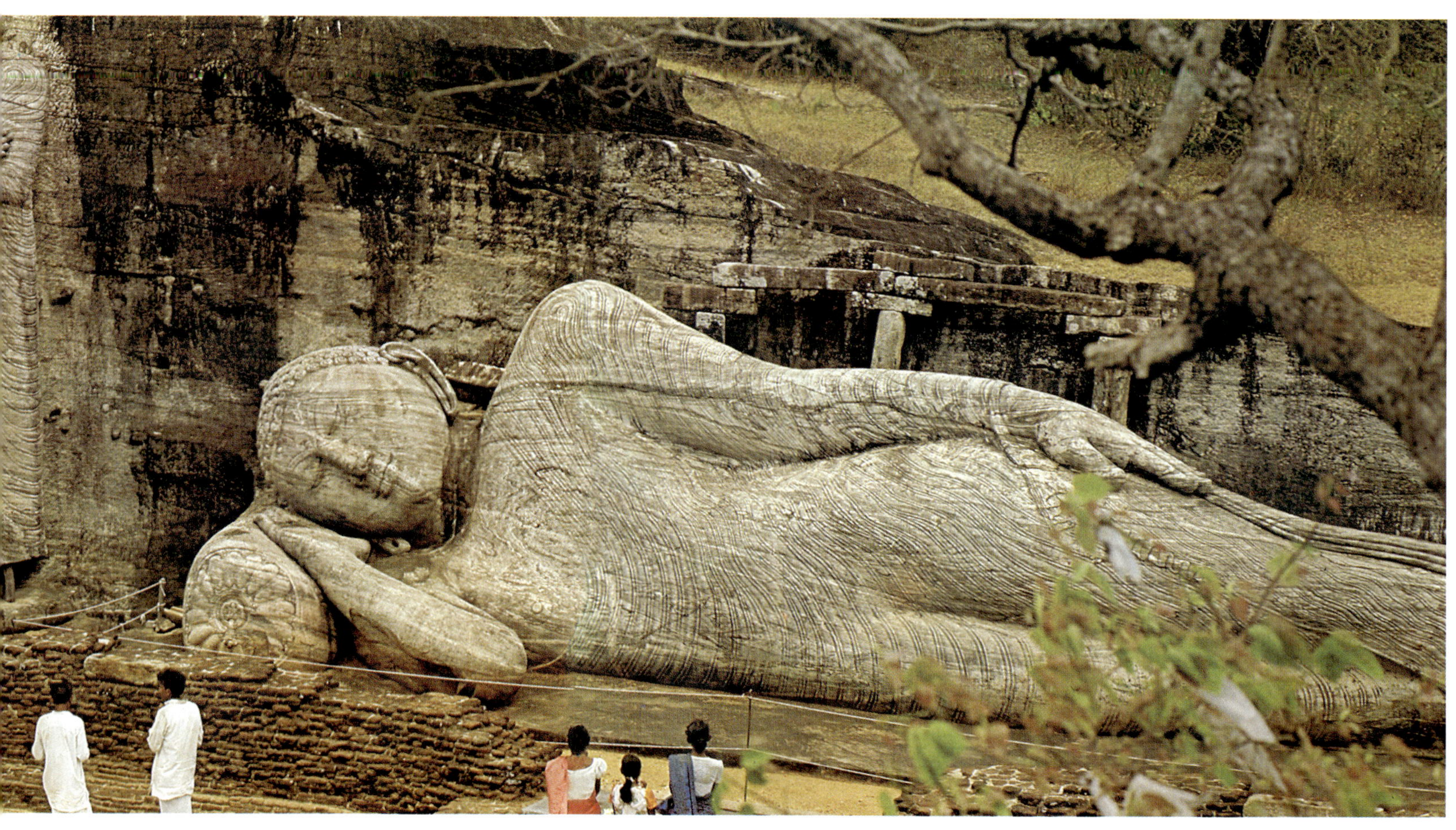

The Spread of Talismans

Figures carved in stone usually represent divinities. The devout offer gifts before them, receiving their power in exchange. The ritual culminates with a trembling lip or fingertip touching the cold stone. Why not prolong this contact by taking a small stone from the site? And why not trace on the stone the shape of our protector or the object of our desire?

Hundreds of small female statues, smoothed by friction and representing bodies shaped by motherhood, have spread throughout Europe and Asia over the last 25,000 years. Did belief in their protective power facilitate pregnancy, through suggestion perhaps, or was that belief the cause of pregnancy for those who were ignorant of natural law?

Anatolia, once agriculture had been mastered, was a matriarchal society where we find small marble guitar-shaped talismans. These are representations of the Mother Goddess and, paradoxically, the more abstract and ineffable the design, the closer and more tangible the pull of their power.

The Sumerians also left us small sculptures with eyes that show the internal tension of someone aspiring to the ineffable. These are votive figures that now step in for humans so that, as is written on one of them, "they will intercede for me."

Did the same desire lead to the stylized white marble figurines of the Cyclades, once covered in red, that retain the industrial-looking cut of tools that might seem modern? Their themes tell us about daily life, their forms captivate us, and the power of their art reaches us.

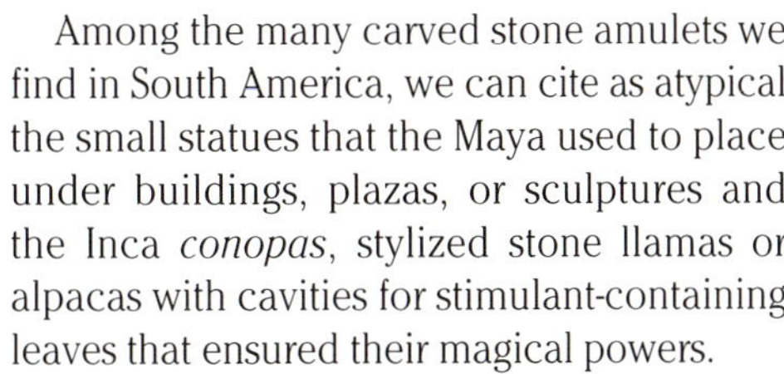

Among the many carved stone amulets we find in South America, we can cite as atypical the small statues that the Maya used to place under buildings, plazas, or sculptures and the Inca *conopas*, stylized stone llamas or alpacas with cavities for stimulant-containing leaves that ensured their magical powers.

In the Orient, the Tantra views sexuality as a mystical experience and symbolizes primordial union, the *Cosmic Egg—the Self-Created Lingam* in small, highly polished oval stones.

Meanwhile, over the remains of the Chinese emperor a jade disk conjures, as it would in life, the cosmic forces symbolized by its abstract appearance.

But earlier, in Mesopotamia, divine power was being replaced by human power. Glyptics were invented, seals in the shape of buttons, rings, or cylinders that indicate ownership of merchandise or the authenticity of a royal message or the identity of someone bringing offerings to a shrine. They are also an amulet for anyone who owns them, and their imprint on clay or papyrus—the paper of China—increases their influence. This art flourished among the Persian nobility who used stones of great beauty, often set in gold; it developed among the Chinese dynasties and spread through India and Vietnam.

The ancient Egyptians used palettes, small reliefs with cavities used first for grinding sacred ointments and later for cosmetic purposes. Thus, the solemn became everyday and even an object of trade. Little by little, commerce created new talismans—these stylized sculptures, abstract or zoomorphic, that were the first coins and ancient currency.

These small talismans carved from stone radiate not only occult powers but tangible powers as well and, when they are well executed, the timeless power of beauty.

◀ *Grimaldi Venus.* Upper Paleolithic. Circa 25,000 B.C.E. Soapstone. Museum of National Antiquities. St. Germain-en-Laye (France)

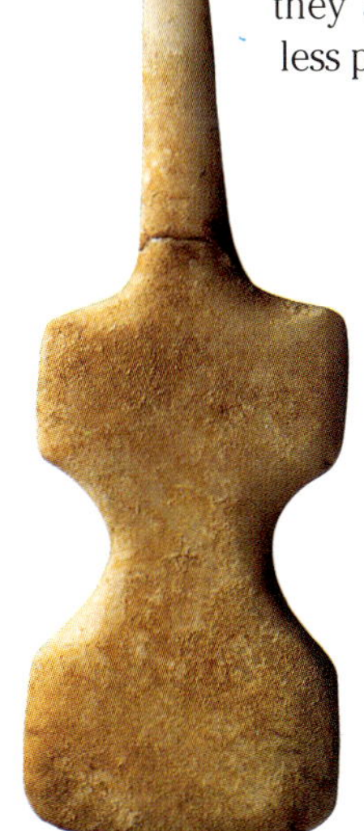

◀ Votive figure 3000 B.C.E. Marble. Museum of the Cicladas, Athens (Greece).

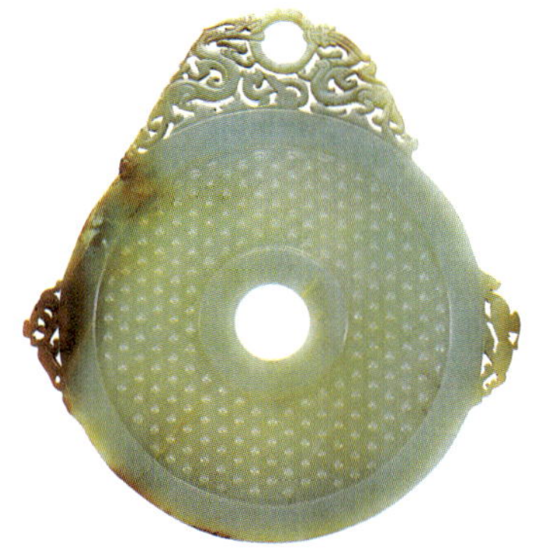

▲ Chinese ritual disk. Second century C.E. Jade. Dingzhou City Museum (China).

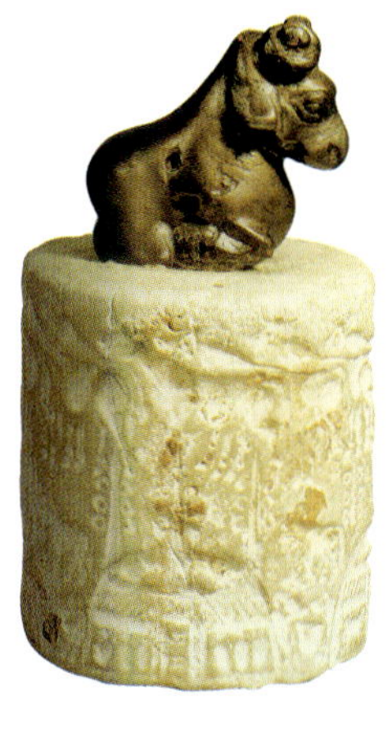

▲ Sumerian seal from Uruk. Circa 3000 B.C.E. Ashmolean Museum. Oxford (United Kingdom).

▼ *Ebih-il, the Superintendent of Mari.* (Syria). Circa 3000 B.C.E. Alabaster. The Louvre, Paris (France). In their eyes . . . the tension of someone aspiring to the ineffable.

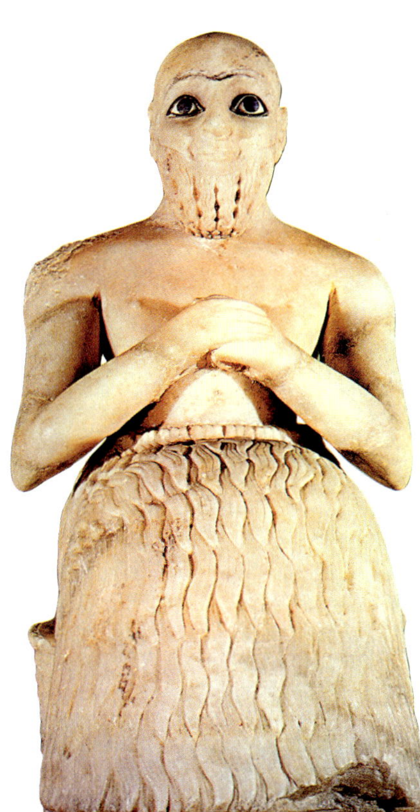

Written in Stone

After mythic times when recorded history began, light entering the caves robbed their sculptures of life. Some mortals then wanted to leave a record of their time on earth and, starting in the fourth century, seeded the countryside with erect stones. At first, these were crude, voluminous menhirs. Later they were obelisks, stelae, or granite columns.

Viewing them, any lay artist can grasp their meaning because they are sculpture and sculpture speaks a universal language. We see in them a civilized expression of the territorial instinct of animals and we hear in them the cries of those who built them: "I built this. My power is great. This is my land."

But sculpture also has dialectical forms and it is then that we need the historian to validate our interpretations. Behind the menhir, a phallic symbol that India would stylize and call the *lingam*, lie hidden the first attempts to establish a social order. Placed in circles or rows, they seem like scenes for the rituals of an incipient priestly caste. Behind the perfection of an obelisk we glimpse mathematics, astronomy . . . the civilization of Egypt.

About 2150 B.C.E. in Sumeria, black stones—diorite or basalt—from remote regions were carved into images known as Gudeas that show the power contained in the original stone and seem devout yet complacent. The letters inscribed on them send an egocentric message to future generations: "I am the shepherd beloved by my god." This is the false modesty of the priest-king, organizer of these first civilizations, reinforcing his influence by claiming divine powers.

In Mesopotamia there were also stelae with reliefs showing leaders with baskets, measuring sticks, cords, and so on. They wanted history to remember them as city planners or, in the case of Hammurabi, as lawmakers. The explicit slogan is "God supports me." Anticipating the future, they cursed those who would destroy them or usurp their name, "Let Shamash pull out his roots, scatter his seed."

The blasphemous stela of Naram-Sim (2250 B.C.E.) is on exhibit at the Louvre in Paris. Its Sumerian warrior challenges the Acadian star gods who will punish him with a short-lived dynasty. New warlike and cruel kings will exalt their manliness by fighting beasts. Around 850 B.C.E., when the subtlety of the Sumerians had been lost, we find writing next to well-known reliefs at the British Museum in London: "I am the king, I am the owner, I am divine, I am all-powerful, I am the judge, I am the prince, I am a hero, I am the conqueror, I am powerful, I am manly, I am Asurbanipal." However, the sculptor and the times betrayed him and today we have more sympathy for the wounded lion than for the arrogance of that hieratic hunter who, to enhance his lineage, had himself drawn with the rigidity, hairstyle, and clothes that had been the fashion 2,000 years earlier.

Another bloodthirsty personage, Asoka, the unifier of India (third century B.C.E.), paradoxically left us the greatest defense of pacifism and tolerance. He erected throughout that immense Asian land hundreds of stambhas, cosmic lightning rods in the form of very tall columns, on which he published 14 edicts urging that everyone be guided by their dharma or conscience. Some symbolic animals crown the columns. It is precisely one of these capitals, depicting lions and made of sandstone, that is the symbol of modern-day India.

The column of the warlike Trajan, erected in 113 C.E., is purportedly a historical document, but rather than extol the power, religiosity, intelligence, or humanity of an individual, as in the above cases, it extols these characteristics in an entire empire.

The desire of the Maya to control the passage of time is not reflected only in their sometimes pyramid-sized calendars. They also mark its passage every five years with ritualistic building of large black stone stelae in the southern part of their territory.

▼ *Trajan's Column* 113 C.E. Marble. Rome (Italy).
A chronicle more lasting than the library that stood next to it.

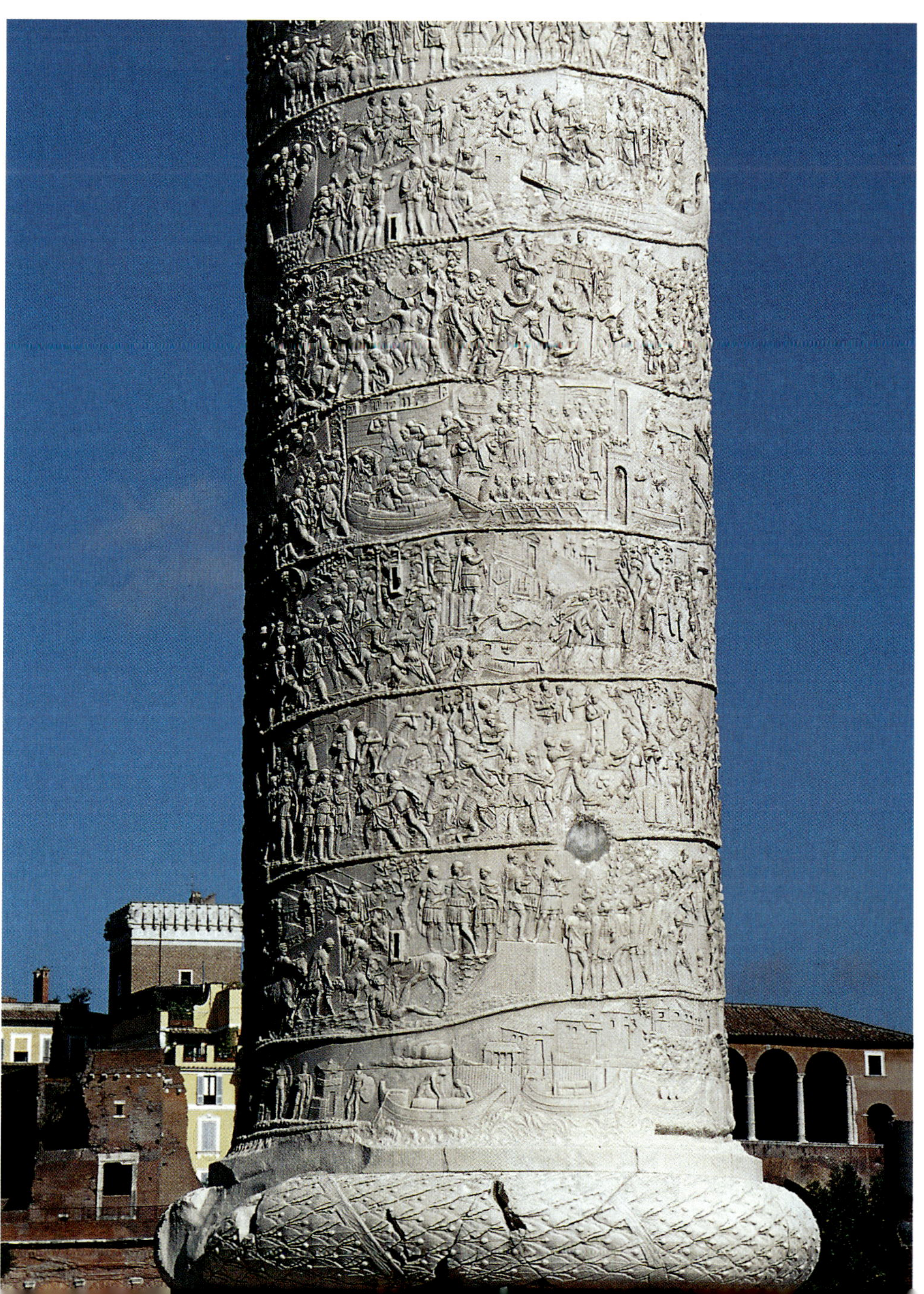

In the center of present-day Turkey, besides bas-reliefs carved directly into the rock we find monolithic blocks and zoomorphic pedestals of very hard rock such as basalt. Here the sculptor was able with apparent simplicity to combine meticulous detail and the force of the rock mass. Thus, the Hittites who dominated Anatolia and sacked Babylon survive to this day. Their kings, protected by the storm god, wanted to leave a record of their empire, especially at the doors of the cities they had conquered. Even without knowing of the Hittites, other peoples would later imitate them.

Ramses II, who formed an alliance with the Hittites in 1271 B.C.E., again promoted colossal undertakings, following the Pharaonic tradition of expressing power in stone. He finished the impressive temple of al-Karnak, built the Luxor Temple, erected many statues with his own effigy, and an endless number of sphinxes, but he never surpassed *the* Great Sphinx of the Ancient Empire, a name the Greeks feminized. Only one other imperialist, Napoleon, would dare to destroy his visage. However, Egyptian sculpture is much more than colossal works. When viewing it, our silence is a sign of admiration and continuing surprise.

With the passage of time, other empires rose and fell. Little remains of them but immense winged bulls with human heads, humbled under the roofs of Europe's two great museums. We also have the ruins of their buildings, architectural remains that the whims of history have transformed into sculpture, as in Persepolis, where Medes and Persians, now without their "King of Kings," would continue to mount guard and where the bull-shaped capitals, like the Hittite capitals, no longer support anything.

Time has also turned into sculpture the *Caryatids* of Tula (Mexico), conceived as temple columns. However, earlier in Mexico the Olmecs had left a record of their power, transporting colossal basalt heads in which the obsidian chisel respected the roundness of the mass. Later, among the Aztecs, a people whom Bartolome de las Casas characterized as having "no wickedness or duplicity," the priests secured their power with representations of their macabre nightmares transformed into gods. Like Egyptian sculpture, the powerful pre-Columbian sculpture must be studied in greater detail than we can provide here.

In the sixth century B.C.E., the Greeks tried to apply the naturalist tendency of the Asurbanipal reliefs, in round masses, to the effigies of the Olympian conquerors known as *Kouroi*. But does this have any association with power? It is not a coincidence that this phenomenon occurred during eras with populist tyrants who vanquished aristocrats rather than beasts. They transferred their feats to the figure of the athlete, as Florence would later do with *David* after defeating the Medici, or Mussolini would do with the athletes in the Olympic stadium, so stylistically similar to the *Kouroi*.

In Rome, the triumphal arches seem to recall that the power of the empire is greater than the power of a victorious general passing through the arches, triumphant yet unarmed. We wonder whether the aqueducts, built when the theory of communicating vessels and lead piping were already known, were not also an expression of power in the form of an abstract sculpture that could be justified based on its utility.

Among all the arts, it is sculpture that most lends itself to the expression of power, gratuitous power as opposed to the utilitarian power of architecture. And this remains true in our own times with the metal Statue of Liberty, the marble Lincoln Memorial, or the stony faces of presidents on Mount Rushmore that witness disdainfully the fall of Stalin's granite form.

Evoking the demolition of statues from the latest empire to fall and (excuse the frivolity) the works of *Obelix*, we note other forms of power associated with sculpture. Xerxes I transported a colossal statue from Egypt to preside over the entry of his palace in Susa. The medieval church converted obelisks to Christianity. The Popes collected Egyptian sculpture and, shortly after condemning the belief that the sun is the center of the universe, installed an obelisk, symbol of the sun, in the center of Saint Peter's Square, the image of the universe. Another obelisk, the one missing at Luxor, reached the Place de la Concorde in Paris in 1836, in exchange for a clock destined for the Great Mosque in Cairo. As sculpture and power seem to be synonymous, if it was impossible during a popular uprising to destroy the image of the tyrant, at least one could break the nose on his portrait.

▼ Olmec head. Before 600 C.E. Basalt. La Venta, Villahermosa, Tabasco (Mexico). Empires fell; all that is left is the roundness of their sculptures.

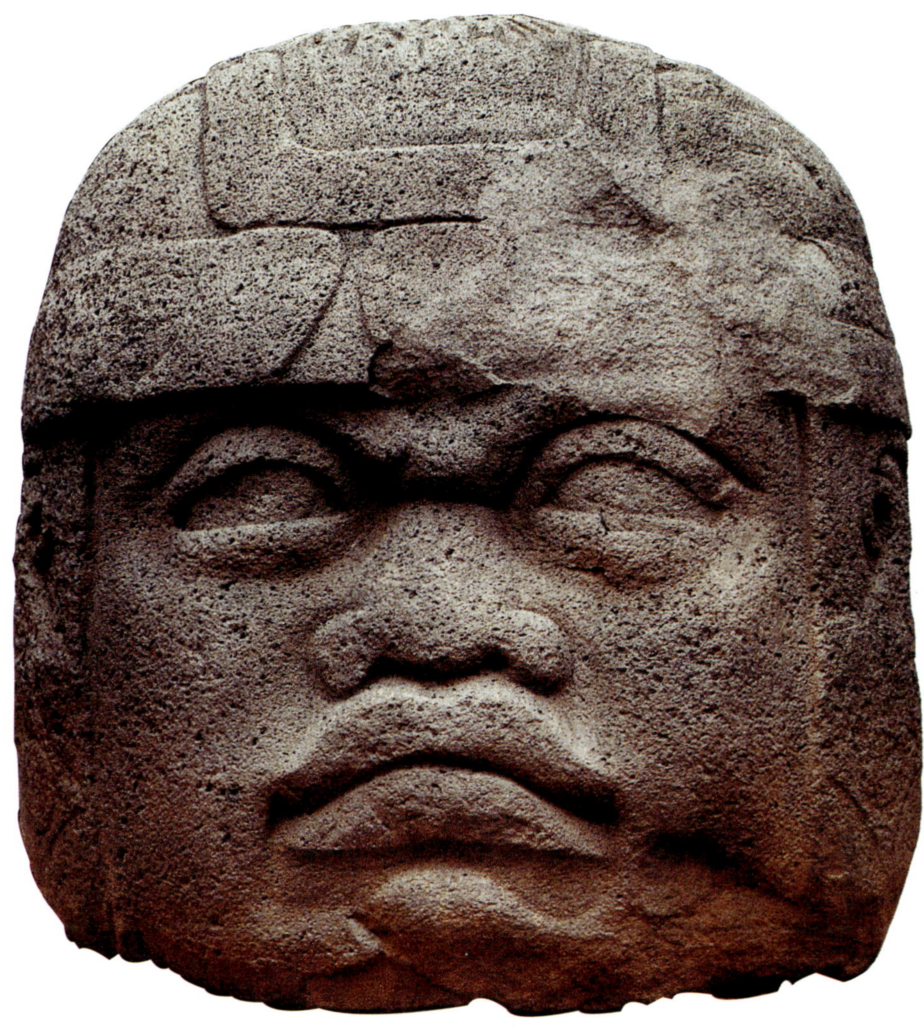

Your Glance Turned to Stone

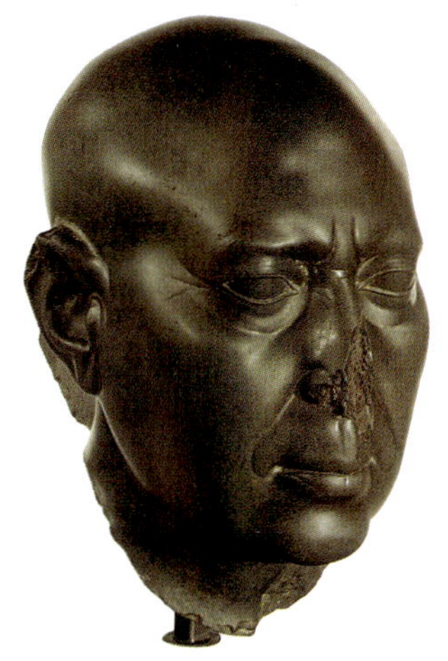

▲ *Priest.* First century B.C.E. Green schist. Egyptian Museum, Berlin (Germany). Sure of his personality, he doesn't hide it.

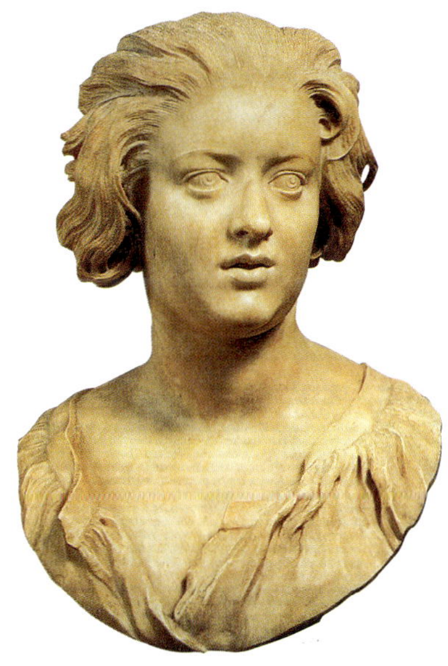

▲ Bernini. *Constanza Bonarelli*, 1637. Carrara marble. National Museum of the Bargello, Florence (Italy). They say that Bernini's subjects look like their portraits.

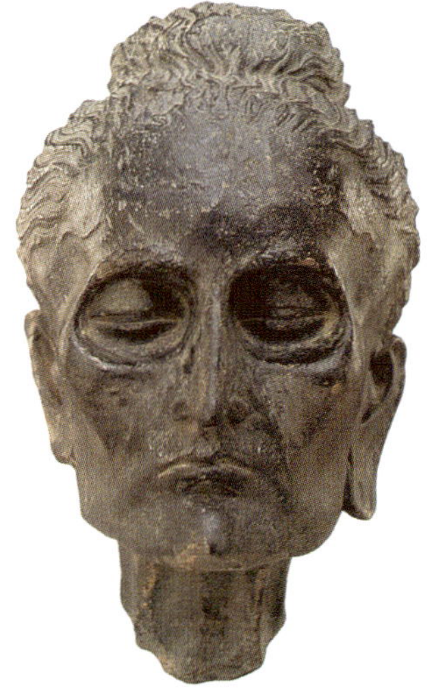

A portrait, a statue emphasizing the expression of personality, also gives us a glimpse of history, but in a more intimate way. Thanks to the sculptor's art, we are able to converse with people removed from us in time and to understand that their concerns and achievements are not unlike our own.

Although there are Sumerian precedents, it was clearly the Egyptians who were history's great portraitists, followed closely by the Romans. In both cases, the origin or excuse is funeral art. We use the word "excuse" because according to Egyptian beliefs, the *Ka* or soul of the deceased, in the shadows of the tomb, penetrated the new stone body guided more by the name than by any similarity to the living person.

Of the Egyptian portraits, we admire not so much the portraits of pharaohs who needed to demonstrate their status or divinity for posterity, but rather the portraits that reflect the humanity of scribes and functionaries. When we look for more information on those portraits whose psychological depth most surprises us, we find that they all belong to high officials, the "image consultants" of the pharaoh of the moment. Acting as the power behind the scenes, they were sure of themselves and did not need to hide their personalities. There is the portrait of Tiyi, the mother of Amenophis IV. It was perhaps she who promoted a religious reform transforming the Egyptians into monotheists. It is possible that this short-lived reform disconcerted the sculptors of Akhenaten. Perhaps feeling the need to be realistic, they invented the caricature so that they could continue to set the pharaoh apart, and idealized his wife Nefertiti. We find plaster casts in the workshop of the sculptor Tutmosis, an indication of his naturalist concerns.

While the Greek philosophers debated whether a portrait should embody the subject's *ethos* (character) or *pathos* (emotions), the Greek sculptors vied to display ideal physical beauty. Lisippo, portraitist of Alexander the Great, combines the three aspects. Although the emphasis is on character when thinkers are portrayed during the Hellenic period, *pathos* became the rule in a world dominated by the Romans, until reaching the extremes of a cruel naturalism. The bust became independent of the body and in the *hermas* the body was replaced by a tall pedestal on which only the genitals protrude.

◀ *Siddharta.* Second century C.E. Schist. Bharat Kala Bhavan, Varanisi (Pakistan). The sculptor advertises the silent interior world of the ascetic.

The Etruscan tradition of representing married couples joined by death and their cult of family ancestors, or Manes, popularized the use of portraits in Rome. Since this was a privilege of the patrician class, an *ius imaginum* had to be enacted to allow the populace, even the shoemaker, to create images of their ancestors from wax impressions of the faces of the dead, who presided over the funeral rites of their descendants. Thanks to these portraits, today we know about a Roman world dominated by pragmatic farmers who in their private moments honored the coiffures of their matrons.

But the image of the emperor may represent advertising rather than reality. Claudio, who was already old and lame, appears as a huge Jupiter; Vespasian, who was given to increasing taxes, looks kindly; Caracalla, who legislated on the rights of citizens, looks like a despot. However, we note an evolution of Augustus' personality in the 80-plus portraits of him found in Rome alone.

Thanks to the system of replacement heads, invented by the Egyptians of the fourth dynasty, the visage proclaiming the policies of the new ruler was transported throughout the empire and thus, sculptures in the provinces periodically had their heads redone.

The portrait tradition survives in medieval Europe, although in latent form. It developed during the Gothic period, flourished in the fifteenth century, and exploded with the discovery of America. It was precisely the news of the New World that led to the first sculptural manifestations of cultural pluralism. Among some 3,000 heads, 320 portraits of different ethnic groups and social classes cover the sacristy of the cathedral of Sigüenza (Spain).

With the Renaissance, the old concept of fame that was the portrait's motivation was reborn. Once again, molds of living subjects were created by applying wax casts to the subject's face. Among the best pieces of sculpture at the Bargello Museum in Florence (Italy), two busts stir restlessly—and one night they will wake up the other marble figures. They are Michelangelo's energetic *Brutus*—an allegory of Lorenzo de Medici, the assassin of Duke Alexander, oppressor of Florence, and Bernini's vibrant *Constanza Bonarelli*. Physique, *pathos*, and *ethos* blend in the air of thoughtful spontaneity, accented by the fresh texture carved by claw and flat chisels. The portrait tradition survives to this day, as we will see when we consider later periods.

The Cold Embrace of Marble

Sculptors strove to conjure cosmic powers or magnify the force of the powerful, but above all to conquer, if not death, oblivion. It is surprising to see how the most universal theme, death, has led to such a diversity of sculptural forms and themes—from pyramids to urns, from urban gravestones to the *Moai* on Easter Island. The treatment is also varied, ranging from the exaltation of pleasure to the macabre.

In the ancient world the corpse, although not necessarily present as it was among the Romans, was wrapped in sculptural forms, surrounded by sculptural objects and framed in enclosures—dolmens, *navetas*, mastabas, hypogea, pyramids—where sculpture creates architecture.

Although cremation has produced little stone sculpture, we cannot forget the compact and sober sculptures found in Iberian necropolises and that the spirit of one of them, such as the matriarchal Lady of Elche (National Archaeological Museum in Madrid), is contained in human ashes.

In Neolithic Europe, the new farmers placed markers at the sites where they sowed corpses in the hope that, like seeds, the corpses would be reborn. Meanwhile, the Egyptians used the scarab as their model and studied human metamorphosis. That persistent search, which impregnates all Egyptian art, produced both the delicate alabaster vases guarding the viscera of the dead, and the anthropomorphic basalt sepulchers, which were copied in marble by the Phoenicians and in live rock by Christians in the High Middle Ages.

The reliefs of the Greek stelae speak to us more of the beautiful recall of the ephemeral nature of life than of an uncertain existence in the kingdom of shadows.

In Trajan's Rome burial became popular. This fostered the development of sarcophagi decorated with reliefs that overused the trepan to make the hair and pupils stand out. In these reliefs, mythological episodes alternate with scenes from daily life and the values of stoicism are exalted. Faithful to this tradition, the early Christians gave shape to the martyr's heroism and incorporated their own symbols or adopted symbols such as half-open doors or images of the Good Shepherd.

During the European Middle Ages, the nobility and clergy preferred to perpetuate the moment of transition to the other life with a serene and placid image and had themselves sculpted recumbent atop their sepulchers. But naturally they were depicted clasping their swords or crosiers, the symbols of their power in life, and accompanied by animals proclaiming the virtues of their sex and condition: fierce lions for men and faithful dogs for women. Despite its small size, the impressive tomb of Philippe Pot seems to ring the death knell of the medieval period. In contrast, the skeletal effigy of Catherine de Medici seems to presage the Baroque (both at the Louvre).

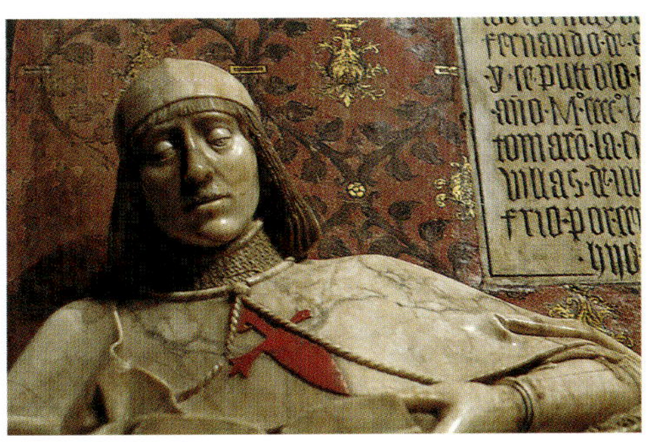

◀ Sebastian de Almonacid (?). *Tomb of Martin Vazquez* (detail). 1497. Alabaster. Cathedral of Sigüenza (Spain). The dead warrior, like a melancholy poet, sits up in a pensive pose.

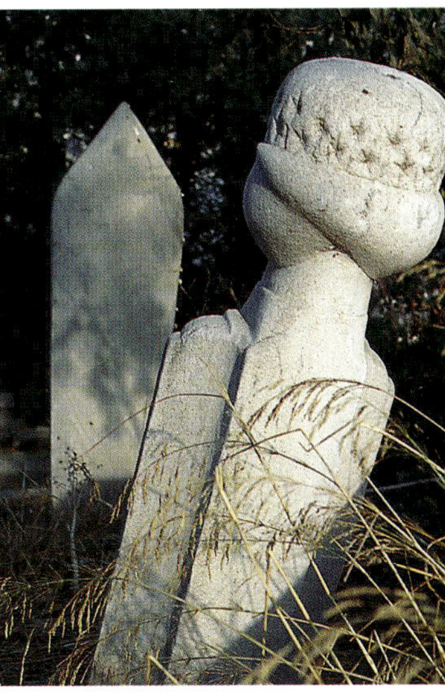

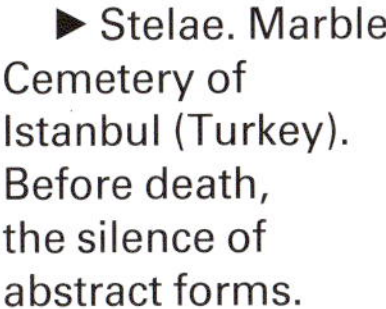

▶ Stelae. Marble. Cemetery of Istanbul (Turkey). Before death, the silence of abstract forms.

In the Tomb of Martin Vazquez (Cathedral of Sigüenza), the once recumbent sculpture is now sitting up in a pensive pose in the Etruscan style and gives way to new Renaissance values that reached their apogee with Michelangelo's sculpting of the Medici Chapel in Florence. There sculpture takes on so much life that we forget, on one hand, the deceased whose pursuit of fame motivated the work, and, on the other, that place for family trophies that the funereal Renaissance chapel became.

Soon came the Baroque and what before was moderation now became grandiloquence and technical virtuosity. Atop the tomb of Richelieu (the Sorbonne, Paris), personages spread out in a theatrical display. In the Vatican, the polychromatic marble tomb of Alexander VII terrorizes us with the theme of *sic transit gloriae mundi*.

However, even in Europe there were other cultures that, while desirous of an afterlife, faced death quietly and expressed their reticence in abstract silhouettes and bas-reliefs. This trend is exemplified in sober Celtic, Viking, or Hebrew stelae, and particularly in the Islamic stelae with their silhouettes that express only the sex or initial status of the deceased.

In the East, the belief in the *sánsara*, which causes reincarnation, demythologizes the place of interment, which is sometimes marked by a simple pile. If it contains relics of the Buddha, it becomes a *stupa*, that unique representation of the vault of heaven with profusely decorated *toranas*, or gateways with three thresholds.

The China of Confucius, where funeral rites were given great importance, left us a legacy of great subterranean mausoleums, replicas of an afterlife city foreshadowed on the exterior by stone functionaries, warriors, or animals flanking the "path of the spirits."

In Monte Alban (Mexico) as well, stelae with reliefs of dancers indicate the entries to the Zapotec tombs. The Maya, whose gods linked death and life, also honored these rites, as evidenced by the crypt at Palenque (Mexico) and the jade mask covering the face of a corpse.

It seems that in the treatment of death, the perception of sculptural language is subordinate to cultural prejudices, in that outside one's culture, funeral sculpture does not produce that shudder that would seem to be intrinsic. But there is something universal. All these sculptures proclaim with more or less irony the inscription that was written, according to the Greeks, on the tomb of Cyrus the Great at Pasargadae: "Oh Man, I am Cyrus, who founded the empire of Persia, and was king of Asia. Grudge me not therefore this monument."

▼ Limona. Tomb. Marble. Arenys de Mar (Spain). The modernist longing for times past.

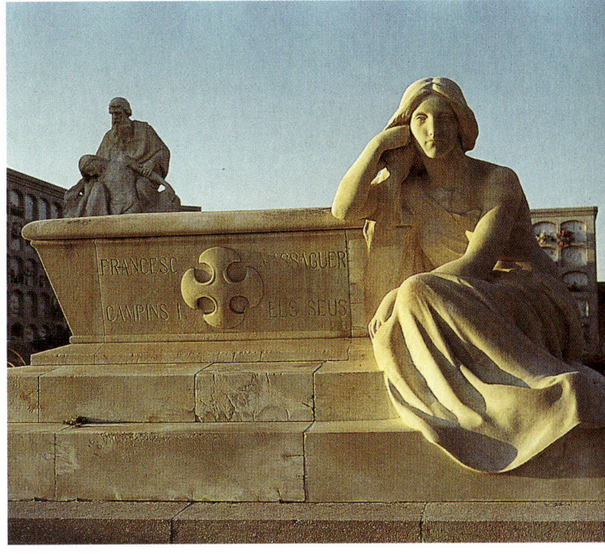

Culture and Ritual

It is in Buddhist Asia and above all in Hindu Asia that we find the greatest quantity, quality, and variety of stone sculpture. Before approaching this subject, those of us who are unfamiliar with these cultures must rid ourselves of aesthetic prejudices if we want to capture something of their true dimension. Otherwise, we may enjoy volumes, textures, and colors, or offer psychological, sociological, and historical interpretations but will have understood little more than the surface of traditional sculpture (as well as Roman, European, or pre-Columbian sculpture), which is not satisfied with feeding decorative ambitions, providing visual sensations, or proposing stylistic models. Its reason for being is to provoke understanding, to answer the needs of the soul. In comparison with this utilitarian goal, taste or aesthetics are secondary issues.

As tradition and the sacred texts already know the best "foods for the spirit," the sculptor, like the orchestra director, does not invent the score but only interprets it. However, when interpreting the score, the sculptor recreates and enriches it. Thus, the sculptor's profession becomes a ritual that requires first "seeing" in a mystical sense and later reproducing that personal vision of what is known by all and what will serve to replenish understanding.

However, the ritual function of sculpture lives on. The finished object is merely an aid to contemplation—whether it's called *dyana*, *ch'an*, or *zen*—and contemplation reveals not only subtle thought but also transforms the personality of the admirer into that which is admired.

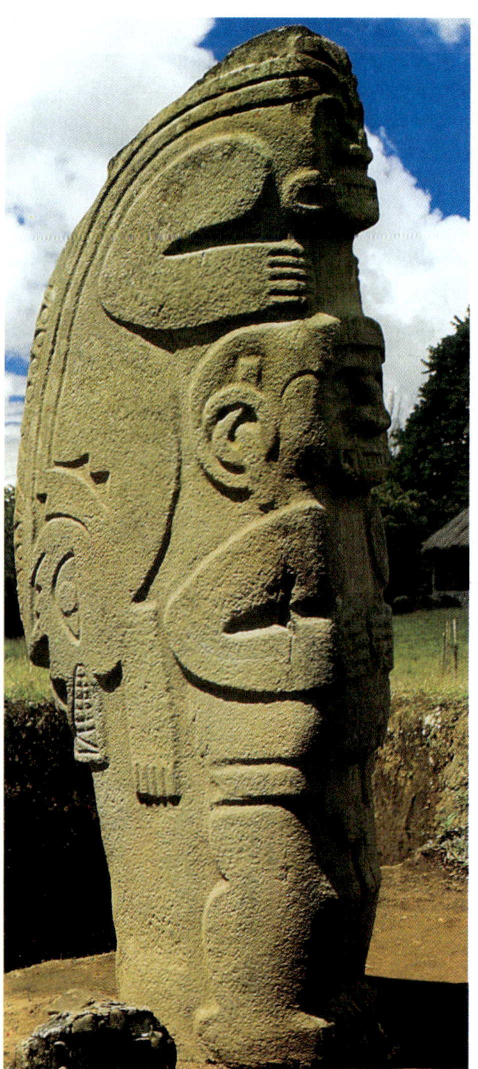

◀ *Doble yo.* Circa 400.
San Agustín, Huila (Colombia).
Is this an invitation for an alliance with the forces of nature?

Quetzalcoatl

It is possible that some of the rich and varied pre-Columbian sculpture, particularly that designed by the various priestly castes, served this purpose. In first century B.C.E., we already find in the Chavin de Huantar area of Peru geometrically shaped representations of felines with snarling teeth that sometimes appear with superimposed snakes. This geometry is conscious and cannot be explained merely by submission to the block of stone. Fearsome subjects will be a constant in subsequent cultures.

It is among the Aztecs that these representations are more frightening. They culminate in the *Mother of the Gods*, a sculpture composed of interwoven snakes, griffins, hands, and human hearts, flaunting a skull on its chest (National Museum of Mexico).

Can representations like this be considered "food for the soul" if they seem rather to ask that we prostrate ourselves in fear? Or do they seek to make our souls stronger by confronting our most intimate fears, fears now under control thanks to the geometric shape they are given? Perhaps their intent is to form a bond with the enemy so as to propitiate its powers, as the enchanting character known as *Doble yo* (San Agustín, Huila, Colombia) seems to be doing. It is possible that they point to a path of human perfection based on the union of opposites, as suggested by the Aztec representations of the divine hero Quetzalcoatl, whose human face is sculpted emerging from the jaws of a plumed serpent—symbols of heaven and earth—and displaying on its chest equally contrasting allegories of water and fire.

The Vedas

India also seeks immunity against a fear worse, if possible, than death, the fear of incarnation. It does this through the contemplation of sculptures of Siva, the most terrible face of Brahma who is the only God according to the sacred Vedic texts but has been displaced by Siva in popular fervor.

Siva, in bronze, but in stone as well, transmits vitality, dancing the dance of life and death. Although he represents destruction, his three faces, his graceful and sometimes androgynous body, his whirlwind of arms, his tranquilizing gesture, and ignorance at his feet as a small bell, invite us not merely to lose our fear of the great transformation but to even desire it.

On the walls of his temples and particularly in the Tantric temples (Khajuaho, circa 1000 C.E.), Siva is carved copulating with Parvati. This image calls for generational and spiritual renewal, in that the body is not considered the prison of the soul as Pythagoras argued, but rather its root from which arises and grows the Kundalini, the libido, carved and adored as a serpent, transforming physical energies into spiritual ones.

Presaging this mentality are the two small statues at the National Museum in New Delhi, known as the Torsos from Harappa (2000 B.C.E., earlier than the sacred texts). These statues express sensuality in their forms and sexuality in their attitudes, now censured by time.

From that period comes the cult of the *lingam* that to this day constitutes the *sancta sanctorum* of Hindu temples and is represented, with the best stones, by pure geometric forms, stylizations that contrast with the surrounding baroque style.

Associated with the cult of Siva, we find enormous carvings of his bull Nandi, transmitter of power; of his son, the god of fortune, the beloved Ganesh with his elephant head; and of his wife Parvati, sometimes seductive, sometimes cruel.

Vishnu, the friendly aspect of Brahma concerned with preserving the living, awakens the desire to fight for what is good when, sculpted with the head of a wild boar, he rescues the Earth from the bottom of the ocean. But he also calls for the serenity of a wakeful spirit when he reposes over Amanta, the cosmic multiheaded serpent holding up the universe.

But these figures are only some of the themes that the Hindu worldview proposes for meditation among the many figures that cover their sculptural temples or the pyramidal towers of the sanctuary cities of the south where the great epics of the Hindu tradition, symbolized in Mount Meru, dwelling of the gods, have been shaped since the fourteenth century.

In these images the sculptor, while remaining faithful to the codes indicated by the Vedas and explained in the *Silpa-sastras*, incorporates popular tastes and contributes his own particular sensibility, as we see in the exquisite temples of Belur and Halebid (Mysore, twelfth century), sculpted in chloritic schist, a material that is easily worked in the quarry but becomes hard and takes on basalt-like tonalities when exposed to the air.

Buddhas

Contrasting with the superabundance of sculptures and the tumultuous agitation of Vedic forms that, recalling the liturgical dance, evoke the *sánsara*, the eternal flow of life, we have the stolid Buddhist calm whose images show the path to nirvana.

Although it is more recent than Hinduism, Buddhism has left us more ancient sculptures because, from the time it was imposed in India in the third century B.C.E., it chose stone over wood. Since that time and up to the seventh century, as it spread throughout the East, it eclipsed Hinduism but at the cost of accepting its popular mythology. It had to incorporate goddesses such as Yakshi, a tree divinity and the ideal of beauty, carved by the sculptor as a figure hanging from the tree of fertility or as a caryatid. The sculptor also carved scenes of local customs such as those that embellish the *toranas* of Sanchi (Bhopal, India, first century B.C.E.).

Buddhist iconography integrates other cultures and becomes confused with Hindu iconography, when it is dynamic, and with Jainist iconography, when it is quiet and self-absorbed. Nonetheless, it is characterized by an aristocratic air that reflects the support it received from the dominant classes.

Some dynasties—Indian, Chinese, Japanese, those of Sri Lanka or Java—promoted the art of grottoes or colossal statues of Buddha and his warriors. Other monarchs favored the stylization of forms.

Noteworthy among the latter group are the Kushans, middlemen on the Silk Road who around 150 C.E. supported the expansionist reform that promoted the Gandhara school. Then, images of Apollonian Buddhas were sculpted in schist or basalt, following the style of the Greeks who reached their borders along with Alexander the Great. Even princes, identifiable because of their mustaches, were depicted as boddhisatvas whose compassion led them to renounce nirvana. This statuary helped to extend Buddhism but was relegated to awakening aesthetic rather than religious sentiments.

With the patronage of the Gupta—335 to 476 C.E.—the culture of northern India reached its apogee, and although they were Hindus who revered Vishnu, they favored the development of the Buddhist school of Samath, which presents reliefs of tactile Buddhas and boddhisatvas with a Hindu sensibility who, in barely insinuated clothing, emerge from the sandstone and transmit a sensation of immateriality.

Among all the images, it is the representations of Buddha that usually resonate more with our interior being. This is no coincidence, in that in the two dynasties cited—the Kushans and the Gupta—the sculpture of Mathura codifies even the most minute details of their iconography. Six measures, four postures, and four attitudes are established. Each part of the body, by analogy, seeks to provoke the same sensations as certain natural elements: neck—musical shell, torso—lion, arm—elephant's trunk, legs—palm tree, hands—flowers, fingers—pea pods. The shape of the eyes varies according to the emotion that one wants to arouse in the subconscious and, on a more conscious level, the position of the hands, clothes, and adornments transmit teachings of the Buddhist dharma.

Thus, the Orient gave sculpture an elevated sense of responsibility that goes beyond the mere display of power, desire for survival beyond death, or magical actions discussed earlier. However, paradoxically, the submission to certain rules and the repetition of themes does not exhaust its aesthetic criteria, which continue to develop ritually like the seasons.

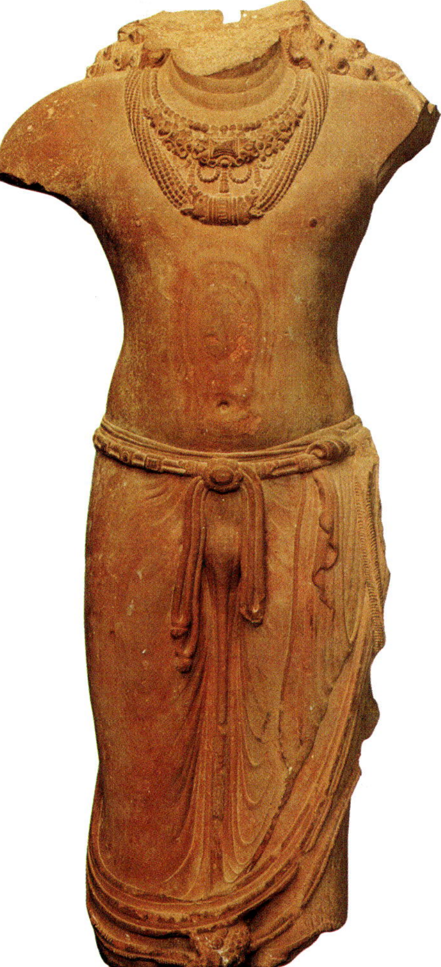

▲ *Vishnu* (?) Fifth century. Sandstone. Government Museum. Mathura (India).
Under apparent calm, subtle hints: chest—steadiness, legs—strength, folds—potency—*kundalini*.

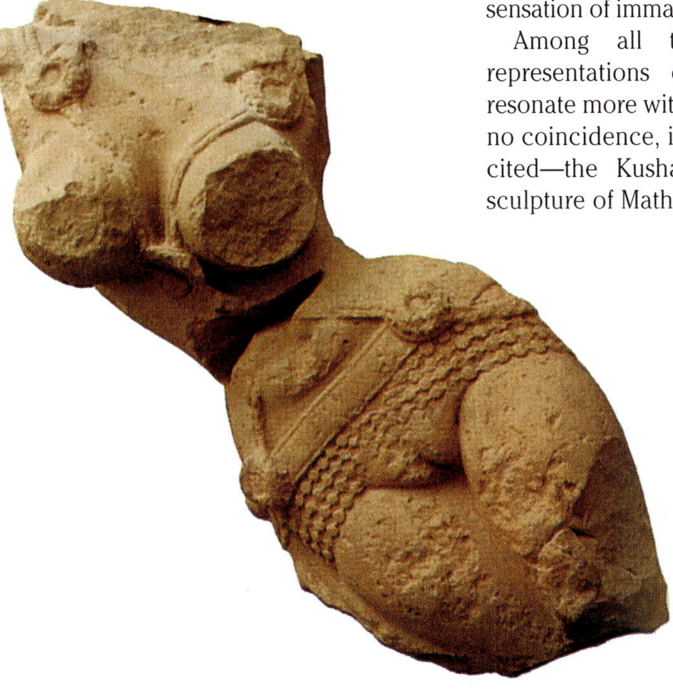

◀ *Yakshi.* Fifth century. Sandstone. Sanchi Museum, Madya Pradesh (India). Incorporating Hindu sensuality, Buddhism becomes popular.

The Marble Polis

During the middle of fifth-century Greece, myth and history, philosophy and art come together in a single science: humanity. This is evidenced by marbles denuded of their original polychromatic tones and copies of sculptures lost to time.

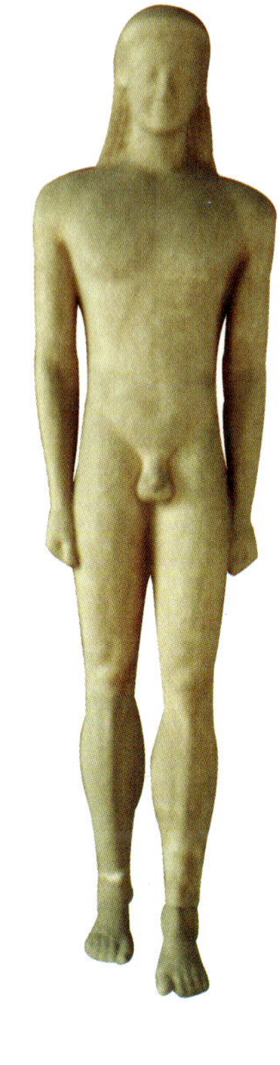

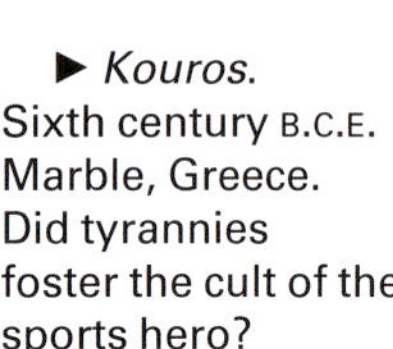

► *Kouros.*
Sixth century B.C.E.
Marble, Greece.
Did tyrannies foster the cult of the sports hero?

▼ Phidias. *Dione and Aphrodite.*
437 B.C.E. Pantellic marble.
British Museum, London (United Kingdom).
How can we differentiate between gods and mortals when Phidias immortalized both?

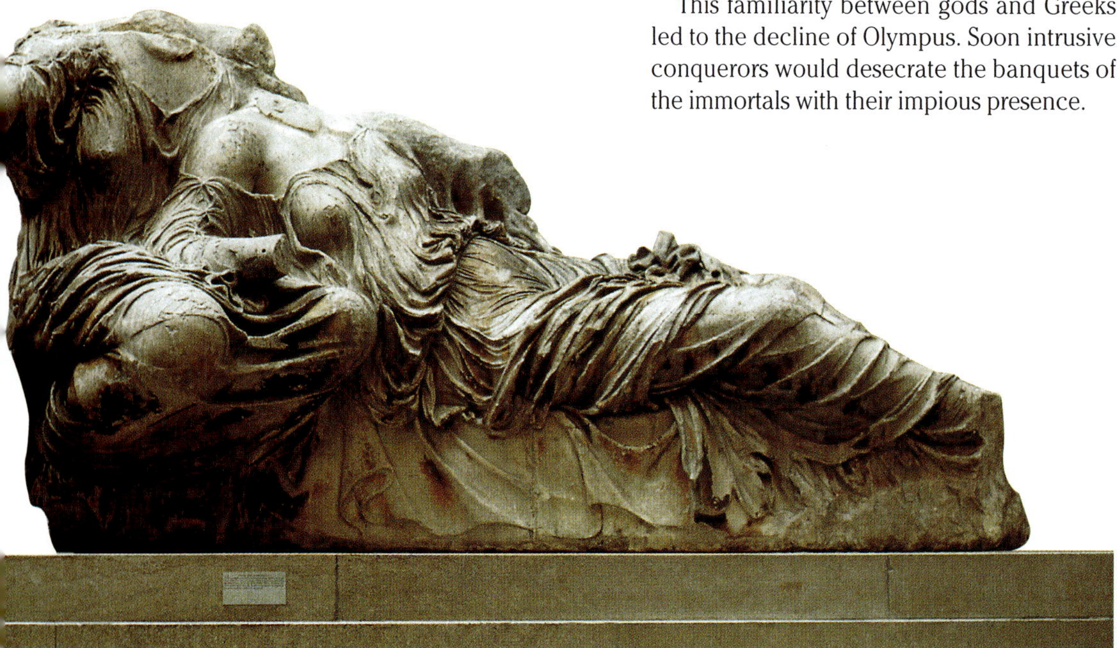

Myth

Myth and daily life merged after the victory over the Persians. The Acropolis at Athens was the scene of success for Phidias and his school of sculptors, the chroniclers. The polis of the League of Delos, to its regret, financed it. On the pediment of the temple dedicated to her virginity, Athena, intelligence of Zeus, was reborn in marble as an adult. This occurred at the dawn of reason when the horses of the sun were arriving and the chariot of lunar intuition had not yet been obscured. Gods and Athenians, witnessing the event, posed for the sculptor Phidias; only he could capture their serene magnificence. Soon, on the rear pediment, the astute Athens-Athena conquers the rough seas and expels the Persians-Poseidon from her city. In one or the other scene, women, gods, giant-vanquishing men, and horses, centaurs, Amazons, and Trojans pass by with processional dignity.

How can we differentiate between gods and mortals at the Acropolis when Phidias immortalized both? Is a pensive Athena using Pericles' helmet or is Pericles dressed in Athena's clothing? Is it the most graceful of Athenian women who is having trouble with her sandal or is it Athena herself?

Imitating the god of wisdom, other gods moved from Olympus to the Acropolis on the Aegean and chose sculptors to humanize them. Apollo, Dionysius, and Aphrodite looked to Praxiteles and, with his help, are embodied in marble sensuality. Envying human tones, they hired the painter Nicias to brush on their makeup.

This familiarity between gods and Greeks led to the decline of Olympus. Soon intrusive conquerors would desecrate the banquets of the immortals with their impious presence.

Elbow to Elbow with Philosophy

Continuing with Greece, historic time elapsed parallel to mythic time and reason opened a path in the minds of the philosophers, in the words uttered in the theaters and in the sculptures that gave life to the city, always governed by the criterion set out by Protagoras: "The individual is the measure of all things . . . ," and this included the gods.

The same interest in physical reality that led to philosophy pushed the evolution from the *kuoroi*, Egyptian in appearance, to the Doryphoros. Uneasiness over the organization of the polis, *including reliance on a tyrant*, is evident in the sculptor's exaltation of the hero. Myron expressed Heraclitus' affirmation that "everything flows" by checking the movement of his *Discus Thrower.* The bronze version of this work has been lost but we have been left with some Roman copies in marble.

After the Egyptians, Pythagoras began to see the mathematical structure of the universe and the sculptor Polycletus saw it reflected in the canon, the proportions that beautify the human body, which he considered divisible in seven "heads," each of which is divided into three parts.

It is said that Socrates regretted the loss of human passion in sculpture. Soon the sculptor Scopas and later the Hellenists would give shape to pain and pathos.

While the hedonists defended an ethic of small pleasures, Praxiteles voluptuously polished his marbles.

What better scenario could there be for preaching stoicism than the bronze monument, or its marble copies, erected by Attalus I in honor of the Gauls who, although they were his enemies, demonstrated moral fortitude in defeat?

If in the ancient world the sculptor showed respect for power and religion, in Greece the sculptor broke bread and drank wine with the philosopher. While contemplating ephemeral human beauty, he philosophized and his work was enriched and evolved along with thought—archaic clarity, classical equilibrium, Hellenist baroque style—and he asked questions that transcended his era. Does realist sculpture imitate what we see (Socrates), what we idealize (Plato), or what we interpret (Aristotle)? The echo of these questions resonates over time and it is in time that the answer will come. Rome will try out naturalism; Neoplatonism will inspire the young Michelangelo's first *Pietà* (Vatican); and baroque sculpture will manipulate some forms to compensate for our deficiencies of perception. But let us continue the chronology.

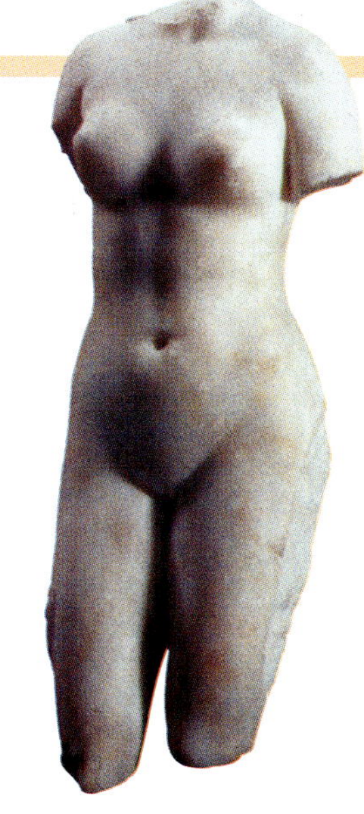

▲ *Venus of Badalona.*
First century B.C.E. Carrara marble.
Municipal Museum, Badalona (Spain).
Romanized Greek gods reach the far limits of the empire.

In the Hands of Politics

Rome was interested above all in the art of politics. Thus, Virgil himself noted, "Others will know better . . . how to carve living faces in marble . . . ; you, Roman, do not forget that your art is to govern peoples, to extend the rule of peace. . . ." The genius of Rome, which is evident in its code of law, not only subordinated sculpture to the art of good government, it considered sculpture work for Greeks. Despite this disdain, we must recognize that the Roman sculptors were masters of the portrait and of relief.

With great practical sense, but starting from a solid Etruscan tradition that, as we have already said, valued naturalism and the portrait, Rome eclectically absorbed everything the conquered peoples developed throughout their history, and appropriated Greek culture, which it soon discovered in *Magna Grecia* in southern Italy.

Curiously, except in Nero's time, until Constantine Rome did not allow itself to be seduced by bursts of Hellenist grandiloquence like the *Colossus of Rhodes*. It was more attracted by the tragic expression of *Laocoon* or the dynamism of the *Winged Victory of Samothrace*.

After the conquest of Greece, shiploads of sculpture and Greek sculptor slaves reached Rome. Soon, free Greek sculptors also immigrated to Rome to work in the workshops that were opening up. Their works, originals or copies, lent prestige to the houses of the patricians and adorned the city. Thus, numerous Aphrodites became Venuses, Zeus became Jupiter, and Apollo became the emperor. These painted marbles dwell in temples, preside over the forum from high columns, or loom from the arches of the Coliseum and reach the far limits of the empire over Roman roads.

Rome valued realism, particularly in sculpture. Whether a statue depicted a dog or a bust, the best critique would be that it "seems real," "alive." Inheritors of Hellenism and lovers of the portrait, they also valued the expression of sentiments. Pliny criticized Myron for not knowing how "to express the emotions of the mind," but Roman sculpture sometimes enjoys external expression and takes pleasure in the grotesque.

Fewer but more influential are those who value classical weightiness and their opinion can be seen in official works from the time of Augustus. Hadrian would be the principal exponent of this Hellenistic current. Perhaps he wanted to revive Greek classicism in Rome, and he achieved this in his own villa. Pursuing a platonic ideal, he obsessively commissioned the best sculptors of his era to create effigies and busts of the mythologized memory of his deceased lover Antinous, depicted as a Greek god and even as an Egyptian god.

In Rome, the relief proliferates in commemorative monuments, such as columns or triumphal arches, and replaces mythological themes with history. Structure becomes narrative, technique is perfected to achieve different depths, and anecdotes are included. However, what is most important is that the relief becomes an instrument in the service of politics, Roman art *par excellence*.

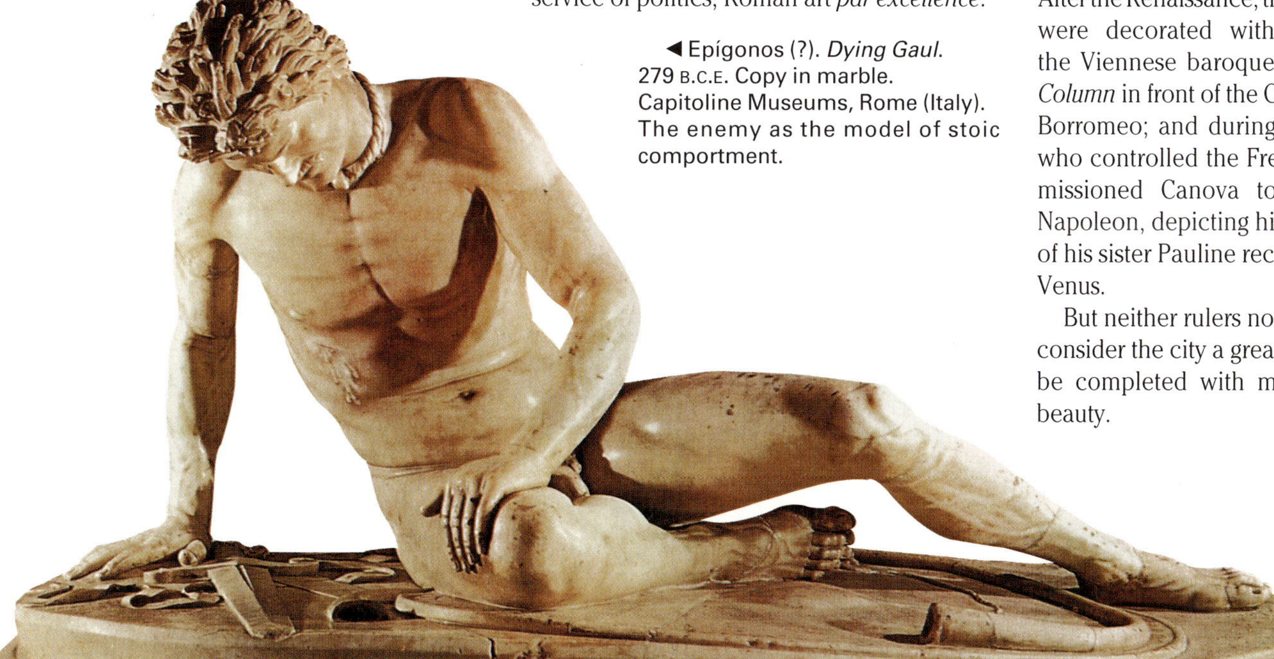

◀ Epígonos (?). *Dying Gaul.*
279 B.C.E. Copy in marble.
Capitoline Museums, Rome (Italy).
The enemy as the model of stoic comportment.

This is what happens in *Trajan's Column*, the *Arch of Titus*, or the *Altar of Peace*, a smaller version of the altar at Pergamo, built by Augustus to publicize his peace-making work. Its reliefs, as earlier in the Parthenon, blend myth, allegory, and history, but here the historical characters can be identified by their names and regions.

The political use of Roman statuary is ambivalent. Augustus and his successors used it to show their superiority, presenting themselves to the people as soldiers, magistrates, pontiffs, or gods. However, following the Greek codes, the politician was accessible to the citizens.

In later centuries, a taste for the classical characterized politicians of a different stripe. After the Renaissance, the gardens at Versailles were decorated with Roman mythology; the Viennese baroque reproduced *Trajan's Column* in front of the Church of Saint Charles Borromeo; and during Neoclassicism those who controlled the French Revolution commissioned Canova to create portraits of Napoleon, depicting him as a new Caesar, or of his sister Pauline reclining like a seductive Venus.

But neither rulers nor citizens would again consider the city a great common dwelling to be completed with memories, ideals, and beauty.

The *Pórtico de la Gloria*

"And behold there was a throne set
in heaven,
and upon the throne One sitting.
And he that sat
was to the sight like jasper
and the sardine stone. And there was
a rainbow . . .
four and twenty ancients sitting . . . and
four living creatures . . ."

That is how Chapter 4 of the *Apocalypse* describes the end of time that was expected to occur in the year 1000 or 1033. When it was postponed *sine die*, the sculptor was charged with reminding us of the imminence of this event at the gates of the churches.

After the dissolution of the Roman Empire, Christianity, the new ideology dominant in Europe, dispensed with statuary in an effort to avoid resurgences of paganism. However, with the change of the millennium, the mindset changed as well. This happened at a time when Vikings and Muslims were terrorizing Christianity but at the time same infected it with a wanderlust that would manifest itself in crusades and pilgrimages, providing routes for the spread of the new Romanesque style.

It was architecture itself that reserved a place for sculpture, primarily around windows and doors and on the capitals. Decorating them challenged the imagination of the stonemason who, in such a limited space and with some predetermined shapes, had to breathe life into biblical or allegorical characters.

It is in the portals of churches where the architect allowed more collaboration from the "master of live stone," and where the theologian determined content and form. At the foot of the images in the plaza, some animal might appear, an allusion to passions that would best be mastered. At the doorjamb, figures might appear, models of an exemplary life. At the mullion, the patron saint of the church might appear to welcome the faithful. In the archivolts, biblical stories might appear to frame the great central theme of the tympanum: the *Maiestas Domini*, the embodiment of the apocalyptic vision where one glimpses fear and the hope of being judged by a Master who is more just and powerful than the feudal lords. In the tympana of the secondary doors, scenes from the life of Mary began to be represented.

The reliefs on the capitals, particularly those in the cloisters intended for the erudite public of the monasteries, soon acquired a freedom of anatomical shapes that respected only the architectural profile. Themes that were at first religious, with the excuse of allegory, were transformed into circus scenes or examples from a fantastic bestiary. Because such scenes were removed from their moralistic purpose, they were criticized by Saint Bernard, promoter of the Cistercian Order, who called them "grotesque monsters, a disarray of deformed beauties and aesthetic oddities." Nonetheless, there is much underlying artistic quality in these sculptures.

All the churches house religious statues but they are generally made of wood, with a few exceptions, such as the perfect *Marededeu del Claustre* in Solsona, Spain. Mary is often depicted as the throne of the Savior.

After centuries of avoiding sculpture in order to distance itself from paganism, how could Christianity codify a style that would express the divine and the human coexisting or fighting with Jews and Muslims who honored the biblical prohibition on making statues? Although in border areas sculptural decoration was limited to plant motifs, Christian lands adopted, with greater permissiveness, the solution of the sister church of Byzantium when confronted with the iconoclastic wars, a solution known to them through codices and tales of the Crusades.

Thus emerges an iconography that respects the sacred but can be understood, that does not renounce the rounded shape as in the Orient, but emphasizes the frontality of the principal figures who are placed in the center of the scene and given a size that is hierarchically superior to other figures. A hierarchy is also established for the parts of the body in order to stress the two great qualities of the soul: intelligence—head and will—hand. Volumes are emphasized, shapes are given geometrical proportions, and the rhythmic folds of clothing are emphasized to give the religious image an otherworldly air. Through other routes, Romanesque Europe created a style of its own that has certain parallels to the style of some Buddhist school as in Saint Martin de Plaimpied (France).

◀ *Pórtico*. 1150. Sandstone.
Saint Mary Magdalene, Vezelay (France).
The breath of the Spirit animates any being with a soul.

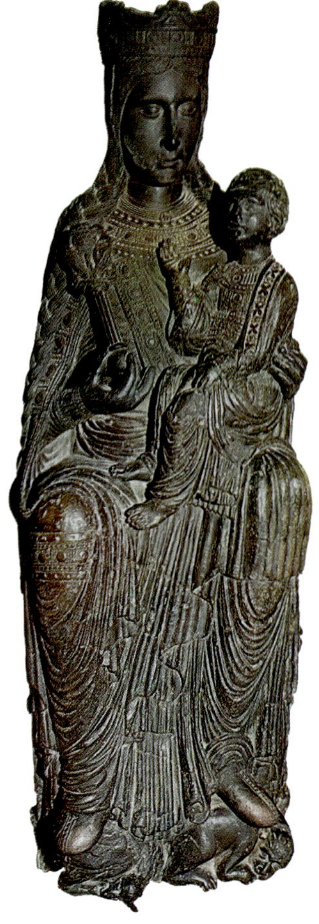

▲ Gislebertus (?) *Marededeu del Claustre*.
Twelfth century.
Limestone. Cathedral of Salsona (Spain).
Mary, perfect throne for the Savior.

These are the general characteristics of a sculpture that extends from Kiev or Constantinople to Oslo or Coimbra, although it is, of course, adapted to each local school. Thus, in Italy sculpture is set apart from the rest of the building by being carved in marble, while in other areas they use the same stone, although it is polychromatic, as that used in the building. The style seems dramatic in Moissac, while it is very dynamic in Vezelay, and in Chartres, the stylized and sweet figures of the doorjambs advocate the Gothic style. Evolving toward naturalism, the sandstone saints in Oviedo and San Vicente de Avila (Spain) establish human relationships among themselves.

All these paths lead to the *Pórtico de la Gloria* of Santiago de Compostela, where the peaceable image of the saint welcomes the pilgrims who, seeking the apocalyptic *Finis Terrae*, find themselves with some relaxed prophets made so lifelike by Master Mateo that the popular imagination invented sardonic dialogue for them.

The Gothic Smile

The Romanesque pilgrimage to the end of the world has a return path on which the enchantment of the simple and ingenuous is rediscovered. Those who were looking for beauty in the storm would be entranced by a smile. Thus, Gothic sculpture emerged after a period of Cistercian purification. This change occurred when Romanesque culture offered mature fruits, while still in the seventh century. The Cistercian Order imposed its pruning but after his criticism Saint Bernard would initiate a new reverence for Mary that would expand the thematic repertory to include femininity: the virgin birth, the Annunciation, pregnancy, maternal tenderness, suffering before the Cross, coronation, and so on.

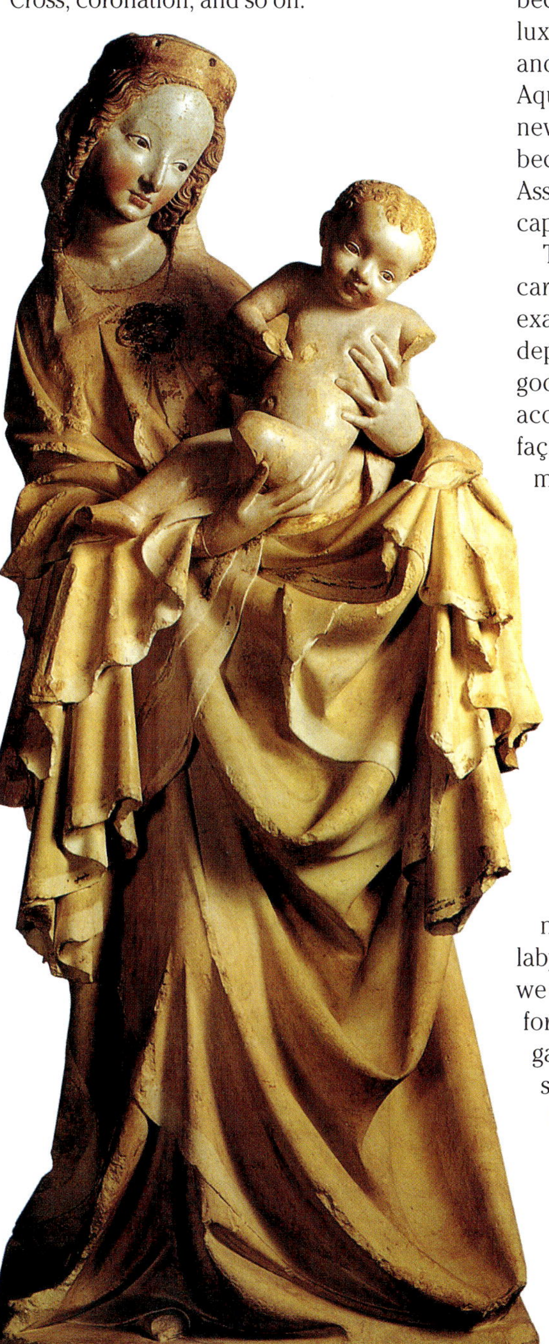

◄ *Virgin of Kruman.* Circa 1400. Polychrome stone. Kunsthistorisches Museum. Vienna (Austria). Tenderness, simplicity, ingenuousness . . . the mysticism of family pleasures.

The new style promoted by the refined and influential abbot Suger in Saint-Denis soon spread to Chartres, Paris, Amiens, and Rheims, and shortly thereafter to all of Europe. The change was abrupt, as if the humanist ghost of Greek classicism, that urge to represent the human figure just as it was, had suddenly been released from the codes that had been imposed. The new style spread and evolved rapidly; its initial restraint soon became lively and sinuous until it took on an assurance that highlighted the individualization of the face while the surroundings became baroque.

As living conditions in the new cities became gentler, society could allow itself the luxury of competing for superfluous things and financing sculpture. While Thomas Aquinas and the incipient universities placed new value on knowledge, Christ the Judge became the Divine Teacher. While Francis of Assisi intoned canticles to Brother Nature, capitals were decorated with plant motifs.

The most humble religion, devotion to the carpenter's Son, as spread by fishermen, exalted its humanity with Gothic sculpture depicting daily pleasures and pains. As the gods did earlier in the Parthenon, the saints acquired limestone bodies and adorned the façades of cathedrals. Yet again intrusive mortals occupied positions to which they were not entitled. Utilizing correlations between scenes in the Old and New Testaments, the sculptor carved kings, presumably the antecessors of Christ, who subtly exalted monarchies that, hoping to obtain support from the cities in order to combat the feudal powers, placed the foundation stones of various cathedrals, such as, Naumburg, Germany.

When we stand before the profusely elaborate statuary of a Gothic temple and then examine it more closely, we do not know where to look. Fleeing from the labyrinth of saints dressed in medieval fashion, we find ourselves delighting in the abstract forms of the pinnacles or the monstrous gargoyles, a fascinating representation of the stonemason's imagination. However, if we look carefully, we can see the imprint of distinct stylistic touches on the same façade, revealing different hands and periods. For example, we can contrast the relative rigidity of the *Annunciation* and *Visitation* series on the main door at Amiens with the treatment given to the same themes at Rheims, where the Virgin and Saint Elizabeth reclaim the sculptural life of the classical world and the Angel smiles mischievously. We will return later to amuse ourselves by observing portraits of daily life, decapitated saints, devils seducing noble ladies, astrological signs, burros playing the vihuela, wise men from antiquity wearing spectacles, and so on.

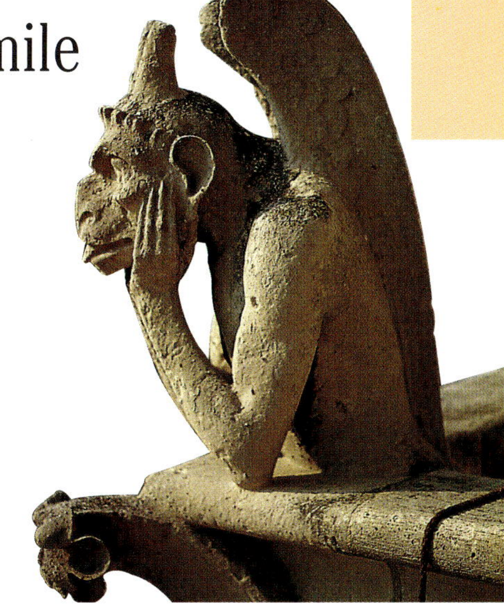

▲ From the towers of Notre Dame, mockery watches over the city of Paris.

However, when we pass through the portals of a Gothic cathedral, subdued by the grandeur of its architecture, we might overlook the reliefs of the retrochoir, an alabaster altar, or the pulpit that seems to be an entity unto itself like some exempt piece of sculpture. We might admire, entirely apart from the architecture, a delicate image of Mary smiling or playing with the Holy Child (for example, the *Virgen Blanca* of Toledo in polychrome marble), often depicted leaning over as if recalling the curves of the ivory tusks from which the first virgins were carved. If we descend to the crypt, we will find, like a foundation from the Gothic world, a Romanesque sculpture that perhaps supplanted a pre-Christian mother goddess.

The relationship between architecture and sculpture would become even closer starting with the construction of the Carthusian monastery in Pavia (Lombardy, 1491). Its entire façade is covered with reliefs and carvings and its style announces the transition to the Renaissance. This new more decorative than sculptural style prospered in Castille and Portugal, where it is known as Plateresque and Manueline.

Al'antica

The rapid evolution of medieval European sculpture is surprising, particularly if we consider that it was in the service of a single ideology, Christianity. With the arrival of Gothic currents, Romanesque hieratic images became naturalistic; they lost solemnity but not decorum and continued to be modest. If the artist carved a nude, whether it was Adam, Eve, Mary Magdalene, or Saint Sebastian, his purpose was to relate it to sin or suffering.

By 1506 the situation had changed to such an extent that Pope Julius II acquired the recently discovered *Laocoon*, restored by Michelangelo and later by Bernini, to adorn his gardens. This Hellenistic work would become the prototype for Renaissance sculpture and the slogan *al'antica*—as in antiquity—would become the cry of modernity. But with this, the snake of paganism slithered toward Saint Peter's Cathedral and years later would provoke the division of Christianity.

Renaissance sculptors considered clothing an expression of something trivial and subject to passing fancies. Influenced by Neoplatonism, they sought to shape a more durable beauty. They retrieved, perhaps without intending to, the Romanesque idea of the human being as *imago mundi* and, when they tried to shape the splendor of the Divine Beauty they saw reflected in the perfection of the human body, they elevated Gothic religiosity, which had been overly preoccupied with daily life.

As the male nude came to symbolize heroic virtue, they sculpted nudes confronting evil, like David or Christ himself (Cellini, the Monastery of El Escorial, Spain). The less frequently depicted female nude was synonymous with beauty and, paradoxically, with chastity. Later, for Bernini, it became synonymous with truth (*Truth Unveiled by Time*, Borghese Gallery, Rome, Italy).

The Prince—some popes and cardinals could be seen as such—was surrounded by refined people and sponsored sculptors, painters, or poets, elevating in this way the social status of artists to the point that they were felt to have a special divine inspiration. It is said that Charles V himself stooped to pick up Titian's paintbrush. In sculpture, Gonzaga ordered a commission unheard of up to that point. He asked Michelangelo "to create a sculpture to his own taste . . ." because what he wanted was "only a work of his own inspiration." For the first time, the artist's signature and the idea were worth more than the finished work.

Sculpture then ceased to be considered a trade, as Michelangelo's father and Leonardo da Vinci himself had feared, and became a liberal art. What was valued in art was the mental process, but sculptors mastered technique and did not disdain manual tasks. In this setting, the sculptors of Florence became independent of the guilds by decree of the Medici, and Giorgio Vasari created an autonomous group that he called the Academy, after the philosophical school of Plato.

The origins of this new mentality could already be found in fourteenth-century Siena and Pisa. But it was in fifteenth-century Florence that the greatest innovations occurred.

Donatello, who first carved a nude David in bronze, anticipated in his disturbing and searching work later developments in sculpture. Already in *Saint George*, a work commissioned by the Armourers' guild, Donatello synthesized the ideals of the Renaissance—volume, stable form, and exaltation of the ideals of youth: naturalness, strength, and beauty. But his work evolved notably in the statues of the prophets he created for the niches of the bell tower. In them the dignity and grandeur seen in *Saint George* combined with expressiveness and psychological depth.

An adolescent and forger of ancient sculpture protected by Lorenzo the Magnificent brazenly signed the *Pietà* (Vatican) at the young age of 23. His name was Michelangelo Buonarotti and in this work he sublimated tragedy, transforming it into absolute beauty and balance, faithful to the Neoplatonism then in vogue. He planed, shaped, and polished a single block of Carrara marble, finishing even the most insignificant details and eliminating any trace of the chisel.

Four years later, in 1501, he shut himself in with an immense piece of marble that had been roughly hewn and twice abandoned in the past by other sculptors. He stayed in isolation until he saw "the image imprisoned inside the block." It was then that *David* and his myth was born.

Michelangelo also received a commission to create the 12 Apostles for the cathedral in Florence but the restless traveler barely began to carve Saint Matthew when he abandoned the project to paint the Sistine Chapel and design the tomb of Julian II, the great illusion and the great failure of his life. He was able to complete only the *Moses*, the archetype of the enraptured mystic holding idolatry at bay, and the two *Slaves* now found at the Louvre (Paris, France). The other *Slaves* would be abandoned.

Back in Florence, he again failed to finish his masterpiece, the Medici Chapel, which he sculpted "more moved by fear (of the Medici) than by love." In these nudes with their contrasting poses—allegories of *Dawn*, *Twilight*, *Night*, and *Day*—sculpture reached its zenith. The strength of the man and woman in their anatomical fullness is accentuated by their serenely restrained expressions and relaxed muscles subtly captured in the first three sculptures in the series.

In his old age, after demonstrating his genius in painting and architecture, Michelangelo returned on three occasions to the theme of the *Pietà*, carving the Palestrina *Pietà* from a block dating back to ancient Rome. However, what he truly wanted and was unable to achieve because of his exacting standards, was no longer to express beauty but rather to express pain and internal suffering, the fruit of his religious repentance, a desire more suited to the Baroque.

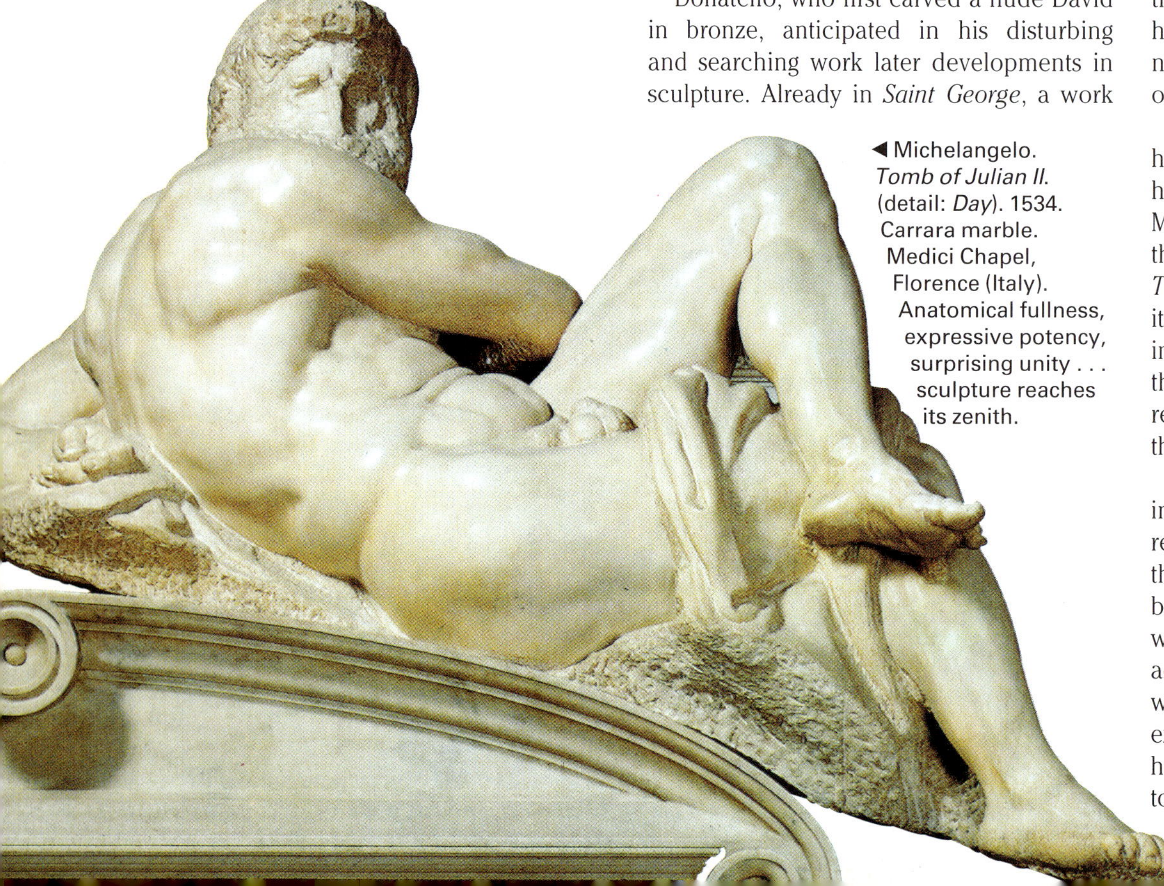

◀ Michelangelo. *Tomb of Julian II.* (detail: *Day*). 1534. Carrara marble. Medici Chapel, Florence (Italy). Anatomical fullness, expressive potency, surprising unity . . . sculpture reaches its zenith.

But Is It Moving?

Would it be possible to surpass Michelangelo, considering that he himself was unable to do so, having abandoned numerous sculptures? His successors, known as mannerists, tried to surpass him by demystifying the importance of the preferred point of view, a Romanesque legacy, and seeking to express movement. These were times when the ideas of Copernicus were maturing in the mind of the young Galileo.

Cellini, thinking about his bronzes, theorized that the viewer must move around the sculpture. Thus, the sculptor must consider an infinite number of viewpoints. Giovanni Bologna showed this in the *Rape of the Sabine Women*, a sort of sculptural tornado that broke not only the tense equilibrium of Michelangelo but also the unity of the block, and forcibly fit different marbles together using what Vasari called "crude patches." Later, the most picturesque stones would be assembled, paying homage to Baroque virtuosity.

Another balance achieved by Michelangelo was also broken. The "mental" disdained the "manual" and sculptors, who now and then visited the practitioners in the workshop, became maquette makers who thought themselves original because they interpreted the rules issued by the increasingly dominant academies.

Europe also shifted and changed. While the reformed churches gave priority to music, the Catholic Church, faithful to the Trentine principles of "instructing the people," opted for a type of sculpture that could "stir and thrill" in order to move the "passions of the soul." The Platonic search for ideal beauty is replaced by the desire to shape real beauty as preached by Aristotle. "Nothing is beautiful but what is real; only what is real is pleasing." The Baroque ideal was formulated and its missionaries, the Jesuits, expanded their sphere in Latin America.

In the seventeenth century, power became centralized in an absolute monarchy that paid the sculptor to glorify the sovereign, whether king or pope. Support was given to sculpture that, in order to attract attention, combined marbles of different colors; in order to stir the emotions, expressed extreme situations from tragedy to ecstasy; and in order to affect souls, went in search of viewers and if possible surrounded them.

The gardens of Versailles or Saint Petersburg, the capitals of the kings and the entire world were considered a great treasure where the sculptor directed the performance. The most important drama of all was staged in Versailles. Galileo supplied the plot: the earth's revolution around the sun. Louis XIV embodied the starring role and the sculptors designed the scenery.

In this context, another genius with marble emerged: Gian Lorenzo Bernini, who remained faithful to his principles of recognizing and becoming inured to beauty and to hard work. In his father's workshop, he learned to model clay and work marble. At the Vatican he "saw" the classics and became "accustomed to beauty." At the age of 24, he sculpted the perfect *Martyrdom of Saint Lawrence*. Soon he achieved maximum virtuosity in still mannerist works such as *Pluto* and *Proserpina* or *Apollo and Daphne*, where marble becomes fleshy as it yields to the pressure of Pluto's or Apollo's fingers.

Bernini reinterpreted the theme of David by adding muscular tension to emotional tension. He "petrified" the expressions to such an extent that, as a contemporary said, "the subject looked like his portrait." His study of sculpture's relation to space and light led him to decoration, architecture, and urban planning.

It is difficult to pass through Rome without coming upon some trace of Bernini, such as the Angels of the Santangelo Bridge or amazing fountains carved in Travertine marble. In the best known of these, the *Four Rivers* fountain, or in the *Elephantine*, using an anachronistic style, we could say that he recycled obelisks and linked them to his sculpture.

Anticipating the psychology of perception, he believed that "in order to imitate what is natural well, one must do what does not appear in nature." Thus, in order to correct optical distortions, for example, he sculpted a subtly larger hand suspended in the air or reflected the effects of the mystic being pierced by the arrow before the angel had let loose the arrow.

The Cornaro chapel (1647–1652), the fascinating scene of the *Ecstasy of Saint Teresa of Avila*, is his masterpiece and synthesizes the Baroque ideal. In it he composed and contrasted individuals, expressions, and poses. In the central theme, the lightness of what seems to be more Cupid than Angel contrasts with the Saint, whose heavy body floats among clouds. The clothing transmits spiritual agitation and the face transmits the placidity of ecstasy. Bernini modified the architecture to achieve his preferred top lighting and completed the scene—behind the back of the viewer—with some distracted figures framed in a balustrade of brightly colored marbles against a ground formed by a relief that best creates the illusion of depth. As a whole, the scene allows for erotic as well as skeptical connotations. Of the eight *witnesses* to the miracle, not one of them looks toward the altar.

Bernini also worked in France, having been introduced by the cardinals who supported Louis XIV. There his work influenced such sculptors as Falconet, Girardon, or Coysevox, the court's great portraitist. The mark of his style is evident in Puget, especially in his *Milo of Crotona*, attacked by a lion.

After the Baroque, the Neoclassicists—Canova is the most admired of these—again took inspiration from classical antiquity. Their workshops, thanks to a system of reproduction by points, began to create an enormous amount of work of impeccable manufacture. However, although they sought to follow Winckelmann's method of "ardent sketch and phlegmatic execution," they did not achieve his objective of "imitating the Greek statues in order to be inimitable," and their delicate marbles that did not incorporate the optical corrections urged by Bernini transmit more a sense of the fragility of porcelain than the strength of stone.

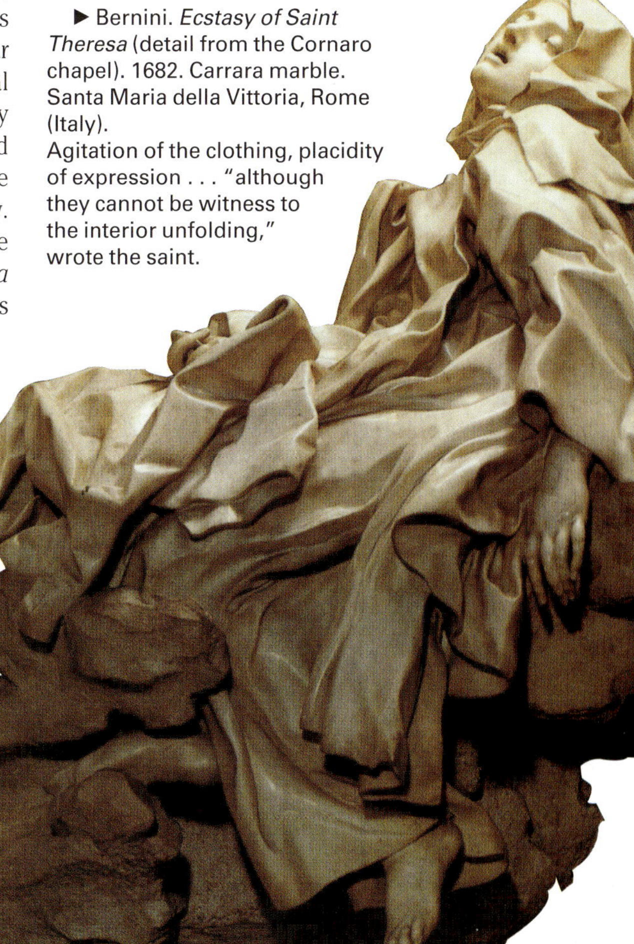

▶ Bernini. *Ecstasy of Saint Theresa* (detail from the Cornaro chapel). 1682. Carrara marble. Santa Maria della Vittoria, Rome (Italy).
Agitation of the clothing, placidity of expression . . . "although they cannot be witness to the interior unfolding," wrote the saint.

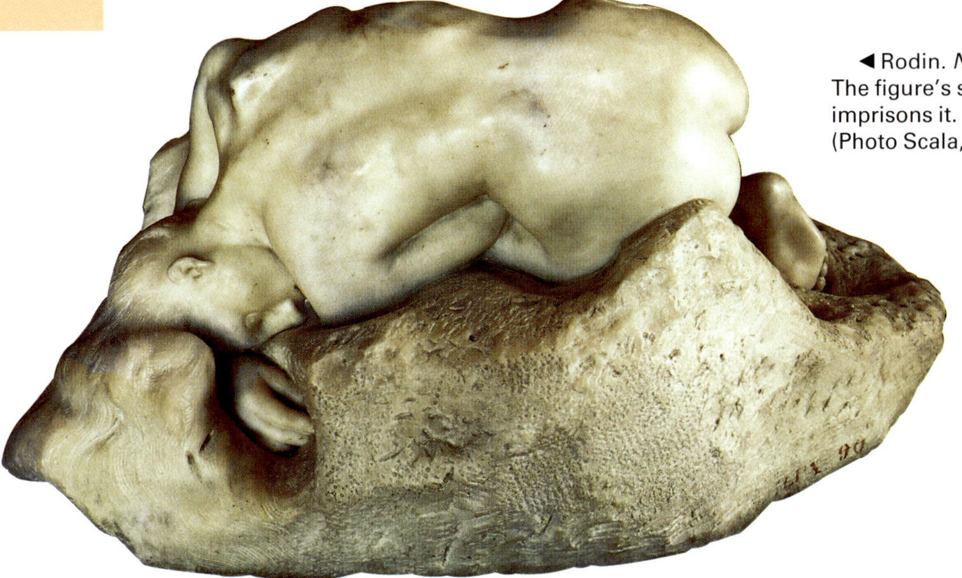

◀ Rodin. *Naiade*. Circa 1889. Marble.
The figure's struggle to free itself from the marble that imprisons it.
(Photo Scala, Florence).

Following the French Revolution, the collapse of absolute monarchy and the authoritarian Napoleon, sculpture was left bereft of a Mecenas and weakened. Moreover, the new fashion declared it antiromantic until 1832 when Rude carved the passionate and revolutionary *Marseillaise* for the Arc de Triomphe in the middle of the Place de l'Etoile in Paris. Its figures, taken from mythologized history, advance with grandiloquent expressions, stridently urging the people to rid themselves of resurgent absolutism, relying on the bourgeoisie. As the middle class increased its power, it built monuments on the thoroughfares of cities for the glory of its new heroes and built public parks that emulated the private gardens of the toppled monarchs.

The Waning of the Academies

While Nietzsche was announcing the death of God, sculpture fled the churches and populated the new cemeteries with sadness, melancholy, and despair. Following the great wars, funeral monuments returned to the cities but became more bellicose than intimate.

Nietzsche also foretold the coming of a Superman who would be born Communist or Nazi well into the twentieth century. Their masters, old men enamored of power, would commission sculptors to broadcast, in hard granite, the portrait of the supposed New Man, from the Olympic stadium in Rome to the Moscow metro. The style of Rude remained alive in these sculptures, although the worker protagonists, taking destiny into their own hands, became hardened and more contemporary. However, after World War II and the end of the Cold War these gods in turn would fall and with them their statues.

If we forget grandiloquent expression and return to the workshops of the nineteenth century, we will find Carpeaux capturing the expression of joy (*The Dance*) or Blai portraying abandonment and absolute human frailty (*The First Chills*) in stone. Then followed years of controversy; the Eiffel Tower and the new technologies called into question the millennial aesthetic that was reluctant to die. Modernism, despite its name and some attempts by Bourdelle, Metzner, or Gargallo later taken up by Art Deco, became folkloric but, because it was still considered too innovative, with the dawn of the twentieth century the focus again turned to classical themes.

A conception of sculpture that simple people could understand and be moved by was reaching its twilight and was perhaps buried in 1919 with the exposition of the last work by the young Julio Antonio, the *Lemonier Mausoleum*. Perez de Ayala described the event: "From the sovereign to the artisan, the entire population of Madrid came to see the marble and bronze statue."

Material, Form, and Space

In 1834 the Academy in Florence decided to remove Michelangelo's unfinished *Saint Matthew* from storage at the cathedral and exhibit it so that "the entire world could admire the potent fantasy of . . . the artist who knew how to rise from the material to the idea."

When the adult Auguste Rodin, who was rejected three times by the School of Fine Arts in Paris, traveled to Italy in 1875, he was infected by the sculptural spirit of Michelangelo. Upon his return, he divided Parisian criticism that failed to recognize his worth until 1900 when his first individual show challenged the traditional sculpture that packed the Grand Palais. Although his works exude the symbolic religious poetics of the period and, like Medardo Rosso and the Impressionists, explore the effects of light, what remains is his figures' struggle to free themselves from the block of marble that imprisons them. All sculptors have witnessed the precise moment when the material releases its secrets but only Rodin knew how to check the work of his laborers at the moment of maximum tension.

The Florentine Academy's decision to reclaim Michelangelo's unfinished work was the prelude to a new conception of sculpture but, as would later happen with Rodin, the authorities did not dare to fund it because the public at large was divorced from the hermeticism of the critical world. In addition, because of some forgeries of Michelangelo's work, direct carving was mythologized and necessarily limited ideas and size.

The principles of modern stone sculpture are strict. Ultramodern artists are practically unaware of it. In addition, the U.S. dollar, the major engine of modern art, trades in the new painting as it trades shares on the market and overlooks recently carved stone while it buys, packs up, and transports medieval churches and cloisters.

And so it goes. New stone sculpture hides in workshop catacombs. When it comes to light, it is timid and small and backed by the prestigious signature of artists who, researching other materials as well, cleanse art of mythical and literary elements in an effort to make sculpture, like art, relate directly to feelings.

While Camille Claudelle, who was so close to Rodin, gave free rein to the emotions, energetically rending forms, Gauguin imported from Tahiti a fresh, original, free, and culturally unfettered style. Derain and later De Creeft would continue to be faithful to the primitivist aesthetic and direct carving of stone. At the same time, others took Gauguin's contribution in the direction of expressionism or neo-expressionism with forms that no longer pursue beauty but rather a catharsis that is more individual than collective.

In contrast, the painter Cezanne, with his enthusiasm for eliminating the transitory to concentrate on the permanent and his geometric conception of nature, would open up new directions for sculpture: cubism, constructivism, and so on. Epstein, Lipchitz, Archipenko, Zadkine, Modigliani, or Giacometti, pursuing abstractionism, simplified forms, repeated them to create rhythms or emptied them out. Among this group, Brancusi set himself up as the obsessive prophet of pure form.

The theories of Freud supported the work of Arp, Miro, or Bourgeois, who preferred to give marble voluptuous shapes without renouncing the abstract, which had become the dogma of a sculpture that claimed to be antidogmatic. Despite this, decades later Mitoraj would recover classical forms and reinterpret them, taking inspiration from dream worlds.

But public statuary distrusted abstraction. Gropius was the only architect who dared to build a fully abstract monument, although it was in concrete. In isolated fashion, Brancusi anticipated the unrest of the end of the century and built a totally abstract three-part series in Tirgu Jiu (Romania, 1938) that redefines nature. His collaborator Noguchi proposed more daring urban projects but could not find anyone to finance them.

By 1953 the new sculpture was sufficiently mature to rise up in a competition organized in London to pay homage to the unknown political prisoner. Then a new dogma arose—the subject limits creativity; the creator's intuition precedes the commission. A composition by Barbara Hepworth made of different types of marbles was among the finalist maquettes.

Starting in 1958 when UNESCO commissioned Henry Moore, abstract sculpture has taken hold of cities and transformed landscapes with such intensity that Moore himself, a fan of local stone, turned to bronze as a substitute in order to meet the demand.

Soon municipal governments grasped the emblematic significance of public sculpture and, with criteria more suited to eras of illustrated despotism, hired prestigious firms, perhaps unaware of concrete projects. And if the people continued to look for literature in abstract stone, the very critics who would not give sculptors this license would facilitate it for the people.

Fortunately, sculptors have known how to respond to this confidence and have carved pure forms (Max Bill, Minimal Art) or cyclopean monuments (Dodeigne). They have competed with architecture (Newman), have created habitable spaces (Singer), have opened pathways of stone, light, and water (Karavan), or have exported the serenity of the Japanese garden to asphalt cities (Noguchi). Others, recovering impoverished landscapes (Long) and designing quarries (Chillida), have warned us of a new death—the death of the planet (*Land Art* and *Arte Povera*).

At the dawn of the twenty-first century, the sculptor has already shown that he is qualified to work elbow to elbow with the architect, the sociologist and the urban planner. In the age of virtual reality, more than ever we need to reaffirm our human identity in the shelter of solid rock, magnetized by its power.

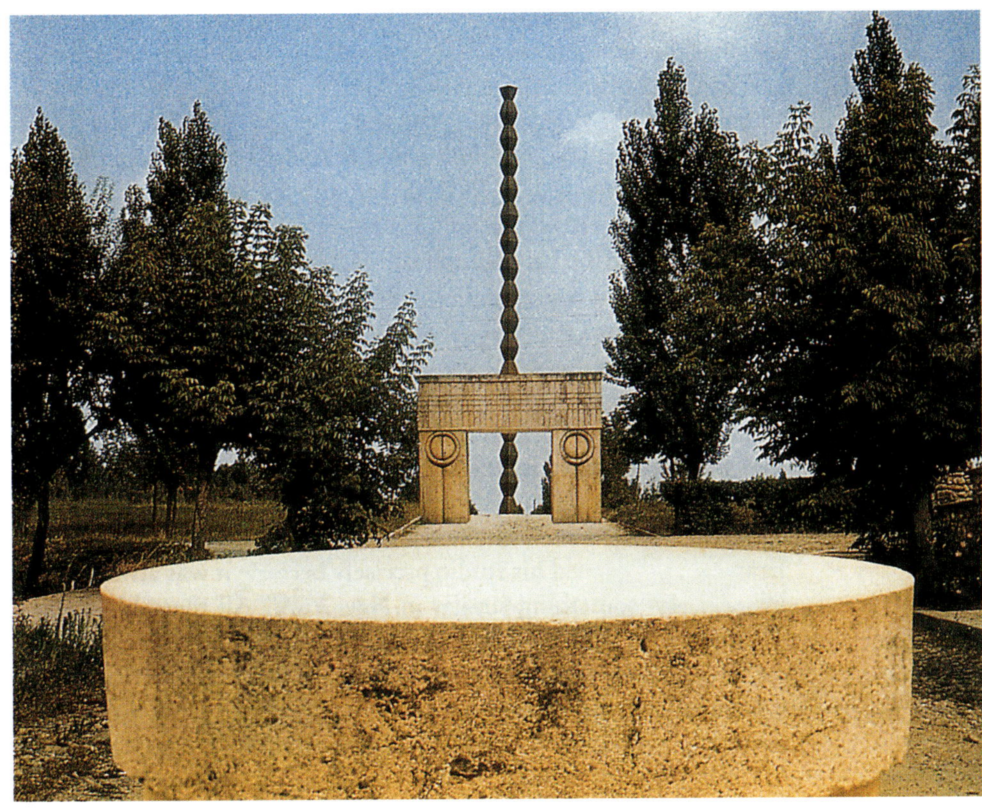

▲ Brancusi.
World War Memorial. 1938.
Tirgu Jiu (Romania).
Composed of: *Table of Silence*, limestone.
Gate of the Kiss, Travertine marble.
Endless Column, metal.
Sculpture, taking shape in open space, transforms the environment.

▼ Noguchi. *Energy Fountain* (detail from California Scenario). Circa 1983. Granite.
Costa Mesa (United States).
The trajectory of this artist shows that the sculptor and urban planner must work together.

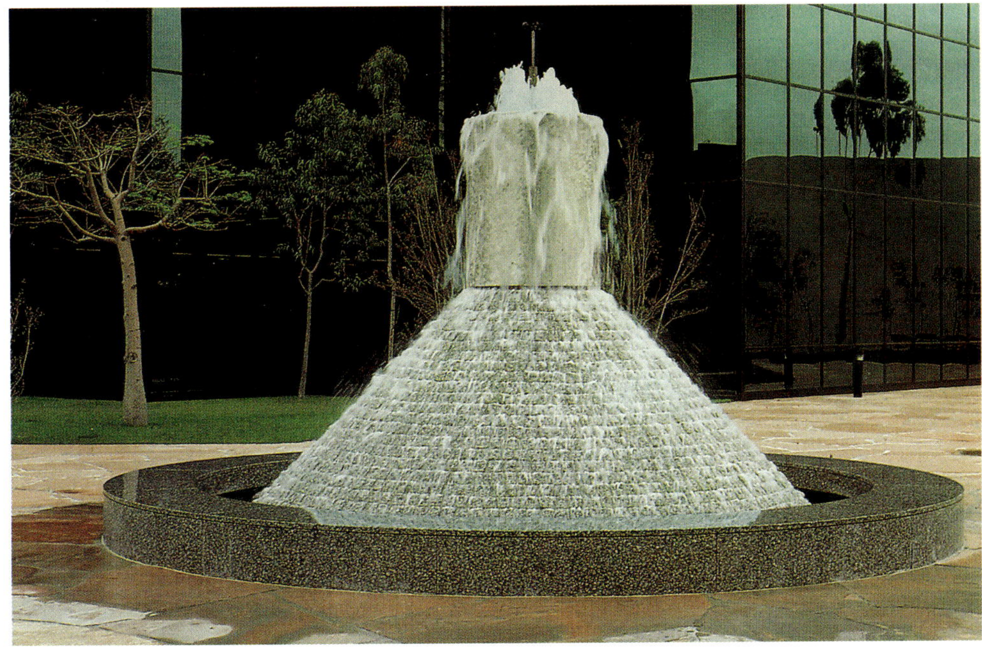

Sculpture over Time

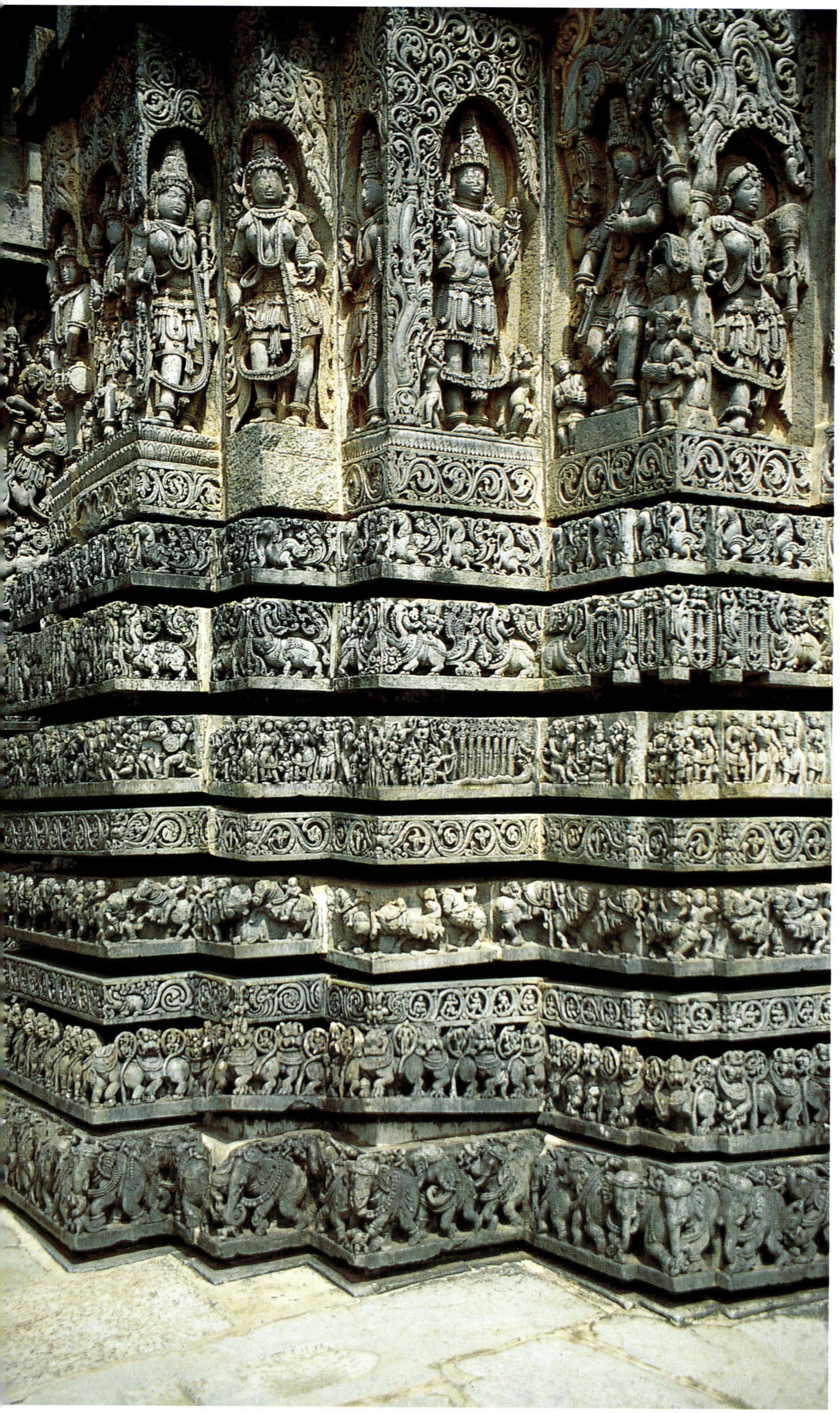

◀ Detail of the Dravide temple at Halebid.
1141. Chloritic slate.
Halebid, Mysore, Karnataka (India).

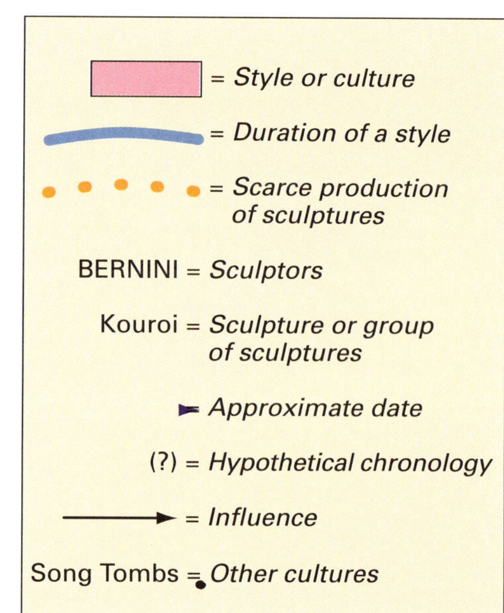

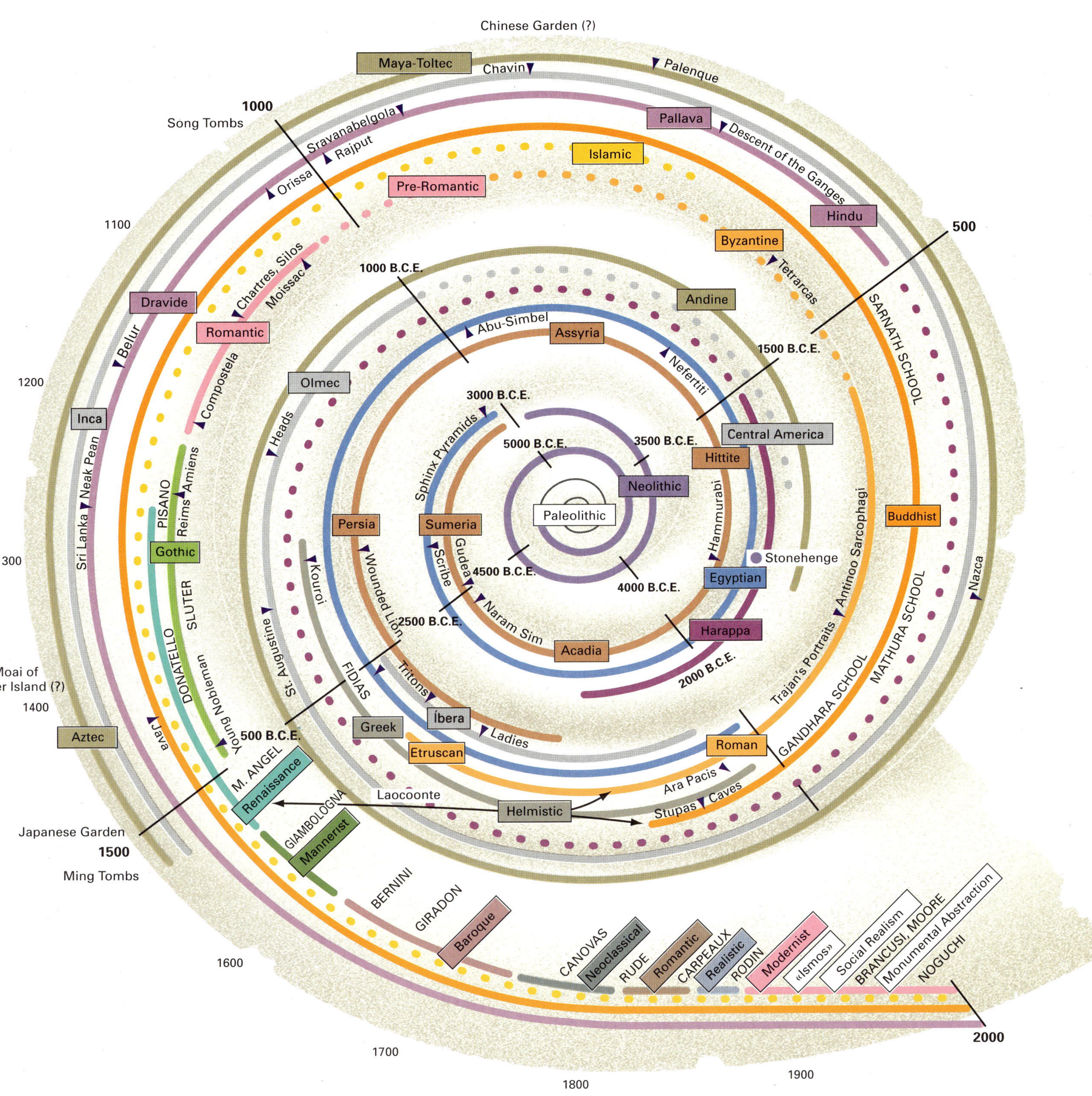
Chinese Garden (?)
Maya-Toltec
Chavin
Palenque
1000
Song Tombs
Sravanabelgola
Rajput
Orissa
Pallava
Descent of the Ganges
Islamic
Pre-Romantic
Hindu
500
Byzantine
Tetrarcas
1100
Chartres, Silos
Moissac
Dravide
Belur
Romantic
Compostela
1000 B.C.E.
Abu-Simbel
Assyria
Andine
SARNATH SCHOOL
Nefertiti
1500 B.C.E.
1200
Olmec
Inca
Neak Pean
Heads
3000 B.C.E.
Sphinx Pyramids
5000 B.C.E.
3500 B.C.E.
Central America
Hittite
Amiens
Reims
PISANO
Neolithic
Paleolithic
Hammurabi
Persia
Sumeria
Buddhist
Gothic
Sri Lanka
Kouroi
Wounded Lion
Scribe
Gudea
4500 B.C.E.
4000 B.C.E.
Stonehenge
Egyptian
Antinoo Sarcophagi
Nazca
1300
SLUTER
St. Augustine
Naram Sim
2500 B.C.E.
Acadia
Harappa
2000 B.C.E.
DONATELLO
Young Nobleman
FIDIAS
Tritons
Trajan's Portraits
MATHURA SCHOOL
Moai of
er Island (?)
1400
Aztec
Java
500 B.C.E.
Greek
Ibera
Ladies
Etruscan
GANDHARA SCHOOL
Roman
M. ANGEL
Renaissance
Ara Pacis
Laocoonte
GIAMBOLOGNA
Helmistic
Stupas
Caves
Japanese Garden
1500
Mannerist
Ming Tombs
BERNINI
GIRADON
Baroque
1600
CANOVAS
Neoclassical
RUDE
Romantic
CARPEAUX
Realistic
RODIN
Modernist
«Ismos»
Social Realism
BRANCUSI, MOORE
Monumental Abstraction
NOGUCHI
2000
1700
1800
1900

Stone

Before carving the stone, the sculptor should know about its characteristics so that his work will be more productive. Therefore, in this chapter we include some geological information, particularly information that we believe might prove useful to us regarding stone formation, composition, structure, and so on. It is also important to anticipate carving problems and be knowledgeable about the great variety of stones that are available so that we can choose the most suitable stone. Thus, we provide information and images of the stones we recommend; however, for practical reasons we will describe their use in the market rather than classify them in scientific terms. In addition, we will provide information on the work done in quarries and will end the chapter with a map locating major beds and natural sculptural landscapes.

Do you know why I prefer marble?
Especially for the way it radiates light,
its toughness, precision, and response to the Sun.
Barbara Hepworth

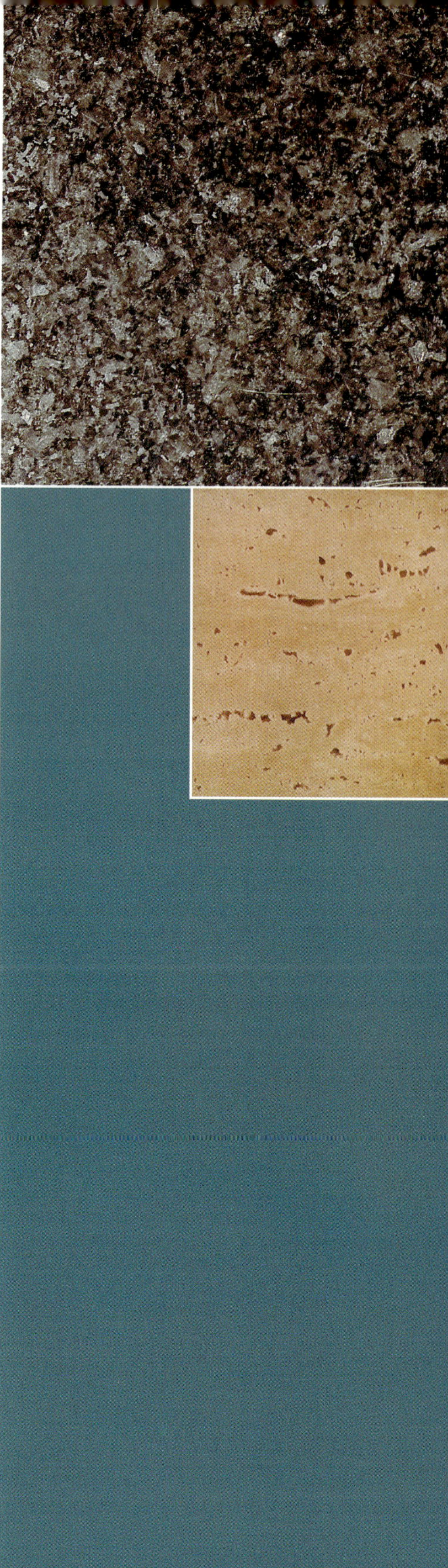

► One of the quarries next to the mythical Carrara (Italy).

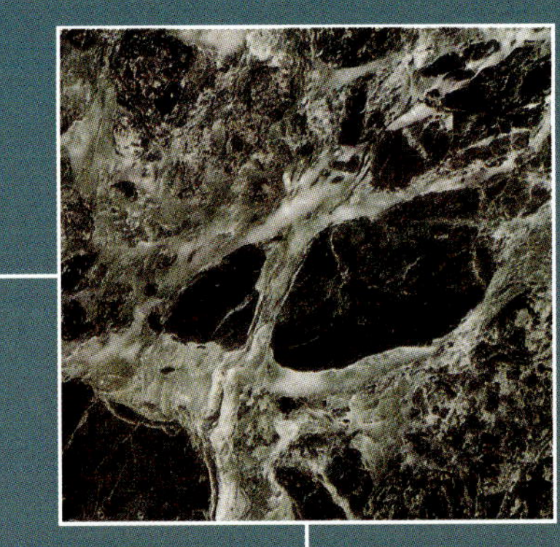

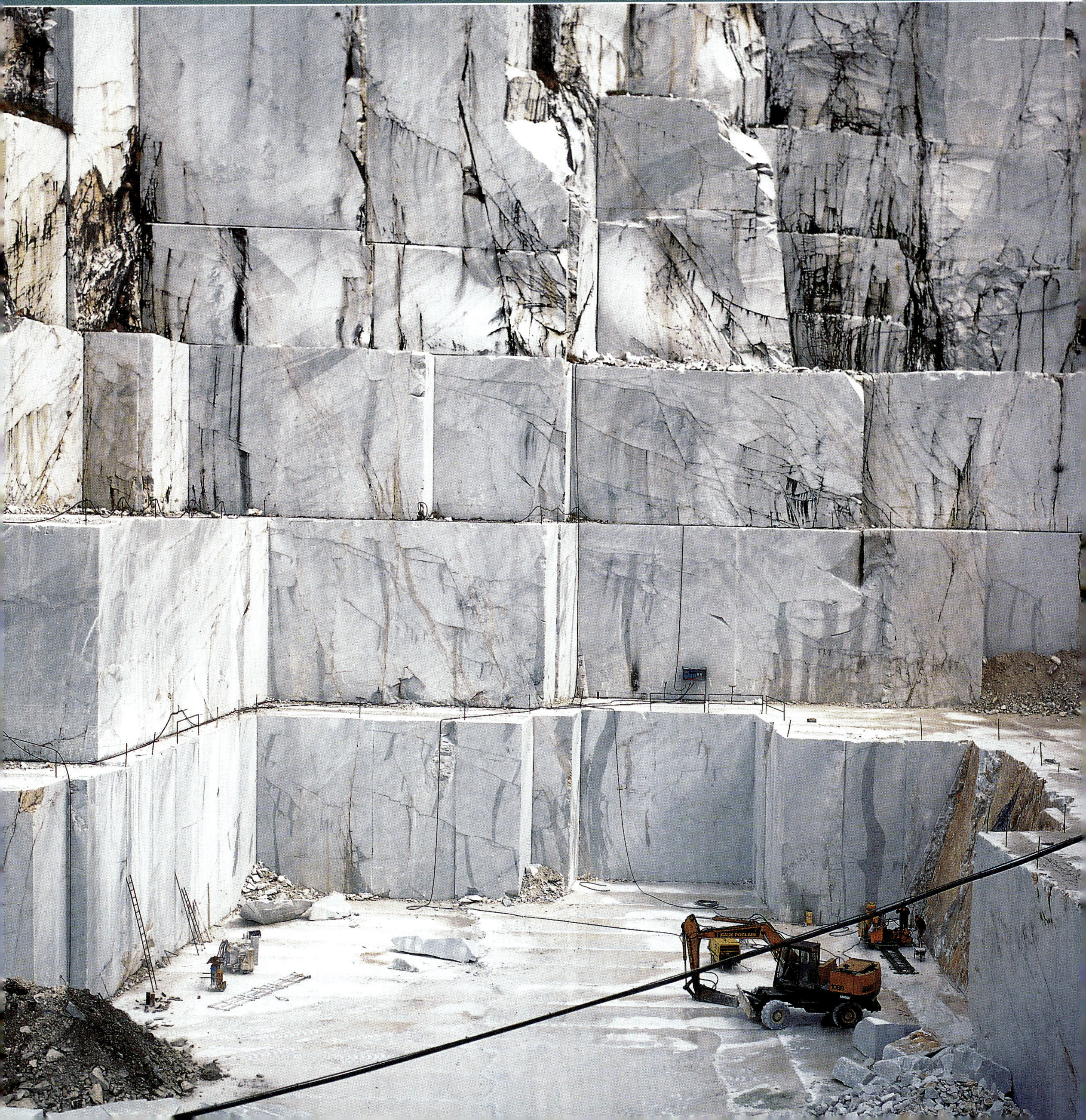

Tu est Petrus

Before carving a stone it is best to know not only its physical characteristics but its emotional characteristics as well. The greater our involvement with the material, the greater the artistry we can wrest from it.

Stone symbolism is present in all cultures. We have already seen that menhirs have been erected since prehistoric times. Religious historians explain that this is because of the belief, in Neolithic Britain and in animist Africa, that upright stones pacified and retained the souls of ancestors and their presence fertilized the soil and attracted beneficial rain. They also mention the Vietnamese belief that stones harbor protective spirits that ward off evil influences. In addition, they describe similar rituals among the Bretons and Hindus who called on the menhir or lingam to cure sterility.

The dolmen, with its uterine references, is considered the dwelling of ancestors who fertilize it. Perforated stones with a similar meaning appear in ancient Asia or Australia and serve as symbols of the cosmic female principle. Rituals are performed before them based on the belief that they regenerate, fertilize, or protect from harm the part of the body that it is inserted in them.

Another very widespread custom, in the Peruvian Andes or in Siberia, over Hebrew tombs or Islamic hills, is the stacking of stones. They usually have a ritual character but even when they indicate pathways, boundaries, or wells, they are surrounded by an aura of respect in that they symbolize the collective will, the power of the group multiplying the power of the individual.

Before reaching their goal, both Muslims on a hadj to Mecca and Christians on a pilgrimage to Santiago de Compostela hurl stones in a specific spot as part of a purification ritual. This custom of transferring evil to stone is a practice common to many of the world's peoples and is frequently used to curse someone shunned by the community, either directly by throwing stones or with fetishistic rituals.

The power of stone survives as a symbol of the divine presence in the great religions. The Ark of the Covenant of the Hebrews rested on stone. In Delos a stone marked the navel of the Greek world. Jesus of Nazareth changed Saul's name to Peter (*Tu est Petrus* in the Vulgate) to indicate that Peter would be the cornerstone of his church. The Roman mass was traditionally celebrated on a marble altar. Even in the rationalist eighteenth century a basilica was built in Zaragoza (Spain) to house a small sacred pillar.

Various tribes in Australia, Indonesia, and North America believe that quartzite consists of fragments that have fallen from the celestial throne, and their shamans use it as a tool of prophecy. In effect, among all stones, it is stones that "shine" or meteorites that are most honored because they are imbued with the sacredness of the stars. Thus, the black stone of Pessinus (Asia Minor), the expression of Cybele, the mother goddess of the Phrygians, was transported to Rome with great ceremony and installed on the Palatine. It is said that the Holy Grail was carved from a stone that had fallen from Lucifer's forehead. Preserved in Tibet is the stone that the Dalai Lama received from the "King of the World," and in Mecca millions have sworn fidelity to the Ka'ba, the right hand of Allah.

Based on falling meteorites, many peoples have speculated on the formation of the heavens and an immense crater was discovered in China. For this reason, Taoists prepared potions of immortality with the stalactites hanging from replicas of the great cave of the universe.

Although all religions confer spiritual powers on stone, none of them idolizes it because for them stone is merely a receptacle of the power it symbolizes or houses. Nonetheless, there has always been speculation regarding the beneficial powers of some stones, particularly precious stones, and many people attest to their efficacy. However, since different cultures attribute different powers to the same stone, we feel that all stones have strong powers of suggestion that are even capable of activating the immune system.

People have also theorized about the symbolism of stone, particularly in Europe of the Middle Ages and specifically among the Masons. It is said that stone is synonymous with knowledge, stability, balance, and even, when not carved, with freedom.

Thus, the sculptor has in his hands a material that can be imbued with his emotions and transmits them to others. Given this responsibility, before cutting into the natural shape of stone, we should ponder the biblical warning: ". . . if you wield your tool on it, you will profane it" (Exodus, 20:25).

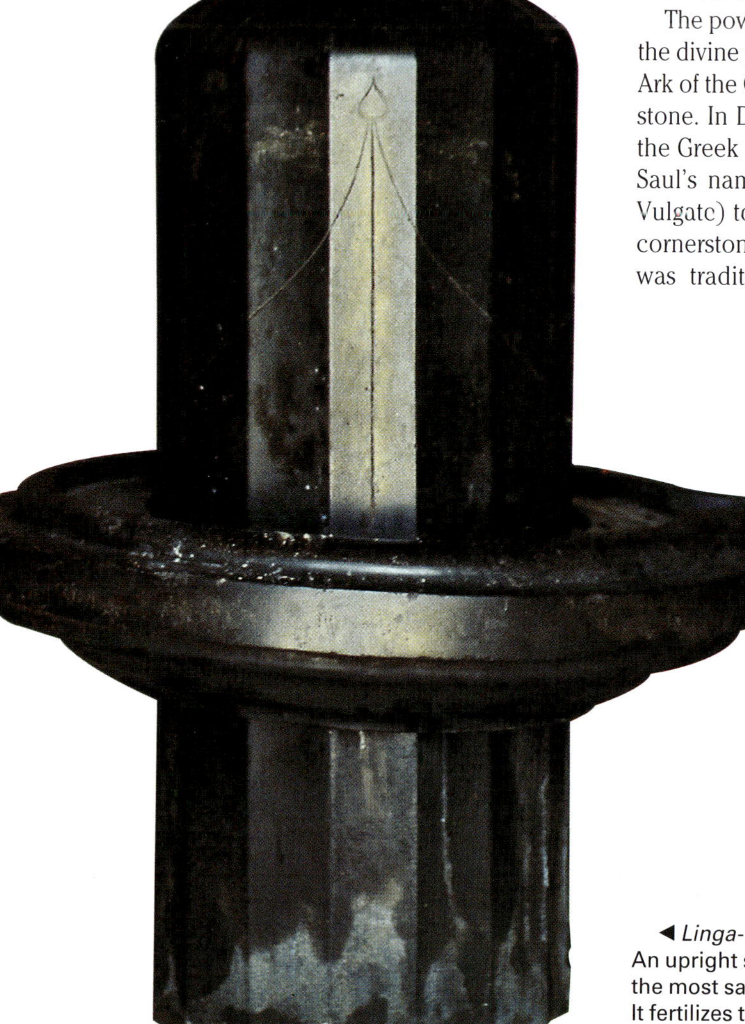

◄ *Linga-Yoni.* Mahaballipuran (India). An upright stone, symbol of Siva, occupies the most sacred place in Siva's temples. It fertilizes the space and regenerates the cosmos.

Every Stone, a World

The solid crust of the earth's surface consists of large rocks called stones when they are fragmented. Each rock is the result of a random combination of minerals, so that it is practically impossible to find two rocks exactly alike. Even two rocks formed of the same minerals may have been subject to various chemical, magnetic, or eroding influences that make them different.

Given the infinite variety of these combinations, geologists distinguish between the essential minerals that make up rock (the most abundant), accessory elements, and accidental elements (the remainder). The sculptor is interested in knowing about the essential minerals of the stone he is carving, as any difficulty in carving is due to those minerals. Hard but brilliant silica and malleable limestone are the most abundant of the statuary stones. There may be other minerals mixed in with them that provide texture and color. For example, marble is primarily limestone (essential), but it may also contain arabesques of dolomite or graphite (accessory) and fossil remains (accidental) or be tinged with iron oxide.

Based on the essential mineral, we classify the stones in the table into two large groups, silicates and carbonates, according to their composition. This will help us to understand their similarities.

The stone industry operates in a demanding construction market, to which it supplies precise data on the chemical composition of each stone it offers, providing additional information on density, resistance to bending, impact, compression, and friction, ability to absorb moisture, normal lifespan, and so on. However, among these data that are difficult to interpret because there is still no universal yardstick, the sculptor is primarily concerned with:

Specific weight: Often calculated in kg/m^2. A simple list of stones ranging from lightest to heaviest would be: basalt, granite, marble, limestone, sandstone.

Hardness: Knowing this is important so that you can use the most suitable tools. The conventional and unscientific *Mohs' scale* does not help us very much because all statuary stones would fall between 3 and 5 on this scale. Stones that contain quartz, the most compact stones, heavy stones, and fine-grain stones are the hardest.

Resilience or impact resistance: Hard stones tend to be resilient and soft stones to be fragile but this is not always the case. The same stone may turn out to be resilient when hit in a direction opposite to its growth pattern and fragile when its layers, visible in the form of seams, are separated.

Workability or ability to be carved and polished: Soft, compact, and fine- and uniform-grain stones such as alabaster or marble are most generous to the sculptor. All recently quarried stones are worked more easily because they become harder later as they lose moisture.

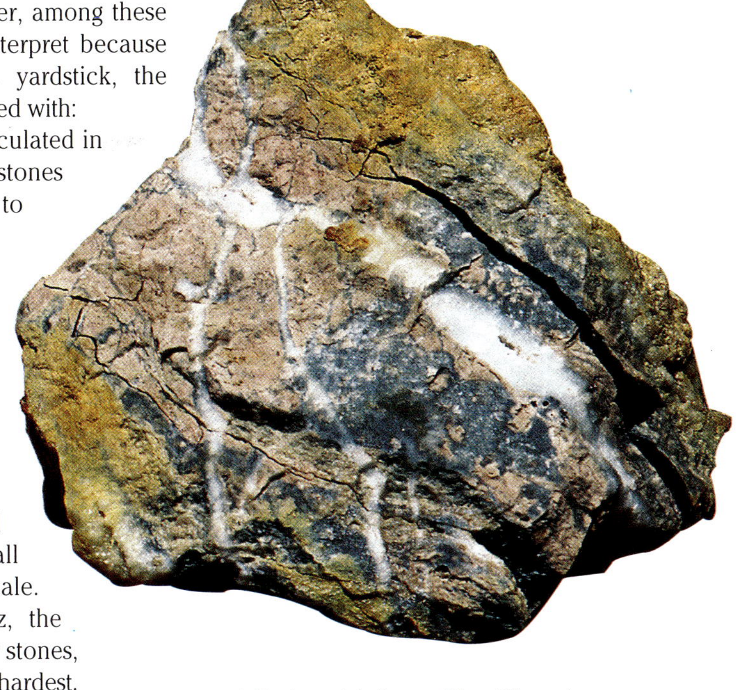

▲ Each rock is formed by different minerals and undergoes a continuous, although slow, process of transformation.

But, always with a view to carving, classification according to essential minerals is not enough because sandstone behaves more like limestone than granite. In addition, the characteristics we have mentioned are also the result of the rock formation process and it is thus advisable to know the origin of the rock.

GROUP	VARIANTS	EXAMPLES	CHARACTERISTICS
Silicates	Silica	Granite, quartzite, sandstone	Vitreous
	Feldspars	Basalt, gabbro	
Carbonates	Crystallized	Diamond, graphite	Not suitable for sculpture
	Amorphous	Living organisms	
	Petrified	Limestone, alabaster, marble, travertine	Easy to carve

The Life Cycle of Stone

The earth's crust is constantly evolving and the same mineral may melt deep inside the earth and then freeze when it reaches the surface (igneous rocks). In this process, it may change stones that come into contact with it (metamorphic rocks). Wind and weather will erode any mineral, but over millennia its particles may recombine until they form a new rock (sedimentary rocks). Thus, the same mineral, quartz, for example, may give rise to stones that are as different as granite and sandstone.

On the following page we include some charts to help you understand these processes since they determine what quarrymen and sculptors call *law*, a concept that defines the order in which stone grows, which should not be contradicted when carving.

Based on their evolution, rocks are classified as follows:

► Section of mountain opened up for a highway. You can see how the sedimentary strata changed direction when a new range rose up, in this case the Iberian System.

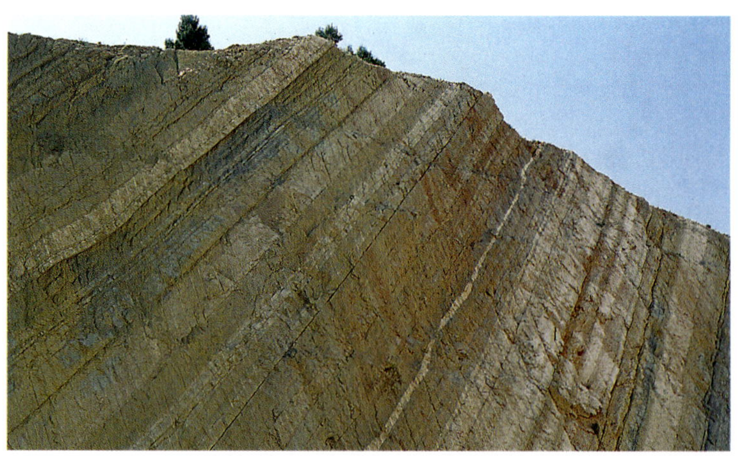

► Recently sedimented clays. The material carried along by different floods, some longer lasting than others, form strata that over time become compacted until they form sandstone. However, an abrupt change in temperature or pressure could also metamorphose these clays and transform them into slate.

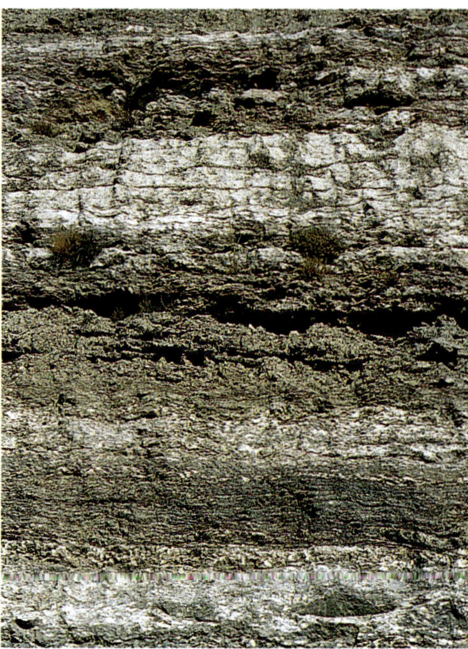

GROUP	VARIANTS	FORMATION	EXAMPLES	CHARACTERISTICS
Igneous	Intrusive	Slow cooling inside the earth	Granite, diorite, obsidian	Vitreous, dense, very hard, solid, good polish
	Extrusive	Rapid cooling on the surface	Basalt	
	Seamed	Magma introduced in fissures in other rocks	Porphyry	
	Eruptive	Abrupt cooling	Tuff, pumice	Limited workability
Sedimentary	Detrital	Agglomeration of sand	Sandstone	Cannot be polished
	Organic	Remains of marine organisms	Limestone	Easy to carve, porous
	Chemical	Precipitation of salts	Alabaster, travertine	Irregular, can be polished
Metamorphic	Orthometamorphic	Igneous, metamorphosed	Gneiss, serpentine	Very hard
	Parametamorphic	Sandstones	Quartzite	
		Clays	Slates	Splintery, not suitable for carving
		Limestones	Marbles	Ideal for carving

▼ Another form of sedimentation more characteristic of carbonates; salts dissolved in water bind together and form curious shapes that are overlaid after every period of rain.

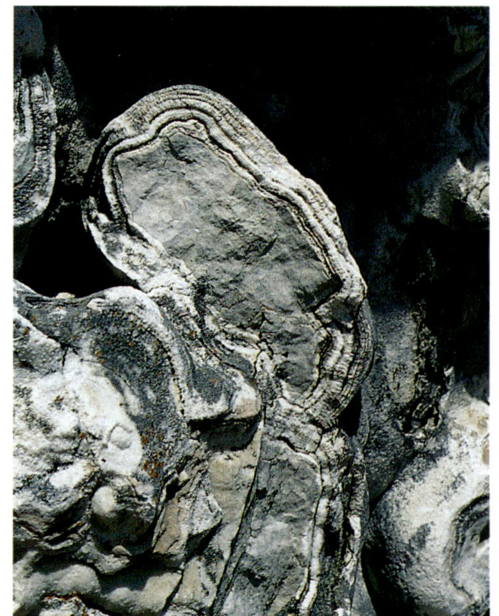

► Schematic drawing showing the location of the different types of stone in an imaginary landscape. After a magma eruption, pressure and heat intensively metamorphose the closest sedimentary rocks, but have a lesser effect on rock that is farther away, sometimes making it difficult to distinguish between marble and limestone, for example.

Alabaster and travertine are created by the precipitation of salts dissolved in water. This is similar to the way that stalagmites are formed. The difference is that travertine solidifies only in sulfurous water.

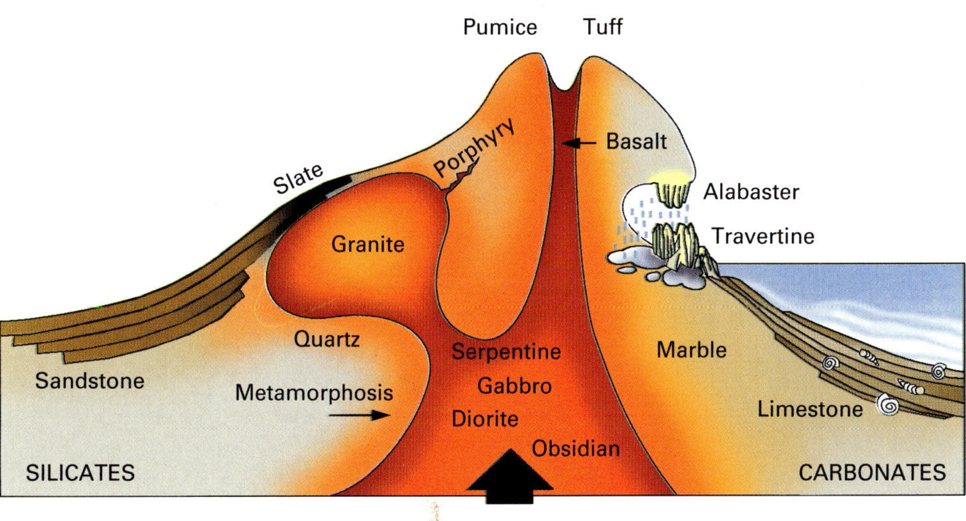

► Evolution of the same landscape after millions of years of erosion. Igneous rocks are more resistant and give rise, for example, to basaltic needles. The accumulation of sand or clay, rock waste, and organic detritus, particularly of the sea, will create new sandstone and limestone.

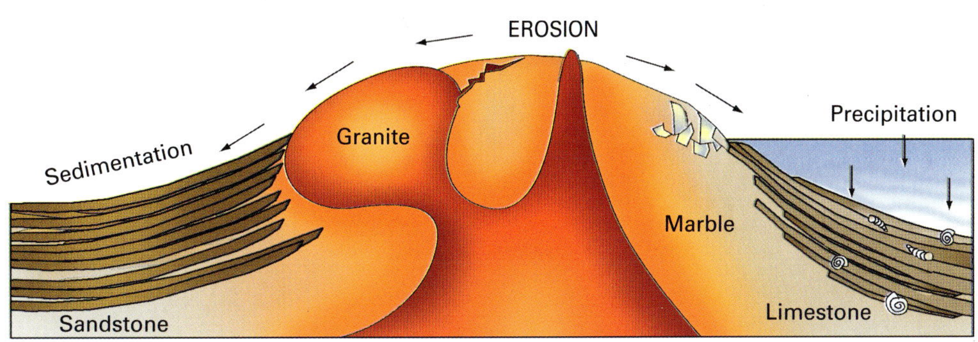

► What happens most often is that we find landscapes where the rocks do not appear in their original location. The emergence of new mountains and continental drift lead to pressures that move or fracture the rocks, particularly soft rocks, forming folds or faults.

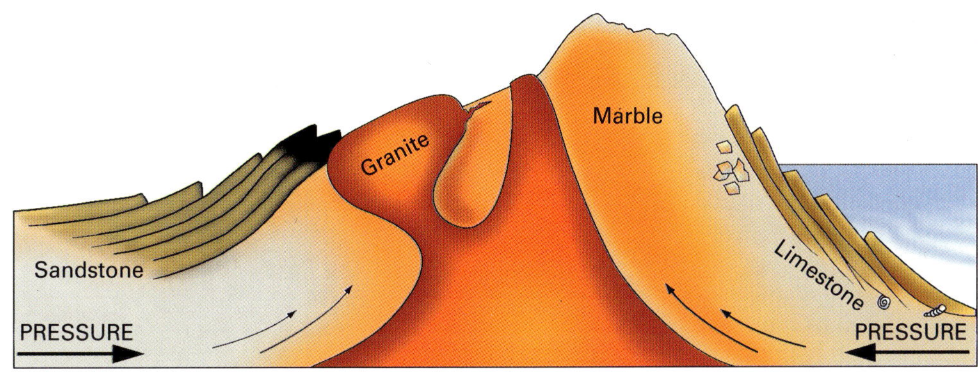

Carving the Earth's Crust

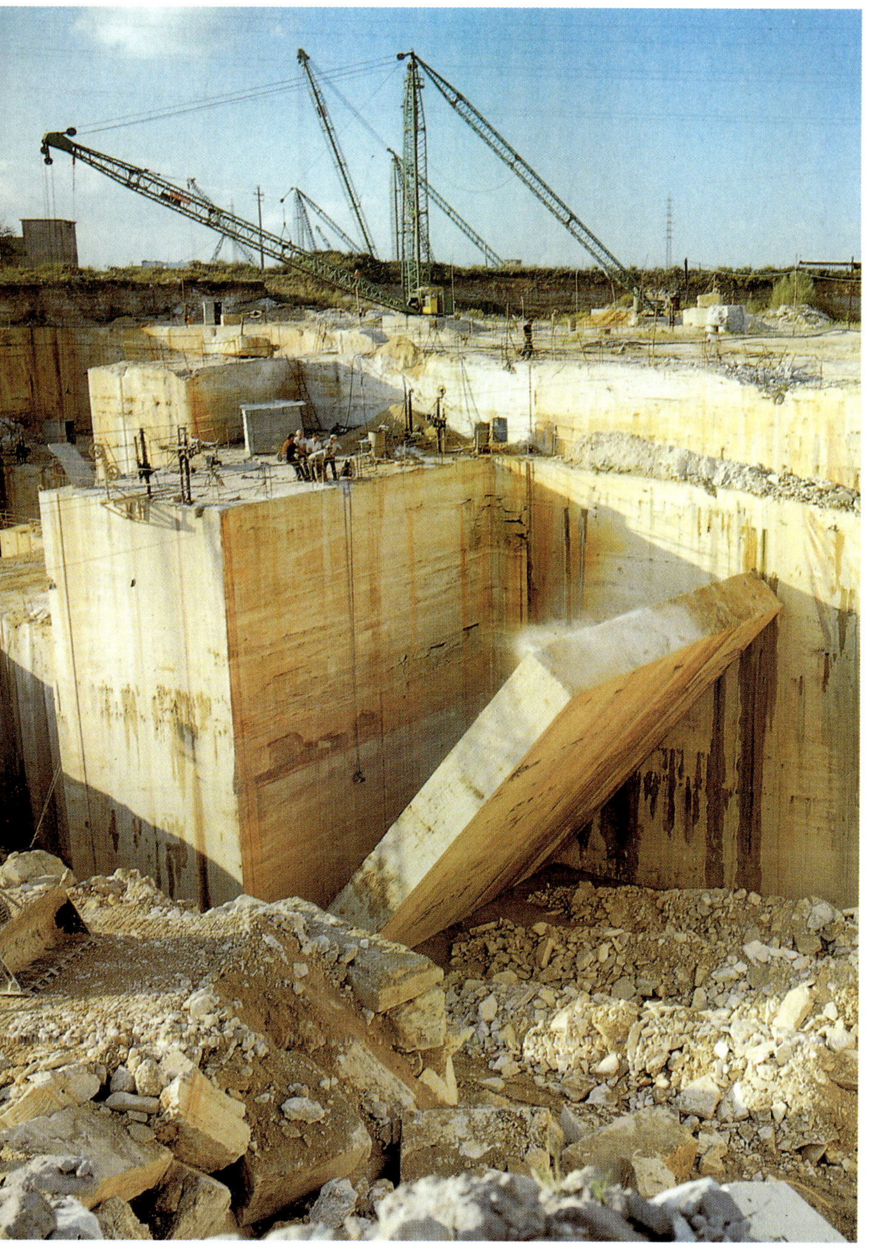

◀ Tivoli (Italy). Moving a slab of travertine.

As a result of the geological processes described, some of the world's areas have rocky formations of a quality that has since ancient times led humans to exploit them. These areas are called quarries.

Once these areas are found and the characteristics of the bed are defined through complex calculations, the work begins to clear away the surface layer and lay bare the rocks that will be sold.

Most quarries are excavated in the open air. However, after removing various layers of better-quality rock, it is possible to open up deep series of wells or follow a seam to dig out wide caverns inside a mountain.

A single bed may provide rocks with similar composition but varying quality. The general practice is to use all the material but for different purposes. Among marbles in particular, the purest stone is defined as statuary stone. When quarry workers find a good vein they follow it, in the belief that, as they say in Carrara with a fever reminiscent of gold fever, the best marble is right behind the marble being removed.

In ancient times, people broke up blocks of rock by inserting wooden poles that swelled with water and cracked the rock. They also planted orderly rows of certain trees with roots that served the same purpose. Although flint, picks, and metal poles have now replaced wood, success always depends on the quarry worker's skill in drilling into the rock at the right spot, as the goal is to split it at its weakest point, according to its pattern of growth.

In such cases it is enough to open up a few grooves or openings in the shape of a V following the direction of the vein and ease each wedge's movement with iron strips. Each wedge is hit with a mallet until the rock "sounds hollow." Levers are then used to remove the block from the rock.

After Nobel invented dynamite, special mass blasting was done for hard rock but this turned out to be uncontrollably hazardous. The method was later perfected by inserting small charges in the holes drilled with pneumatic hammers placed vertically and horizontally.

More recently, complex machinery that slides along rails has been installed in quarries. This machinery notably reduces the manpower needed and also produces perfectly square blocks, making the best possible use of natural resources. Some machinery, such as immense power saws, abrade the rock with a carborundum- or diamond-toothed chain that hangs from a movable arm. Another type of machinery moves a double set of enormous cutting disks placed vertically and horizontally. But the machinery used most often operates a pulley that pulls a continuous iron thread with or without diamond teeth, depending on the hardness of the rock. These thread saws allow for a clean cut with a minimum of wasted material.

▼ Carrara (Italy). Open-air marble quarry.

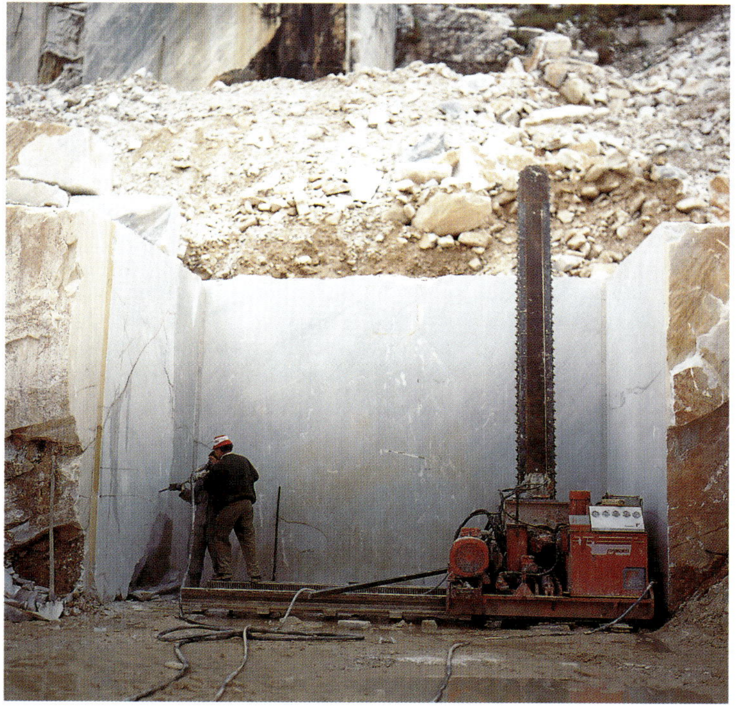

A thermal lance can be used to cut igneous rock with abrasion. Also under study is the use of laser beams, electron beams, ultrasound, or pressurized water jets.

We are far removed from the time when Michelangelo went to the quarry to select and direct the cutting of a block of stone. Today's sculptors must usually be content with the stones offered on the market before being sawn into thin architectural sheets.

Next to large quarries there are usually important industrial complexes that prepare stone according to market requirements. To pay off the machinery, they import huge blocks of stone from lesser quarries located in distant locations since ease of transport, particularly by sea, allows them to do this. For example, we shouldn't be surprised to find blocks of South African granite in the port of Carrara alongside native marble, or the green marble from India we obtained in the quarries of Macael (Spain), which we will use later in one of the exercises.

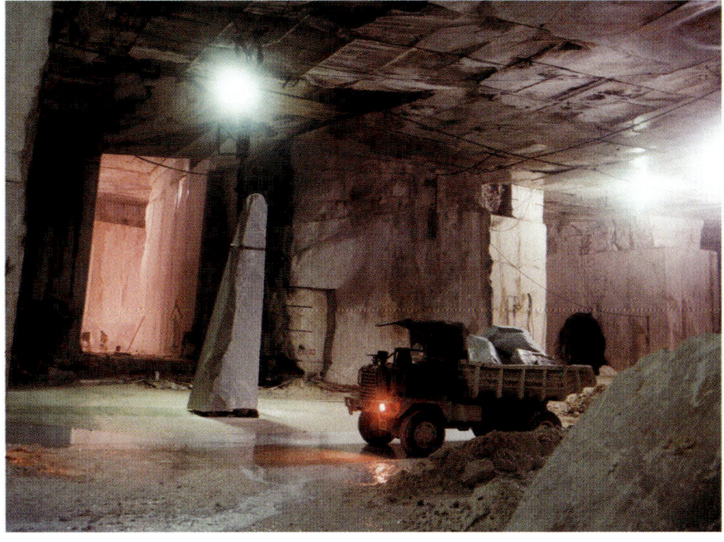

▲ Carrara (Italy). Underground marble quarry.

▼ Carrara (Italy). Marble quarry pit.

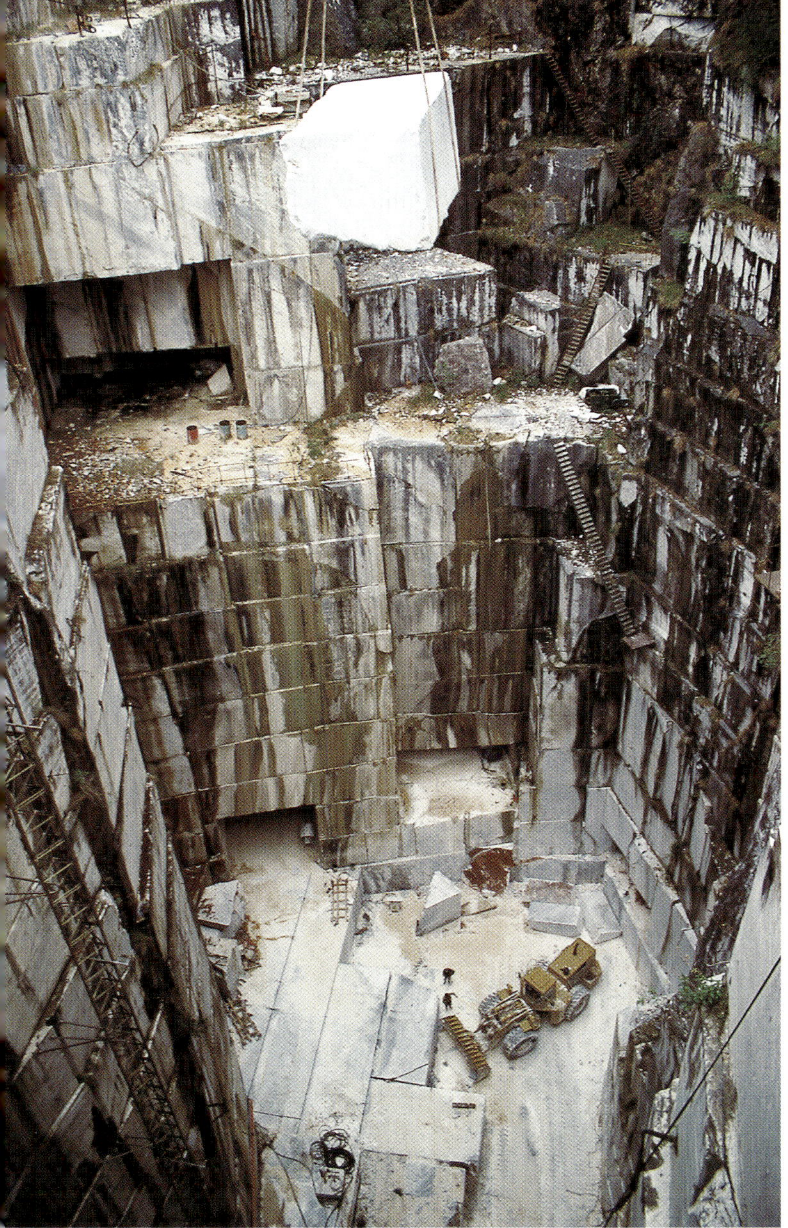

Among the most famous quarries in the history of sculpture are the quarries of Mount Pentelicon, near Athens, which gave life to the Parthenon, and the mountain quarries the Romans called "lunar" because of their color and that are now known by the name of the city that sells most of this stone: Carrara.

Obviously not all rocks are used for decoration or statuary. For example, mountains with alabaster are mined for gypsum and thus, explosives are still being used in these quarries. In addition, each quarry tries to make the best use of its resources. Thus, lower-quality marble can be broken up for mosaics, crushed for surfacing façades, or used as powder to cover the cement reproductions that are replacing original sculptures in the plazas of Italy. However, marble also strengthens our bones when we drink it dissolved in calcium-enriched milk.

▼ Port of Carrara (Italy). Stones from all around the world are stored here alongside the local marble.

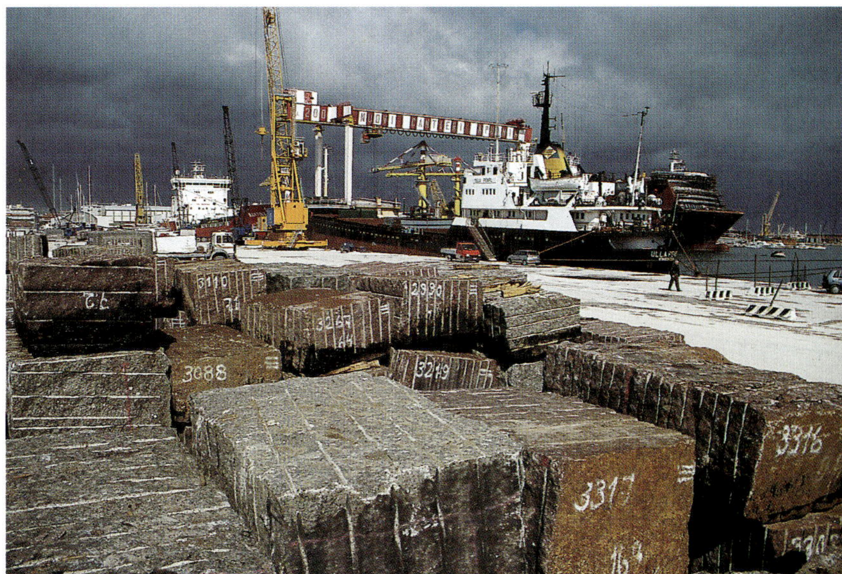

Stones

Under the general name of *stones*, the market supplies different rocks that generally coincide with what geologists call sedimentary rocks. A microscope reveals their structure, which is usually amorphous as they are the result of the overlapping of grains. When strata are separated, the break is usually flat, but it may also be uneven if the sediments were dissolved in water.

As an example of their variety, we show some polished stones and other stones as they appear when broken spontaneously. However, we recommend that you visit a warehouse or, even better, a sculptor's workshop to gain more detailed knowledge.

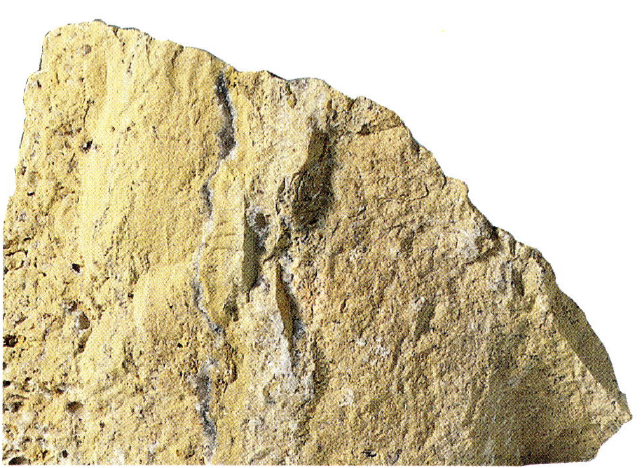

▲ Travertine.

▼ Limestone.

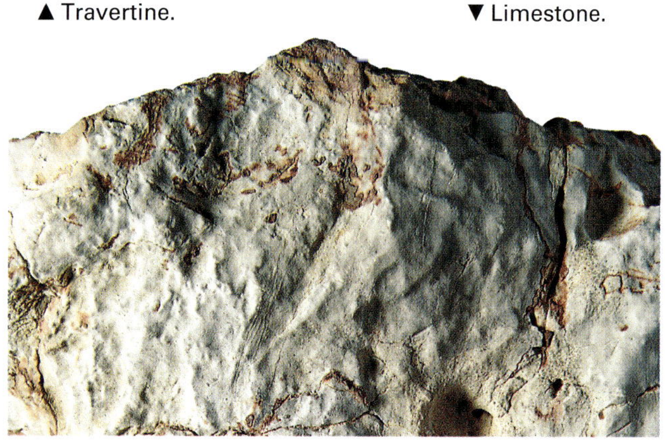

▼ Sandstone.

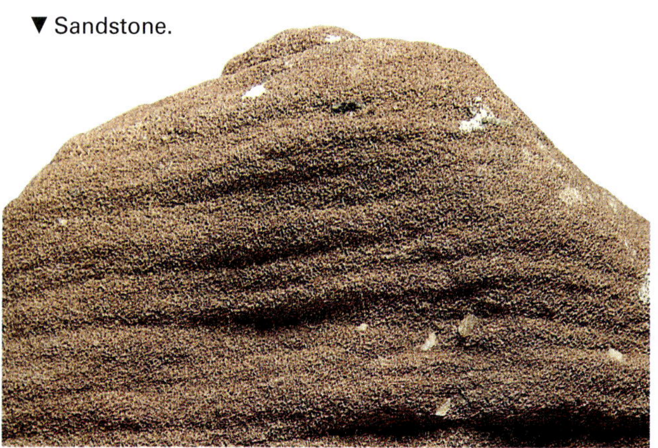

Alabaster

Alabaster is a generally white, veined, soft, translucent, and compact but fragile stone that is formed when calcium dissolved in water settles. It is similar to marble but lacks its consistency because it has not undergone metamorphosis. It is most often recommended for making the initial carving because it is easily worked and polished. However, because any knock can damage it, it is advisable to remove the more superficial layers of the block and the layers near the impact of the point chisel.

Alabaster was used in Egypt to carve containers for viscera. England exported numerous altars during the Middle Ages and during the Renaissance a *Transfiguration of Christ* by Berreguete topped the choir of the cathedral in Toledo (Spain). Chillida prefers alabaster for its luminosity, but other sculptors have stopped using it because its beauty draws our attention away from sculptural forms.

Travertine

Although we have described chalky alabaster, there are also limy alabasters such as stalactites or travertine that formed when calcite settled near a geyser among sulfurous water and organic remains. It has internal cavities and gray-brown, cream, rust, or reddish veins that make it unsuitable for realistic sculpture. It is more earthy, hard, and compact than alabaster but it also has a fine grain and shines when polished. It colorfulness captivates us easily, making it suitable for beginning direct carving.

The Romans named it *lapis tiburtinus* after the ancient city of Tibur, today's Tivoli, and used it to lend prestige to some public buildings. Later it would be used in the construction of Saint Peter's Basilica in the Vatican. Several fountains in Rome are carved in travertine and Moore reclaimed it for modern sculpture.

Limestone

Limestone is composed primarily of the mineral calcite and is formed when organic detritus settles on the ocean floor, usually in relatively shallow waters. It is white or cream-colored when pure, but can also be reddish, gray, and even black, as in Calatorao stone from Spain, which we will use in the fourth step-by-step exercise. It frequently contains fossil remains. Although there are many varieties of grain and stratification, it is usually easy to carve and polish.

Lithographic limestone is the finest-grain limestone. *Dolomite* may contain quartz, which makes it hard. *Oolithic* limestone has a characteristic spheroid structure formed by concentric layers.

The more naturalist sculptures of Egypt (*Nefertiti* or *Seated Scribes*) are usually of polychrome limestone. Limestone is also the stone most frequently used in Gothic cathedrals.

Sandstone

When it disintegrates, any rock becomes sand and when the sand hardens it creates a new stone, sandstone. Thus, the color and composition of sandstone varies depending on the original rock, although earthy or grayish types predominate. Sandstone usually has grains of quartz. This provides resiliency and shine but wears down tools, which is why some sandstones are used for sharpening. If they contain silicates, they can be harmful if breathed in. The strata of sedimentation—their law—is easily detected. Thus, smoothing work is easy, since once they are separated large chips can be lifted. Their granular texture does not allow for polishing.

Sandstone was used a great deal during the Roman period and gave shape to numerous Buddhas in the Orient. It is easily worked and its warmth, particularly at dusk, lends character to towns and cities such as Salamanca (Spain).

▼ Limestone from Boñar (Spain).

▼ Limestone from Aguilar (Spain).

▼ Sandstone from Aguilar (Spain).

▼ Sandstone from Brañosera (Spain).

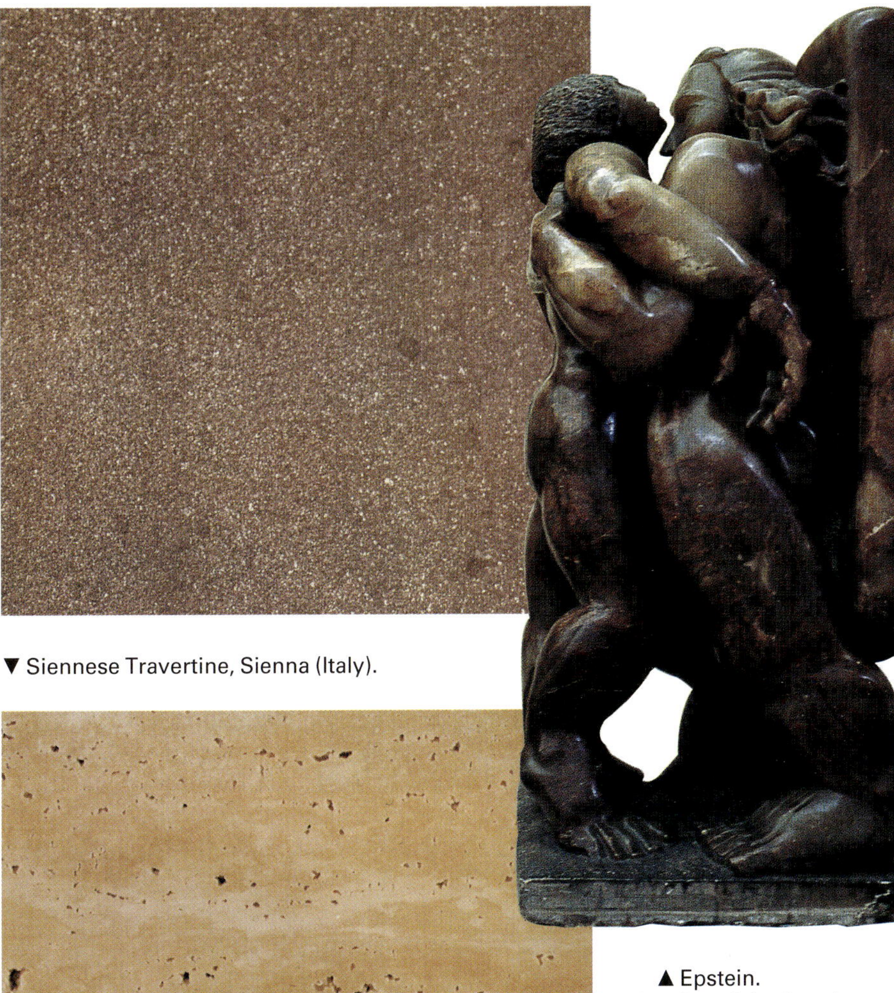

▲ Epstein. *Jacob and the Angel.* 1941. Large block of rose alabaster. Tate Gallery, London (United Kingdom).

▼ Roman Travertine, Rome (Italy).

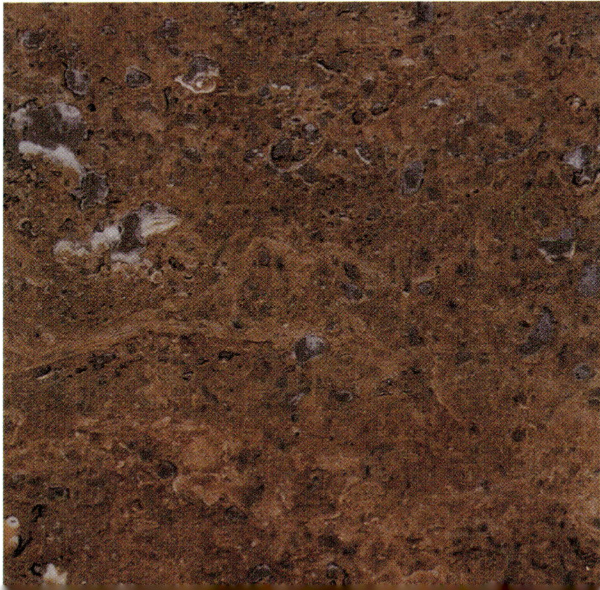

▼ Siennese Travertine, Sienna (Italy).

Marble

Marble is ancient limestone recrystallized by heat or pressure. Sculptors prefer it because they can control it easily since it is resilient but not too hard. In addition, it can be worked in all directions because its structure is uniform. This happens when it has undergone intense metamorphosis. However, if metamorphosis was limited, the stone may retain strata and fossils that will impose their law on the carver. Marble is usually fine- or medium-grained with a sugary appearance and can be perfectly polished and shined.

Calcium carbonate is the essential mineral in marble. When not mixed with other materials, it gives marble a uniform white color that is ideal for realistic sculpture because it does not detract from form. Thus, the most valued *statuary stones* are marble. However, what usually happens is that the limestone already contained other accessory minerals, has undergone oxidation, or become mixed with sand, lime, or clay during metamorphosis. This leads to a wide range of colors that sometimes combine to form fanciful tracings in the form of waters, veins, or arabesques.

The most famous marble comes from the Apuan Alps and is known as Carrara marble for the city that has sold it since Roman times. Carrara was the marble most often used by Renaissance, Baroque, and Neoclassical sculptors.

Of the marble-producing countries, Greece follows Italy, which sells many varieties of marble. The most characteristic Greek marbles are *crystalline* from Naxos and *pentelic* from Athens, which was used to build the Acropolis. *Blanco Macael* embellishes the Alhambra in Granada (Spain). It is also very pure and thus suitable for sculpture; it is quarried in the Sierra de los Filabres of Almeria (Spain).

Although these white marbles have the longest tradition, every day new quarries begin commercial operation all around the world. The color mosaic that accompanies this text gives an idea of the variety of this malleable material.

However, the beginner should not be seduced by color alone as colorful marble may contain internal impurities that will alter the shape of the stone.

▼ Blanco Macael. Almeria (Spain).

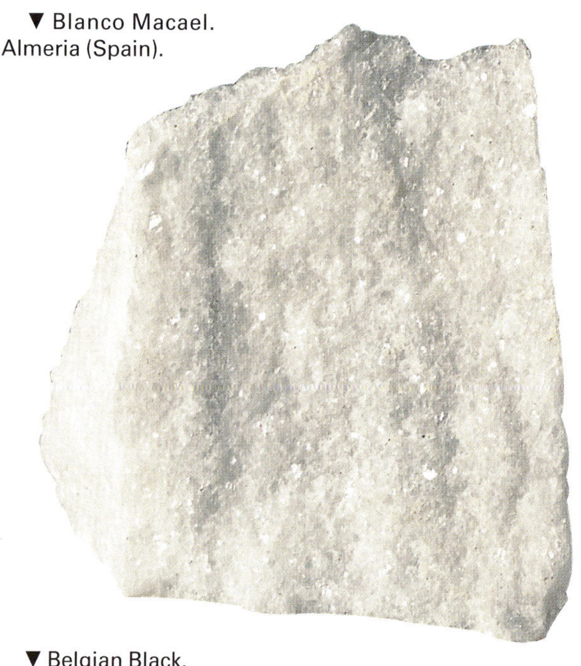

▼ Peralba Rose. Belluno (Italy).

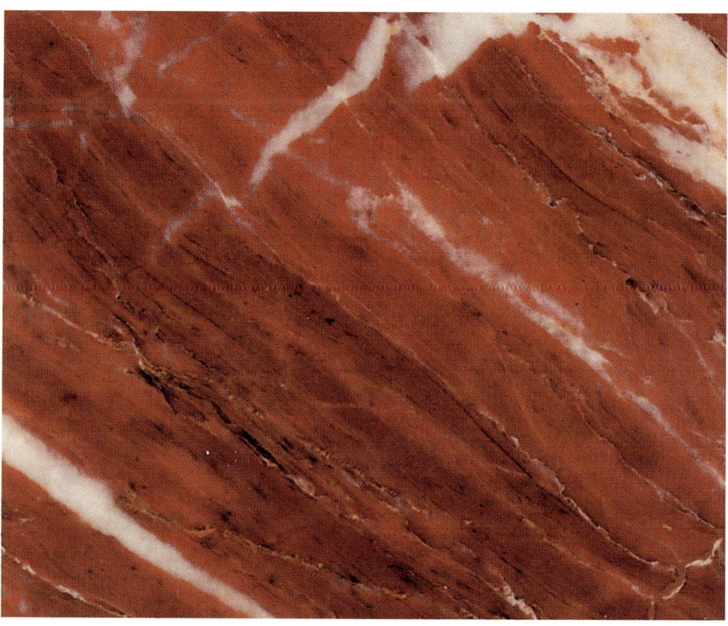

▼ Belgian Black. Belgium.

▼ Apuan Cipollino. Lucca (Italy).

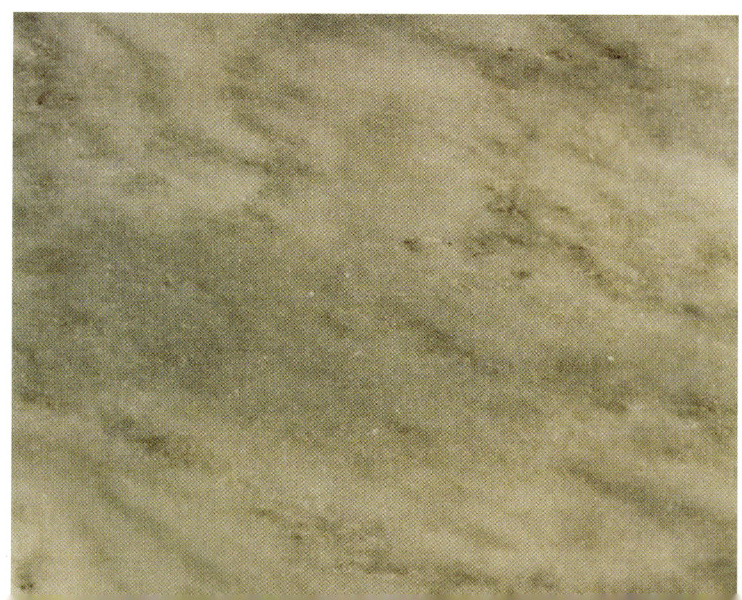

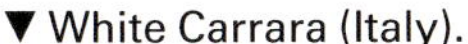

▼ White Carrara (Italy).

▼ Fiore Urdine (Italy).

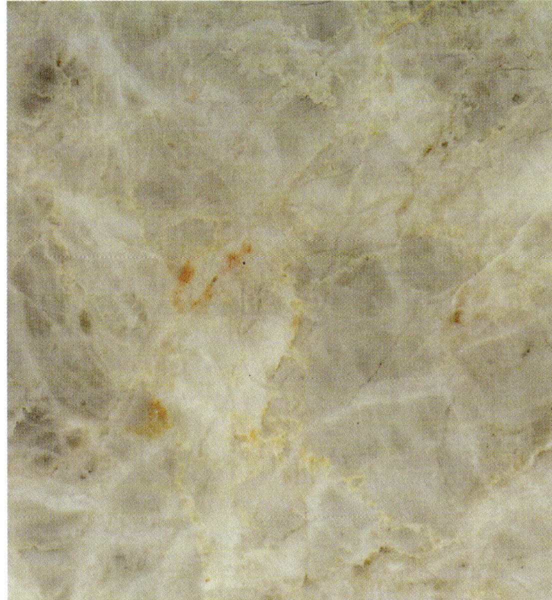

▼ Bardiglio Imperiale. Lucca (Italy).

▼ Rosso Magnaboschi. Vicenza (Italy).

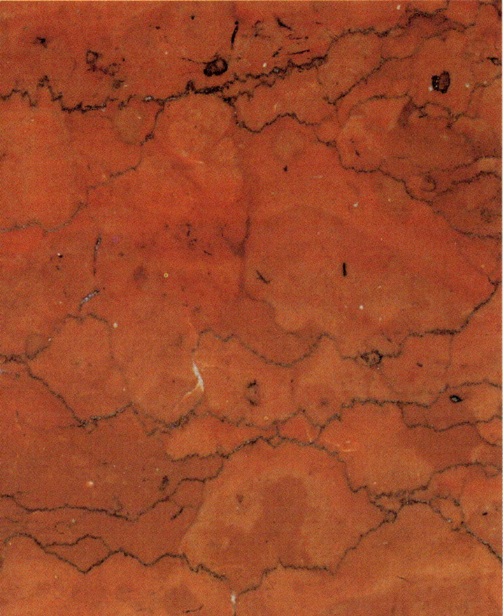

▼ Rosso Rubino. Lucca (Italy).

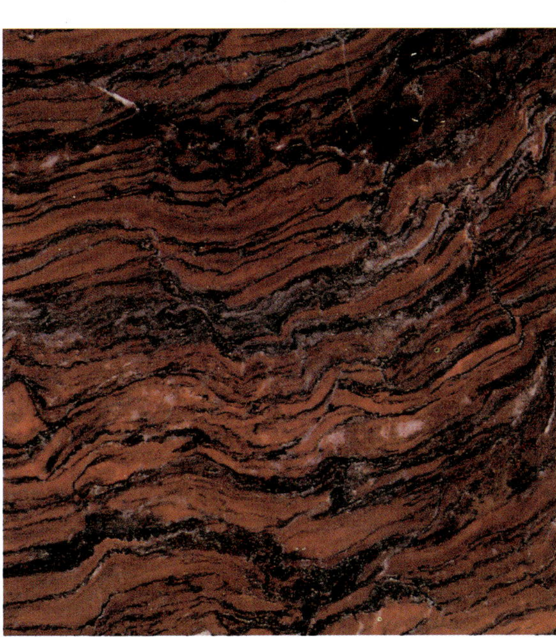

▼ Verde Issogne. Aosta (Italy).

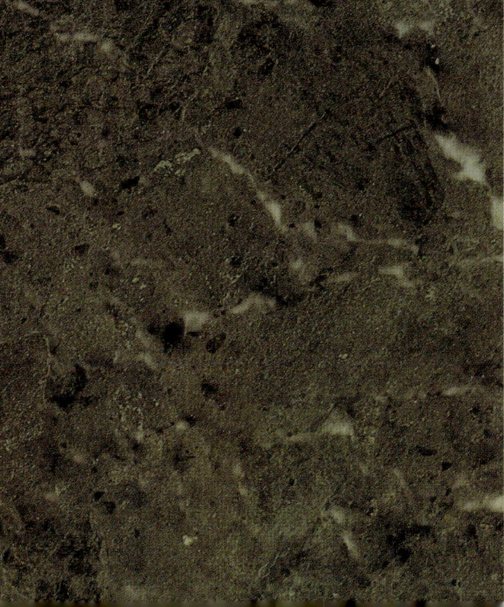

▼ Verde Issore. Aosta (Italy).

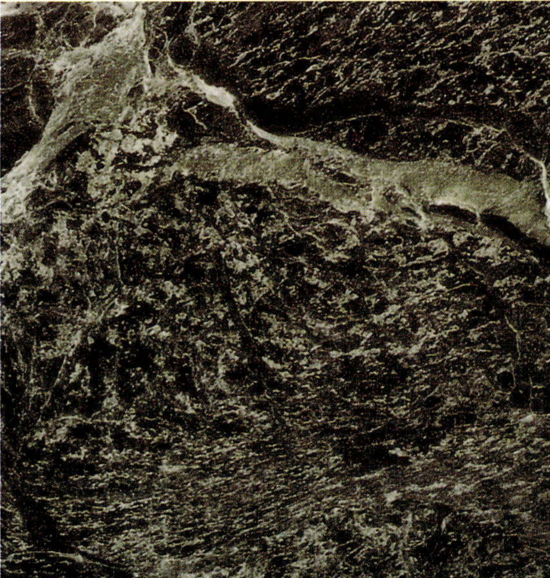

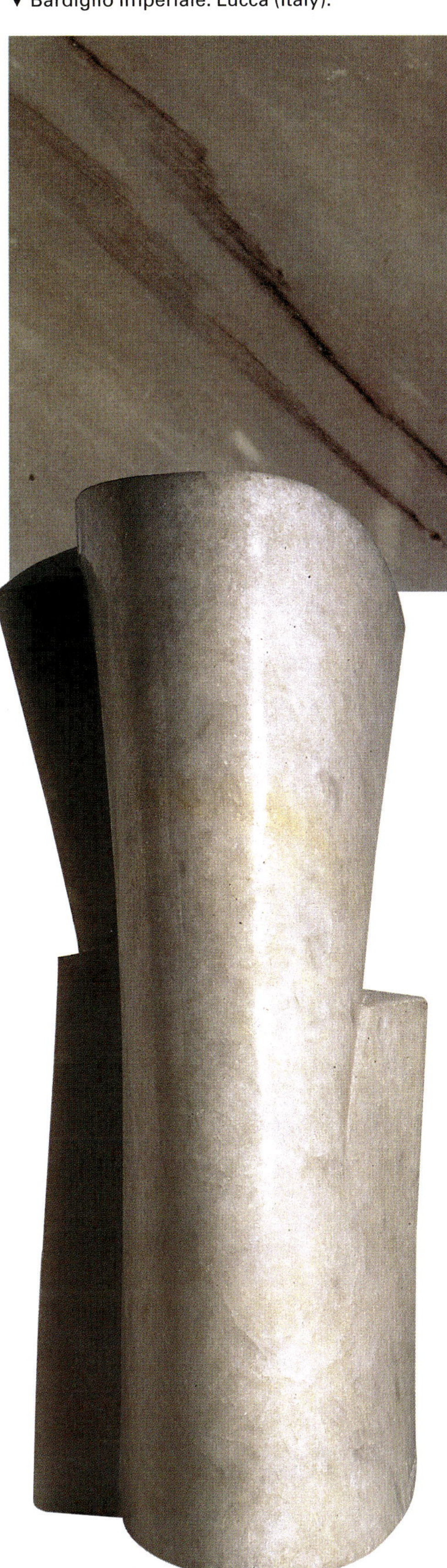

▲ Camí.
La ductilitat del fets, 1983.
Pentelic marble.

Granite and Other Very Hard Stones

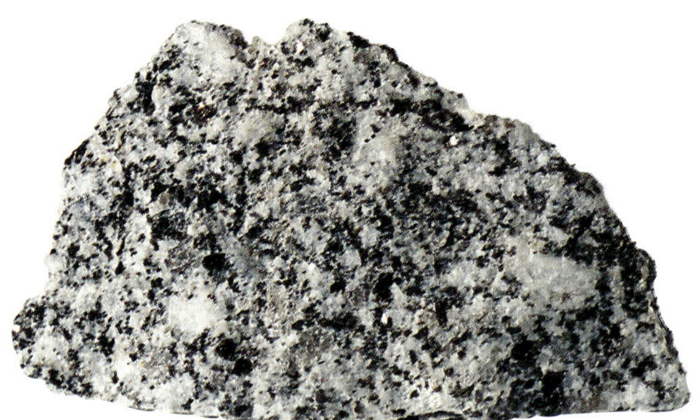

▲ Granite.

▼ Blue Aran. Lleida (Spain).

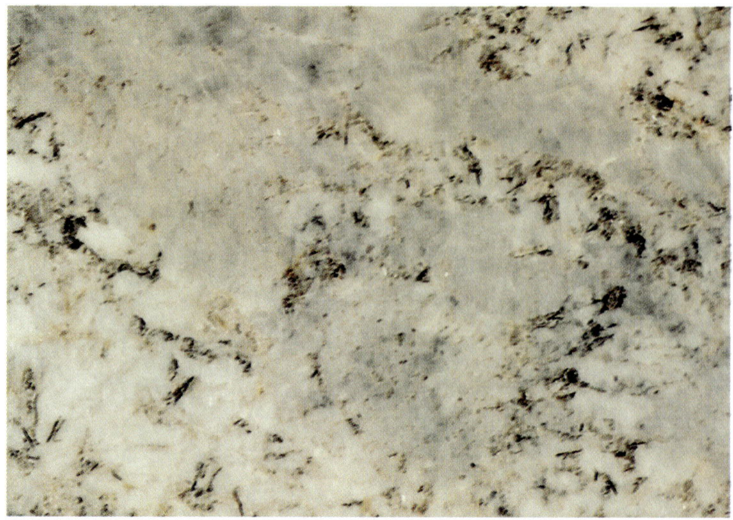

Granite

When magma inside the earth cools, it forms very hard rocks. The most abundant rock is granite, which is composed of various minerals, primarily white or pink feldspar, which acts as an agglutinant for hard quartz and mica, in addition to other ferromagnetic minerals that provide color.

Granite has a homogeneous structure although it may have druses, cavities with well-formed quartz or feldspar crystals. The grain is coarse or very coarse, but constant. Extraordinary polish and shine can be achieved with patience.

The quartz in granite wears down tools. In addition, great perseverance is required to work granite because it is a very hard stone. When trimming granite, it is advisable to make closely spaced parallel cuts and then break off the peaks with a point chisel.

France, Italy, and the Iberian peninsula, where granite was used to build the aqueduct at Segovia and the El Escorial monastery, supply varied and high-quality granite. Also worth noting are the red granites of Sweden, Finland, and Argentina, the black granites of Uruguay, South Africa, and Brazil, and the great variety of colors offered by granite from India and South America.

▼ Yellowish cream. Madrid (Spain).

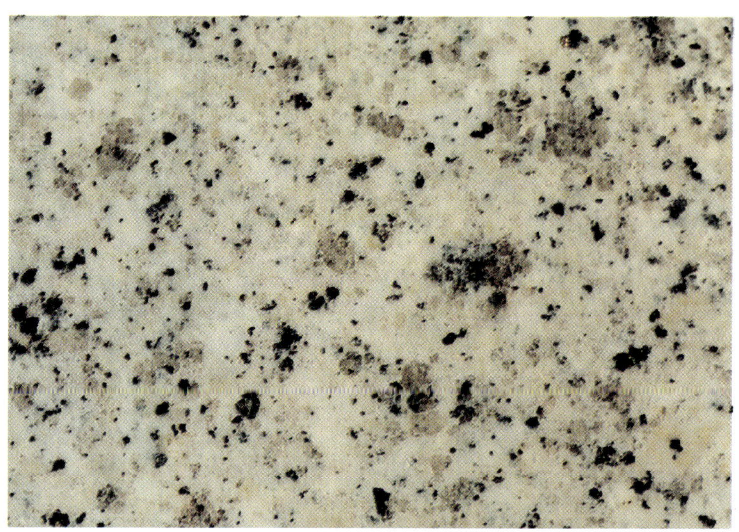

Other Very Hard Stones

Among the great variety of igneous stones, the following are notable for their beauty. **Basalt** may be black, gray, bluish, greenish, and even reddish. When polished well, it can take on a metallic shine. **Syenite** is similar to granite but contains less quartz and is easier to carve. It may be rose, violet, green, or gray. **Porphyry** is a dark reddish color, has feldspar crystals, and is difficult to carve. **Diabase** varies from dark green to a gray that is nearly black and is easier to polish than to carve. **Diorite** is a hard, black stone that was highly valued in Mesopotamia in the time of Gudea. **Gabbro** is a grayish rock that when altered takes on white and greenish tones. **Obsidian** is glassy black with metallic reflections, was formed by lava, and is brittle because it did not crystallize.

▼ Syenite.

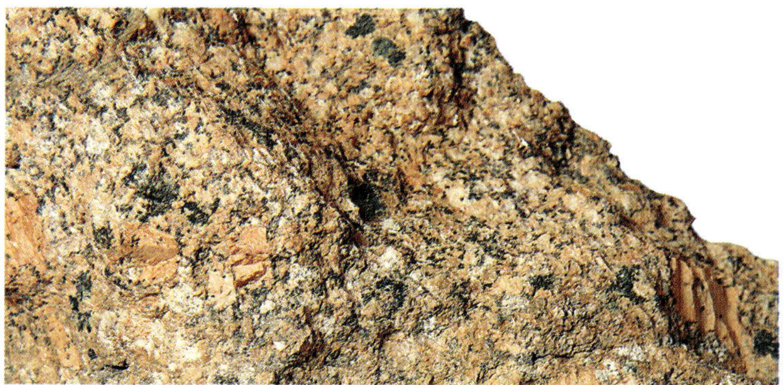

▼ Diorite.

▼ Extremadura Blue. Caceres (Spain).

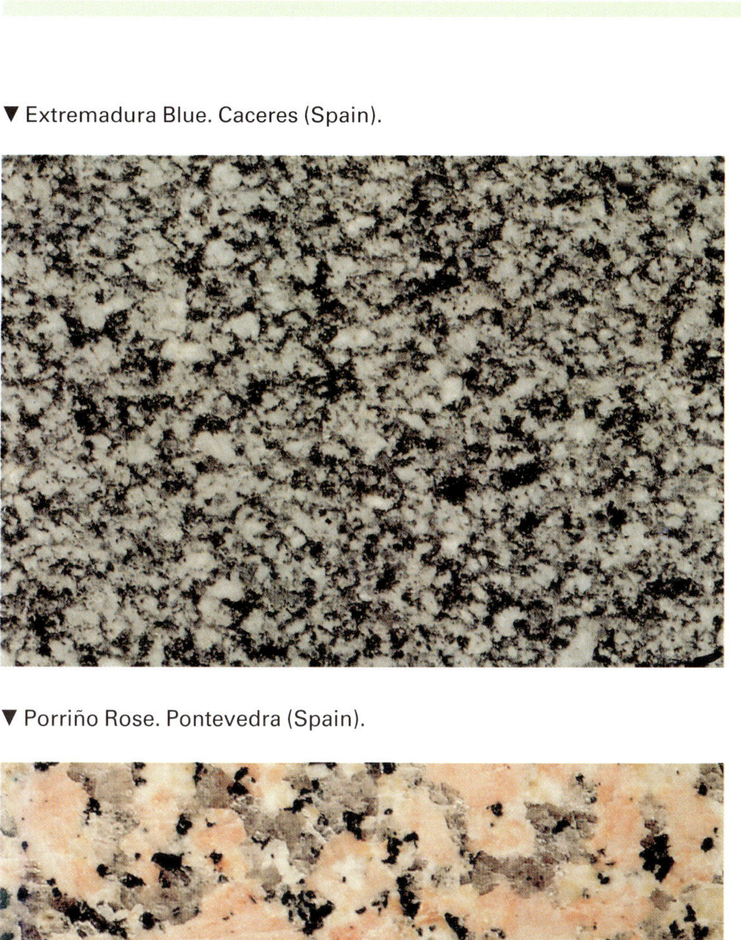

▼ African Black. South Africa.

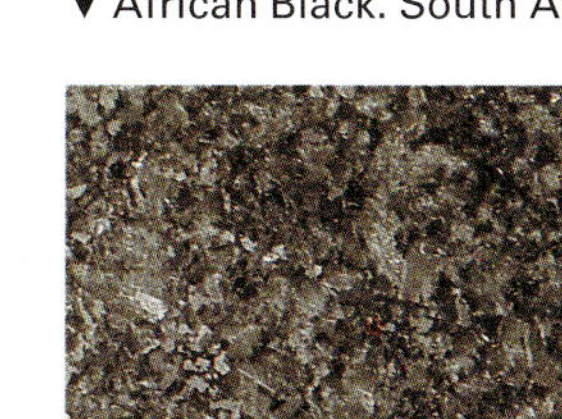

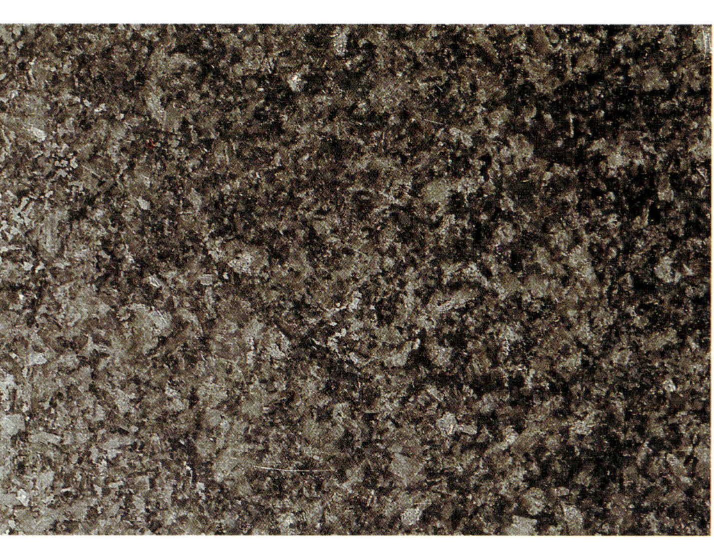

▼ Porriño Rose. Pontevedra (Spain).

▼ Imperial Red. Sweden.

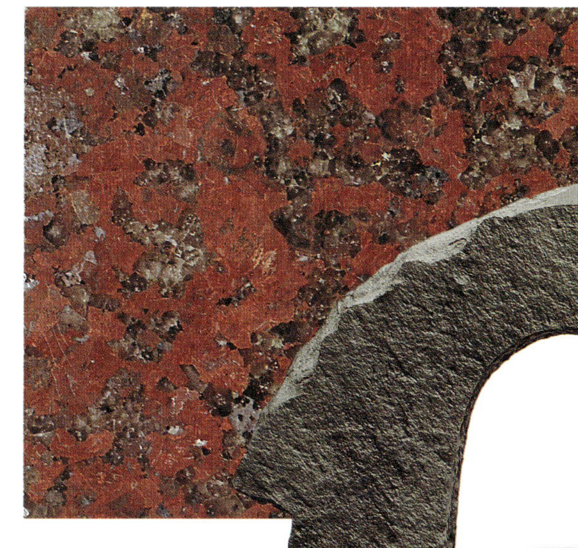

▼ Porphyry.

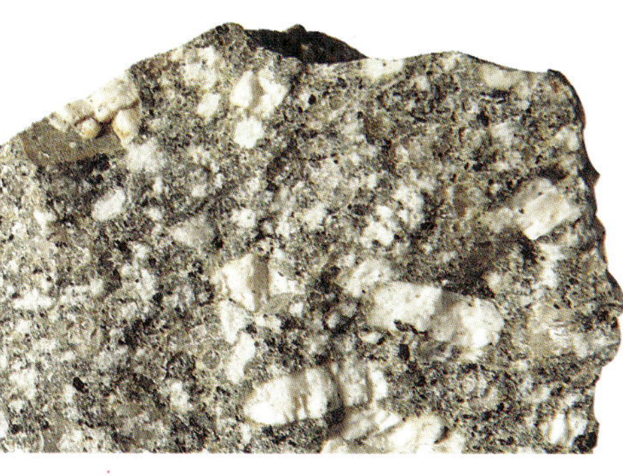

▼ Diabase.

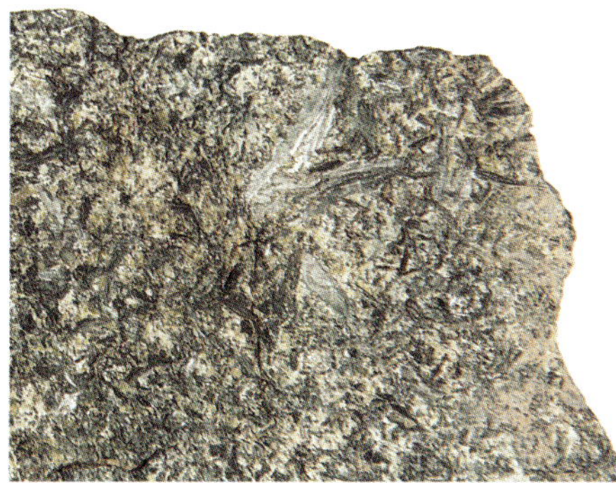

▼ Gabbro.

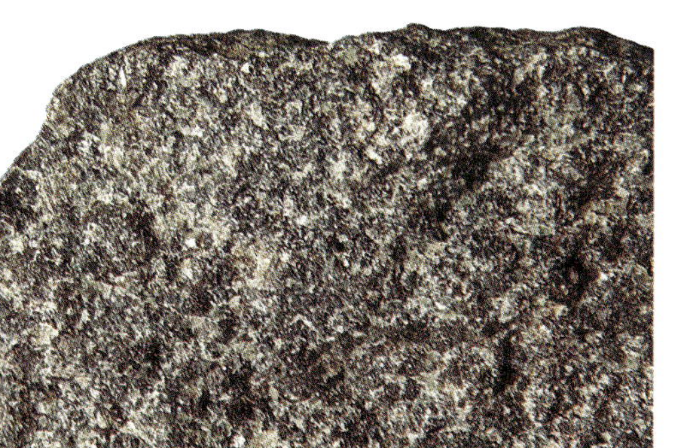

▼ Obsidian.

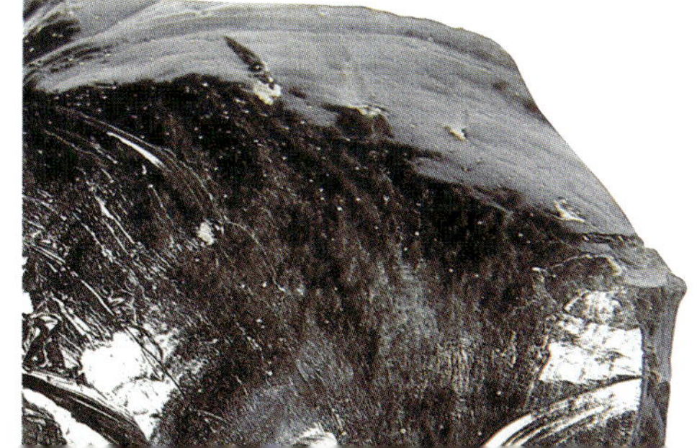

▲ Mariano A.V.
Eclipse, 1997. Basalt.

Stones from around the World

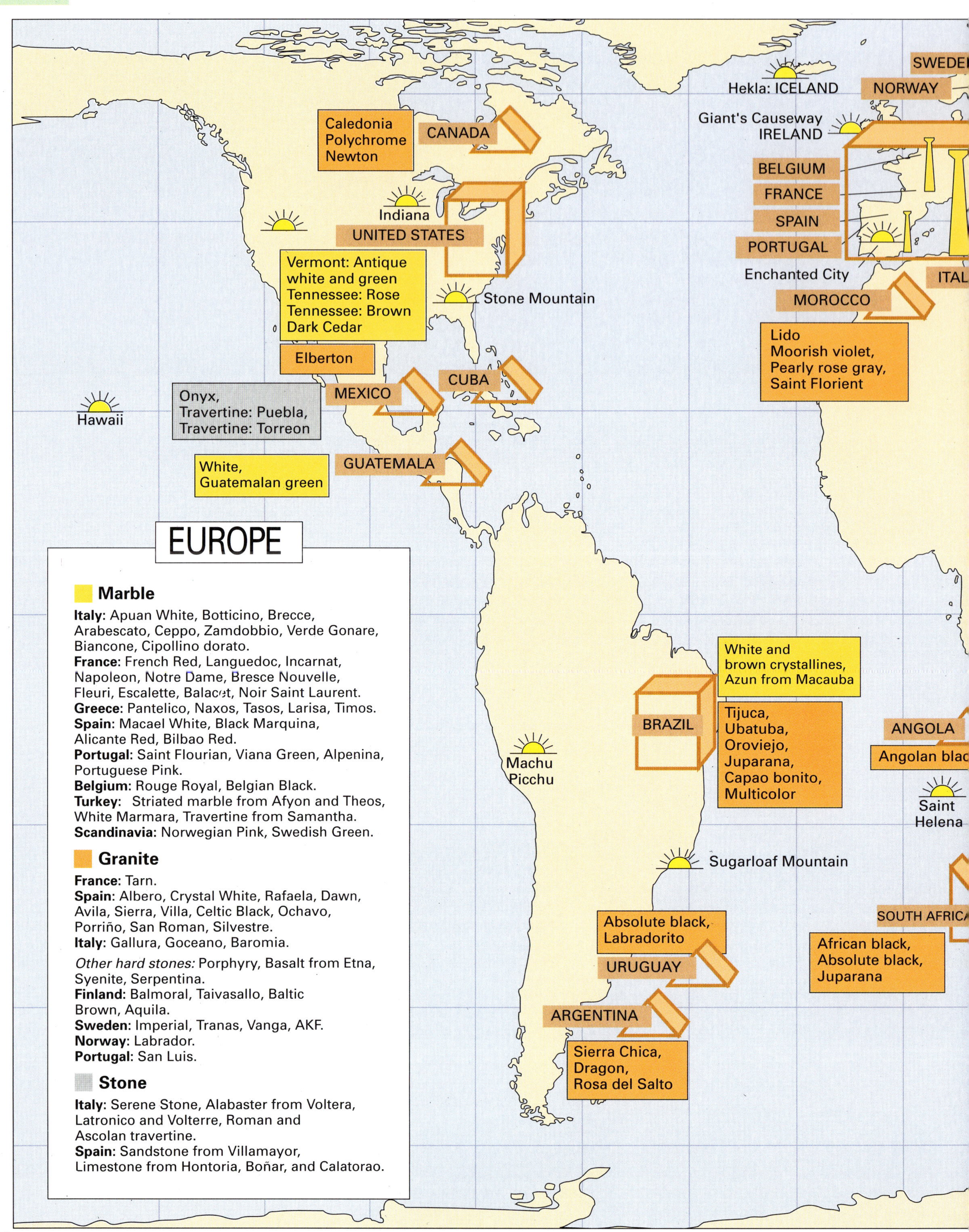

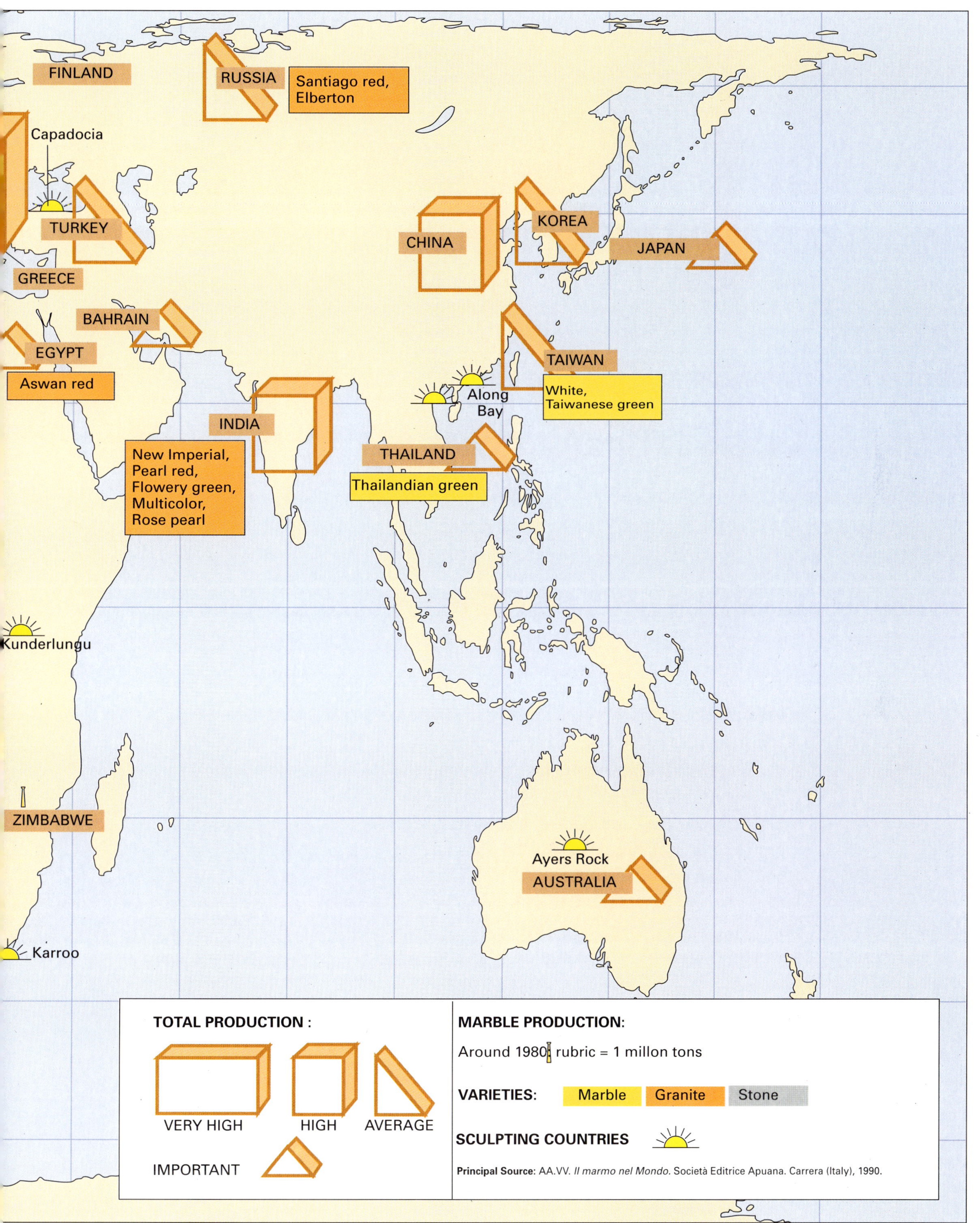
FINLAND
RUSSIA
Santiago red,
Elberton
Capadocia
TURKEY
GREECE
BAHRAIN
EGYPT
Aswan red
CHINA
KOREA
JAPAN
TAIWAN
White,
Taiwanese green
Along
Bay
INDIA
New Imperial,
Pearl red,
Flowery green,
Multicolor,
Rose pearl
THAILAND
Thailandian green
Kunderlungu
ZIMBABWE
Ayers Rock
AUSTRALIA
Karroo
TOTAL PRODUCTION :
VERY HIGH
HIGH
AVERAGE
IMPORTANT
MARBLE PRODUCTION:
Around 1980 rubric = 1 millon tons
VARIETIES:
Marble
Granite
Stone
SCULPTING COUNTRIES
Principal Source: AA.VV. Il marmo nel Mondo. Società Editrice Apuana. Carrera (Italy), 1990.

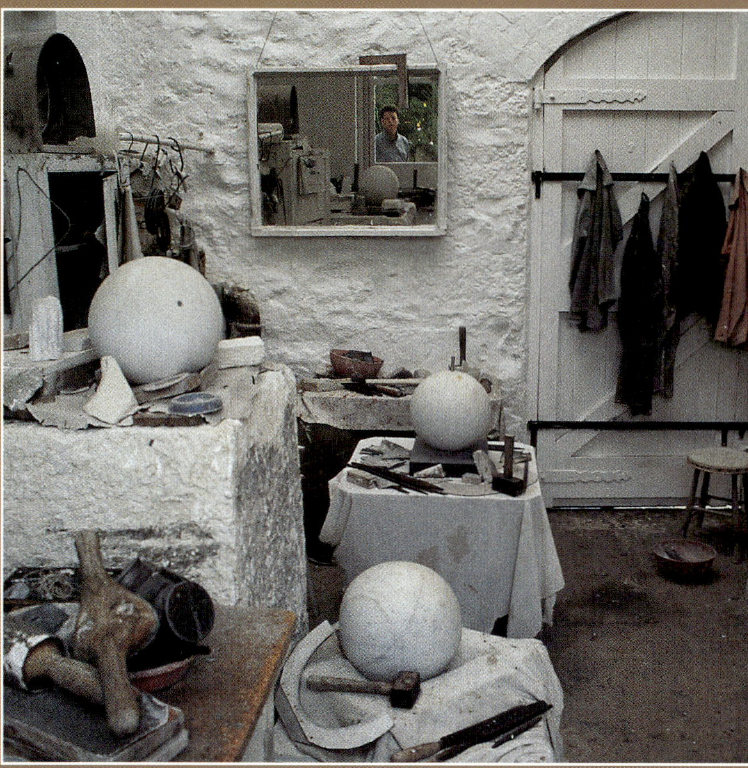

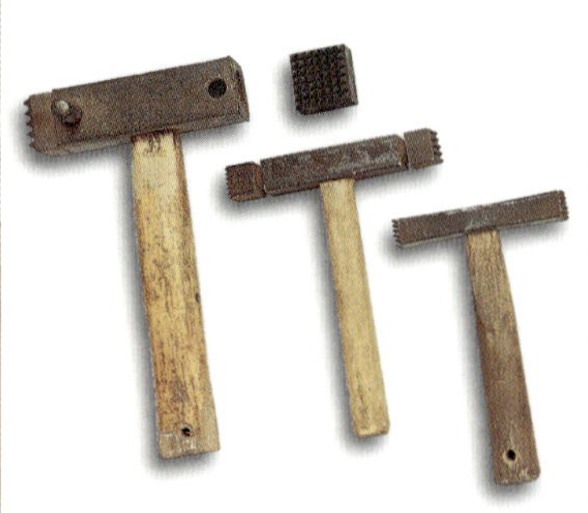

In the next pages we will discuss the characteristics of the sculptor's workplace and the tools used to carve stone. However, we should first consider some aspects of the sculptor's studio as a place for inspiration and drawing sketches. We will also list some tools used to design and make maquettes through addition and subtraction. We then describe different types of workshops and classify tools in three basic groups: basic, specialized, and professional. Before concluding, we will show the equipment used to polish and shine a piece of sculpture.

It was a custom with Apelles, to which he tenaciously adhered, never to let any day pass, however busy he might be, without exercising himself by tracing some outline or other—a practice which has now passed into a proverb.

Pliny the Elder

The Workshop

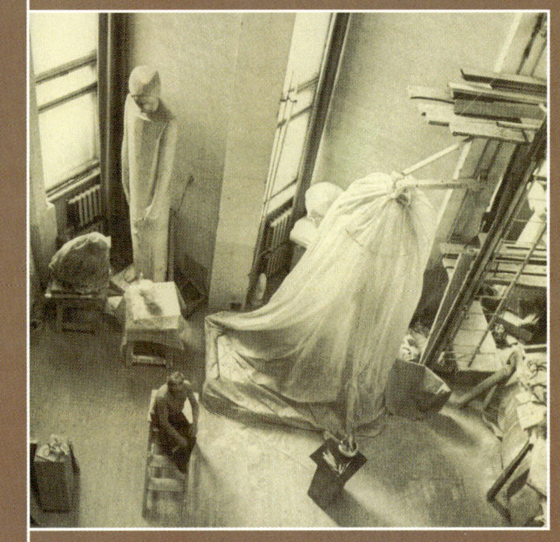

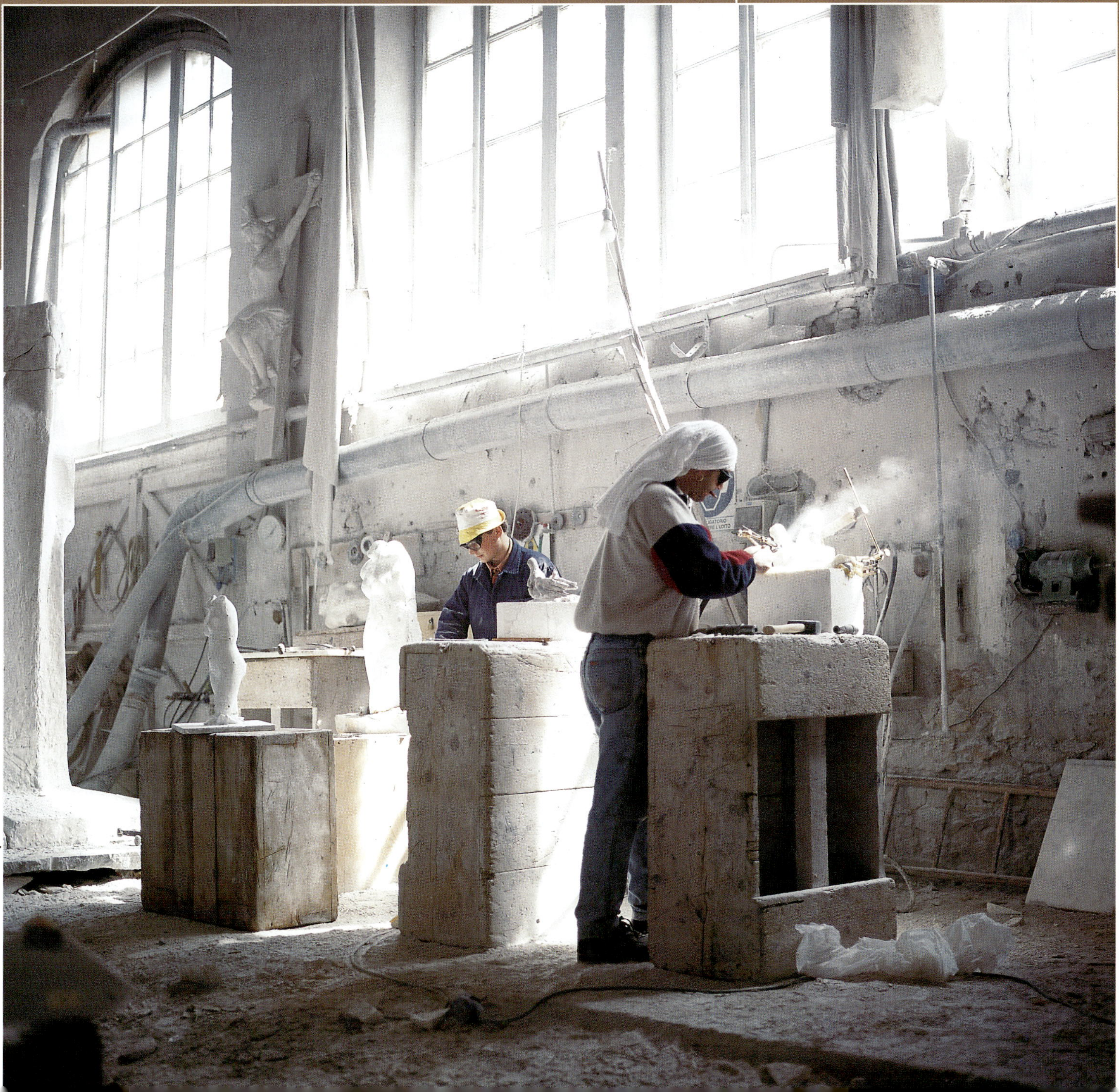

The Sculptor's Studio

Several people may be involved in the process of creating a sculpture, but the initial concept usually comes from a single person who, having conceived an idea, has to capture it so that it will take on provisional shape and volume. To do this, the sculptor needs a place to work and some materials with which he designs, draws a sketch, and then builds a maquette to capture his inspiration.

Inspiration may come at any time, whether we're visiting a museum or hiking on a mountain path, so we should always carry a camera or a simple notepad on which to draw a sketch.

Over time many sculptors, without planning to do so, manage to collect different types of objects with evocative shapes that, sooner or later, influence their creativity. If we use these objects to create an environment in our studio or give them their own special area, they will carry on a dialogue with our subconscious and create new shapes. It is also helpful to keep catalogs, books, photographs, or a record collection that lets our imagination fly on the subtle wings of music.

Once the shape of the sculpture is conceived, we will need material to give it form. Although many sculptors use a drawing or a three-dimensional computer program, we prefer to approach the mass of stone directly because of its immediacy compared to the unnecessary abstraction required by one-dimensional representations.

Wax or potter's clay were traditionally used to create maquettes but today plastecine and modeling clay are easier to use. If possible, the color should be similar to the color of the stone chosen so that we can better approach an understanding of the final work.

After preparing the sketch, we recommend the intermediate step of getting used to the technique of preparing a maquette, using a soft material such as porexpan, pumice stone, or fiber cement. This will help us develop skill in the irreversible subtractive process that carving stone involves.

We have listed the basic requirements needed before carving—finding inspiration and making maquettes—because these requirements will determine the characteristics of our studio. Our own skills—drawing, modeling, or carving—will determine whether we will need a water outlet so we can create maquettes with potter's clay or plaster of Paris.

The essential elements needed in the work space are good lighting and a comfortable work surface, if possible a revolving stand that will allow us to construct any volume.

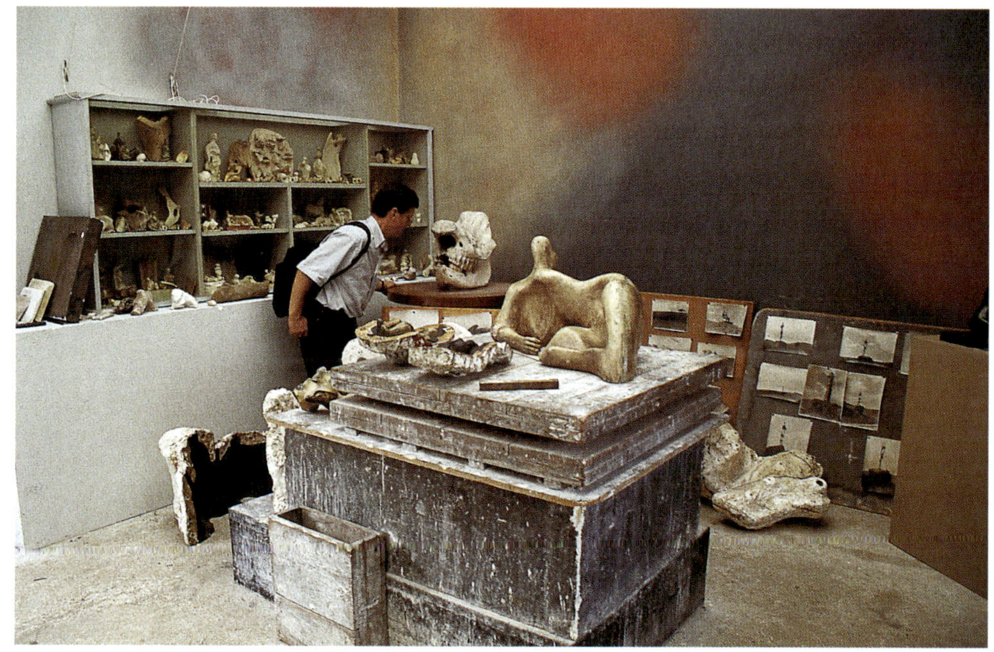

▲ Photograph taken in 1982 of one of the studios where Henry Moore conceived his projects. Mixed in among his sketches we see flints, bones, and even an immense skull.

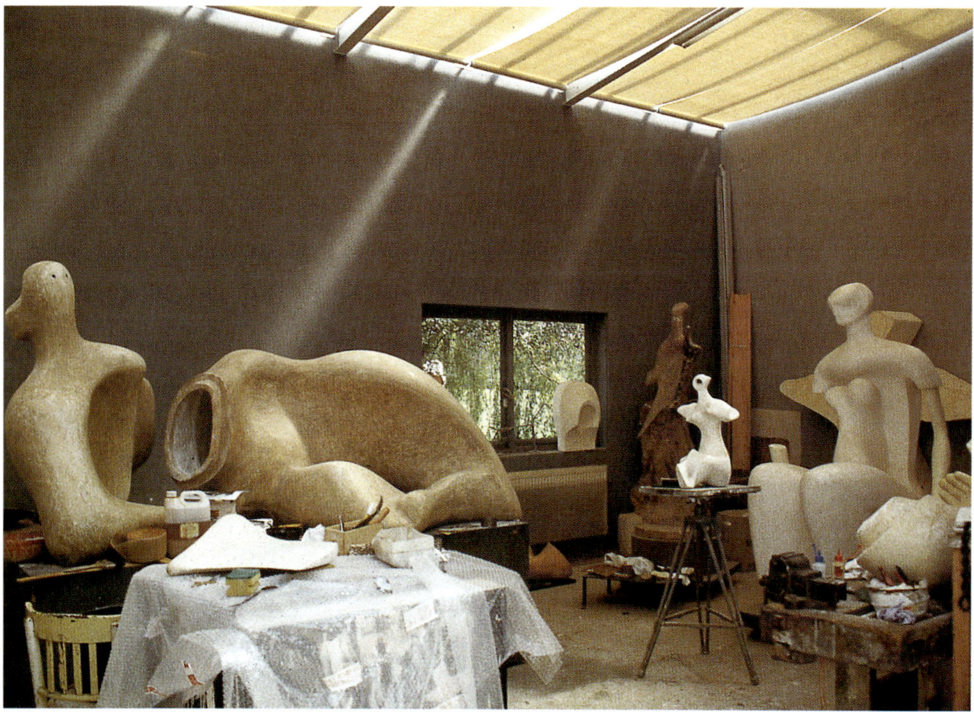

◄ One of the spaces where Moore's sketches are transformed into maquettes. The filtered top lighting bathes the shapes and heightens volume.

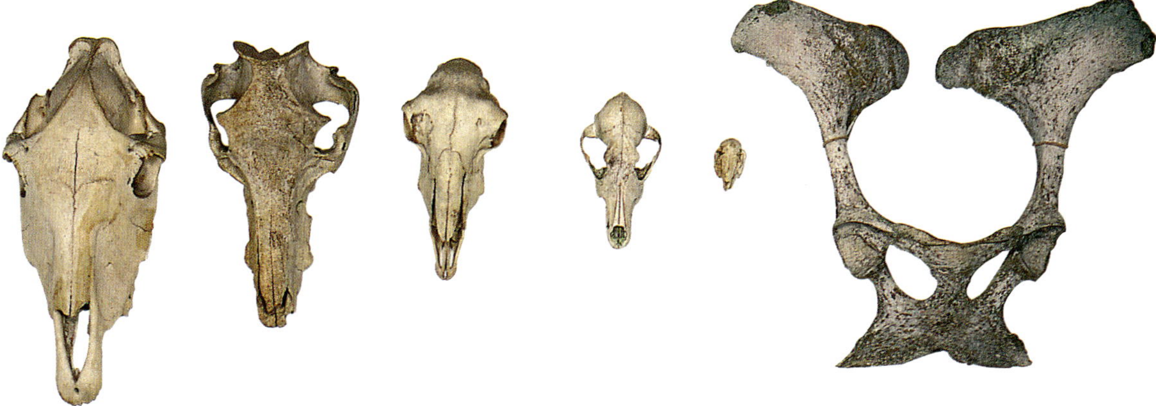

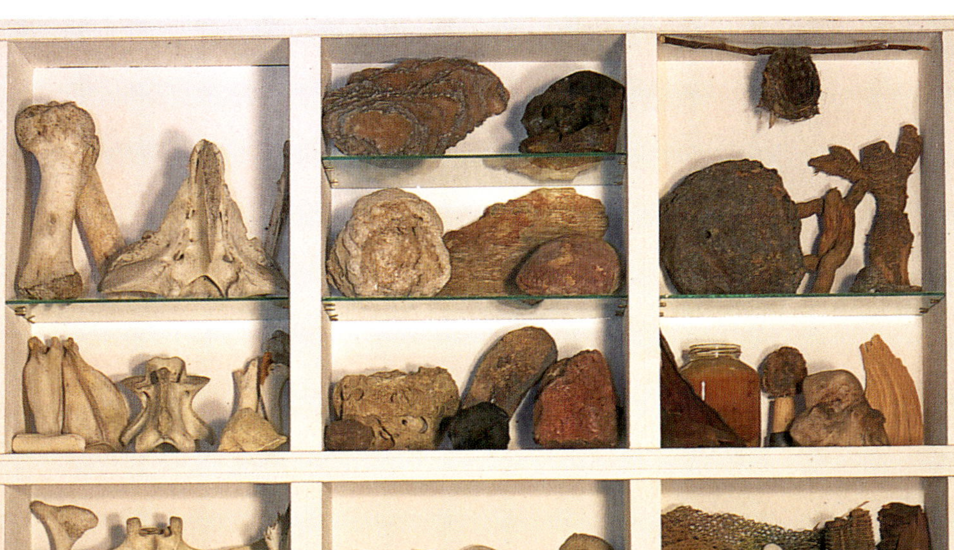

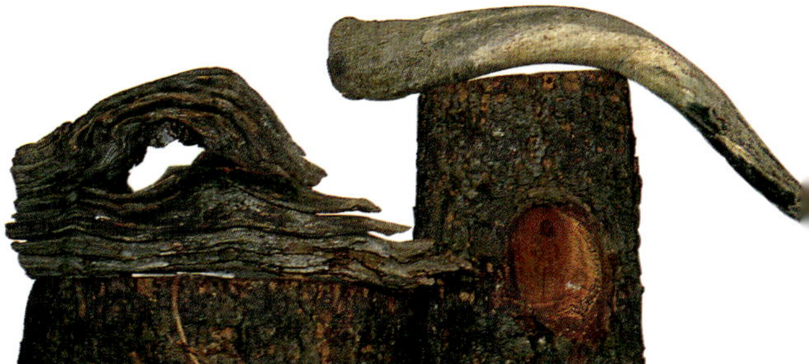

◄▲ Some niches in Camí's studio where objects have accumulated. Their shapes still recall the life they had. They are not there to be copied but rather to help us to capture the subtle traits that infuse life into inanimate objects, like the sculpture we would like to create.

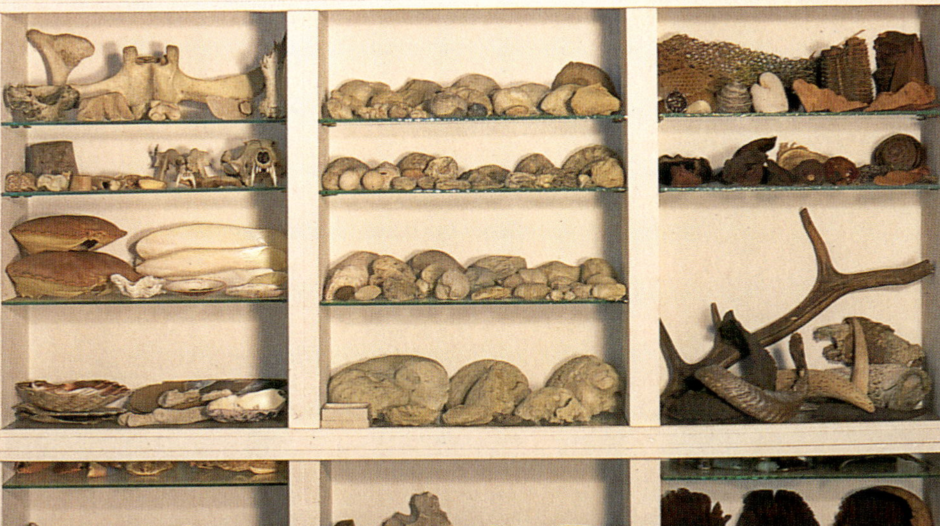

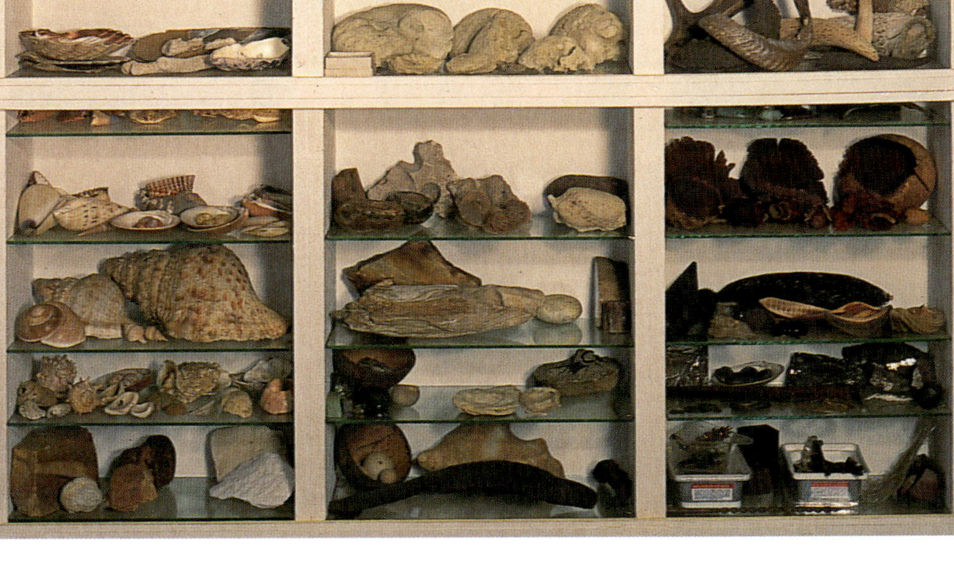

▼ Having a good professional library does not necessarily mean slavishly following the dictates of technique or fashion.

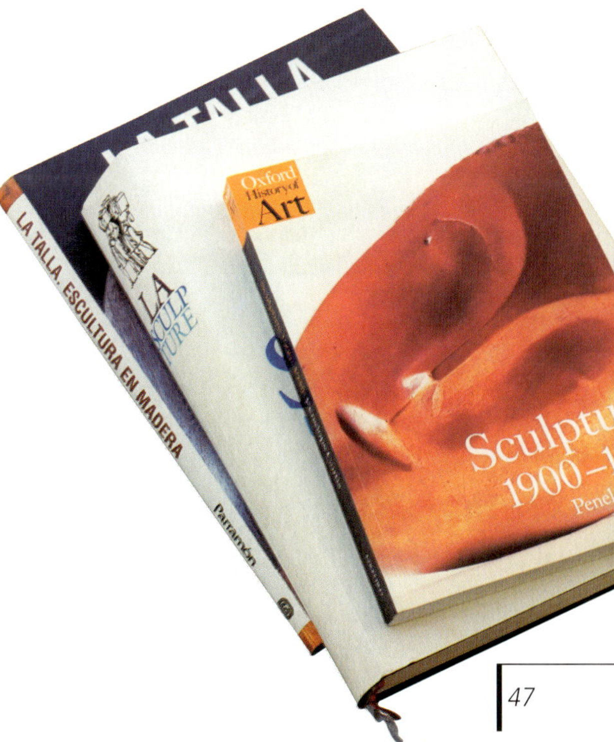

Material for the Studio

So as not to lose time, which could easily hinder the creative flow, we should equip our studio with the materials we will need to develop projects. Here we list different tools, more as a reminder than as a list of requirements, as each person must select the tools most suited to his or her work method.

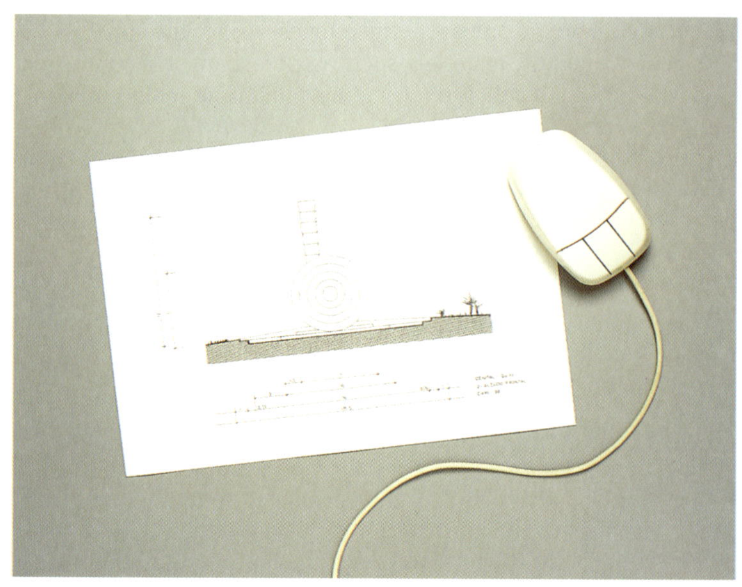

► Those who opt for two-dimensional representation will find it useful to have pencils, rulers, squares, a triangle, a transparent box for tracing, a compass, a flexicurve, a Polaroid camera, a computer, and so on.

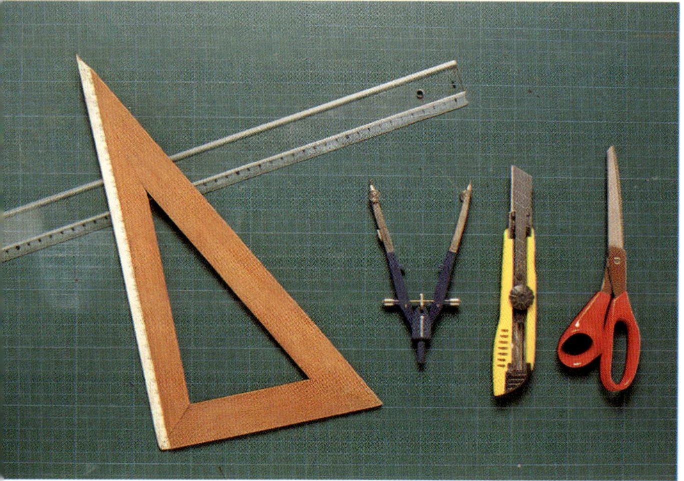

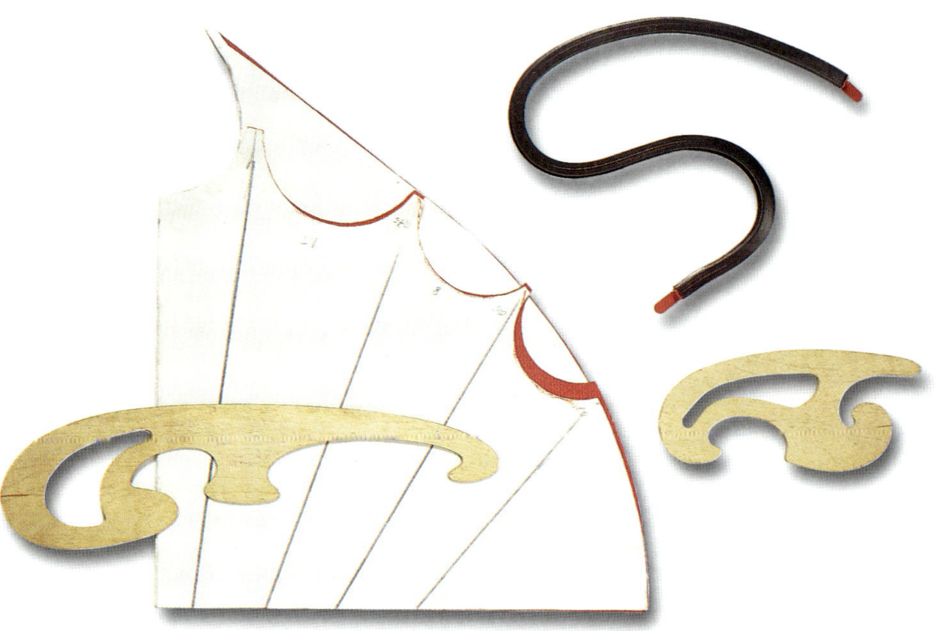

▲ ► A square rubber base is useful after designing the sketch. Together with a mat knife, scissors, and glue, it allows us to build cardboard templates either for making the maquette or for transferring measurements to the final work.

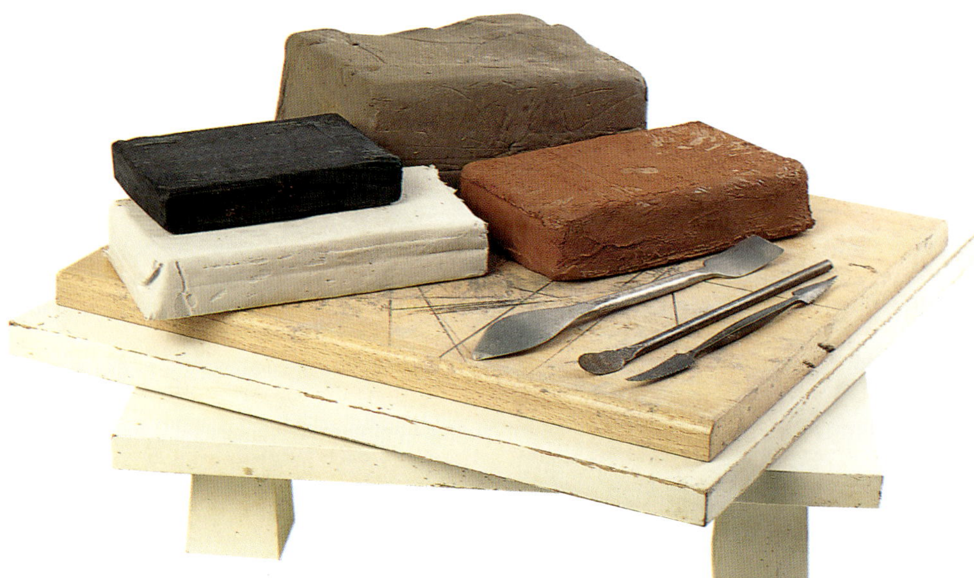

◄ However, sculptors conceive of their forms in terms of volume and it is preferable to get used to this idea. If we're going to make maquettes using the process of addition—allowing us to add and remove material freely—potter's clay, plastecine, and modeling clay are some suitable materials. It is advisable to work with metal picks and a palette knife, use a revolving platform, and prepare the maquette on top of a board and not directly on the stand.

We recommend preparing maquettes using the process of subtraction and soft materials such as porexpan or fiber cement because cutting back the stone and being unable to replace material will teach us how to sculpt stone.

▼ Porexpan, specifically medium-density porexpan, is particularly suitable for carving maquettes. To work it, we can use a cutter, a craftman's knife, and sandpaper.

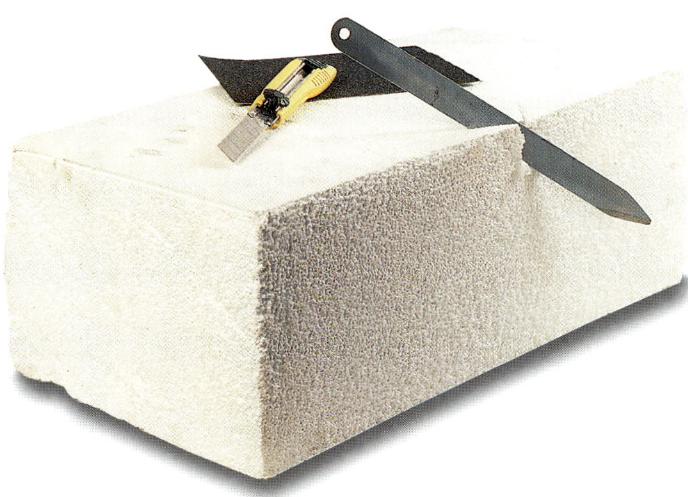

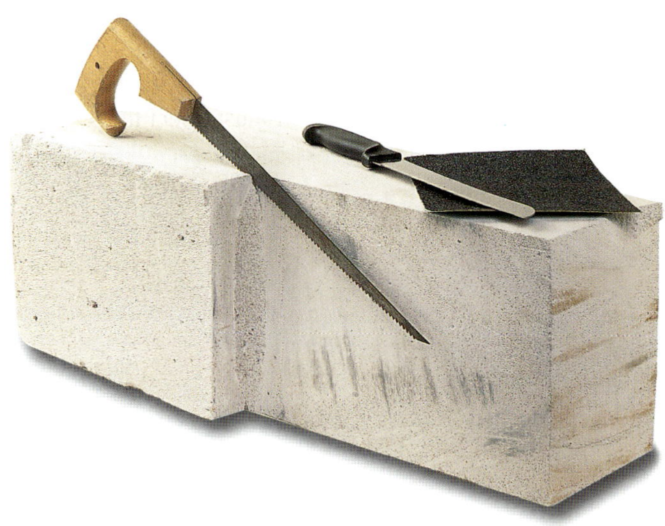

▲ Fiber cement, the artificial material that is most like stone, can be sawed easily. It can also be roughed out with a kitchen knife and molded with sandpaper.

► Plaster of Paris has many applications. It can be used to build blocks to be carved once it has hardened. It can also be molded around a structure or used to correct a maquette made of porexpan or fiber cement. You will need a rubber bowl to prepare it and palette knives to apply it.

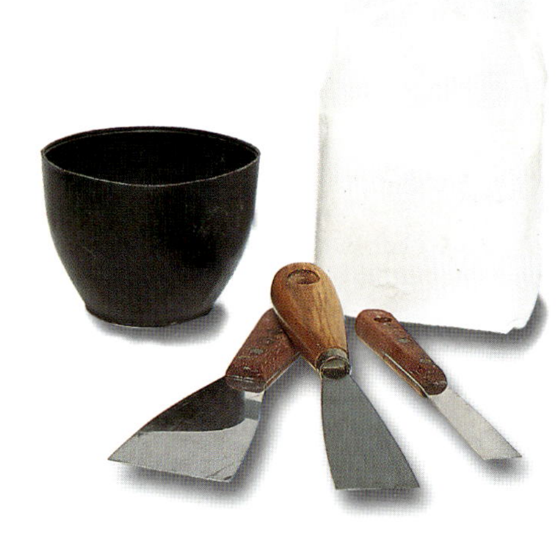

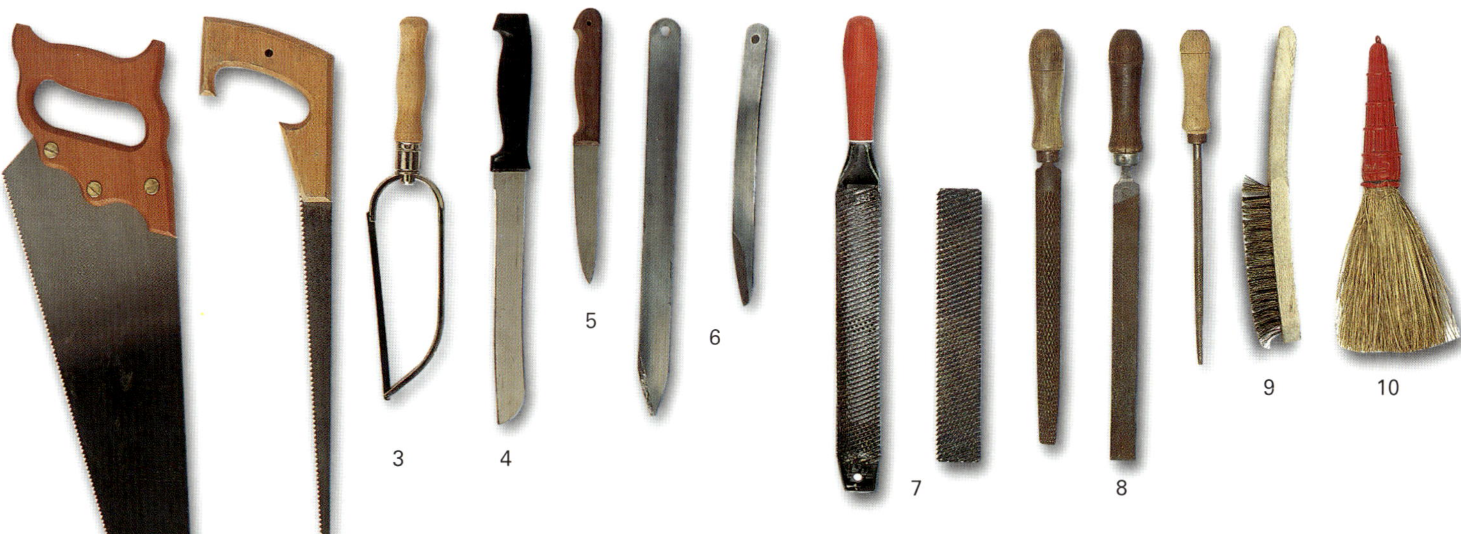

▲ You may also find it useful to have the following tools for working these materials: (1) backsaw; (2) compass saw; (3) marquetry saw; (4) serrated-edge kitchen knife; (5) smooth-edge pointed kitchen knife; (6) curved craftsman's knives; (7) changeable sheet large-toothed rasp; (8) flat, half-round and rattail rasps; (9) scratch brush for cleaning rasps; and (10) brush for cleaning the block.

Workshops

Before we choose a place where we will work with stone, we should at least anticipate the basic necessities. Like any workshop, it should be functional, well lighted, safe, and welcoming, and it should put us at ease so that we can be productive and carving will be a pleasant task.

Stone is a very heavy material and our workplace must have easy access. If we don't find a level ground floor space, we should at least be sure we have a freight elevator and that the floor is strong enough to bear the weight of the stones we will be storing. It would also be practical to have a stand on wheels and a revolving platform. Height will depend on the block we are carving, so we will have to adjust as needed by adding small pallets.

The characteristics of the space and the type of installations will vary according to the tools we will be using. We can choose manual, electrical, or pneumatic equipment. Pneumatic tools completely replace manual or electrical tools and require the installation of a compressor, which in turn requires appropriate electrical outlets.

Noise will be inevitable in our work, particularly if we use electrical equipment or a compressor. If our workshop is near inhabited buildings, it must have soundproofing. If not, we will have to limit ourselves to working during hours that will not disturb our neighbor's sleep.

When we cut with a circular saw, or even when we polish manually, we produce dust. Even if we sweep it into a corner, it would be wise to choose a space we can air out and to install a cabinet where we can store our tools.

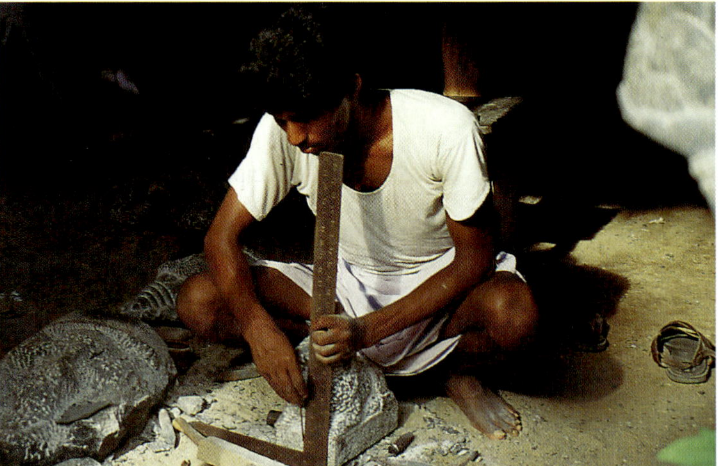

◀ Carver in Mahaballipuram (India).

Although there are many types of workshops, the common and perhaps most important characteristic is that they should suit the needs of the individual sculptor. Thus, at one extreme we have the artisan who works with great skill and a bare minimum of tools, shows his work to tourists, and sells sculptures he carves on the bare soil. At the other extreme, there are huge industrial warehouses that mass-produce sculptures or use sophisticated machinery.

Outside cemeteries or on the outskirts of small cities, we often find a marble cutter who combines a workshop, showroom, and stone warehouse. Others work in marble for decorating kitchens and bathrooms. Their advice and materials may be useful.

Although the stoneworkers' trade unfortunately is dying off, we can find one of their workshops in towns that sell local stone. They generally have covered workshops, but many prefer to work in the open air when the weather permits, and they are great experts on the local stone.

There are also workshops of sculptors who, in addition to doing their own work, do sculpture on commission. Their discretion means that they go unnoticed. Their workshops are among the best equipped and, like the enthusiastic members of the profession that they are, they usually have a warehouse full of stones or know how to get them. One might learn more from them than from an art school.

In Carrara, Italy, rather than sculptors' workshops, we should speak of a sculpture industry because there are more than 50 firms there. Some of these have been in existence for 100 years, while others have been in business since the 1920s. Many of the twentieth century's great sculptors have worked there. The nearby city of Pietrasanta has taken up this tradition and now surpasses Cararra in the number of its workshops. Sculptors from all over the world go there to create their works or improve their technique.

Some ambitious sculptural projects, such as the *Sagrada Familia* in Barcelona or the erection of any public monument, require that a workshop be set up on site and equipped according to the specific needs of the project.

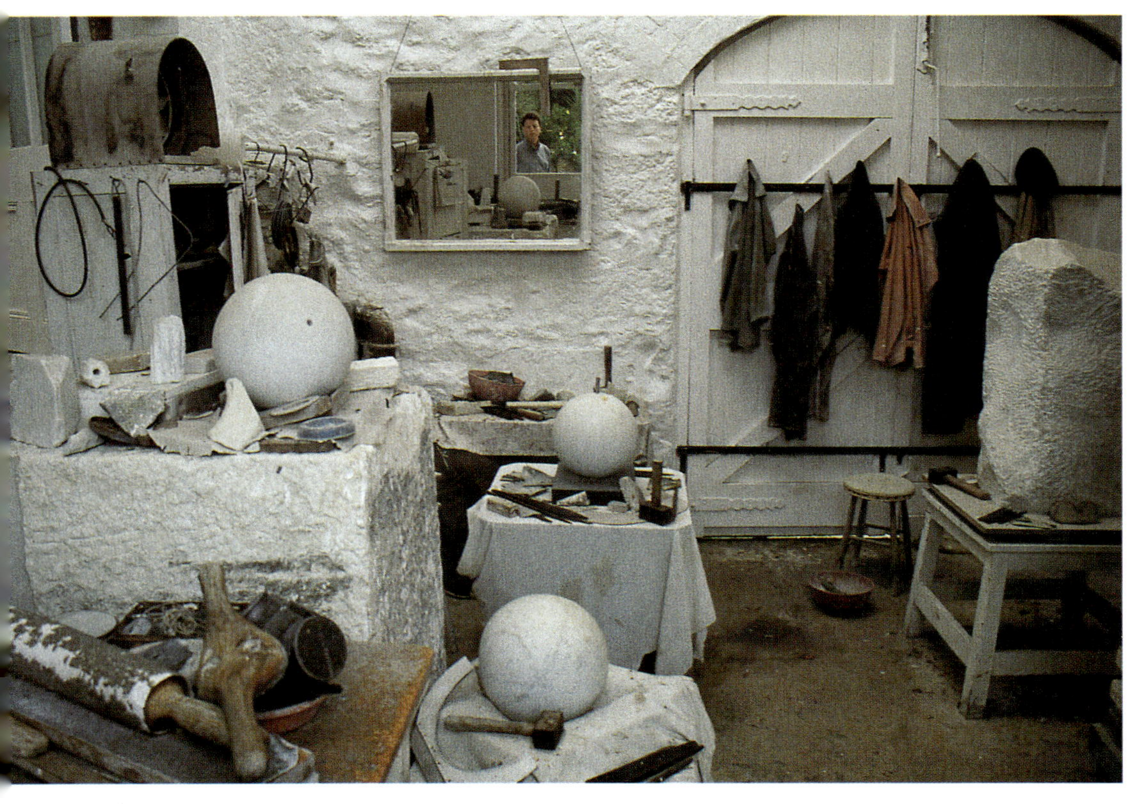

◀ Workshop of Barbara Hepworth in Saint Ives (United Kingdom), preserved for history.

To finish, we should find the workshop of a specific sculptor. Many cities preserve the workshops of prestigious artists, having transformed them into foundations or museums. They are often cozy houses with gardens, better set up for small projects than for carving large blocks. For example, we can visit Zadkine's and Bourdelle's workshops in Paris, and Rodin's workshop in nearby Meudon.

Briefly summarizing the history of workshops, we note that an excavation found the workshop of Tutmosis, the official sculptor of Akhenaten, a large part of which is now on exhibit at the Egyptian Museum in Berlin. In addition to allowing us to admire the fascinating face of Nefertiti, perhaps a prototype intended for reproduction, this exhibit shows us the techniques and tools belonging to the great sculptural tradition of the Egyptians.

In second-century Rome, workshops reproducing Greek statuary proliferated. During the Middle Ages, stonemasons set up shop in front of cathedrals. The Renaissance *bottega* included a shop and housing for the master and his disciples. The workshops of later great sculptors were set up for working on equipment with the most ingenious contraptions for reproduction and expansion. It is said that Bernini hired workers based on the commissions he received and Rodin, in his most prolific phase, ended up with some 150 collaborators.

Thanks to what is left of unfinished pieces of sculpture, we can deduce the type of tools that were used in the past. More primitive sculpture was carved by cutting into the stone with other harder stones and polished by rubbing with sand. The discovery of metals fostered the great advances in sculpture in Egypt and Mesopotamia and we could say that carving tools have barely changed since then. It has been shown that the ancient Greek *kouroi* were carved with a point chisel. In Naxos, they began to polish with emery and during the Hellenic period the trepan was used to impart lightness to hair. There are also clear signs that tooth chisels were used in seventh-century India, while in pre-Columbian America, where metals were unknown, colossal sculptures were carved primarily with slow abrasive techniques.

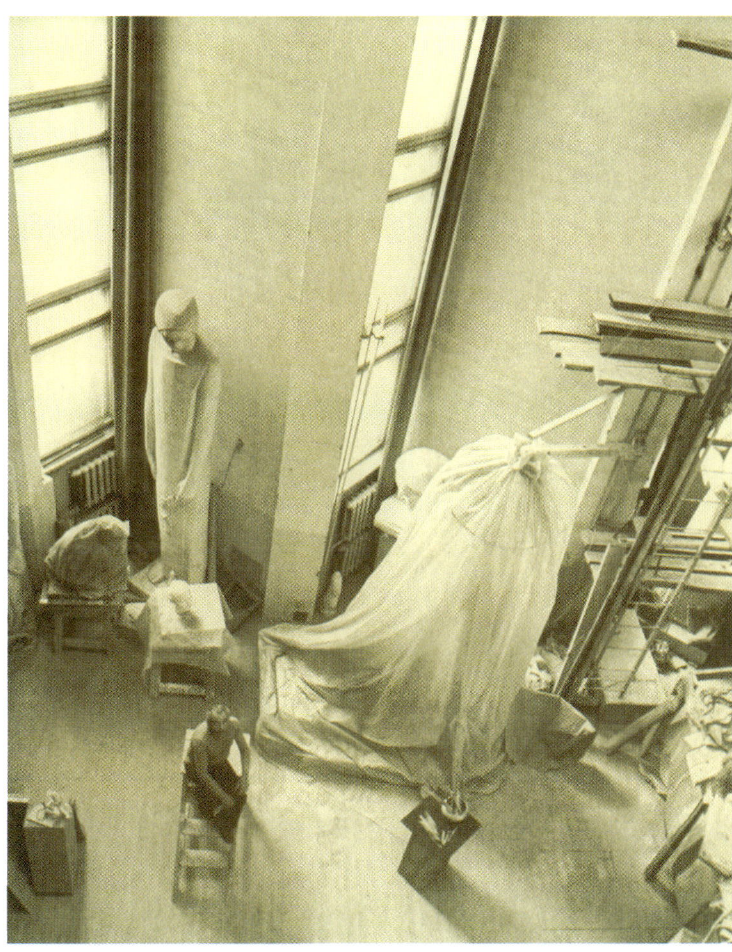

▲ Workshop of the Ukrainian Ryabichev, in the time of state sponsorship.

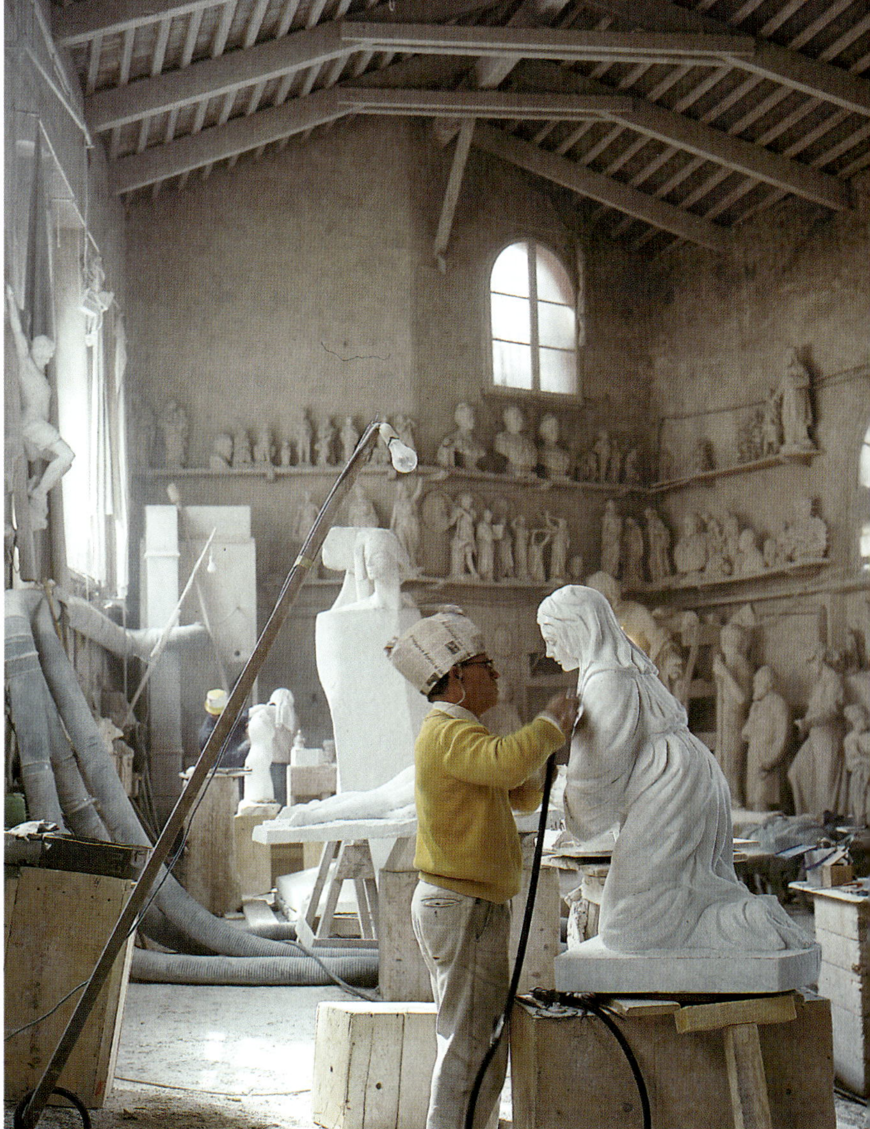

▼ *Rigoli* workshop in Carrara, active since 1878, where portions of the works of Moore, Karavan, Pistoletto, Cardenas, Mitoraj, and Cesar, as well as others, have been carved.

Tools for Roughing Out and Measuring

Accident prevention should be a priority when setting up our workshop. In addition to the usual items, our first aid kit should contain eyedrops in case the dust from the stone irritates our eyes and an analgesic in case we hit our fingers rather than the stone. Of course, it would be better to prevent these mishaps altogether by using goggles, a mask, gloves, and earmuffs.

Having noted that safety comes first, we list some of the tools used most frequently in the workshops of today's sculptors. However, since some of these tools can be used for similar tasks, it is not essential to have all of them before beginning our first sculptures. We start by noting tools used for roughing out and carving. On the following pages we will show tools for modeling and finishing.

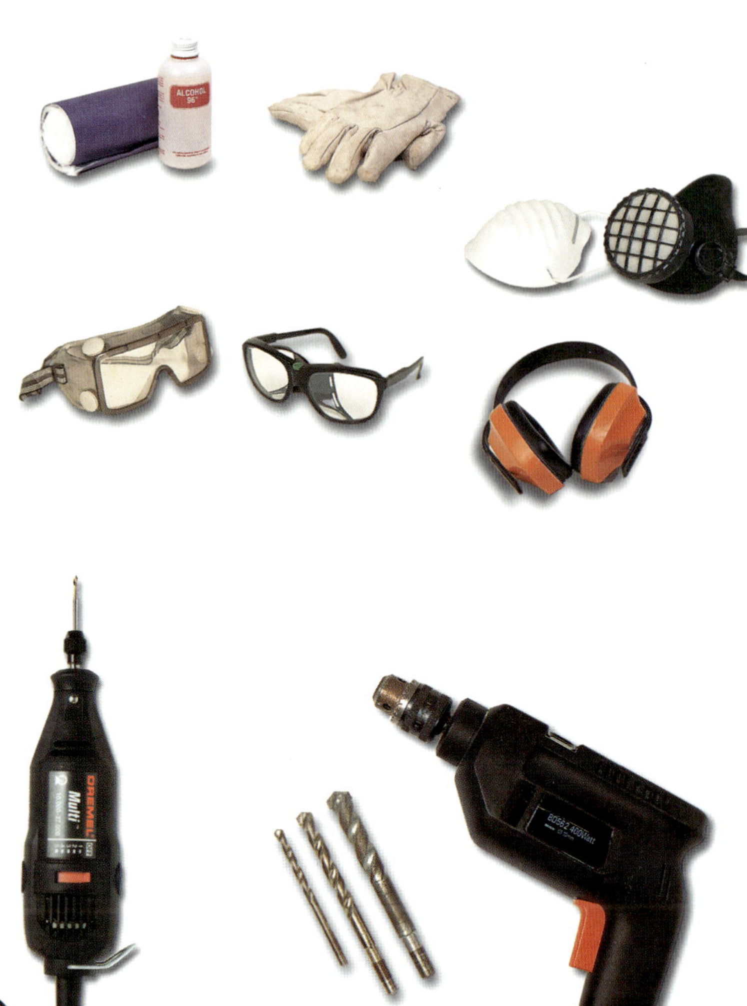

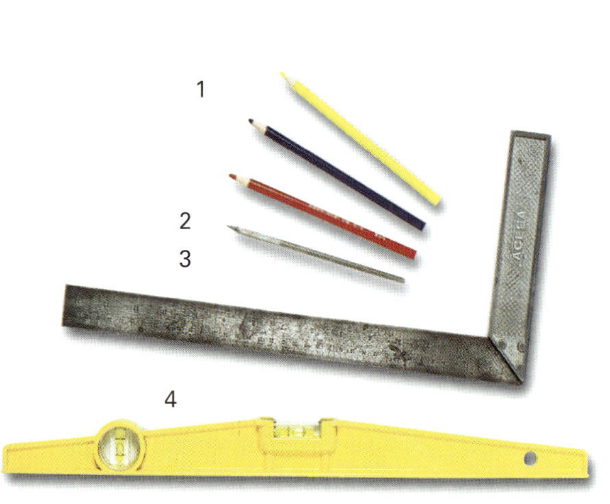

▲ Even for direct carving it would be useful to have tools for measuring and projection as they will be necessary if we plan to do enlargements with a square or template. Most often these include: (1) special colored pencils for stone; (2) a plotter, a type of metal pencil that etches grooves in the stone; (3) a metal square; and (4) a level.

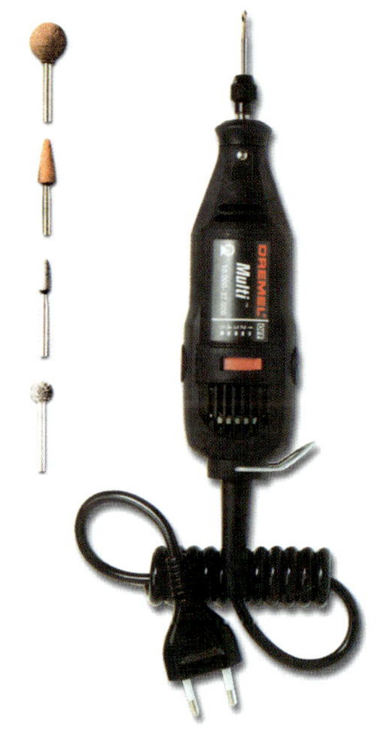

▲ Do-it-yourselfers have small machines with numerous attachments for working different materials. Some of these attachments can be used to do detail work in stone, but if we want to go further with sculpture, it is preferable to invest in more durable equipment.

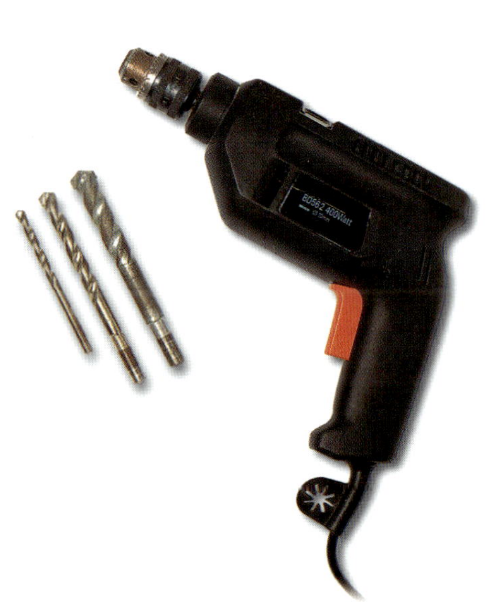

▲ Of the do-it-yourself tools, the drill is most useful for sculpture. Tungsten carbide bits replace the traditional trepan. Later we will see other tools for finishing.

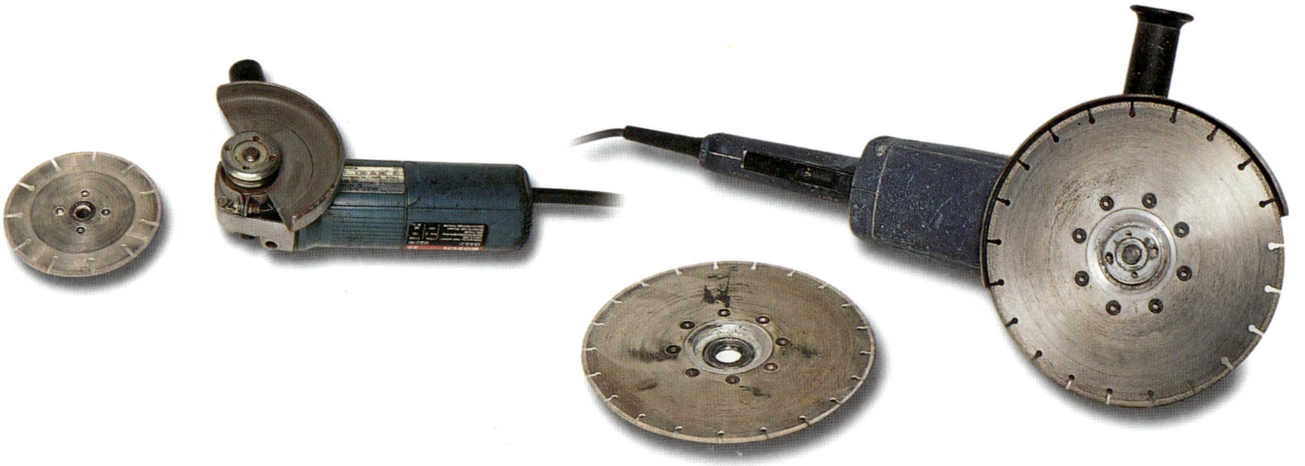

◄ If we plan to spend many hours carving, we should have a small or medium-sized circular saw to which we can attach different diamond blades for cutting and roughing out. We can even use it for modeling if we use a carborundum blade.

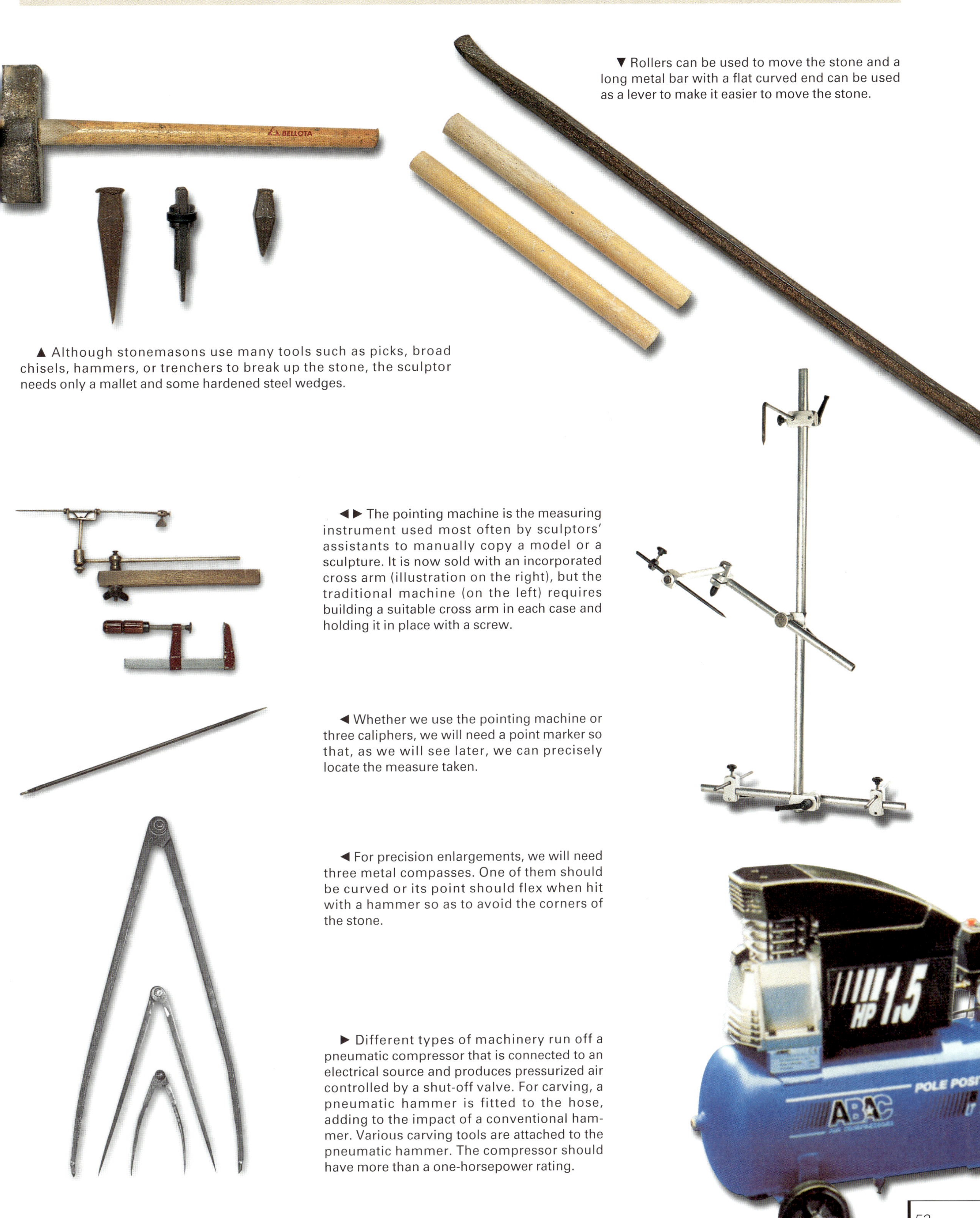

▼ Rollers can be used to move the stone and a long metal bar with a flat curved end can be used as a lever to make it easier to move the stone.

▲ Although stonemasons use many tools such as picks, broad chisels, hammers, or trenchers to break up the stone, the sculptor needs only a mallet and some hardened steel wedges.

◀ ▶ The pointing machine is the measuring instrument used most often by sculptors' assistants to manually copy a model or a sculpture. It is now sold with an incorporated cross arm (illustration on the right), but the traditional machine (on the left) requires building a suitable cross arm in each case and holding it in place with a screw.

◀ Whether we use the pointing machine or three calliphers, we will need a point marker so that, as we will see later, we can precisely locate the measure taken.

◀ For precision enlargements, we will need three metal compasses. One of them should be curved or its point should flex when hit with a hammer so as to avoid the corners of the stone.

▶ Different types of machinery run off a pneumatic compressor that is connected to an electrical source and produces pressurized air controlled by a shut-off valve. For carving, a pneumatic hammer is fitted to the hose, adding to the impact of a conventional hammer. Various carving tools are attached to the pneumatic hammer. The compressor should have more than a one-horsepower rating.

Carving Tools

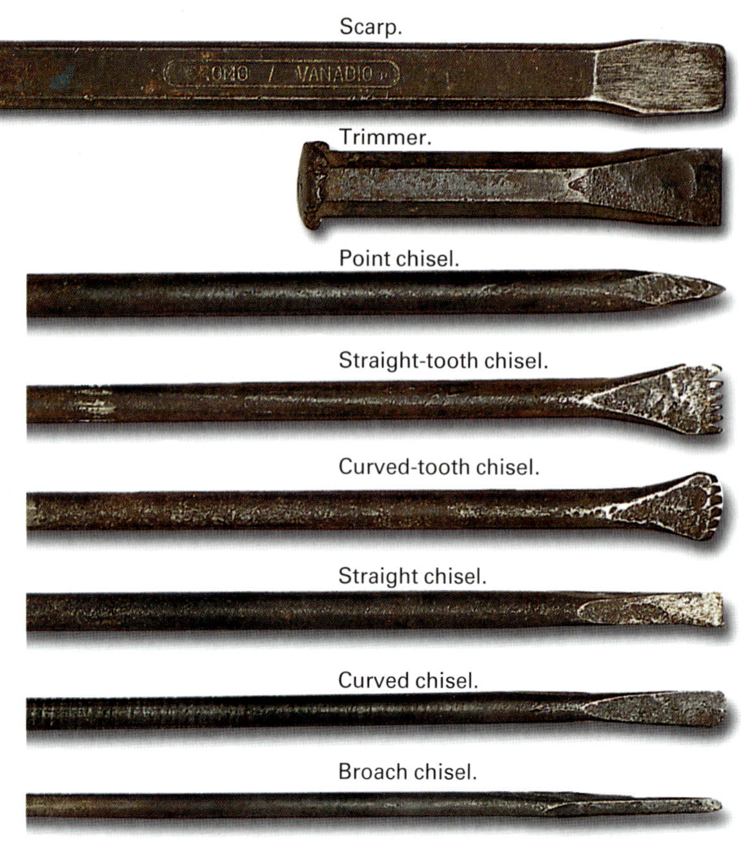

On this spread we show a selection of carving tools specifically used by sculptors. Those on the left are traditional hardened steel tools, plus mallets used as manual hammers. On the right are their pneumatic counterparts with tungsten carbide edges and heads adapted to the compressor hammer. Alongside each we show their outline and body width; the tungsten carbide appears darker. Between the manual tools and the compressor tools we show, in outline, the most common blade widths, valid for all of them.

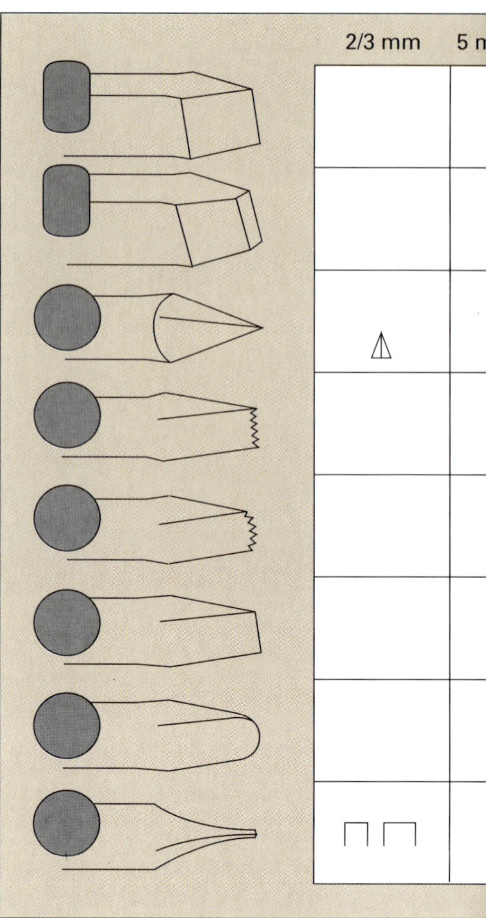

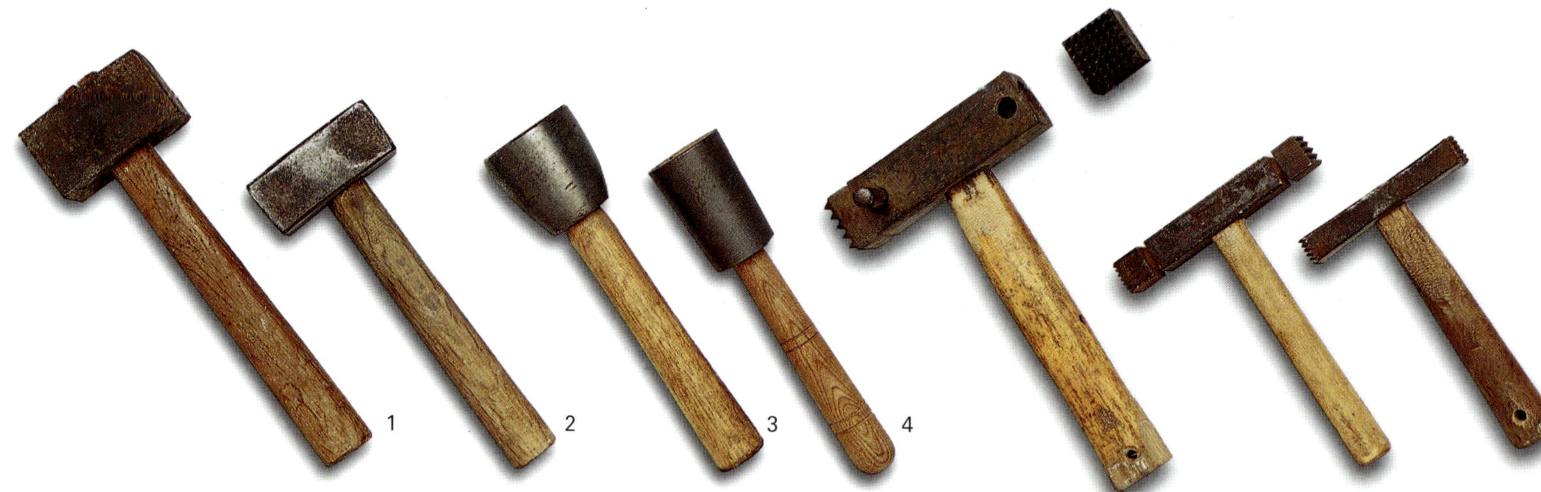

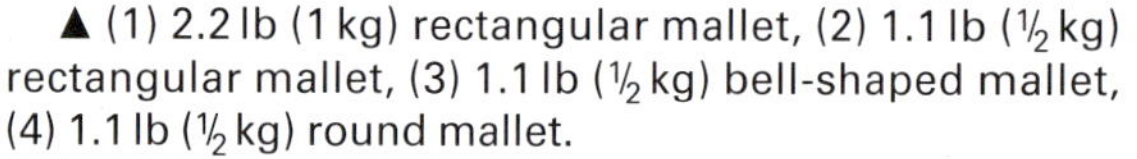

▲ (1) 2.2 lb (1 kg) rectangular mallet, (2) 1.1 lb (½ kg) rectangular mallet, (3) 1.1 lb (½ kg) bell-shaped mallet, (4) 1.1 lb (½ kg) round mallet.

▲ Bushhammers: large and medium with changeable head and small traditional bushhammer. On the right, the outline of their pyramid-shaped teeth.

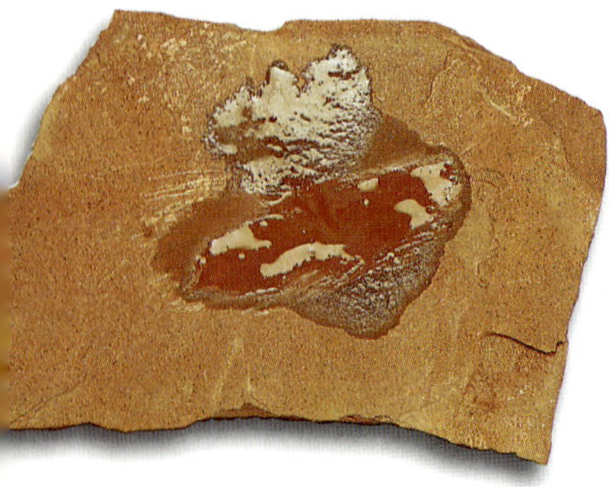

◄ The edges of these tools wear down with use. It is therefore advisable to have a whetstone on hand. To grind point or plain chisels when the tip has broken, we use a grindstone or, since the procedure is a delicate one, we take them to a professional who straightens them out and tempers them again.

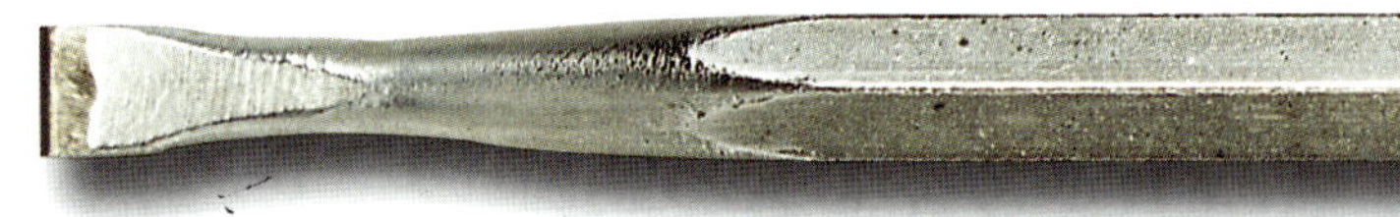

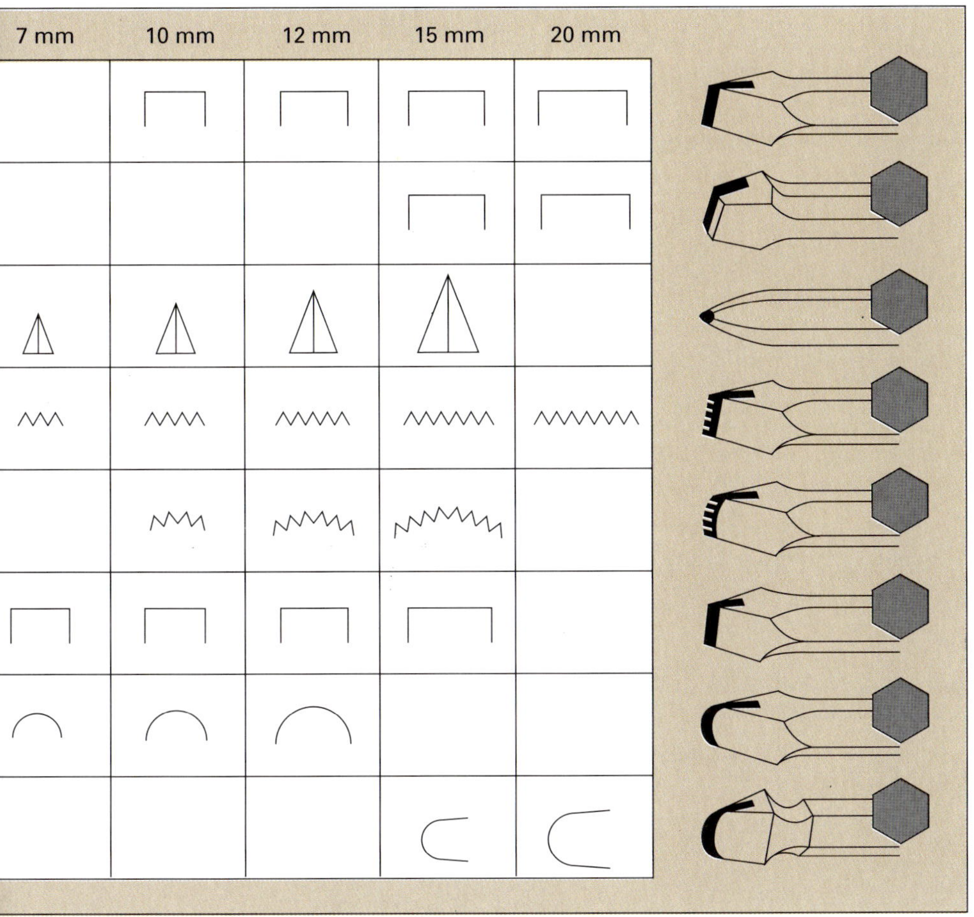

◀ Although there are tungsten carbide scarps, moles, and point chisels, they are rarely used.

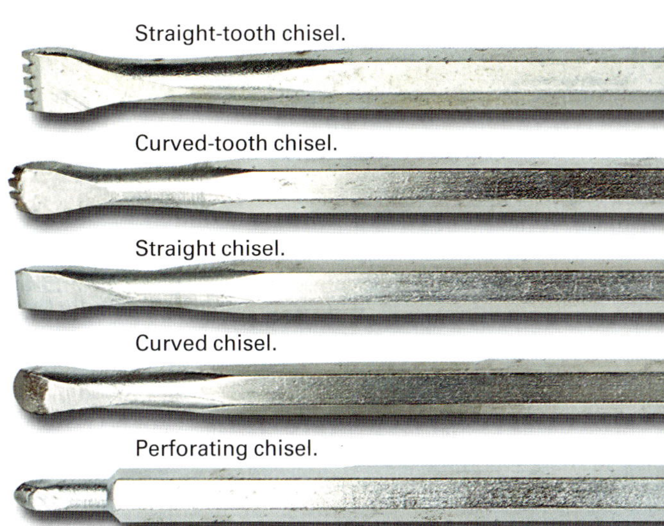
Straight-tooth chisel.
Curved-tooth chisel.
Straight chisel.
Curved chisel.
Perforating chisel.

▼ Pyramid-shaped teeth of the bushhammer and bushing tool, viewed from above and from the side.

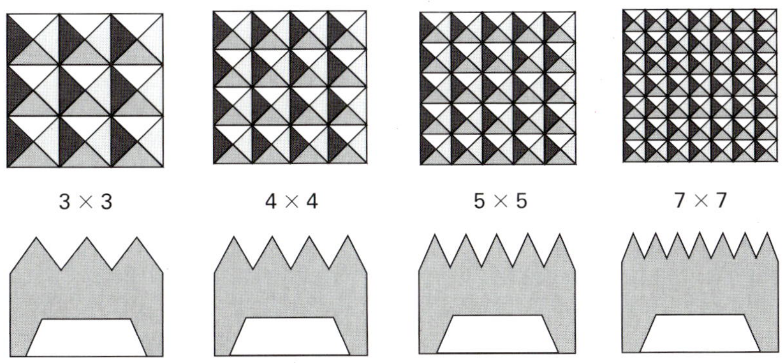

▼ The bushing tool, which replaces the manual bushhammer and has similar teeth, is attached to the pneumatic hammer, which makes it turn and move back and forth, allowing us to mold a plane, concave, or convex surface.

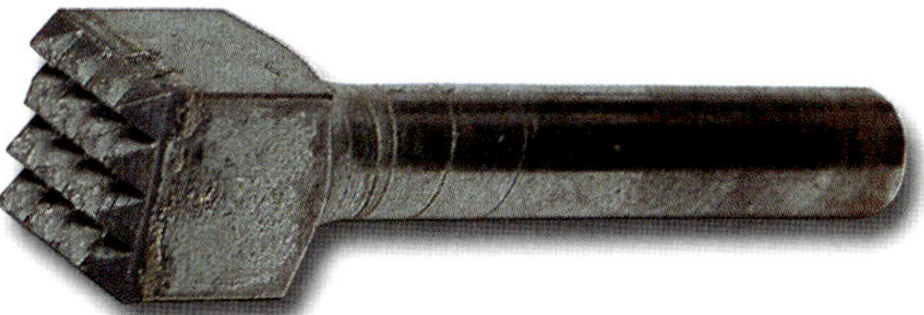
▲ Square bushing tool.

▲ Cylindrical bushing tool.

▼ Pneumatic hammer with tungsten carbide chisel attached, life size.

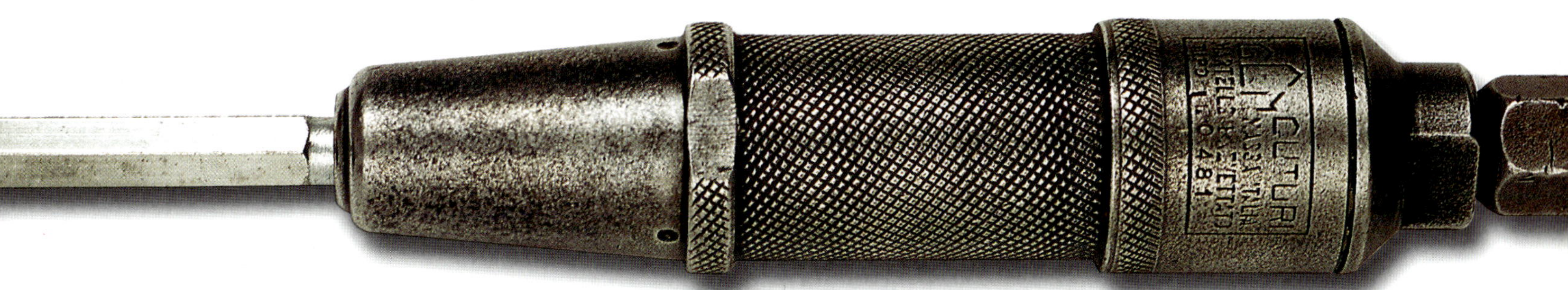

Finishing Tools

We understand finishing as the process of sculpting details, smoothing or evening out surfaces, and polishing until the stone becomes glossy and then shining until we can see light reflected in the stone. We can do all this by hand, by attaching accessories to a drill, or by using special machines.

Hand Tools

These are some of the items most commonly used to hand finish a sculpture: rifflers, carborundum stone, and rasps.

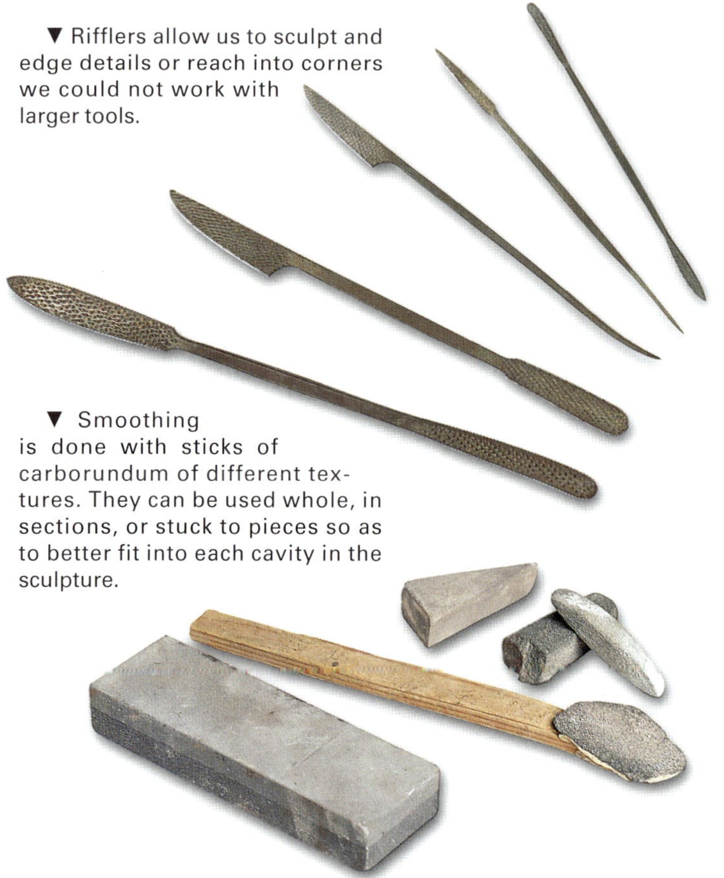

▼ Rifflers allow us to sculpt and edge details or reach into corners we could not work with larger tools.

▼ Smoothing is done with sticks of carborundum of different textures. They can be used whole, in sections, or stuck to pieces so as to better fit into each cavity in the sculpture.

▼ Sandpaper or emery, which we can reinforce with a block of wood and use to even off surfaces is used to smooth soft stones such as alabaster but can also be used to polish the corners of other harder stones (A). Another type of sandpaper is moistened with water and used to shine limestone and hard stones (B), rolls of ordinary sandpaper (C), and sandpaper for use with water (D).

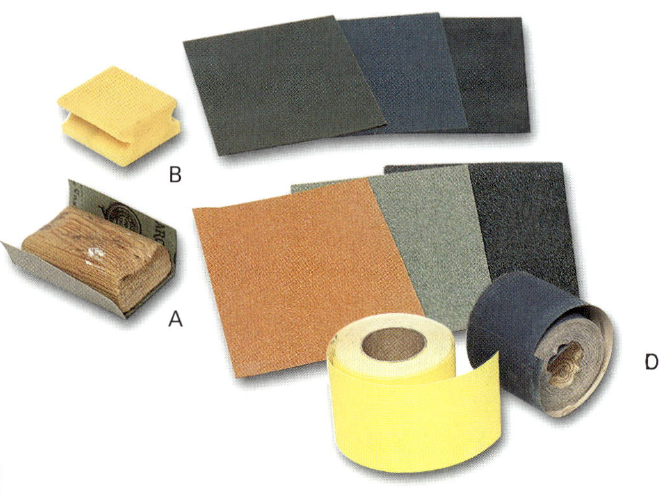

Other Ways to Use a Drill

We can speed up the process of finishing details by attaching carborundum cutters to the drill. To polish these details, we can also fix a rubber support to the drill plus small filing attachments. We can polish large surfaces by attaching sandpaper disks to the same rubber plate.

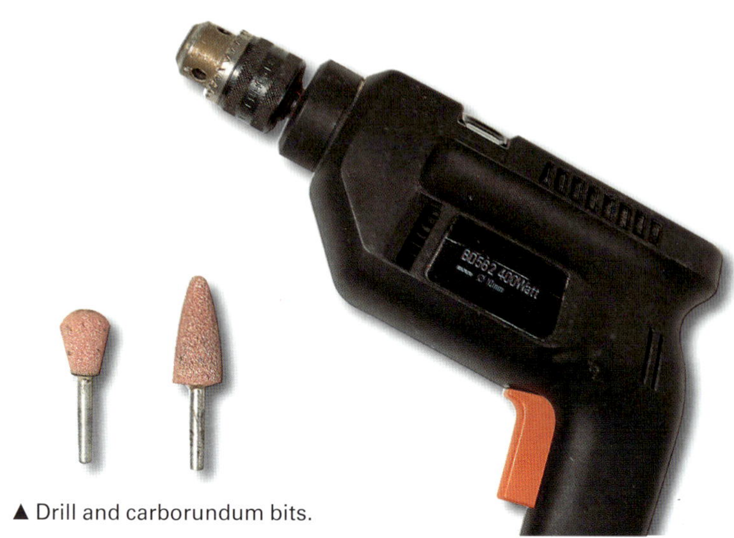

▲ Drill and carborundum bits.

▼ Small filing attachments and rubber supports.

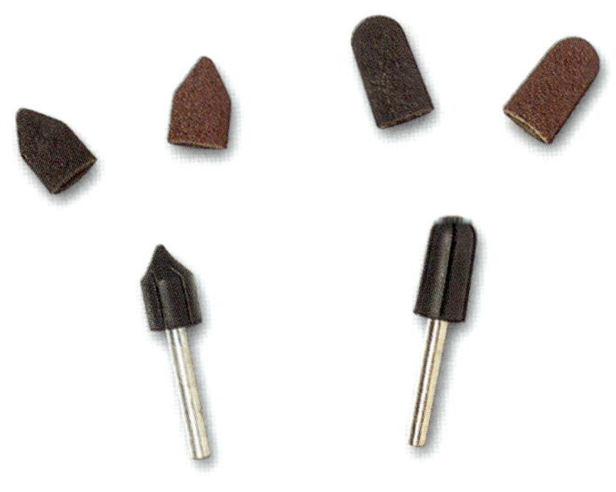

▼ Rubber plate (A) and different sandpaper disks that, when attached to the drill, allow us to polish flat surfaces.

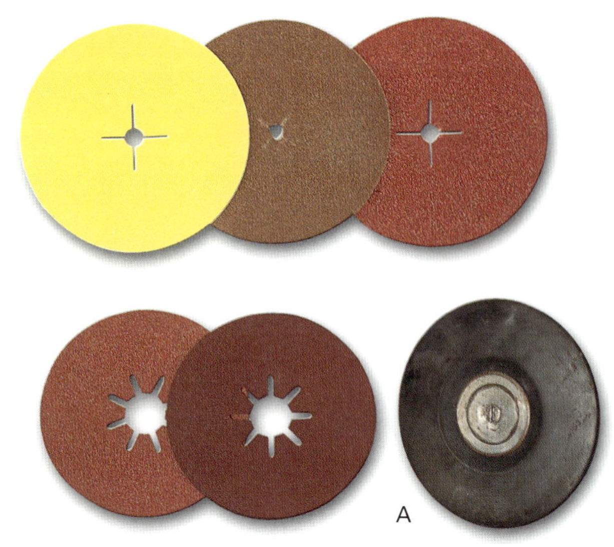

Specific Machinery

If we have an electric or pneumatic drill, we can attach small disks and diamond cutters that allow us to carve and smooth out details even on hard stone. If we attach a very fine cutter we can also make linear incisions and even sign our work.

There are also electric polishers that are more powerful than a drill. Carborundum or diamond disks are attached to them over a rubber plate for shaping, and if the disks are very fine grained, they can also be used for polishing.

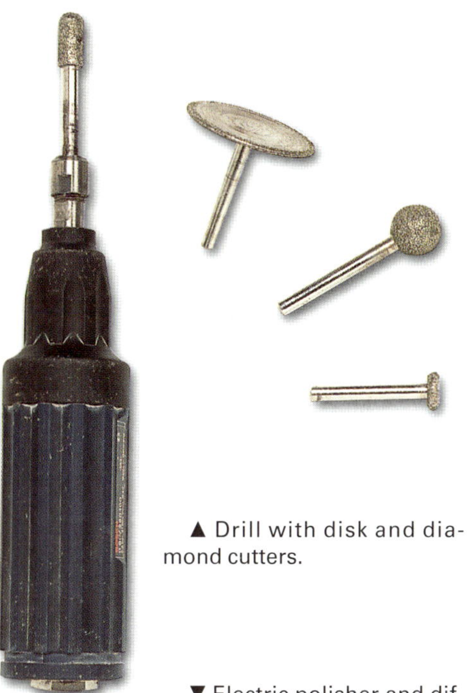

▲ Drill with disk and diamond cutters.

▼ Electric polisher and different carborundum and diamond disks.

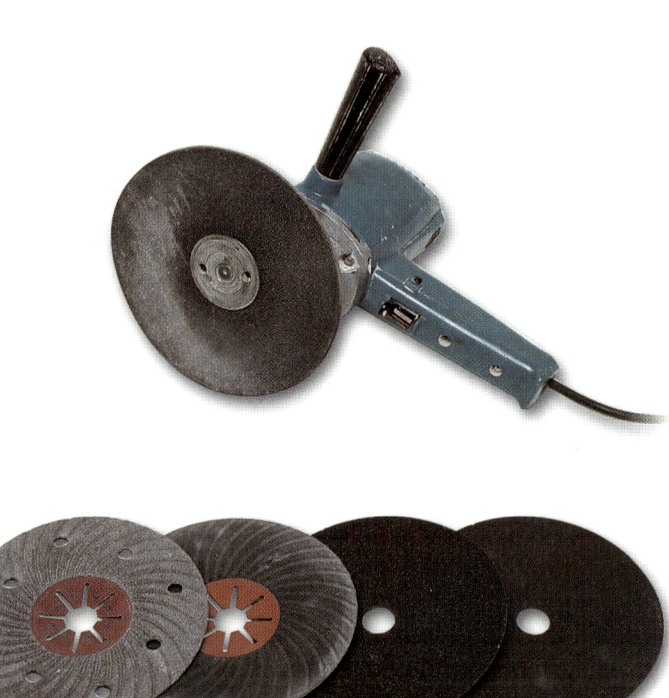

Brightening

If we want to give more light to stones that allow for it, once we have polished the stone with any of the preceding methods, we can highlight its shine with fabric disks attached to the polisher or by applying specific products offered on the market.

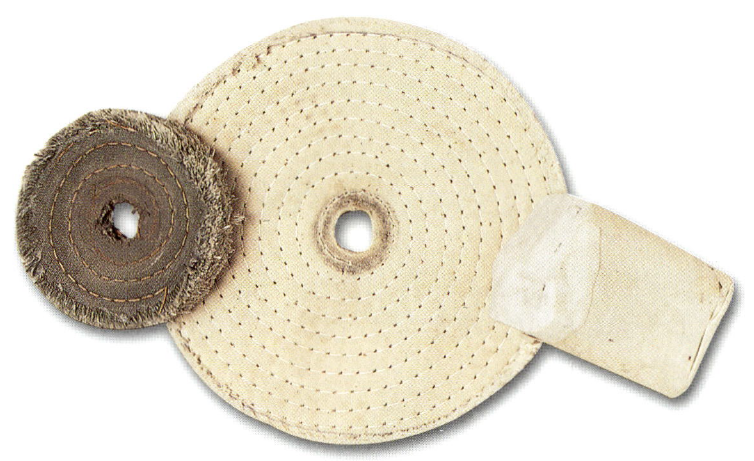

▲ Fabric disks suitable for attaching to a drill or polisher and polishing paste.

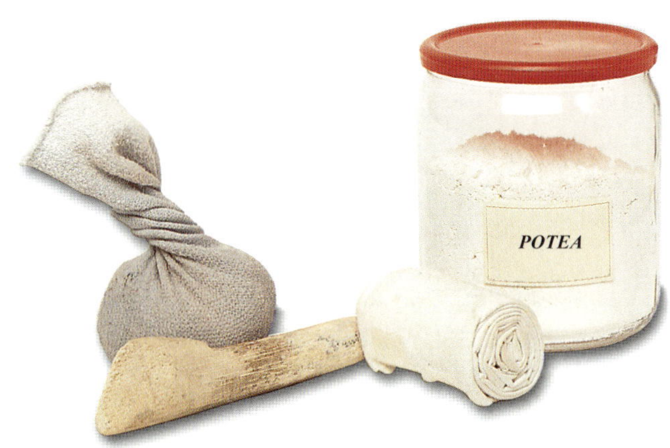

▲ Specialized stores provide recommendations on the most suitable products for shining each stone. The usual method is to soak a rag with one of these products and rub it in by hand. We can also use a palm leaf fiber to reach into corners.

Industrial Machinery

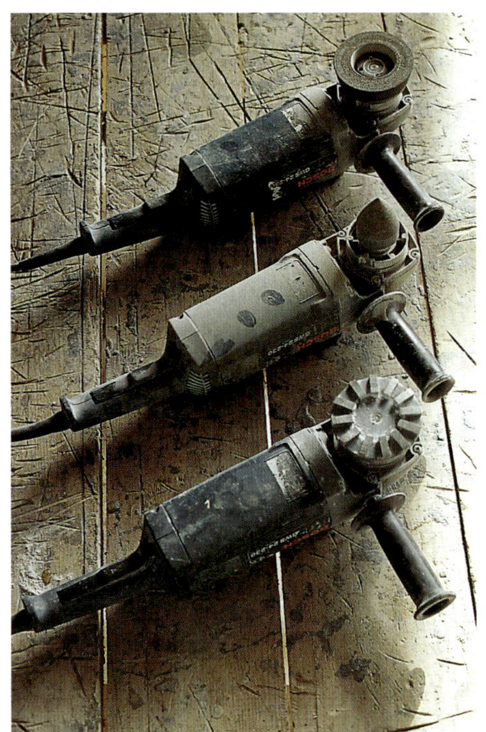

We should remember that industries that are well equipped to work large blocks of stone are usually set up next to large quarries. Given that their principal clients are involved in construction, what is most in demand are slabs for covering buildings and therefore, these industries spend most of their time preparing blocks of stone. However, the machines they have can be of use to the sculptor who is planning a monumental work and who wants to save himself some hard roughing-out work by having the block shaped for him or asking them to polish a side of the sculpture that doesn't need to be carved.

In these industries, we can find anything from the most traditional quarrying tools to the most sophisticated, computer-guided lathes, copiers, or carving machines.

If we focus on the tools we already know about, such as circular saws or polishers, we will note that in the industrial versions the cutting surface is parallel to the motor and not toward the front. This and the fact that they are very powerful makes them more suitable for long jobs during which they will have to support a lot of weight.

Another characteristic of industrial cutting and abrasive tools is that they are set up so that a hose can be attached for wetting down the stone so that the blades don't overheat.

We can also see some welding machinery that is used in a process in which a broad surface of the stone is overheated. This causes cracks in the most superficial layers of the stone and makes it possible to imitate natural erosion.

▲ ► Industrial polishers and cutters.

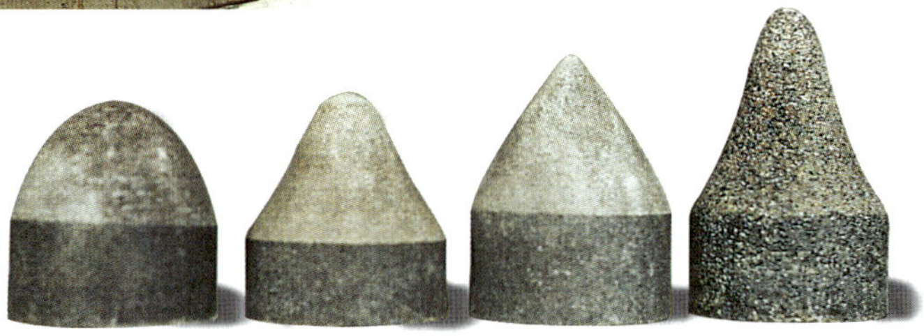

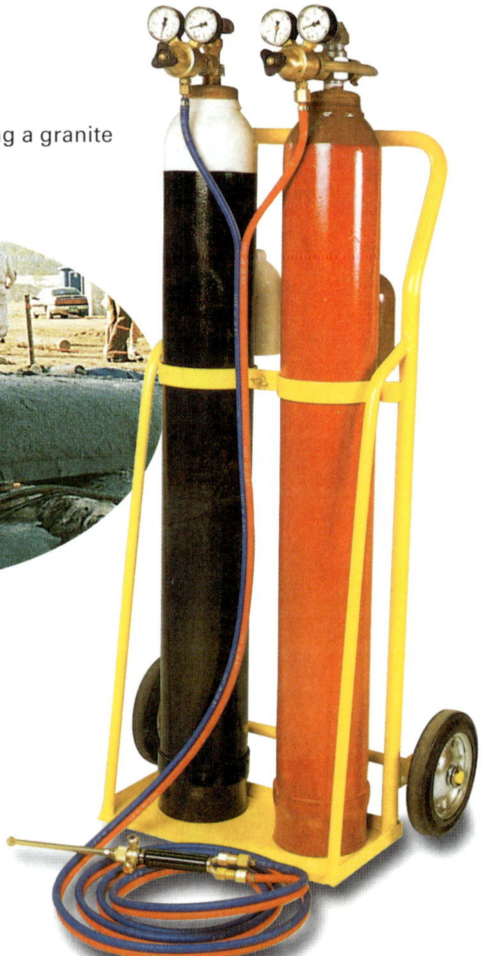

▼ Flaming a granite sculpture.

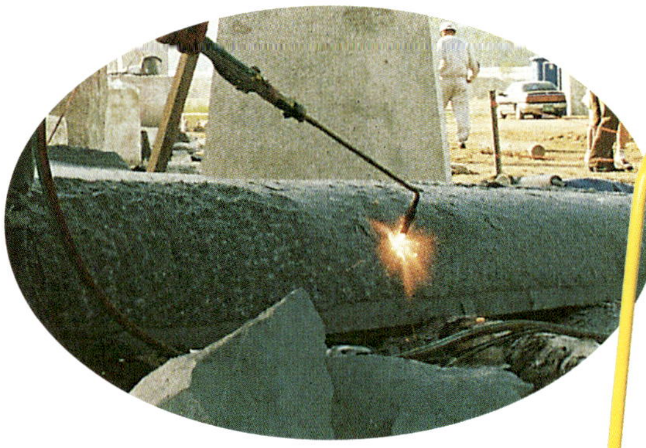

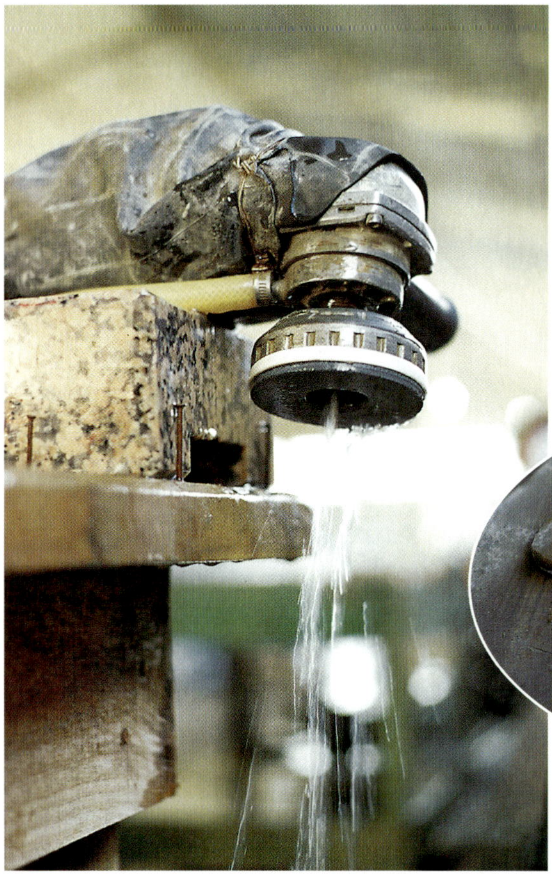

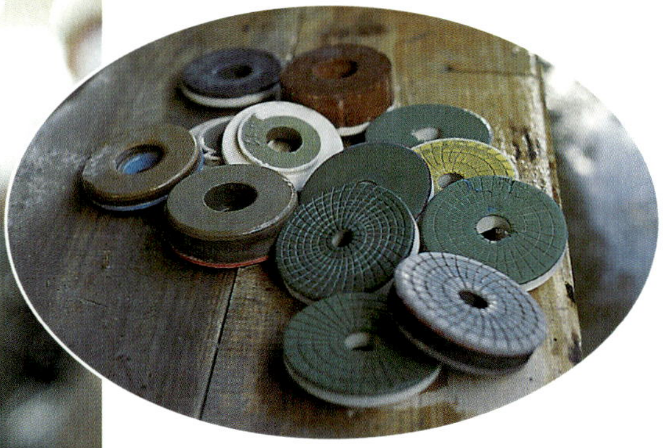

◄ ▲ Abrasive and polishing blades that have been fitted to a hose.

▲ Welding equipment used to flame a stone in order to simulate erosion.

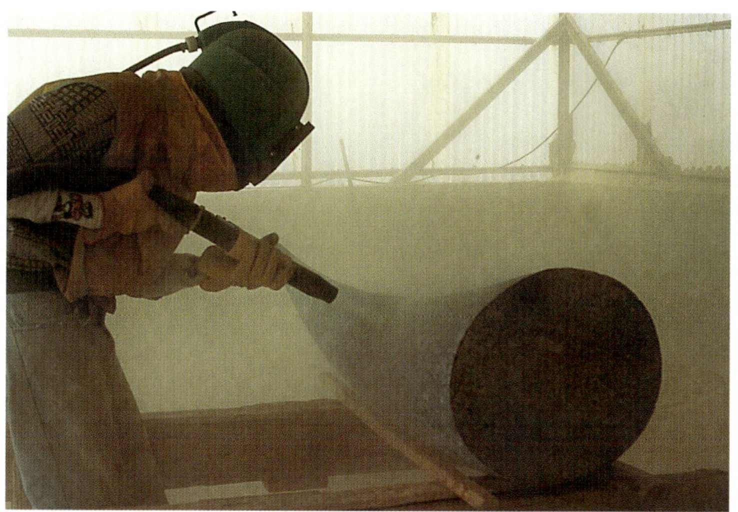

▲ Process of "sanding" a sculpture.

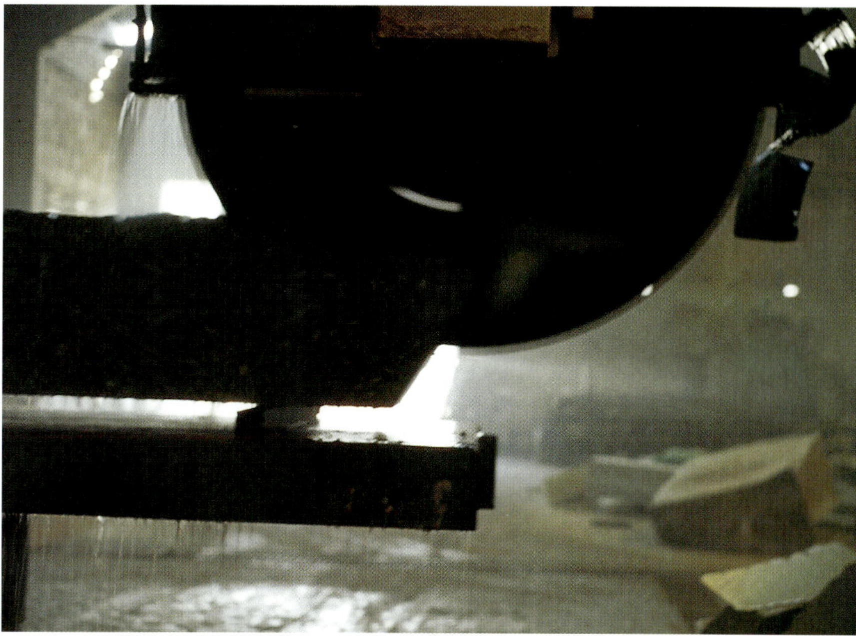

▲ Diamond blade at the *Artangola* workshop in Barcelos (Portugal), smoothing a piece of granite $1\frac{1}{2} \times 1\frac{1}{2} \times 15\frac{1}{2}$ feet ($0.5 \times 0.5 \times 5$ m).

Another way to simulate erosion consists of blasting the stone with a jet of sand under great pressure. In addition to the right machinery, this requires an appropriate location and the use of a face mask to prevent potential injuries.

In this type of industry, it is surprising to see how insignificant the great blocks of stone seem under the huge blades or on top of the immense polishing platforms.

Another more complex machine uses a diamond thread that slowly but at a constant rate gives the block a shape that has been designed in advance.

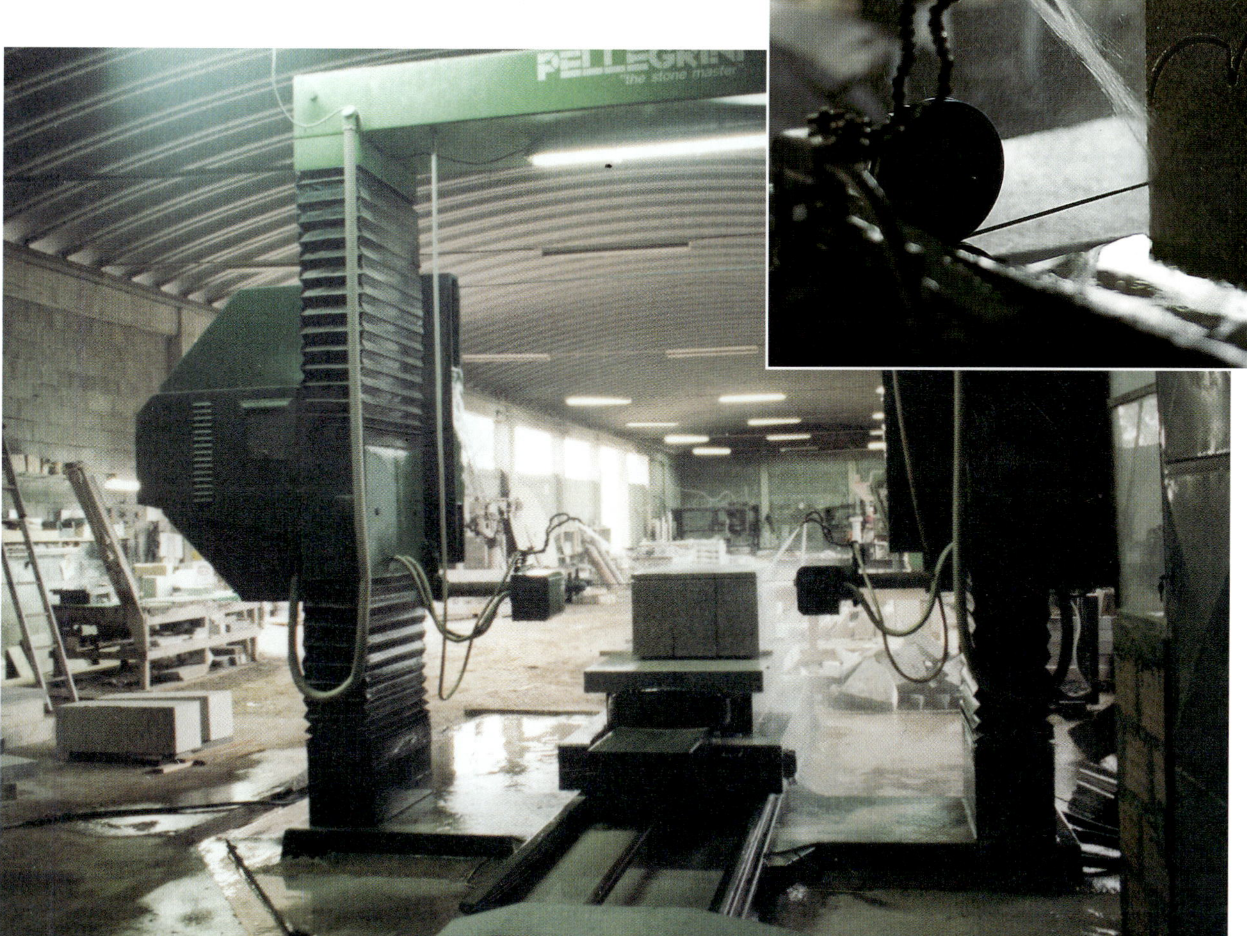

◄▲ Diamond-threaded outlining and detail machine, also at the *Artangola* workshop.

The Project

The initial drawing of a sculpture determines the quality of its outcome. In this section, we present several ideas that will help achieve the quality we are looking for. We then give a step-by-step demonstration of how to cut a maquette and we discuss large-scale projects. We conclude the chapter with a section describing the way in which several collaborators worked together to produce a highly complex work.

The aesthetic views of individual artists are more important than precepts posited by experts . . . Just as adhering to dogma does not make one a believer, slavishly following the rules of art does not make one an artist.
Rabindranath Tagore

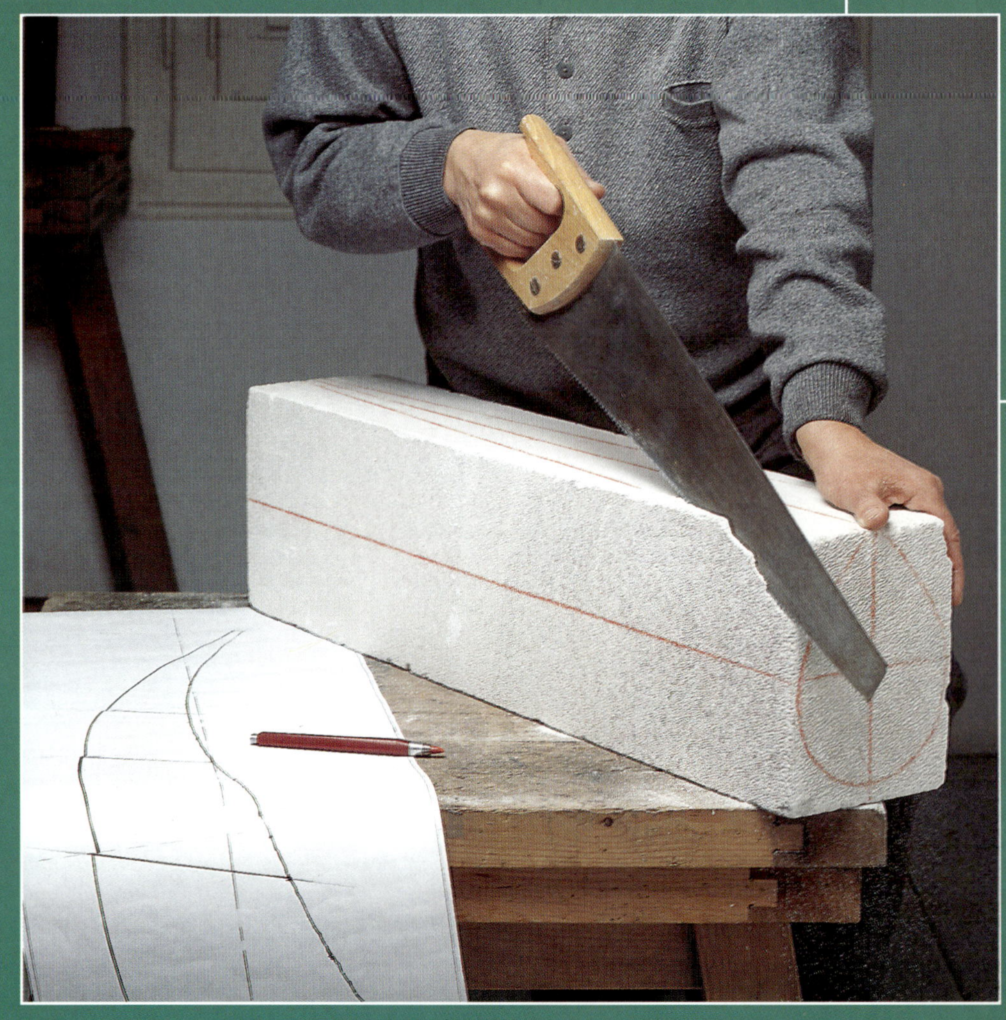

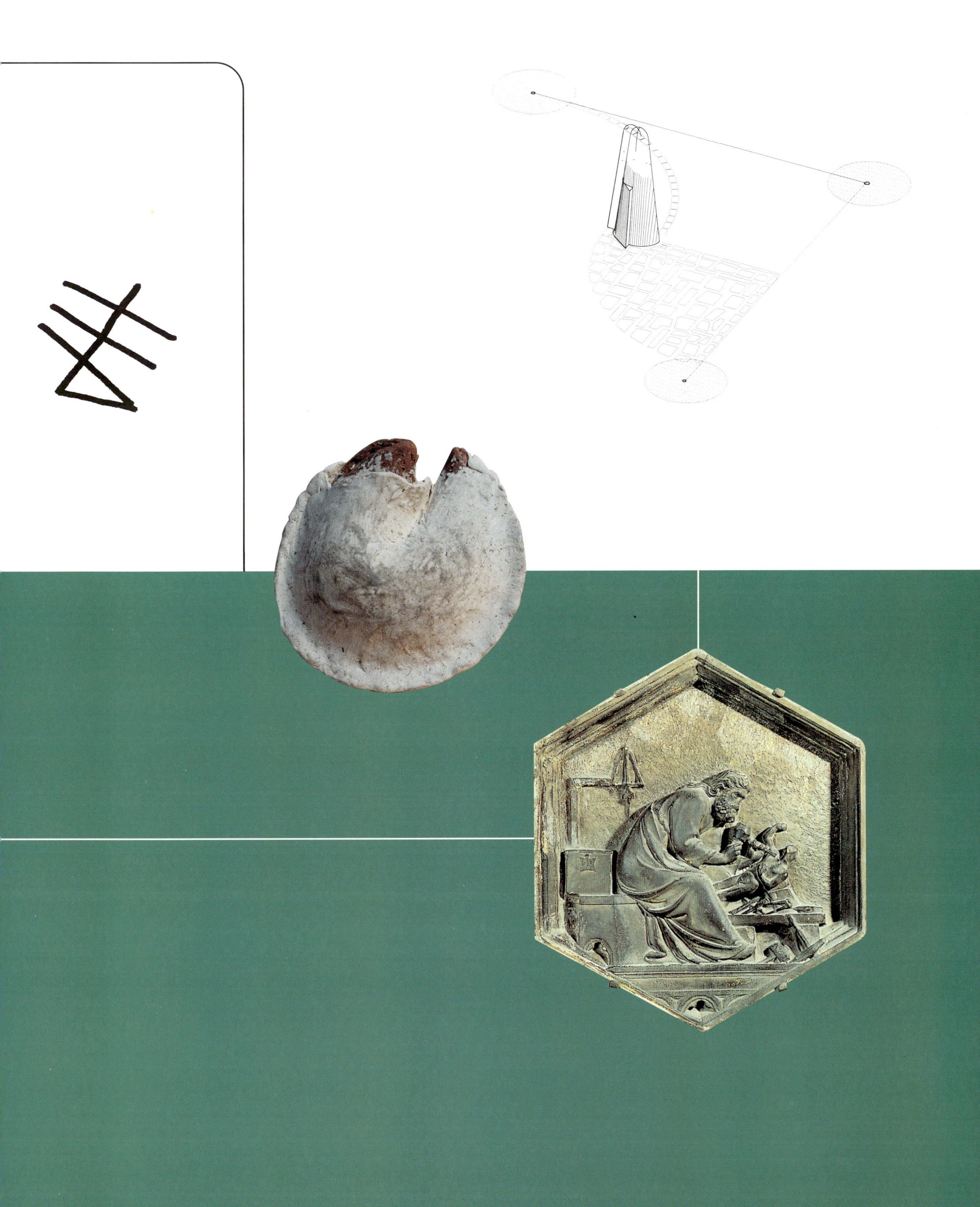

The Philosopher's Stone?

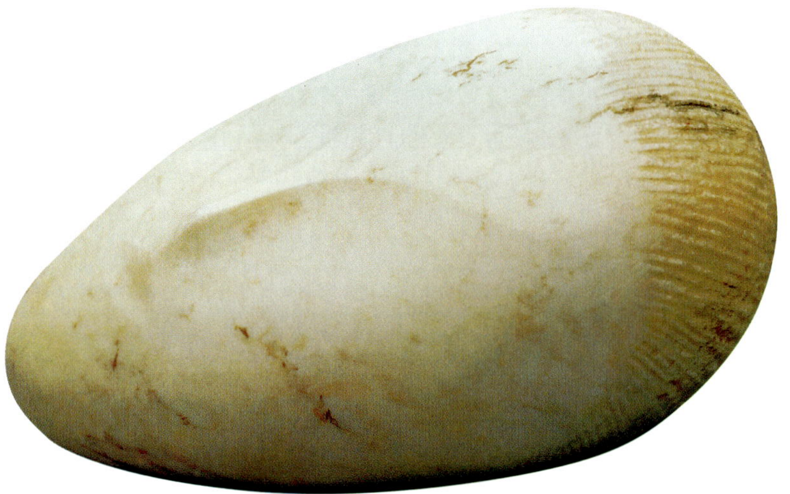

◄ Brancusi. *Sleeping Muse III*, 1918. Marble. Private Collection.

No alchemist or sculptor has ever found the philosopher's stone, that element capable of turning everything it touches into gold or art. However, notable advances have been made in chemistry thanks to alchemists, and present-day artists have benefited from the experiences of sculptors in the past. Before beginning any project, it is helpful then to look back in time to avoid the mistakes made in the past and surpass the accomplishments.

In the chapter entitled "Carving" in our earlier book—*Carving. Wood Sculpture*, Parramon Editions, Barcelona, 1996—we presented several considerations for qualifying a work as art. We endorse our previous ideas and restate them here as we provide some concrete answers to several sculpting questions. We will begin with those that offer aesthetic solutions to technical problems.

The fragile or delicate nature of a subject can be rendered while still preserving its poise and harmony: Greek athletes posed "casually" alongside a stone or trunk of a tree; the folds in many sculptures, though they represent fabric, are made of marble and serve as a pretext for providing volume to a work; in the Medici chapel, Michelangelo discretely highlights the Virgin's foot by allowing it to overhang the pedestal, and so on.

If a stone, because of its characteristics or shape, can set its own standards, why shouldn't we set ours? Many sculptures end up being overwhelming because they are unable to break free from the marble block from which they were carved. We have much to learn in this regard from the Hittite, Mesopotamian, or pre-Columbian sculptures.

Although we can always choose a stone that best suits our purpose, it is better to subordinate our modeling ideas to the characteristics of the stone, such as its crystallization, fossil traits, and, in particular, the direction of its veins.

The *wet cloth* technique, starting from a model with wet clothes clinging to the body, allowed Fidias to combine reverence for his ceremoniously dressed goddesses with the beauty of the feminine form. It also created a sweeping sense of serenity on the faces of a Buddha or a Roman Pantocrator. If we set aside the folds or focus on the exterior of figurative sculptures, we will understand that the taste for abstraction has remained dormant for centuries.

Classical sculptures intended to be viewed from a distance also convey a certain expressiveness. This becomes clearer when the work is placed closer to the viewer, as happened with Michelangelo's *David*. Should we not, then, deliberately use disproportion as a means of expression, following the example of the Roman sculptors and the primitivism reclaimed by Gauguin?

Realism also conceals slight distortions in the anatomy, precisely to give it a more realistic appearance—the size of a sculpted body needs to be a little larger than a human body to compensate for its lack of movement. Carracci suggested that Bernini draw muscles in the style of Michelangelo until he was able to render them as an integrated whole. To avoid optical distortions, Bernini preferred to sculpt long legs and a small head and feet, and to enlarge the muscles of the male while shrinking those of the female.

Learning from existing theories on sculpture, we should point out first of all that the evolution of style is a continuous cycle: hieratism—sobriety—ornamentation; or the inverse: expression of feelings—equilibrium—purity of forms. This evolution is also evident, albeit imperceptibly, in the work of the most unsettled sculptors. Being aware of this evolution opens the way to self-criticism and keeps us from falling into areas that we otherwise would reject.

The diversity of opinions on the *law* governing the ideal proportions of the human body undermines the dogma of absolute classical beauty. The law not only relates to European concerns about the proportion of the head with respect to the body or, in the case of the colossal Olmec heads, to facial expressions, it also deals with finer details such as the length of toes, something that is different in Mediterranean and Hindu cultures.

Though it would seem unlikely, the complex studies on the *golden* section, the ideal balance between the representation of strength and volume, is not limited to realistic sculpture. Concern for the mathematical structure of forms is at the root of contemporary art as well. It was a topic of study at the Bauhaus, and Brancusi had it in mind when he conceived his *Gate of the Kiss*, a work we referred to earlier. Gestalt psychologists have also studied the effects of balance on perception. Their conclusions about the emotions a work of art can arouse in our subconscious are added to already existing conclusions on balance or tension between lines and dominant volumes in a sculpture.

Sculpture in the twentieth century taught us respect for material, as we infused it with our own personality. It also taught us to pursue pure forms without yielding to excessive ornamentation; to value the internal or surrounding space of a sculpture while keeping the human scale in mind; and, above all, to capture the essence of sculpting without giving in to mimicry of forms.

Brancusi was obsessive in his pursuit of pure form or what we have been referring to here as the philosopher's stone. We can see this in his many ovoid forms rendered in wood, bronze, and various kinds of marble.

Unlike the alchemists, some sculptors have discovered the philosopher's stone. Their discovery was more intuitive than empirical and, what is more, not replicable. Imitating good art has always been part of the learning process during both the classical and abstract periods of art. In fact, training in many art schools includes working in the style of recognized artists. These schools believe that students who are inspired by the work of others will eventually develop their own personal styles. Results are often questionable, oftentimes even for those sculptors who want to imitate successful works of their own. Can this not be explained by the fact that they copy the results and ignore the questions that, if raised, could provide inspiration for new forms?

When criticizing our own work or that of other artists, it is helpful to keep in mind the different schools of philosophy that have studied aesthetics. These range from the classics or Quintillian's Asian school to the Apollonian or Nietzche's Dionysian school. One can assess whether a sculpture is a piece of handicraft or a work of art, a copy or an original; whether it is imbued with formality, symbolism, allegory, or expression; whether it exalts beauty, the sublime, the trivial, or the hideous. However, it is not enough to merely classify a sculpture. The idea behind Tagore's words, which we cited at the beginning of the chapter, apply here as well: Adherence to a religion, ideology, or trend is not enough to judge a person's worth. Assessing artistic value is, perhaps, more intuitive than rational. The right side of our brain may be able to capture this value, while the left side is barely able to grasp any of its anecdotal characteristics.

We conclude the chapter by recalling Bernini's formula, which we believe still applies today, for discovering the philospher's stone, which we believe also still holds true today. It states that we should "contemplate beauty" in the broadest sense of the term as something that torments and stirs us from within; "become accustomed to it" until it is fixed in our subconscious and colors your view of life; and "work hard." This last note calls to mind Vasari's story about Filippo Lippi, the painter who, when accused by his patron of working too slowly, defended himself by saying that his works are "celestial forms not beasts of burden." We find no contradiction in the words of the same historian who, when referring to the works of Michelangelo, affirms: "Works inspired in poetic frenzy are the only true works, superior to those born out of intense labor." Indeed, persevering in one work enables us to create another, first in slow, logical progression and, when we least expect it, through those intuitive leaps that characterize "poetic frenzy." As Picasso would later say: "Inspiration, when it arrives, should find us hard at work."

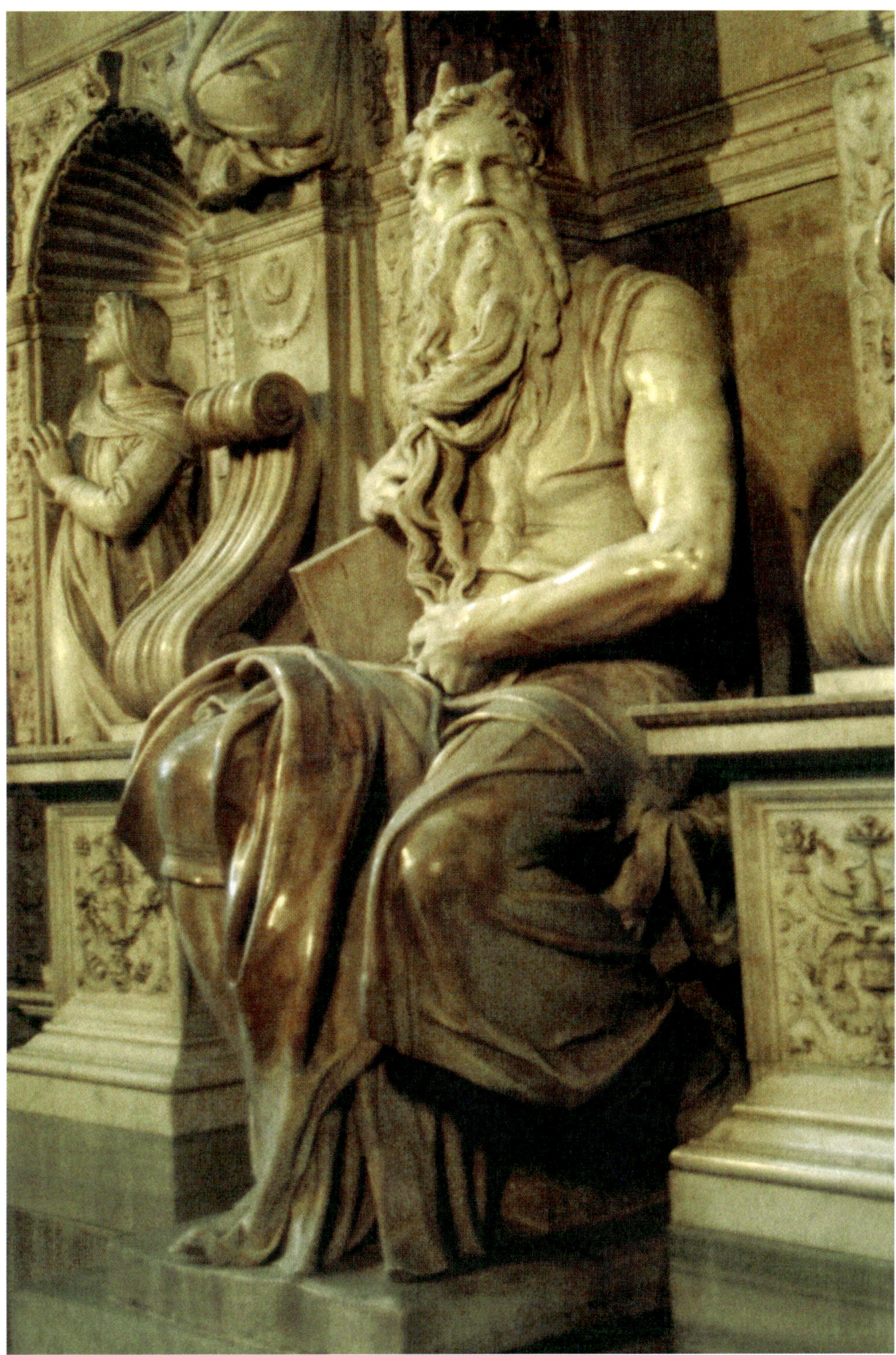

▶ Michelangelo. *Moses*, 1513.
Carrara marble.
Saint Peter in Vincoli, Rome (Italy).
"Why don't you speak?" the artist demanded.

Inspiration in Gestures

Poetic furor does not happen by chance and when it does, it may leave just as quickly. Therefore, it is advisable to always have on hand materials we might need to plan new works that may not be our most creative, but that we take on for the mere pleasure of sculpting.

Copying shapes might perhaps allow us to acquire the technical skills we need to eventually master the basics in stone carving. However, it will be our own life experiences that will ultimately drive our effort to convey in stone what we easily sketched on paper. This is provided, of course, that "inspiration, when it arrives, should find us hard at work."

The human figure is one of the most recurring themes in sculpture. On the one hand, it enables us to exalt the beauty of the body and its defects and, on the other, to convey inner emotions through its stance.

The figurative sculptures on these pages are not necessarily intended to be used as models. Rather, their purpose is to help us look back at the same source for renewed inspiration—the human being; that is, our neighbors, with all of their sufferings and triumphs.

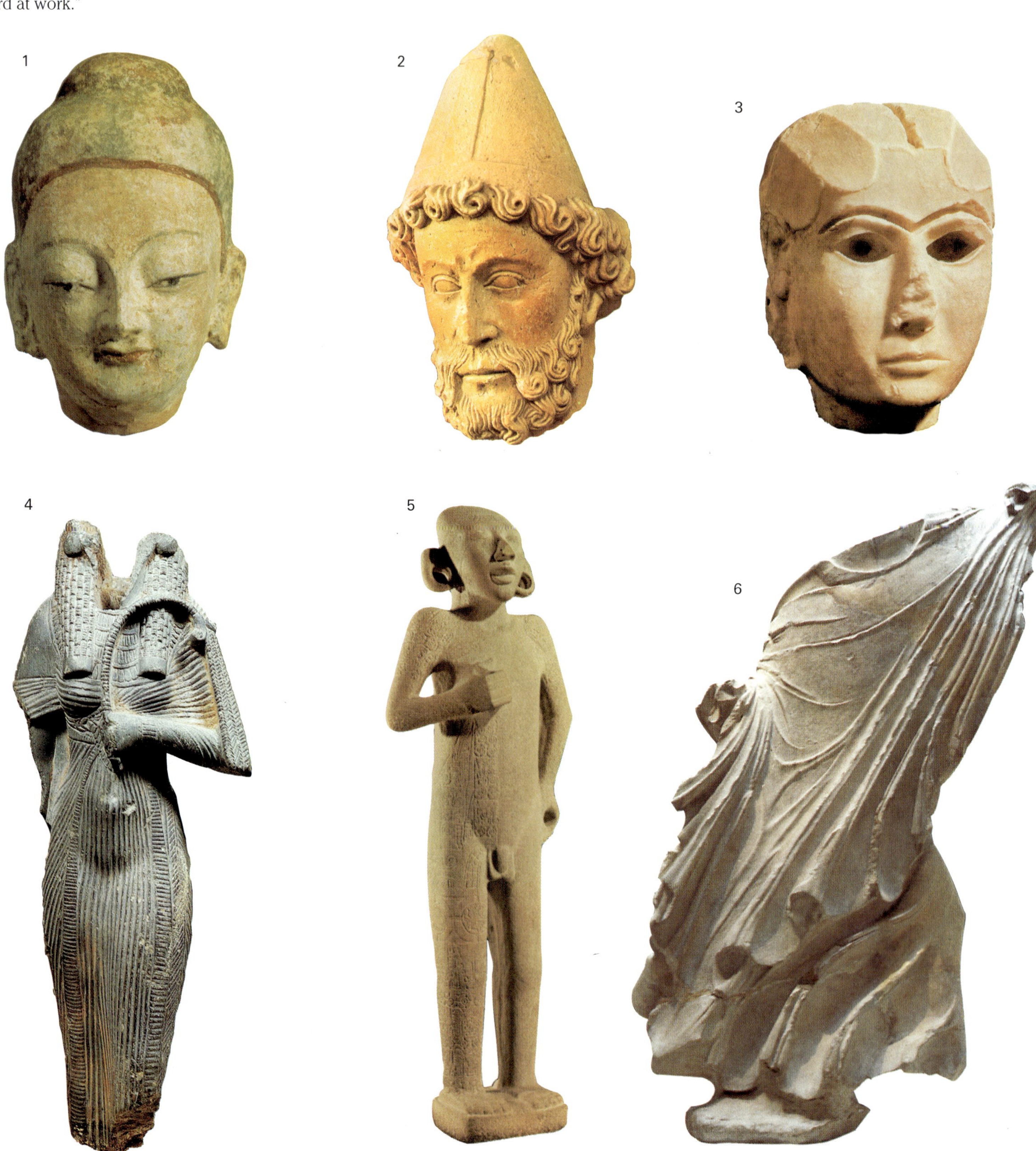

7

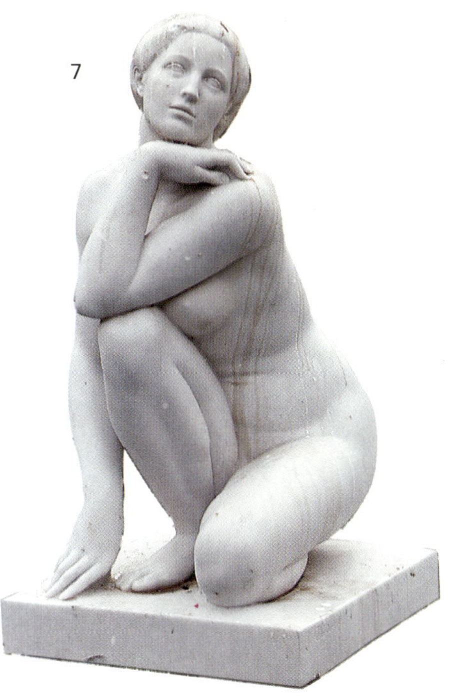

8

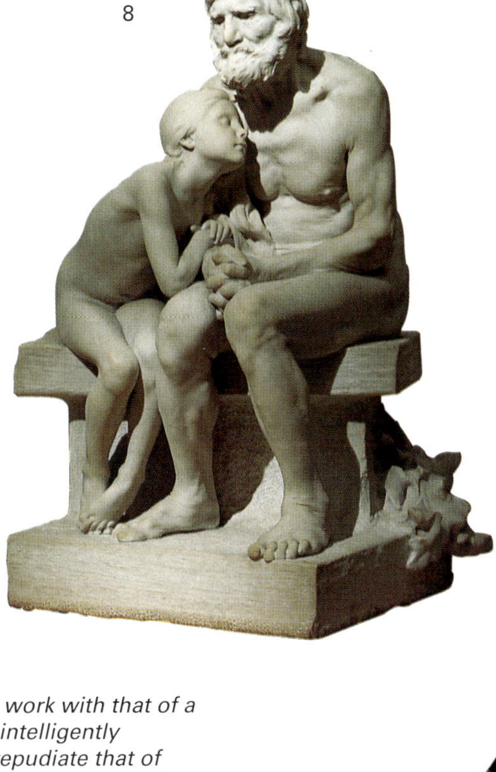

9

One advantage we have is that we can compare our work with that of a thousand others who have come before us. We can intelligently continue in the tradition of Scopas or unabashedly repudiate that of Praxiteles.

Marguerite Yourcenar

Art that is the result of fleeting inspiration should be viewed quickly because it lacks depth and character. On the other hand, art that is structured, complex, and mature is based on analysis and can be contemplated forever.

Josep Clara

1. *Head of Buddha.* ninth–eleventh centuries. Polychrome stone.

2. *Head of Pope.* Circa 1300. Sandstone (?). Musée du Tau, Reims (France).

3. *The Lady from Warka.* Circa 3000 B.C.E. Marble. Museum of Iraq, Baghdad (Iraq).

4. *Egyptian Queen (detail).* 1250 B.C.E. Polychrome Stone. Cairo Museum (Egypt).

5. *The Adolescent from Tamuin.* Circa 900. National Museum of Anthropology, Mexico D.F. (Mexico).

6. *Nereid of Xanthos.* 380 B.C.E. Marble. British Museum, London (Great Britain).

7. Clara. *Goddess.* 1910/1928. Marble, Copy, Placa de Catalonia, Barcelona (Spain).

8. Blay. *The First Cold.* 1892. Marble. National Museum of Art of Catalonia, Barcelona (Spain).

9. Campeny. *The Dying Lucretia.* 1804. Marble. Chamber of Commerce, Industry and Navigation, Barcelona (Spain).

10. Chac-mool. Circa ninth century. Yucatan (Mexico).

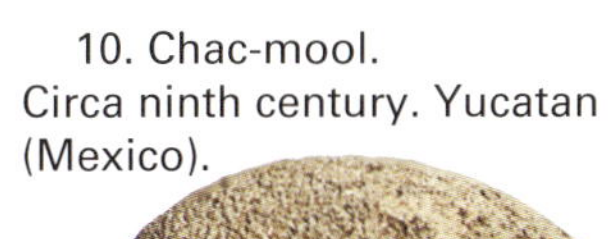

10

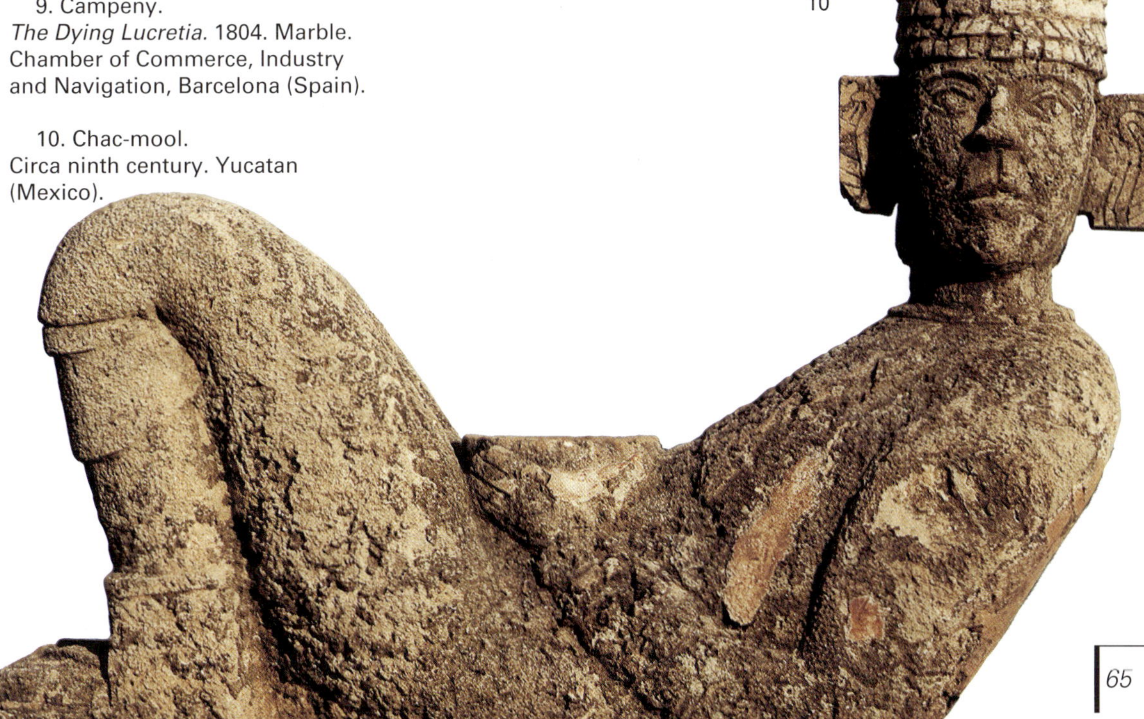

Free Forms

Nature surrounds us with capricious shapes springing from the edge of human feelings and that either delight or disturb as we look at them and, therefore, also serve as a source of inspiration.

Many sculptors have, throughout the centuries, transformed stone into what are commonly known as abstract sculptures. Kant refers to these as "free beauties," a term we also like to use because it expands the concept of beauty to everything that might cause a stir in us.

Though freely formed, these sculptures have their own rules—some imitate organic forms that reflect living things; others the geometric structure of minerals. There are even those that evoke the dream world and are totally abstract, that reduce the anecdotal element to capture what is essential.

Some of these free forms can be highly evocative, the greatest measure of aesthetic value in ancient China. This happens when one object subtly conjures up another so that, when perceived subliminally, it evokes vital situations or moments that are passed down in our collective subconscious and expressed in the form of archetypes.

Many birds and a multitude of fish in the sea are beautiful in their own right even if they have no particular usefulness or purpose. They are naturally pleasing in and of themselves. The same is true for Grecian frets, foliage used to fashion frames, or colored bits of paper, and so on, that have no meaning, represent nothing, and have no utility based on any particular concept, but that are spontaneously beautiful. These fall in the same category as what we refer to in music as fantasy (having no theme) and even music without words.

Immanuel Kant

All good works of art incorporate abstract and surreal elements, order and surprise, intelligence and imagination, science and the subconscious.

Henry Moore

1. Vaulted niche from the Nungsan-ri Temple, Puyo. Sixth century B.C.E. Granite (?). National Treasure, Puyo (Korea).

2. Mora. *Paperina gran.* 1994. Senia limestone. Private Collection.

3. Fragment of Queen Tiyi's Head. Circa 1417–1379 B.C.E. Yellow Jasper. Metropolitan Museum of Art, New York (United States).

4. Archeological Remains from Nemrut Dagi (Turkey). First century C.E. Limestone.

5. Nahara. *Mandala.* 1993. Diabase. Private Collection.

6. Mitoraj. *Augen des meeres.* 1984. Marble. Private Collection.

7. *Hera de Samos* (coré). Circa 570–560 B.C.E. Marble. Louvre Museum, Paris (France).

8. Arp. *Female Torso.* 1953. Marble. Ludwig Museum, Cologne (Germany).

9. Laurens. *Woman with a Guitar.* 1919. Limestone. Private Collection.

10. Louise Bourgeois. *Cumul 1.* 1969. Marble. Georges Pompidou Center, Paris (France).

11. Camí. *Fragment of Strength.* 1985. Marble.

12. Han, Chang-Jo. *Genesis of Language.* 1990. Butress granite. Private Collection.

1

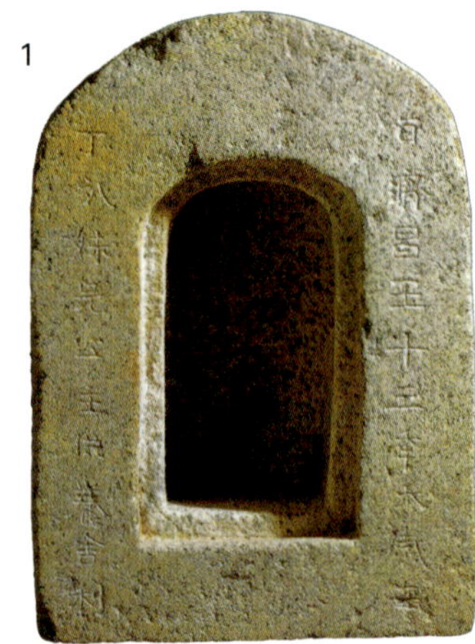

2

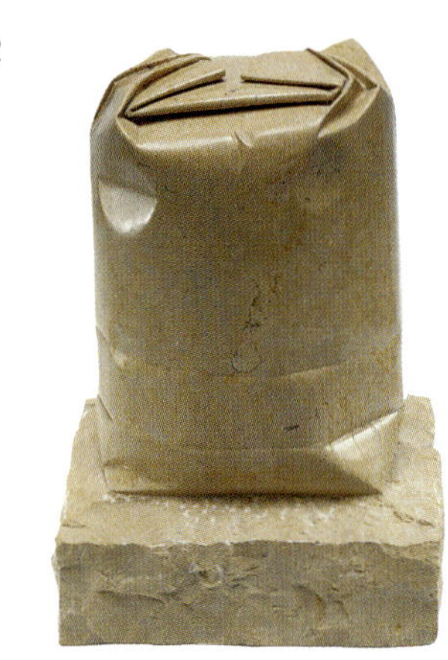

3

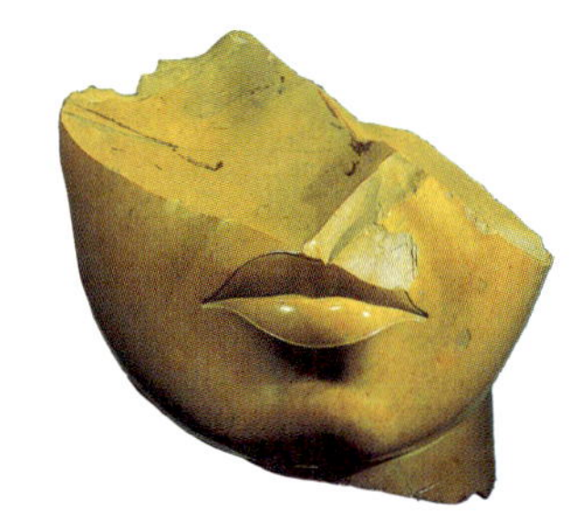

4

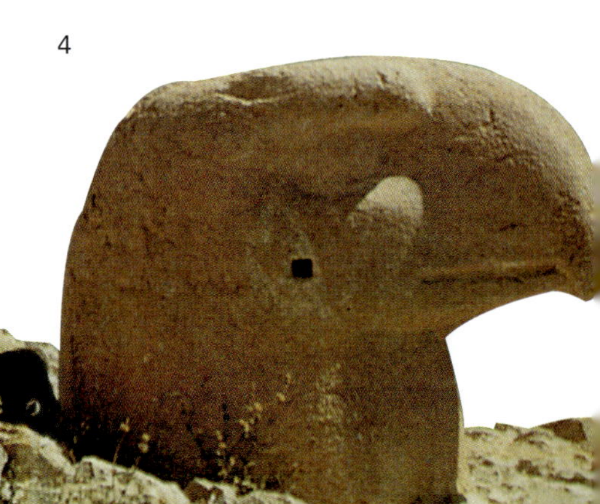

5

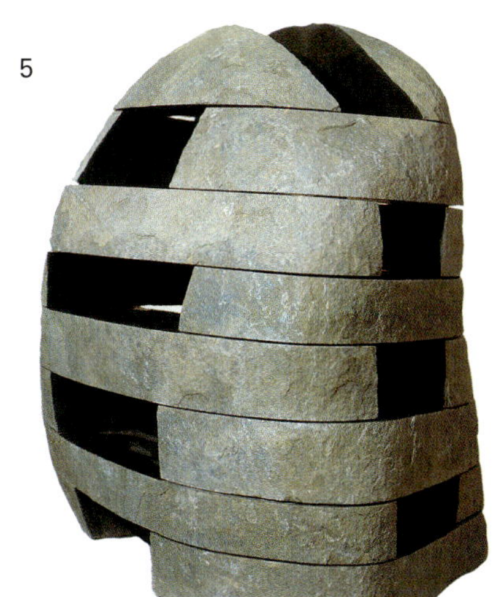

6

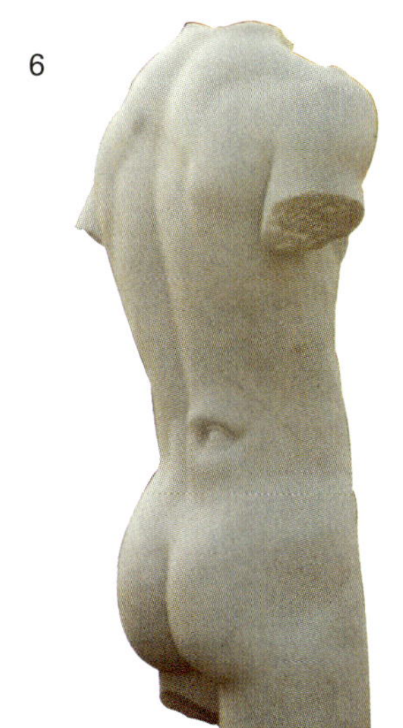

7

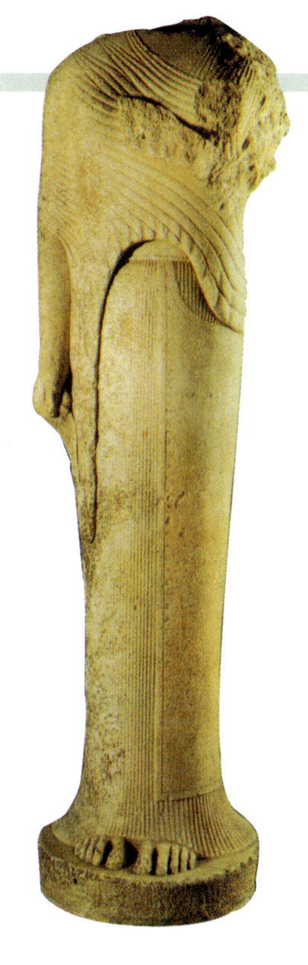

8

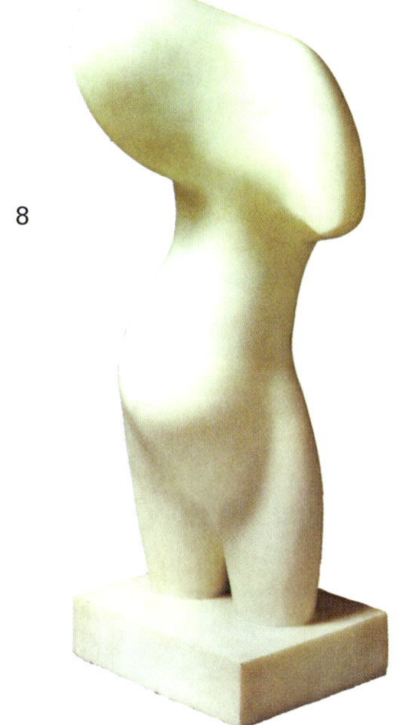

9

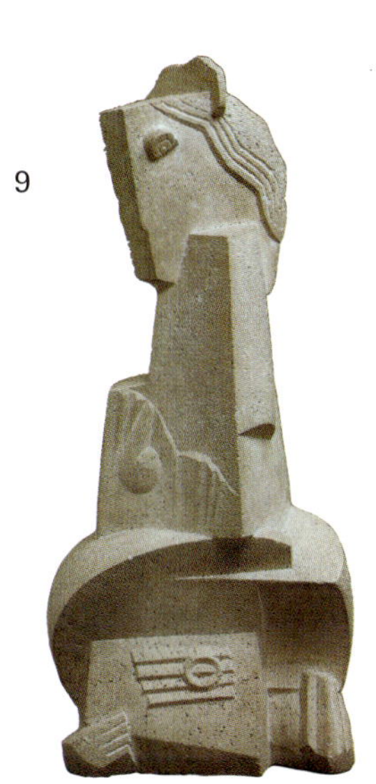

10

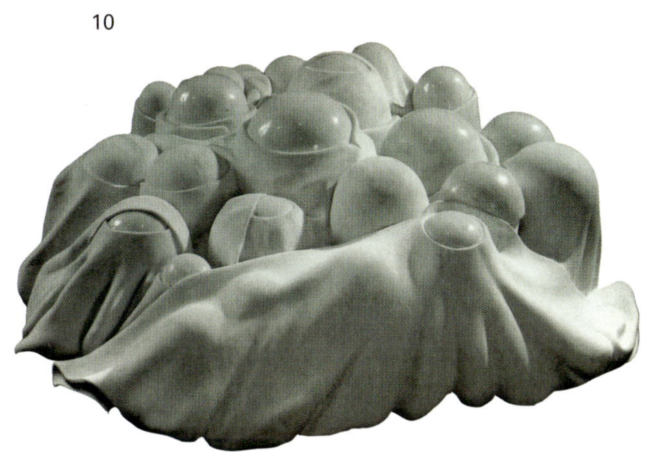

11

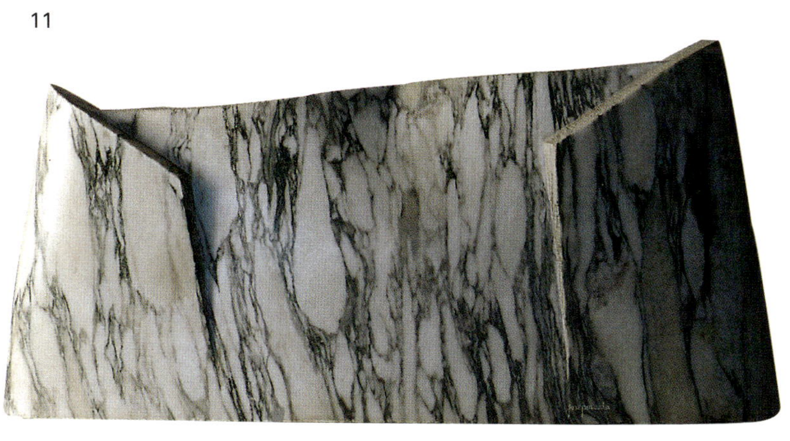

12

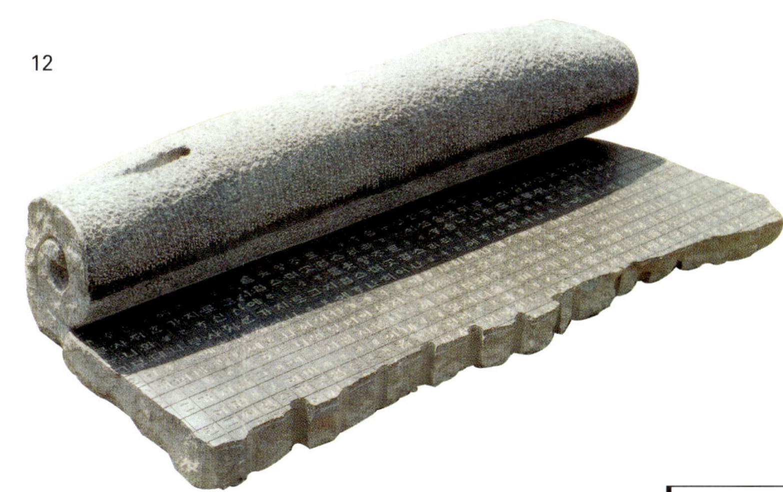

The Outline

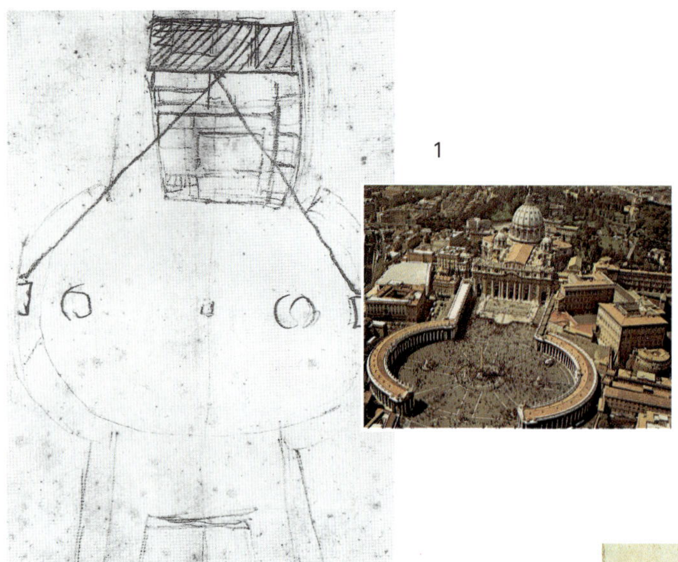

1

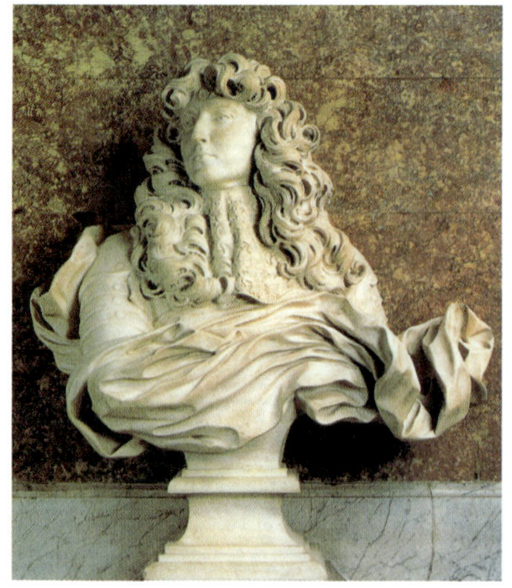

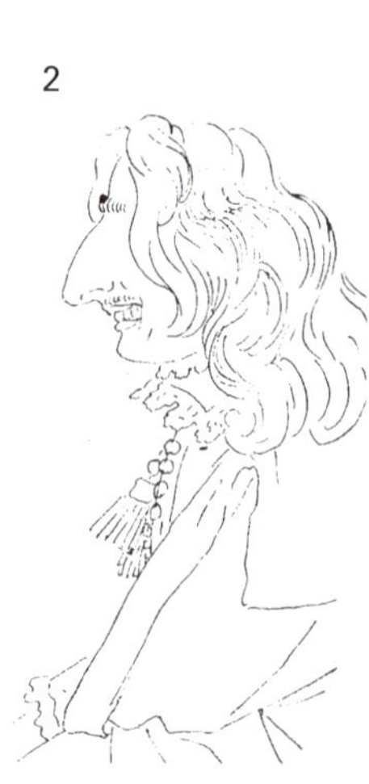

2

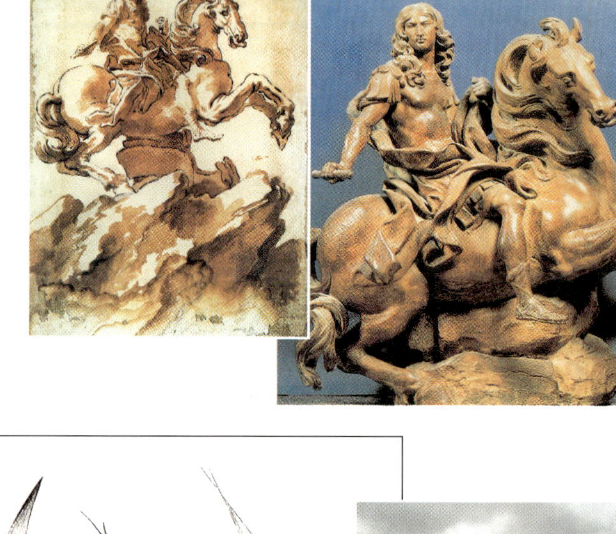

3

Once an idea is conceived, it should be jotted down quickly before it fades from memory. The best way to do this is through a quick sketch. We can perfect the sketch later or proceed directly to the material using outlines to help us better understand the volumes we need to define. Rodin said: "When I started my career, the sculptor Constant gave me the following advice: in the future, when you do your own sculpting, don't perceive forms as flat, but rather as surfaces with depth. . . . So, instead of visualizing the different parts of the body as more or less flat surfaces, I always thought of them as projections of internal volumes. . . ."

Here are three examples of how Bernini expressed his ideas:

1. Schematic outline for remodeling the Vatican square. What is important here is the distribution of the dominant volumes in this urban sculptural complex.

2. Caricature of a Frenchman by Bernini drawn while he was designing the Louvre Palace and carving the portrait of the Sun King. To carve the bust of Louis XIV, Bernini relied only on a front and a side sketch he made of the king. Bernini may have invented caricature as a way to memorize the dominant features of a face. He started work on the bust of the king in 1665, using three separate stone blocks because he mistrusted the quality of French marble. The bust is preserved today in the Palace of Versailles.

3. A more protracted and less successful effort Bernini undertook was his commission for an equestrian statue of the king. Neither the drawing, nor the maquette, nor the sculpture that Girardon altered before it was finally placed in the gardens of Versailles were approved by King Louis XIV's advisors.

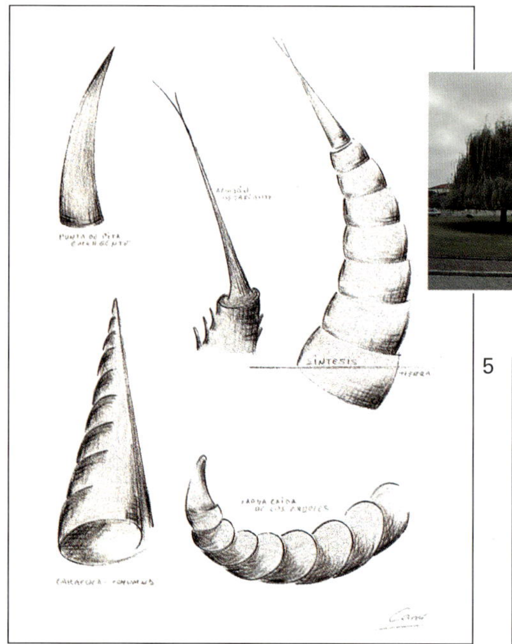

4

5

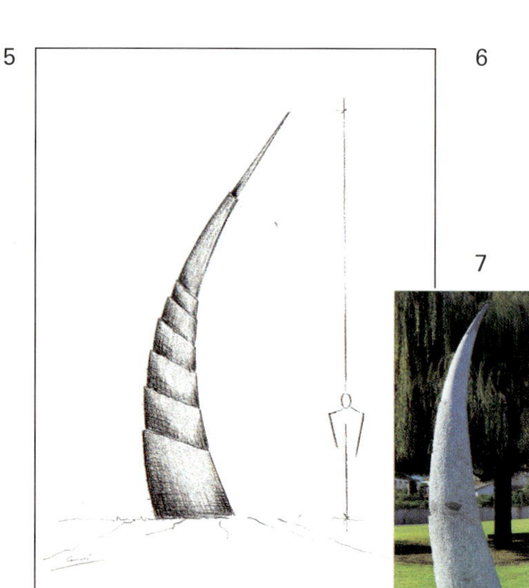

6

7

The final shape of a work often comprises several ideas. Before starting work on a granite sculpture to be placed under a willow tree (4), Camí draws several rough sketches (5), which he then combines into the first drawing of *Fito* (6). The evolution of this sculpture will be described later in this book (7).

8 9 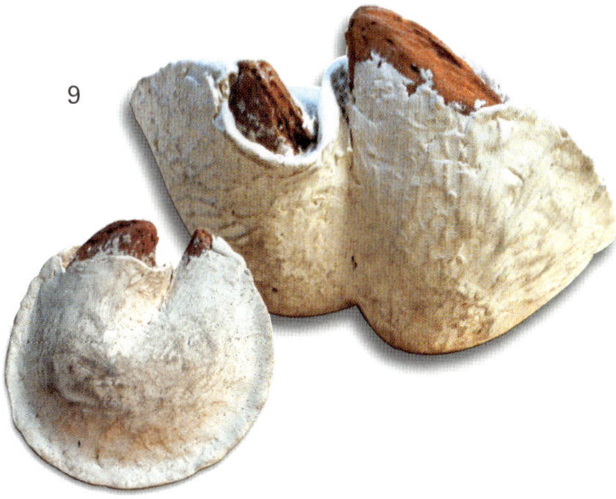 10 11 12

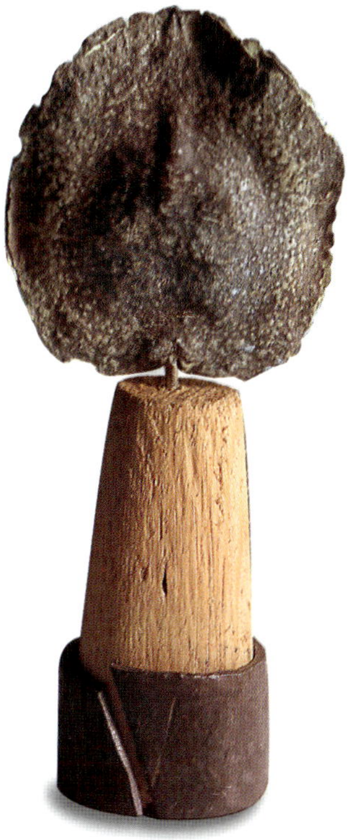

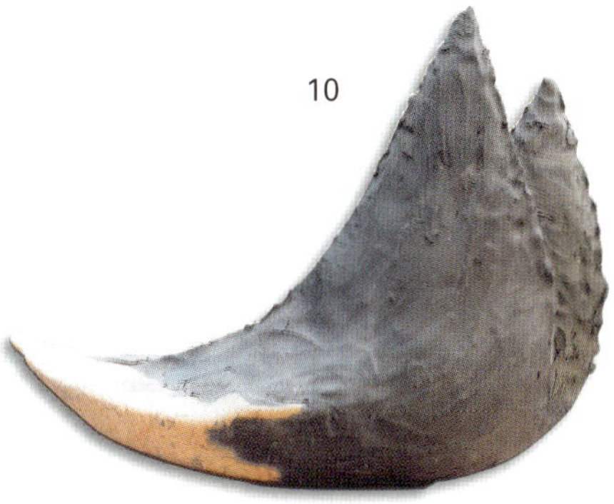

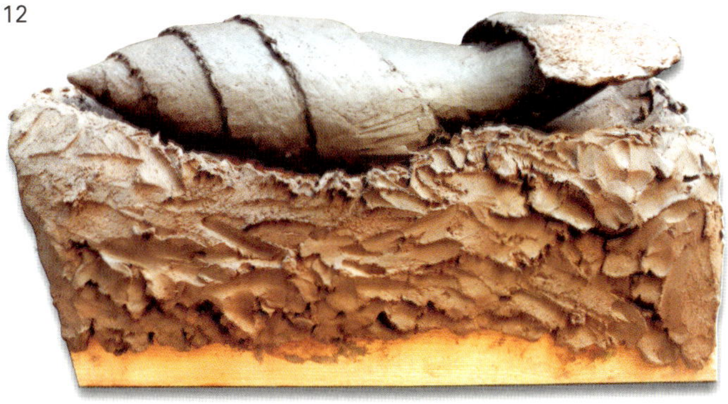

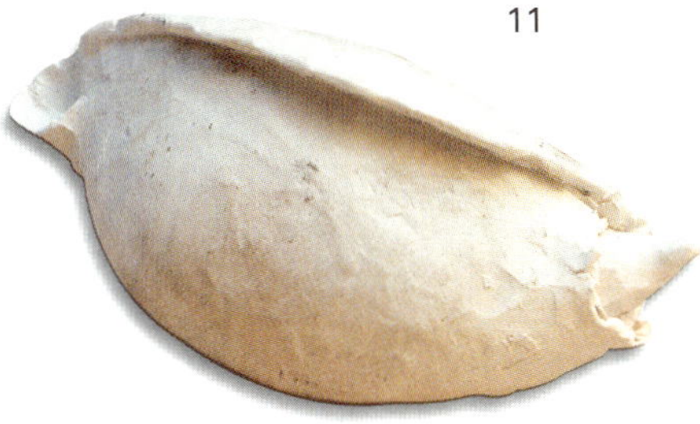

Any material can be used to make a model, since it will be for our exclusive use only. For example, we can make a model using recycled objects (8) or we can finish it in wax, plaster of Paris, or modeling clay. Here we use plasticine, two almonds (9), a piece of wood (10), and a wooden egg as a core (11). However, the most suitable material is still modeling clay (12).

Before reaching its final form, a maquette may undergo several changes. However, before it actually gets converted into a sculpture, it must wait for the right moment and be adapted to the characteristics of the stone. It is not unusual to find in some corner of a sculptor's workshop maquettes that are waiting their turn, or as the saying goes, *ars longa, vita brevis* (13).

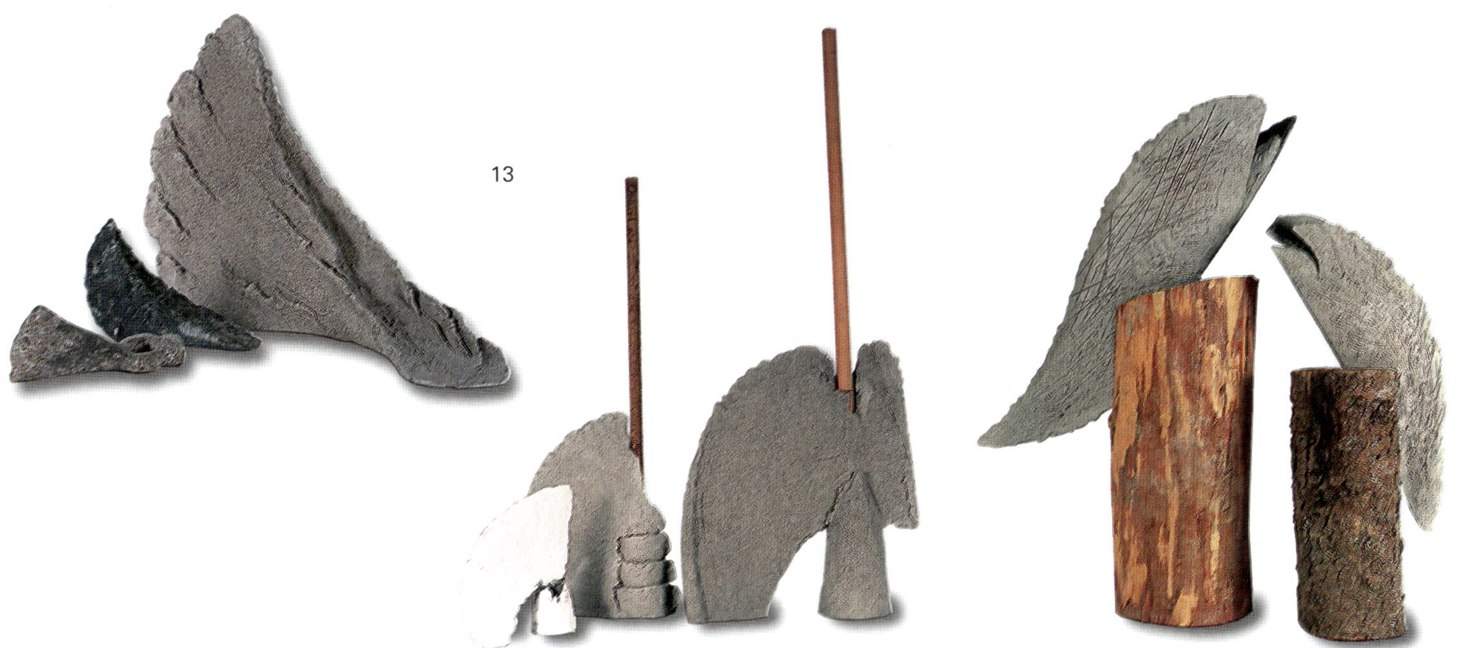

13

The Maquette

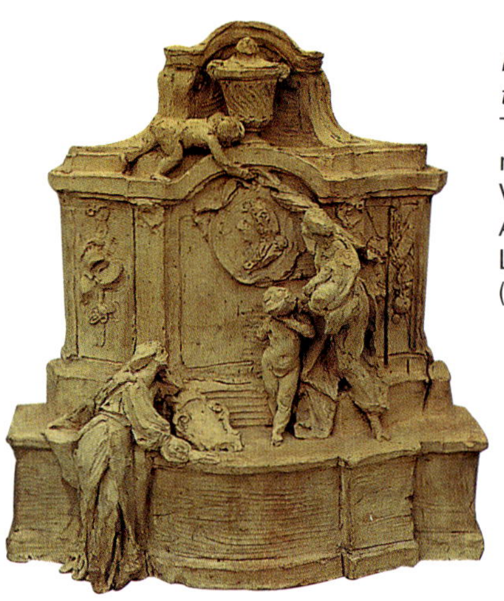

◀ Roubiliac. *Monument to John I*, 1750. Terracotta maquette. Victoria and Albert Museum, London (United Kingdom).

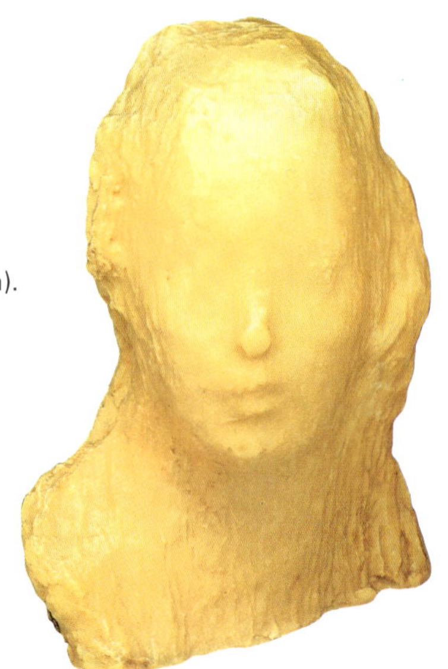

▲ Funeral Mask of Lorenzo de Medici, 1492. Wax cast. National Museum of Bargello, Florence (Italy).

◀ Merardo Rosso. *Behold the Boy*, 1906. Sculpture, wax over plaster. Private collection.

If we are planning to do direct carving and are sure of our idea and have mastered the technique, then a simple sketch is sufficient to begin roughing out the stone. Afterward, the stone itself will guide us; however, it is still better to make a maquette that is as close as possible in proportion, color, and material as the intended sculpture. Although this procedure is more time consuming, it will save time in the end.

In complex works, as for the monument illustrated here, the sculptor makes different large-scale maquettes for the details he considers most important. Here, Roubiliac made different maquettes of human figures. Some sculptors, like Rosso, use maquette-like materials for their final work.

To reproduce sculptures and parts of the human body, a mold is made, a technique most suitable for casting. After the mold is filled with plaster, it is used as a model to make copies. Human masks are made by casting warm wax on an oiled face. Death masks in particular have had a significant role in the history of portraits.

If we buy the maquette along with the finished work, we will note how frequently changes are made. Modifications may be made to satisfy the requests of the client, in response to criticisms and, above all, to meet final size requirements. Adjustments to the maquette for *Dance*, a work conceived for the façade of the Paris opera, allowed new figures to be introduced. Three years after its completion, which also took three years, the sculpture was labeled a "major disaster" and "an insult to public morality."

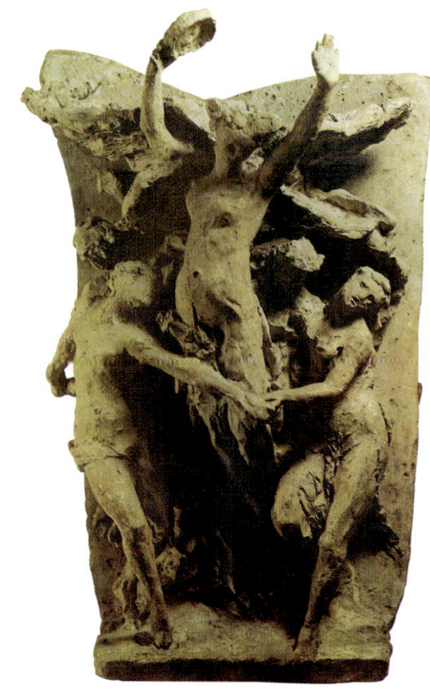

▲ Carpeaux. The *Dance*. 1869. Terracotta maquette. Louvre Museum, Paris (France).

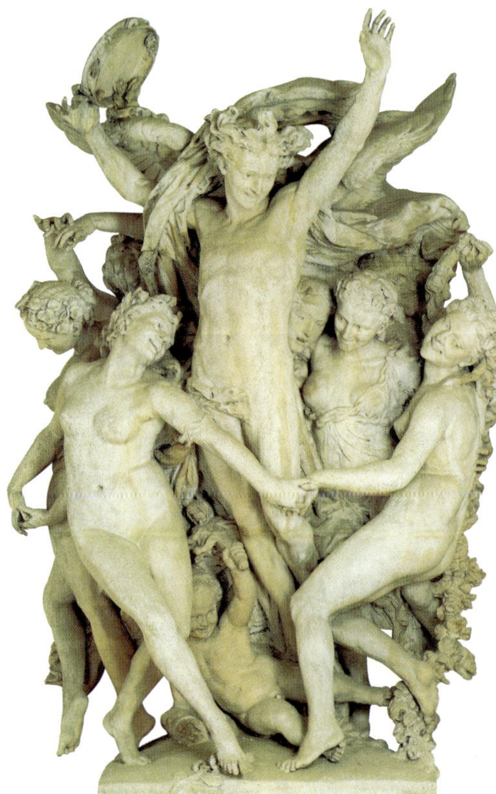

▲ Carpeaux. The *Dance*, 1869. Stone sculpture. d'Orsay Museum, Paris (France).

▲ Bartolini. *Tiziano's Venus*. Plaster model. Galleria della Academia, Florence (Italy).

When an exact reproduction is intended, the maquette is enlarged to actual size, frequently in plaster, and is then called the *model*. It is clear that this sculpture of *Venus* was copied using the point system. The marble work is on display at the Fabre Museum in Montpellier (France), while this and many other plaster castings of the nineteenth century are found next to Michelangelo's *Slaves* and *David*.

It is best to use the subtraction process for carving a maquette. This brings up problems that might occur when working with the stone. Here we demonstrate how to carve the Fito maquette using a block of fiber cement.

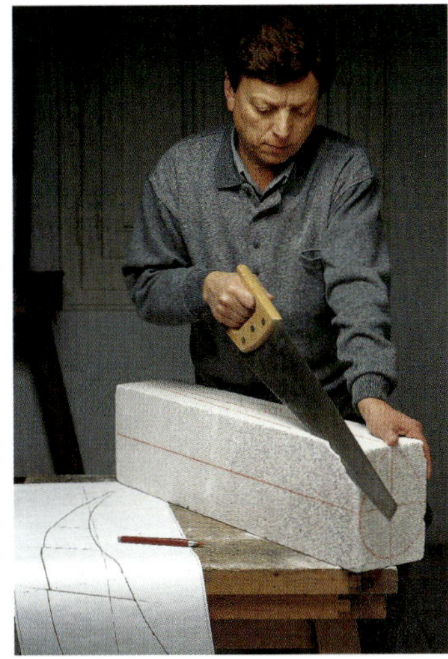

► 1. Using a diagram as reference, we draw a set of axes on the fiber cement block. Then we use a backsaw to cut the block.

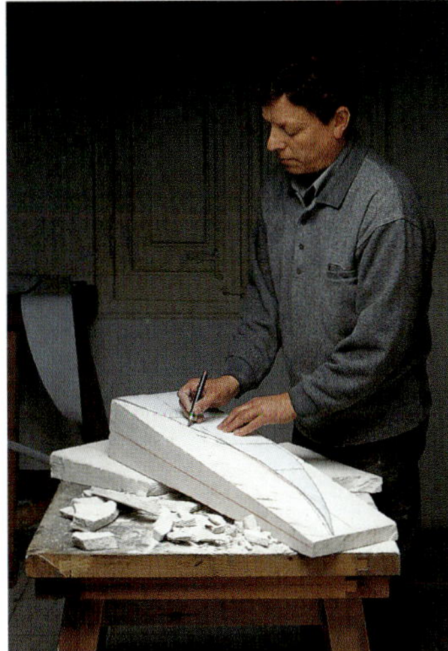

◄ 2. Using the same cutout template, we draw the largest outline possible on the two main sides of the block.

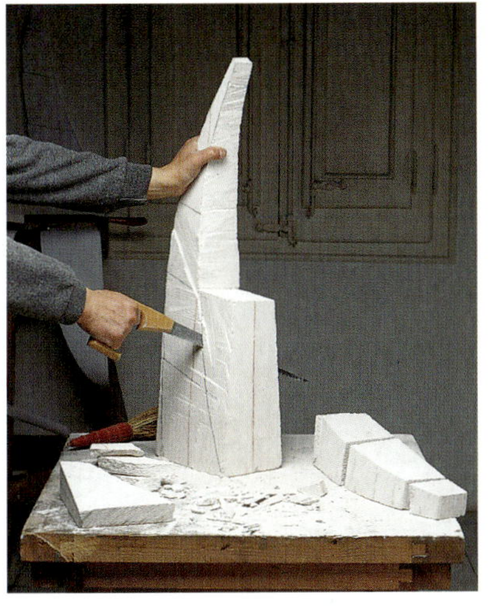

▲ 3. With a pointed saw, more flexible than the previous one, we cut out the maquette's silhouette. For better control, we prefer to cut away excess material in sections.

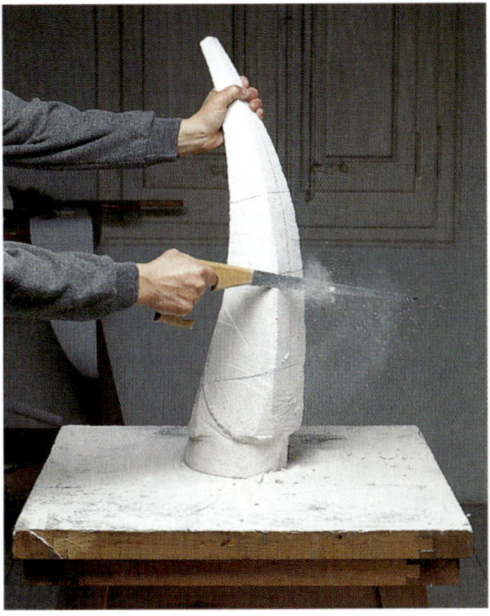

▲ 4. With the same saw, although we could also use kitchen knives, we continue defining the maquette's volume. As we model, we continuously rotate the maquette so as not to lose overall vision of the work.

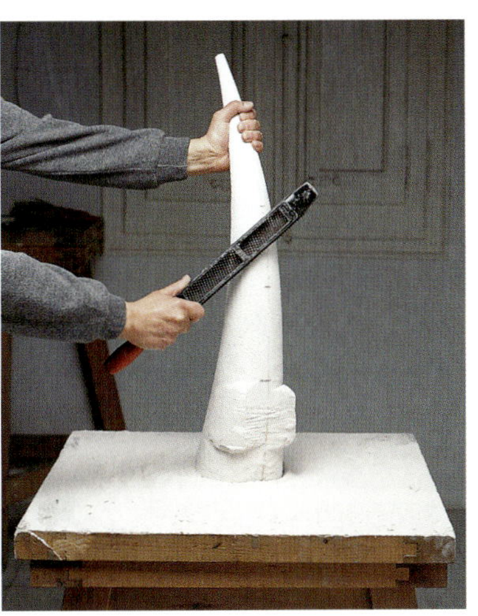

▲ 5. To even out the surface, we file it down with a rasp into a conelike shape. We still have at the bottom the section that was not touched by the saw, which coincides with the border of the original block.

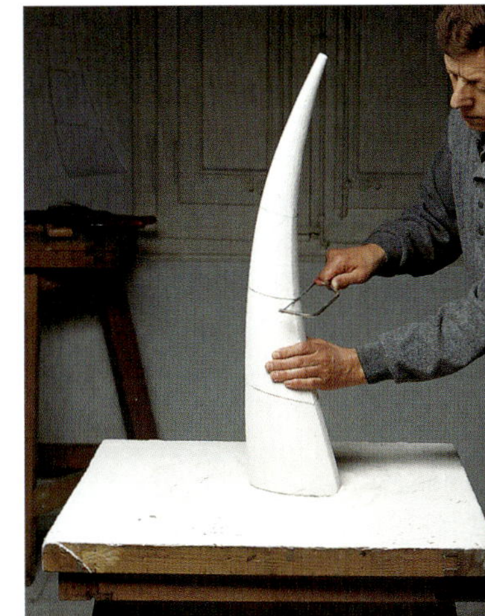

▲ 6. After drawing in the three sections shown on the diagram, we cut into them with a marquetry saw.

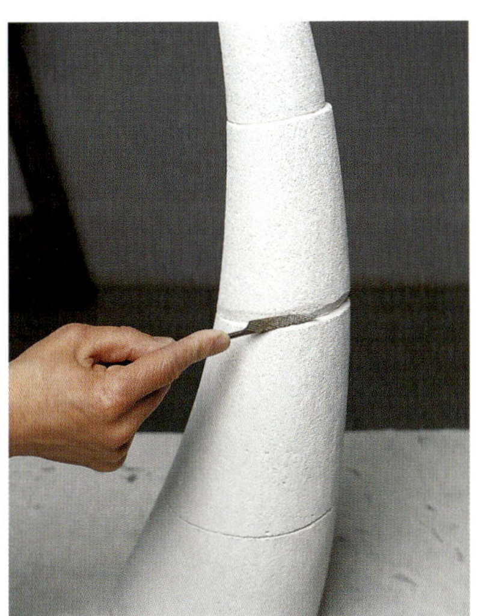

▲ 7. We model these sections with a riffler in order to simulate the progression of organic growth.

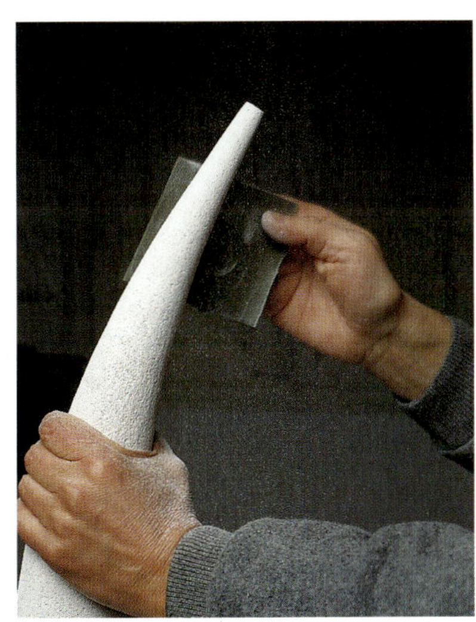

▲ 8. We use sandpaper to even out the rough spots left on the surface by the other tools.

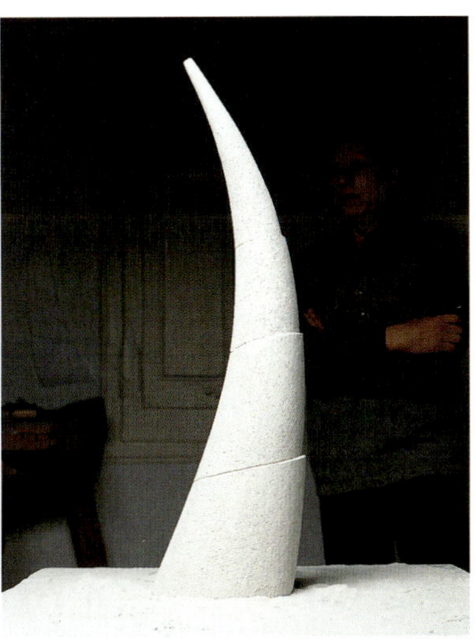

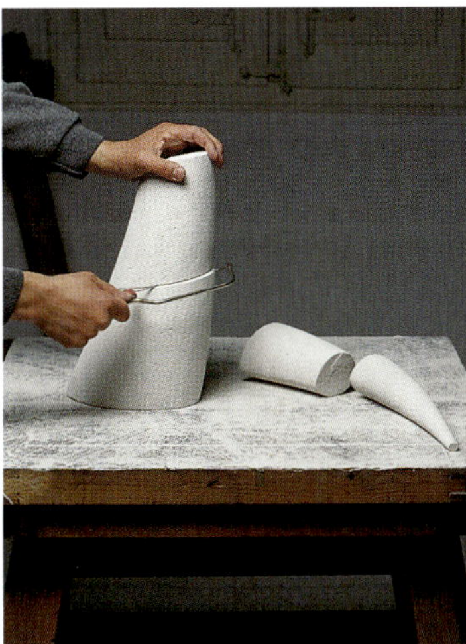

▲ ► 9. This is our maquette, which we later break apart in order to calculate measurements for the section templates, since the model will be enlarged tenfold before being transferred to granite.

Monumental Projects

If our sculpture is going to be seen in public or requires the collaboration of several professionals to build it, we would express our project in diagrams, maquettes, and if appropriate, in photographic collages that would help clients and collaborators understand it more easily.

We believe that all aesthetic designs intended for public consumption should rest on solid ethical principles that combine the personal integrity of the sculptor with the social expectations of the space the work will ultimately "invade." If we are attune to the concerns of the public entities that finance the sculpture through taxes, or if we allow them to participate in our project by providing them with adequate information, we will have gained loyal supporters who ensure respect for our work in the future. It is our belief that we should put to rest once and for all, together with the history of the twentieth century the stains of enlightened despotism, resulting from the mythification of artistic endeavor.

In addition to advice from psychologists and public relations experts, we should also rely on the support of geologists and urban planners to provide information on the characteristics of the site in question. We should also rely on the help of engineers or architects to assess the weight, balance, and anchor of the sculpture, ensuring that it will not pose a threat to the public safety.

It is also important, from an aesthetic point of view, to consider the orientation of the sculpture, since the sun's trajectory will determine where shadows fall on it. We should also be mindful of the environment in order to decide whether the sculpture blends in harmoniously with the surrounding buildings and landscape. If what surrounds the work is colorless or insignificant, then we should also assume the responsibility of making our work its own point of reference.

To cover as much information as possible, we will think about the shape of the sculpture and will choose the stone that is most appropriate for the location and community where it will ultimately be placed, at the same time remodeling the environment, if appropriate. To firm up our idea we will, as before, rely on outlines and maquettes, but this time we will lay out our plans to scale, section, elevation, and perspective. A good detailed design will make our work easier and allow us to see its many planes in three dimensions.

Together with the plans and the maquette, we will present to the sponsors a written report of the work that will include descriptions, techniques, and conceptual ideas that will clarify any questions that might arise.

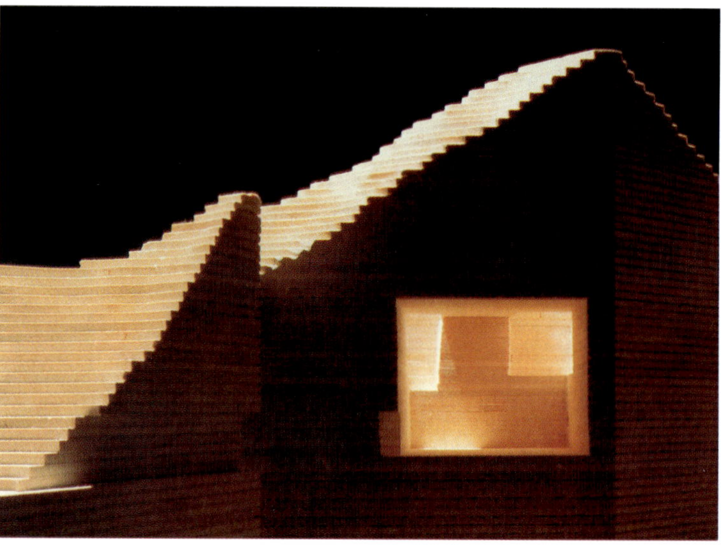

◀ Chillida. Tindaya Mountain. 1996. Fuerteventura, Canary Islands (Spain).

A sculptural project that proposes to combine respect for the shapes of a mythical mountain with the economic interests of those wishing to quarry it. In an effort to attain a consensus before undertaking this monumental task, the government of the Canary Islands has published a splen-did book with the collaboration of several prestigious architects and engineers.

Before presenting the final proposal, we will summarize the costs for our contractors: stonemasons, practitioners and assistants, moving contractors, publicists, and so on. We will calculate insurance and tax costs, establishing a margin of foreseeable errors, and we will add our own fees, including the time we will devote to the design, and the procedure on how we will carry out the work.

Before agreeing to delivery dates in the contract, we will carefully estimate how much time we will need, keeping in mind that some activities, such as site remodeling, publicity, or permits, are activities that can be done simultaneously. However, most of the tasks need to be carried out consecutively, and a delay in any one of these will set the schedule back.

CONSIDERATIONS FOR PROPOSING A PUBLIC SCULPTURE

1. Pre-project Information
- *Sociological Report:* basic needs, community values, cultural concerns, background on public works, concrete proposals of children and adults.
- *Urban or landscape environment.*
  — Installations of subsoil, ground that could be affected or could alter the vision.
  — Architecture, public utilities, traffic, and vegetation.
- *Geological characteristics.*
  — Subsoil: underground currents, hardness of ground.
  — Ground: direction of the streams, trajectory of sun for maximizing volumes.
  — Climate: levels of humidity and rainfall, which could oxidize color, thermal variations that might preclude use of soft stones.

2. Scope of the Project
- *Theme and form*: Realism, abstraction, free forms.
  Symbolic, suggestive, subtle, abrasive, provocative.
- *Selection of the stone:* local, imported, subject to erosion, incorporation of other materials.
- *Environment:* centered, haphazard, construction in a respected place.
- *Hiring of contractors:* helpers, practitioners and assistants, moving contractors, stonemasons, technical engineering supervisor.

3. Proposal
- *The sculpture:* project time and materials, execution of the work, contributors, packing, transportation, placement, artistic fees.
- *Site remodeling:* building, landscaping, lighting.
- *Other:* publicity, permits, insurance, taxes, contingencies, margin of error.

4. Maintenance
The sculptor is not responsible for any subsequent damage caused by vandalism. However, he can help reduce the incidence of these acts by lobbying for neighborhood respect for the work as a well-deserved patrimony, and by avoiding in the sculpture those elements that require close supervision, such as nooks, small fountains, delicate edges, and so on. Is it daring to say that a sculpture of quality can defend itself alone?

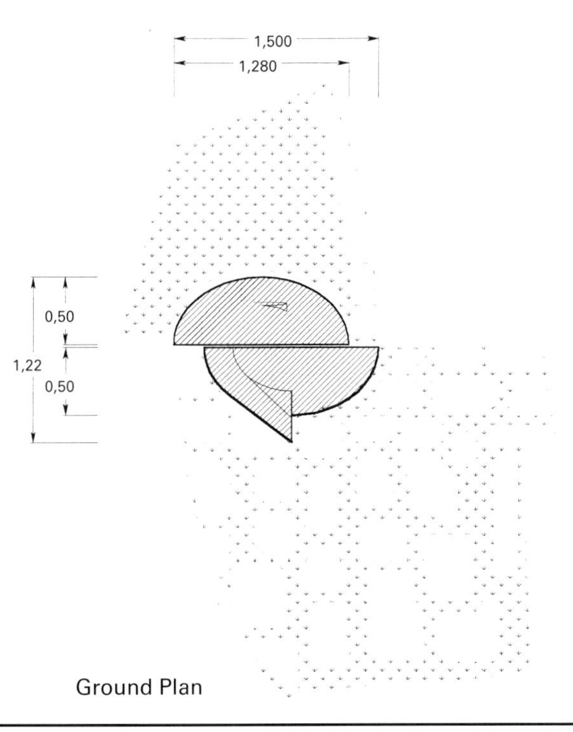

Ground Plan

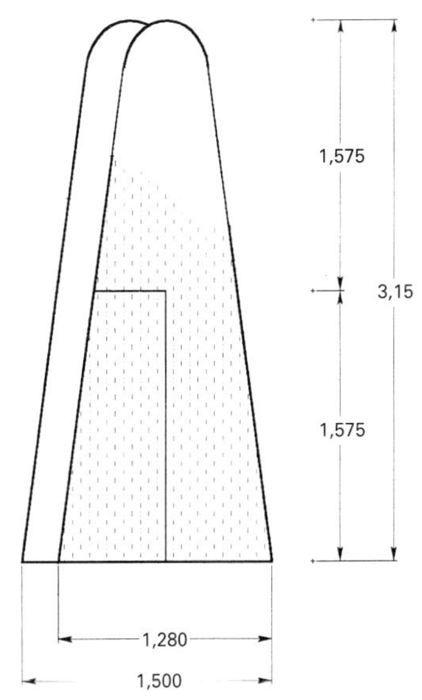

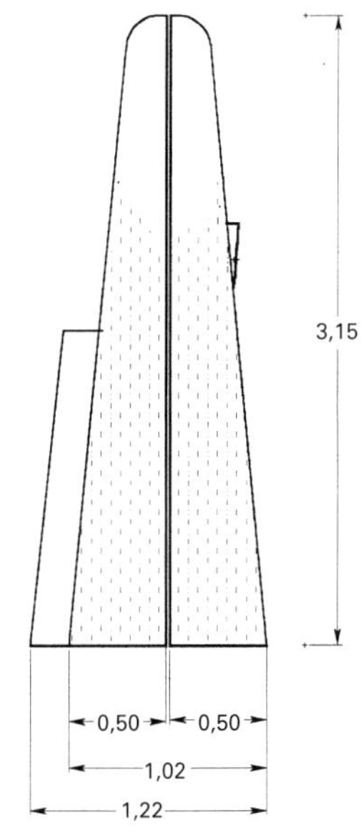

Elevation

▲▶▼ Camí. 1999.

Plans of the ground, elevation, and virtual perspectives of the *Father's House* project, the procedure for which we will show in the last step-by-step exercise of this book. The remodeling of the environment is inspired in the yin-yang symbol and the idea of the whole attempts to capture the theme proposed by the township of Puyo (South Korea): *Unity, love, and eternity, a prayer for the unification of Korea.*

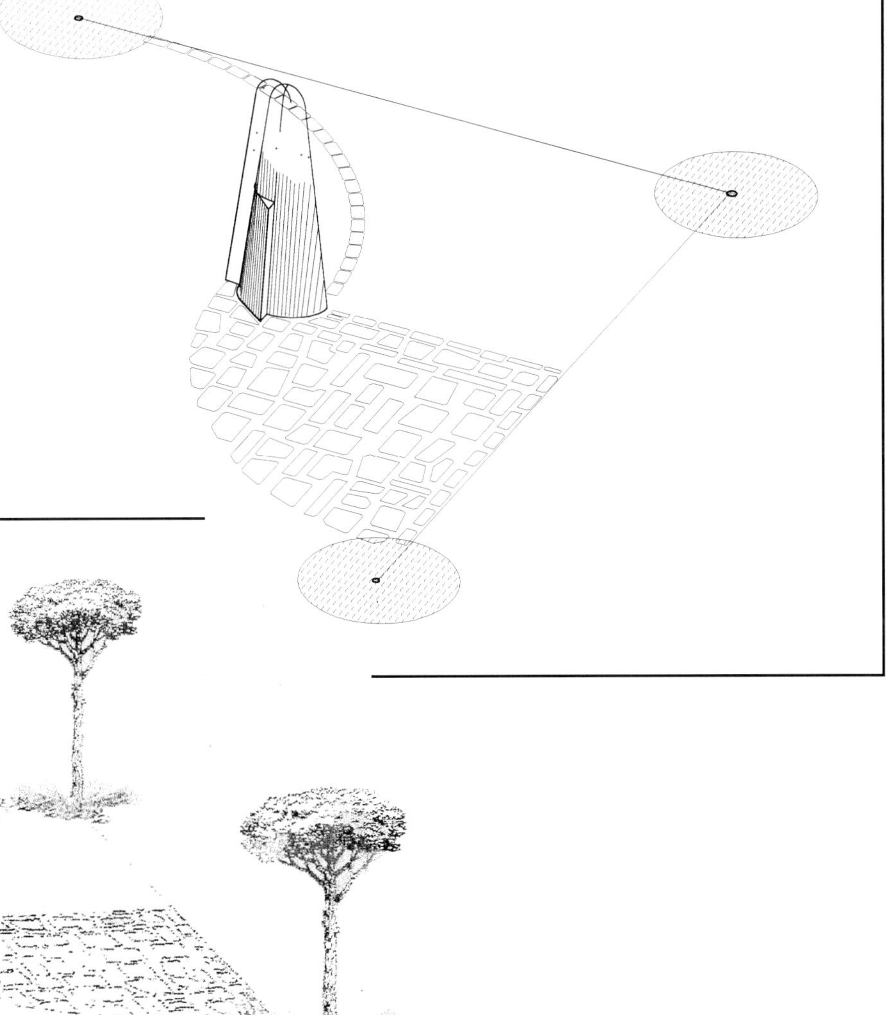

Sculptors, Practitioners, and Patrons

According to modern opinion, Rodin did not belong to any of the above classifications. He is recognized as a talented, at times genial, modeler of forms, but only as such. Personally, I think this argument lacks merit and, furthermore, that it is inappropriate. After all, what matters is the end result.

Jacob Epstein

The polemic raised by the fraudulent work of Jonchery, a collaborator of Rodin, became so heated that several critics, after learning that some craftsmen were reproducing in marble what the master had shaped in clay, wanted to strike Rodin's name from the roster of sculptors.

This outdated romantic notion replaced, in avant-garde times, the polemic revolving around the paternity of works, and was perhaps partially responsible for the belated emergence in our cities of abstract sculpture, since monumental works obviously require a team effort.

This right of authorship was always denied to anonymous artists, but these expert artisans or **practitioners**—whether called workers, trimmers, laborers, carvers, assistants, freemasons, or stonemasons—used their technical prowess, effort, and dexterity to extract shapes that others designed from the stone.

All that remains of their identity are the enigmatic inscriptions they left behind, such as the masonry markings found in old Persia. Evidence that they possessed individual criteria is found in the stylistic differences apparent in the same Gothic frontispiece, such as the one in Orvieto, Italy, for example. It is absurd that sculptors do not pride themselves on recruiting the collaboration of practitioners. This is not the case in other artistic areas such as film, for example, where a mediocre film director can enhance his reputation and work by working with a well-known actor.

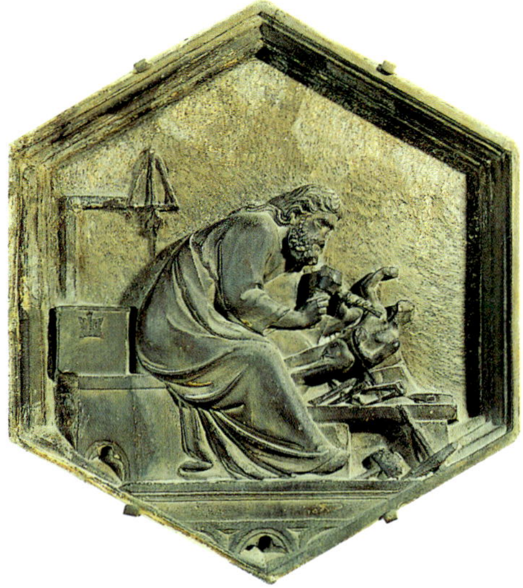

► Giotto—Andrea Pisano. *The Sculpture.* Circa 1340. Museo della Opera del Duomo. Florence (Italy).

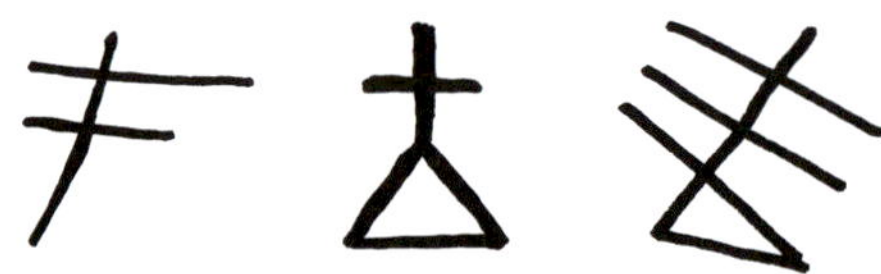

◄ Quarry markings of the Martin family: Felip, Felix, and Feliu; Feliu would later carve one of our works.

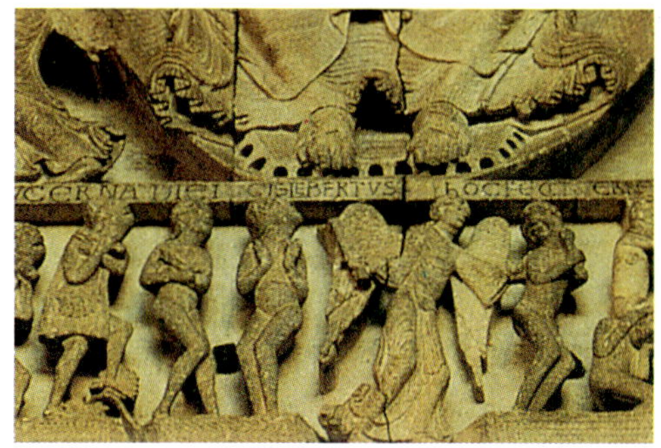

▲ Gislabertus' "discrete" signature in the center of the kettledrum in the cathedral at Autun (France).

As for practitioners, let's not forget that Giotto designed and Andrea Pisano carved 21 panels for the bell tower of the cathedral in Florence, and that Donatello, a genial sculptor, was a *scarpellino* (stone carver), a job that Leonardo da Vinci and Lorenzo Buonarotti disdained. Buonarotti granted the tutorship of his adolescent son to another Lorenzo, *the Magnificent* of the Medici family, when the latter convinced him that sculptors should not perform hard work.

The **sculptor** or *artifex*, who is sometimes accorded the name architect—*magister lapidum, mastermason* has traditionally received credit for the work, not so much for its execution as for its design. The word *design* was transformed by Renaissance artists into *segno di Dio* (sign of God). In those times, however, a maquette was needed to finalize a contract, whereas previously a sketch was sufficient.

The Egyptian master sculptor who hired artisans, enjoyed a certain social prestige but did not achieve more than guest status among the dominant classes. On the other hand, the names of the *technicians* (designers and craftsmen) are included in Greek history.

In twelfth-century Europe, when anonymous artists and influential clergymen such as Abbot Suger designed sculptures, in Italy, the sculptor signed the work discreetly, but in the Autun cathedral, Gislabertus leaves a highly visible mark on his *Last Judgment.* Centuries later, in 1500, Michelangelo would also brazenly carve his initials on the *Pietà* to dispel rumors that the work was done by artists from Lombardy. Another way of expressing paternity for a sculptural piece is by including a self-portrait in it. This is exactly what Pilgram and Parlen the Younger, among others, did in the Vienna and Prague cathedrals, respectively. The question remains as to whether the face of any Michelangelo or Bernini sculpture belongs to either of the artists. Other types of signatures include those that are preceded by *fieri fecit* or *is prefecit opus*, which refer to the sponsor or benefactor.

▼ To whom do the faces of Nicodemus and David belong?

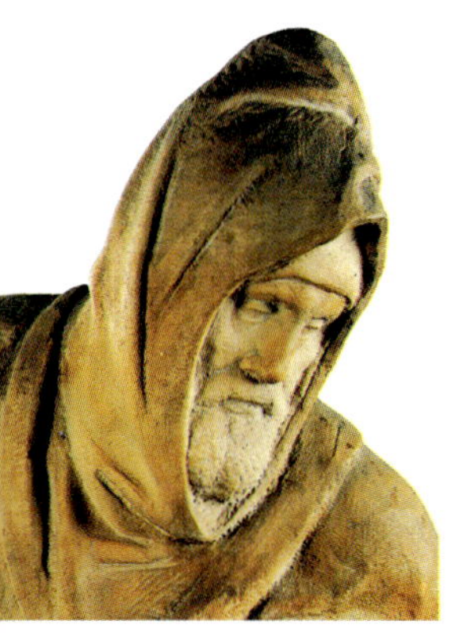

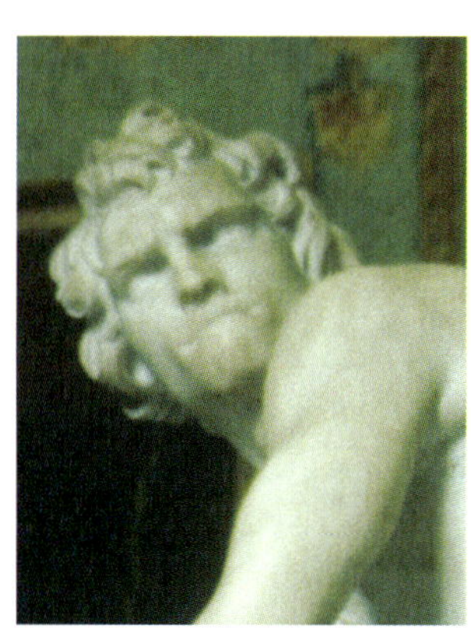

My sculptors customarily got confused; the most mediocre ones fell somewhere between blandness and strength.

Adriano's Memoirs.
Marguerite Yourcenar.

It would be naive to believe that the opinions, either tacit or expressed, of those who finance a work of art are of no consequence. Thus, even the **patron** contributes to the outcome of a work.

With few exceptions, production of massive stone sculptures have been sponsored by either religious, political, or economic authorities who used them as vehicles for spreading ideologies or as a show of power: to this day, Egypt proclaims the power of Ramses II.

In the great ancient civilizations, sculptors had to submit to rigid codes set by the leading intellectuals and priestly classes. In Egypt, these rules changed only during the reign of Akhenaton whose master sculptor, Bek, proclaimed himself "Disciple of His Majesty." When looking at history, we are also reminded of how August's imperial system used marble structures as a propaganda tool. Asoka, the Kushana, the Andhara, or the Guptas in Asia used sculpture to promote the spread of Buddhism in their kingdoms. Baroque Catholicism used sculpture in the war for patronage against reformist churches and, before the invention of television, liberals, Fascists, and Communists used it to spread their ideologies.

At the same time, people of opulence such as Caius Cilnius Maecenas, advisor to Emperor August and patron of poets Virgil and Horace dedicated, either purposefully or on a whim, a portion of their wealth toward the promotion of sculpture.

The love of art for art's sake, a concept attributable to the patrons of art, arose during the reign of Emperor Adrian who commissioned for his villa near Tripoli, among other works, replicas of Greek sculptures that he most admired during his numerous trips.

However, the best-known patrons were those who promoted Renaissance sculpture: the Medici, Florentine arms dealers and populist bankers. Cosmus the Elder financed Donatello's works and various religious orders "for penitential and expiatory reasons because of his prior violent political behavior and gains acquired in a less than meritorious manner." Lorenzo the Magnificent, poet, philosopher, diplomat, and epitome of the ideal Renaissance man, promoted Leonardo da Vinci and Verrocchio who also enjoyed the patronage of the Rucellai and the Martelli. And let us not forget that Pope Leo the Tenth and Clemente the Tenth were Medicis who were more concerned with keeping the undisciplined Michelangelo in rein than with trying to understand Luther's arguments.

In another example, the Borghese, Paul the Sixth and his nephew Scipione supported Bernini—son of a practitioner under the patronage of Urban the Seventh—who was tied to their family by a kind of *servitu particolare* (special bondage) that forced him to reside in Rome all of his life, except during a six-month stay in exile at the court of the Sun King. Influenced by the powerful, the middle classes also became clients of sculptors from whom they commissioned busts. Another contributing factor to the proliferation of patrons was that the town hall in Florence raised or lowered taxes benefiting the guilds, including the sculptors' guild that outfitted the vaulted niches of Orsanmichele, their church.

Academies, which Catherine the Second introduced in Russia, became fashionable when the Bourbons came to power and promoted salons and art exhibitions. Their influence was not limited to setting aesthetic doctrines and they strictly oversaw official purchases and commissions. They even went so far as to prohibit sculptors from opening personal ateliers. This gave rise to the emergence of a merchant class that Diderot defined as "dealers of all things and makers of nothing." Among them promptly stood out Le Brun whose client was Marie Antoinette. We might also recall the sculptor-client relationship between Napoleon and Canova.

When American buyers—except for Paul Getty who collected classical sculptures—emerged on the scene, they provided the sole criterion that allows competition on an even keel with European sophistication. "The goal of all art is to be fully alive in the actual moment," said Gertrude Stein. Stone sculpture escapes this dictum, but the goal of these new lovers of art, along with their Russian and French counterparts, is not to live the aesthetic pleasure precisely in *the actual moment* without making an investment in the future. At times they do it by chance, as was the case with businessman Andre Level and his associates from The Bear's Skin, who in 1914 catapulted the concept of the auction. Others, the Guggenheims, for example, needed the advice of the artists themselves or their closest critics to know whether they liked a sculpture or not. But all insured their investments, following the advice of Raymonde Moulin, who gave publicity to artists in an effort to sway public opinion. The works of Rodin, Maillol, and Bourdelle became collectors' items with the Cognacqs: Ernest, a businessman who without ever visiting a museum, gave one to the Parisians, and his nephew Gabriel, who was more involved in art than politics.

Today, merchants and gallery owners, who are sometimes guided by their business sense and other times by their aesthetic sensibilities, direct their attention to sculpture, this following the emergence of abstract art. Noting how large companies are sponsoring more popular activities, several of these merchants and business owners have replaced the work of the patron.

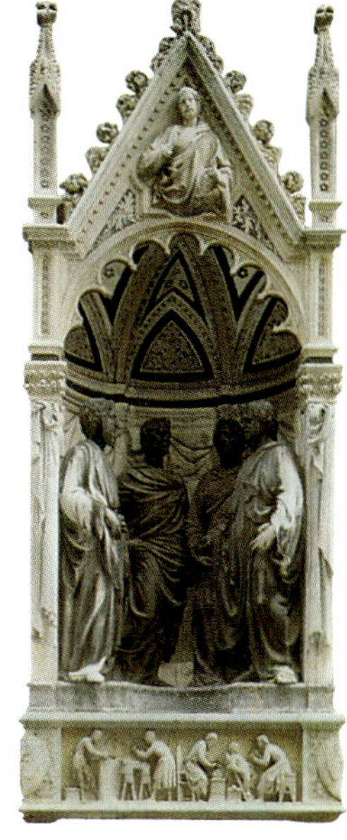

► Vaulted niche of Orsanmichele in Florence, financed by the sculptors' guild in memory of four fellow members suffering martyrdom during the time of the Roman Empire.

Public institutions, city halls in particular, after periods of building up and tearing down monuments of famous people who ceased to be so after a political change, dedicate a small percentage of their urban budgets to dress up their cities by outfitting them with abstract sculptures. They often delegate their aesthetic preferences to art critics or commissioners, who, like those in the academies of the past, can influence the paternity of a sculpture or the direction of an artistic trend.

▼ Personal work of sculptor Mariano Andres Vilella, our assistant, who is posing here with a colleague.

Wind Sails, 1997. Cabra limestone. Alcudia (Spain).

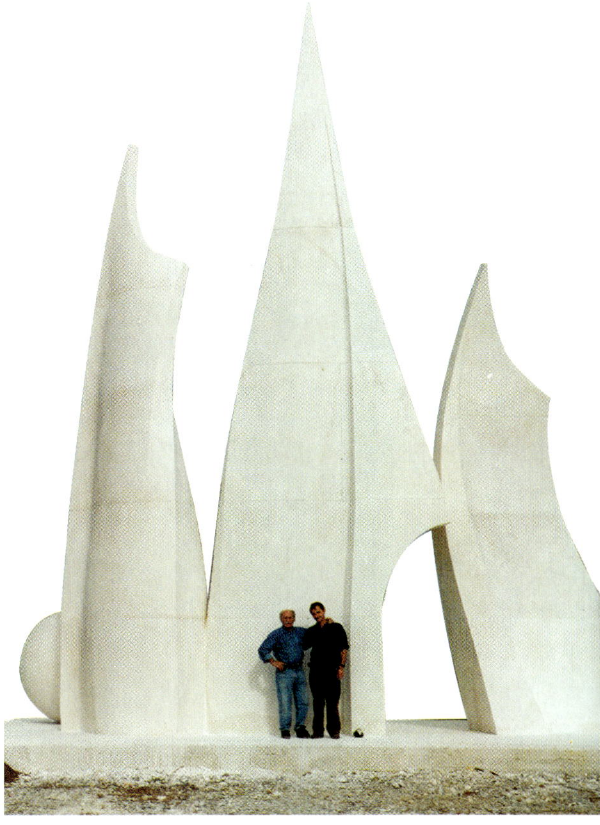

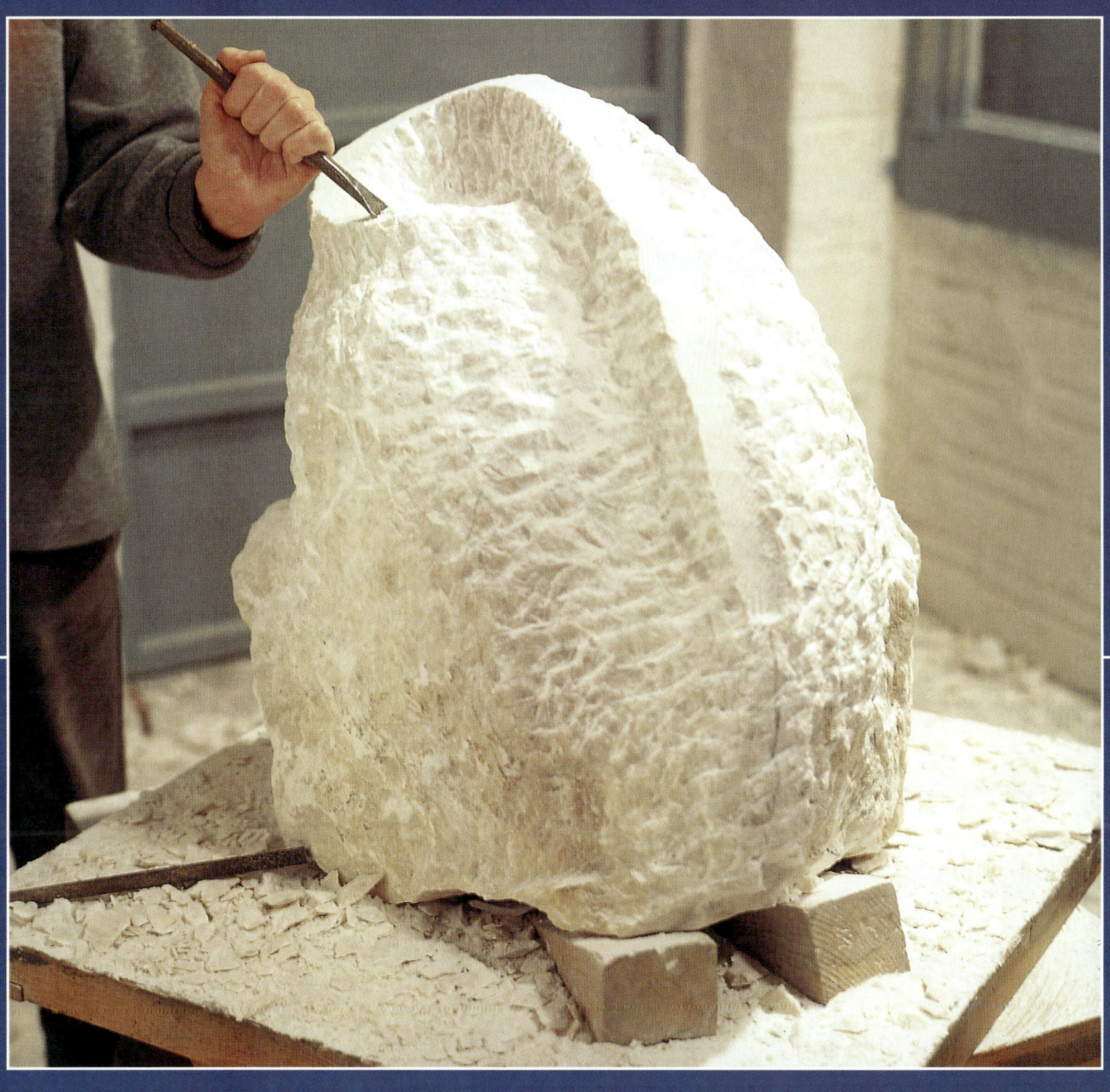

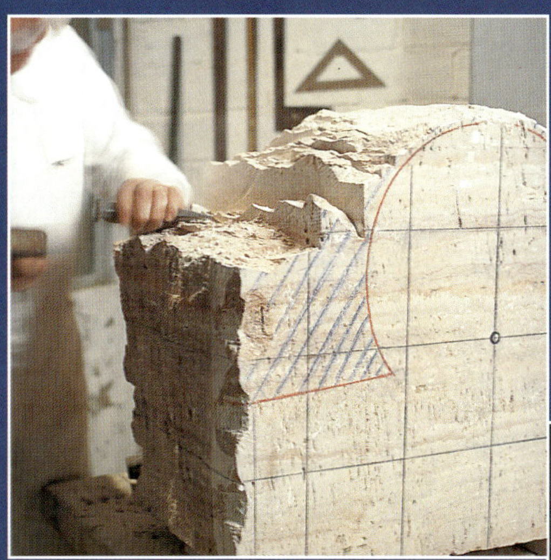

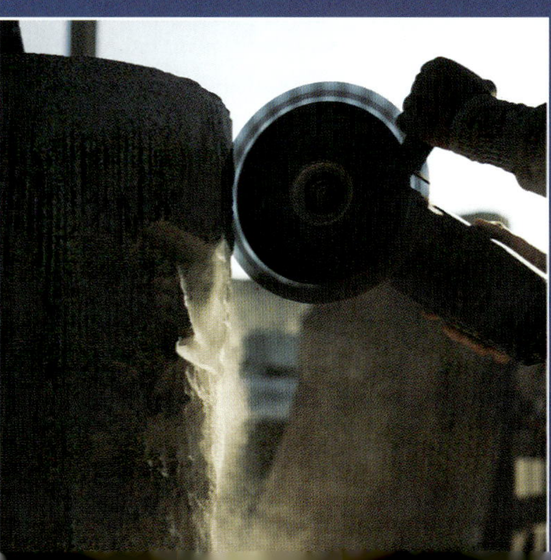

Direct *Carving*

In this section, we will discuss the basics necessary for those who wish to begin to carve in stone. First, we will present several aspects that can help to facilitate the work and handling of tools. We will then show you how to prepare some of the most commonly used templates. We will gradually move into the realm of volume until we have arrived at two of its most defining features: smoothing, which determines volume, and modeling, which defines it. We will conclude by illustrating the various textures produced by different types of tools so that you may choose the one most appropriate for finishing a sculpture. Keep in mind, however, that our purpose here is to highlight the essentials; we will expand on each and show its application in the step-by-step exercises that follow.

Don't waste your time trying to establish mundane or political relationships. You will see many of your colleagues wrapped up in the allure of fame and fortune. They are not true artists. However, this does not mean that they are not intelligent and if you choose to become part of their struggle, you'll waste as much time as they; that is, an entire existence; you will not have one second left to be an artist.

Auguste Rodin

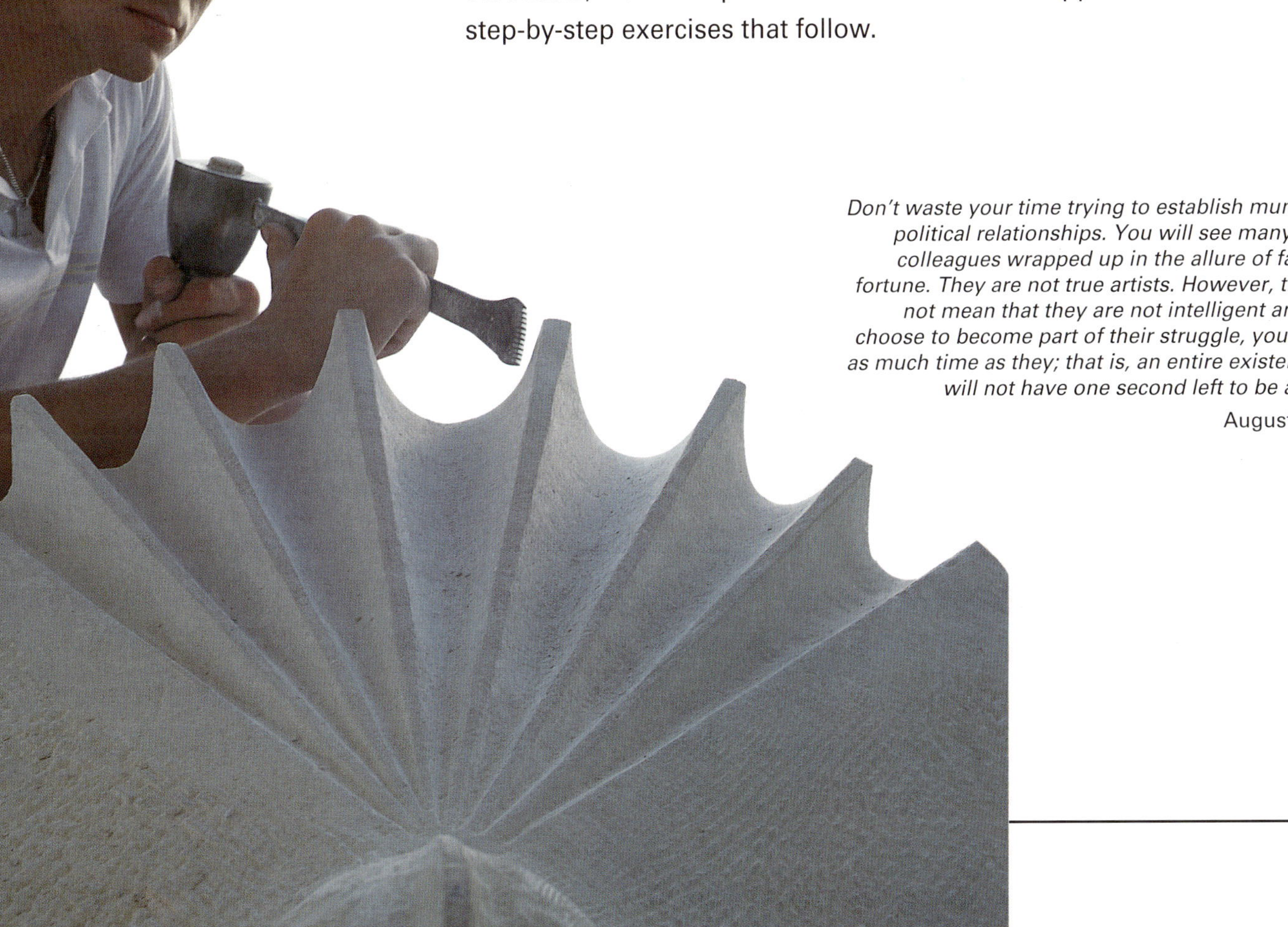

Preliminary Activities

Once we have decided on a project, we will choose the most appropriate stone. For figurative sculptures, we will choose a stone that is uniform in color, but for free forms we might choose a stone with veinings. We avoid hard stones if we don't have the proper machinery to work them, and sandstones if we plan to polish any part of the sculpture.

After we have decided on the type of stone most suitable for our purpose, we go to a stone shop, marble dealer, stonecutter, or stonemason to select the stone. Our main concern is getting a block that is solid enough that it won't crack as we work it. Even rocks that have a good outward appearance can have internal fissures that might weaken it. These fissures are often difficult to detect, so we have to trust the experts. However, even they cannot always give us the guarantee we want; we also rely on our own intuition.

If we compare rocks containing clay, which in their natural state are really incipient "sandstones" that the kiln converts into "metamorphic" stones, we see that, like sandstone, these rocks may not break apart when dealt hard blows, but can break down and develop imperceptible cracks at their weakest points. We reject stones that have very fine cracks, even those as fine as a shaft of hair. We call these kinds of cracks *hair fissures*. We also usually discard stones that show fine fissures as we carve, because subsequent impacts will cause the stone to split again at its weakest point, which is usually where the different strata overlap.

Fortunately, though, not all stone irregularities are dangerous cracks; the huge oven deep inside the earth that has baked the rocks might also have trapped bubbles inside of them or, because of a sharp rise in temperature, created invisible cracks, both of which can be treated by the same process.

When we buy a small ceramic or glass vase—another "artificially fired stone" whose main mineral is silica—we tap it with our knuckles to see if it sounds broken. So why not take a hammer to a stone so that we may reject it if it emits a low-pitched sound or select it if its high-pitched "ring" tells us that it is well formed?

Moving the Stone

Weight is an obstacle that can stop the sculptor and his client from choosing a particular stone if they are unaware of certain techniques that can be used to handle it. Long before cranes were invented, Archimedes had already realized that with the appropriate lever one could raise the world. The lever that is best suited for this task is a metallic crowbar with a flat end that fits under the stone. There are also other little tricks one can use to streamline efforts, some of which are illustrated in the pictures on this page.

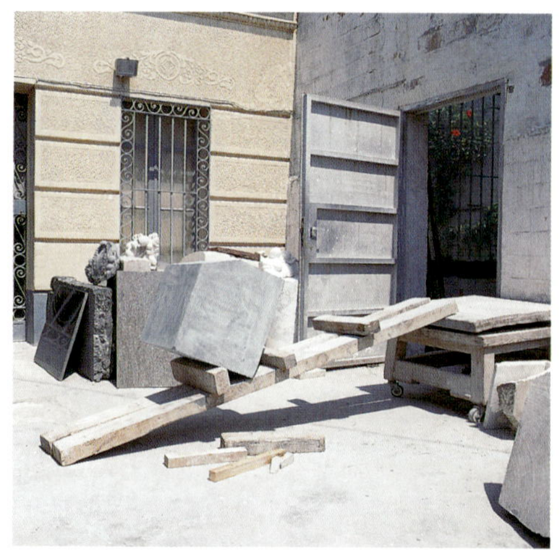

▲ To lift the stone onto the worktable, we can build a ramp with planks of wood and slide the block on it or, depending on its shape, we can roll the stone over the strips of wood. The strips prevent the stone from sliding and also help it roll. If we have help, we can also tilt the workbench and lean it against the stone on the floor and, keeping both in balance without letting them slip apart, bring them to an upright position.

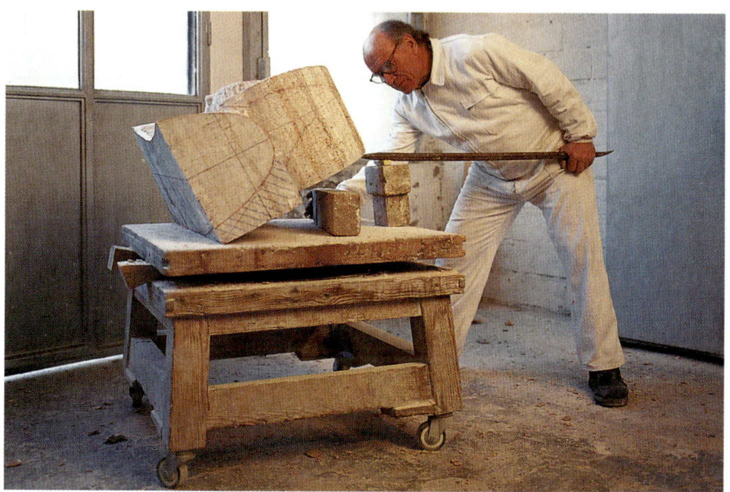

▲ If we have to stand the stone up in a vertical position, we will use the crowbar with the flat end. Each time we apply pressure to the crowbar to lift the stone, we will push a wooden support under it until we can easily turn the stone over. If necessary, we can raise the crowbar's leverage point with two or more wedges that we place on top of each other.

► A sawhorse on wheels will help us move the stone at each step of the process to the appropriate place in the workshop. A rotating platform will avoid the need to change our work posture. To turn the stone over, we will move it over a piece of wood that unsteadies it and makes it easier to move.

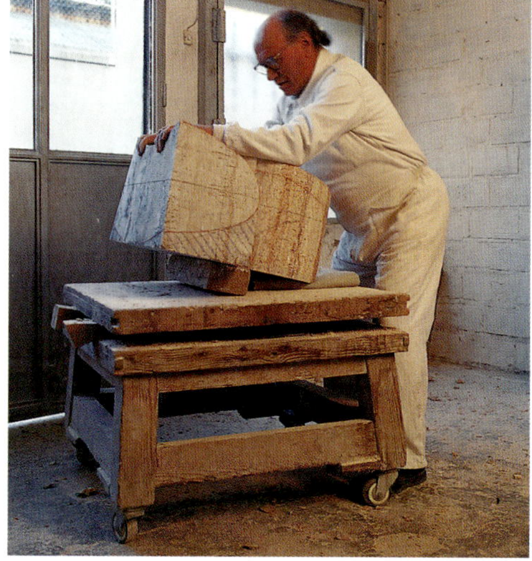

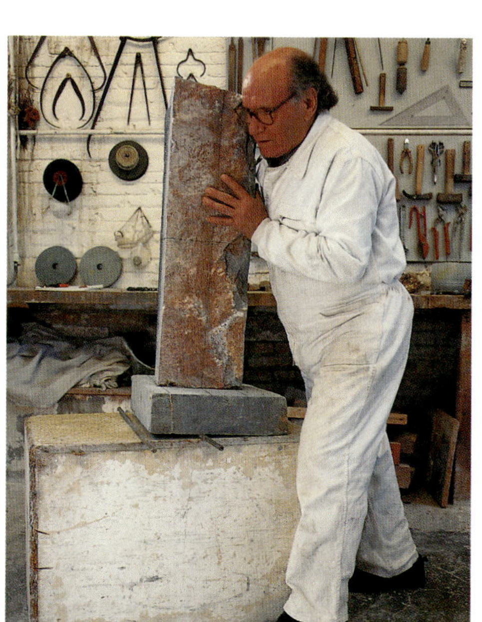

◄ We can use bars to slide the stone on the floor, on a ramp, or on the worktable. However, if we need to turn it only slightly, we merely have to sprinkle sand on top of the worktable before we place the stone on it.

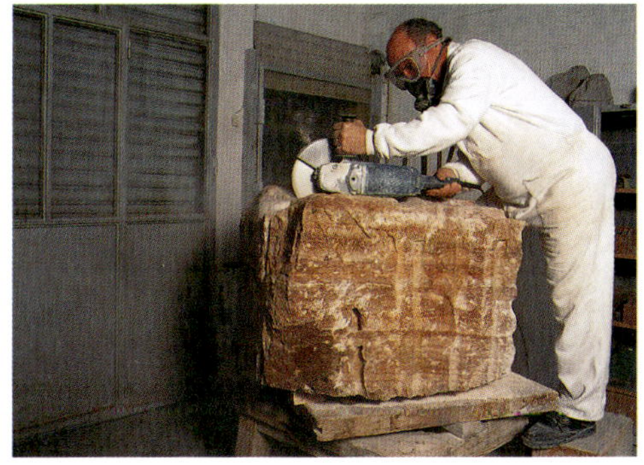

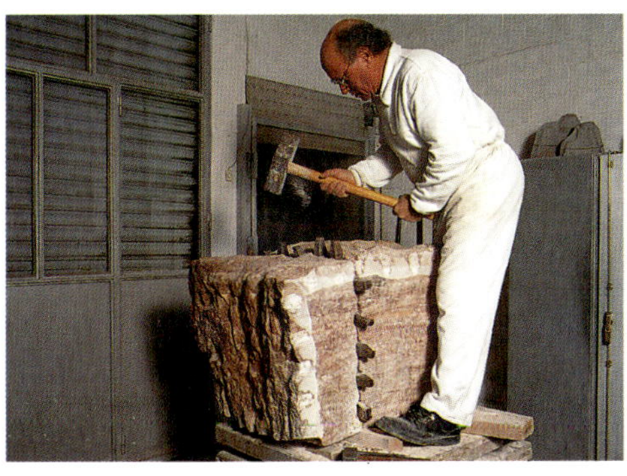

Fracturing

Since it will be difficult to find a block that exactly matches the desired size of our sculpture, we must either modify its design or pare down the stone. For very large blocks, we rely on a technique traditionally used in quarries and that is illustrated below.

▲ **1.** We use a ruler and a plotter to mark the break line, respecting safety margins. We chisel a groove along this line or we score it with a circular saw, as shown here, and then deepen it with a point chisel into a V-shape. The punch holes should be driven perpendicular, so as to accommodate wedges whose proximity will depend on the hardness of the stone. It will be easier to slide the wedges if they are flanked by small pieces of thin steel with lightly filed edges.

If the groove is aligned with the stone's vein texture resulting from sediment stratification, we have to score only one face of the rock to crack it. Fracturing will occur naturally, but not always in the way we expect it to.

If, as in this case, however, we try to split the rock perpendicular to its vein structure, we will have to insert wedges on all visible sides of the stone.

▲ **2.** We will chisel the groove to a perfect V to make the wedges fit better. Then we insert the wedges using light strokes of the mallet, making sure not to hit one harder than the other. If we get a dull sound on one of the wedges, we know that it isn't placed properly and that it could fall out. Before this happens, we make the hole deeper and reinsert the wedge.

We have already placed a strip of wood that will serve as a separator below the cut line. We have placed it in such a way that the piece of stone that we want to break is raised up. In this way, the weight of the stone itself will help to break it off.

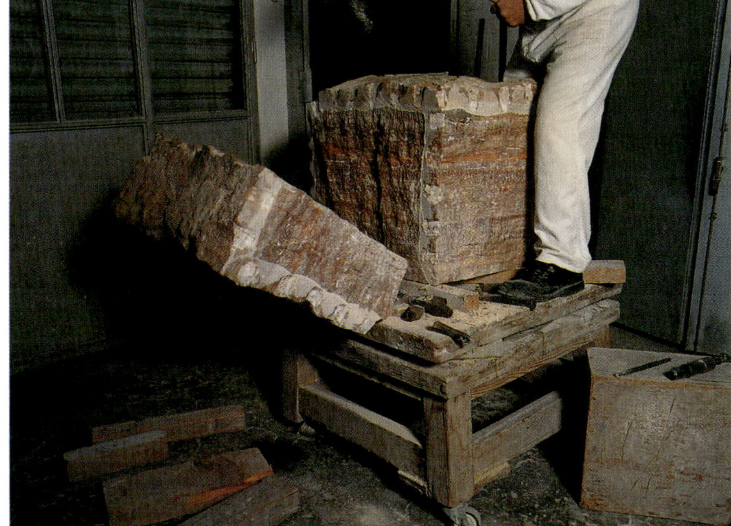

► **3.** After a series of hammer blows to the wedges, the increased high-pitched sound tells us that we can deliver the final blow . . . and we split the rock. Several pieces of wood will cushion the fall of the split rock. Though it may be a spectacular site, it is better if we don't allow the rock to fall from the worktable. The best way to do this is to work on the floor on wooden planks that are placed crosswise beneath the separating strip of wood.

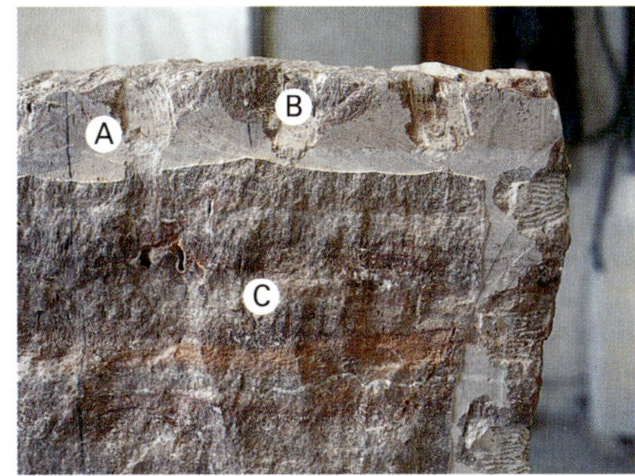

▲ **4.** This is how the surface of the cut looks. You can see (A) the area that was cut by the circular saw, which, if it were chiseled, would only need to be deepened by $1^1/_2$ inches (4 cm); the marks left by the wedges (B); and the fractured surface (C).

Consolidation

When carving, it is important for the block to be resting on a solid base so that it doesn't move when we hit it. If the base of the block is smooth, its own weight will immobilize it; otherwise, we can stabilize it with wooden wedges. If the stone is small, we can glue it to a larger one and secure it to the worktable with clamps.

► ► If we want to work on a block in a vertical and, therefore, unstable position, we will glue it with plaster of Paris to a base stone to steady it. When the sculpture is almost finished, a few strategically placed chisel strikes will be enough to break away the plaster and free the stone from its base.

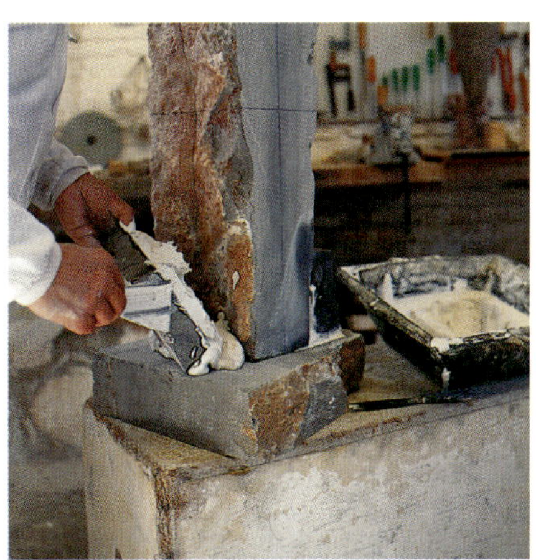

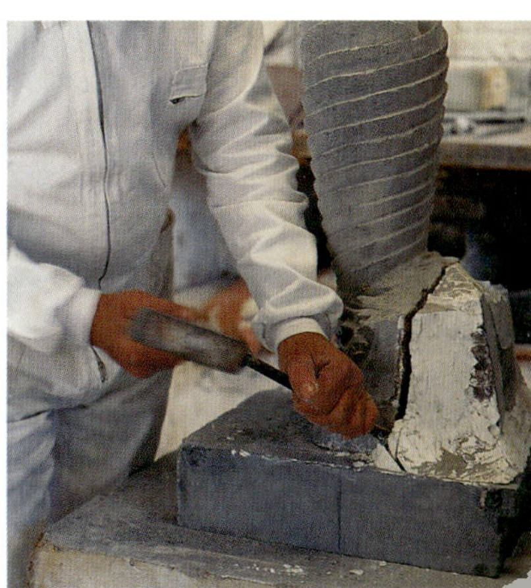

Becoming Familiar with the Tools

Before starting to carve, and with the maquette and block in front of us, we visualize how the former will be totally enclosed within the latter, making sure that the sculpture's salient points easily fit within the size of the block. We should repeat this exercise each time we look at the stone. When this becomes a habit, we will see how the process spontaneously reverses itself; when we look at the stone we will visualize the maquette.

But before we "immerse ourselves" in working the stone, we recall Michelangelo's well-known adage, "the experienced artist does not conceive an idea that cannot fit within a single block of marble, from which only the hand that obeys intellect can free it." Before continuing, we suggest you inspect all of the block's surfaces and familiarize yourself with the tools.

Each type of stone and each stage of the carving process requires tools that are often designed by the carvers themselves. Basically, tools differ in the shape of their tips or chiseling areas, while their grip handles or points of contact with the hammer look the same.

The hardness of a rock determines the size of the cutting blade. This will be wide for soft stones and narrow and hardened for hard stones. The same criteria also apply to the different stages of carving—narrow blades to remove big chips, and wide blades, which carve surfaces more accurately, to shape final surfaces.

Although a wide variety of tools are used in quarries, the most common ones used by sculptors are manual and electronic tools.

▲ If we wash the stone, its vein texture will become visible. The texture's orientation will provide us with information about the stone's formation. If flaws are not detected by tapping with a hammer, we will thoroughly inspect the stone for minor cracks. If a crack is detected and we are unsure about its significance, the humidity trapped inside may provide us with a clue since, in the case of a marble slab, it will show on the slab's opposite side. When in doubt, a strong hit and we will likely have two perfectly good stones.

Manual Tools

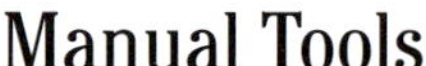

Among the tools most commonly used in sculpture are the **trimmer** or **mole**, which enables us to smooth out large surfaces; the **bushhammer**, for wearing down or evening out surfaces; the **tooth chisel** and the **flat chisel**, used in shaping, and the **rasp**, suitable for smoothing out small rough spots.

All of these tools are generally made of tempered steel. While the bushhammer is used as a hammer, the others need to be used with a mallet and have cylindrical shapes. The exception is the trimmer, whose rectangular shape prevents it from spinning in the hand when hit.

The pictures illustrate the application of each tool.

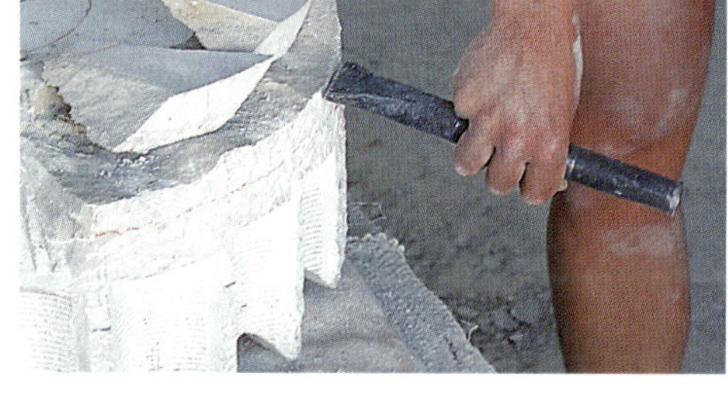

▲ The trimmer, also called the "mole" because, like the animal, it works under the surface, enables us to break off large chunks of stone when used at the spot of sedimentation or on ill-formed rocks, as is the case in slate rocks. We can also use it to chip off large pieces of hard rock regardless of where on the surface we apply it. Bricklayers find this tool especially useful for detaching all mortar that adheres to the brick with one solid blow.

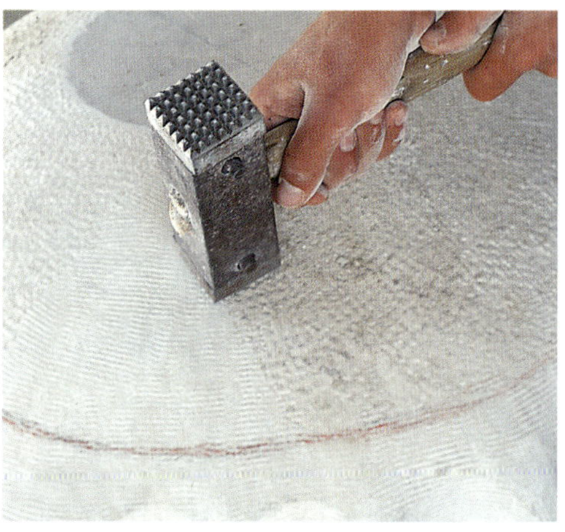

▲ The bushhammer, a type of hammer that can have between 9 and 49 teeth, is used to even out surfaces in order to detect irregularities in the stone and to redraw grids or reference lines.

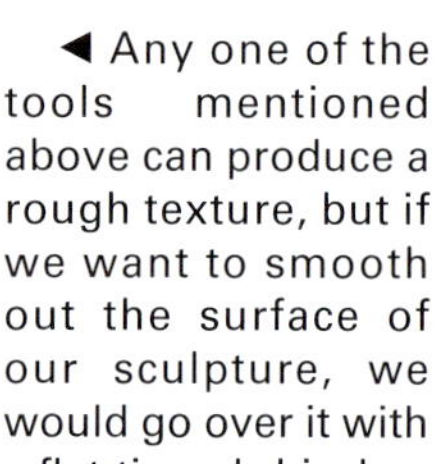

◀ Any one of the tools mentioned above can produce a rough texture, but if we want to smooth out the surface of our sculpture, we would go over it with a flat-tipped chisel.

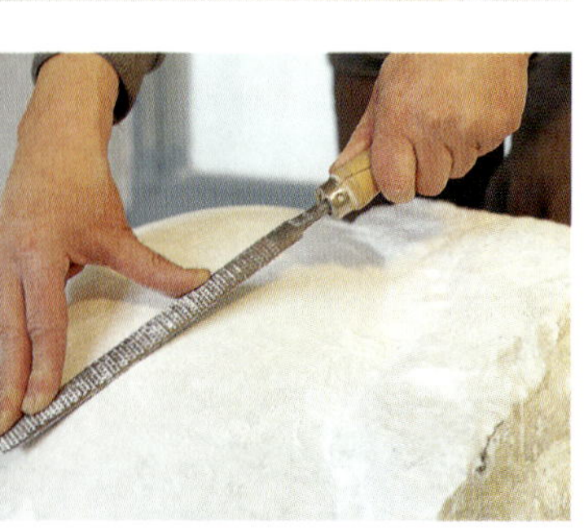

◀ Finally, we use the rasp to smooth out the markings left by the chisel. This tool can also be used on soft stones such as alabaster.

▼ The point chisel can also be used to break off large pieces of stone if we hold it in the same position we would a trimmer for impact. We can control it better and use it to break off smaller pieces if we hold it at a lower angle.

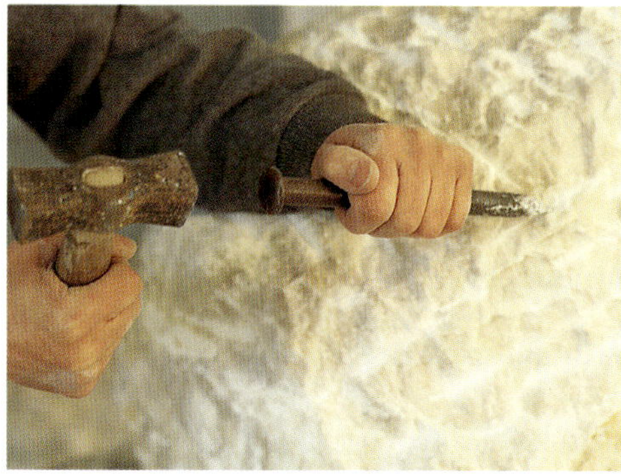

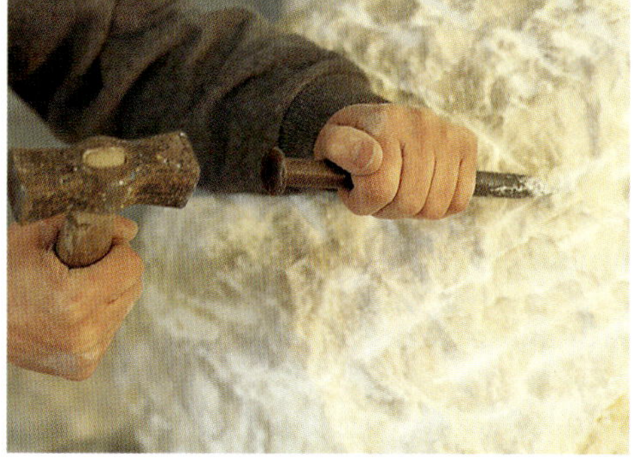

▼ The tooth chisel is the most common sculpting tool because it allows for detailed shaping. The ridge grooving creates a subtle play of light that Michelangelo was so fond of creating. He always used this type of chisel. Some historians who have forgotten this technique confuse this "refinishment" with the *non finito* of his unfinished sculptures.

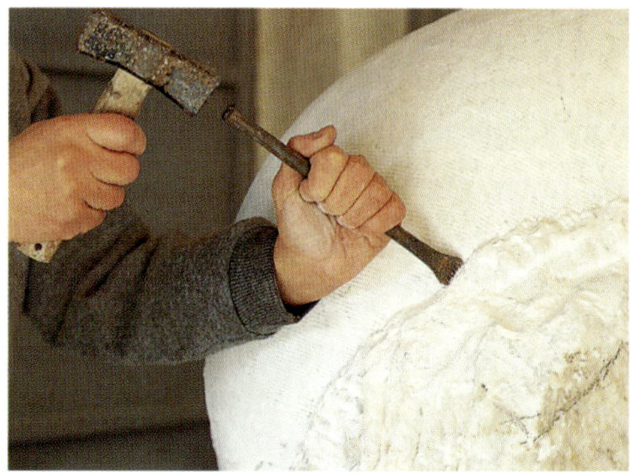

Electric and Pneumatic Tools

Electricity supplies the energy needed by the stonecutter's hammer. In some tools, such as the **circular saw**, the **polisher**, and the **drill**, it does so directly, while the **compressor** generates compressed air that also activates similar tools. However, the compressor is mostly used to move tooth and flat chisels by means of a pneumatic hammer.

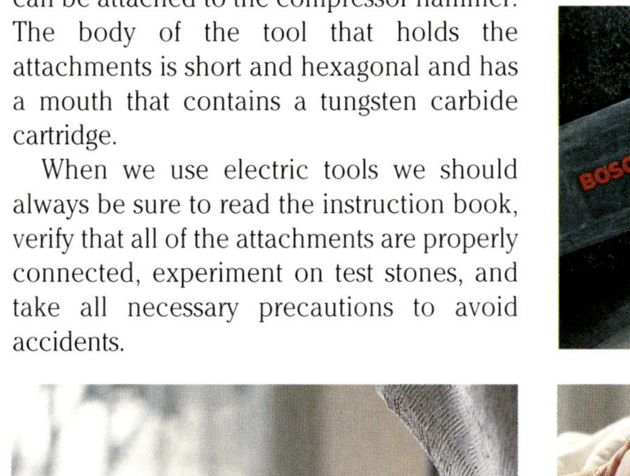

A wide variety of diamond disks for cutting, and bits of sandpaper and fabric disks to clean and shine can be attached to the first group of tools. All of the manual tools can be attached to the compressor hammer. The body of the tool that holds the attachments is short and hexagonal and has a mouth that contains a tungsten carbide cartridge.

When we use electric tools we should always be sure to read the instruction book, verify that all of the attachments are properly connected, experiment on test stones, and take all necessary precautions to avoid accidents.

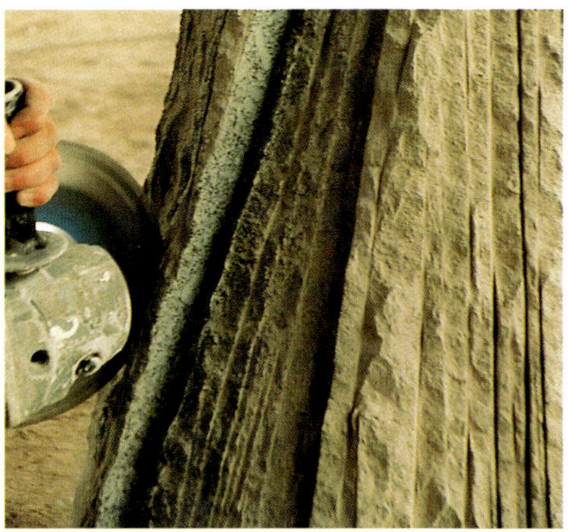

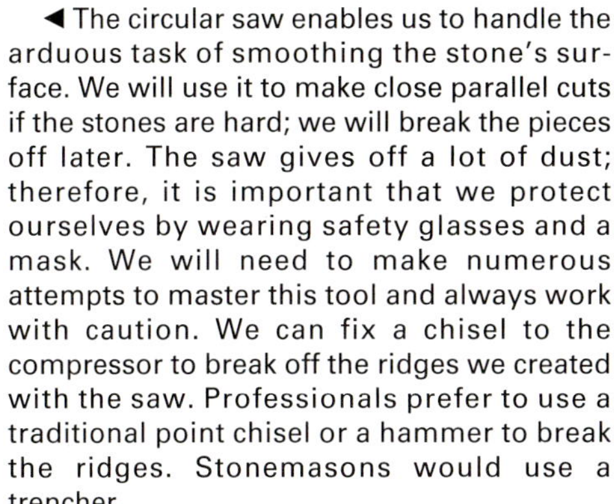

◄ The circular saw enables us to handle the arduous task of smoothing the stone's surface. We will use it to make close parallel cuts if the stones are hard; we will break the pieces off later. The saw gives off a lot of dust; therefore, it is important that we protect ourselves by wearing safety glasses and a mask. We will need to make numerous attempts to master this tool and always work with caution. We can fix a chisel to the compressor to break off the ridges we created with the saw. Professionals prefer to use a traditional point chisel or a hammer to break the ridges. Stonemasons would use a trencher.

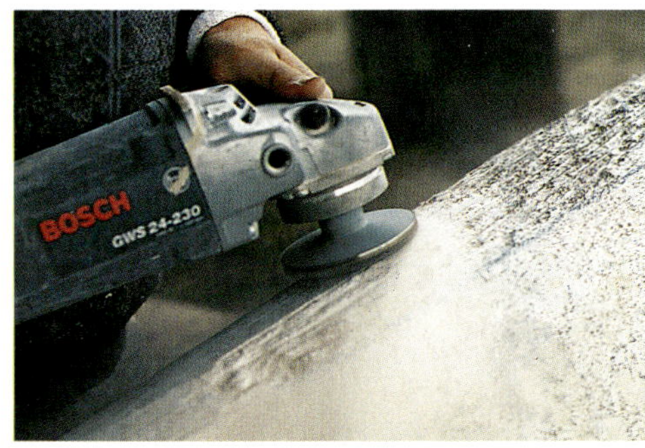

◄ There are a wide range of diamond cutting disks that, when attached to the circular saw, make the shaping and polishing work, including that on curved surfaces, easier.

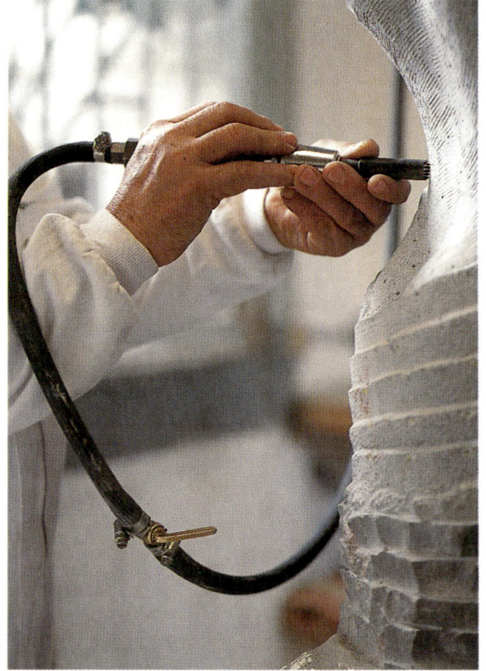

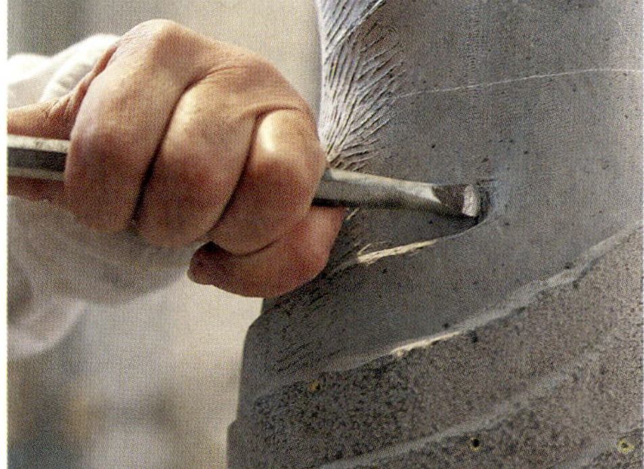

◄ ▲ The compressor acts as a striking mallet, and when in operation, is controlled by a shut-off valve installed on the hose. Tooth and flat chisels can be attached to the pneumatic hammer that is at the end of the hose and in this illustration is hidden behind the hands.

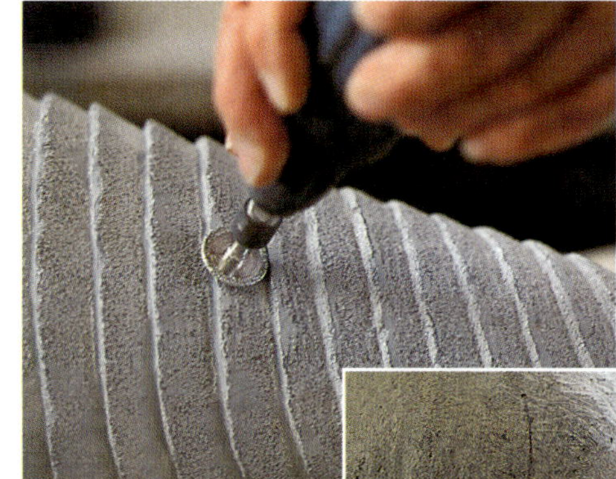

▲ ► To refinish details, we will use a drill similar to the type lapidaries use to power tiny disks or bits.

► In order to clean flat surfaces we use a rubber plate to attach sandpaper disks to the drill. We can also use a polisher, remembering to protect ourselves from the flying dust.

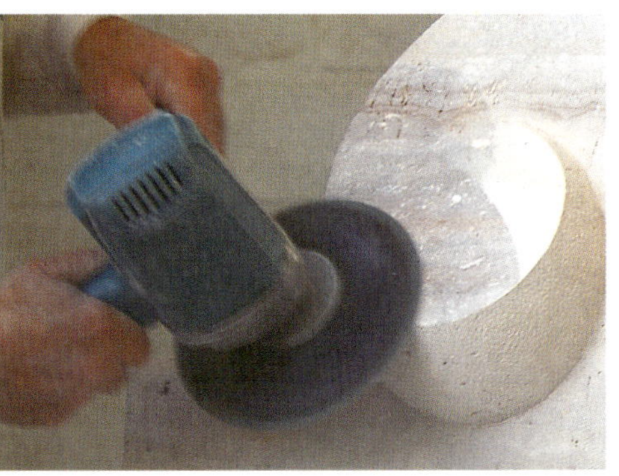

► We shine the stone using a cloth activated by the polisher or drill. We apply the polishing cream pressing the cartridge down on the rotating disk in the direction of the arrow, moving slowing and deliberately in order to prevent the cream from splattering.

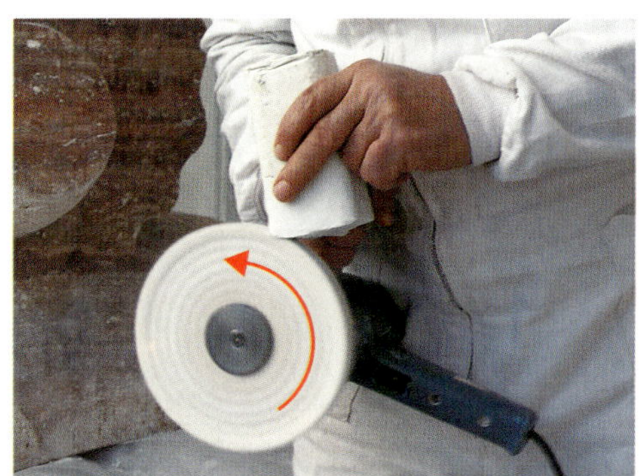

The Complexity of Reliefs

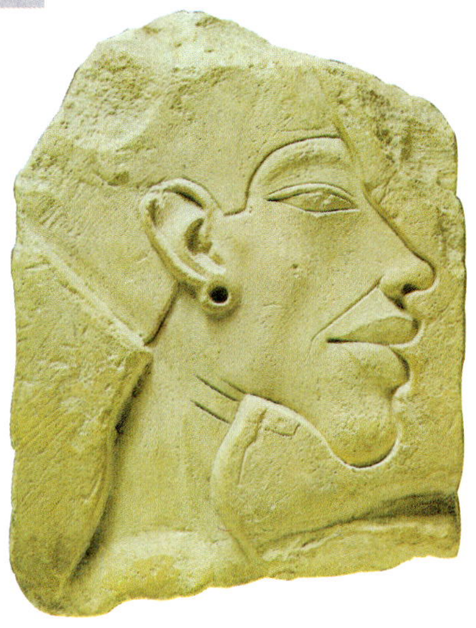

◄ Akhenaton. c. 1350 B.C.E. Limestone. Egyptian Museum, Berlin (Germany). Sunken relief, perhaps a fragment of a bas-relief carving.

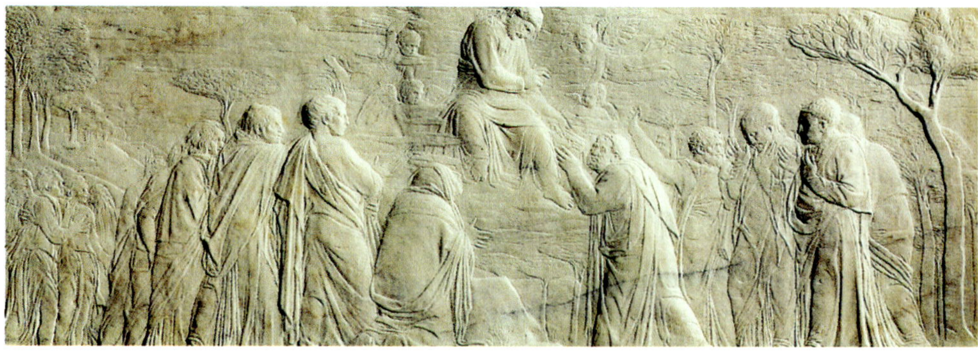

▲ Donatello. *Christ Giving the Keys to Saint Peter.* c. 1430. Marble. Victoria and Albert Museum, London (United Kingdom). Schiacciato relief with geometric perspective.

We need to train ourselves how to use the tools and shape models, starting with simple forms, before we gain the confidence we need to overcome obstacles. We suggest following a set of exercises that will help us gain this confidence. First we want to examine the difficulty central to what seems to be the simplest form of sculpture, but that in reality is not—the relief.

We know that sculpture is divided in two large groups: freestanding volumes, which can be viewed from all angles, and relief, which is usually attached to a wall with its back side unsculpted.

Relief sculptures range from a simple incision or frieze to the most complex representations of perspective that include the collation of different stones.

A relief could adorn the facades of an Egyptian or Hindu temple, bedeck Roman porticos, adorn a neoclassic pediment, give depth to a functional building, provide a picture medallion for a monument or gravestone, as well as for our homes.

To make a relief we can simply score the outlines of the design into the stone's surface. These are known as sunken reliefs or negatives. The process is not very difficult and withstands the passage of time. This type of relief was practiced in Egypt during the eighteenth and nineteenth dynasties and is still used to sign a sculpture.

More frequently, the relief involves removing the background material from the stone to make the sculpted parts stand out, hence its name. A detailed classification of these reliefs exists based on the depth of carving. It is doubtful, though, that the artists had the classification or aesthetic attributions in mind when carving reliefs.

A relief that stands out slightly, similar to an embossed drawing, is defined as *schiacciato* (flattened in Italian). In a *bas-relief* the figures stand slightly out from the plane. In a *medium-relief* half of the volume of the figures is carved out. The carved figures of a *high-relief* or *complete relief* are detached from their background to such an extent that we see the work more as a freestanding sculpture than a two-dimensional drawing.

The relief is one of the most difficult forms of sculpture because it combines the complex techniques of sculpture with the concept of painting. Indeed, although relief is three-dimensional and intended to be viewed from the front, it adheres to two-dimensional criteria similar to those of painting. Sometimes, however, it requires visual corrections depending on the light that falls on it or the angle from which the viewer observes it.

The perspective in a relief also relates to pictorial styles. At times the perspective is disregarded in order to accentuate the narrative elements of juxtaposed images as in hunting scenes of Asurbanipal in the British Museum and in abstract compositions. Other reliefs combine the most salient points of the work in a single image (Egyptian foreshortening). Some invert the lines of escape (Byzantine perspective), arrange themes in a hierarchy according to their importance (Romanesque), or faithfully follow the principles of geometric perspective (Renaissance).

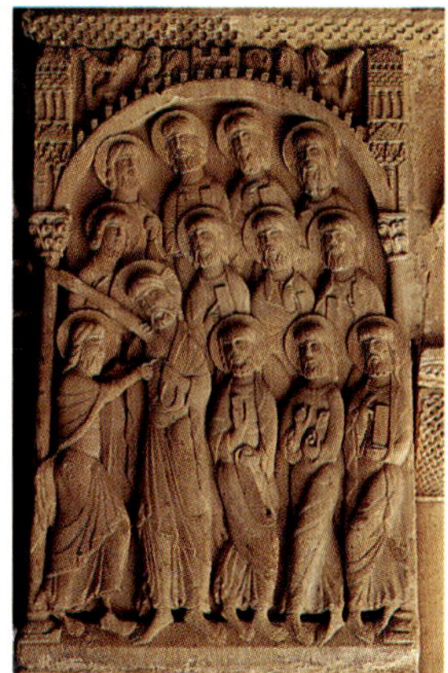

◄ *The Doubt of Saint Thomas.* Twelfth century. Sandstone. Silos Monastery (Spain). Medium-relief with hierarchic characteristics, having Christ stand out more than the Apostles.

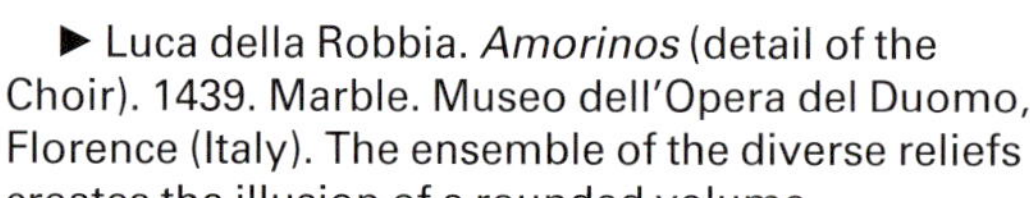

► Luca della Robbia. *Amorinos* (detail of the Choir). 1439. Marble. Museo dell'Opera del Duomo, Florence (Italy). The ensemble of the diverse reliefs creates the illusion of a rounded volume.

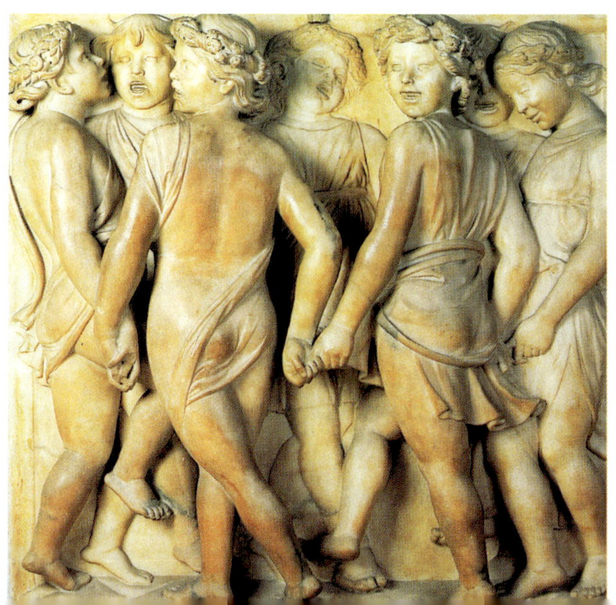

The First Steps

An exercise we propose for those attempting their first carving is to select a slab of marble as thick as a kitchen counter and to practice rounding the edges and digging into it until turning it into a type of rosette.

We have provided a marble worker a slab from Macael (Spain), which is about 1 inch (3 cm) thick; we have also given him a paper template in the shape of a wing to use as a model for shaping the marble.

◀ **1. Half reed.** To round the edges, we will begin by drawing a horizontal axis (A) that will divide the slab into two halves, and indicates the center we need to respect until we finish. Then we will place the marble on a piece of wood so that the side we are working on hangs over.

With a tooth chisel we reduce the top and bottom edges (B) until we form a third plane around the marked line (C). With the chisel, we smooth all remaining corners between surfaces. In this way, we have shaped five cylinders that practically design a half cylinder, better known as a half reed.

▶ **2.** To give the marble a curved shape, we rub the entire edge with a carborundum strip, rubbing diagonally from top to bottom and bottom to top, moving over the center until forming a continuous curve.

If we want to polish and shine, holding the marble in the same position, we rub it with an increasingly finer grain of sandpaper that we use with water.

▶ **1. Concave surface.** Before giving a concave shape to the smooth surface of the marble slab, we lay it on a folded blanket as a precaution to prevent it from cracking when we hit it. The blanket will absorb the force of the blows.

With the marble lying flat, we use a tooth chisel to mold a wide area, working from the outer rim toward the center so we don't chip the edges. Little by little we carve into the marble's surface until we've eliminated the center layer.

▶ **2.** When the curvature is satisfactory, we erase the markings left by the tooth chisel by polishing the entire surface with sandpaper disks of increasingly finer grain, and then, finally, with a rubber disk. We could also smooth it manually with a carborundum stone or sandpaper. To shine the surface, we will rub it hard with sandpaper that we use with water.

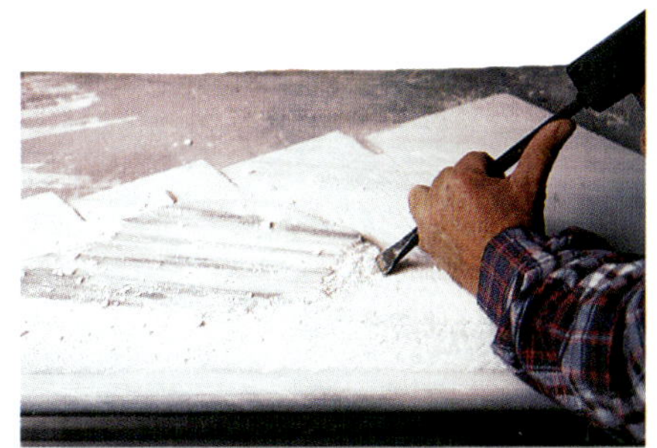

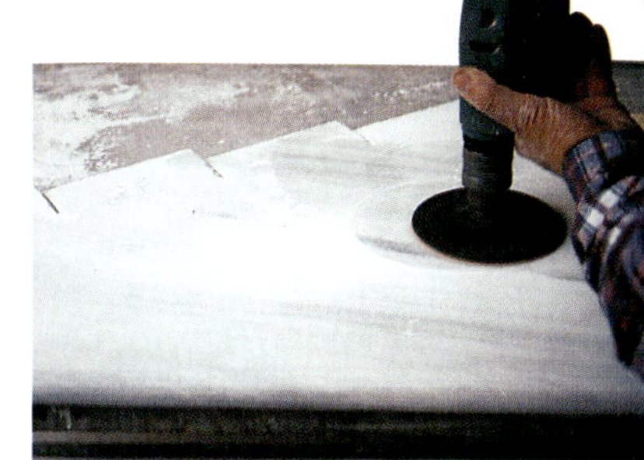

▶ **1. Perforations.** To make incisions, we will place the same marble over two planks of wood to lift it from the worktable and allow the drill to pass through it. Using a drill with tungsten carbide bits, and with the motor running intermittently, we make small holes that we will later enlarge using increasingly larger bits. It is best to start off first using a plotter or a point chisel to make a hole that will accommodate a 3 mm bit.

Here we have made two perforations whose diameter exceeds that of a drill bit. If we take a look at the third perforation, which has just been started, we will understand the process. We drill the contour of the circumference with small bits. Then with the chisel we punch out the material between the holes. Finally, with a rasp we smooth the perimeter of the resulting large opening.

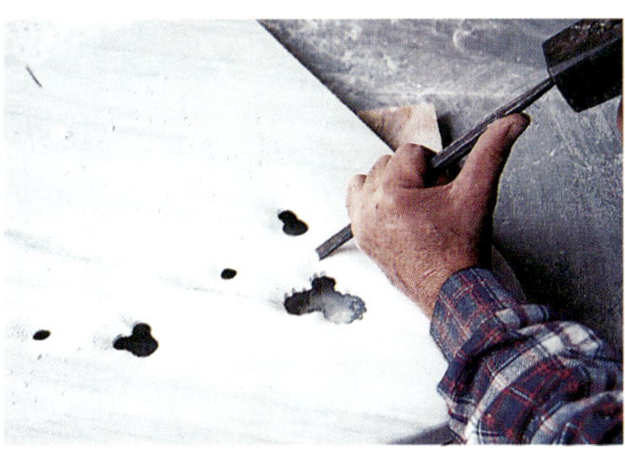

◀ **2.** So that our first rosette(?) is sleeker, and to get more practice using the chisel, we can carve little craterlike cavities around the holes. We use a medium-size chisel, firmly grasped, to trim the edges from the outside in, with light taps applied at an increasingly lower angle the closer we get to the center.

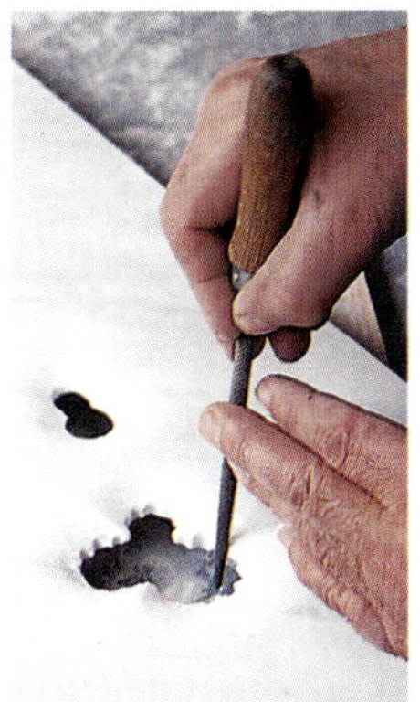

◀ **3.** Finally, with a curved rasp, we smooth out all of the small edges left by the chisel, and with a cylindrical file we smooth the perimeter of the adjoining holes. We will use a carborundum stone to polish the carving and wet sandpaper to shine it.

This simple technique not only enables us to produce this type of stone perforation, but it also allows us to drill along the contours of tracings drawn on a stone slab or block without perforating completely through the stone. Then, with the tooth chisel, flat chisel, and rasp we can smooth the drill marks and complete our first relief.

Mastering Volumes

Here are some exercises, not only to master the carving of round volumes, but also as a basic example of carving any sculpture. In the following illustrations, we will demonstrate how to clean the surface of alabaster and even out its base, and also how to build a hemisphere in sandstone. These two exercises have the added advantage of being able to be evaluated objectively, which will help us measure our own technical progress.

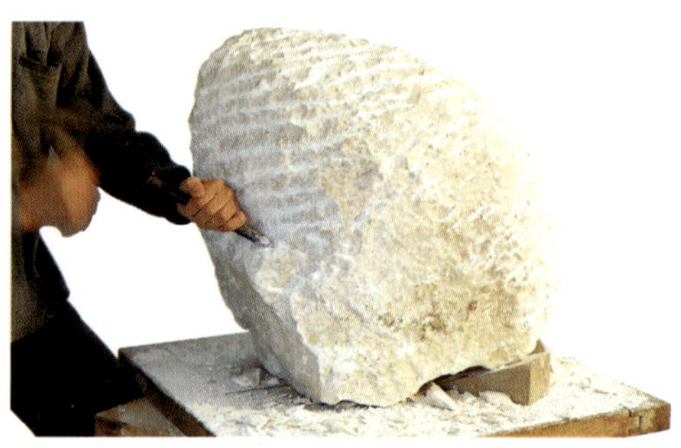

▲ We treat the alabaster by removing its outer layer as if we were peeling a fruit. Here we are doing it by *chopping*, moving the chisel all around the stone. We hold the chisel as parallel to the block as possible rather than perpendicular, thus avoiding any new injuries to it.

Cleaning

Because it is a soft stone, alabaster is the best choice for carving your first sculpture in the round. However, before carving a soft rock that has not been industrially sawed off, it should be treated by chipping off the breakable areas. This operation is essential when working with pumice stone or volcanic lavas, and necessary with alabaster since it damages easily, though superficially, during extraction, transportation, and carving.

Flattening the Base

Once we have treated the stone, the first thing we do is flatten the base on which the future sculpture will rest. In this way the block stays securely in position on the workstand while we carve it. Doing this as a first step avoids damaging the parts we have worked on.

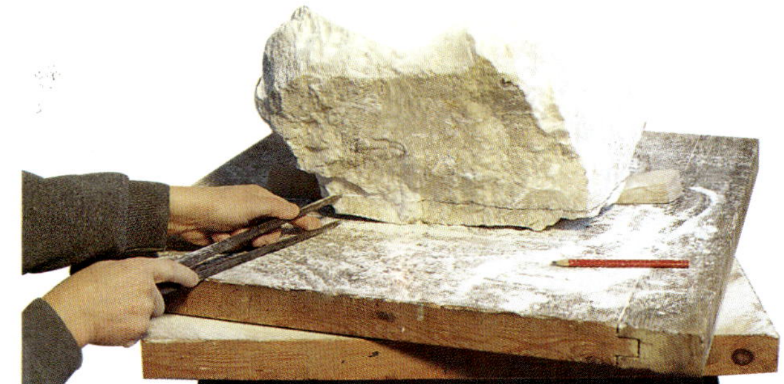

◀ **1.** With one end of a compass grazing the flat surface of the workstand and the other end resting on the stone, we will mark the perimeter of the base to a height that will guarantee sufficient material to work the base.

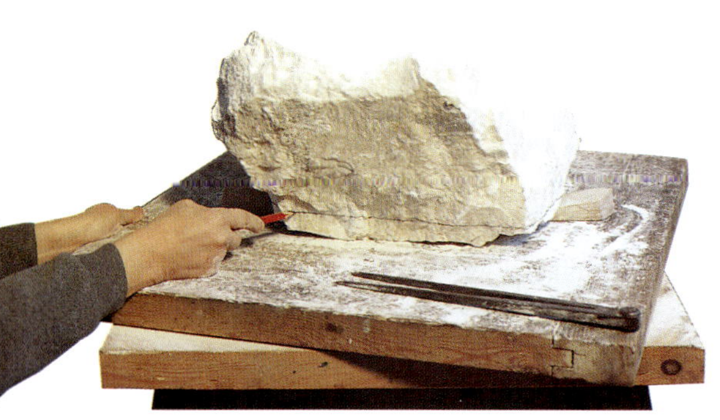

▲ **2.** Then, to highlight this perimeter, we mark over it with a plotter or a thick pencil.

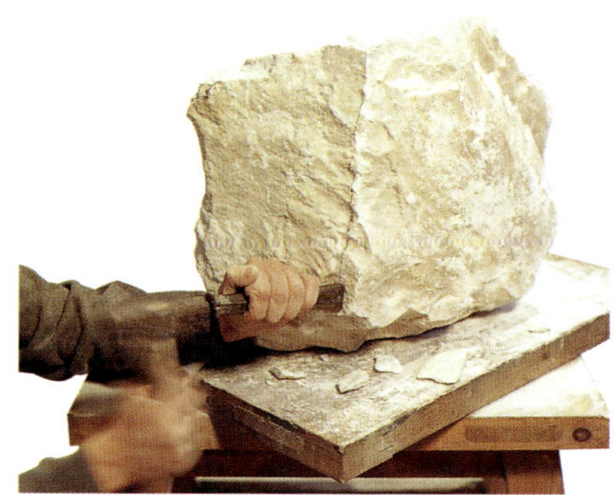

▲ **3.** Next, we use a trimmer along the marked perimeter, chipping off excess material from the outside in.

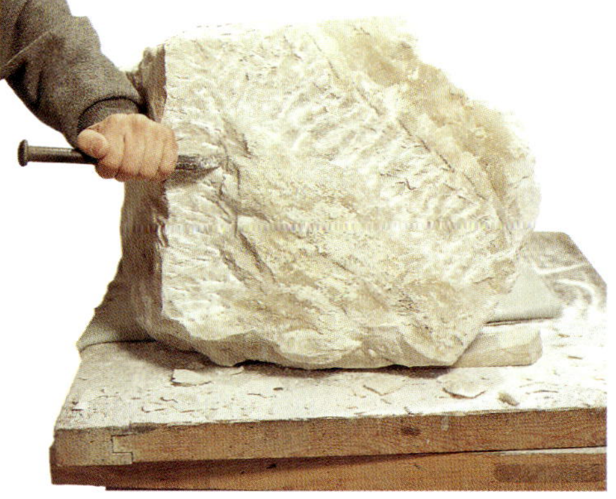

▲ **4.** Starting from the edges, we flake the stone progressively toward the center of the base, ignoring for now the area the stone is resting on, which we will work when we turn the stone over.

▼ **5.** We use a tooth chisel to smooth out the irregularities left on the surface. Because it is close to the marked line, we work on the perimeter area first. We work the area very carefully; it will serve as a guide for smoothing the rest of the surface. This strip, known as the master line, will be the key reference for shaping large volumes as well as details. It is usually smoothed later with a chisel, but in this case we don't think it is necessary.

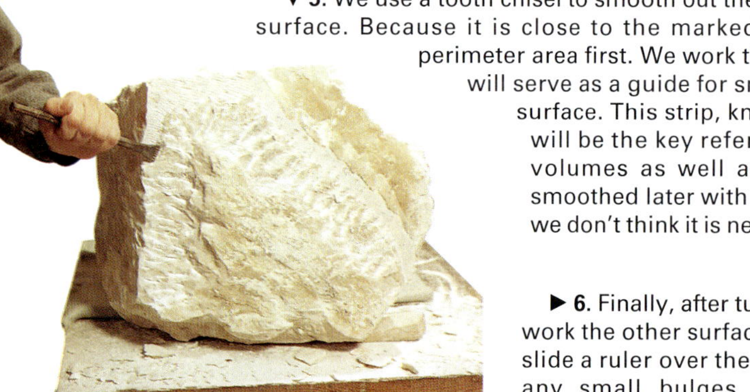

▶ **6.** Finally, after turning the block over, we work the other surfaces in the same way and slide a ruler over the work to see if there are any small bulges left that need to be smoothed out.

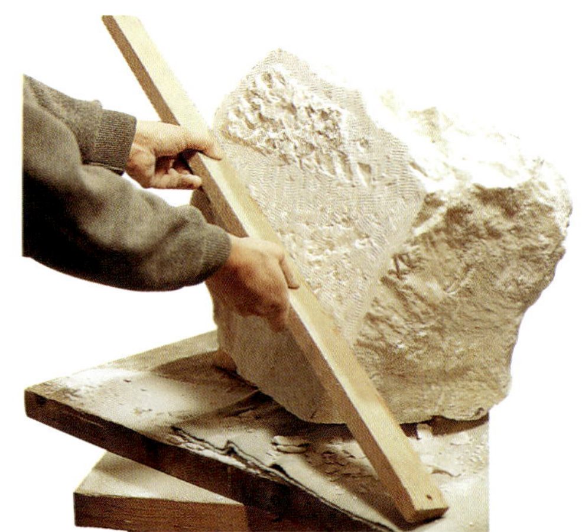

From Polyhedron to Sphere

One of the biggest challenges for an apprentice stonemason is shaping a sphere. Although it may appear to be simple, this exercise forces one to "visualize" the desired form inside the stone block. You have to fashion a perfect cube that would comprise the sphere, and do so using little effort and few tools. You need to ensure that the diameter of the sphere matches the width of the cube or, in other words, that the center of each of side of the cube retains its initial dimension and lies on the surface of the sphere. But the greatest lesson the sculptor learns in this exercise is that the slightest error, making one point too deep, for example, implies making changes to all of the points. Summing up, let's say that the exercise allows us to evaluate the results objectively as well as literally by comparing the diameter of the sphere with the dimensions of the original block.

We demonstrate here the four main steps in sculpting an oblique hemisphere that will constitute a secondary part of a sculpture and whose main side has already been reduced. To understand which steps to follow, we recall our surprise at learning in geometry that cutting off the edges of a cube gave us an octagon, and that a sphere is a true polyhedron with an infinite number of planes.

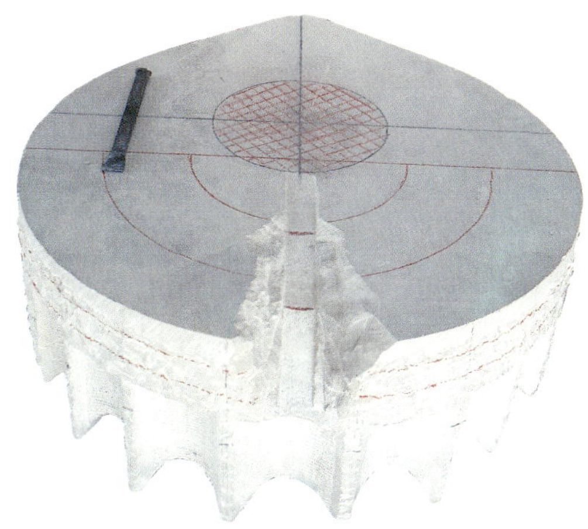

▲ **1.** First, we plot a set of symmetry axes, shown here in black. Once the center of the surface has been located, we mark on the surface several equidistant circles, semicircles in our case. We also draw other circles around the girth of the stone using a compass. We follow the same procedure as before, resting one of the arms of the compass on the worktable. We then use a point chisel and then a tooth chisel to carve a groove connecting the circles around the girth with the ones on the stone's surface—first the top girth circle with the inner circle on the surface, and continuing, the lower girth circle with the outer top circle. This and other similar grooves will guide us later in the roughing-out phase.

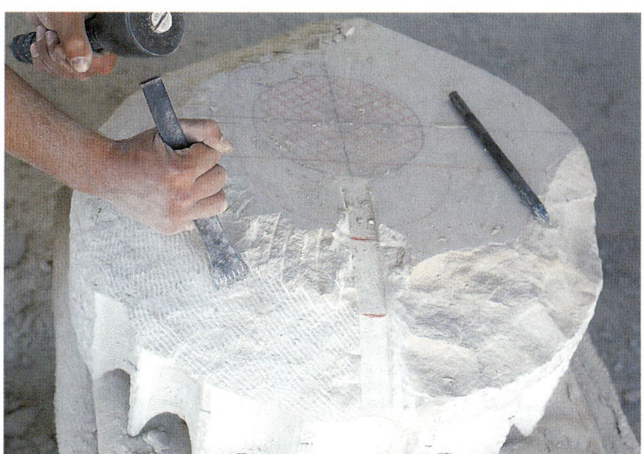

◄ ► **2.** Guided by the master line carved earlier, we cut back the rest using the trimmer and the point chisel when there is a lot of material to reduce and the tooth chisel when we get close to the bottom of the groove.

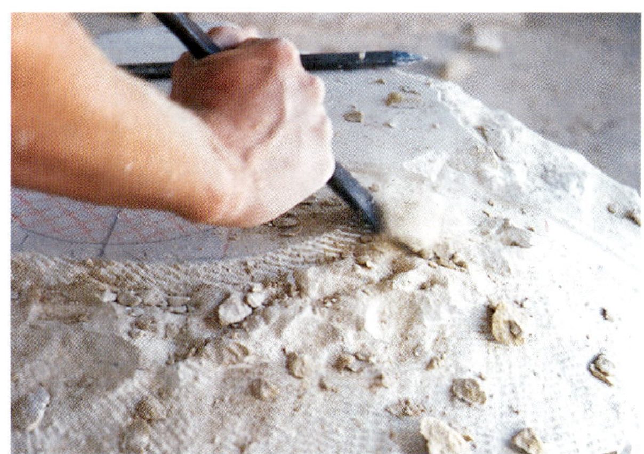

► **3.** As we approach the prescribed dimensional limits, we redraw the circumferences and level the surfaces with a tooth chisel having fewer teeth. Although a spherical shape is already discernible, we must proceed methodically and scrupulously increase the facets of the polyhedron. When the different facets have been carved, the only thing left for us is to trim the edges with the tooth chisel.

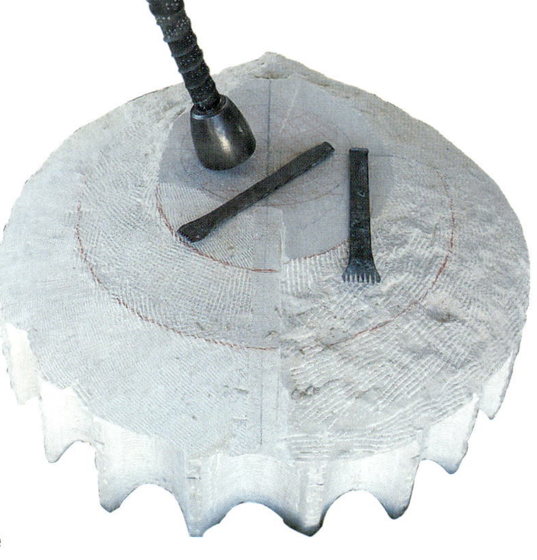

► **4.** Finally, we refinish the entire surface with the tooth chisel, drawing concentric circles to unify the volume. To smooth the surface of the hemisphere, we use a chisel to rub out the small grooves left by the tooth chisel and a rasp to smooth out the chisel markings. We can detect any other irregularities using our touch or a back light.

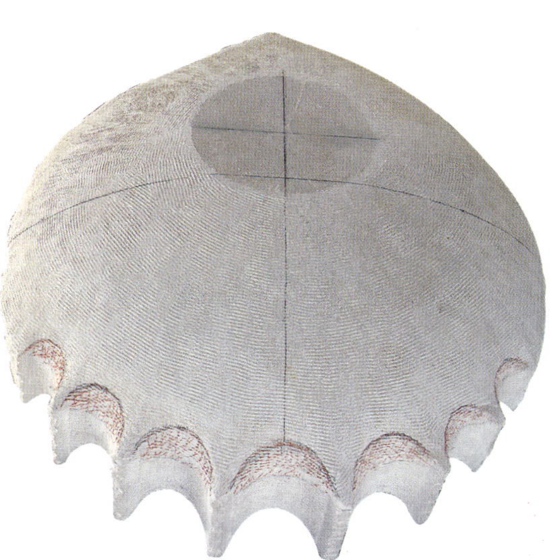

Roughing Out

Direct carving is the true road to sculpture, but also the worst for those who do not know how to walk.
Constantin Brancusi

Though carving is a continuous process of cutting away superfluous material, we divide the process into several phases: **outlining**, reducing the block to basic forms that encompass the desired product; **roughing out**, reducing material until the main volumes emerge; **modeling**, working the surfaces and details; and **finishing**, giving the final texture to the work.

Knowing "how to walk," especially when you are carving directly, implies being able to distinguish clearly between these steps, in particular between roughing out, or reducing, and modeling. After all, sculpture is a game of volumes that begins during reduction and ends when we reach what we figuratively call carving.

For better control when shaping volumes, it is best to reduce the stone from all angles by rotating it, despite the fact that Michelangelo worked his block from the principal point of view. His approach was like that of a person who, on emptying a bathtub, feels that his body is emerging from the water.

Here we demonstrate how to carve or reduce three sculptures, beginning with one in sandstone.

Patterned Reduction

Although we would like to engage in direct carving, we should first learn how to subject the stone to our will. Only then will we be able to speak to the stone and allow ourselves to be carried away unrestrained by its characteristics.

With this in mind, we propose as a first exercise to trim a stone using, on purpose, a simple model. If we trim a sandstone it will also help us comprehend the nature of this stone, which is made up of stratified layers, and that, therefore, will shatter better in one direction than another.

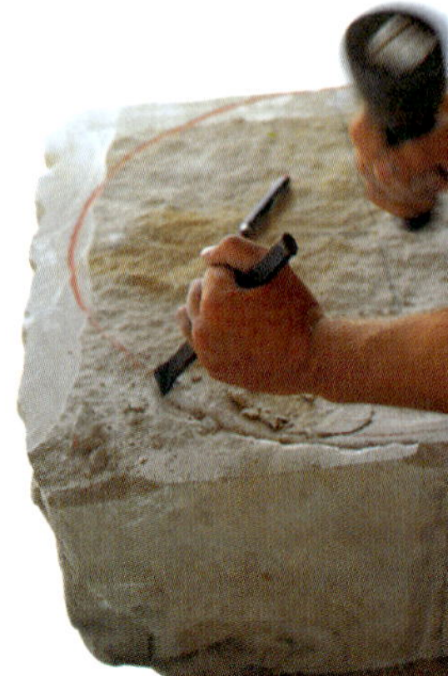

► **1.** To shape a cylinder, first we outline its perimeter with a compass. We then chisel along this outline and pare off all excess material from the top with accurate hits of a trimmer directed from the outside in, and then with a punch, from the inside out.

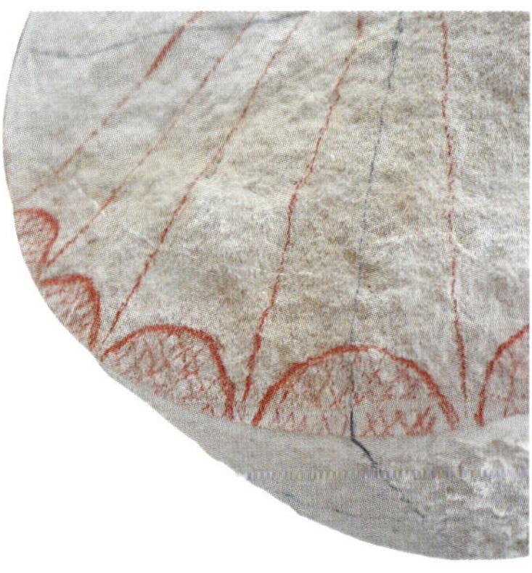

◄ **2.** We then draw in the areas to be trimmed, which are shown here in red.

► **3.** Next, we use first a tooth chisel and then a flat chisel to carve up to the guidelines' marked edges. Being careful not to go beyond these lines, we remove the excess material and with the tooth chisel we smooth the concave semicylinders.

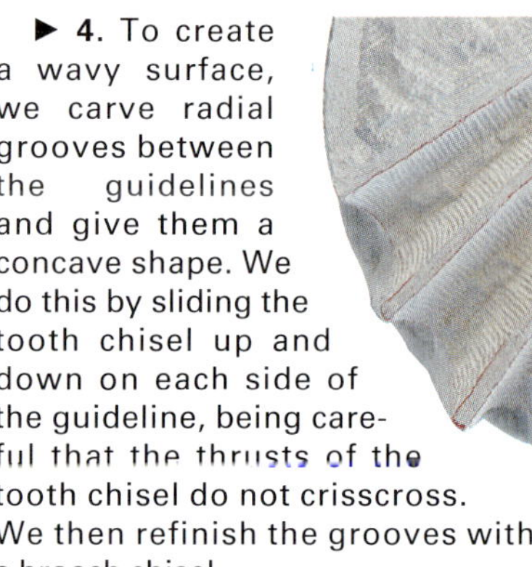

► **4.** To create a wavy surface, we carve radial grooves between the guidelines and give them a concave shape. We do this by sliding the tooth chisel up and down on each side of the guideline, being careful that the thrusts of the tooth chisel do not crisscross. We then refinish the grooves with a broach chisel.

Direct Trimming

Once we master the stone and the tools we can risk carving by improvising or by relying only on a rough sketch. Again we can resort to alabaster whose tractability will facilitate our task.

► **1.** First we outline a suitable volume for the carving, excluding the stone's edges that may hide fractures.

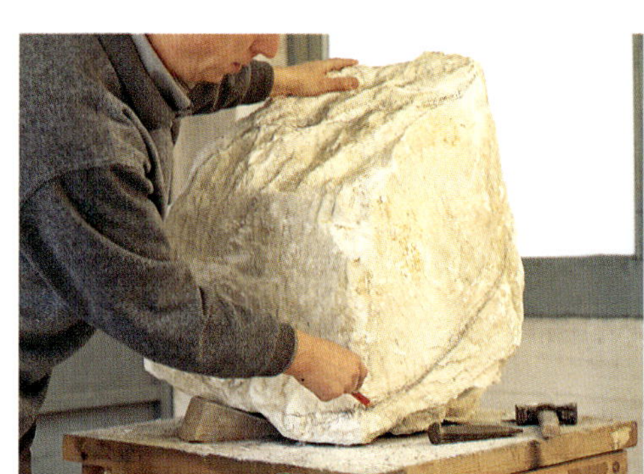

▼ **2.** With the point chisel we trim down the stone's edges and its outer surface. Having pared the stone to an adequate volume for the sculpture, we begin to plan the shape of our sculpture.

▼ **3.** After drawing a guideline, we continue trimming with a point chisel to shape our first conceived volume, which, in this case, is a concave shape.

▼ **4.** Using the same point chisel, we have pared down some areas and rounded other ones until we have achieved the shaping of this sculpture.

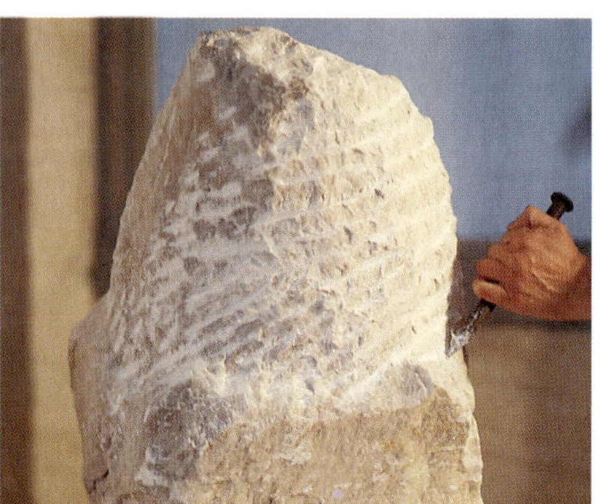

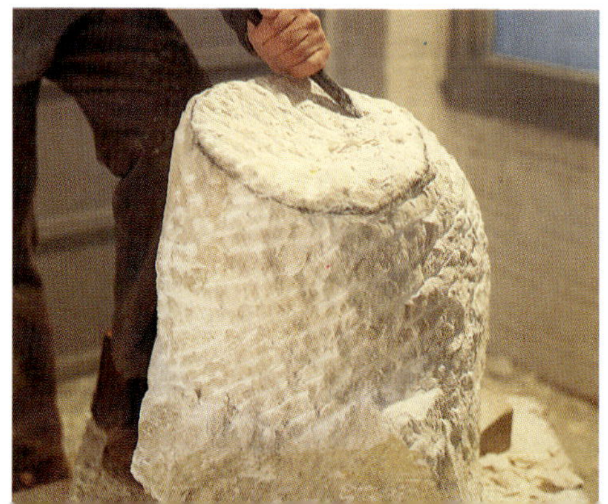

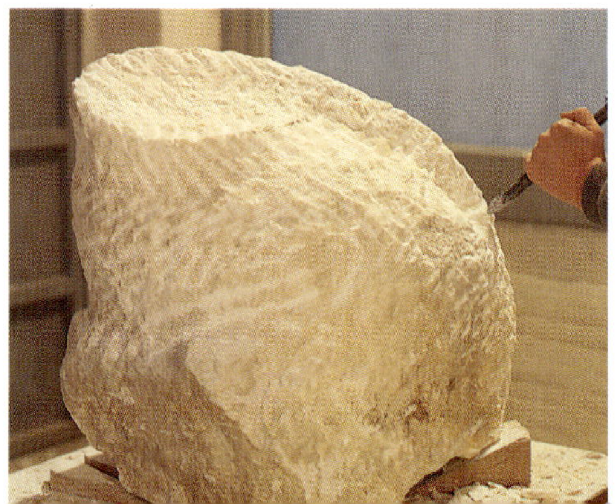

Trimming a Hard Stone

The previous exercises could have been performed using electrical tools. Here we will show you how to use them to carve travertine stone, a harder stone than the previous ones. Because the intended shape of the sculpture is complex, we will rely on the guidelines of a grid.

◄ *Akhenaton and a Queen.* 1340 B.C.E. Limestone. Egyptian Museum of Cairo (Egypt).

Sculpture left unfinished after trimming, perhaps because the sculptor Tutmosis did not like the carving or, more likely, because of the political upheavals that caused the demise of his patron.

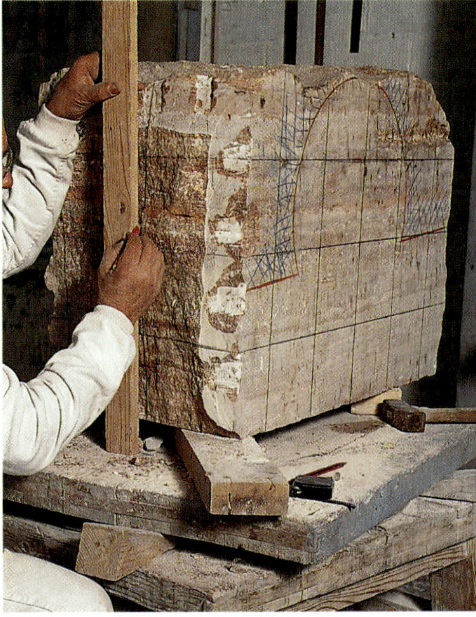

▲ **1.** We begin tracing axes on all sides of the stone with a pencil. We draw grids on the block, and guided by them, we pencil in the complete outline of our future sculpture.

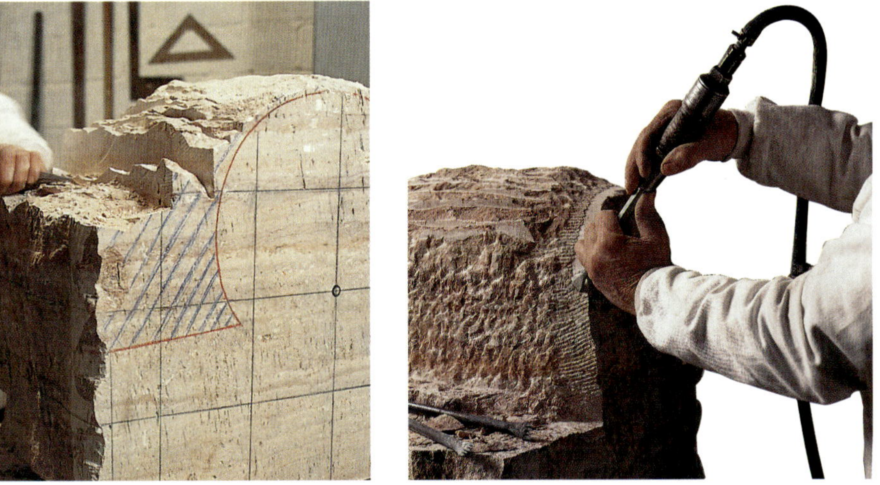

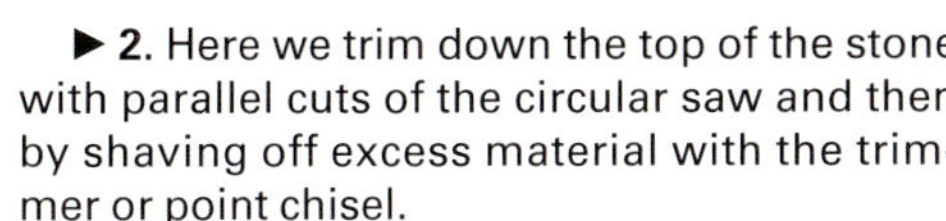

► **2.** Here we trim down the top of the stone with parallel cuts of the circular saw and then by shaving off excess material with the trimmer or point chisel.

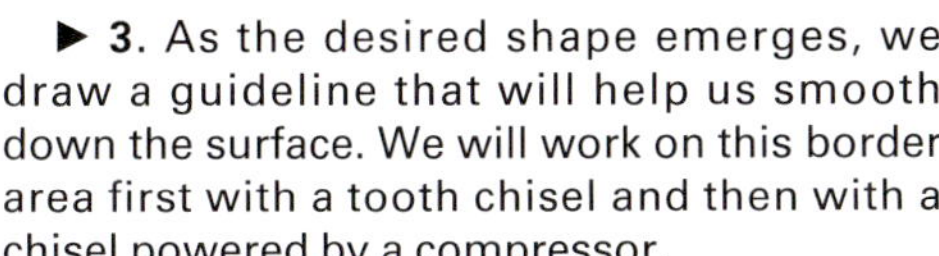

► **3.** As the desired shape emerges, we draw a guideline that will help us smooth down the surface. We will work on this border area first with a tooth chisel and then with a chisel powered by a compressor.

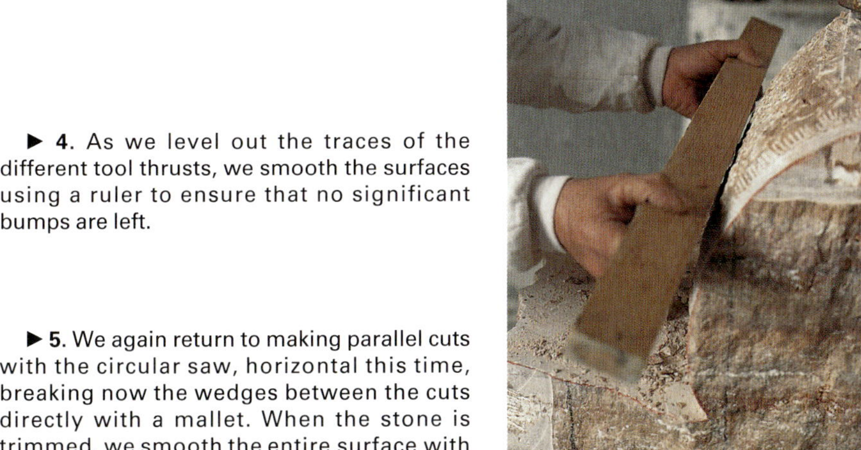

► **4.** As we level out the traces of the different tool thrusts, we smooth the surfaces using a ruler to ensure that no significant bumps are left.

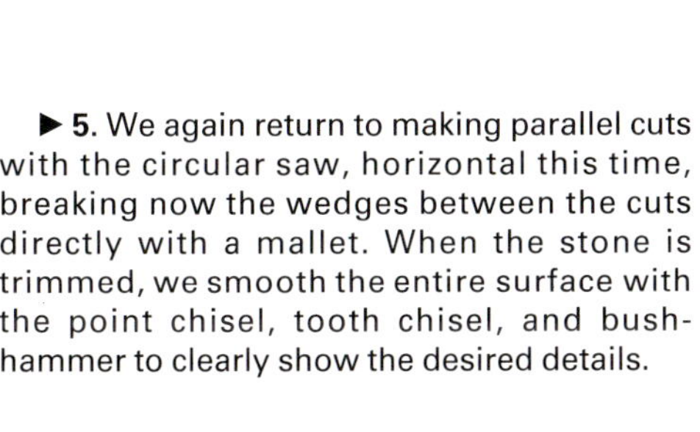

► **5.** We again return to making parallel cuts with the circular saw, horizontal this time, breaking now the wedges between the cuts directly with a mallet. When the stone is trimmed, we smooth the entire surface with the point chisel, tooth chisel, and bush-hammer to clearly show the desired details.

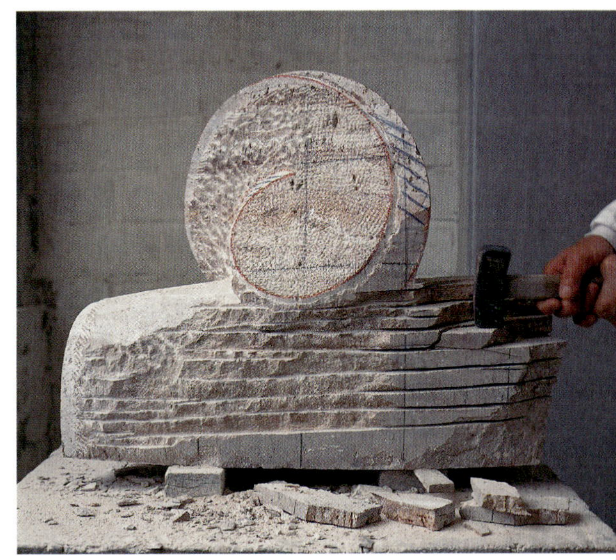

Modeling

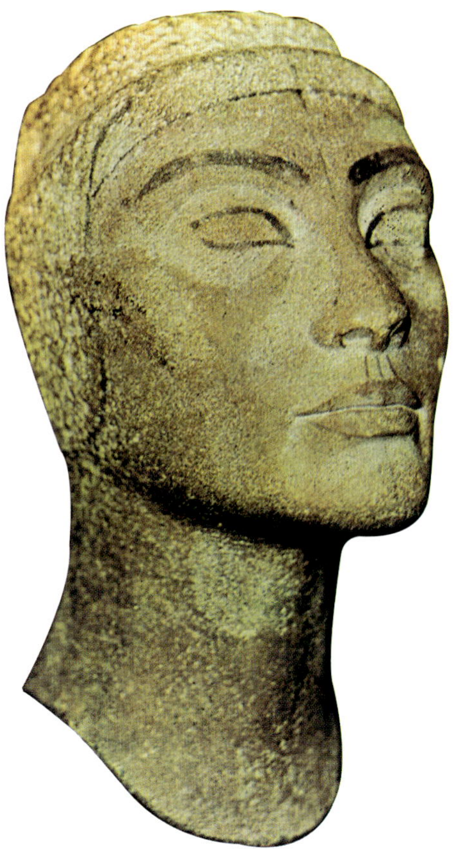

This portrait, left unfinished during the trimming process, enables us to see how the Egyptian sculptor relied totally on symmetry and was meticulous in the elaboration of details. If we observe the left side, we see that during the trimming process an oval area has been preserved on which he drew the eye's outline, which he was also already in the process of doing on the opposite side.

To highlight the most frequent problems encountered during this process, we illustrate the modeling of some details of the three previously trimmed sculptures.

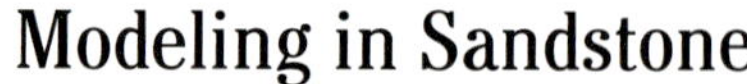

Modeling in Sandstone

After defining the sculptures' main volumes, we shape their details with the graver and chisel. Now we must control the strength of the impacts and work steadfastly, resting the hand on the stone for better accuracy, to peel off small layers of the stone until we near the desired surface level. Because sandstone cannot be polished and is expected to retain a rough surface, the bite of the tools used must be kept consistent.

◀ *Nefertiti*. 1364 B.C.E. Quartzite. Egyptian Museum of Cairo (Egypt).

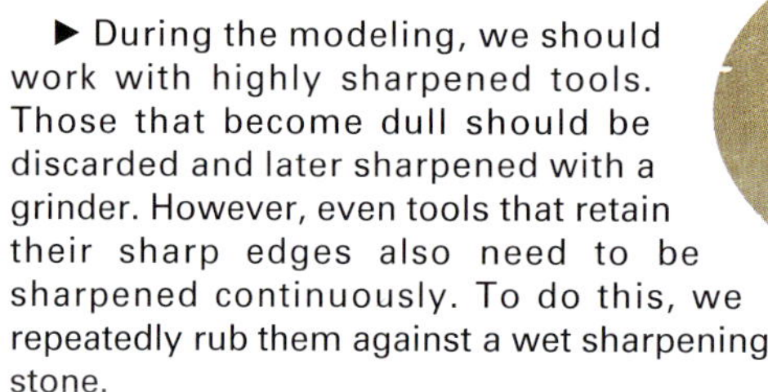

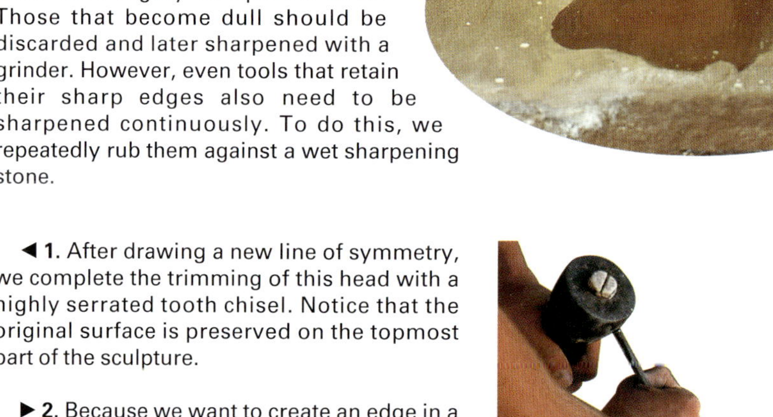

▶ During the modeling, we should work with highly sharpened tools. Those that become dull should be discarded and later sharpened with a grinder. However, even tools that retain their sharp edges also need to be sharpened continuously. To do this, we repeatedly rub them against a wet sharpening stone.

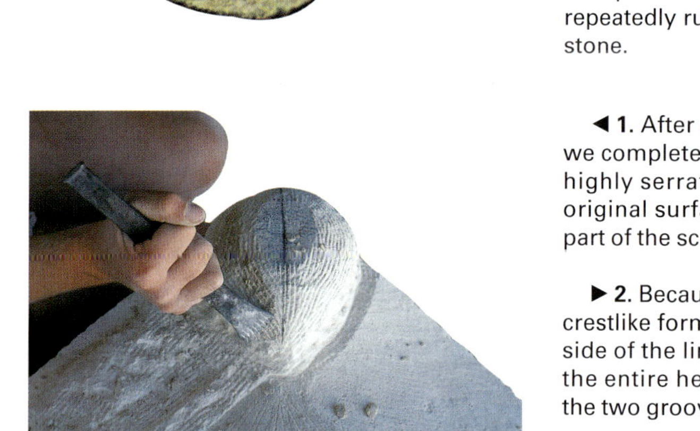

◀ **1.** After drawing a new line of symmetry, we complete the trimming of this head with a highly serrated tooth chisel. Notice that the original surface is preserved on the topmost part of the sculpture.

▶ **2.** Because we want to create an edge in a crestlike form, we chisel two grooves on each side of the line of symmetry and again shape the entire head with the tooth chisel around the two grooves.

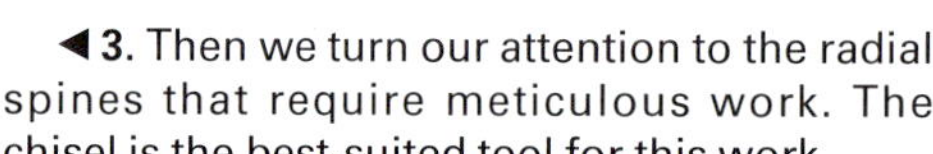

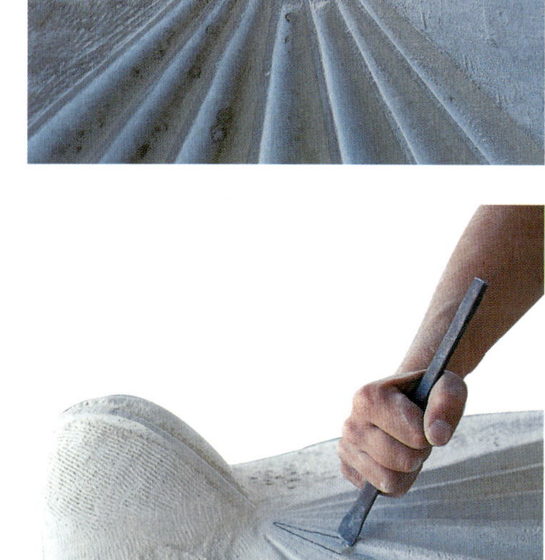

◀ **3.** Then we turn our attention to the radial spines that require meticulous work. The chisel is the best-suited tool for this work.

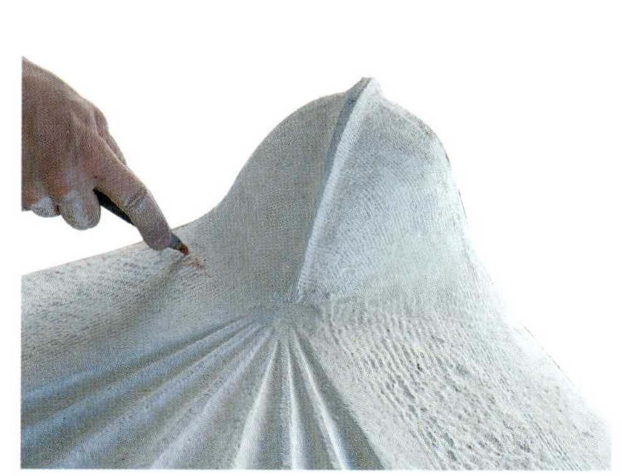

▶ **4.** Before we apply the final touches to our sculpture, we hold it against the light or feel the surface to detect small imperfections in the smoothness of the surface. Then we apply the finishing touches—we use a pumice stone to polish the edges and we use a tooth chisel to smooth some areas and a bushing tool to smooth others.

Modeling in Alabaster

We return now to the direct carving we worked on before. Although we did not start then with a preconceived modeling idea in mind, we recall that each wavy shape, each surface abides by its own norms that cannot be arbitrarily altered. This implies that if we carve more deeply than required into an area, we will have to modify the others to preserve consistency in the sculpture's form. As we reach the depth of the sculpture's final surface, we must keep the tooth chisel as parallel as possible to the stone's surface to avoid scarring the alabaster.

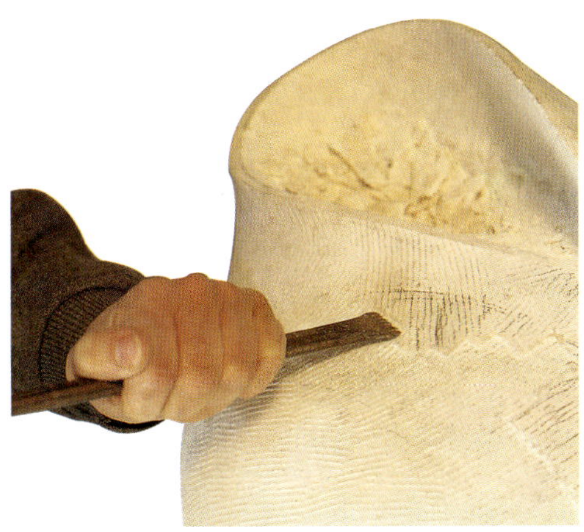

◄ 1. To shape alabaster stone, we remove small layers with the tooth chisel, adjusting the direction of the tool's bite to meet the carving needs at hand.

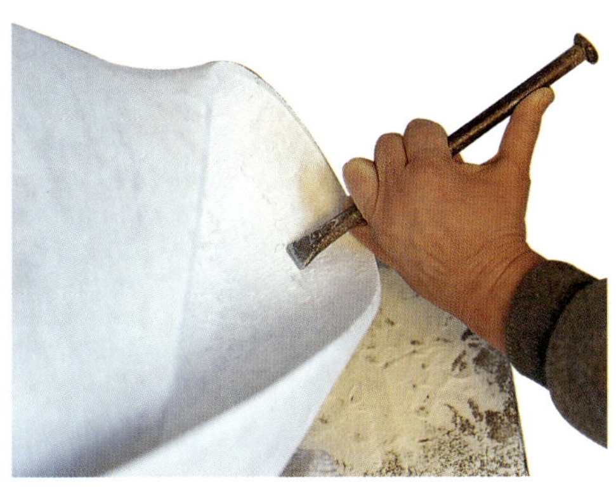

◄ 2. With the chisel we smooth down the work's dominant areas that, in our case, we will later polish. Because the tool's bite should be very precise, we control the chisel with the little and ring fingers, we guide it with the thumb, and, if needed, we will steady the hand by resting it on the stone.

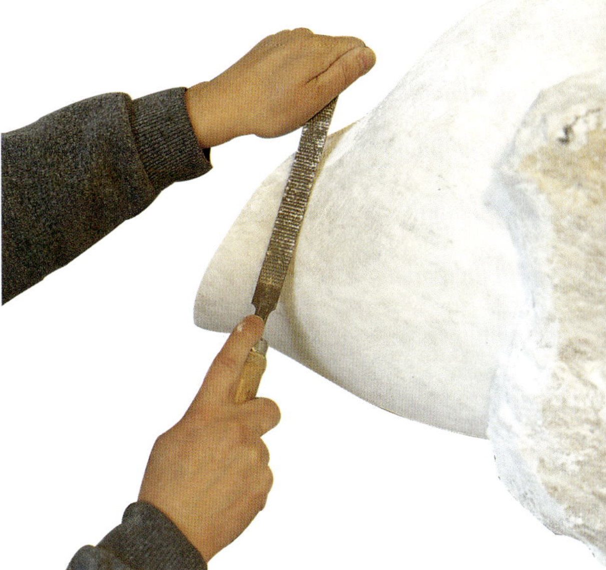

► 3. The softness of the stone, however, enables us to forego using the chisel and we can erase the marks of the tooth chisel directly with a rasp.

Modeling in Travertine Stone

We finally will see how using a compressor can facilitate modeling by freeing both hands to work with the chisel. We also will discover the importance of the guideline in refinishing details.

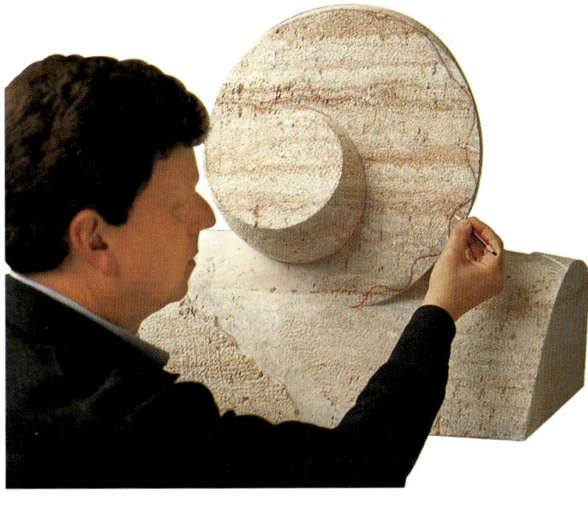

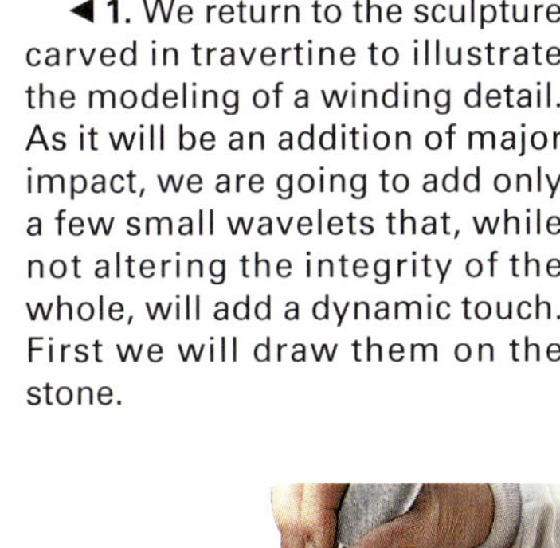

◄ 1. We return to the sculpture carved in travertine to illustrate the modeling of a winding detail. As it will be an addition of major impact, we are going to add only a few small wavelets that, while not altering the integrity of the whole, will add a dynamic touch. First we will draw them on the stone.

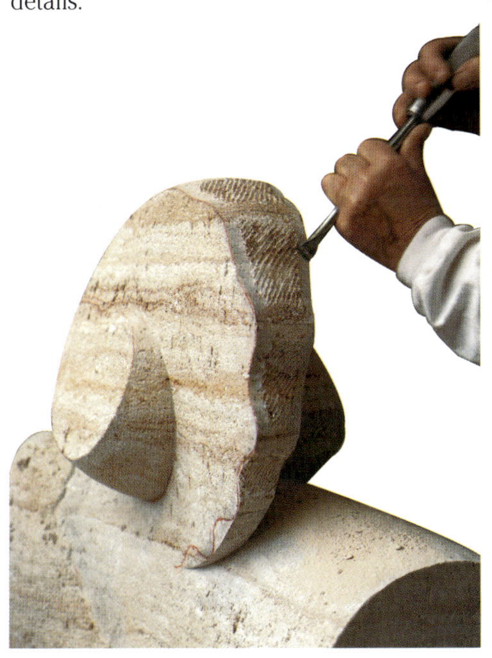

◄ 2. Then we chisel in a few guidelines. Guided by them, we use the tooth chisel and continue modeling the rest in orderly fashion.

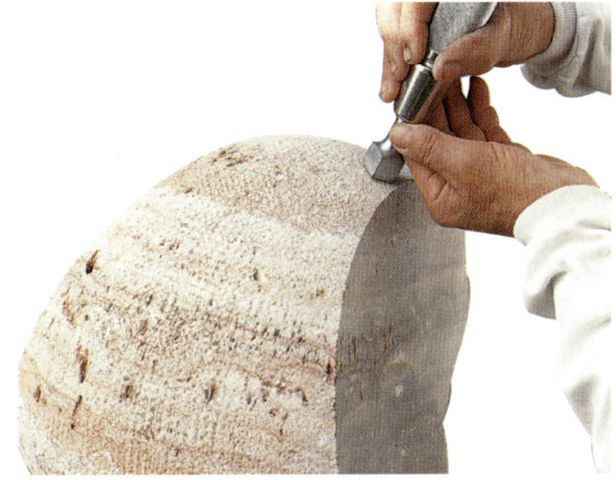

► 3. When satisfied with the results, we smooth out all marks of the tools, this time using a bushing tool.

Customized Textures

Since each tool leaves its own characteristic stamp, we can use all and each of them to customize the texture—from the large workshop augers to the circular saw, to the tooth chisel or rasp. It is important to choose the type of refinishing early so that, while working, we will be preparing the final texture.

Here we illustrate different textures that carving tools leave on the flat surfaces of different stones, not only on those of the stones shown but also on stones of similar hardness.

We recall, however, that each stone is endowed with traits that enable, and sometimes demand, a particular finish—sandstone cannot be polished and salinity deteriorates its surface; limestones are easily dyed; and some igneous varieties of the stone yield many diverse textures according to their finishing.

The shape and size of a sculpture also demand some type of finishes over others—polishing can give a gloss to a convex area, while grooves left by the circular saw can accentuate the sculpture's linearity. On the other hand, to abuse already complex textures can detract from the shape of a small sculpture or enrich the surface sobriety of a large one.

If we want to attain highly polished surfaces, we first smooth them with a rasp, then we rub them with carborundum stone or progressively finer pieces of sandpaper. We polish them with wet sandpaper of progressively finer grain and to shine them we apply specific polishing products. If, in addition, we wish to waterproof the shine for a couple of years or for interiors, we will give it a coat of wax. We can also simplify the process by applying shining paste with a cloth disk attached to a polisher or drill.

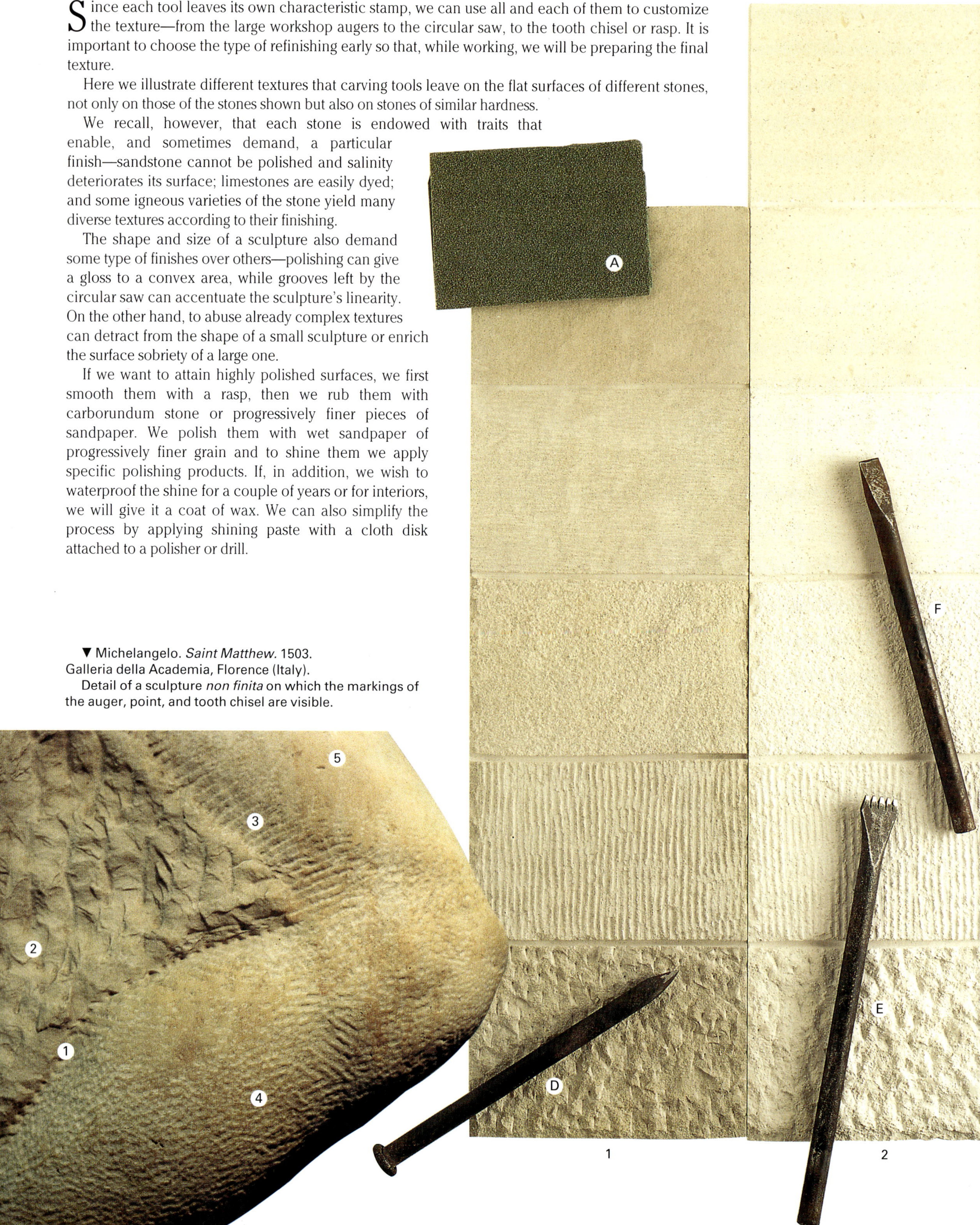

▼ Michelangelo. *Saint Matthew.* 1503. Galleria della Academia, Florence (Italy).

Detail of a sculpture *non finita* on which the markings of the auger, point, and tooth chisel are visible.

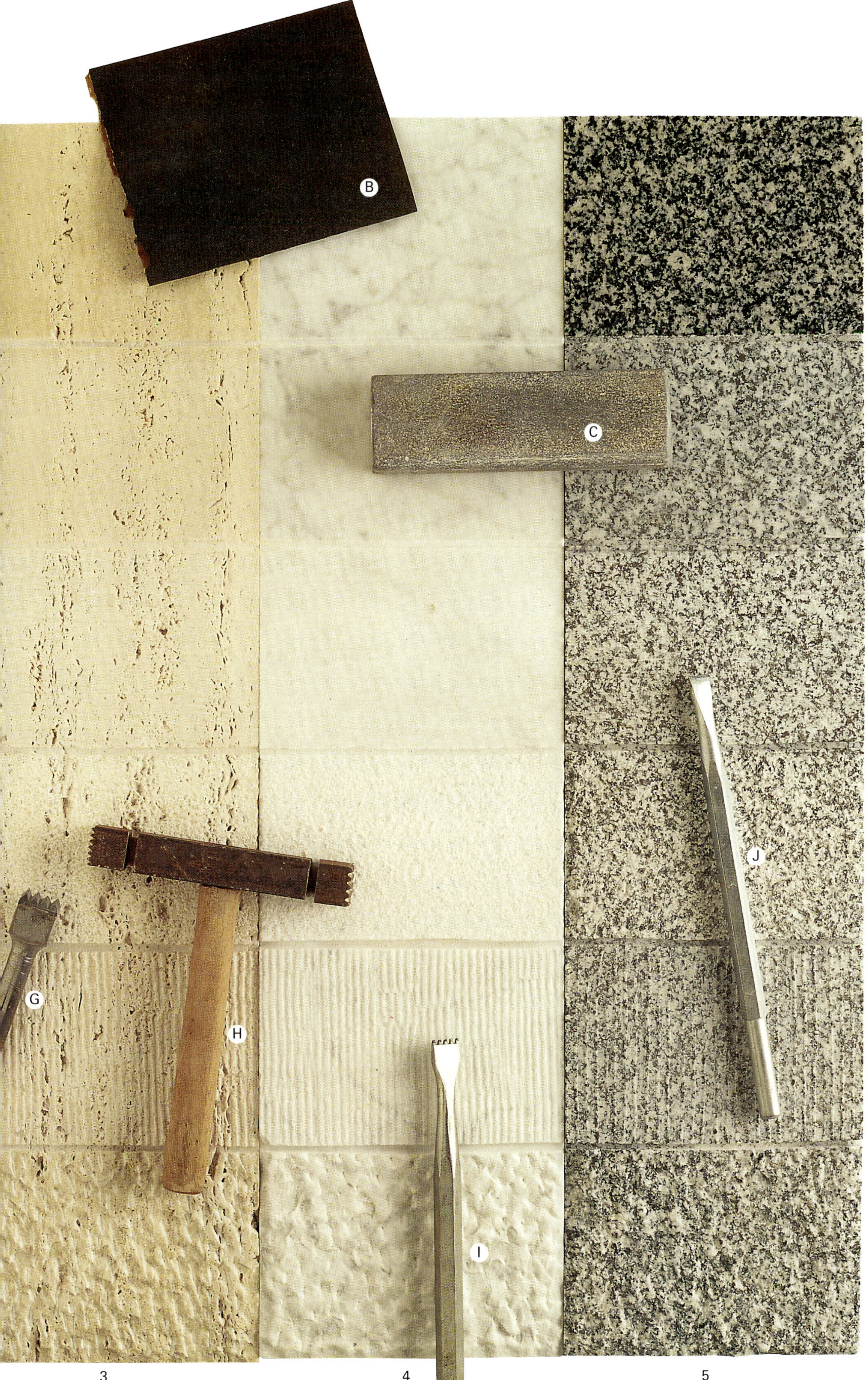

Sandpaper (A). Sandpaper to be used with water (B). Carborundum stone (C). Point chisel (D). Tooth chisel (E). Chisel (F). Bushing tool (G). Bushhammer (H). Tungsten carbide tooth chisel (I). Tungsten carbide chisel (J).

1. Sandstone from Vinaixa, Lleida (Spain).
2. "Cream of Andalucia" limestone, Cordoba (Spain).
3. Roman travertine (Italy).
4. Carrara marble (Italy).
5. "Black ochavo" granite, Badajoz (Spain).

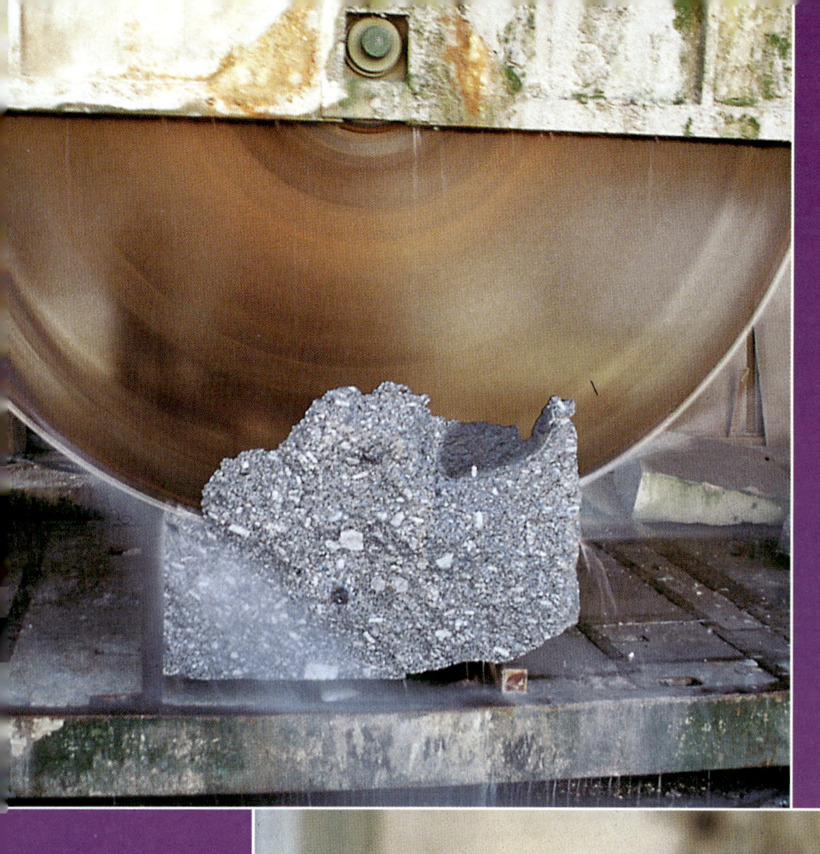

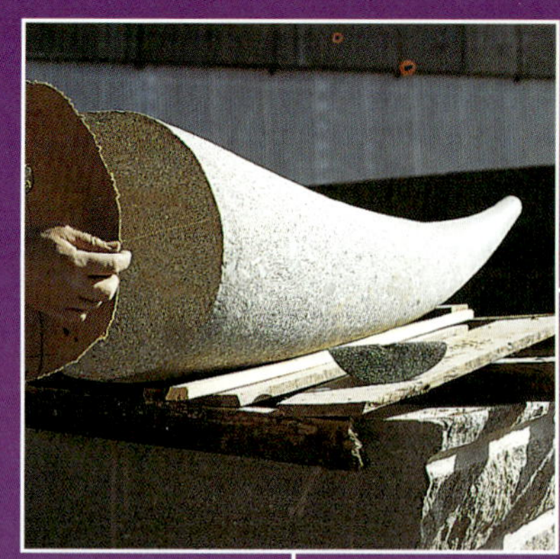

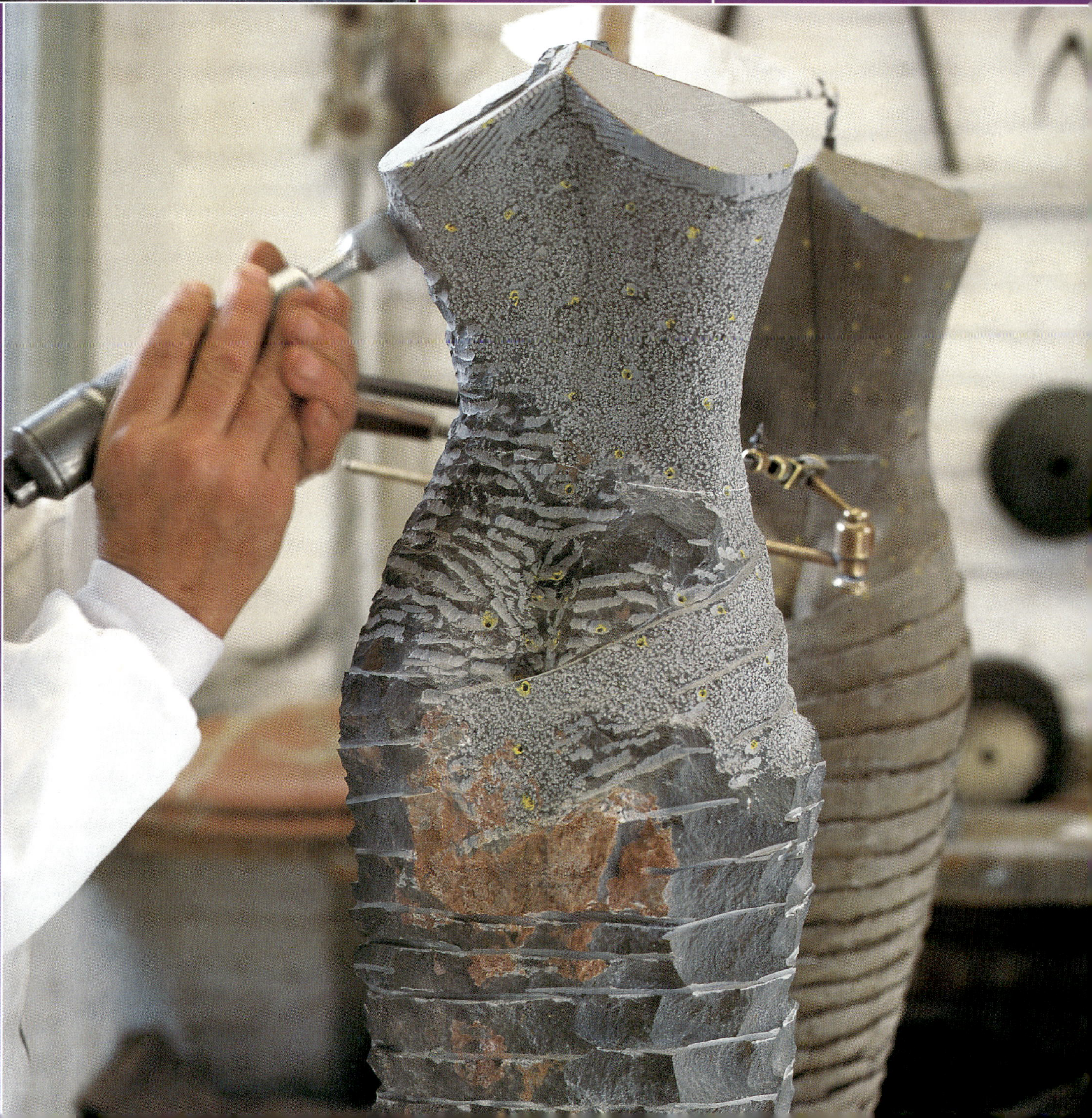

Carving as a Trade

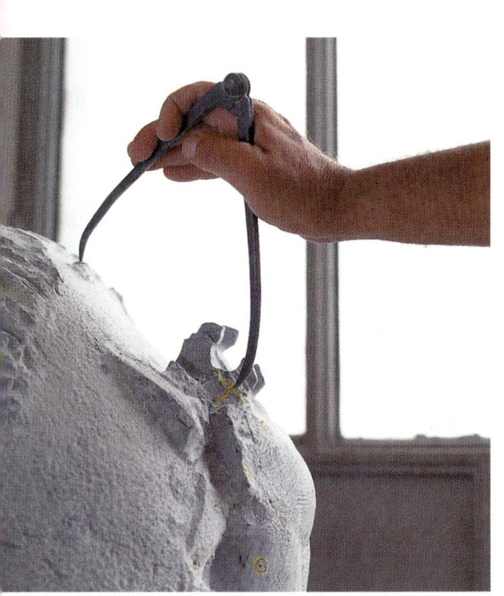

Traditionally, the stone carver has passed on his knowledge through a direct relationship with the apprentice. That is how it has been and, from a pedagogic point of view, that is the way we believe it should be. On the other hand, given that each stone carver has developed his own technique and specialized in a specific type of stone, be it marble, granite, or sandstone, though these carvers may be experts, they are very reluctant to express opinions about issues outside their field of expertise.

We should make a note of this at the start of this chapter. In it we will talk about how to develop maquettes or reproduce models. We will make our explanations germane to topics and, in particular, we will provide recommendations to those who truly wish to learn the trade and who are working temporarily as apprentices with different professionals.

Our intent is to provide information to the sculptor that will make him aware of the resources at his disposal and to impart knowledge about techniques that might expand his creativity. With this in mind, we conclude this introduction and will provide an array of options for sculpting in stone in combination with other materials and other arts.

At work, we certainly will discuss shop topics, since all issues related to techniques, good or bad, are expressed as much in words as in action. This is something like gestures that, involuntarily, accompany what words express . . .

It is just as harmful and mistaken to expect all things from technique as it is to loathe it.

Vincente Navarro

Industry as a Resource

We recommended turning to marble dealers, stonemasons, or stone carvers for the procurement of stones for sculpting medium and small works. However, if we prefer to work with big blocks, we will have to go to the stonemasons or to the big warehouses that are suppliers to the stone industries.

After selecting an appropriate block, we can ask to have it broken down according to the required dimensions. If it is in the quarry, it is most probable that the stone will be broken apart with wedges. It is advisable to witness the operation, not only to learn the technique, but especially to familiarize ourselves with the physical traits of the stone we are acquiring.

In the quarry or in some related plant where they laminate or cut big blocks of stone, they can level off the base of our future sculpture with big circular saws with diamond disks and also shape the block according to its intended configuration. This simplifies the tough task of carving. Also, if our project entails simple geometric shapes, we can ask the workers to process it completely, since they have available machinery for sanding, flaming, polishing, or shining. These finishing touches we can also contract after we undertake the carving and modeling process of the sculpture on our own.

However, since we should keep in mind that the sculptor is only an occasional customer of these companies whose normal clients are architectural firms, it is wise to restrain our demands that may easily raise unwanted curiosity.

Where we will meet a sympathetic response is in the industry that produces sculptures. Here, the workshop staff will help with technical solutions and will even be receptive to us controlling the sculpting process.

Although a vanishing industry, we still can find in most countries stone carvers or sculptors who will carve for us on commission. However, big enterprises provide very limited services and the major sculptors of the world, as we already mentioned, continue to turn for service to Carrara and Pietrasanta (Italy), which enjoy a centuries-long tradition.

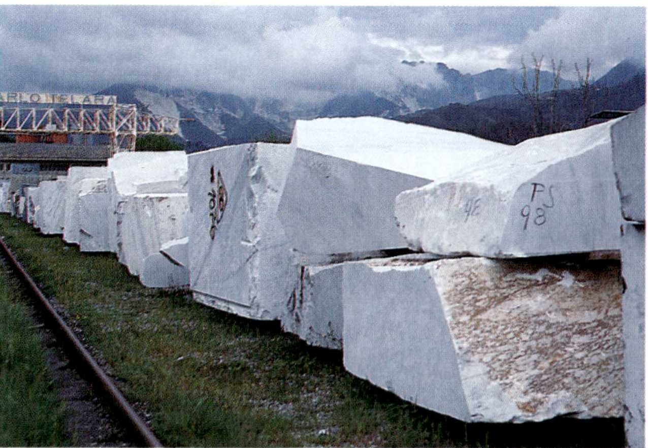

◄ Marble warehouse near the train station of Massa-Carrara where you can also get other kinds of stones.

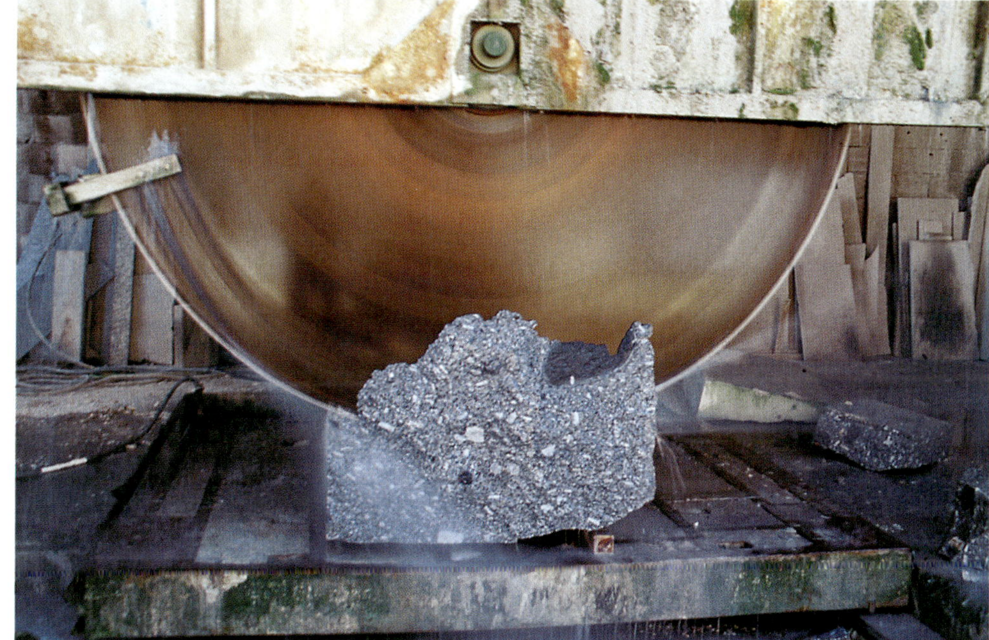

▼ Sawing disk to cut granite. Big companies are equipped with machinery for production of monumental sculptures as well as the processing of medium-size stones.

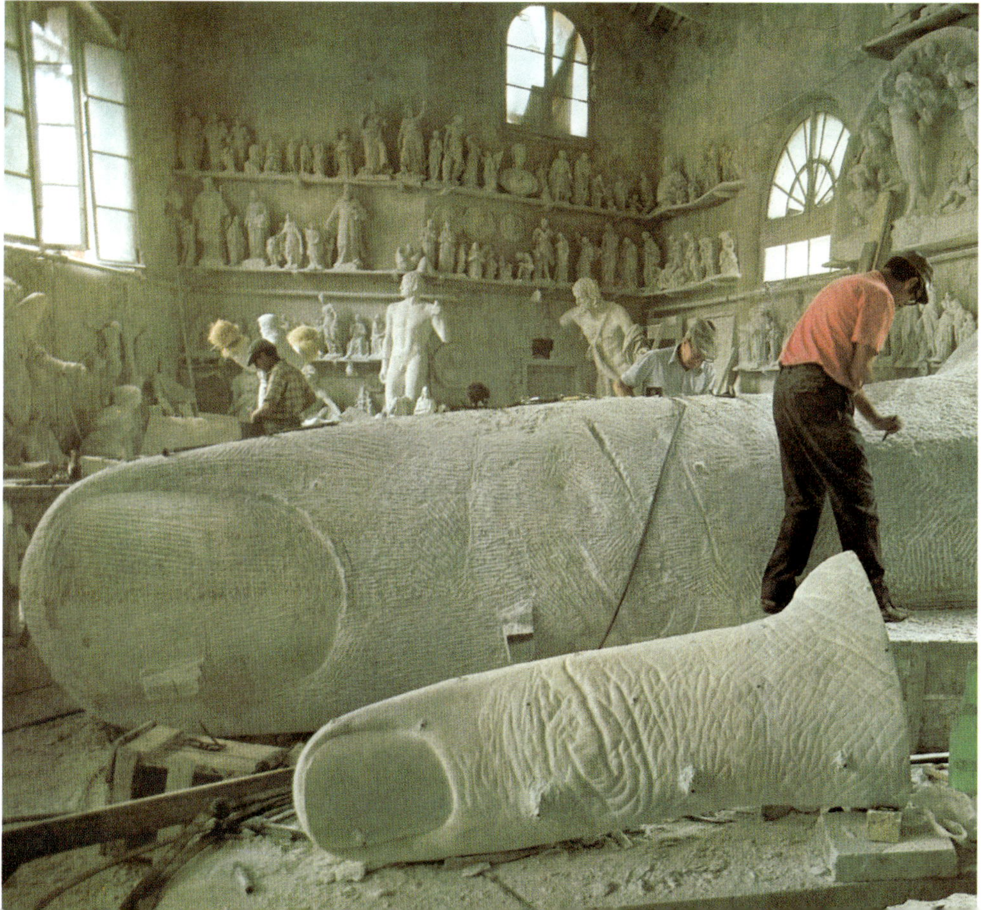

► Reproduction from the publicity brochure of the Rigoli of Carrara workshop, which shows an enlargement process of a sculpture—*Le Pouce*—by the French artist Cesar.

The Power of the Block

When discussing monumental works we cannot ignore the achievements of sculpture in the twentieth century, which by resorting to simple forms, vindicated the strength of stone as a material and created new tension between the sculpted components. The cited industries can make the enormous labor easier for us, meaning that without these industries we could mostly execute works with geometric structures. We could also dispense with machines if, inspired by the Japanese garden, we would want to convey the subtlety and force of stones in their natural state, or, learning from the great Chinese cultural tradition, we would impart meaning to the capricious shaping of erosion and, by manipulating only what is necessary, we would limit ourselves to selecting and combining stones of suggestive shapes.

In this sense, the sculptor, spoiled by his great achievements of monumental works, should compare his might against a sculptor our historic chronicle has ignored: Nature. The true monuments in stone are not works by humans nor have they been corralled within museum walls. We refer here to the immense Ayers Rock in Central Australia, to Colorado's Grand Canyon, or to Utah's impressive National Park, to the Giant's Causeway in Northern Ireland, to the breathtaking landscape of Capadocia or Pamukkale in Turkey, to the stylized lava tube at Saint Helena in the South Atlantic, to the defiance of the laws of gravity at Along Bay in North Vietnam, or to the small islands of South China, to name a few.

We mention this mastery of weather as a sculptor prior to getting into more technical aspects, so that we try to avoid perfection, which sometimes can be sterile when involving dominance over detail. In fact, many of the ideas that have been expressed in stone could have been expressed in other materials, but none of them could surpass the force conveyed by an obelisk or the bluntness of a menhir.

◄ Example of one of the numerous sculptures that nature has sculpted in the *Enchanted City* in Cuenca (Spain).

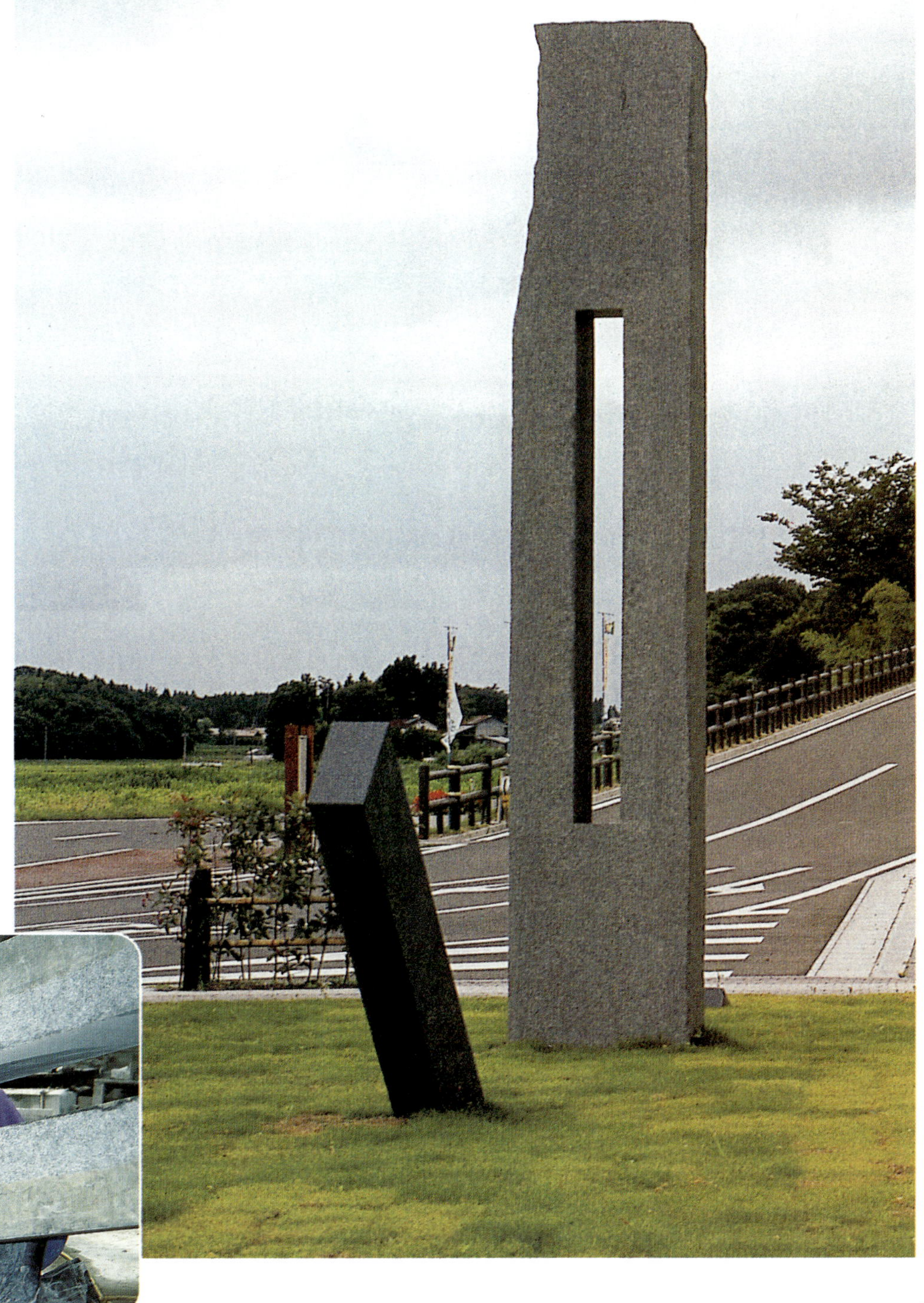

▼ Satoru Sato. *An Unexcluded Space I*. 1992. Blue Granite. Minamikata, Miyagi (Japan). Detail of the work's preparation in the workshop and general view of the sculpture in its final place.

Enlarging by Templates

One of the most simple, but also most effective, means to reproduce and enlarge a maquette consists of drawing it and then cutting its different side views out of cardboard or wooden board. The resulting shapes, when profiled on the stone block, will guide us during the trimming process. If needed, we can prepare more accurate templates for modeling details. The success of our final work will depend on such templates.

Although not a very exact technique, the procedure can impart a sense of security when carving directly, without depriving us of the freedom to reinterpret the maquette or the original design. Its effectiveness is manifested in composite sculptures consisting of multiple blocks joined together.

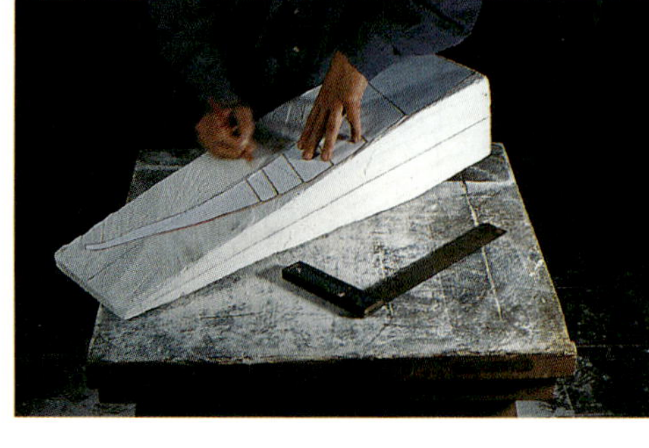

▲ **1.** We can use a template even when constructing the maquette. In this case, we have drawn to scale its main side view. A cutout photocopy of the project serves as our template for tracing the outer perimeter of the model on the asbestos cement block that we will later carve.

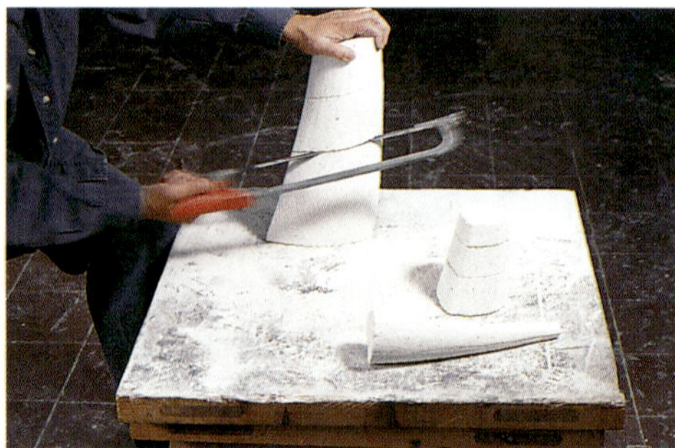

▲ **2.** We have planned to carve this sculpture out of various granite blocks. Instead of relying on mathematical calculations to calculate the size of each block, we prefer to use sections of the maquette to transfer direct measurements to the block's surfaces. We can then enlarge them to actual size and also adjust the templates' final size.

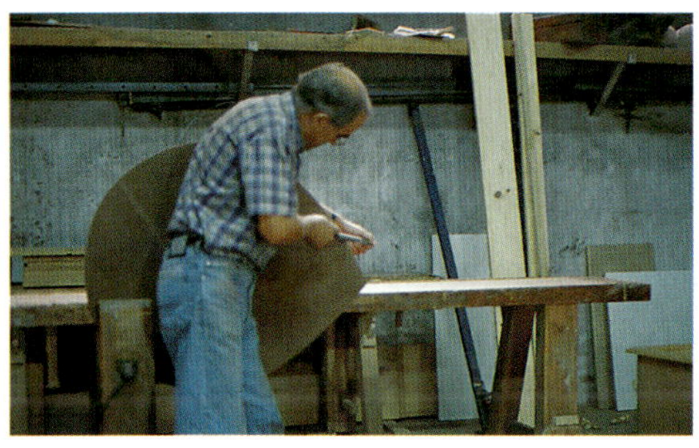

▲ **3.** Because different artisans will be handling the templates, these need to be made of resistant material. Therefore, after drawing them to real size, we will have a carpenter construct them out of a wooden board.

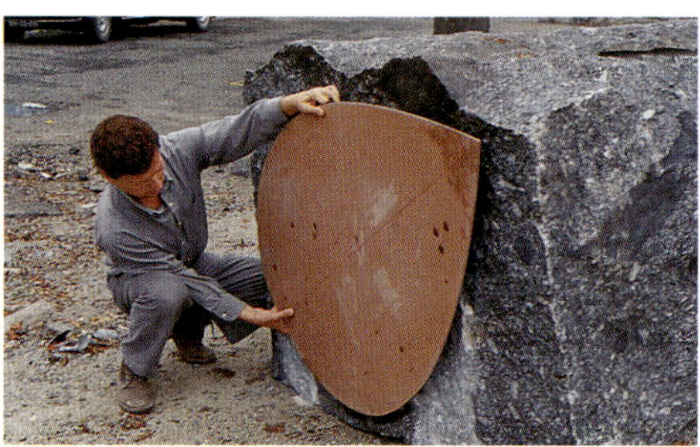

▲ **4.** The template will ensure that the size of the block is appropriate. It will also help us to draw a contour on the block that will reveal the amount of excess material to be trimmed.

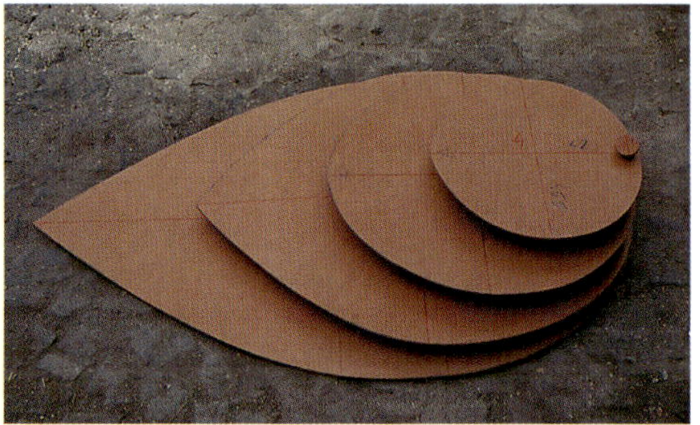

▲ **5.** The sculpture that we will be carving consists of four elements, which by resting on top of each other provide continuity within one form. The three horizontal templates will serve a double purpose; each will define the upper plane of the larger block and, at the same time, will define the base of the ensuing smaller block.

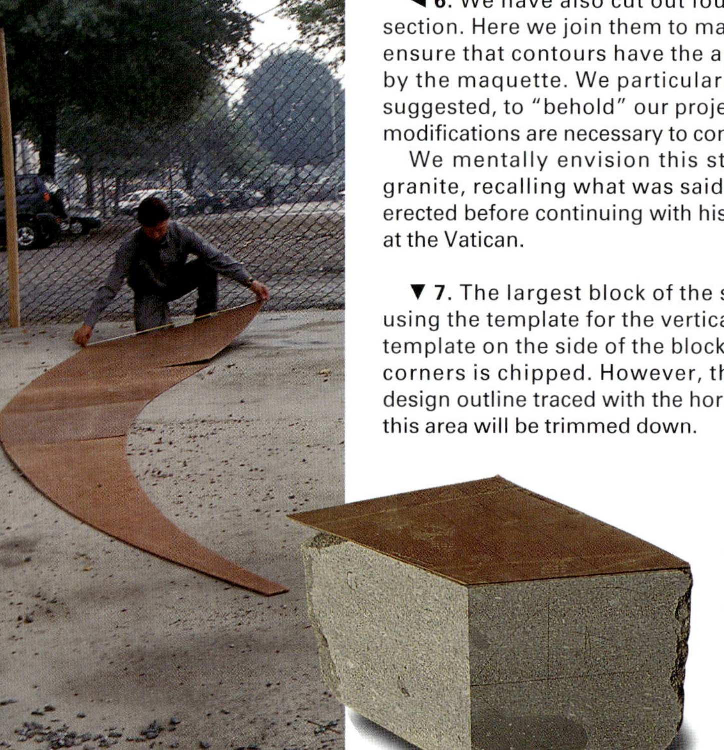

◀ **6.** We have also cut out four vertical templates for the central section. Here we join them to make sure they fit well together and to ensure that contours have the appropriate curvature as prescribed by the maquette. We particularly do so also to be able, as Bernini suggested, to "behold" our project in actual dimension and decide if modifications are necessary to conform with its planned size.

We mentally envision this structure erected and covered with granite, recalling what was said about the test column that Bernini erected before continuing with his construction of Saint Peter's Square at the Vatican.

▼ **7.** The largest block of the sculpture has been cut by machine using the template for the vertical section. When superimposing the template on the side of the block we discover that one of the block's corners is chipped. However, this causes us no concern since the design outline traced with the horizontal section's template shows that this area will be trimmed down.

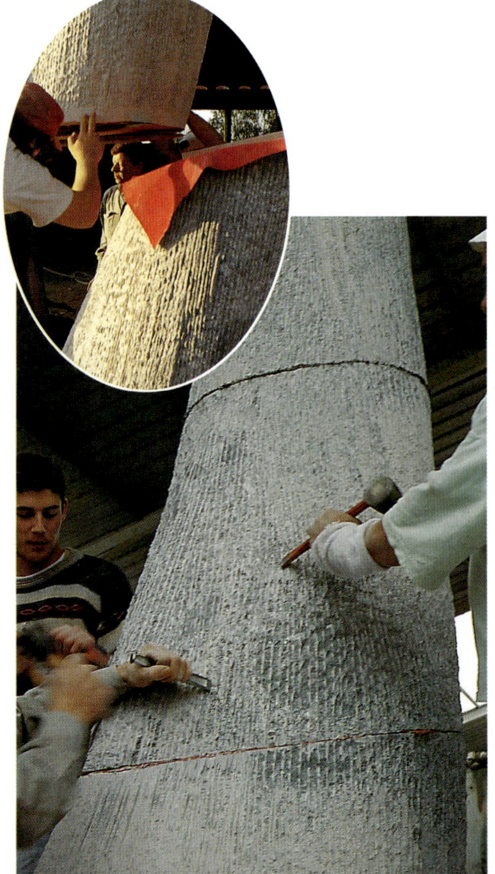

►► **8.** The individual templates have enabled different workers to cut each block separately. They will find out how precise their shaping has been when the blocks are joined together. As this is only a test, we use a piece of carpet to protect the edges of the topmost block and to make it easier to rotate it. Then we smooth with chisels the traces of the cutting saw.

Another technique dating back to Ancient Egypt (as shown in the bas-relief in the picture) consists of using a gridlike framework to transfer the main design features of the maquette to the block. To enlarge the features it will suffice to increase proportionally the size of the grid. This technique is not especially difficult to follow when dealing with flat surfaces such as reliefs. Here, however, we will explain how to apply it in three dimensions.

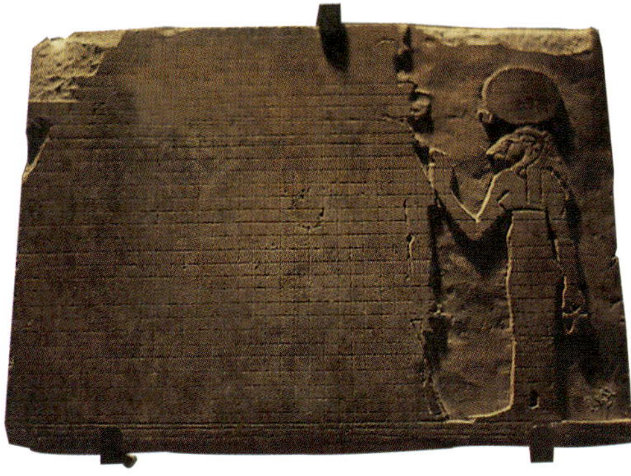

◄ Unfinished bas-relief that shows that the Egyptian sculptor was already using a grid system. From other sources we know that the grid also served to conform to the proportions prescribed by the priests.

► **1.** First we need to trace the grid over the maquette. To do this we start with a baseboard on which we have previously traced a grid and on which we glue the maquette. With a ruler or a carpenter's square we project the baseboard's grid lines vertically on all sides of the maquette, and then we trace parallel equidistant horizontal lines on it. Because the resulting squares are large, we will use them more as guidelines than for exact reproduction of the design. A denser grid network would provide a higher degree of accuracy.

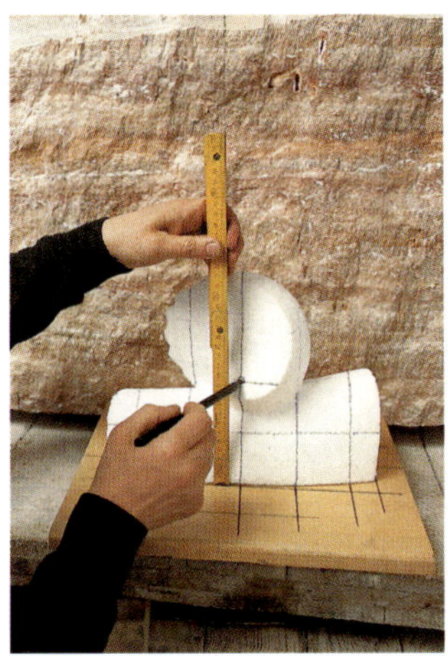

▼ **2.** Given that our block is relatively square, we will have little difficulty in tracing the grid on it. The only precaution we will take is to start the grid layout from a set of central axes. After repeating the operation on all sides of the block, we will transfer the design outline on its sides with the help of the grid squares and the maquette. Most often, we will find that a block's shape is irregular and that we will have to project the grid network on it from a baseboard in similar fashion that we did with the maquette.

► **3.** After tracing the design outline on the block, we redraw the grid lines that have become blurred and we shade the areas that need to be trimmed off. The seemingly distorted shapes resulting from projecting straight lines over curved volumes are of no concern. The elongated circumference that we see in the center of the maquette is only a projection resulting from the extension of the vertical grid lines from the back to the front of the stone.

► **4.** We have been guided here in trimming by the side view drawing shown in the previous photo. Since in the process we have erased a few grid lines, we will have to redraw them.

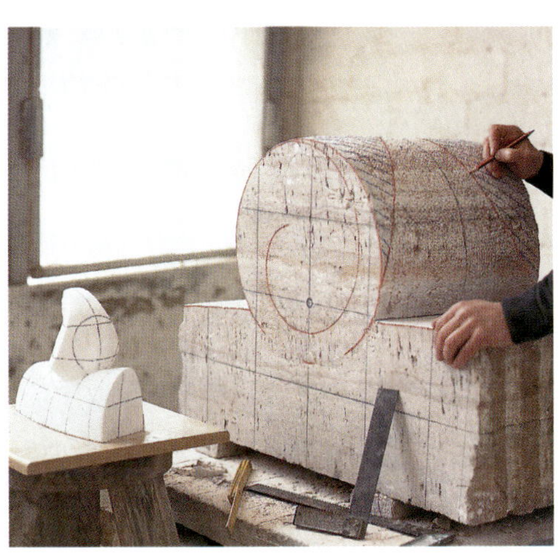

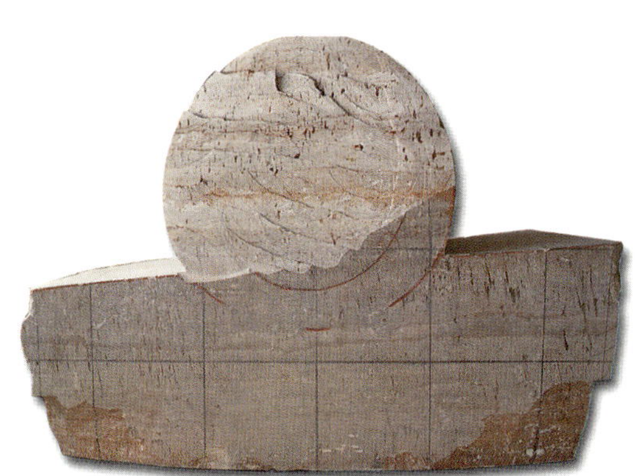

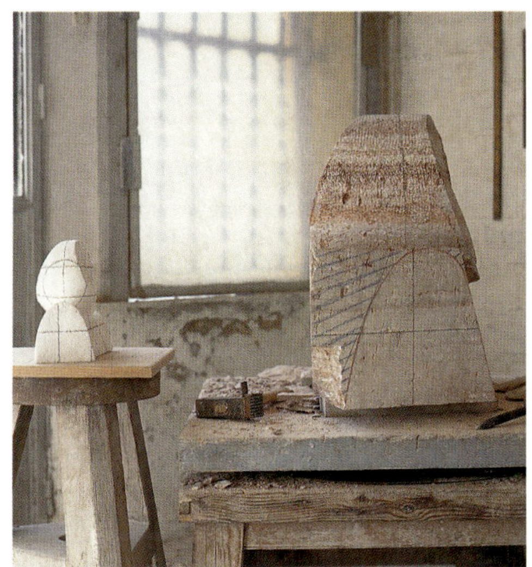

◄ **5.** As we progress with the trimming, the volumes on all sides of the sculpture take shape and we can see with satisfaction that the emerging form gradually resembles the maquette more and more.

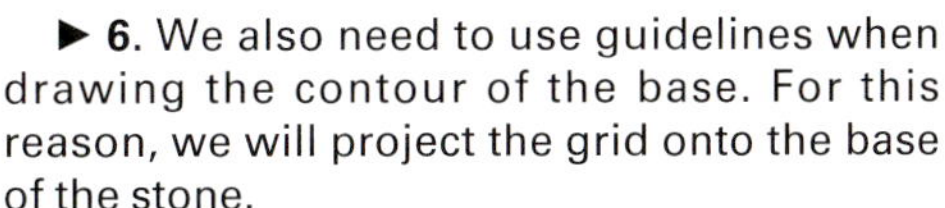

► **6.** We also need to use guidelines when drawing the contour of the base. For this reason, we will project the grid onto the base of the stone.

Some details entail a higher degree of precision. To confidently model them, we can draw in the area of interest a new partial grid with denser squares.

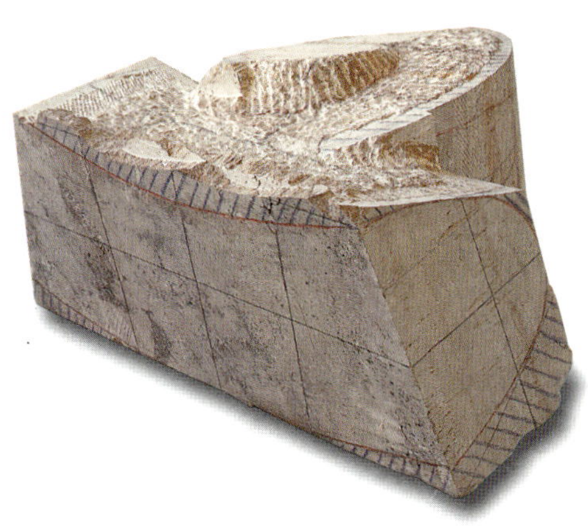

Systems of Reproduction

Recent advances in the information and laser fields could bring about revolutionary technical changes in the ways sculptures are reproduced and maquettes or drawings are copied or enlarged. Current applications, however, are few due to slight demand.

Safeguarding the patrimony of the sculptures in our cities is becoming a priority for many cities and countries. Policies to preserve original art works in museums and replace them with copies on public streets are creating a demand for new techniques as well as for experts who can reproduce original sculptures.

Romans, we recall, had a passion for copying Greek sculptures, but for fundamentally different reasons. When Romans copied Hellenistic bronzes in marble, they technically copied foundry-made sculptures by reproducing them in stone that, often, helped to improve the works' aesthetic expression. This is not the case today since the new copies substitute the original stone with synthetic ones and carving with molding. Of course, ironically, you cannot discern a substitute work from looking at a tourist picture, and explaining reproduction techniques falls outside our fundamental purpose, which is stone carving.

When we described the stone industry we mentioned the existence of complex machinery that could hew the four faces of the stone and trim off much of the excess material under computer control. Demand for this type of work will determine whether such techniques will be improved and become more common.

The Laser and the Pantograph

Advances in the use of the laser in sculpture are also limited. Equipment was recently patented for the first time with the exclusive feature of reproducing perfectly in a stone block each detail of a model by using a laser. This, however, only enhances confidence in the results but does not alleviate the work involved.

Another option for serially reproducing sculptures is through the use of an industrial adaptation of the pantograph, a machine common in wood carvings. However, here demand also is partial to reproductions made by moldings and in synthetic stone. Such statues of little goblins or modest Venuses make certain gardens look infantile.

In 1837 Achile Collas adapted the pantograph used by designers to the carving of relief and, later, to sculpture in general. His machine reproduced surfaces by means of four articulated arms. Sculptors use the pantograph especially for designing medallions and coins. The machine faithfully reproduces each detail of a larger-size model and also permits its enlargement. The movements of a needle smoothly running over the contours of the model are conveyed to a chisel that carves the block and cuts into it to the depth of the model's contour. This machine is more suited to reproduce sculptures in plaster of Paris than ones in stone.

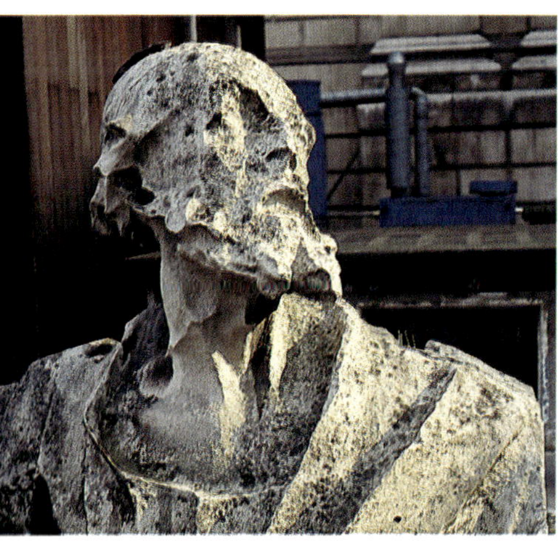

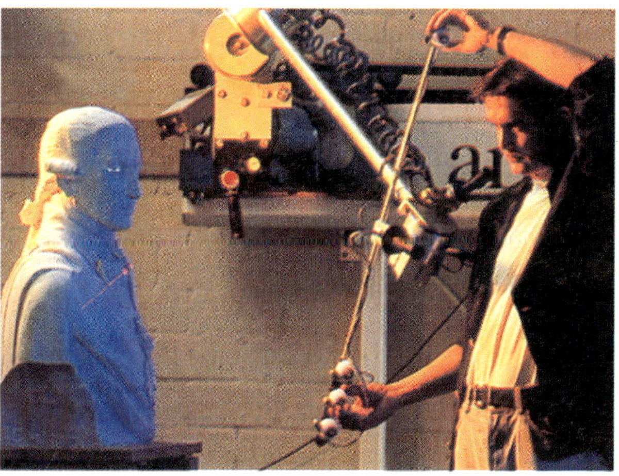

◀ This machine projects onto the stone block a laser ray that faithfully reproduces the contours of the model.

▲ F. Bird. Saint Andrew. 1724. Limestone. Saint Paul's Cathedral, London (United Kingdom). The sculpture exposed to the elements deteriorates and must be restored or substituted by a copy in order to preserve the original work. This raises the question of how to value the shared contribution of the contemporary sculptor who enhances the statue's expression.

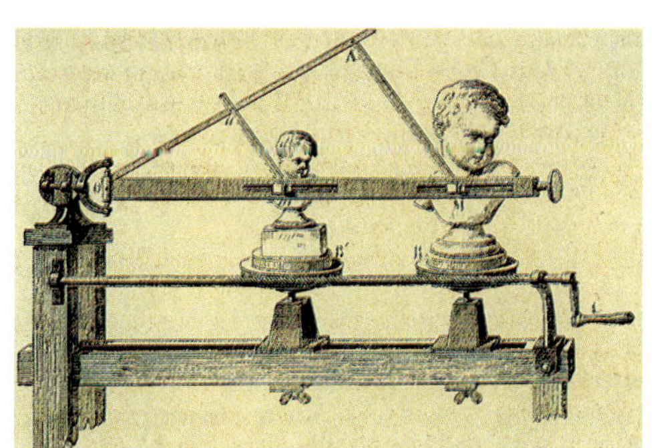

▲ Print from the end of the nineteenth century, which shows how Collas's pantograph enabled him to reproduce a smaller-sized sculpture.

Pointing

It is not surprising that sculptors rely on inventions of the past to make their task of copying, enlarging, or reducing models or maquettes easier. These skills share a common technique known as pointing.

Leonardo da Vinci, the prototype of a multitalented artist—though he reviled sculpture and exalted painting, a fact that Michelangelo interpreted as a justification of Leonardo's inadequacy as a sculptor—clearly describes this system:

If you wish to make a figure of marble, first make one of clay. After you have finished it and let it dry, set it in a box large enough so that after you have taken the clay figure out, the box can hold the block of marble wherein you propose to lay bare a figure resembling the one in clay. Then after you have placed the clay figure inside this box, make pegs so that they fit exactly into holes in the box, and drive them in at each hole until each white peg touches the figure at a different spot. Stain black such parts of the pegs as project out of the case and make a distinguishing mark for each peg and for its hole, so that you may fit them together at your ease. Then take the clay model out of the case, place the block of marble in it, and take away from the marble what is sufficient for all the pegs to be hidden in the holes up to their marks.

Perhaps no one before has used pointing exactly as we do today; however, the technique has been in use since classic antiquity. This is evidenced by writings from the fifth century B.C.E. or by unfinished Hellenistic sculptures such as *Dionysius and the Satyr*, which are displayed at the National Museum of Athens (Greece). The technique's popularization is attributed to Pasiteles and Arqueselad, who Pliny mentions as among the most famed sculptors of the first century. Instead of using boxes, as da Vinci didactically proposes, these sculptors used plumbs and substituted for the rods other ways of scaling such as by compass.

During the Renaissance scaffolds, chassis, and similar devices were used. Alberti, with his treatise *De Statua*, became the top scholar on these techniques. He also invented a stone-trimming device he called *exempeda* and another device for modeling.

In the Baroque period, the three-compass technique, which we will discuss later, was popular. During the Neoclassic period, pointing techniques were so widespread that Wittkower, when referring to the museum workshop of Canova in Possagno (Veneto, Italy), where hundreds of models and castings are kept, joked by saying, "Many of theses castings seemed to have contracted the German measles."

All of the above-mentioned pointing techniques—plumbs, Alberti's degree-marked circle, da Vinci's box of rods, scaffolds, chassis, squares, three compasses, and so on—became obsolete when the sculptor Gatteaux invented, and Durard and Girard patented in 1822, the point-measuring machine or pointing machine. The machine is even today the sculptors' preferred vehicle for copying a model.

When using the pointing machine it is advisable to work with a model made of compact material. Usually the sculptor makes a plaster casting of the original clay model and from the casting he transfers the points to the stone. We will discuss first the use of the chassis system and then, in more detail, the pointing machine and the three-compass system.

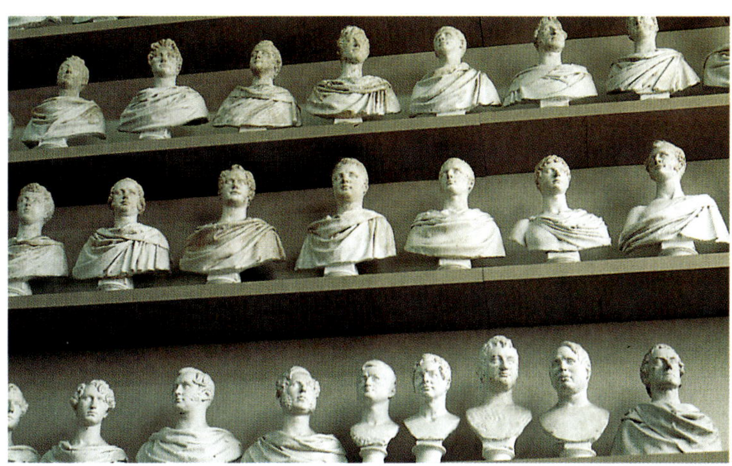

► Copied plaster models in the Galleria della Accademia, Florence, (Italy).

The Chassis System

Here we see, as an example, what one of these ancient methods of relative precision looks like. We will use this system later, as an initial step, in order to locate main reference points that will enable us to work with three compasses, a more precise system than that of the chassis one.

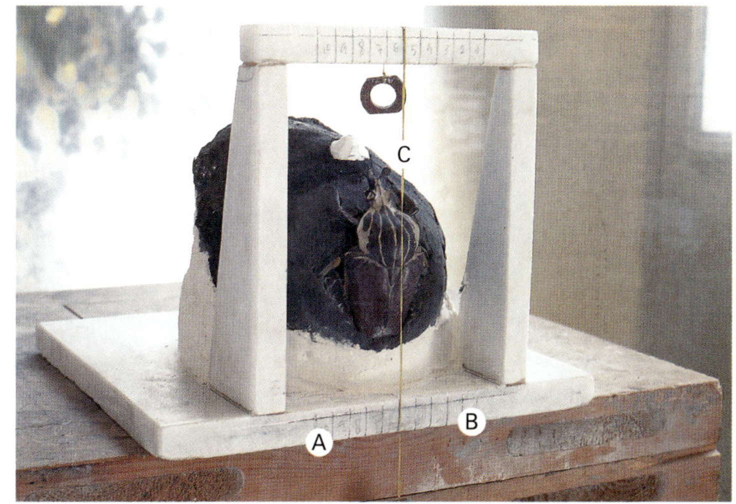

► **1.** We try here only to locate on the stone the spots of the humps of plaster on the top and sides of the maquette. To do so we have constructed with pieces of marble a chassis from which we hang a plumb line. This will allow us to take three measurements with a compass that will locate any point in three-dimensional space. Therefore, the convergence of points A and B will provide the height, and C will indicate the depth.

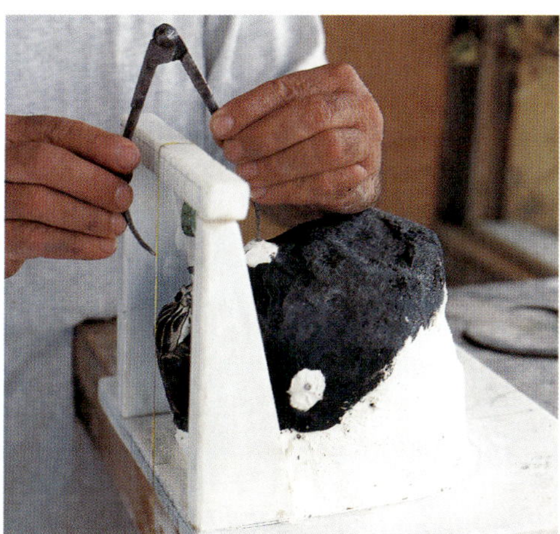

◄ **2.** We will measure the location of the deep point from the plumb line. The inherent lack of precision of the system is evidenced by the limitations of this technique and of similar ones that rely on the plumb line.

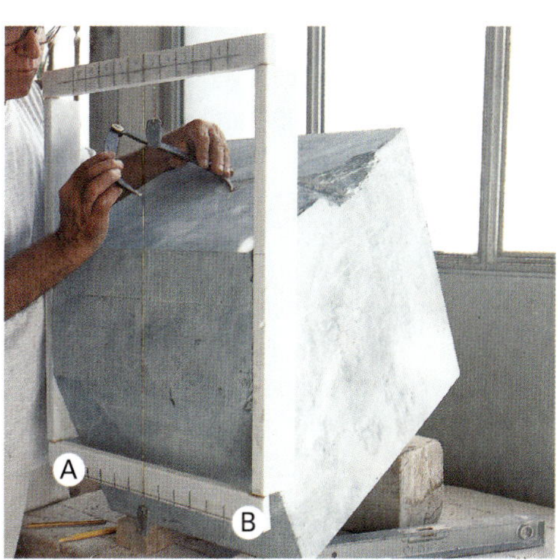

► **3.** To transfer the measurements to the stone we are going to carve, we need to construct a chassis proportionate to the block's size. From the three reference points corresponding to those of the small chassis we transfer the measurements taken after multiplying, by three in this case, the aperture of the compass.

Using a Pointing Machine

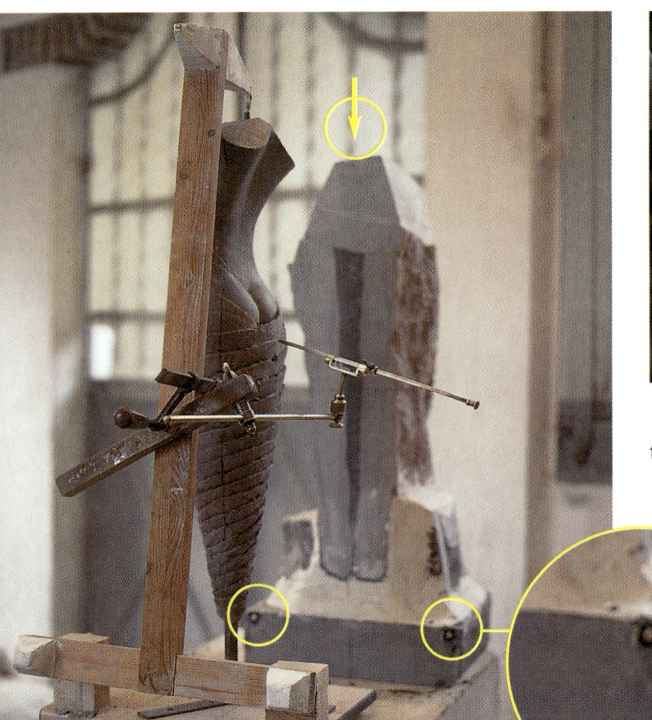

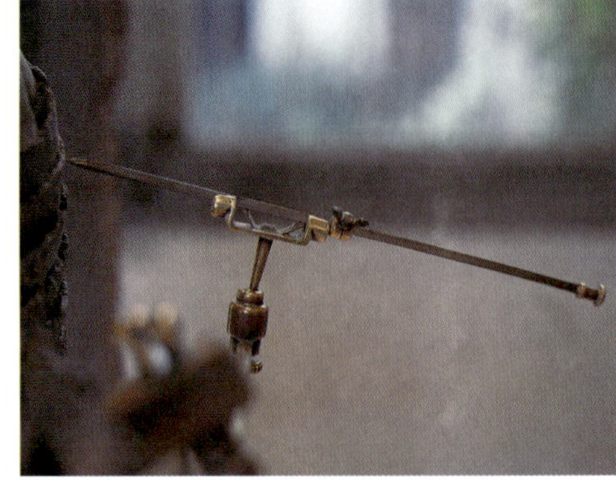

◄▲ **1.** After situating the pointing stick over the model, the tip of the rod's flexible arm will indicate the coordinates of the point we want to identify, while a screw nut in the middle of the rod will measure its depth.

The pointing machine is a three-dimensional measuring device that allows the copying of sculptures of the same size as the model. It is made of a crosspiece in the form of an inverted T, and an articulated arm that supports a rod.

The crosspiece always touches three fixed points on the surface of the sculptures. These points, which are indicated in the illustration by three circles on the block of stone, serve as a consistent reference from which all measurements are made. The arm, being mobile, allows the rod to be freely moved about.

If we first position the pointing stick on the model and place its tip at a specific location and then move the device to the stone block, the pointing stick's tip will show us the coordinate of the chosen point. But let us proceed step by step.

The first step consists of locating the three reference points. With this in mind we mark a point at the top of the vertical axis of the model to be copied, and two at the bottom on its base. Since our model lacks a base, we substitute for it two pieces of wood glued to the platform. After choosing a block of larger dimensions than the model, we repeat the operation. This time, however, we mark the points on the stone ensuring that the relative distance between the three points corresponds accurately to those of the model. This is an easy operation as it is

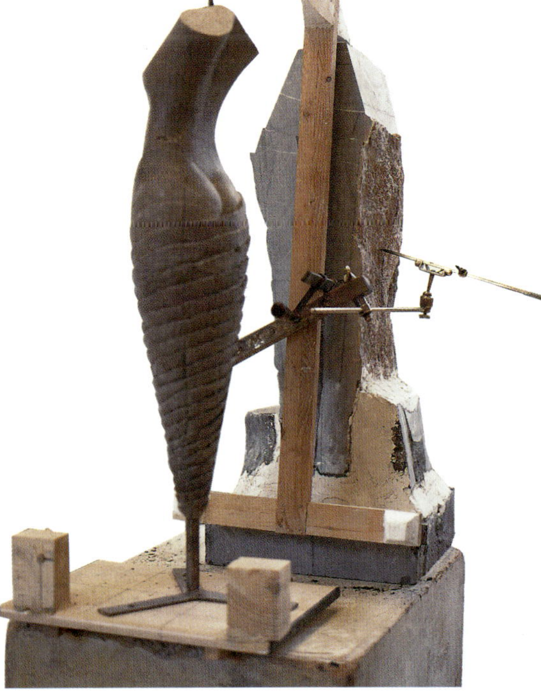

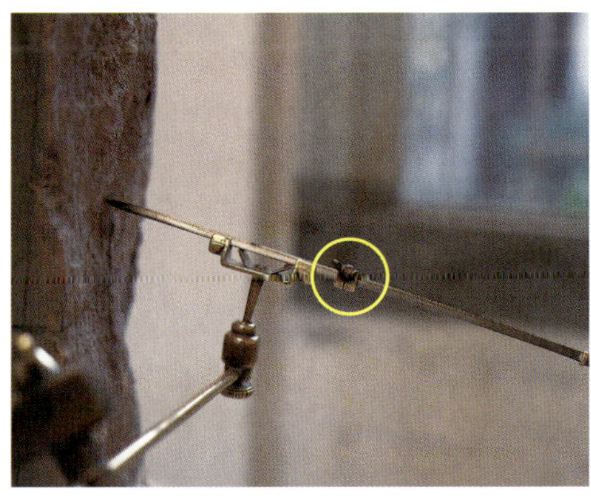

◄◄ **2.** Trying not to move the arm, we transfer the crosspiece to the block. The distance between the nut and the tip of the rod will indicate the depth of the point on the stone more precisely than the way proposed by da Vinci.

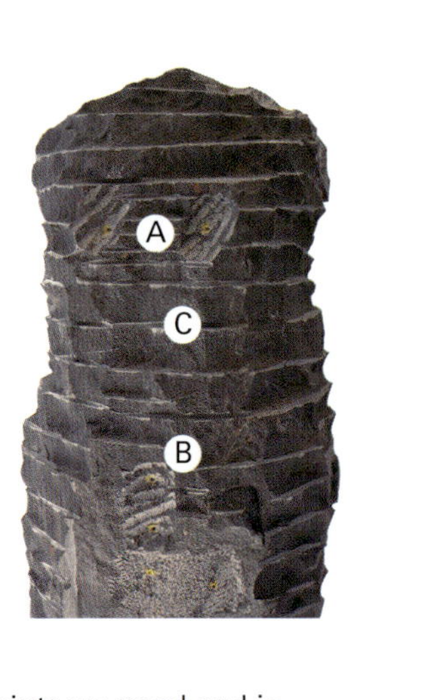

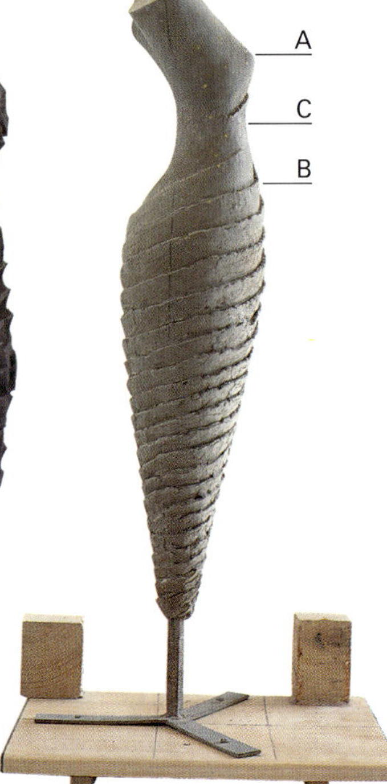

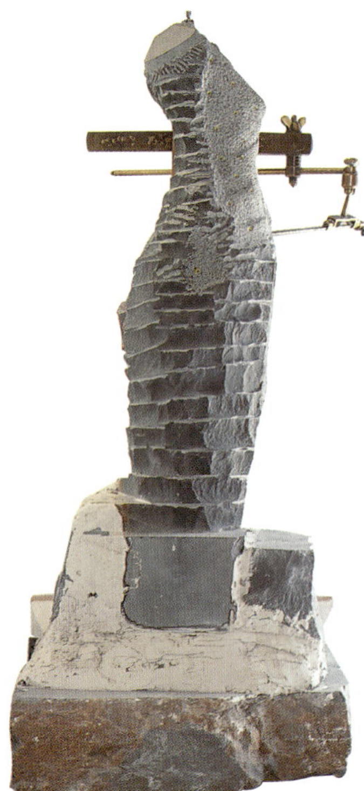

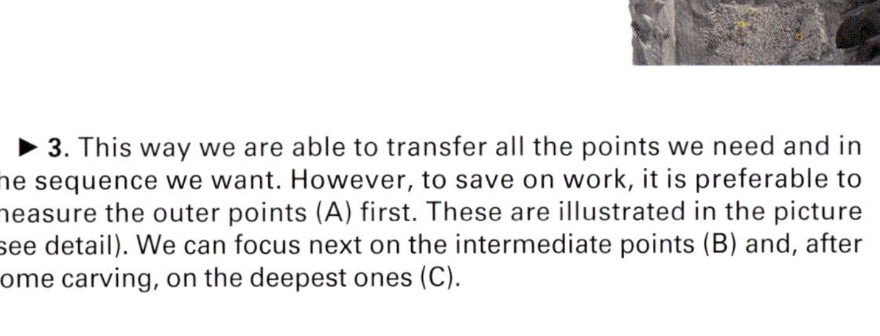

► **3.** This way we are able to transfer all the points we need and in the sequence we want. However, to save on work, it is preferable to measure the outer points (A) first. These are illustrated in the picture (see detail). We can focus next on the intermediate points (B) and, after some carving, on the deepest ones (C).

controlled by the tips of the three pointing sticks supported by the crosspiece. Since during the carving process we will continually have to move the crosspiece from the model to the block, to avoid any involuntary shifts in the reference points, it is advisable to glue a metal washer to the points with an incision in its center that fixes the position of the pointing stick tip.

While the pointing machine is usually sold as a complete unit, the device can be provided without the crosspiece. On page 140 we show how to build such a crosspiece.

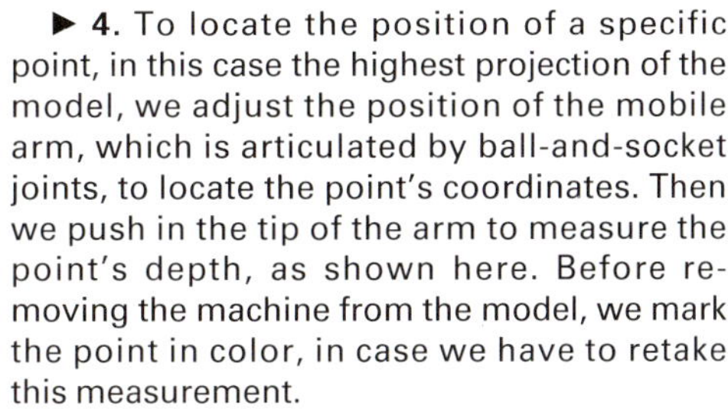
► **4.** To locate the position of a specific point, in this case the highest projection of the model, we adjust the position of the mobile arm, which is articulated by ball-and-socket joints, to locate the point's coordinates. Then we push in the tip of the arm to measure the point's depth, as shown here. Before removing the machine from the model, we mark the point in color, in case we have to retake this measurement.

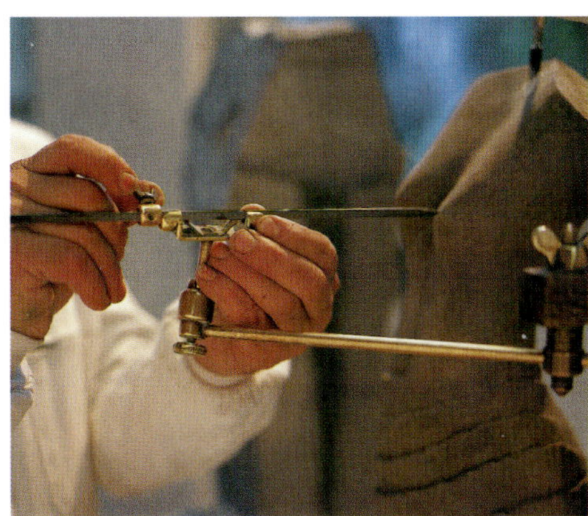

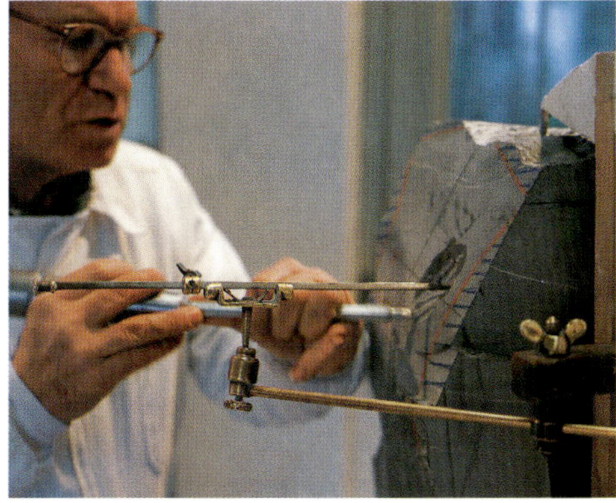

▲ **5.** Then, guided by the tip's position, we reduce the excess material on the stone's surface to approximate the depth measurement of the model.

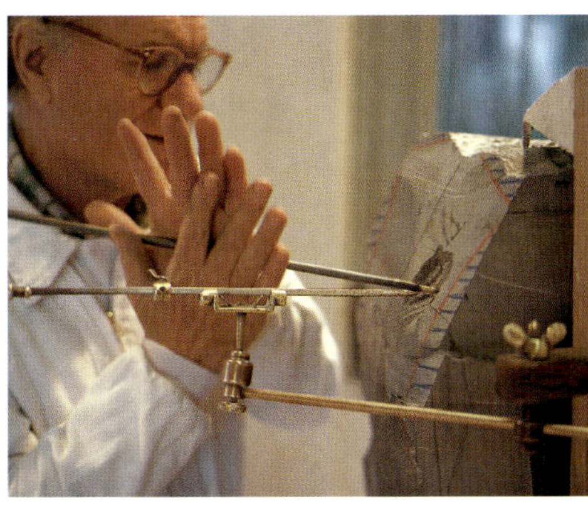

▲ **6.** When we have scraped the material almost to the depth we are looking for and the distance between the nut and the tip indicates that we need to carve between 2 or 3 mm, we carefully trepan with the point marker, rotating it back and forth with both hands.

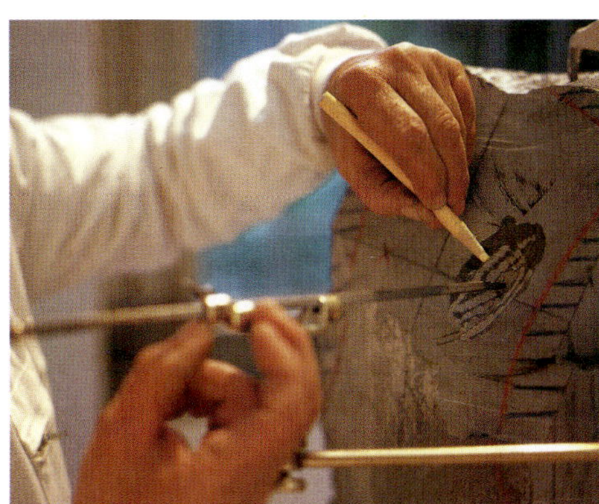

▲ **7.** Finally, once the position of the point is precisely determined, we will mark it for identification in yellow. However, if we are driven by perfectionism, we will carve the points about a hundredth of an inch less than necessary, foreseeing the reduction that will ensue from erasing the points' trepan marks.

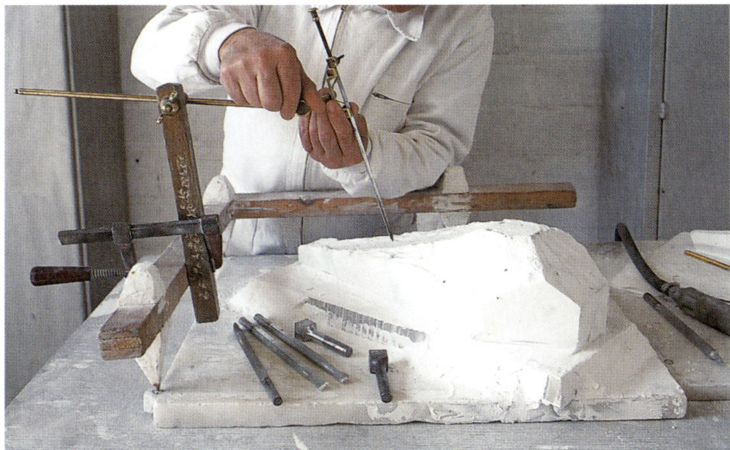

▲ This technique also allows the reproduction of horizontal volumes. In this case, we mark the three reference points on the supporting board, as far apart as possible, and we proceed as before.

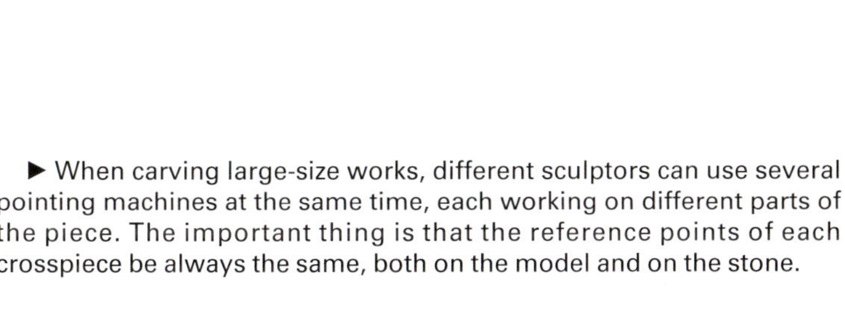
► When carving large-size works, different sculptors can use several pointing machines at the same time, each working on different parts of the piece. The important thing is that the reference points of each crosspiece be always the same, both on the model and on the stone.

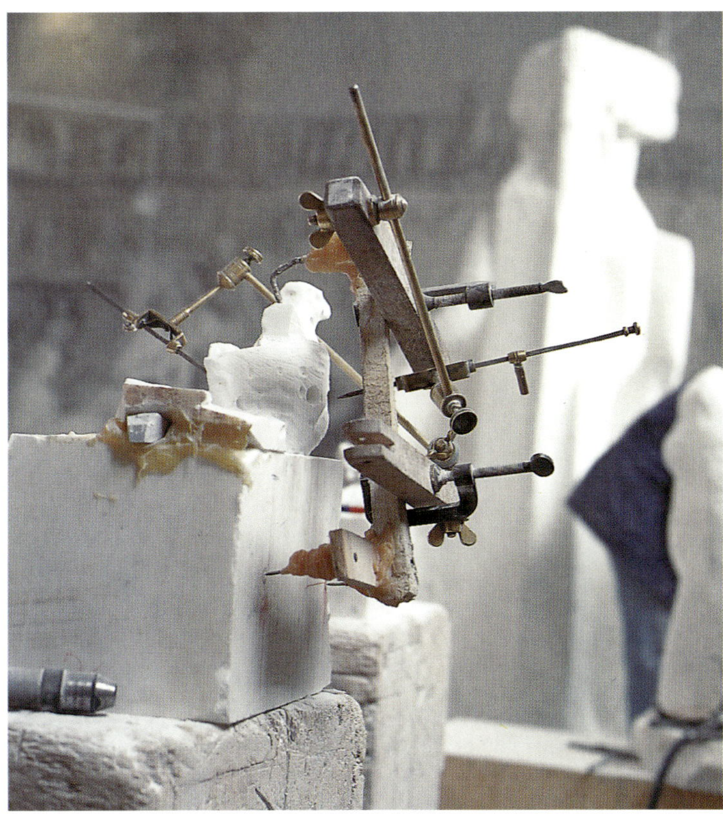

The Three-Compass Technique

The measurement of points with the three-compass technique is as precise as using the pointing machine. Although it requires more patience, the technique allows enlarging or reducing the size of a model. Numerous Neoclassic pediments and later date reliefs were carved with this technique, which is best suited for reliefs.

The Mother Points

The three-compass technique is based on the principle that any point on a volume can be sited by means of three coordinates. The intersection of two compass measurements will determine the height and width, while a third measurement will determine the depth. In order to preserve the relationship among all *reference points* that we locate on the copy, we will need three permanent main reference points, which we will call *mother points*.

The first step in copying or enlarging a model consists of situating three washers on the model's most salient points in order to rest an arm of each compass on them. If, for example, the model is a portrait, the mother points will be located at the top of the head and at the ears. For a relief, one mother point will be located at its topmost site and two at its base's extremities.

Then we must transfer the exact locations of these three points to the block. In doing this, it may be easier to resort to other techniques than the compass method at this initial stage. We have used, in a step-by-step procedure that will be described later—a chassis—but we could also have built a simple crosspiece suitable for the model.

We show how to transfer the mother points with compasses using measurements traced on top of a plaster model that originated from the Galleria della Accademia in Florence. Keep in mind that the last measurement should be the most precise. In any case, after locating the mother points, we must carefully assess our measurements, verifying with a compass that the location of the three points correspond correctly on both the model and the block.

▶ We situate the mother point A in the center of the topmost part of the stone. With the compass we measure the following distances of the model and we transfer them to the block: from A to D; from A to B, and from D to B (the intersection will give us point B); then from A to C, from B to C, and from D to C (the intersection of the three measurements will give us point C).

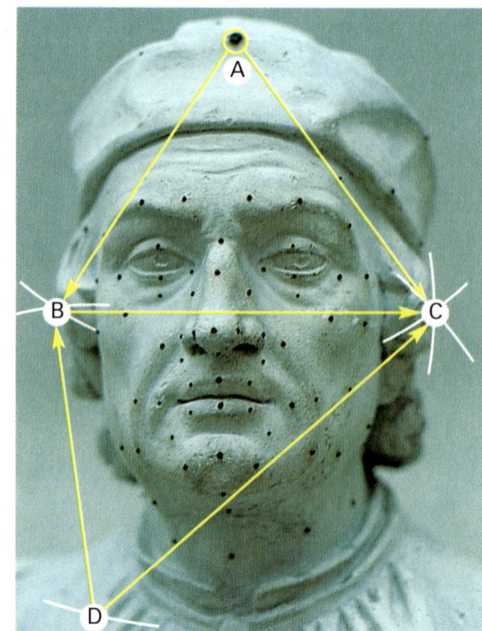

The Reference Points

Once we have transferred the three mother points of the model to the stone block, either by the chassis or the compass technique explained earlier, it is necessary to proceed placing the other reference points on the block. We will describe now how to do this using the compass technique.

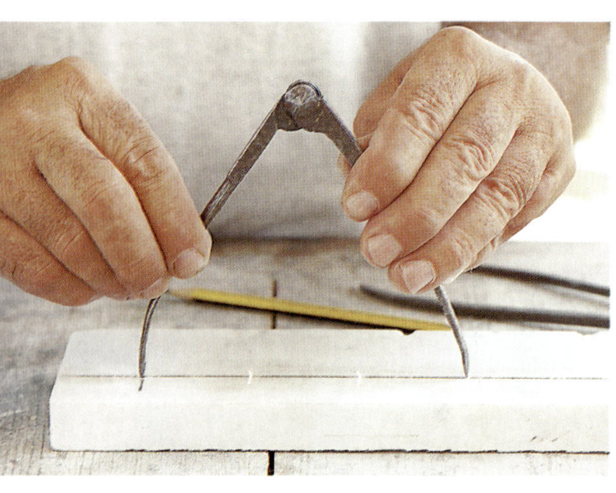

▶ **1.** We choose any point on the model, but here it is advisable to start by choosing the most salient points. We will use the first compass to measure the distance that separates this reference point from each mother point. We then transfer this measurement to the stone and we repeat this operation for the other two mother points. If the compasses' arms are curved, they will better skirt any edges of the model and especially those of the block. The desired point will lie at the intersection of the arms of the three compasses.

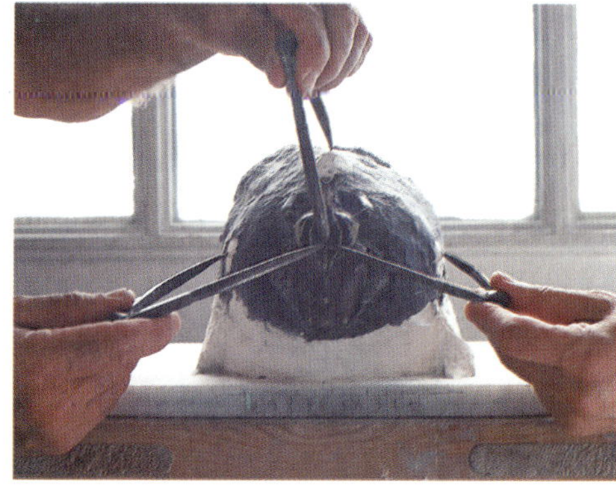

◀ **2.** If we want to enlarge the sculpture over the model's size, we can use as a simple multiplication table a line that we have traced here over a piece of marble. At one of its ends we will place an arm of the compass that is partially open to reflect the measurement taken from the model. We will then displace the open compass along the line as many times, here three, as required by the enlargement. Finally, we attain the enlarged measurement by opening the arms of the compass over the whole enlargement span.

▶ **3.** Although it is known as the three-compass technique, we have used six compasses for the measurements of the model and the block. With the three small ones we take measurements of the model that we transfer to the block by the multiplication table. We then open the big compasses to retrieve the measurements already transferred to the block. The intersection location of the three compasses, each resting an arm at a mother point, will locate a "reference point."

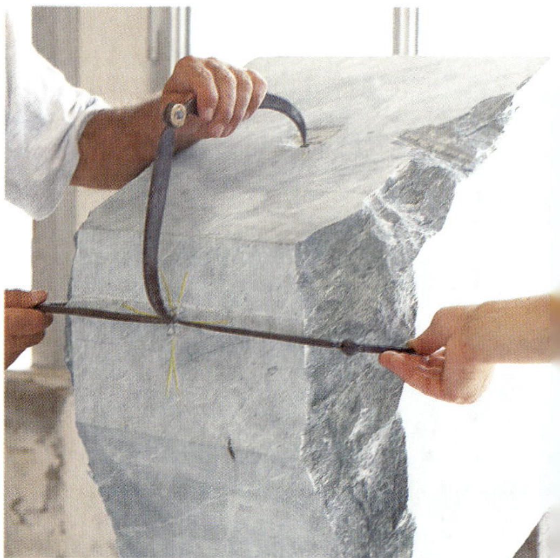

► **4.** Locating the points usually leaves multiple markings on the stone since the three compasses seldom intersect at the same point. If their markings are far off, it indicates that the point's location should be deeper and it tells us that we should trim down this area. The marking of the tip of the compass will vary with the position of the point, which often lies off-center of the intersecting point of the compasses.

► **5.** While we trim the excess material, we note that the markings of the compasses come closer to each other until all three markings coincide. Just before this happens, we will trepan lightly with a point maker, to avoid drilling more than necessary.

▼ **6.** To avoid extra work, we will again duplicate the technique mentioned when discussing the pointing machine: First we locate the most salient points, then the intermediate ones, and finally the deepest ones.

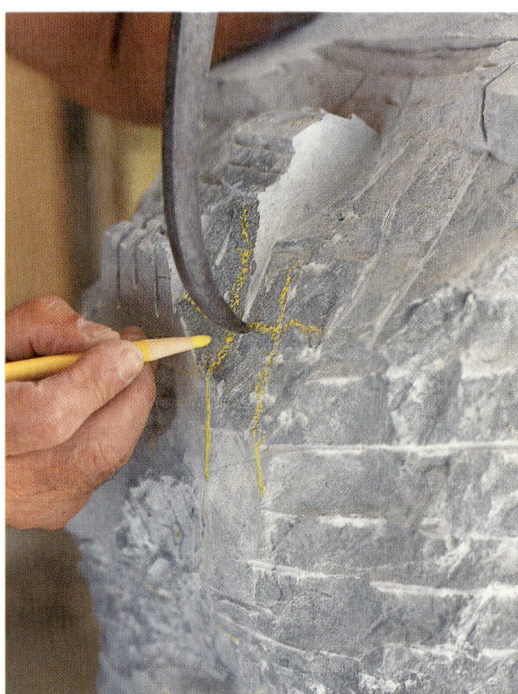

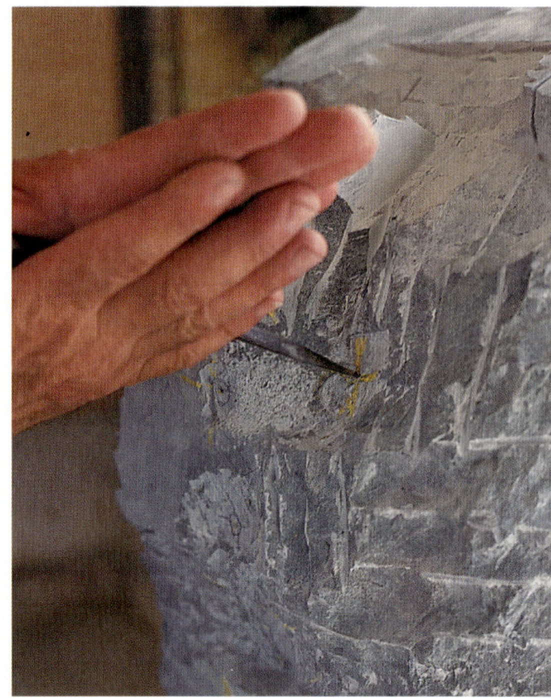

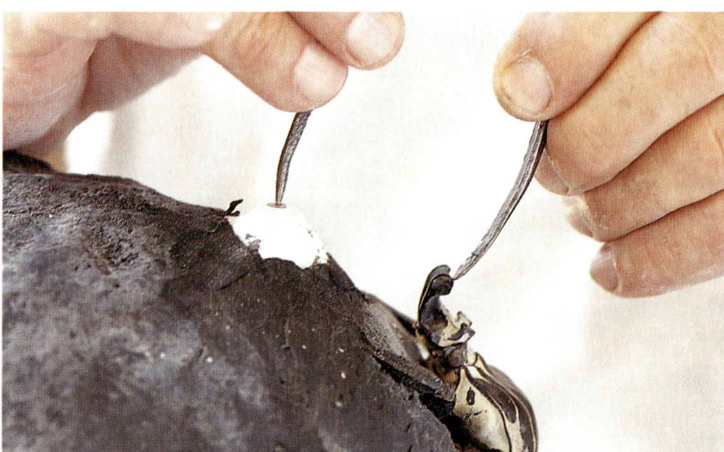

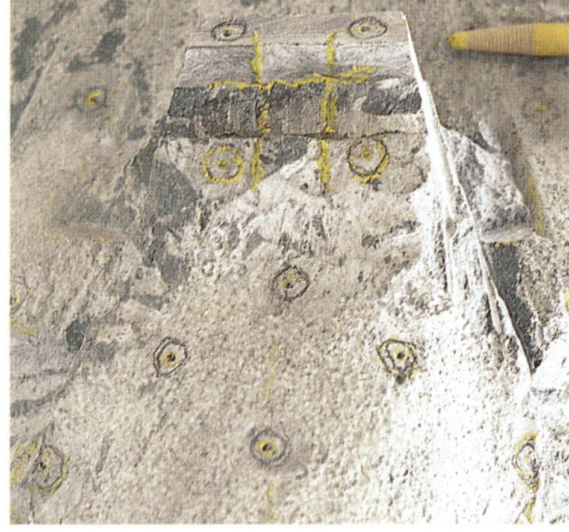

◄ **7.** After locating the most salient points that will help us shape what will become the shell of the beetle, we site one of medium depth that will determine the distance between the antennae.

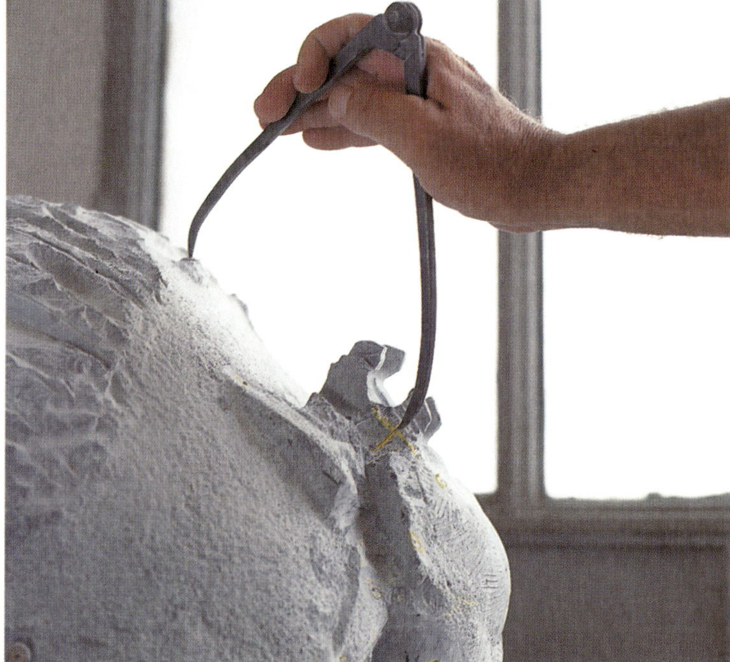

◄ **8.** After transferring all the points and trimming down any excess material, we will verify the accuracy of all measurements.

The Intermediate Points

The three-compass technique can also enlarge large-size sculptures, but with the help of many workers. In this case, several new mother points will have to be dispersed strategically. These we will call intermediate points. Any of the reference points can be transformed into an intermediate point so that, measuring from this point, other new ones can be established until the sculpture is covered by a network of triangles.

Each triangle enclosed by a grouping of intermediate points bounds an area that can be worked on independently from the others.

Mastering the three-compass technique can also prove very useful to the sculptor who wants to work in detail on a specific area of a directly carved sculpture, for example, sculpting a small head on a very large sculpture.

Touches of Color

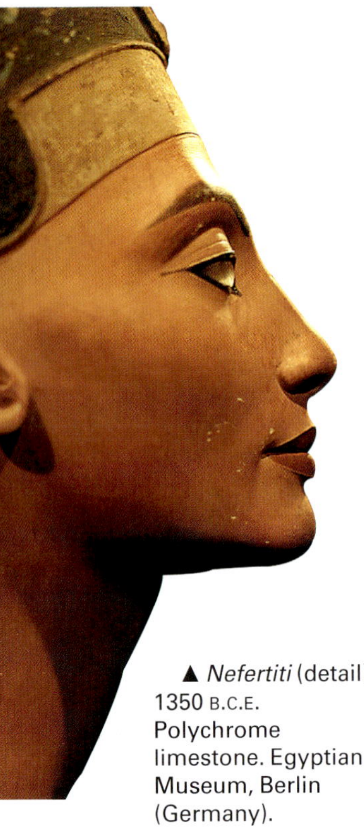

▲ *Nefertiti* (detail). 1350 B.C.E. Polychrome limestone. Egyptian Museum, Berlin (Germany).

Traditional sculpture in stone has frequently resorted to color to give its works a realistic aspect. This has been the case in Egypt, classic Greece, or during the Gothic period, and has also been common in the Orient. Romanesque sculpture has used color as a symbolic element.

Although the passing of time has stripped the majority of sculptures of their original polychrome colors, from their traces we can infer that in primitive art the color was applied directly to the stone and soon afterwards over an underlying coat of plaster. In Ancient Greece the stone was left marked with traces of the point chisel so that the layer of plaster could easily adhere to it, while in the classical period, marble was polished before the paint was applied. However, the painting of the latter statues gradually became more discrete.

Starting from the fourth century B.C.E., polychromy fell into disuse and remained so during the Hellenistic and Roman periods. The custom reemerged, however, during the Renaissance. Following the Middle Ages, when polychromy over stone was widespread, the Gothic period used it only on details at specific sites.

The new sculpture that the twentieth century promoted brought back the color to accentuate expression, as in the case of Gauguin, or to construct the planes and volumes of cubists and constructivists.

Although we are partial to the purity of the natural color of the stone that offers countless possibilities and shades if chosen appropriately, and although we believe that we must respect each material's natural appearance, we cannot ignore the totally legitimate option of coloring it.

From a technical point of view, we must keep in mind that the most porous and bright stones, especially limestones such as alabaster, are most suitable for coloring. However, if we intend to paint an igneous stone we run the risk that the color will be absorbed only by its outer layer and the pigment will wear away with time. In any case, specialty stores can advise us and will point out the most appropriate coloring products. It is, however, more interesting to investigate this ourselves, experimenting with the most basic homemade recipes such as using tea or coffee to give a patina to a recently carved Carrara stone or "aging" a sandstone with ferric chloride. We could also alter the stone's color by means of chemical reactions produced by different minerals in contact with it.

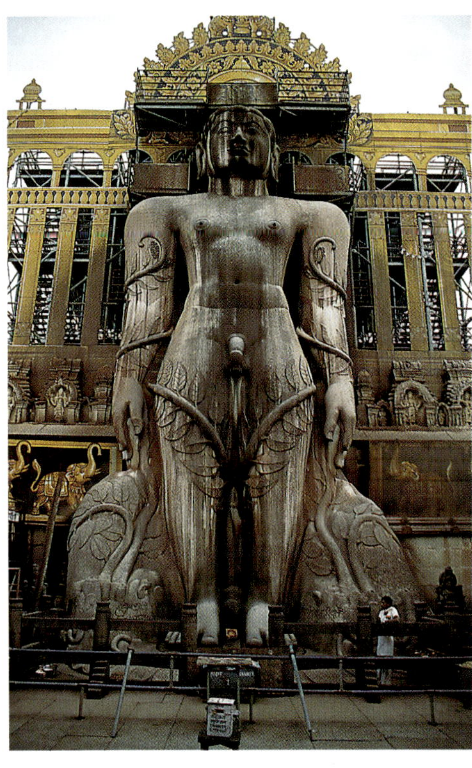

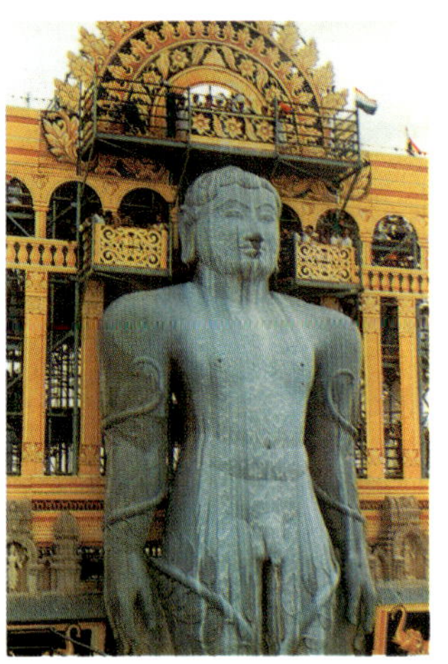

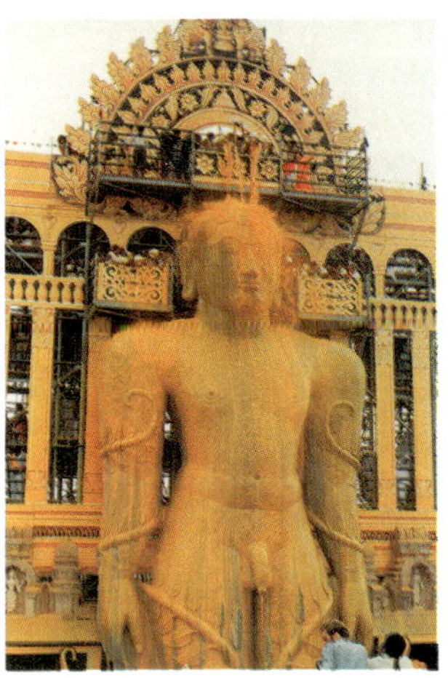

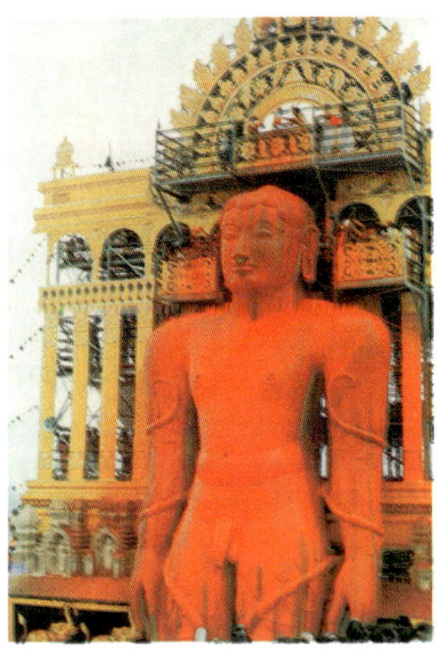

◄▲ *Gomateswara*. 981 C.E. Granite. (17.5 m). Sravanabelgola, Karnataka (India).

Certain cultures endow their religious sculptures with a natural pigment and alter the color with aromatic fragrances and ritual rubbings. The most spectacular case occurs once every 11 years in the south of India. There the Jainists, when celebrating the "Mahavira Jayanti," bathe this enormous image carved in the mountain rock with milk, saffron, pigments, flower powder, and gold powder.

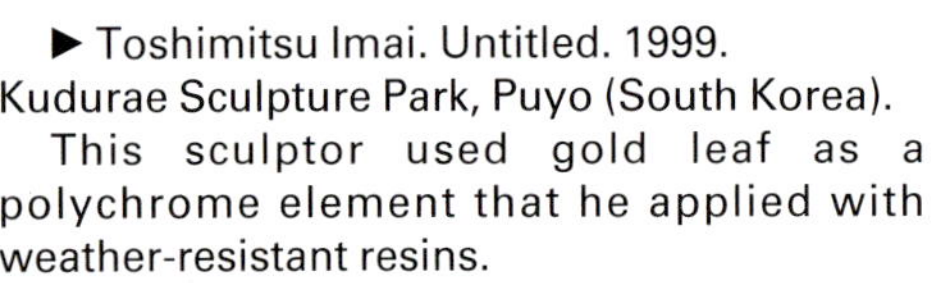

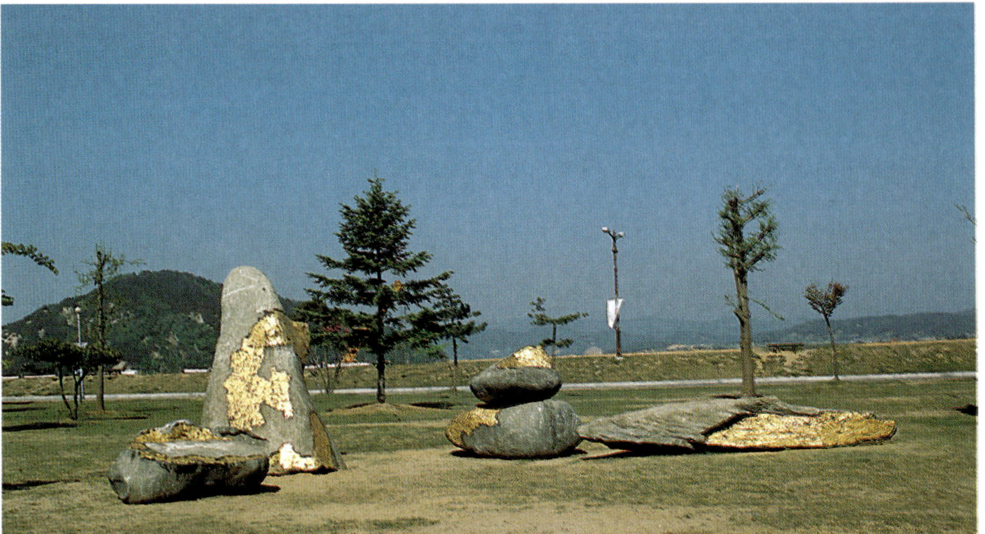

► Toshimitsu Imai. Untitled. 1999. Kudurae Sculpture Park, Puyo (South Korea).

This sculptor used gold leaf as a polychrome element that he applied with weather-resistant resins.

Investigating Other Materials

The only eye of Nefertiti reminds us of the frequent use of inlays that, during the Baroque period, attained technical virtuosity in the mixing of different stones. In reality, thanks to the durability of special glues made for stones, inlays do not present a problem, provided we don't have constraining aesthetic objections.

A stone sculpture can also become more expressive and gain in size if we know how to complete it with diverse materials such as wood, metal, glass, and so on.

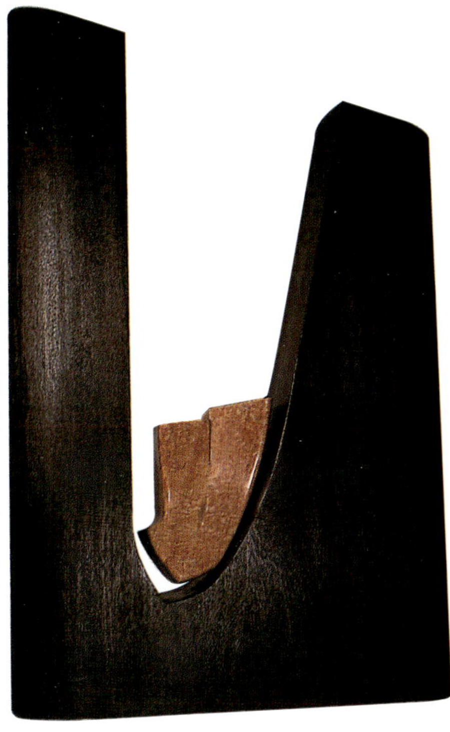

◀ Camí. *Silent Germination.* 1983. Agate and dyed wood.

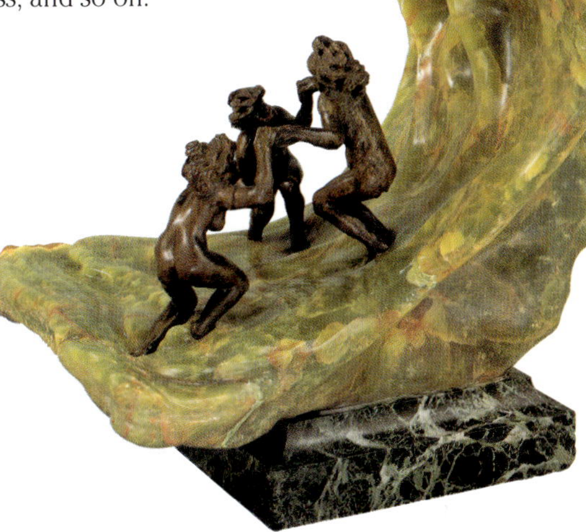

▶ Camille Claudel. *La Vague.* 1900. Onyx and bronze. Private collection.

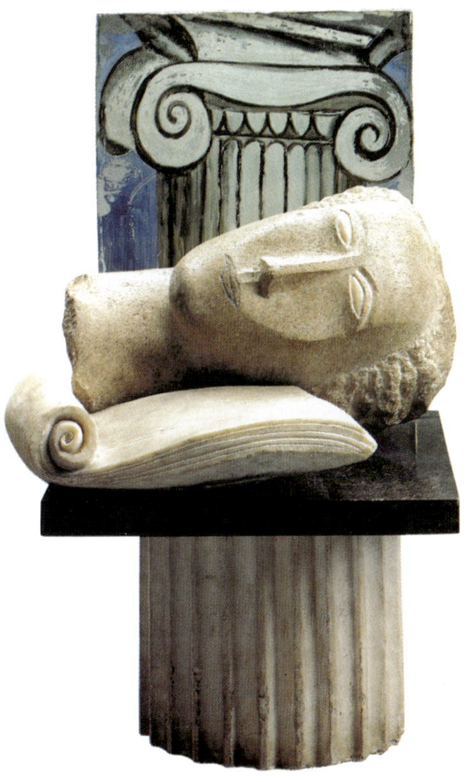

▲ Zadkine. *Espirit de l'Antiquité.* 1927. Marble, stone, and painted crystal. Museum of Fine Arts, Boston (United States).

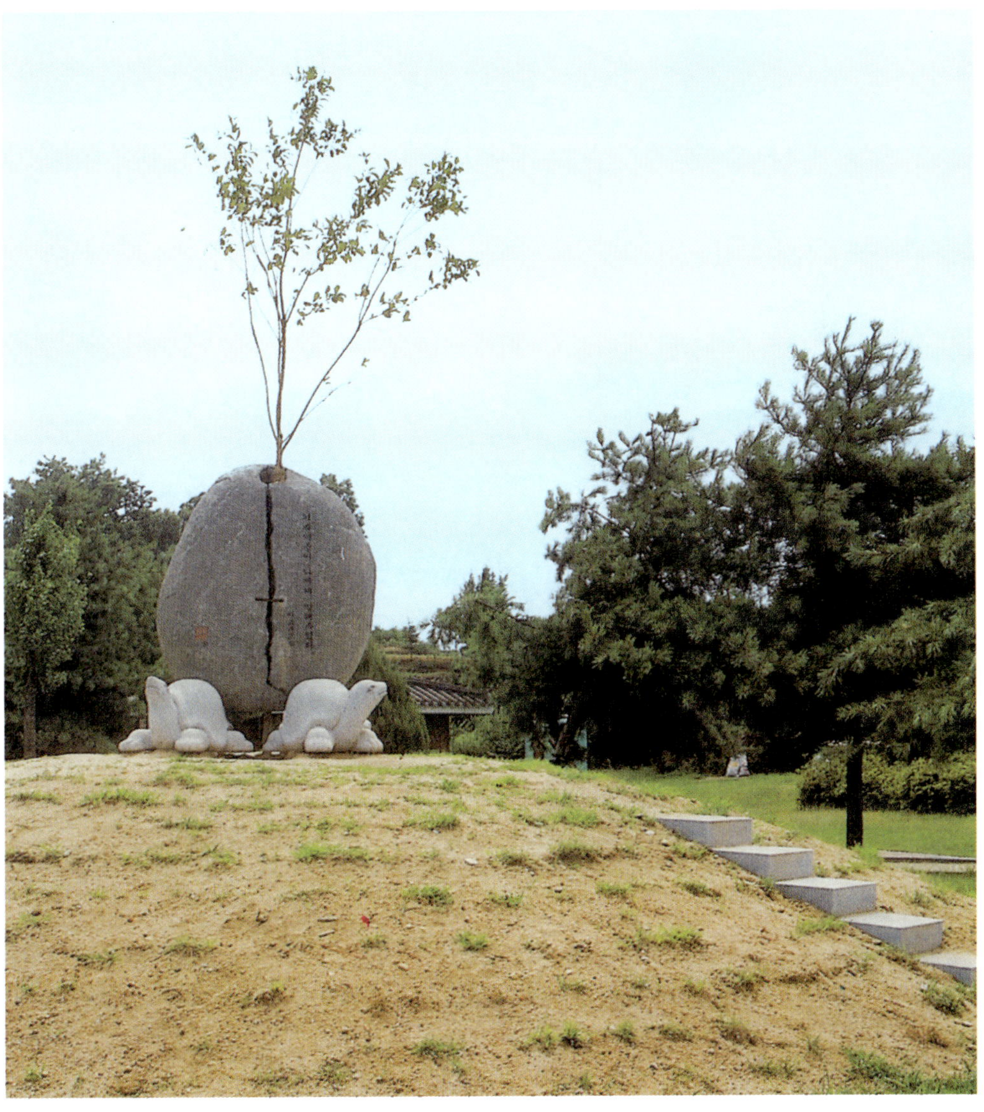

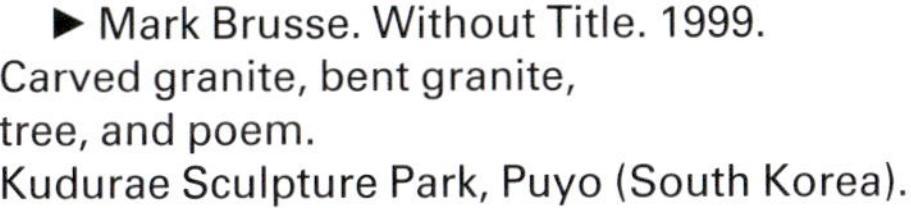

▶ Mark Brusse. Without Title. 1999. Carved granite, bent granite, tree, and poem. Kudurae Sculpture Park, Puyo (South Korea).

Sculpture, Architecture, and Urban Planning

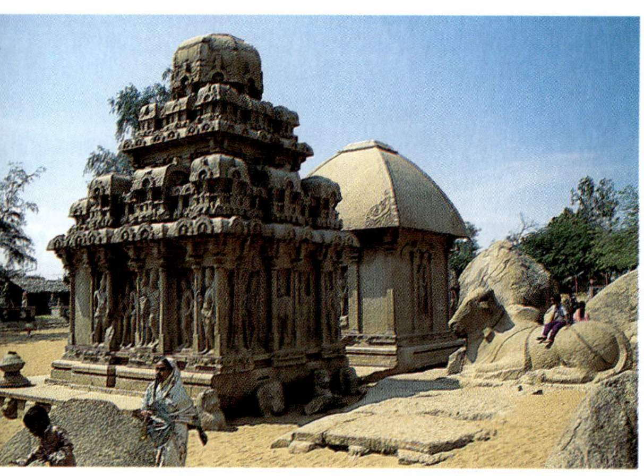

▲ In Mahabalipuran, in Southern India, a sole granite rock displays capricious sculptures that reproduce the forms of temples.

Is it a mere chance that the two greatest sculptors in history also stand out as important interior designers, architects, and urban planners?

When Michelangelo designed the Laurentian staircase in Florence, the dome of the Vatican, or the Capitol square, did he do it to show that as a good Renaissance artist he was a versatile man? Did Bernini, who decorated the interior of Saint Peter's in the Vatican, planned unsuccessfully the remodeling of the Palace of the Louvre in Paris, inspired the construction of squares and bridges in Rome, or constructed Saint Peter's square, forget his sculpture training while applying it? Should the serene but impressive beauty of the Marbles of the Parthenon and of the entire Acropolis in Athens be attributed solely to the architects Ictinos and Calicrates or to the sculptor Fidias? Do we consider the Egyptian and Aztec pyramids sculpture or architecture? Does the purity of lines and the beauty of the different granites of Lenin's tomb in Moscow represent a sculpture that challenges the sculptures of the past or is it just another sculpture in the middle of the Kremlin square? When Noguchi or Caravan organize a space, do they make a sculpture or practice urbanism?

Similar questions besiege us when we contemplate the utopian projects of the Neoclassic architects Ledoux and Boulle or, making a new chronological leap, when we admire the shapes of organic sculpture of Le Corbusier's Notre-Dame-du Haut chapel in Ronchamp (France), or the monumental structure of marble and crystal of Le Grande Arche de la Defense in Paris erected with minimalist criteria as a visual projection of other triumphant arches.

The increasing specialization of different techniques cannot make us forget that human concerns and needs, which art expresses, do not admit these distinctions.

The menhir inspires the obelisk, the minaret, the bell tower, in the same way that the dolmen engenders the dome and the cromlech organizes the space anticipating urbanism.

But all of these human creations, whether called sculpture or architecture, express the same physical need: to orient oneself in space and, if possible, to consecrate it. This focus on winning the central spot has determined during millennia the location of public monuments. It has also influenced human personality promoting models of life on top of mountains, at the crossroads of paths, or in the center of squares, until, it is clear, demystifying times descend upon us and sculpture surprises us in unexpected places.

A misunderstood concept of art unity can ravage us, and it already does so in the realm of public sculpture. With the excuse of interdisciplinary art, discipline experts of the most prestigious social stature—in architecture and gradually less in painting—deem themselves capable of resolving "minor" problems. Furthermore, their proximity to the seats of power facilitate this belief. In this context, public opinion does not react if, with tax money, a monumental sculpture

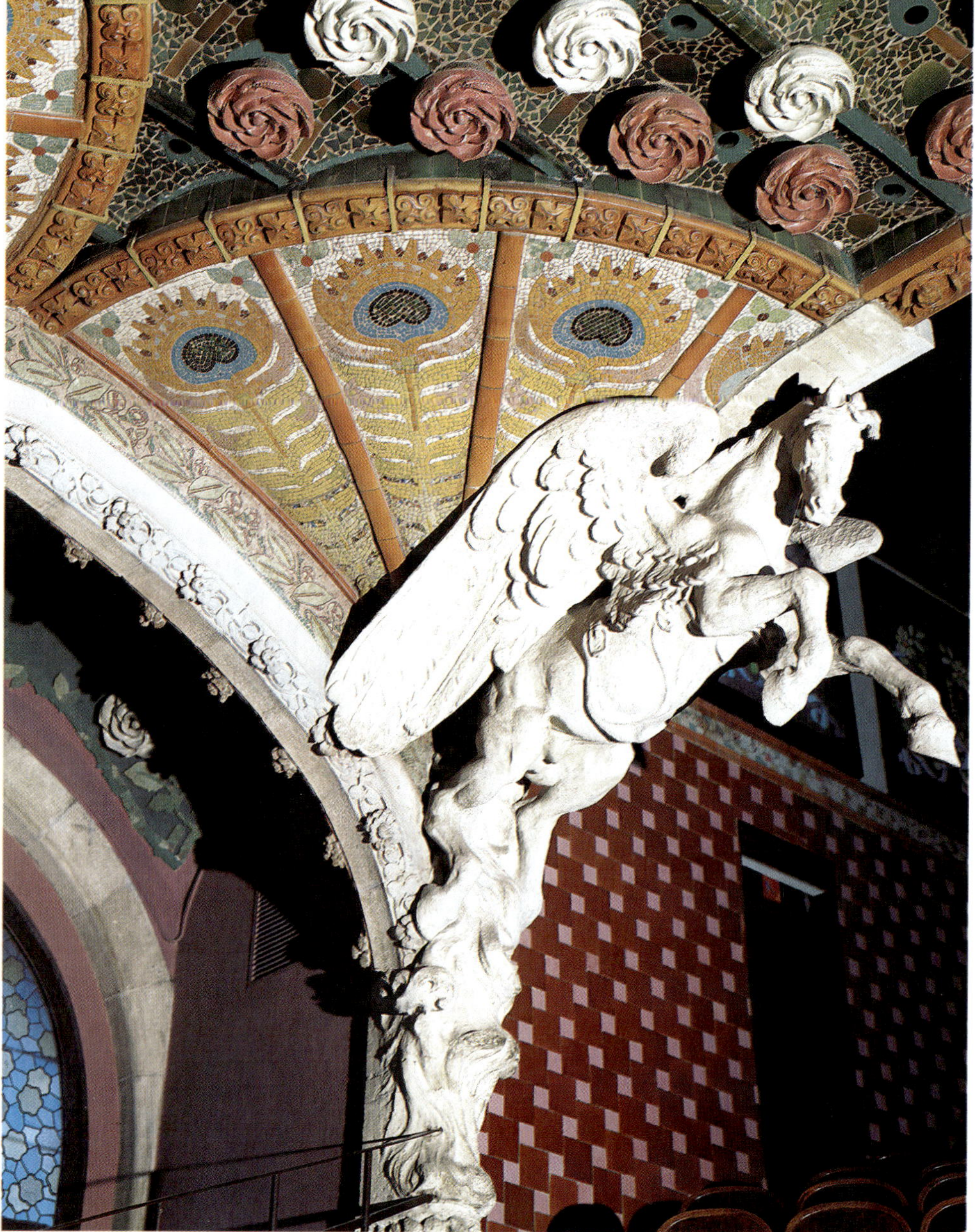

◀ Domenech i Montaner—Gargallo. *"Winged Horse,"* 1908. Toba de Bera. Palau de la Musica Catalana, Barcelona (Spain).

linked to an urban project is assigned to a starving painter or is commissioned to an artist who has never drawn a sketch. But the work itself, with its flat surfaces that the design prescribes, betrays the lack of development of its authors.

We seek unity in the arts that is based on collaboration and teamwork in a way where individuals contribute their concerns or intuitions and experts their technical or aesthetic skills. We base our opinion on historical evidence that, although it has produced few "interdisciplinary" geniuses, has bequeathed a rich patrimony in all continents, making it impossible to determine where the work of one artist begins and that of another ends. Architecture was never more prestigious than during the Gothic period, but even then, architects knew how to relinquish the outer decoration of the cathedral to sculptors and to acknowledge the superiority of the creator of volumes inside the cathedral, glorified by stained glass windows.

This intent to unify the arts acquired a conscience during the Baroque period. An example is the "Transparency" of the Cathedral of Toledo (Spain) where an architect, a sculptor, a painter, and a goldsmith challenged the laws of gravity by harmonizing the different marbles, alabasters, jasper, stucco, and bronzes into a single work that foreshadowed Modernism, another movement pursuing identical objectives.

However this collaboration among artists was not evident only in times of pompous tastes. It also engendered a sober and functional conception of art that touches us even in the most mundane daily activities. We refer to the Bauhaus, a school of art in which designers, painters, sculptors, architects, urban planners, and students collaborated.

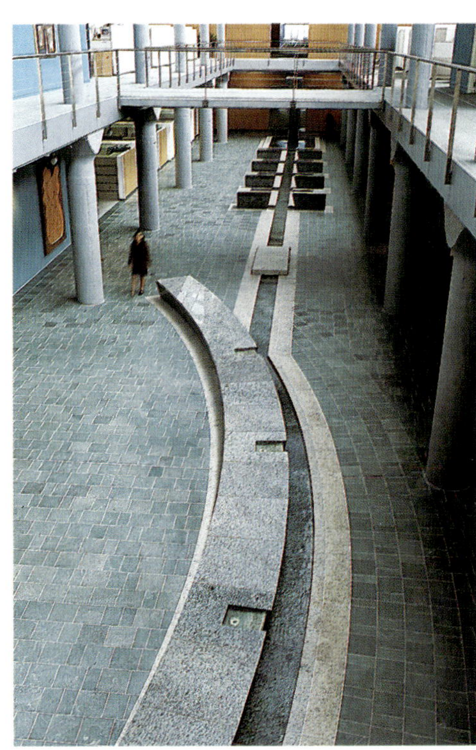

► Murase. Port of Seattle. 1994. Blue granite. Seattle (United States).

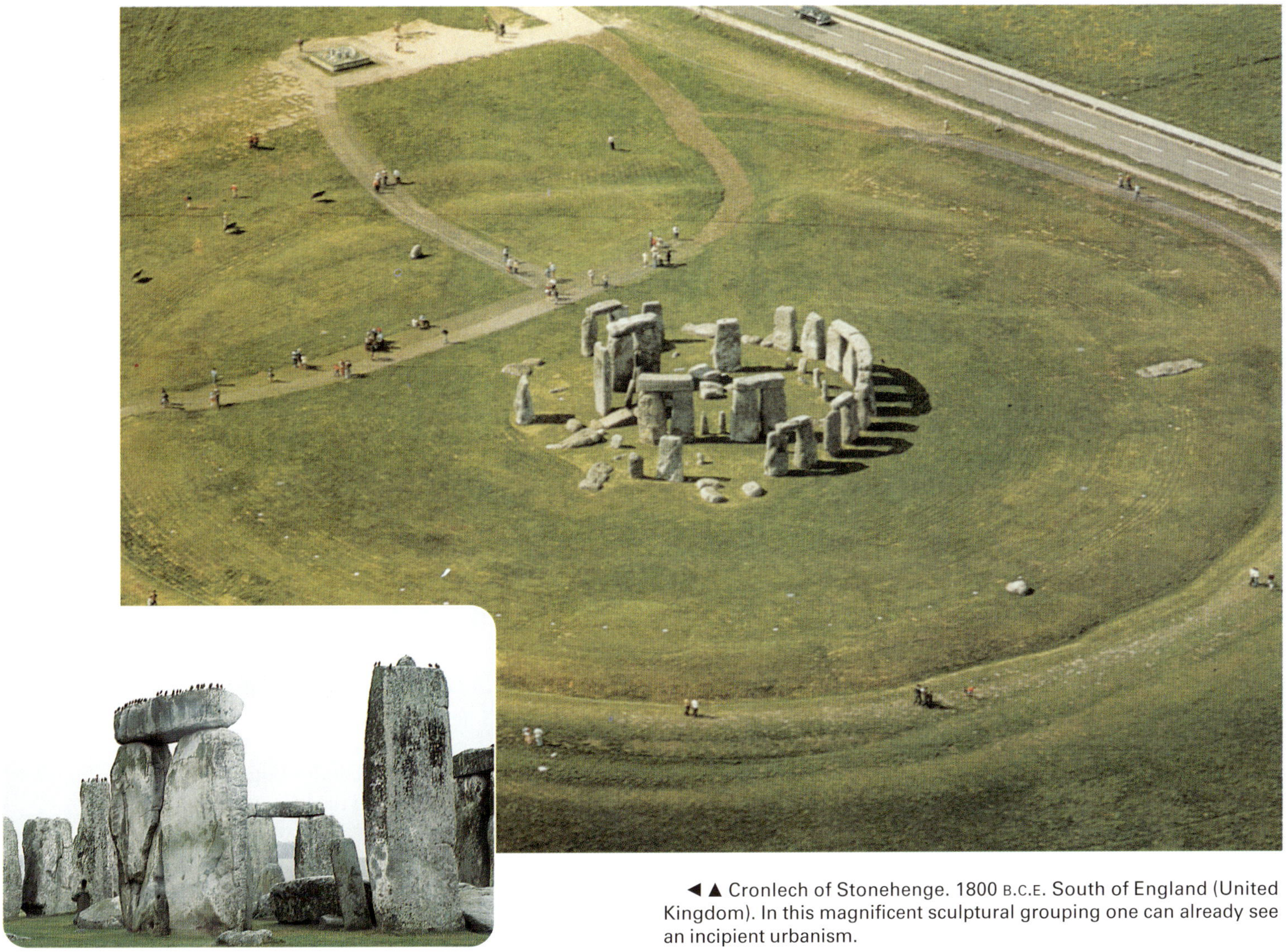

◄ ▲ Cronlech of Stonehenge. 1800 B.C.E. South of England (United Kingdom). In this magnificent sculptural grouping one can already see an incipient urbanism.

Step by Step

After dealing with the basic aspects of stone carving, we will demonstrate in this section the sculpting process, thus putting into practice the principles we have discussed. The following exercises are of increasing complexity: First we show a direct carving in alabaster; we follow with one in sandstone using a template; we enlarge a travertine sculpture using a maquette on which we have drawn a grid; we then demonstrate the use of the pointing machine in reproducing a sculpture in limestone; we enlarge another marble sculpture using the three-compass technique; and, we conclude with two reports discussing the production process of two monumental granite sculptures.

It has already been said that sculpture is often the result of teamwork, a fact that is often ignored. As we wish to acknowledge this reality, one of us, Camí, conceived and directed the carving of all the sculptures illustrated here. However, we assigned the carving of each sculpture to different professionals: a stonecutter from Lleida, a practitioner from Barcelona (Spain), another practitioner from South Korea, and a company in Portugal with expertise in granite carving. In this way our experience will be enriched.

We used manual tools only for the first two sculptures and then we relied on electric, pneumatic, and industrial tools. Although it was not intended that these exercises be imitated, we believe that basically they can serve as examples for stimulating creativity and helping understand the different techniques.

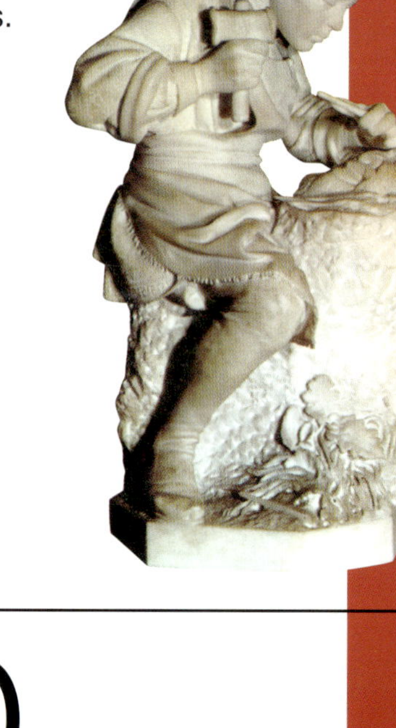

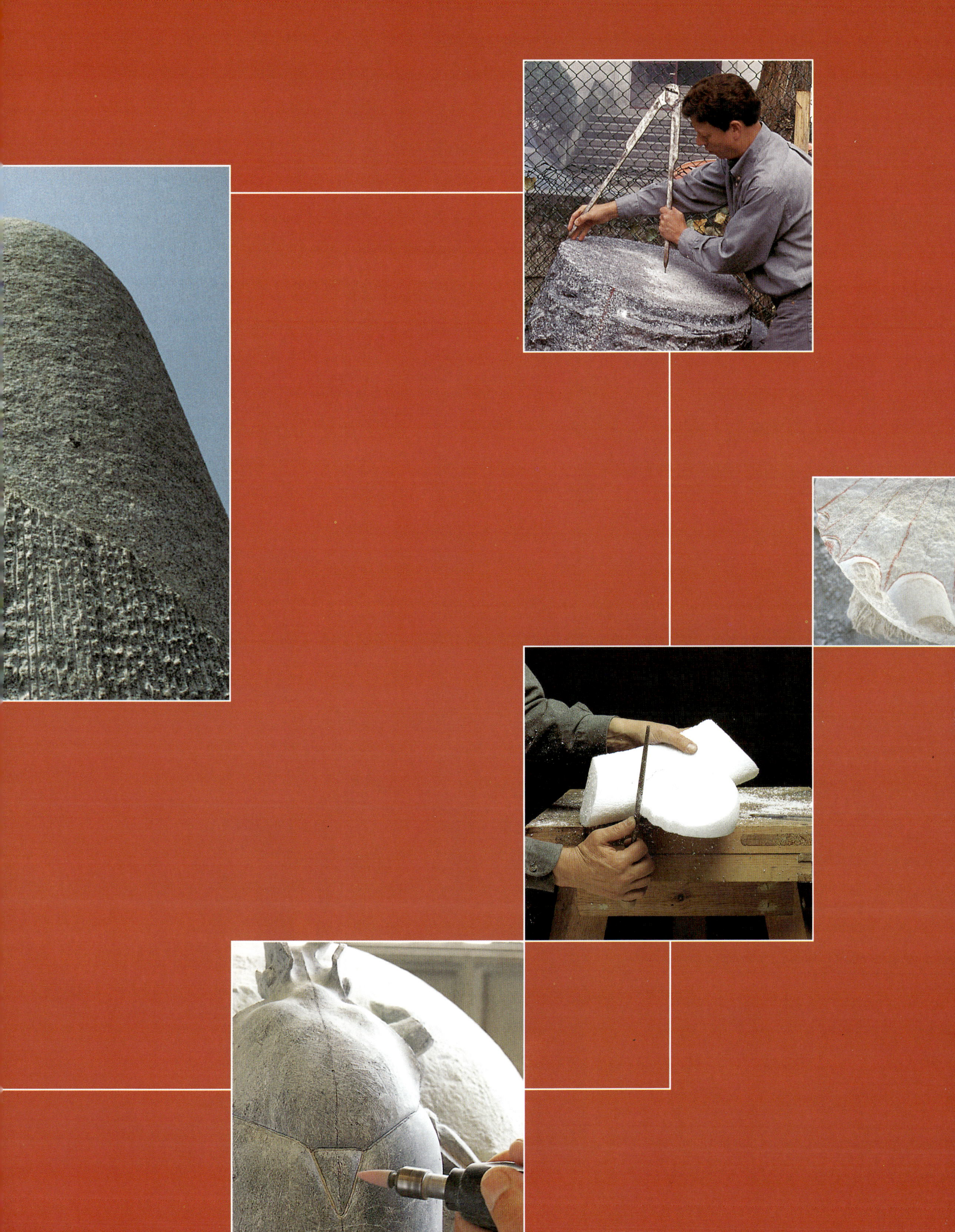

Direct Carving

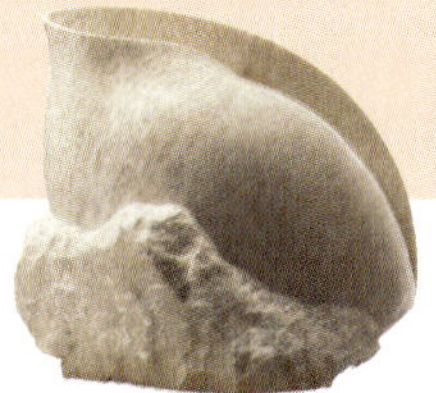

We begin this section by demonstrating how simple it is to carve in alabaster, a stone that is easiest to work with and that we recommend to anyone who is sculpting for the first time. Because we are dealing with a fragile material, we will first treat the stone, then reduce it in size until we have defined the volume, modeled the details, and, finally, polished part of its surface.

We will use a 25 × 20 × 15-inch (65 × 53 × 37-cm) block from Beuda, Gerona (Spain) and will directly carve an organic figure, inspired by the shape of a conch, using traditional tools and without the use of a maquette.

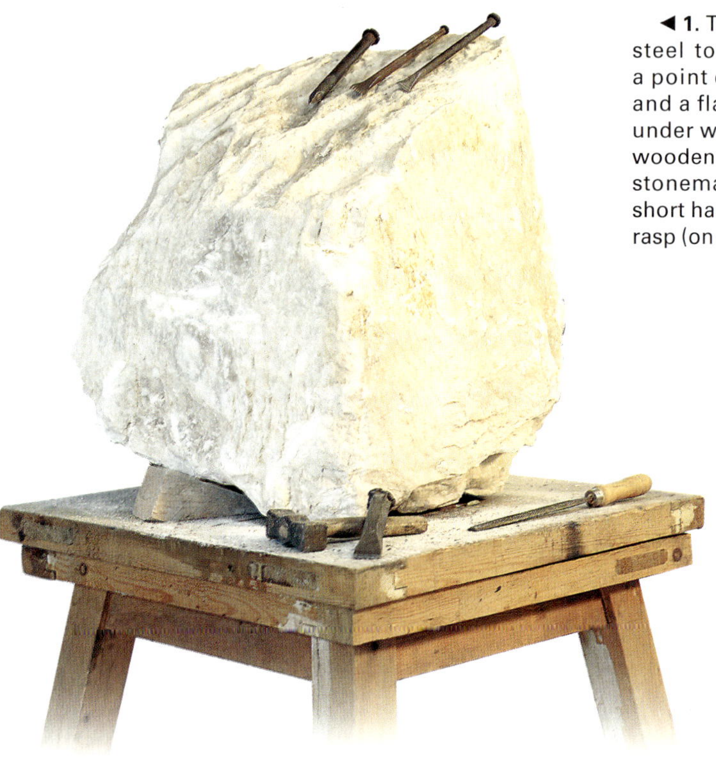

◀ **1.** These are the tempered steel tools that we will use: a point chisel, a tooth chisel, and a flat chisel (on the block under which we have inserted wooden wedges); a trimmer, a stonemason's hammer with a short handle, and a carpenter's rasp (on the work stand).

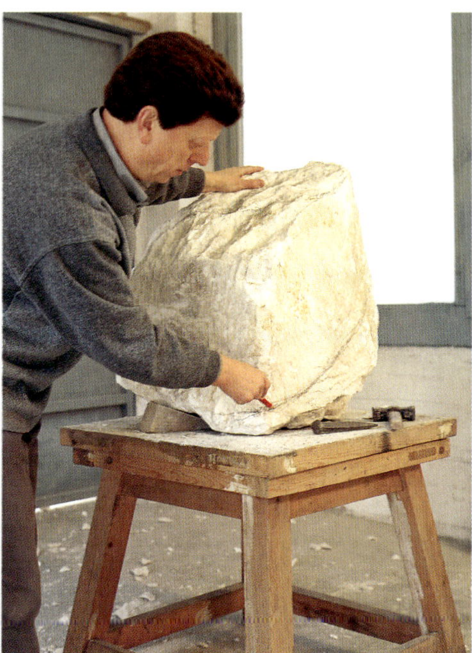

▲ **2.** We begin by drawing the outline of the form chosen for a model, avoiding the surface material that might be damaged.

▶ **3.** Then we pare down the material outside the marked line using a trimmer, though we could also use a point chisel. We try to impact the stone obliquely so as not to damage its internal layers.

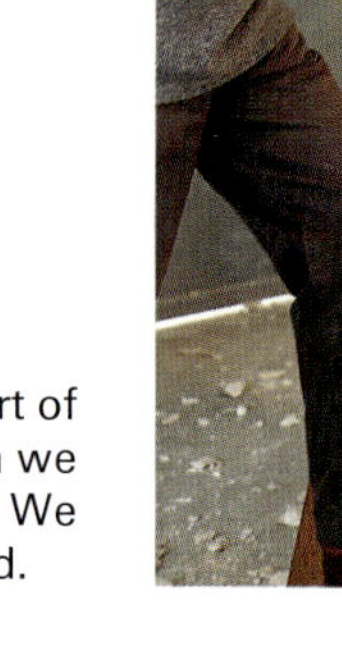

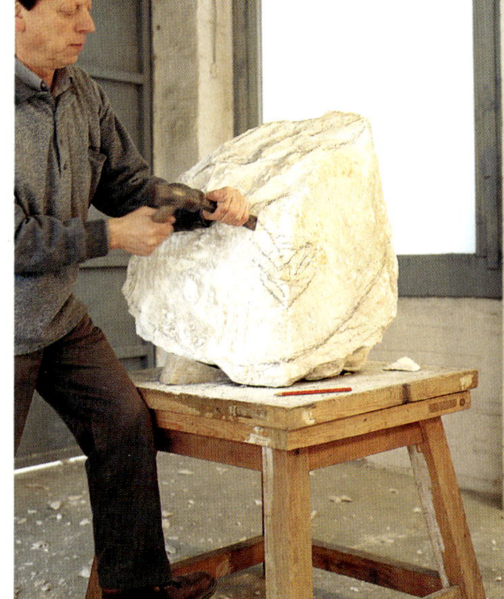

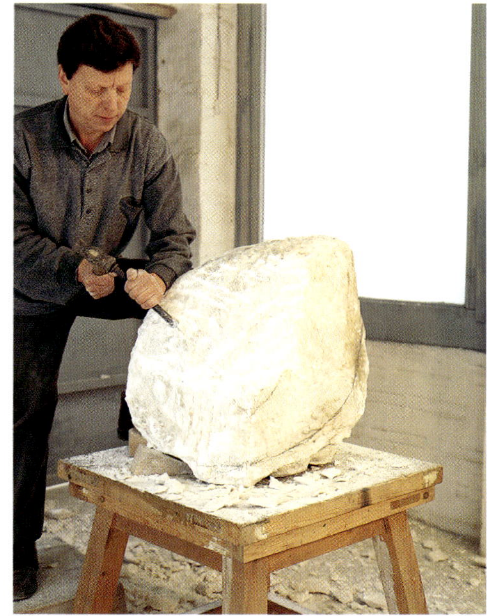

▶ **4.** We continue working the upper part of the stone using a point chisel with which we make wide grooves that stretch outward. We leave the lower part of the stone untouched.

► **5.** When we are sure that there is no risk of damage to the alabaster, we begin the true reduction process and use a point chisel to configure the ovoid shape of the top part of the figure.

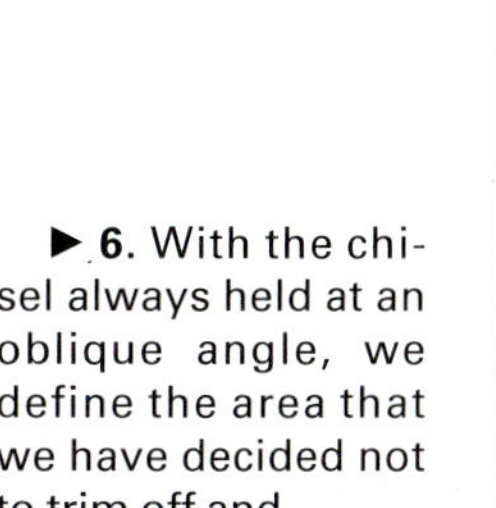

► **6.** With the chisel always held at an oblique angle, we define the area that we have decided not to trim off and

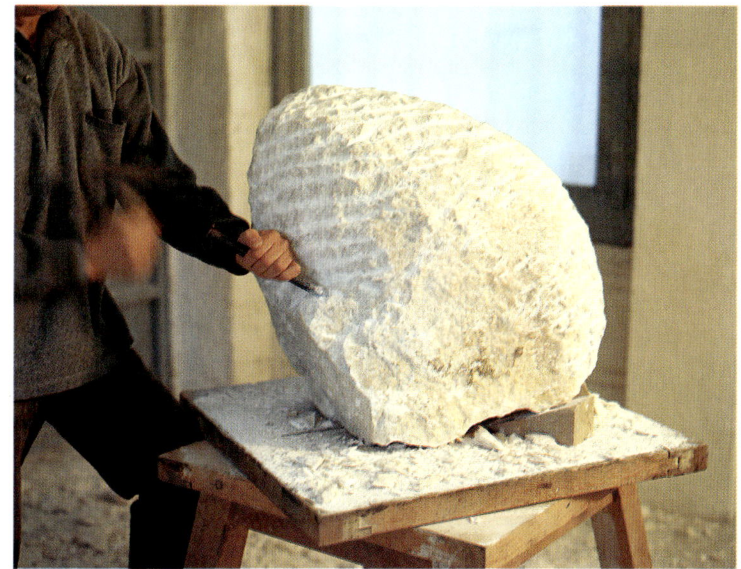

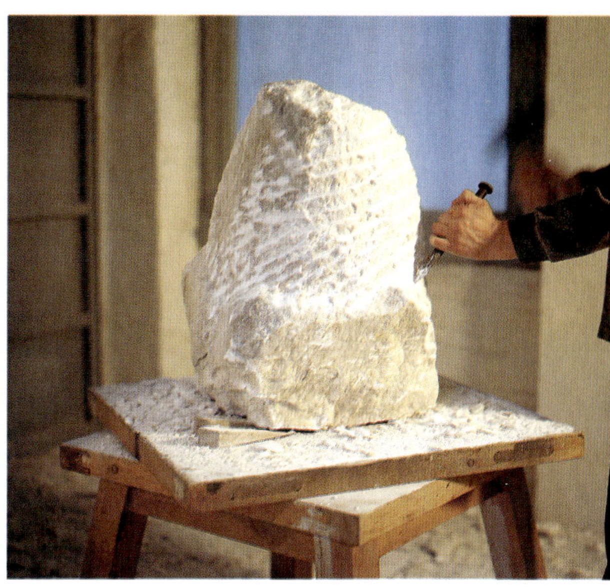

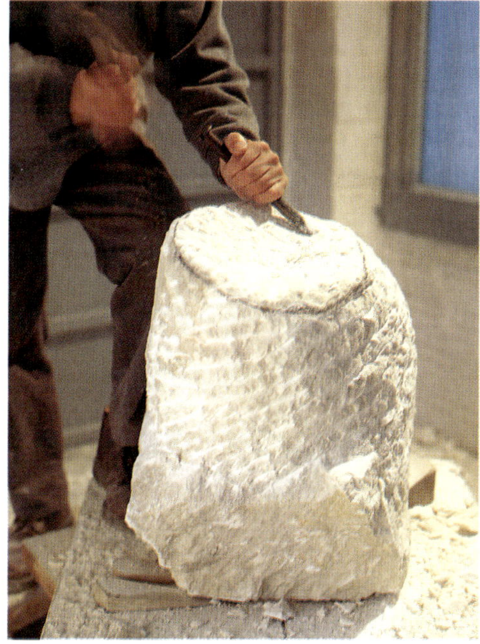

◄ **7.** we focus our attention on the upper part of the figure where, guided by the contour drawn earlier, we carve out a cavity extending from the outline to the stone's center.

► **8.** Using the same point chisel, we reduce one side of the alabaster, conveying the impression that the opposite side has flared up. Now we chip away at the upper area to suggest that the uppermost side is turning over on itself.

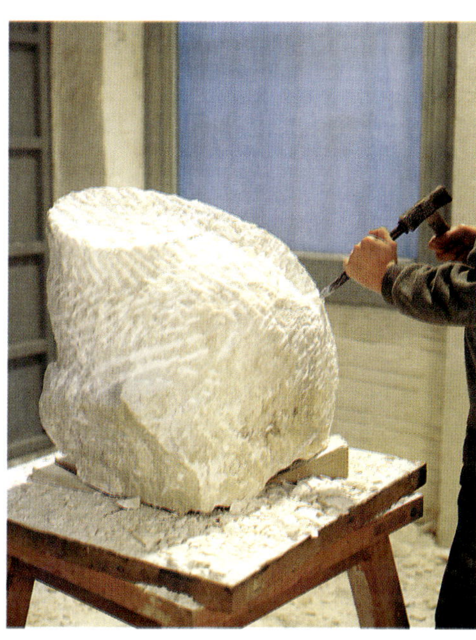

◄ **9.** The trimming has created an edge in the shape of a peaked crest that rises in the center of the block. To accentuate this edge and suggest that the sculpture is freeing itself from the block, we also trim the area that we did not plan to reduce.

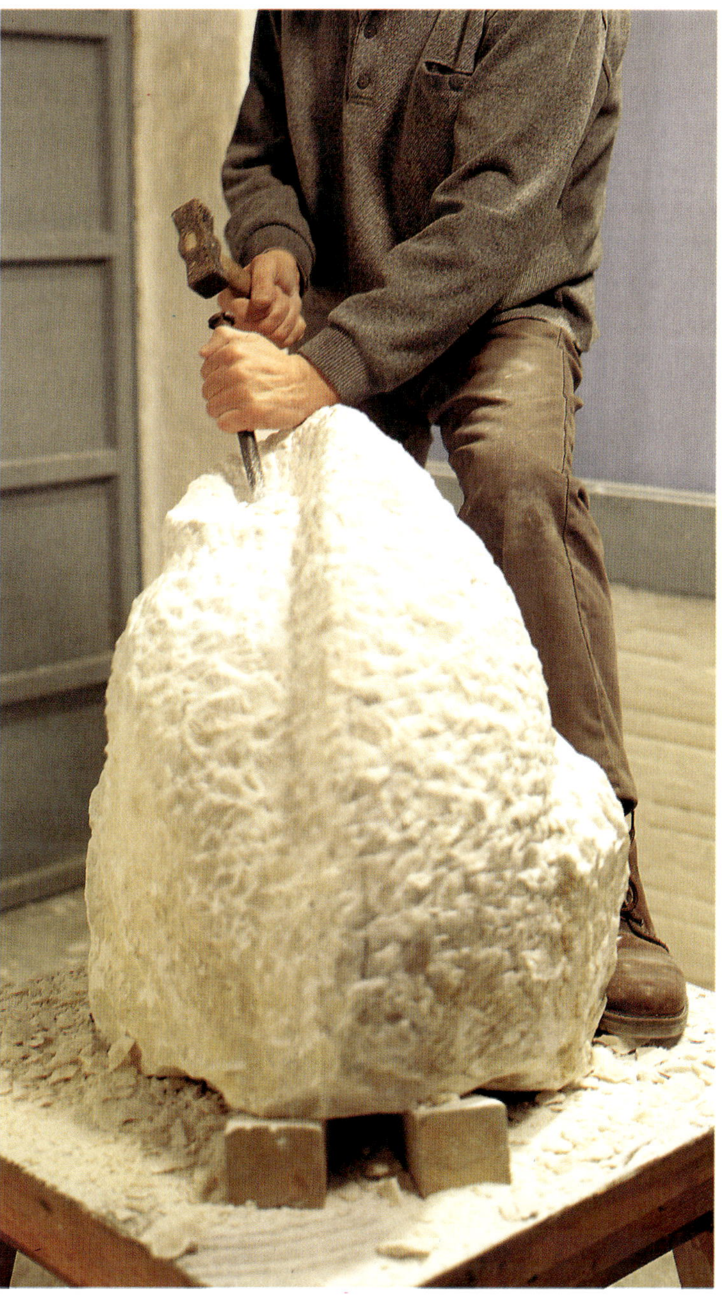

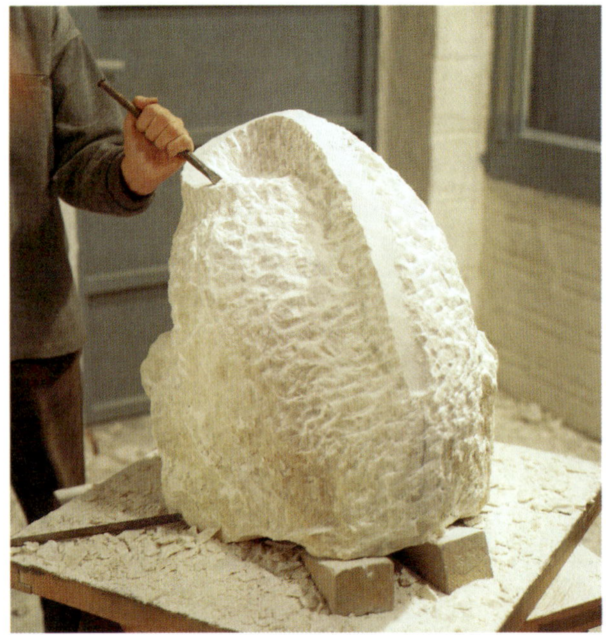

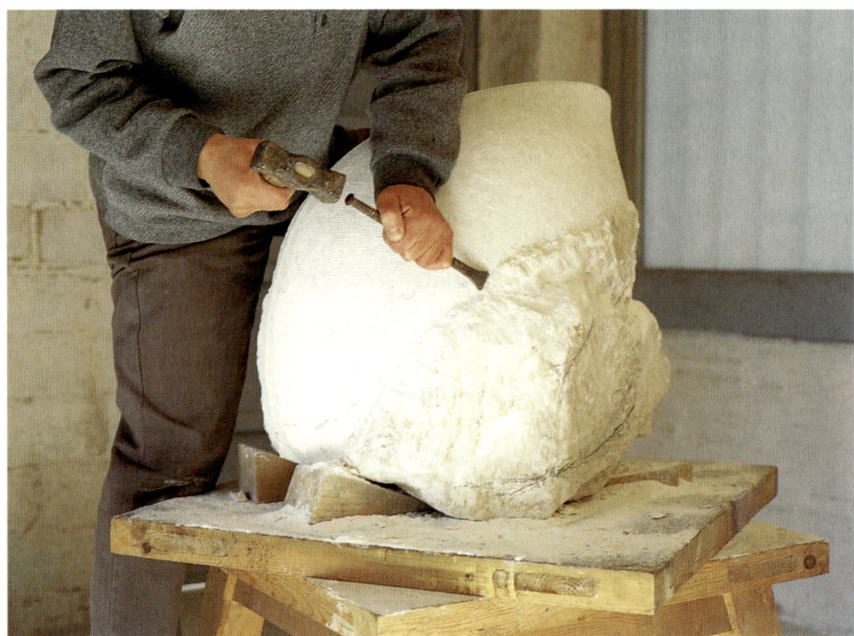

▲ **10.** We start modeling the "crest" with a tooth chisel to rid the alabaster surface of edges that could become damaged under the impact of the point chisel.

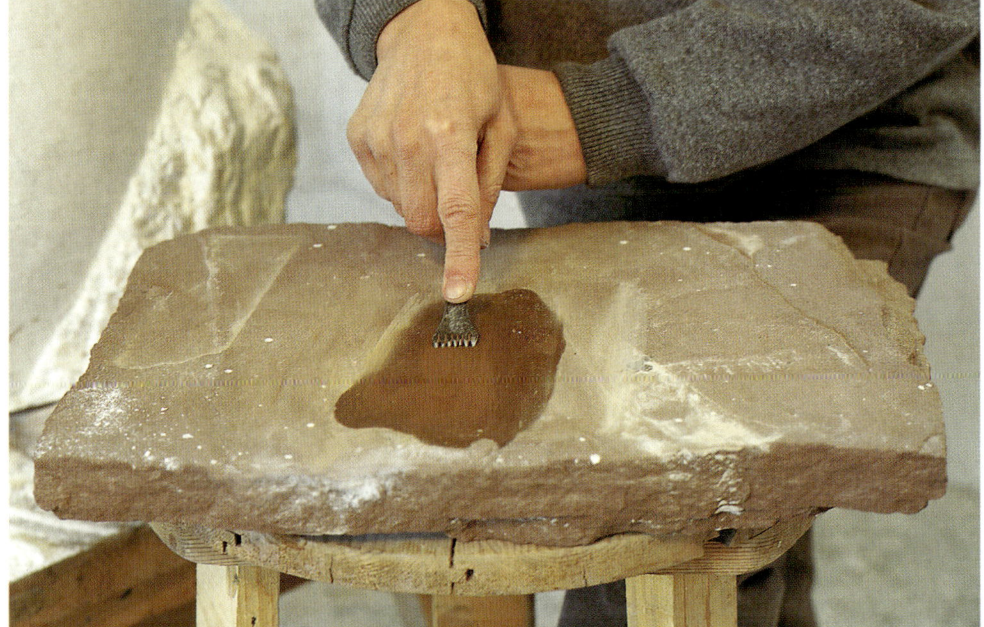

▲ **11.** We then model the back side of the stone with the tooth chisel, from its crest to its base. After this trimming, the stone's ovoid shape becomes more pronounced.

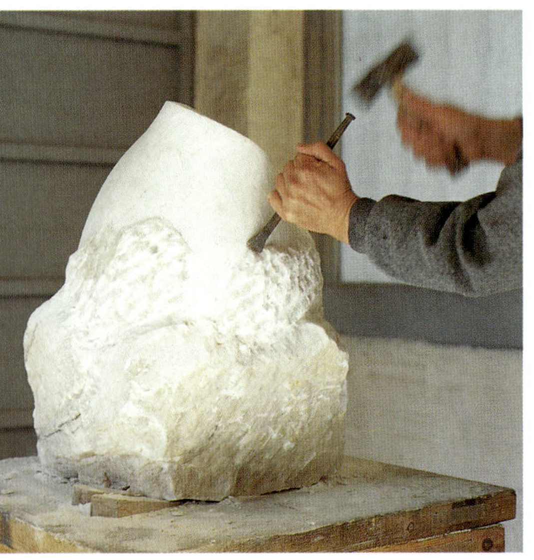

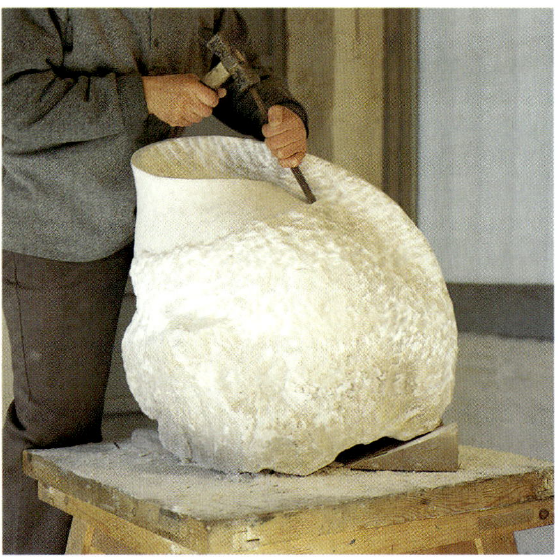

▲ **12.** Because the work now demands added precision, we need to sharpen the tooth chisel from time to time by rubbing it repeatedly over a wet whetting stone, here a sandstone rich in quartz.

◀ **13.** We keep modeling on either side of the stone, trimming the outer surface of the stone with the tooth chisel to erase the markings left by the point chisel.

◀ **14.** To avoid losing overall vision of the work, we continuously rotate the sculpture; at present, we are modeling its back side.

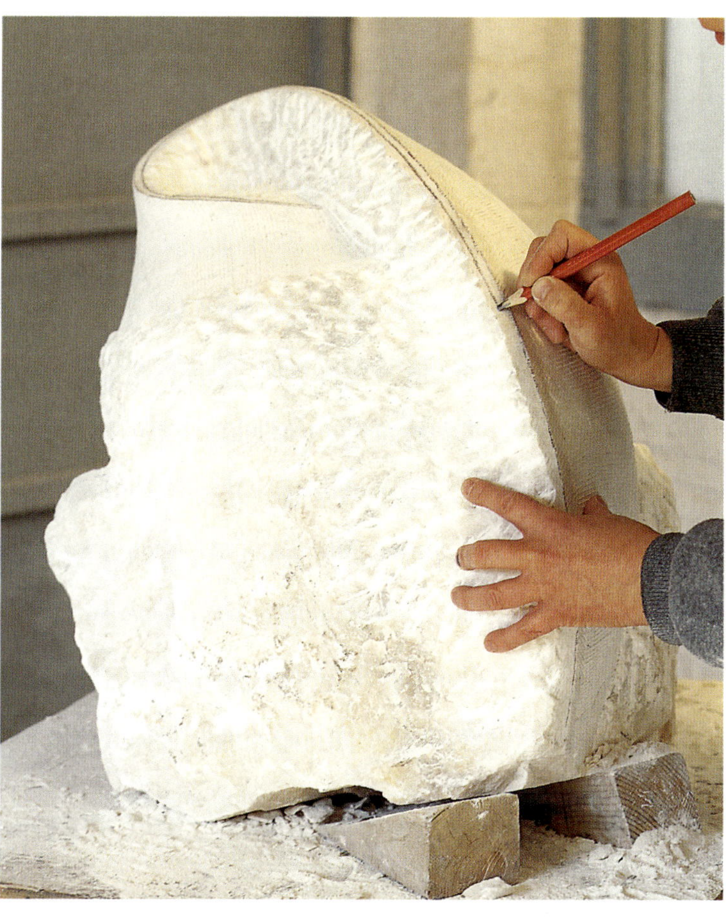

◄ **15.** Before continuing, we use a pencil to delineate the thickness of the crest, leaving a certain safety margin in view of the reduction that will occur later in the smoothing process. Because of the fragile nature of the stone, we do not leave any rough edges.

▼ **16.** We use the tooth chisel to continue modeling the interior of the crest, shaping a vertex running along its entire inside surface. We rest our wrist on the stone to steady our hand when refinishing.

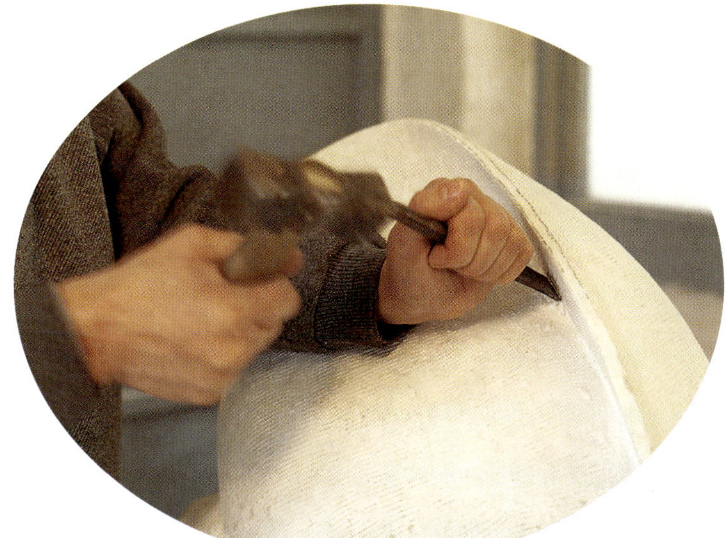

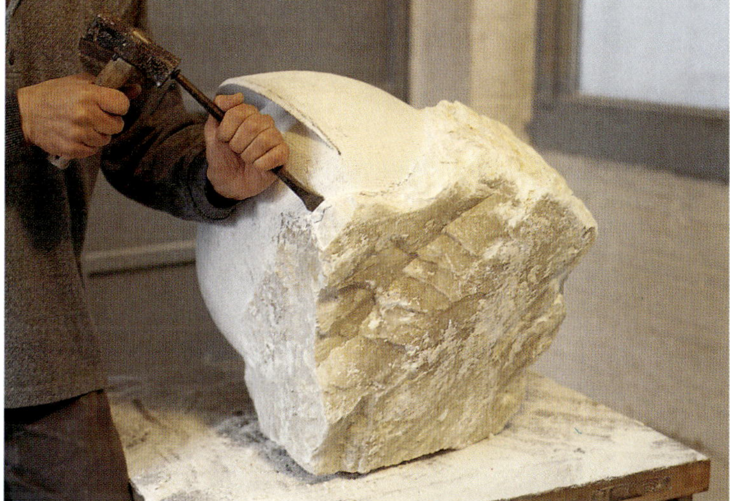

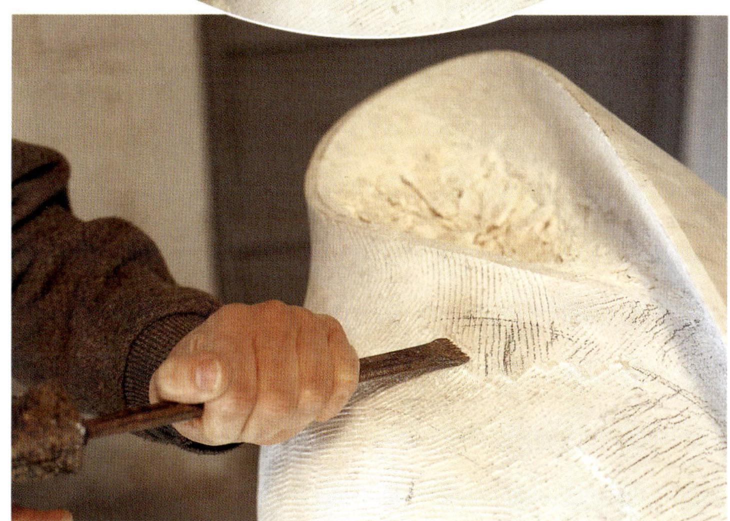

▲ **17.** We turn the block over on its side to make it easier to trim the base. However, when we finish working the base with the tooth chisel and straighten it up, again

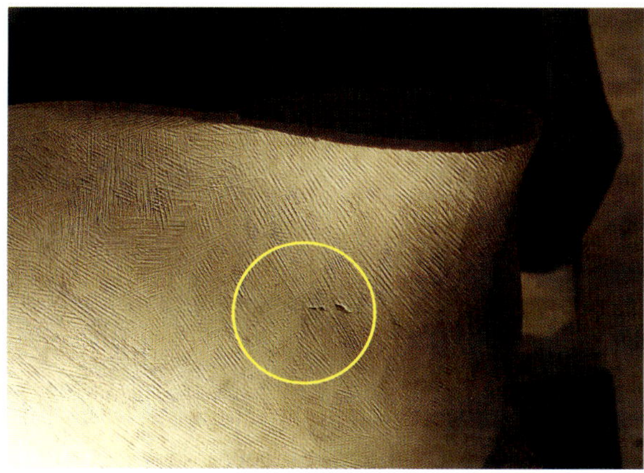

▲ **18.** we detect a surface irregularity that forces us to smooth down an area on the stone's front side. As a result, we use the tooth chisel again to trim down a surface layer about one hundredth of an inch (2–3 mm) deep.

◄ **19.** A tiny hole becomes visible after we file the stone using a rasp. We could eliminate the hole by removing another layer from the area, but we decide to keep it since our goal is to duplicate nature's own forms, including even its imperfections.

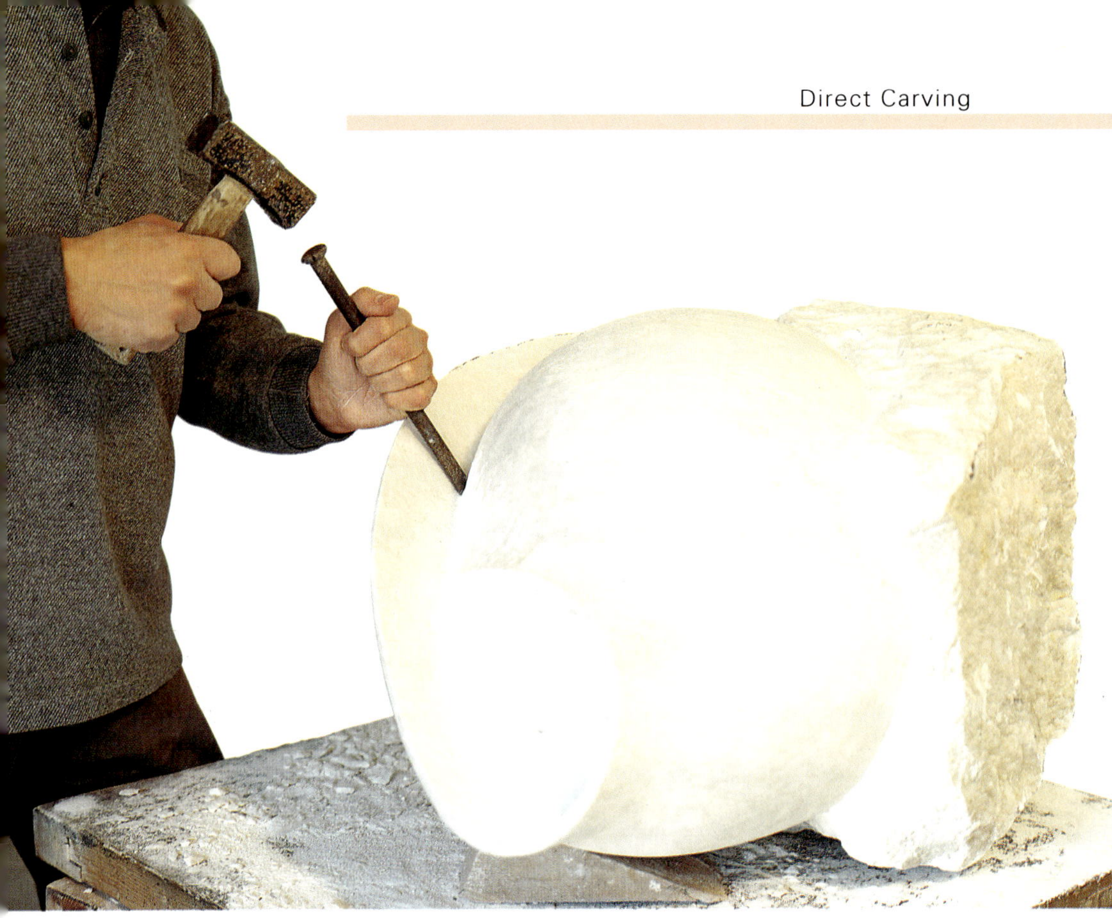

◄ **20.** We turn the block over again making it easier to work, and then we use a chisel to start erasing markings left by the tooth chisel on the inside of the uppermost part of the crest.

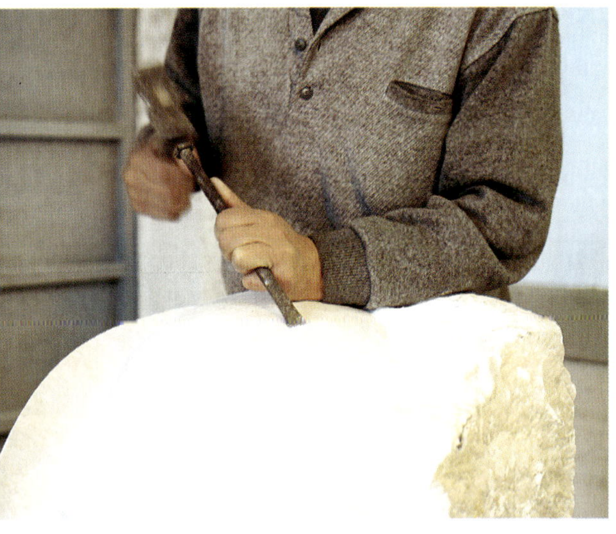

◄ **21.** With the block in the same position, we chisel its front side from top to bottom.

► **22.** We continue doing so until we have erased all of the tooth chisel markings. We do this more out of habit than need since we are dealing with a soft stone and could just as easily use a rasp.

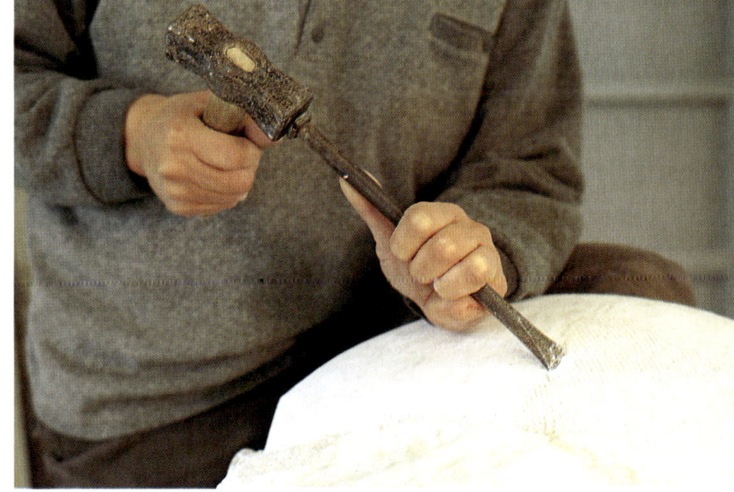

▼ **23.** Then we go on to model the alabaster using a medium-grain carpenter's rasp, starting from the outer side of the top edge.

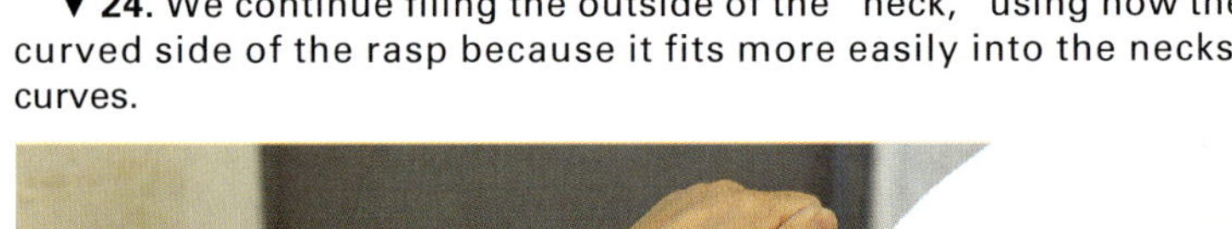

▼ **24.** We continue filing the outside of the "neck," using now the curved side of the rasp because it fits more easily into the necks' curves.

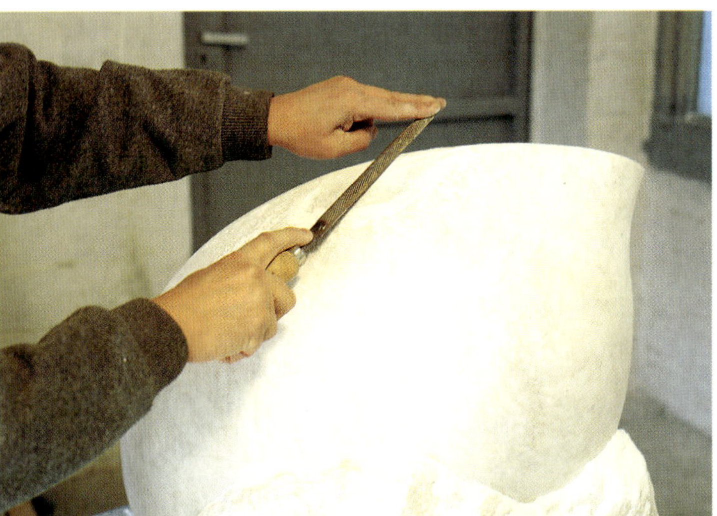

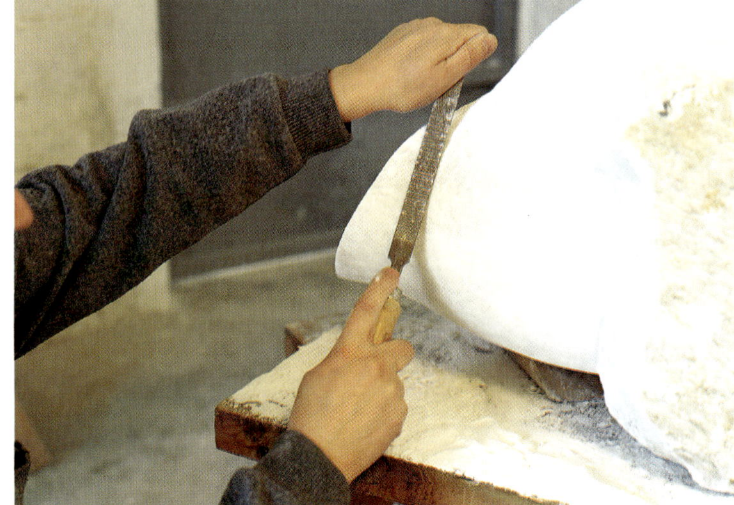

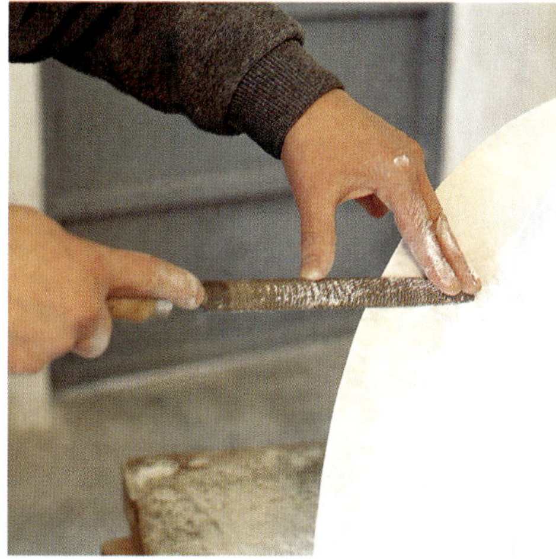

▲ **25**. We also model the inside of the crest's, using here the upper part of the rasp.

► **26.** We finish modeling the lower part of the sculpture rotating the rasp from the inside out.

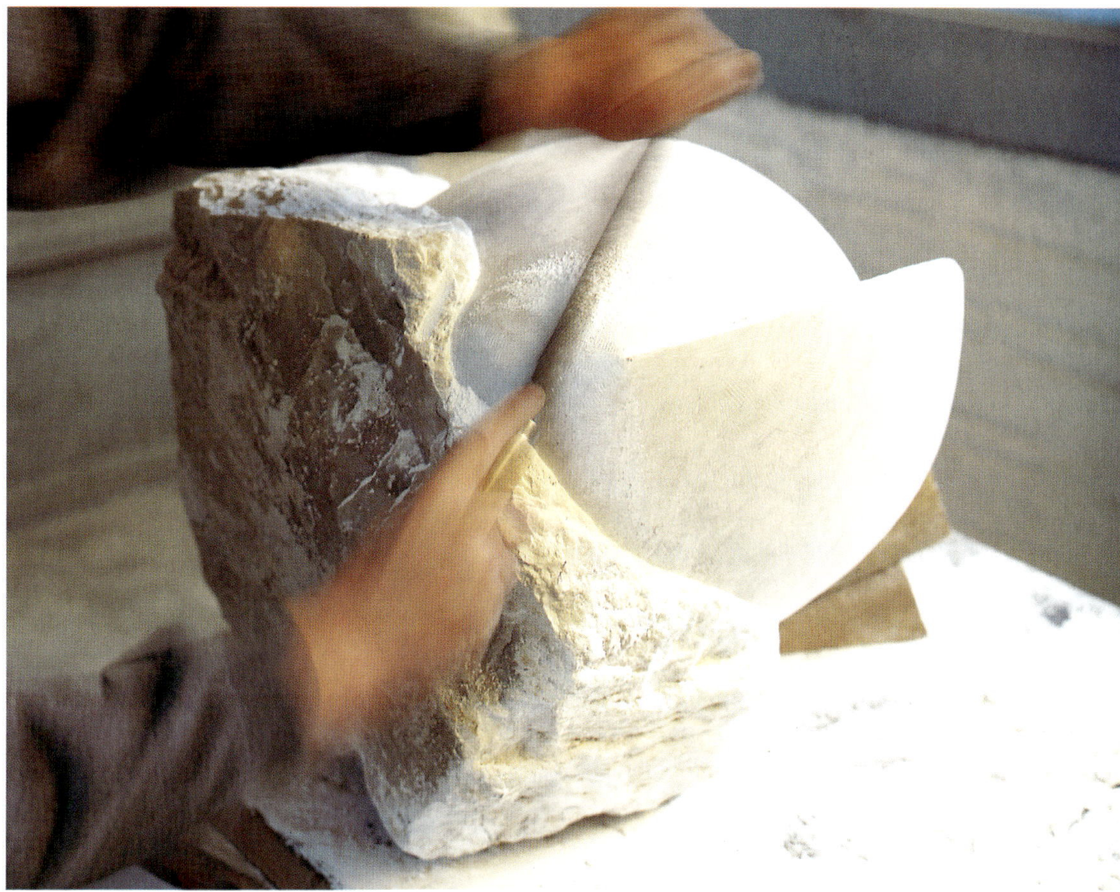

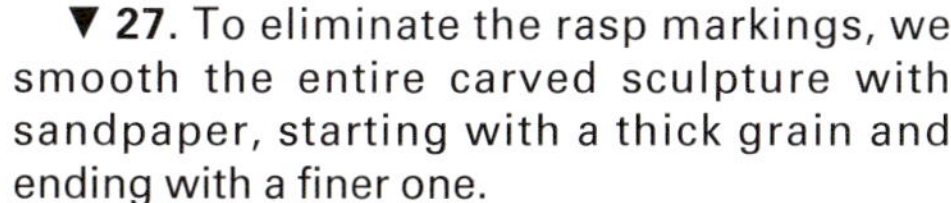

▼ **27.** To eliminate the rasp markings, we smooth the entire carved sculpture with sandpaper, starting with a thick grain and ending with a finer one.

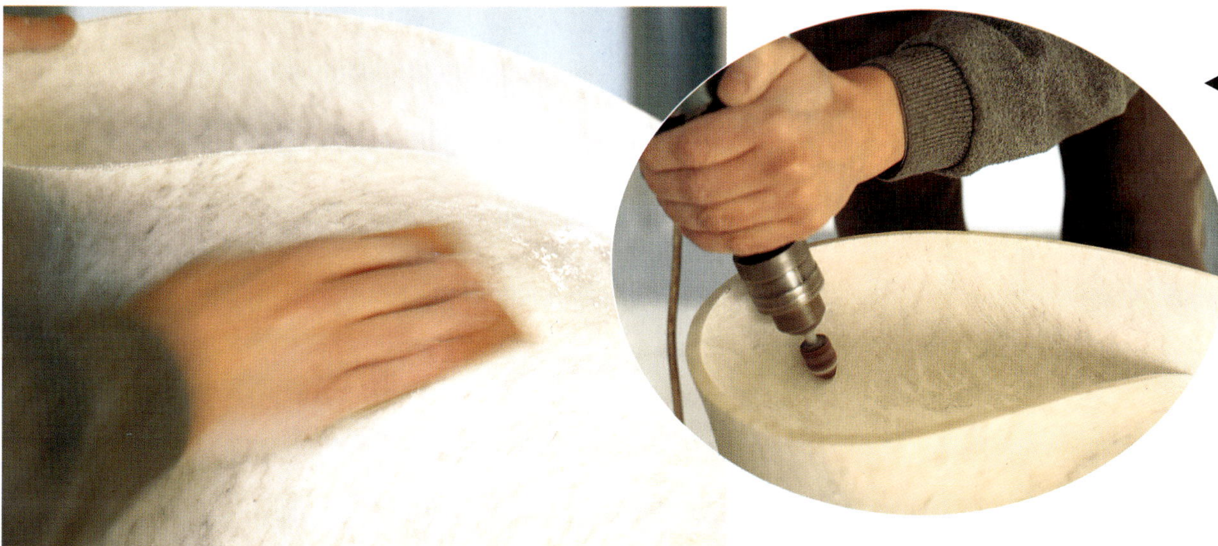

◄ **28**. Now we smooth the inside of the concavity with a drill whose rubber bit attachment has an emery coating. We could have achieved the same result using sandpaper.

► **29.** To give luster to the stone we buff it with sandpaper that we use with water that, in this case, has been mounted on a curved wooden support. At the same time we rub a wet sponge on the alabaster's surface. The alabaster, which seemed to have a consistent color, now exhibits a variety of hues.

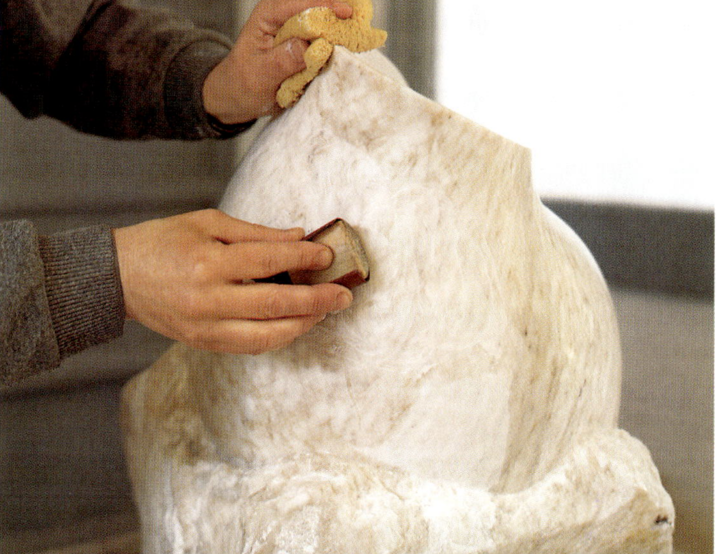

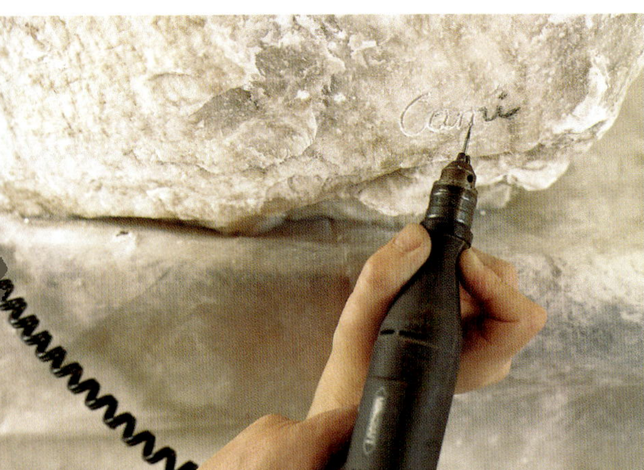

▲ **30.** Although we could sign the work with a chisel, we prefer to do it with a small steel drill bit. When signing a work this way, it is advisable to do a test beforehand, because the drill may be too difficult to control.

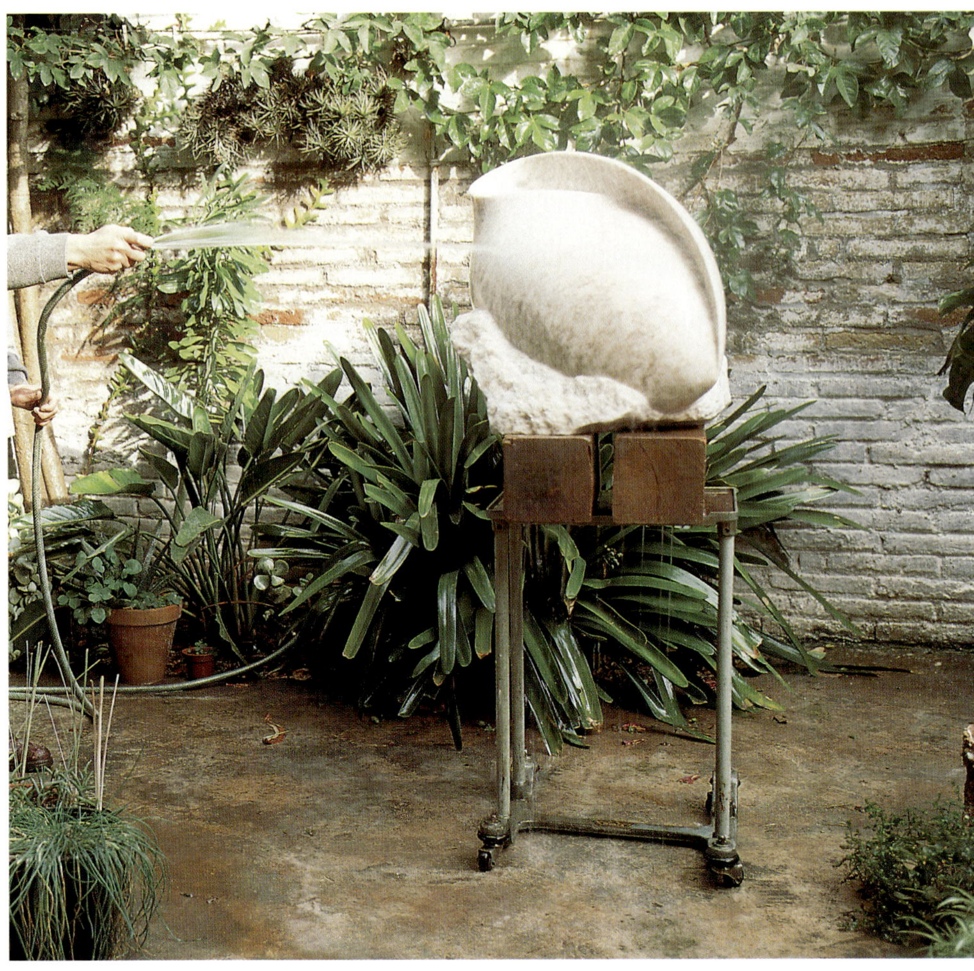

► **31.** The finished sculpture needs to be cleaned with either water or compressed air, which we will do in a follow-up exercise.

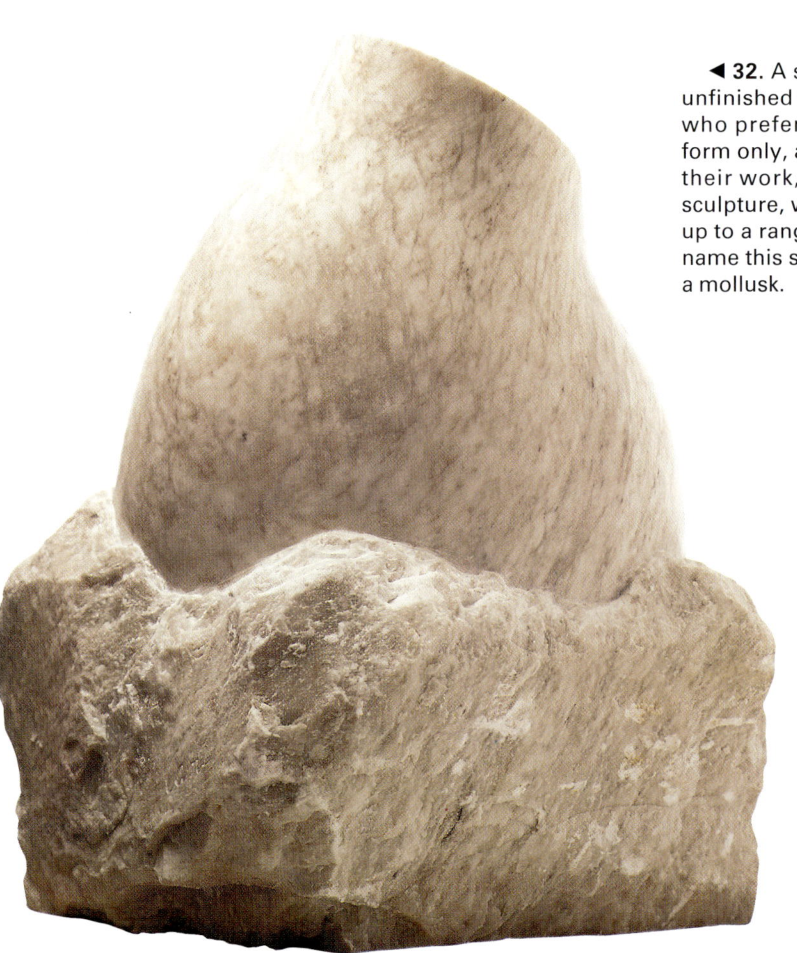

◄ **32.** A sculpture without a title is like an unfinished work. While we understand those who prefer to express themselves through form only, and shy away from giving a title to their work, we prefer to give a name to our sculpture, which, in all likelihood, will open it up to a range of interpretations. We decide to name this sculpture *Limpet*, which is a kind of a mollusk.

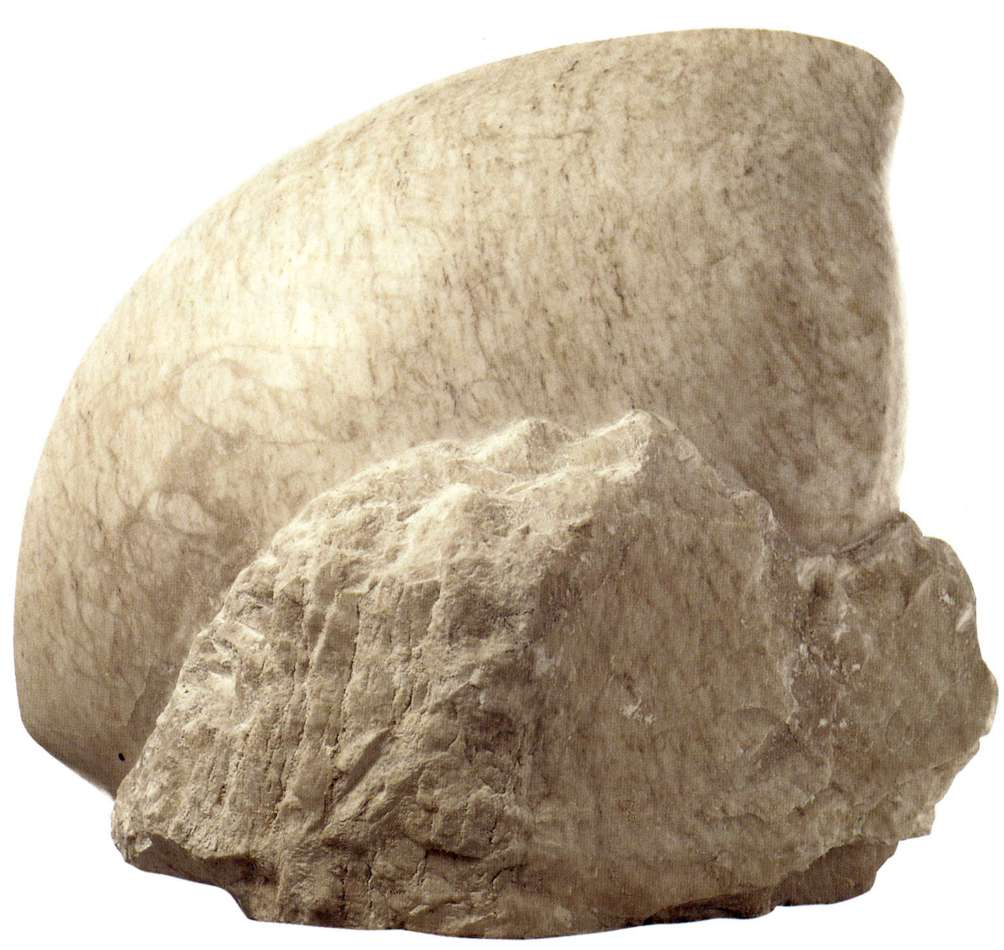

◄ Camí
Limpet, 1998.
Alabaster.
20 × 18 × 16 inches
(50 × 47 × 40 cm).

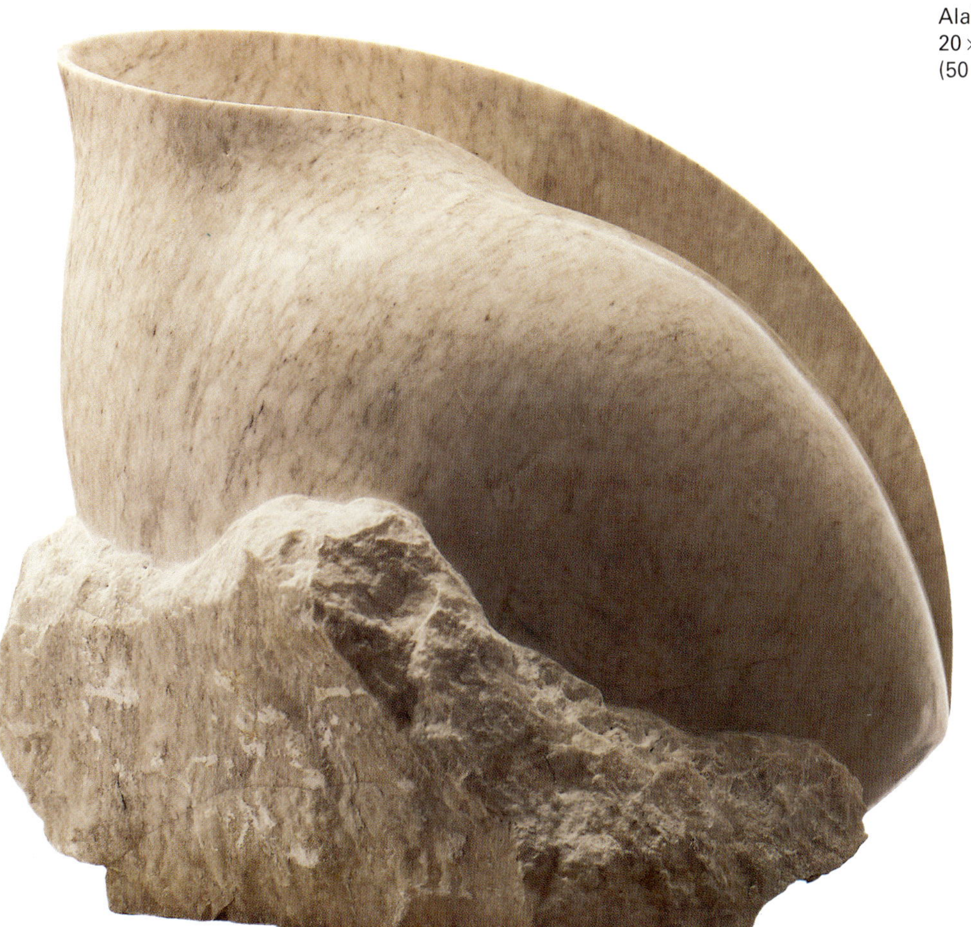

Carving by Templates

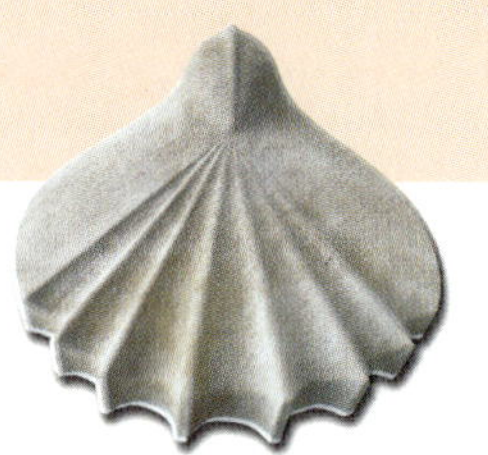

The objective of this exercise is twofold: to carve a stone with the help of a template and to benefit from the expertise of the Feliu stone-cutting studio. Thanks to the studio's various tools, here we will learn how to carve grooves or edges in stone and transform a rectangular block into a hemisphere. These exercises, which represent basic steps in a carver's training, will also help us produce a scalloped sculpture.

The craft of stone carving has been handed down from generation to generation, transmitted as if by a virus. From the hands of master craftsmen have come imaginative Romanesque capitals, heraldic coats-of-arms masterfully sculpted, or baptismal fonts that serve as the inspiration for the sculpture we will carve here.

We pay homage to this noble craft and avail ourselves of its techniques by calling on the Feliu Martin studio to do our carving. Feliu learned how to carve from his father Felix, who learned the trade from his father Felip. He also inherited from them what we can best describe as a "passion" for a job filled with sweat and dust and that to an outsider would seem totally unrewarding.

The Martin family has demonstrated its technical skill in the restoration of Cistercian monasteries. They have also confirmed or refuted theories of learned historians by studying the tool markings of antiquity.

Let's observe now in this step-by-step demonstration how Feliu worked under our watchful eye and that of his elders to carve a sandstone sculpture, using only the sketches and templates we gave him as a guide.

▲ Self-portrait in sandstone of Reynard de Fonoll, master builder at the Santes Creus Gothic cloister in Spain, holding a bell-shaped hammer.

Feliu, who as an adolescent carved a sphere as a test from his father, uses modern carving techniques. However, for this exercise we have asked him to employ traditional ones.

We start by selecting a block that is "live" and large enough for our purpose. After verifying its measurements at 10 × 30 × 25 inches (27 × 75 × 62 cm), we strike the stone and listen for a sound that would tell us whether it's cracked or not. Then we inspect the stone carefully to see whether it has any hairline fractures, in which case we would reject it. With this particular type of stone, we know that the arrangement of its sedimentation layers will tell us the best way to direct the hammer blows.

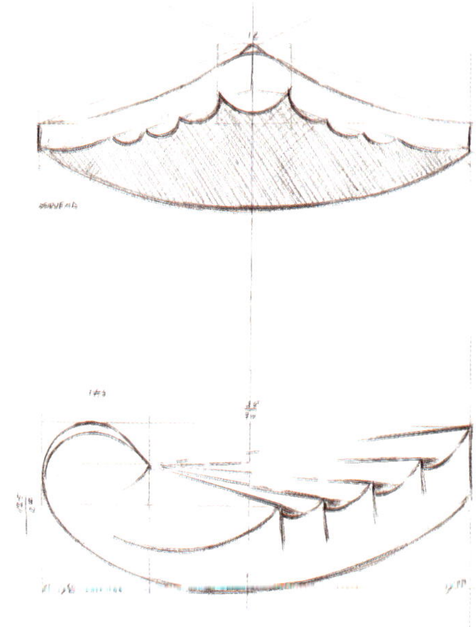

▶ With the dimensions of our chosen block in mind, we have sketched our idea for the model in this drawing and in a template that we have given to Feliu.

▼ Feliu, Felix, and Felip Martin, three generations of a family of stone-carving enthusiasts, will share their expertise with us in a step-by-step demonstration.

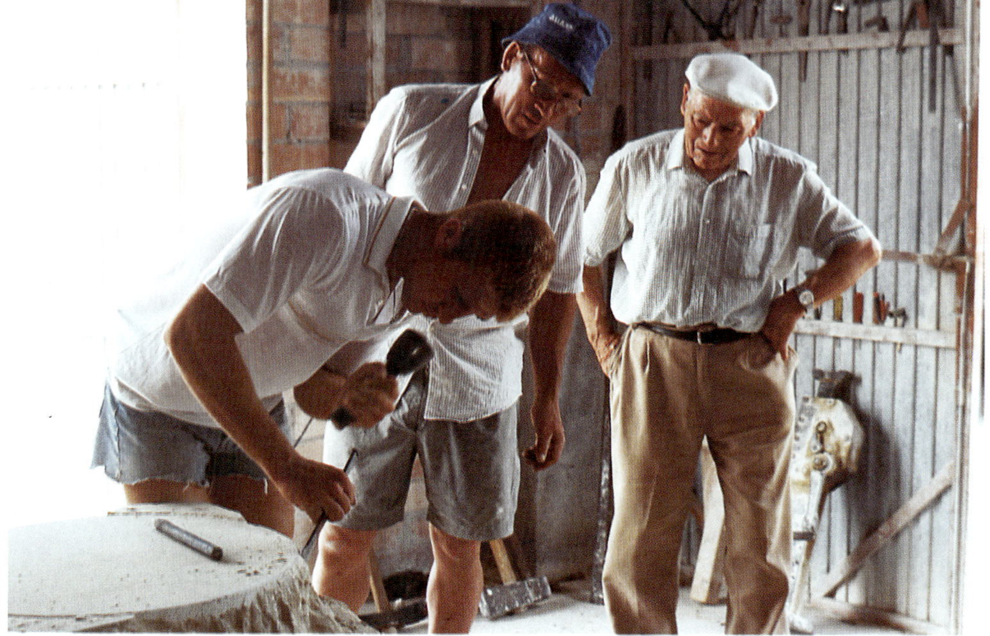

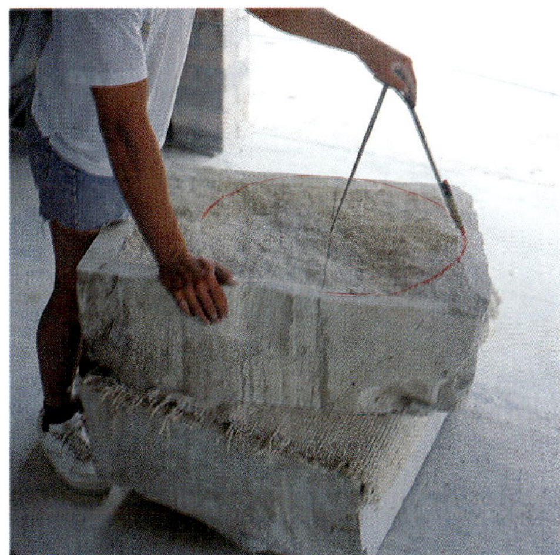

▲ **1.** When we are sure the stone is suitable for the project, we mark the points of symmetry in black and the perimeter in red and begin to outline.

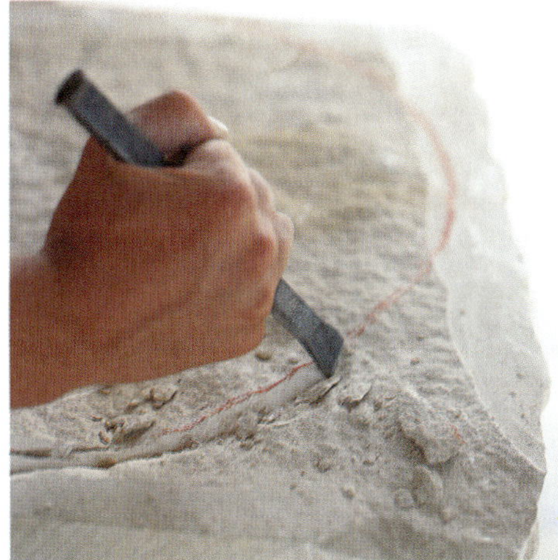

▲ **2.** We go over the outline we drew with a chisel. The resulting groove, or master line, will allow us to rough out the stone later without any fear of crossing over the perimeter line.

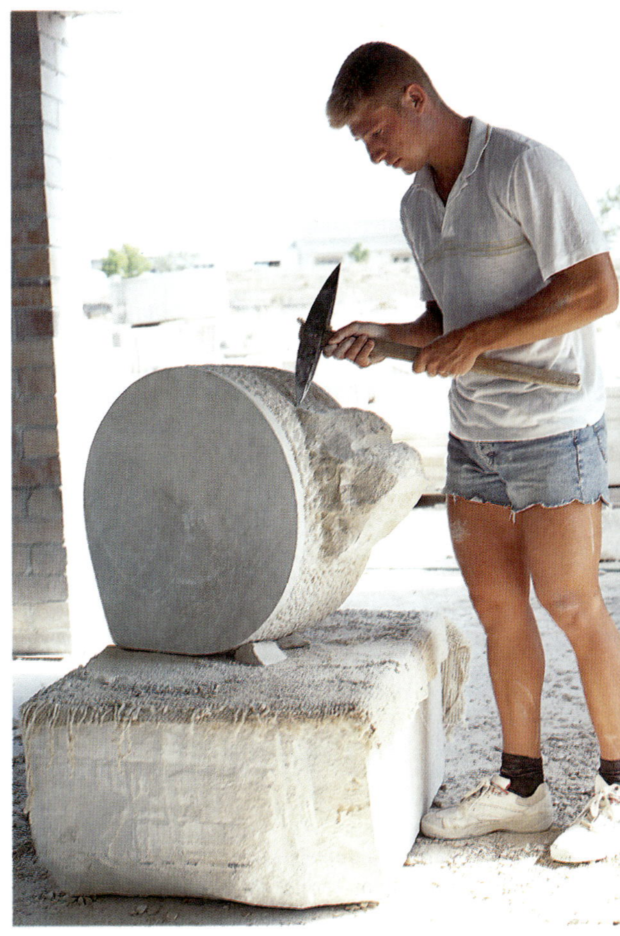

► **3.** Feliu has already cut back the unwanted material using a stonecutters' hammer; others have reduced the stone more slowly using a mallet and a point chisel. The most important thing right now is to stay inside the circle or master line.

▼ **4.** Using a template drawn on a 1:1 scale over cardboard and then cut out, we transfer the silhouette to the stone. The semicircles, marked in red, show us the areas to be trimmed out in order to achieve a series of arcs.

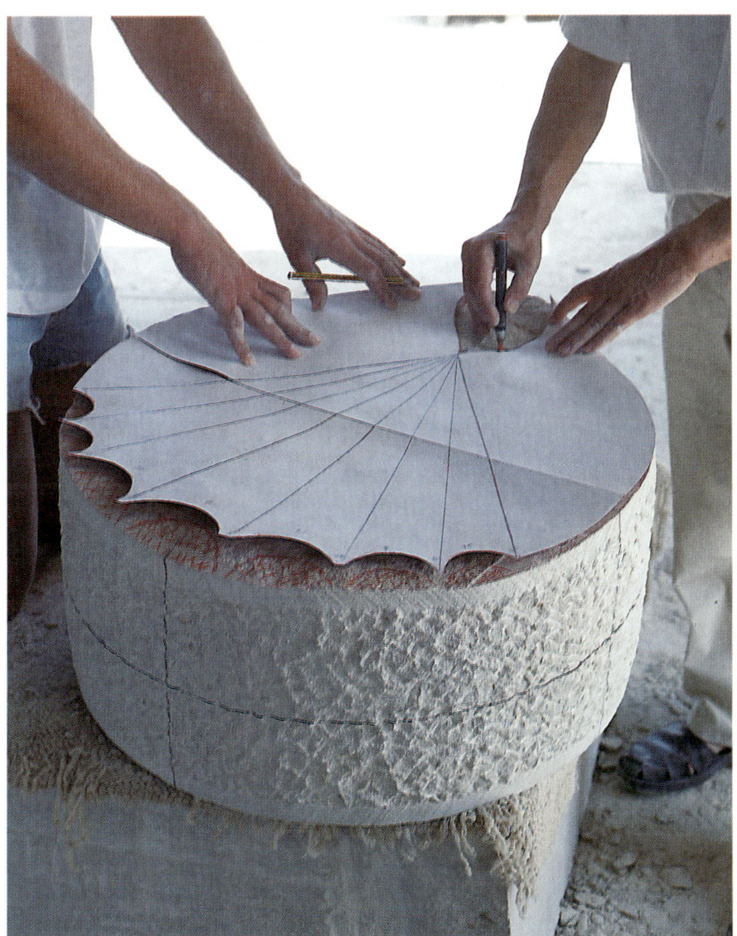

▼ **5.** After theorizing on the calligraphy of the quarry, Feliu tests our understanding. We had to decide which tools were used based on the markings left behind: (1) first, a chisel to mark the master line; (2) then, a point chisel to rough out the stone (the chisel marks are still visible on the middle arc); (3) finally, a tooth chisel to give the largest arc its curved shape.

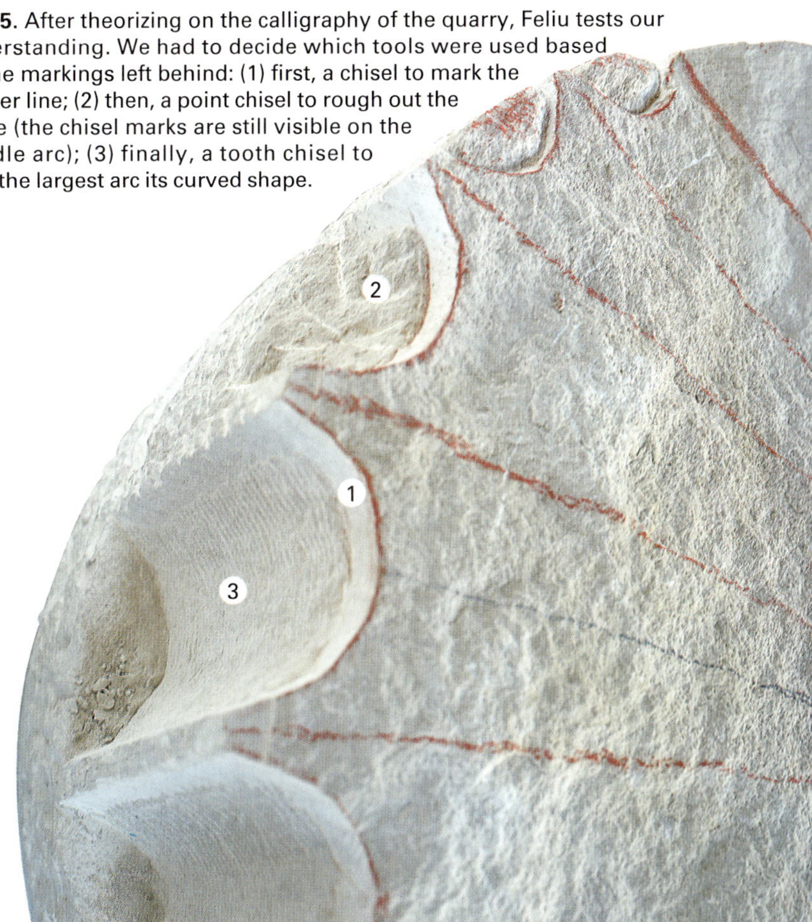

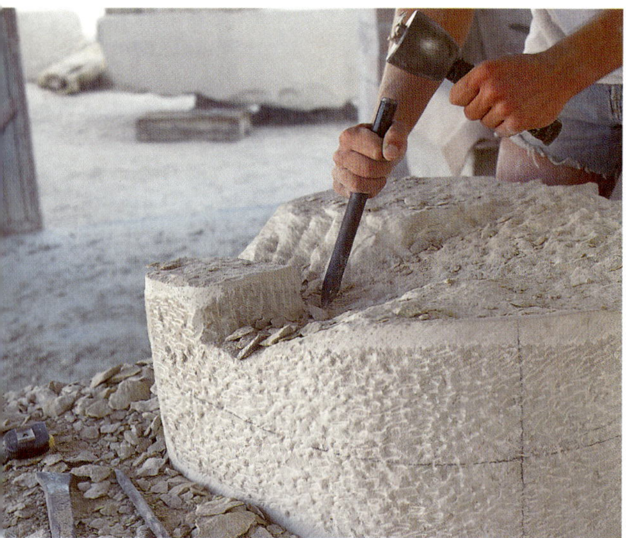

▲ **6.** After using a chisel to incise the master line of what we will call the head, we use a point chisel to carve out the main form until we reach the deepest point to be roughed out according to the sectional sketch. In this way the head takes shape and emerges from the material around it.

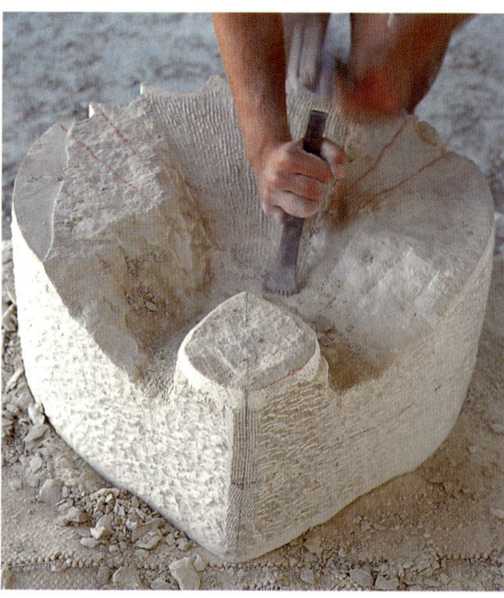

▲ **7.** Next we try to fashion an inclined plane between the back edge and the deepest point of the area next to the head. To do this, Feliu first uses a tooth chisel to carve out a central groove that he now widens. He will then use a stonecutters' hammer or a point chisel to remove the rest of the material.

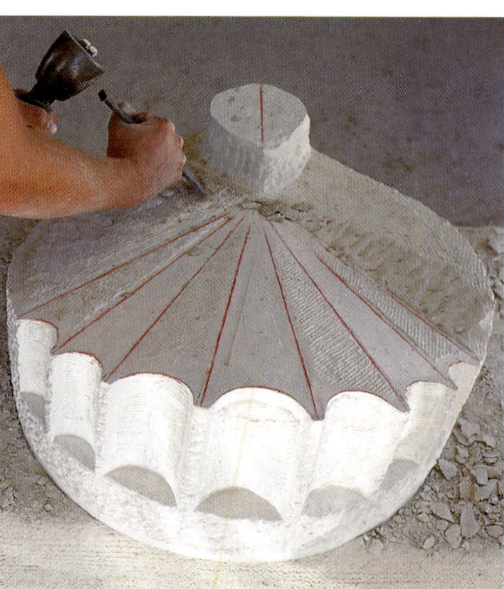

▲ **8.** After fashioning an inclined surface, we chisel out new master lines, whose center will be determined by future edges, and trace over them in red. We will continue roughing out using a point chisel, ignoring the base.

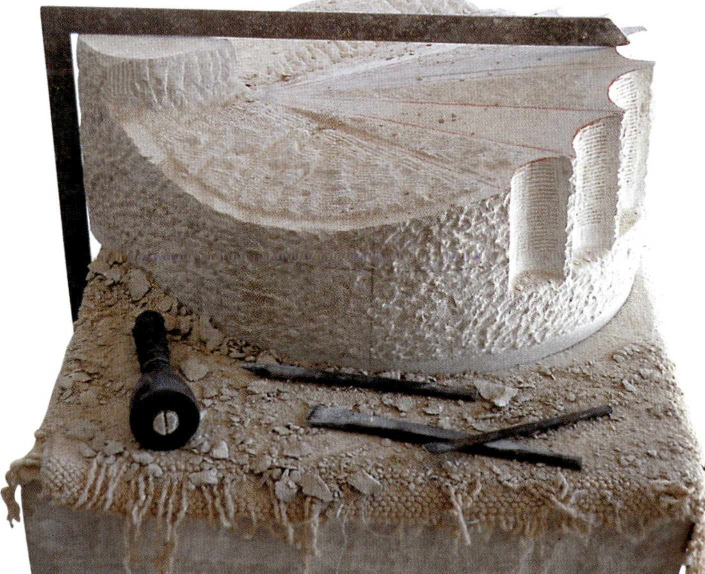

◀ **9.** The uppermost part of the work is now carved. The square confirms that the head and the side opposite it are on the same plane, with the inner cavity showing the roughed-out volume.

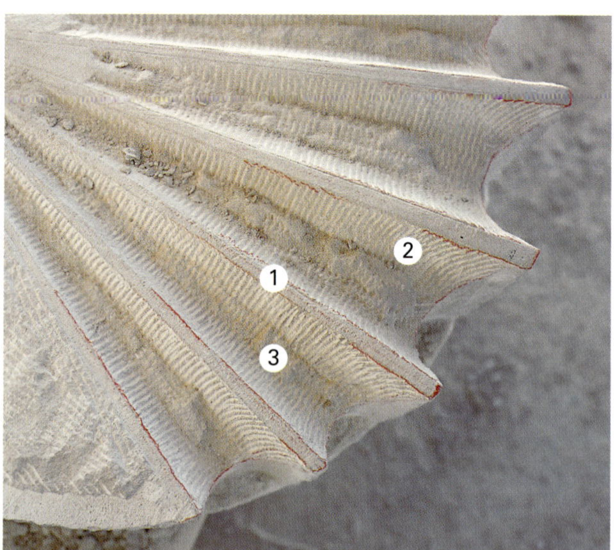

▲ **10.** We use a tooth chisel to give a scalloped shape to the surface, from the edge to its deepest point. Now the master lines, drawn in red (1), suddenly emerge (2), as we carve out the space separating them. At the deepest part (3) the impacts of the tooth chisel have not crisscrossed, something that would require more precision.

◀ **11.** Now we use a curved chisel to clean the inside of the grooves from the outside in, going in as far as the width of the chisel will allow.

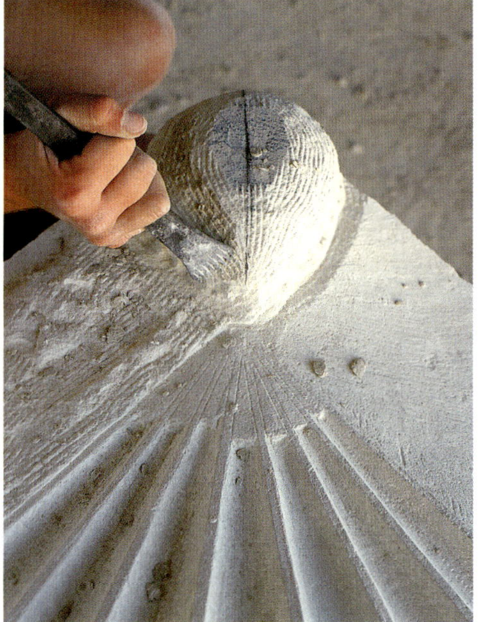

▲ **12.** We use a tooth chisel to carve the head, using the symmetrical center as a point of reference.

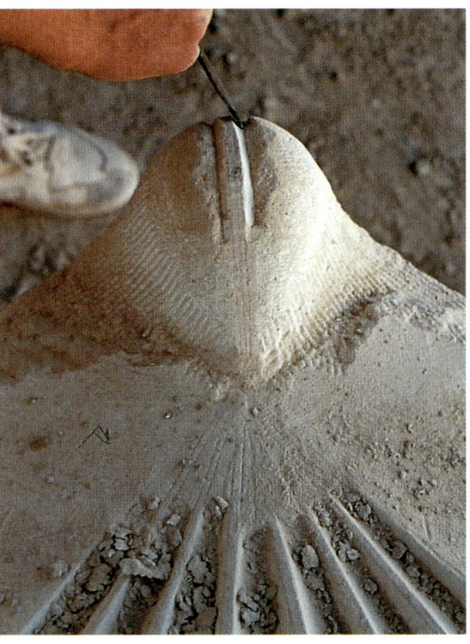

▲ **13.** We chisel out a slice around the axis, which we will later sculpt into the shape of a crest.

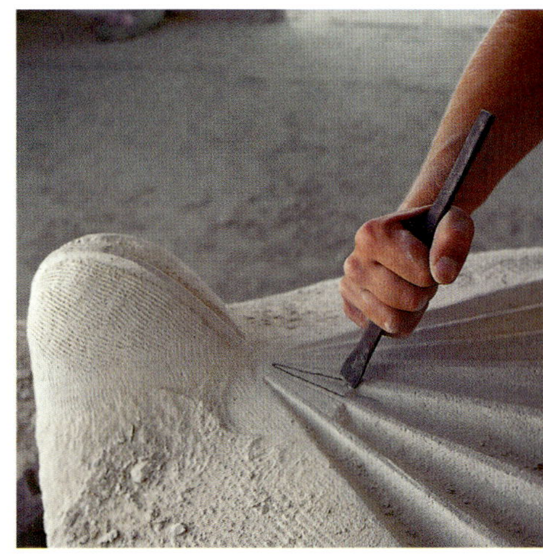

▲ **14.** Since we have already defined the dominant volumes, we turn our attention now to the details, using a chisel to groove the vertices that require greater precision.

► **15.** The crest is now cut; the volumes begin to take shape. Thus, the sculptor and the stonemason vie to find defects that they immediately rectify using a tooth chisel.

◄ **16.** Feliu attends to the final details and meticulously goes over the surface with a tooth chisel; the texture of some areas is already finished.

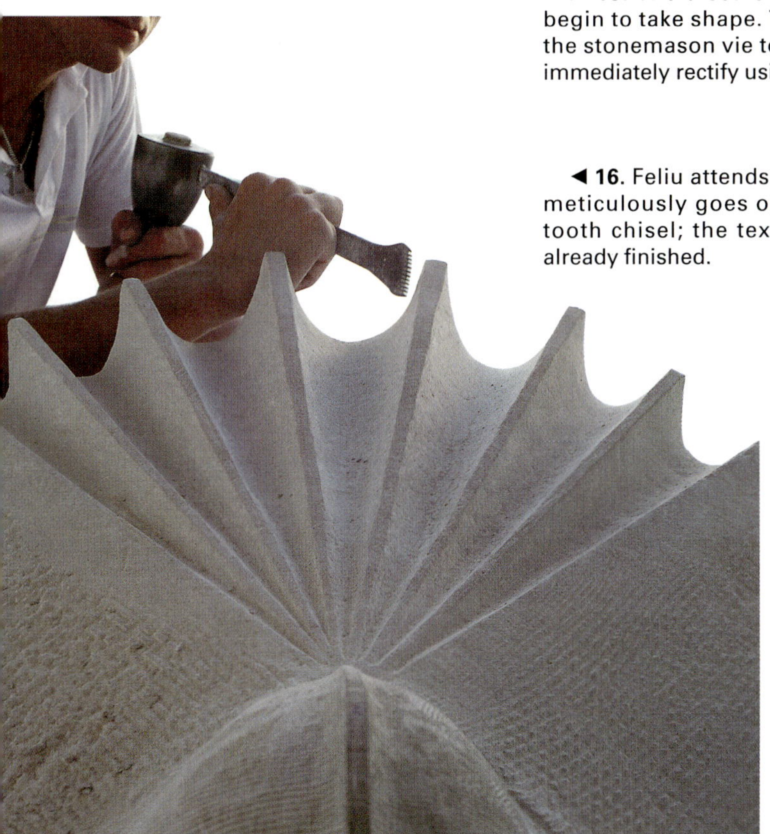

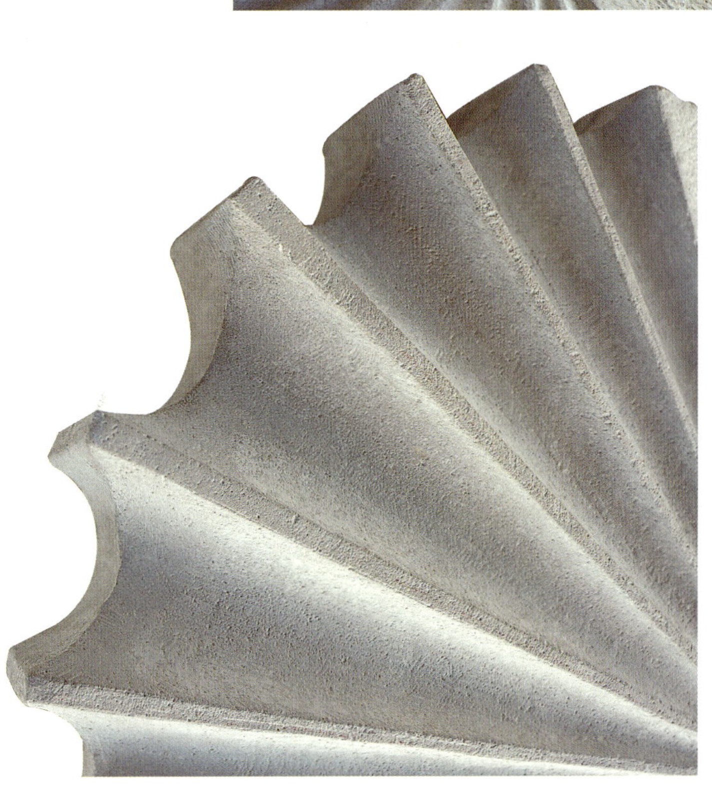

► **17.** We finish modeling the upper part of the sculpture. We still have to sand the edges, but before we do that we want to give the other side a hemispheric shape and leave one support surface flat.

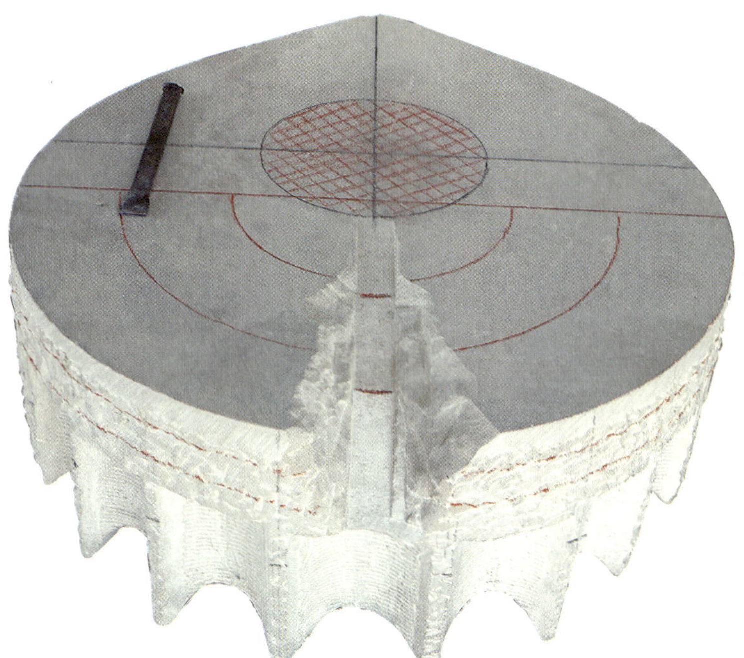

◀ **18.** We start work on the back side by marking axes, some for determining the off-center base (these are marked in red), and others for maintaining symmetry. Recalling what he learned about hemispheres, Feliu draws red half-circles to indicate the depth of the different levels that need to be roughed out. Some are located close to the bottom and others higher up. However, when we use the tooth chisel to carve out a central groove, they meet. This groove will guide us through the roughing-out phase.

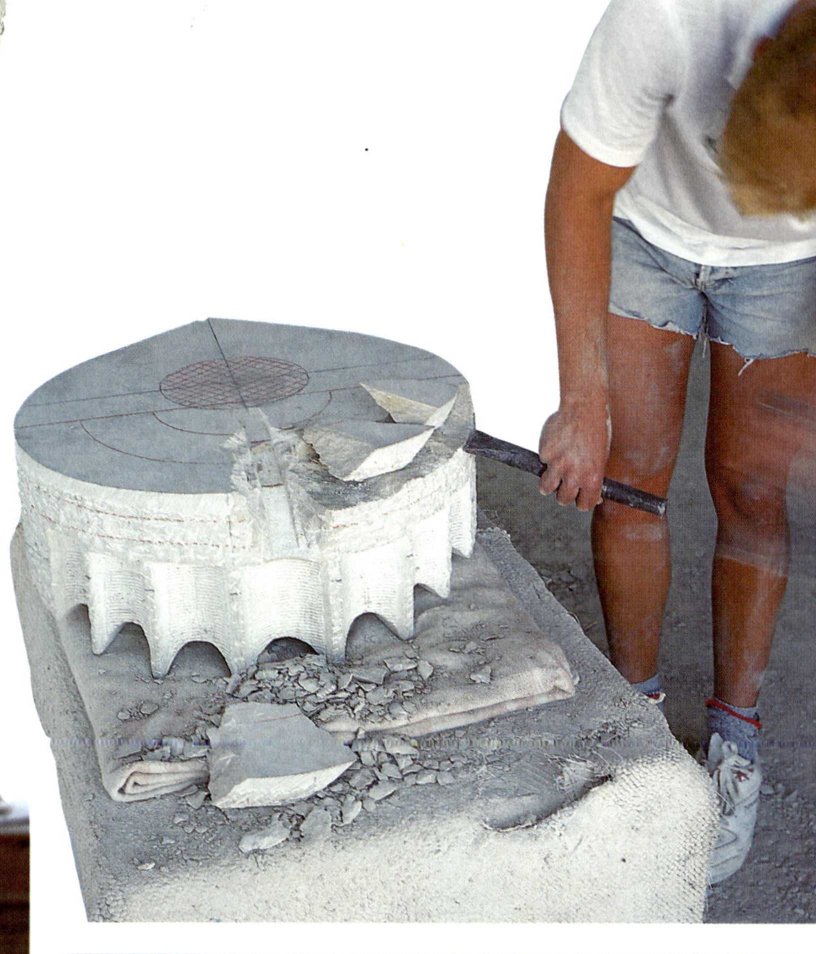

▶ **19.** Finding the polyhedron is the first step toward producing the sphere, and without going beyond the limits of the groove, the stone is reduced. Here is where the skill of a stonemason is fully appreciated; with a good understanding of the stone's law, he knows just the right angle to hold the trimmer and lifts out large chunks of stone.

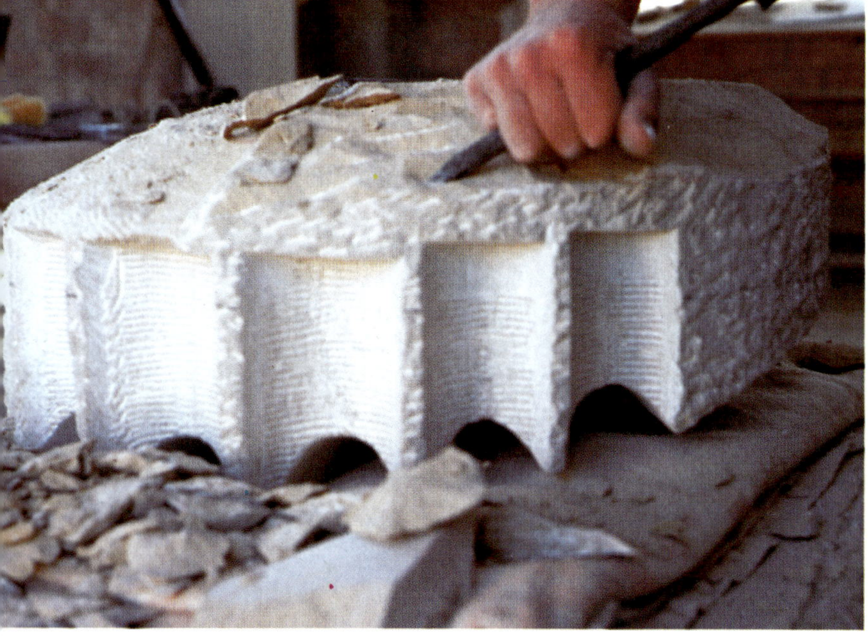

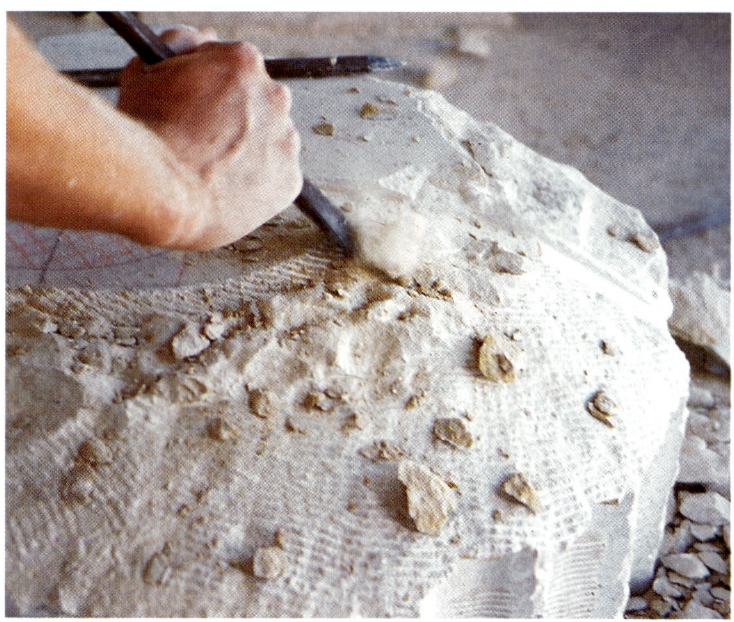

▲ ▶ **20.** For greater precision, we use a point chisel and a tooth chisel.

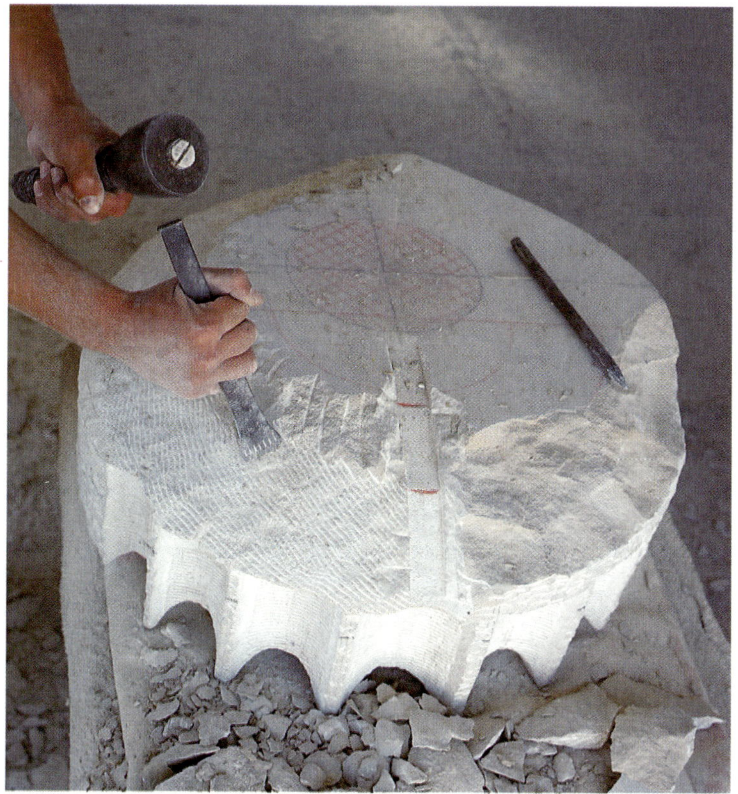

▲ **21.** We worked half of the surface with a point chisel. Now, however, we use a tooth chisel, which is more precise, to smooth out the left half, then we will continue with the rest.

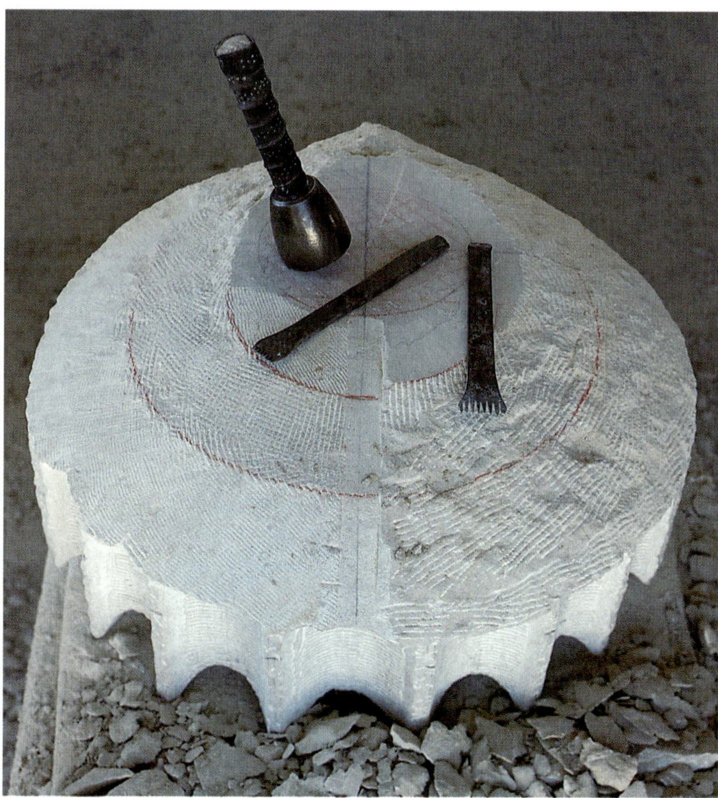

▲ **22.** We have shaped a polyhedron that, through careful gradation, we will later shape into an oblique hemisphere. Then we will use a tooth chisel to trim the edges so that as we even them out, the volume we are looking for will take shape.

◀ **23.** We add a few more touches to the areas marked in red to even out the curved shape. The strata left to be cut is a reminder to us of the depth of our chisel work.

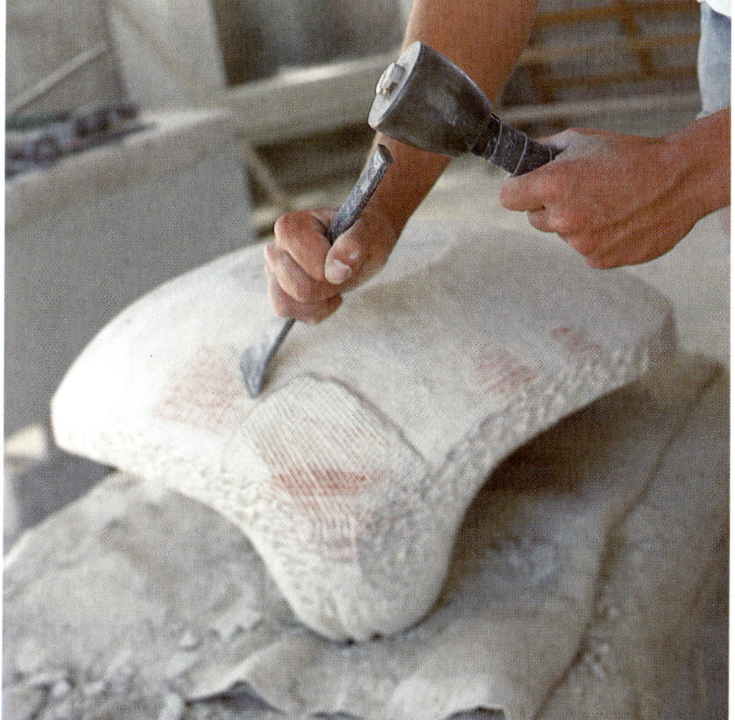

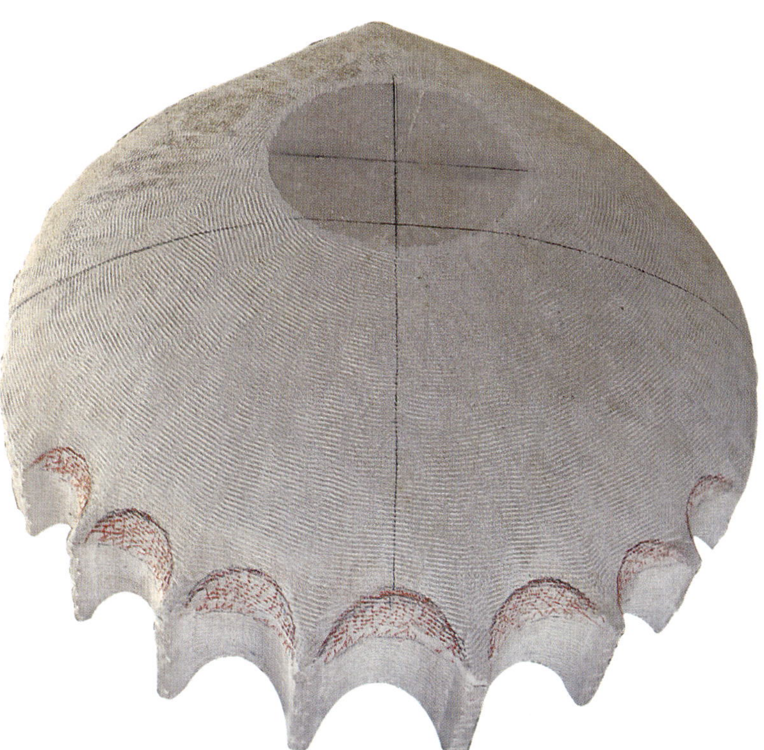

► **24.** We redraw the axes to look for possible irregularities and we refinish the hemispheric surface where we see the fine marks left by the tooth chisel. We still have to model and work the areas marked in red with the tooth chisel.

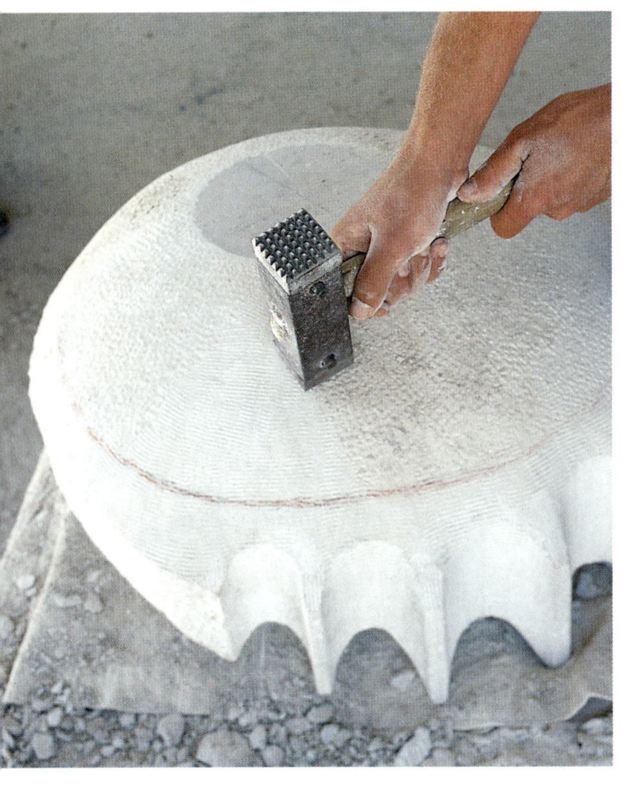

◀ **25**. Feliu works the final texture with soft, rhythmical blows of a bush-hammer; he uses a thick grain for the center and a fine grain for the perimeter outlined in red. After listening to the harmonic sound that is produced, Felix and Felip approve Feliu's work, which has not injured the block during the process. According to both men, the stone "rings clear."

▶ **26**. With a toothed trencher, the hammer commonly used in quarry work, we give texture to the center area of the upper part of the figure. We use a bush-hammer for the rest.

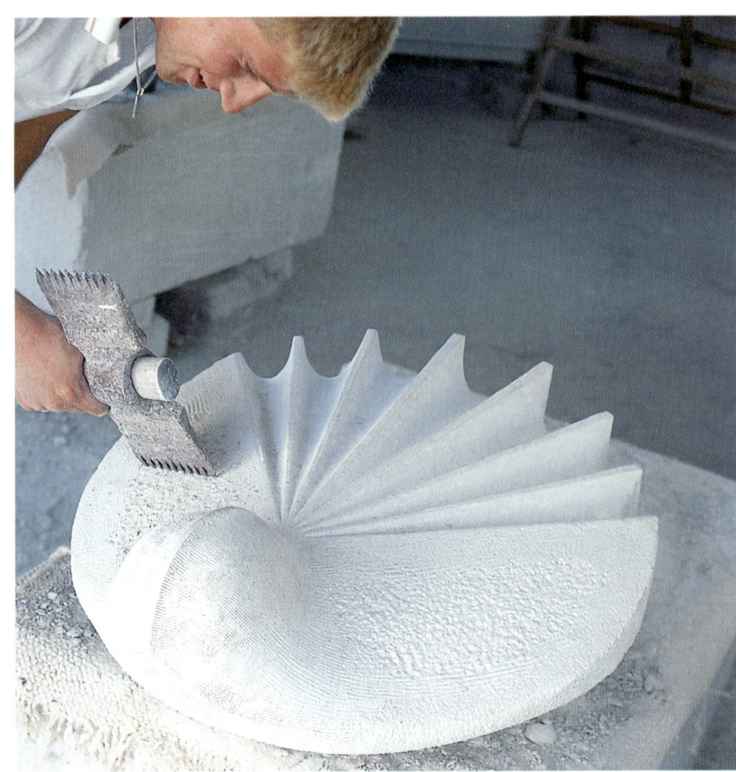

▶ **27**. Final touches: With an abrasive stone and with sandpaper, we trim the edges and attend to the last details. It would have been risky to do this before.

◀ **28**. Finally, we model the half reeds by passing a thick-grained abrasive stone over them lengthwise and polish them with a finer stone.

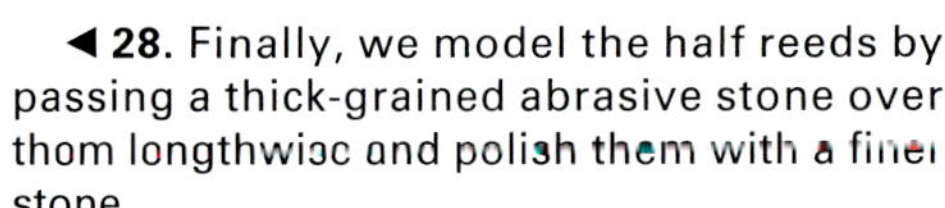

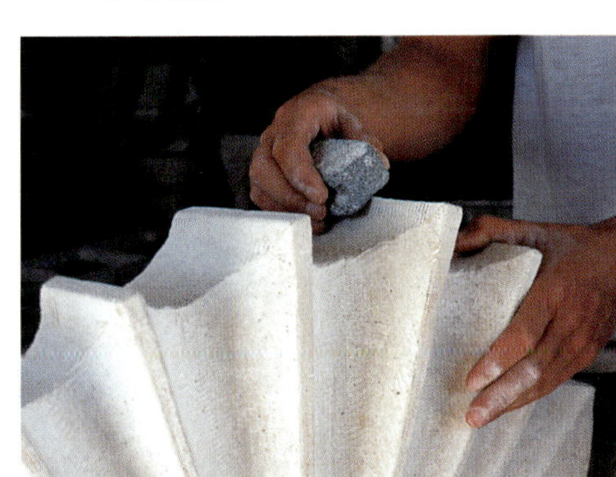

▶ **29**. Both sculptor and stonemason are satisfied with the work, which was done in the town of La Floresta (Lleida, Spain) using local sandstone, and sign the piece with a very fine point chisel. The sculptor signs his name and the stonemason leaves a distinguishing mark based on an ancestral quarry tradition.

▶ **30**. The serene color, firm but soft shapes, and its appearance insinuating a cupola, fossil, shell, dove, and baptismal font suggest the name we give to the work: *Peacemaker*.

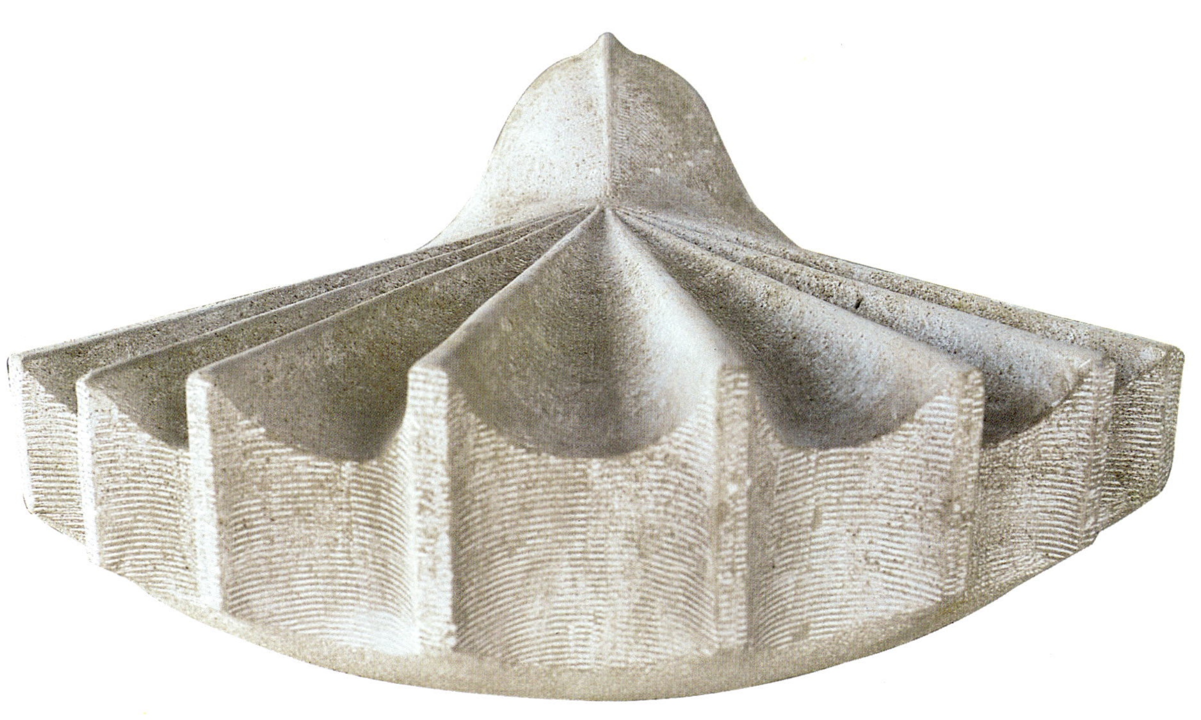

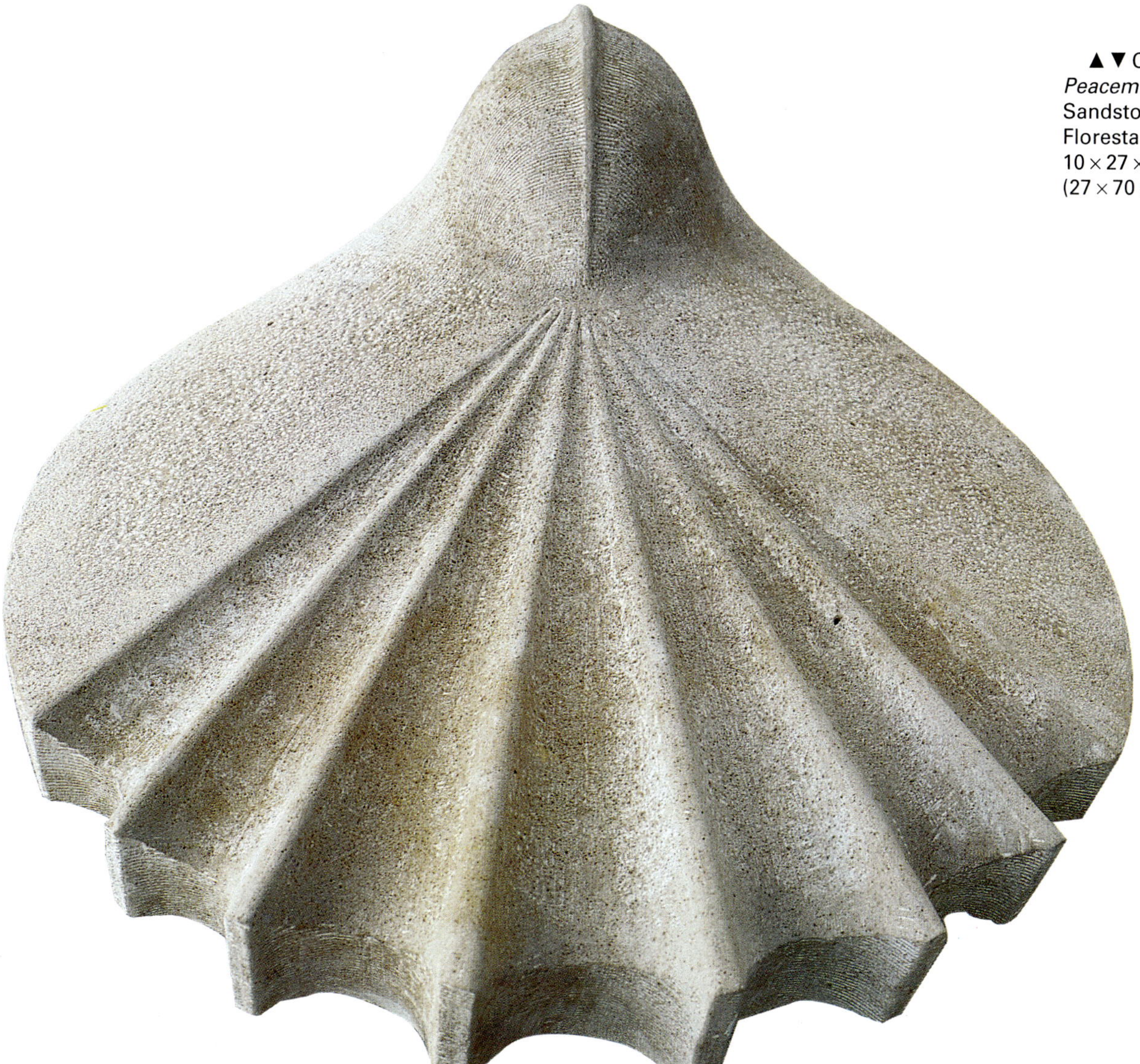

▲▼ Camí
Peacemaker. 1998.
Sandstone from La Floresta (Spain).
10 × 27 × 24 inches
(27 × 70 × 60 cm).

Enlarging by Squares

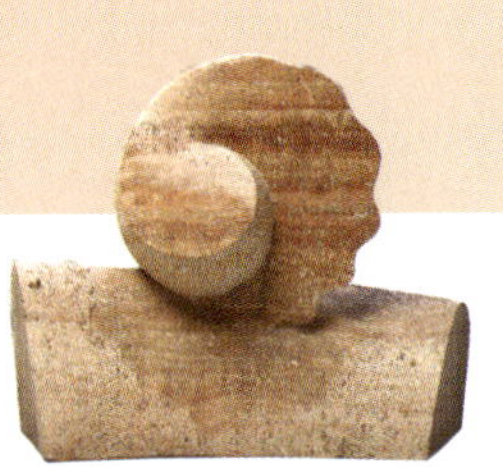

We now begin a two-fold step-by-step exercise that is more complex than the previous one. First we will make the maquette. Then, as he carves the stone, Mariano will triple its size. We will thus see how to subtract a soft material to make a maquette; we will get to know a most basic method of enlarging, used by the Egyptians, and we will become adept at handling a circular saw and a compressor.

We have chosen porexpan for the maquette because it is the best material available for learning how to use the subtraction process and shape volume.

The sculpture that we have conceived falls somewhere between an organic shape and a geometric shape. What we hope to achieve in this sculpture is a union between disparate objects such as a ram's head and a princess, and antagonistic ideas such as irony and seriousness, haughtiness and introspection.

We will cut the final sculpture in travertine stone. Though not usually recommended for carving figures, we have chosen a 22 × 27 × 16-inch (57 × 70 × 40-cm) block of travertine that is veined, reddish, and contains incrustations of quartz. The surprises that the interior of this stone will offer can only enhance the sobriety of our figures.

In this and in subsequent exercises, we will not employ the services of a stonemason to cut the stone. This job will be done by Mariano Andres Vilella, sculptor and recently retired professor of the Faculty of Fine Arts in Barcelona, Spain. As a sculptor, Mariano is quite familiar with the expressive possibilities of stone, and having worked as a sculptor's assistant since his adolescence, he has mastered technique, which he will share with us. Mariano will teach us how to enlarge a maquette using a grid. Since squares are used to draw the grid, the process is also known as *enlarging by squares.* To transfer measurements, we will also use a ruler, a yardstick, and a pencil. We will draw the grid in black, the outlines in red, and whatever else is needed in blue.

We could cut this sculpture using traditional tools only. However, since we've demonstrated their use in the preceding two exercises, we'll allow Mariano to use the more complex circular saw and compressor, and, in the process, we'll learn how to handle them.

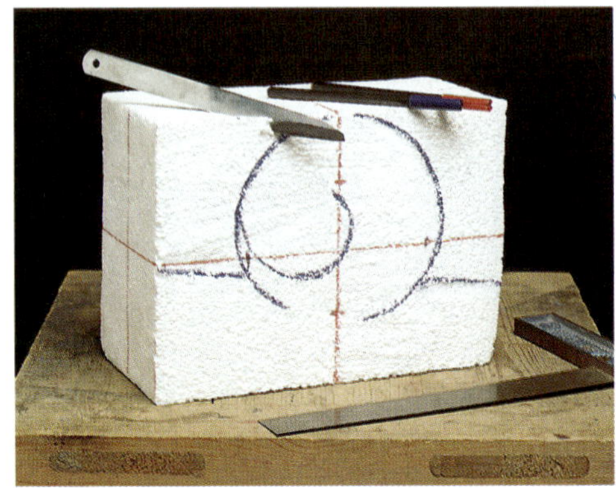

◀ **1.** We are going to cut the maquette from this porexpan block on a rotating stand. We use a slightly curved steel knife similar to the one that craftsmen use to cut leather. We have already marked the axes in red and the outside perimeter of the shape we have in mind in blue.

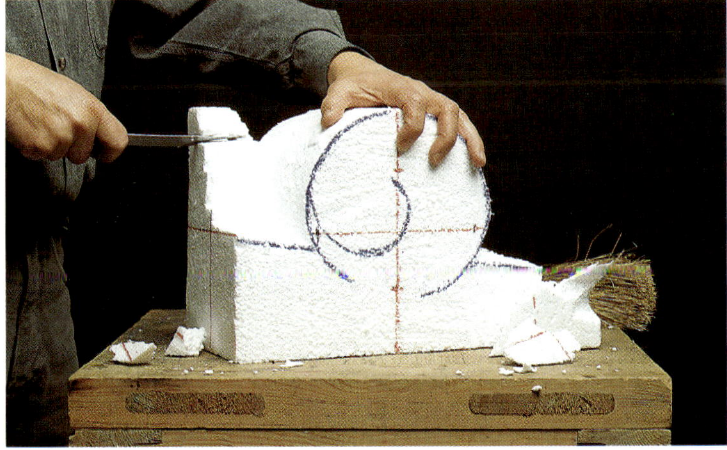

◀ **2.** We use the knife to rough out the rest of the material until we have outlined the outer silhouette. For safety, we always make sure that the hand holding the block is not in the path of the knife.

▼ **3.** We draw lines now on the next area we want to rough out so that we can fashion the front part of our figure in the shape of a snail.

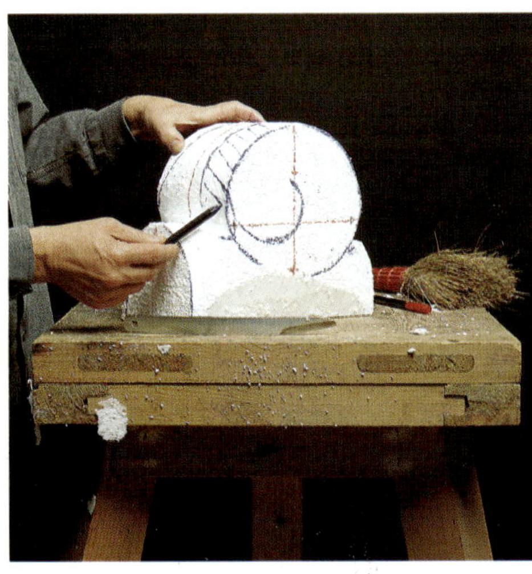

▼ **4.** To begin the roughing out, we rotate the stand or the maquette itself to make it easier to cut the material, always respecting the delineated borders.

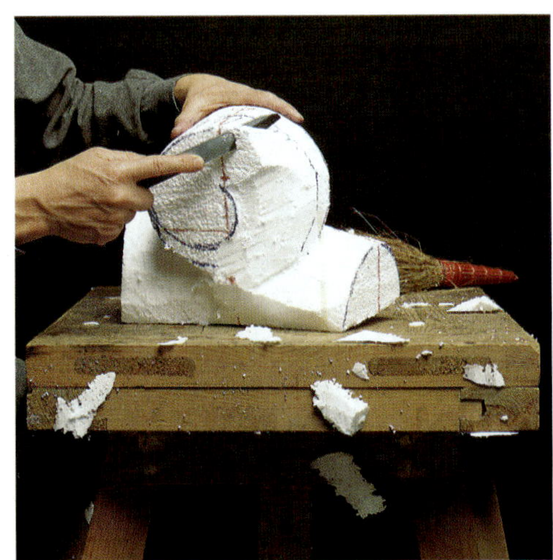

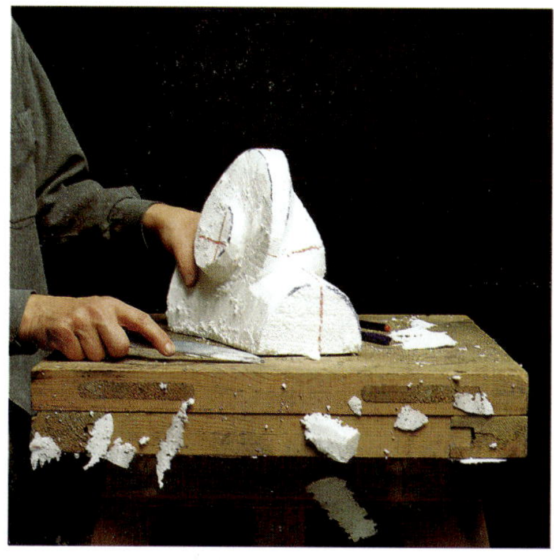

▲ **5.** We have repeated the process on the back side of the figure. We redraw the axes, we draw the new outlines, and we take the maquette in our hand to observe it from different angles and keep the integrity of the entire piece in mind.

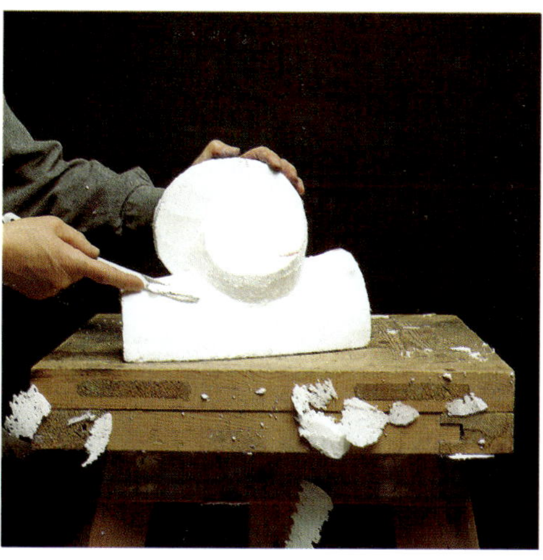

▲ **6.** We go over the back side of the piece to give it the beginning of a continuous diagonal surface that we will later call the shoulder.

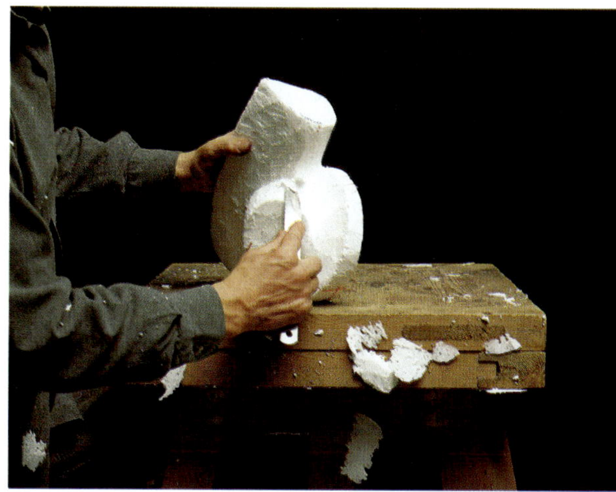

▲ **7.** Because the material is so light, we can work on it from all angles. We finish the modeling carving out a corner.

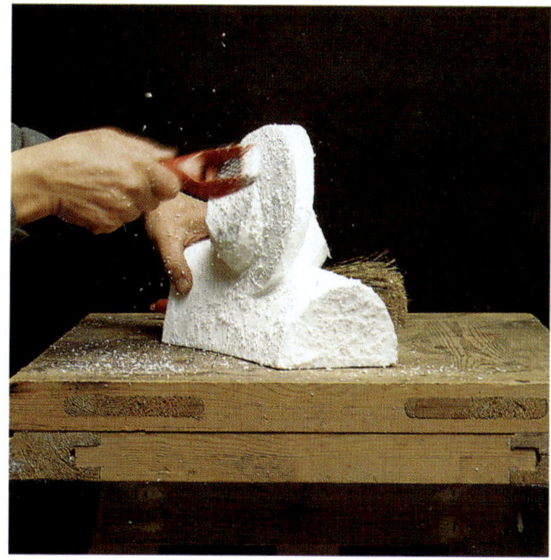

▲ **8.** We use a small rasp with a curved blade to trim the areas that the knife has left and we continue smoothing the surface.

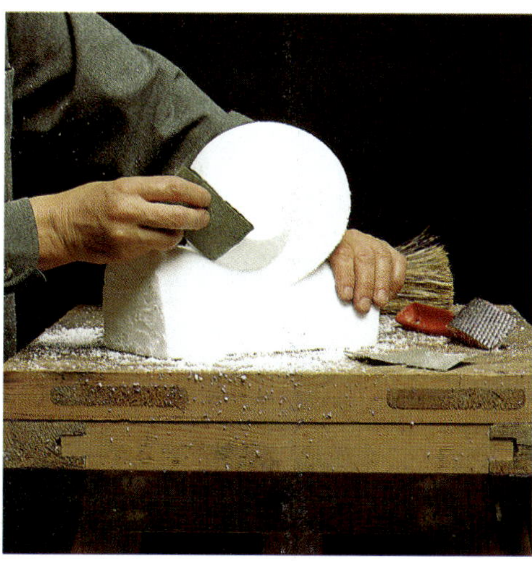

▲ **9.** We use sandpaper to smooth the rough textures that have remained and trim the edges.

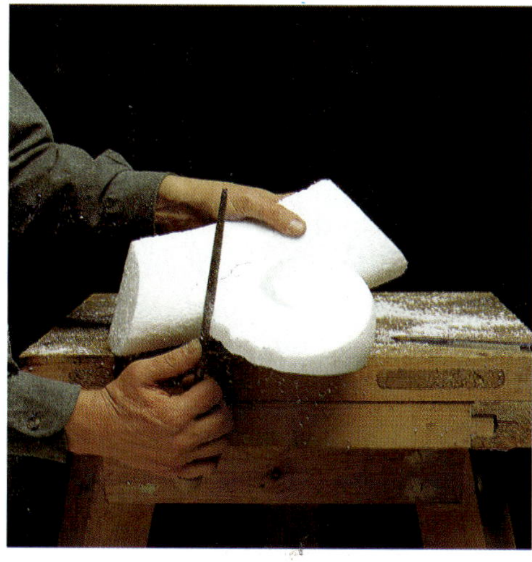

▲ **10.** Once we have given volume to the dominant shapes, we focus on the details. Here, we use a cone-shaped rasp to model some waves that we had also planned for.

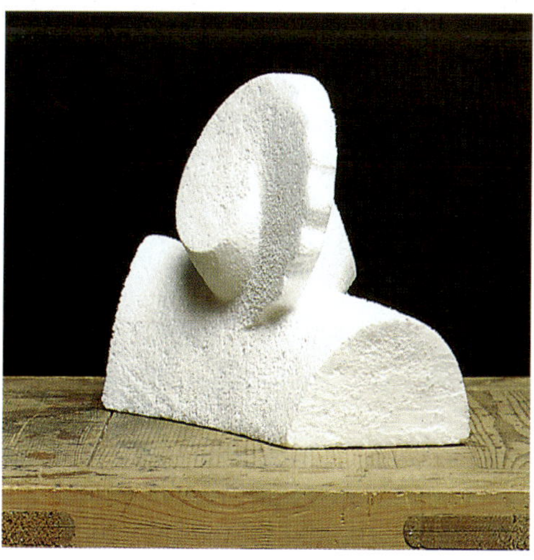

◀ **11.** The maquette is now complete, but it is only a point of departure. To transfer it to the final material and size we have to consider whether the travertine stone needs changes or whether the enlargement needs to be adjusted.

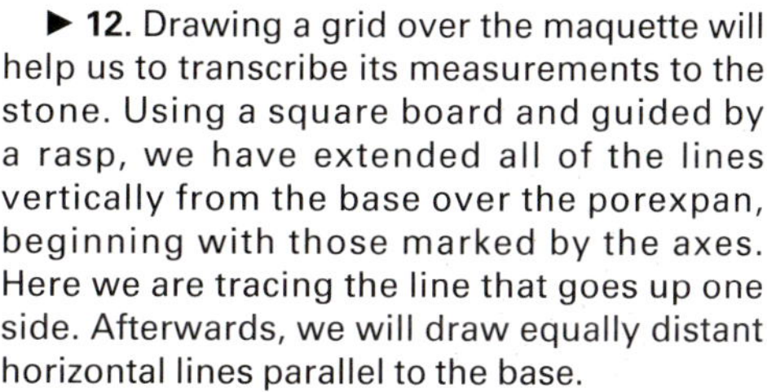

▶ **12.** Drawing a grid over the maquette will help us to transcribe its measurements to the stone. Using a square board and guided by a rasp, we have extended all of the lines vertically from the base over the porexpan, beginning with those marked by the axes. Here we are tracing the line that goes up one side. Afterwards, we will draw equally distant horizontal lines parallel to the base.

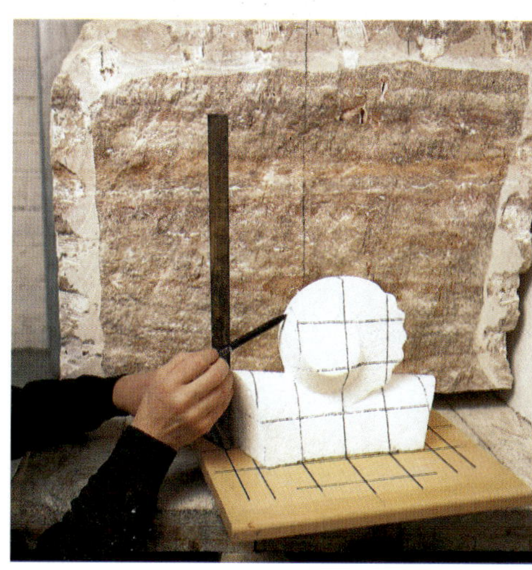

► **13.** We now begin to cut the stone. We multiply the largest measurements of the maquette by three to get the measurements of the block, which we have loosely calculated. Starting from the axes, we draw squares on each one of the sides of the stone, tripling the distances between the lines with respect to the maquette. Then, using the maquette as a reference, we draw the outline and mark the first area to be roughed out in blue.

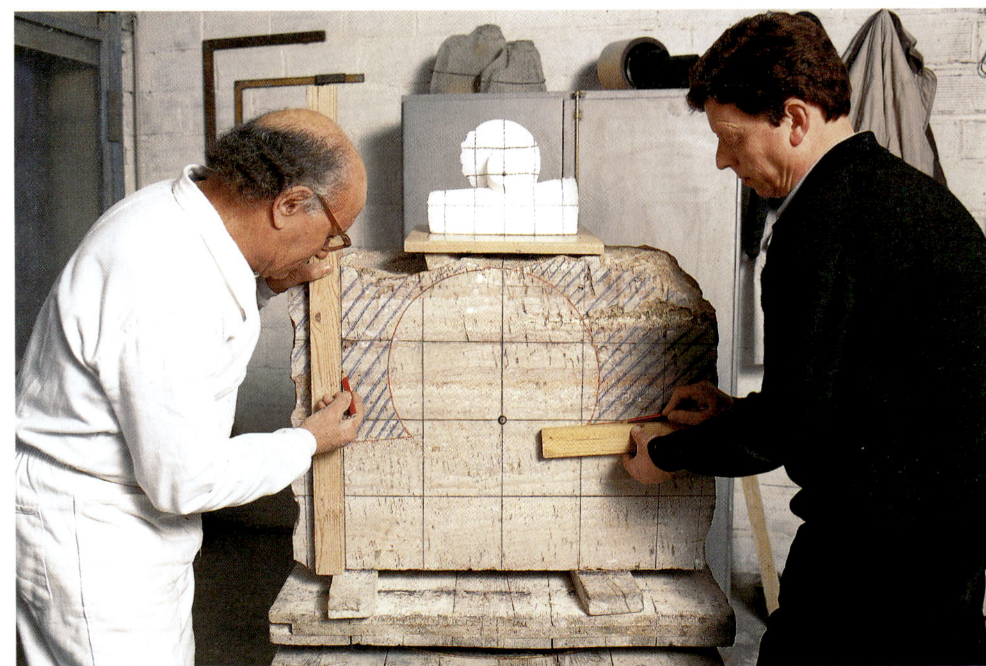

▼ **14.** The roughing out is done in two phases: First, we use a circular saw to cut deep parallel grooves in the stone; the harder the stone, the closer we make the grooves. Then we use a hammer to break them off.

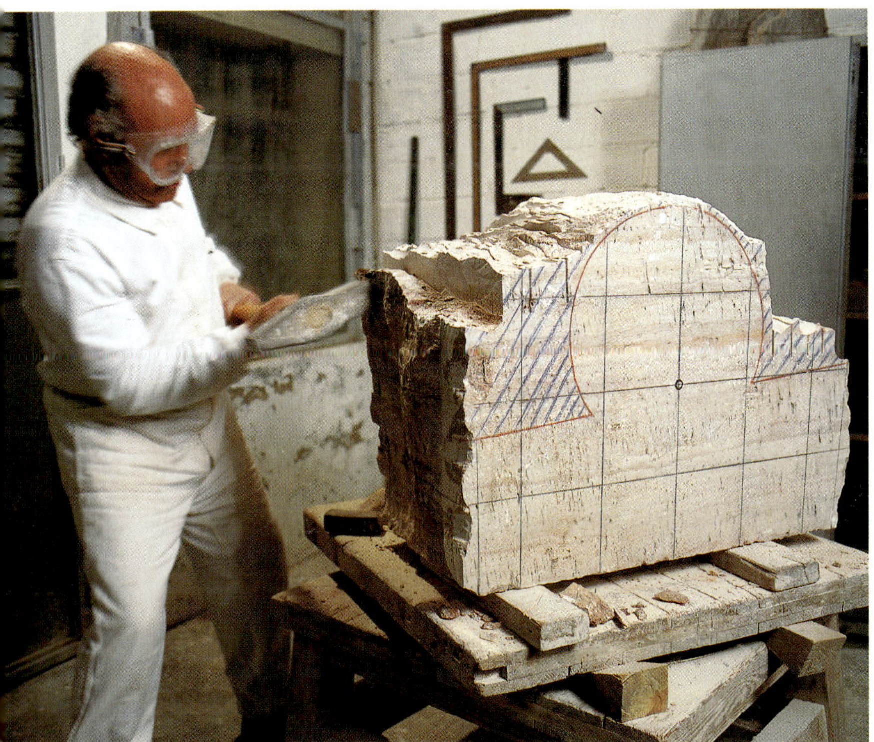

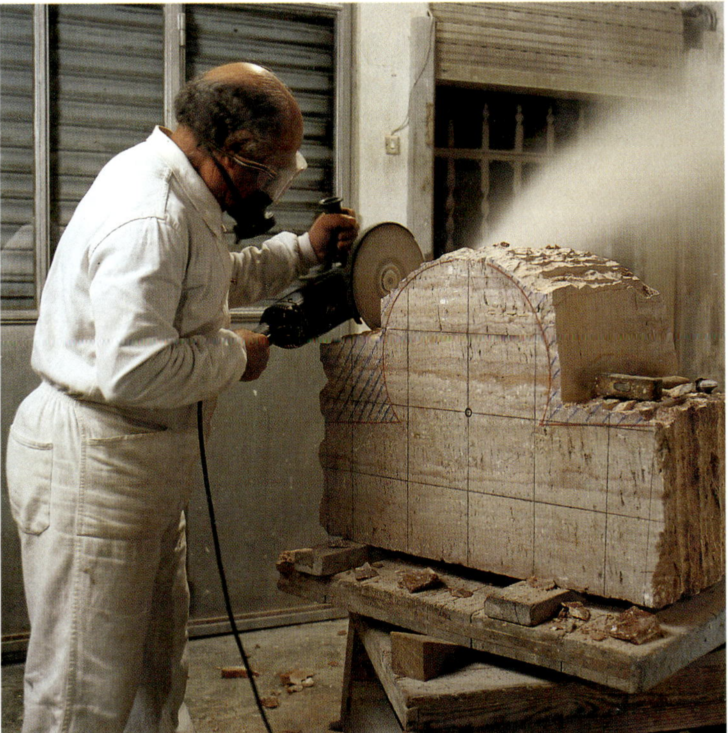

▲ **15.** Again, we use a large diamond-disked circular saw to rough out the marked areas. Pressing down on the saw enables us to cut deeper. We direct the dust the saw makes off to a corner.

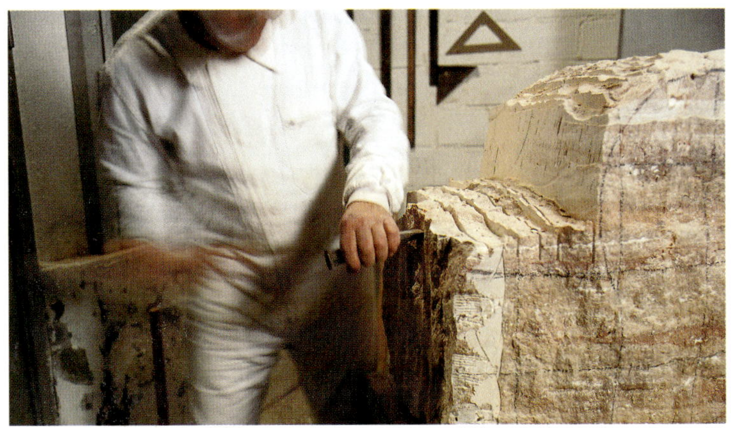

◄ **16.** The closer we get to the end of the roughing-out phase, the more precise we have to be cutting with the circular saw. To prevent chips from bouncing off the stone, we replace the hammer with a trimmer and a mallet, always cutting from the outside in.

► **17.** We are getting closer now to the largest part of the outline. We see at the top some peaks left by the circular saw, and in the center some impressions left by the pointing chisel that was used to reduce the peaks. Before we used a tooth chisel; now we use a chisel attached to a pneumatic hammer to smooth out the first master line. As the compressed air enhances the force of the mallet, we use both hands to guide the chisel.

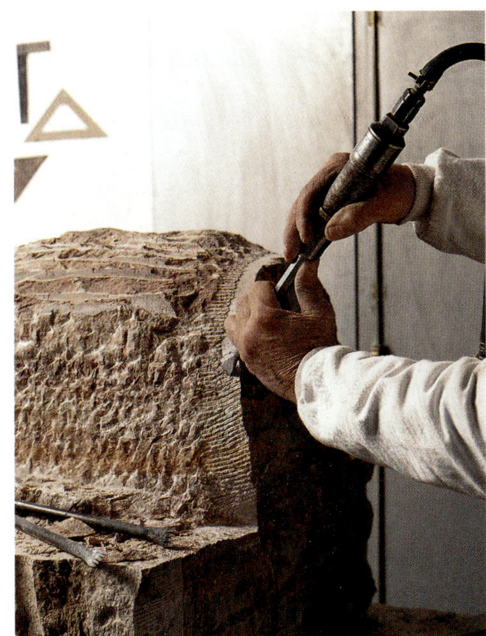

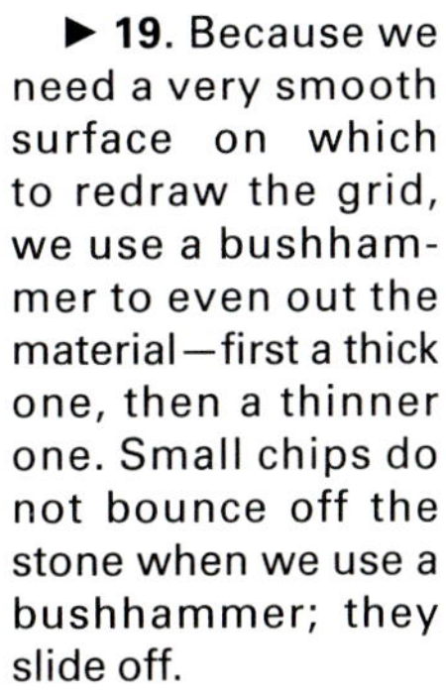

► **19.** Because we need a very smooth surface on which to redraw the grid, we use a bushhammer to even out the material—first a thick one, then a thinner one. Small chips do not bounce off the stone when we use a bushhammer; they slide off.

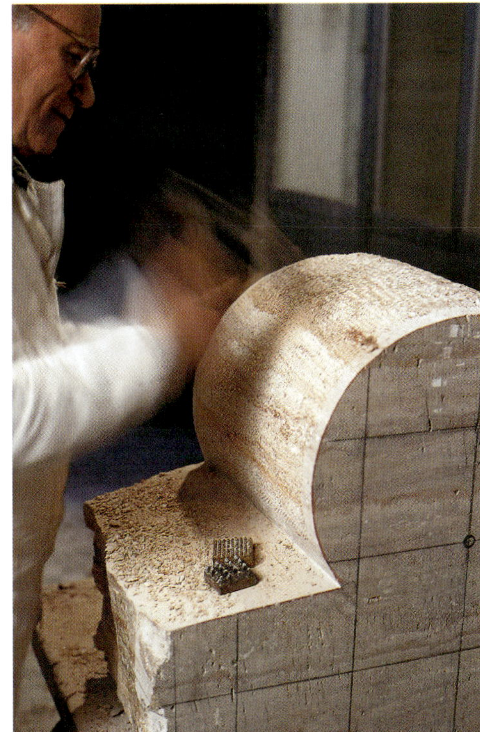

► **20.** We use a ruler to check whether the surface is smooth. We also note that the pointing has left an uneven texture—on top the texture made by a point chisel; in the middle by a number 4 bushhammer; and below, a number 6 bushhammer.

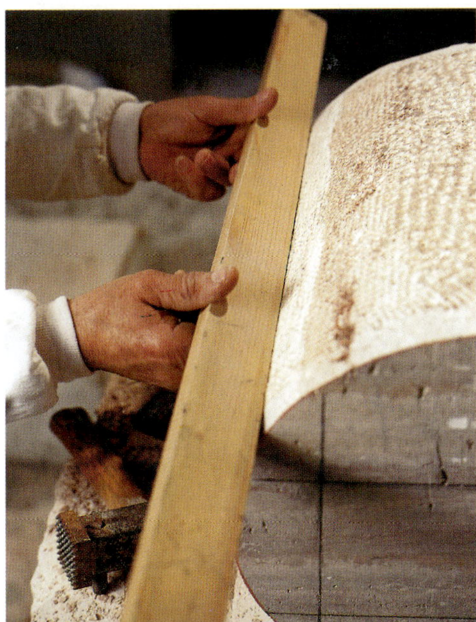

▼ **18.** Mariano has carefully worked the two master lines that define the shape of the figure in this phase. Here he uses a point chisel to break up the peaks left by the circular saw, trying not to reach the depth indicated by the master line. He prefers to use, and suggests that we do as well, the point chisel with a mallet since all we need here are light taps, not the forceful blows of a pneumatic hammer.

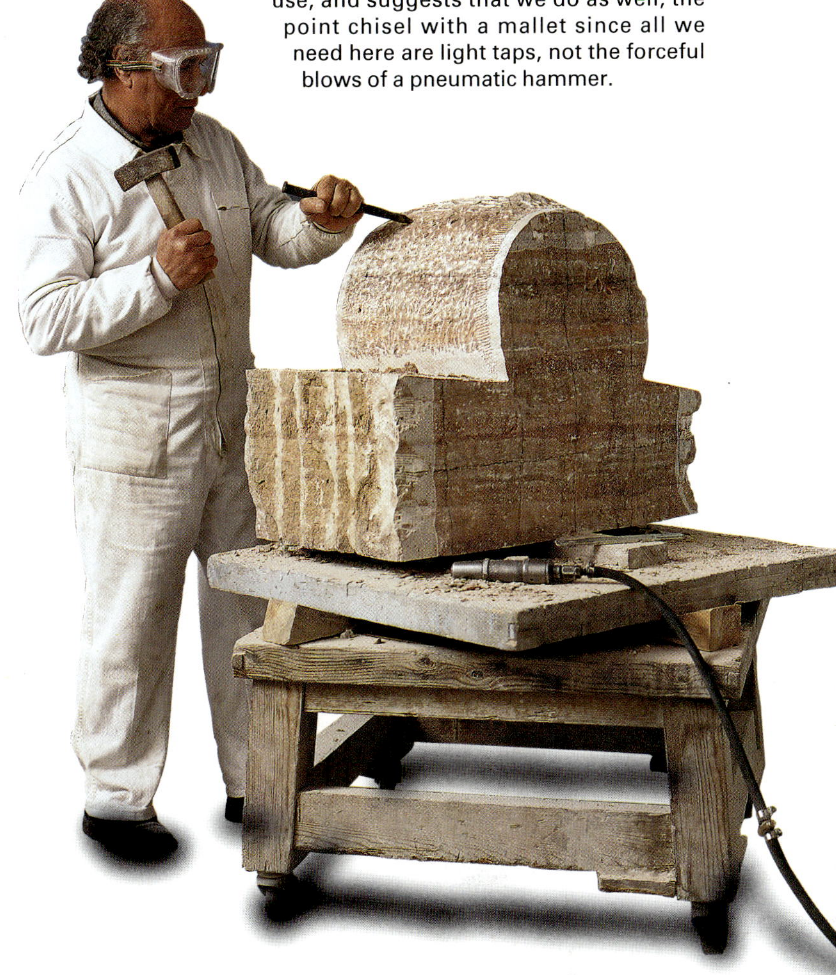

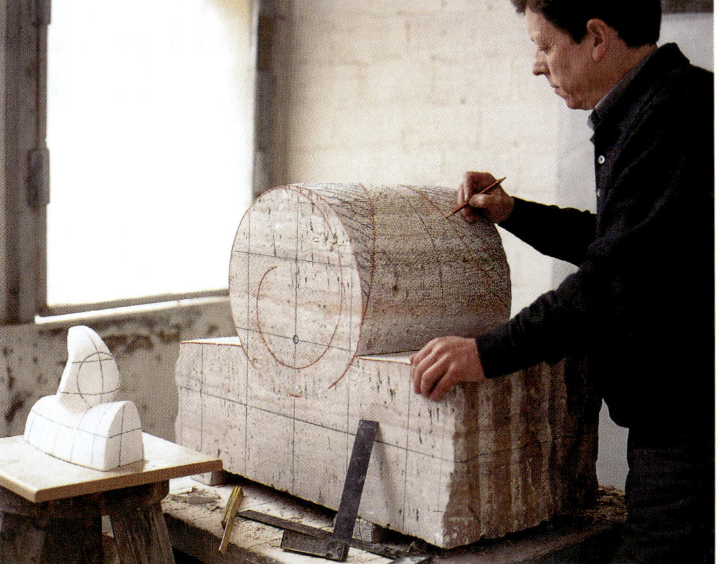

▲ **21.** We draw a grid over the travertine, which is now outlined and, keeping the maquette in mind, we mark our outlines. We use blue lines to indicate the area that needs roughing out in the next phase. The circle that appears on the maquette is simply the extension of a line from a square on one of the hemispheres.

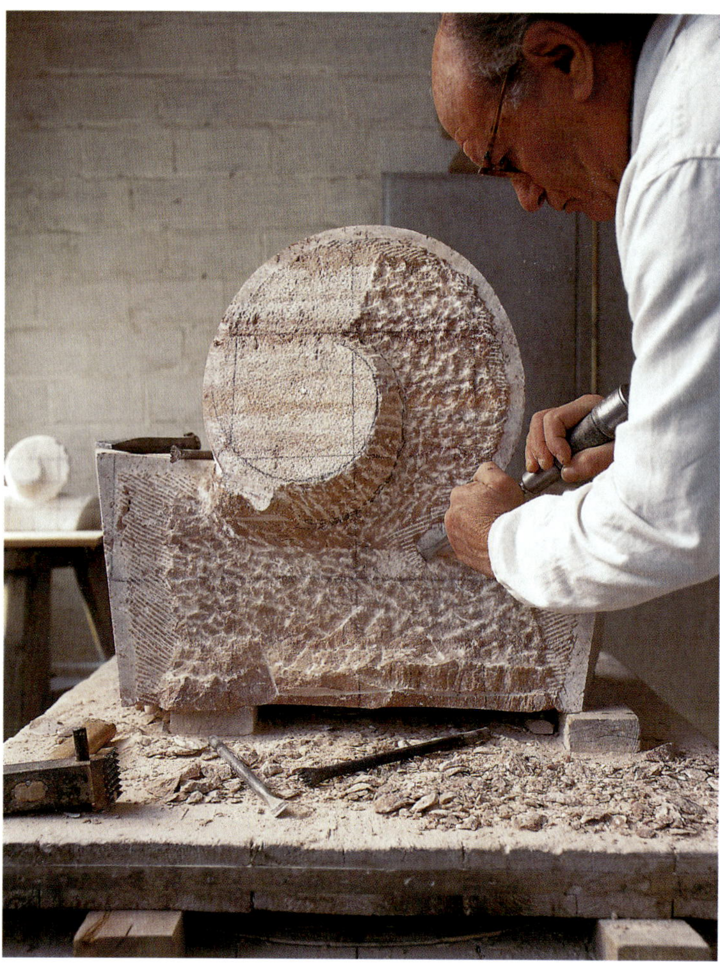

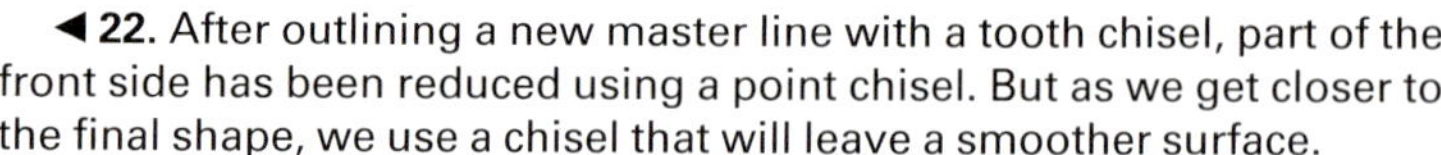

◄ **22.** After outlining a new master line with a tooth chisel, part of the front side has been reduced using a point chisel. But as we get closer to the final shape, we use a chisel that will leave a smoother surface.

▼ **23.** We turn the sculpture over so we can cut more easily. As we work the volume, we need to draw the grid and the outlines on each side, including the base. We continue cutting back the rest of the material.

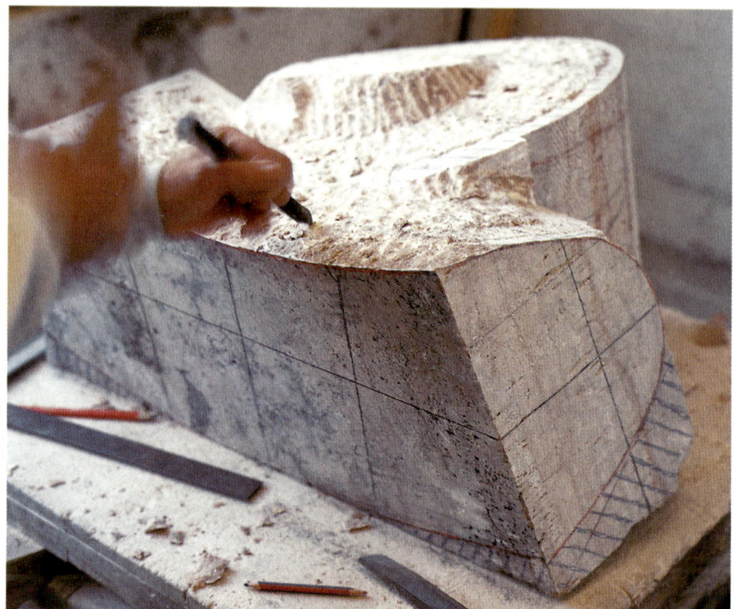

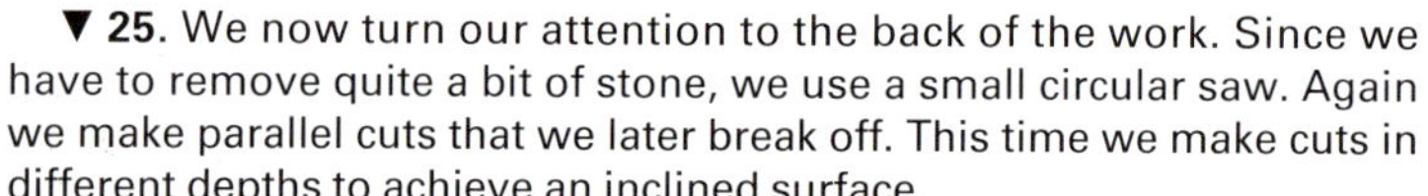

► **24.** Again, as we get closer to the edge of the base marked in red we work the master line, first with a tooth chisel and then with a flat chisel. Note the correct position for detailing. The arm rests securely on the stone, and the chisel, slightly inclined, is held between the little finger and ring finger, and is guided by the thumb so that it works from the outside in.

▼ **25.** We now turn our attention to the back of the work. Since we have to remove quite a bit of stone, we use a small circular saw. Again we make parallel cuts that we later break off. This time we make cuts in different depths to achieve an inclined surface.

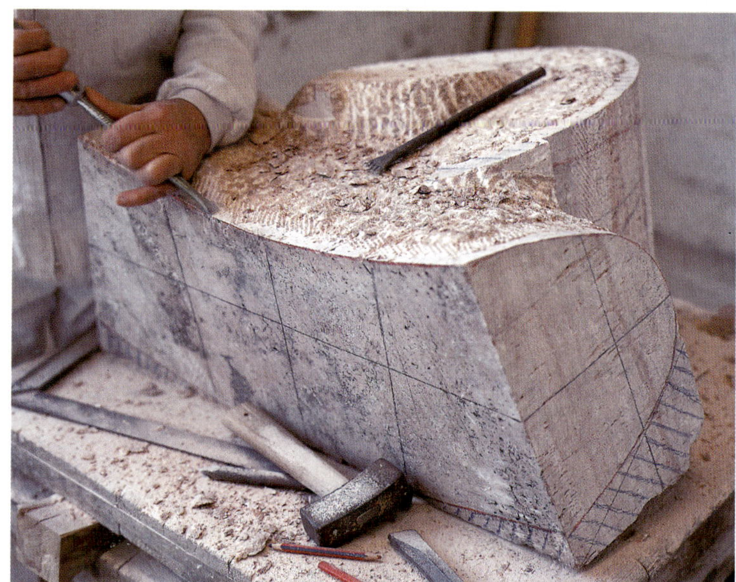

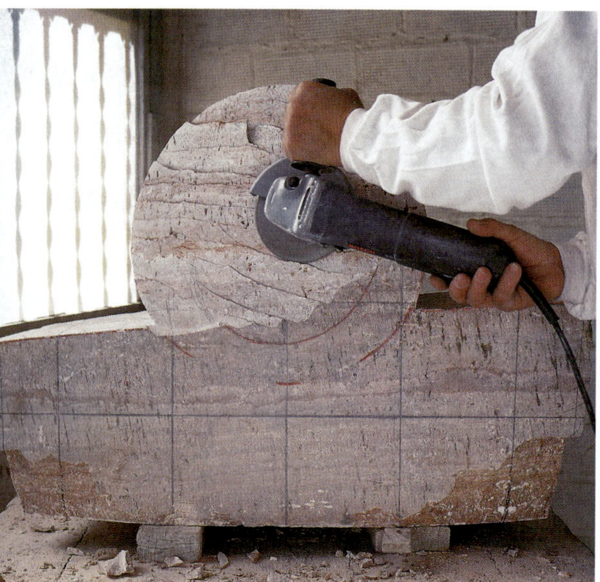

► **26.** Before continuing to reduce, it is best to incise a new master line, first with a tooth chisel and then a flat. Mariano insists that the only way to master the representation of volume is to use lines like these.

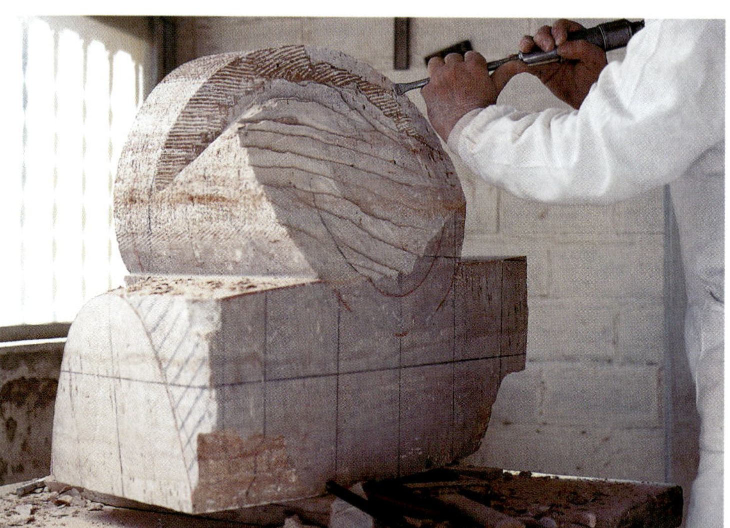

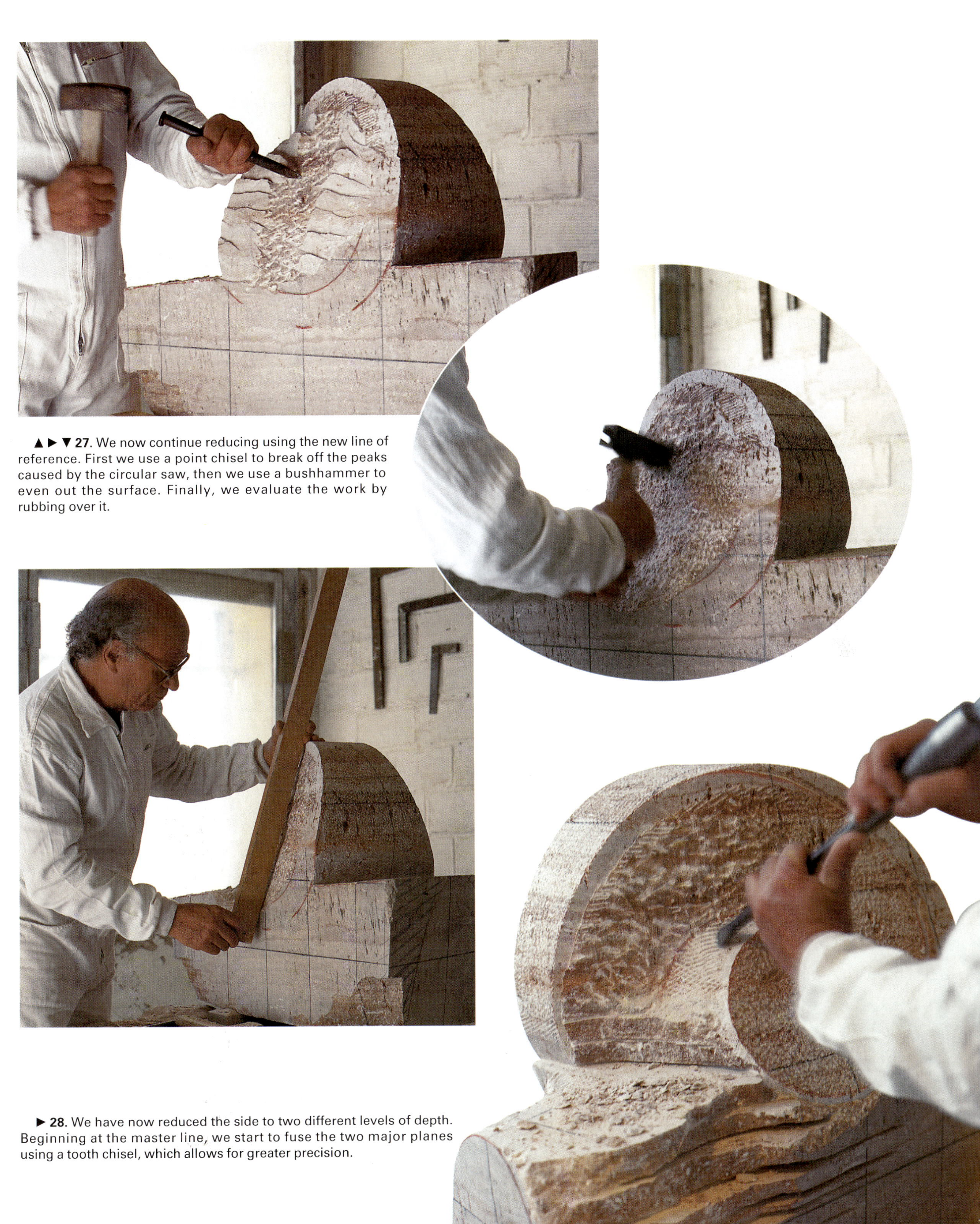

▲ ► ▼ **27**. We now continue reducing using the new line of reference. First we use a point chisel to break off the peaks caused by the circular saw, then we use a bushhammer to even out the surface. Finally, we evaluate the work by rubbing over it.

► **28**. We have now reduced the side to two different levels of depth. Beginning at the master line, we start to fuse the two major planes using a tooth chisel, which allows for greater precision.

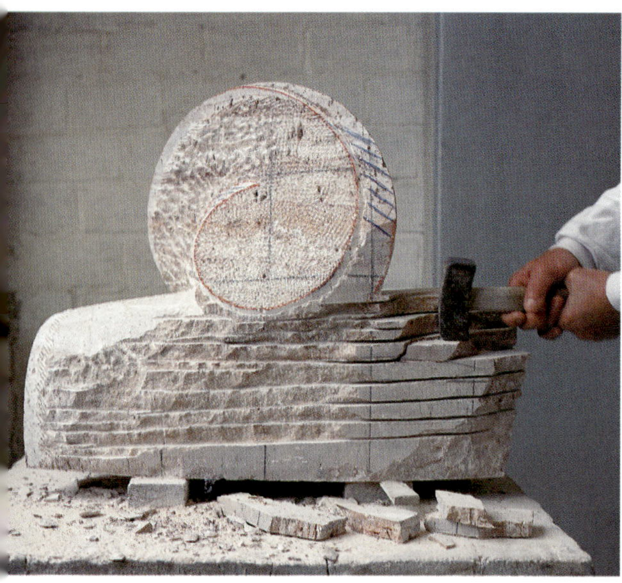

◀ **29.** We now reduce the lower part of the figure. The process, which we have already explained, can be seen more clearly here: parallel cuts using a circular saw, direct use of the hammer to break off large chips.

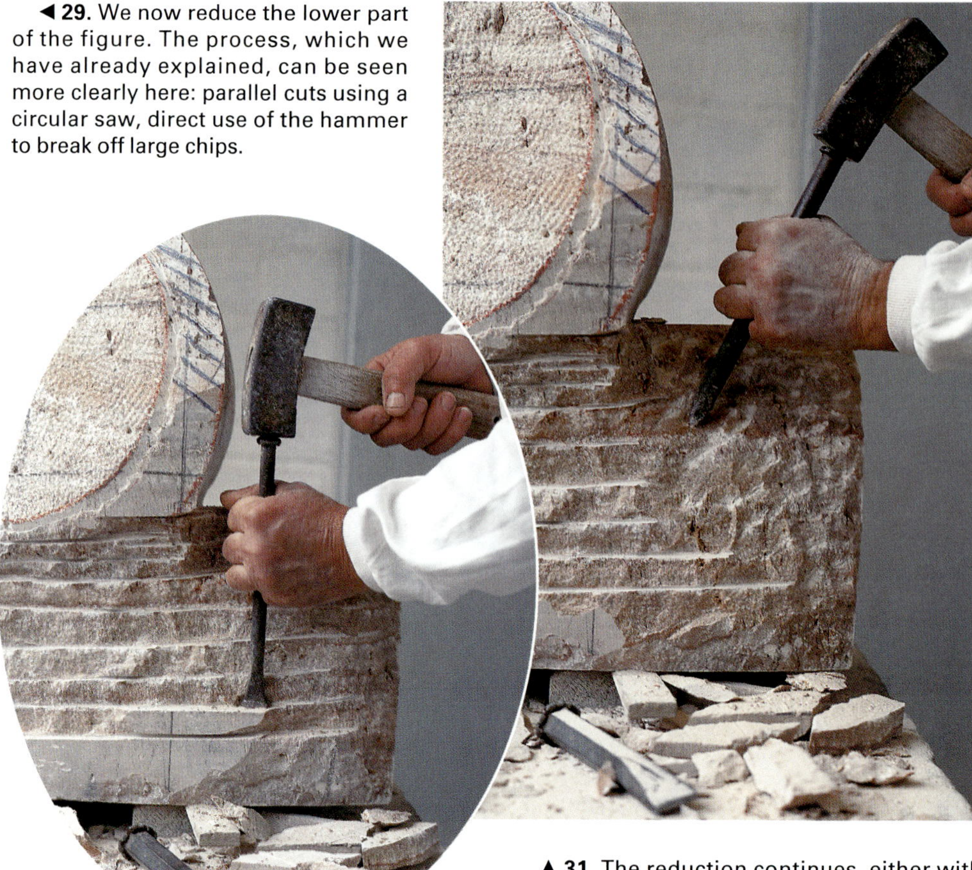

▶ **30.** Note the curved shape of this hammer: It is arched and might very well be an antique. Both Mariano and Feliu before him collect out-of-date tools. The difference is that in their hands the tools become a talisman that transforms their work into a ritual.

▲ **31.** The reduction continues, either with a trimmer, a flat chisel, or a point chisel, depending on which tool is needed at any given moment.

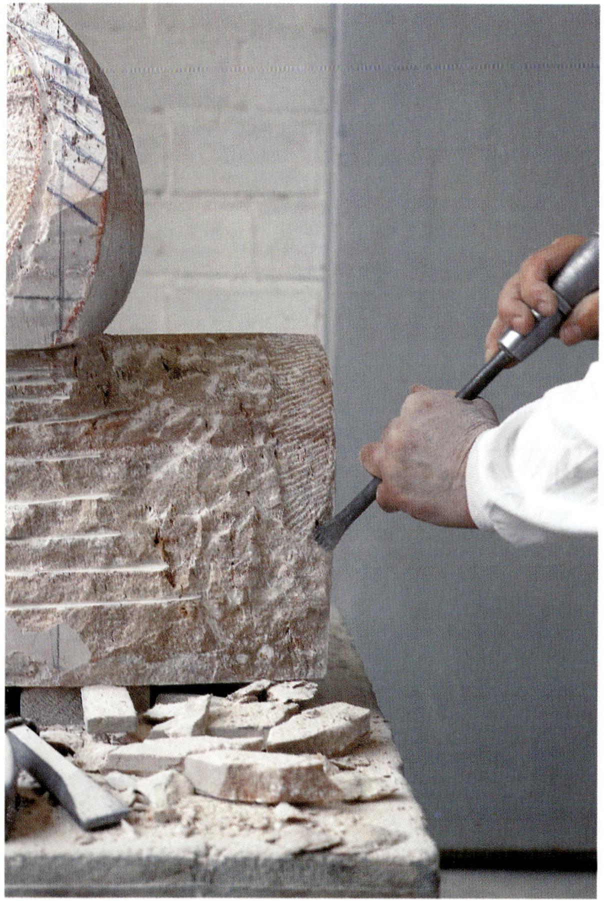

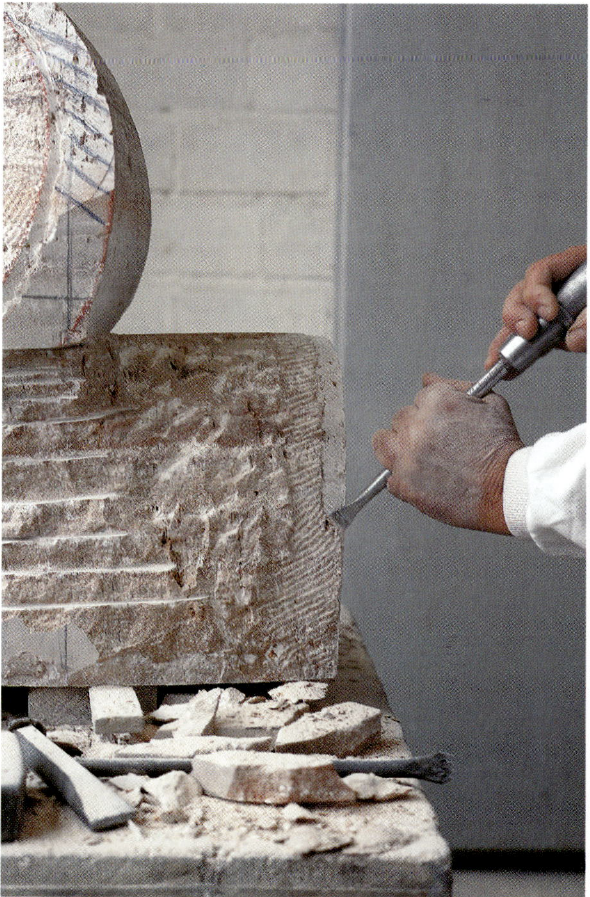

◀ ◀ **32.** We are getting close to the desired shape. It is important, then, to work a new master line for the shape that is nearly finished. As on other occasions, Mariano first uses a tooth chisel to draw the line.

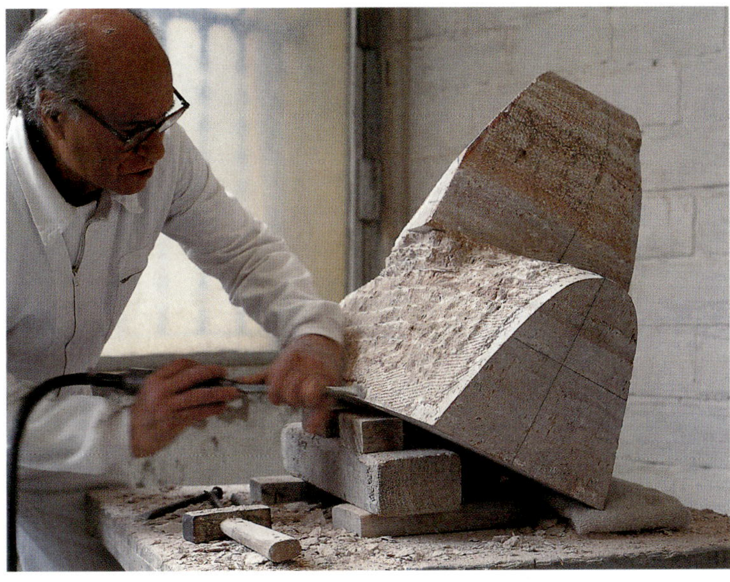

▲ **33.** We see the results of the arduous task of reduction: A form emerges and takes on life. It is important to protect the finished edges with a folded-over cloth and to raise the new work area for comfort. The weight of the stone itself keeps it steady. As Mariano works the master line, inspiration takes hold.

► **34.** As if possessed, he mounts the sculpture to give final touches with the trimmer and corrects any flaws he sees on the top part of the sculpture.

▼ **35.** The point chisel, which is carrying out its last task of reducing the "mane," works here almost in parallel with the stone and leaves large grooves.

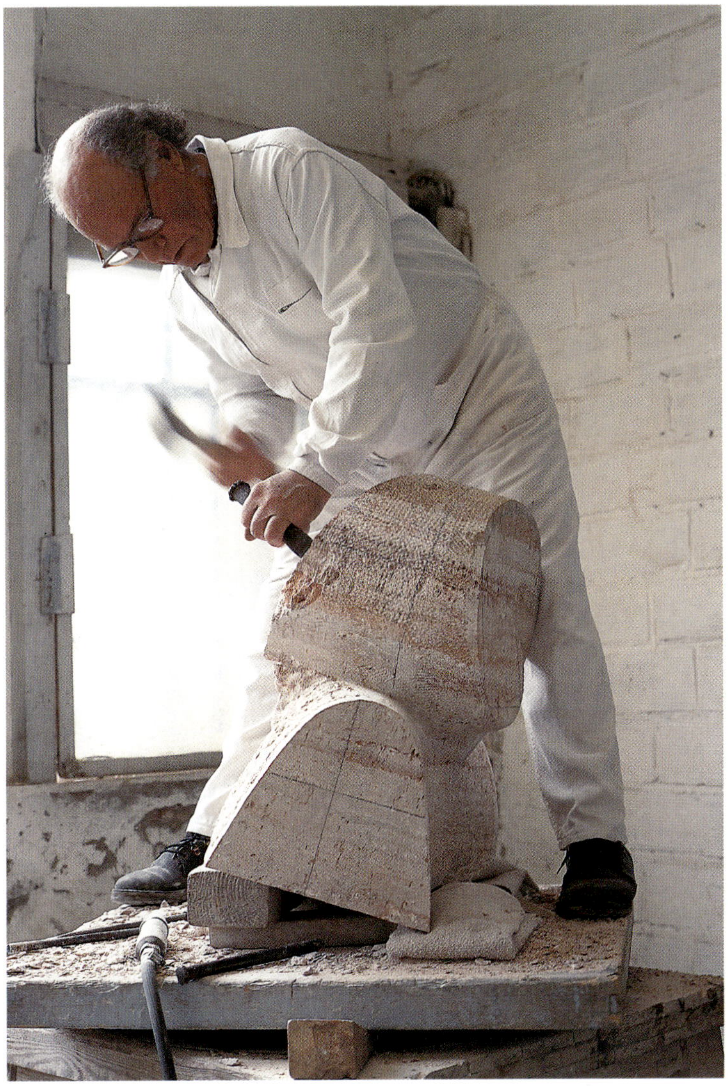

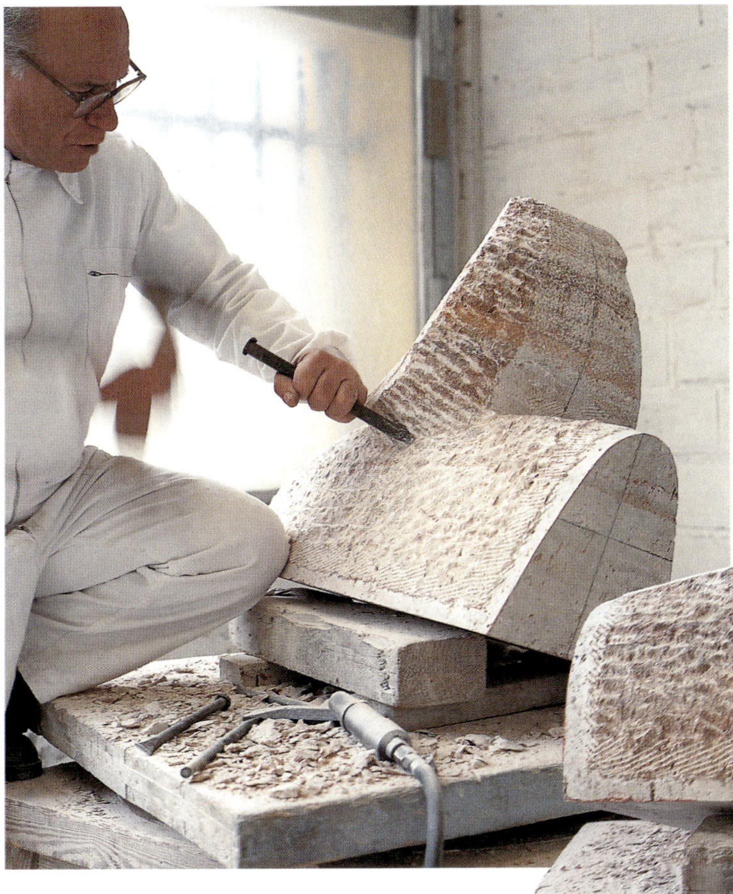

▼ **36.** Here is a frontal view of our fully carved sculpture. The dominant form is now final, which means that the reduction phase is over. All we need to do now is model the surface and square the angles. We use the square to redo the grid; we check to make sure that it closely matches the maquette and if there are any discrepancies we rectify them.

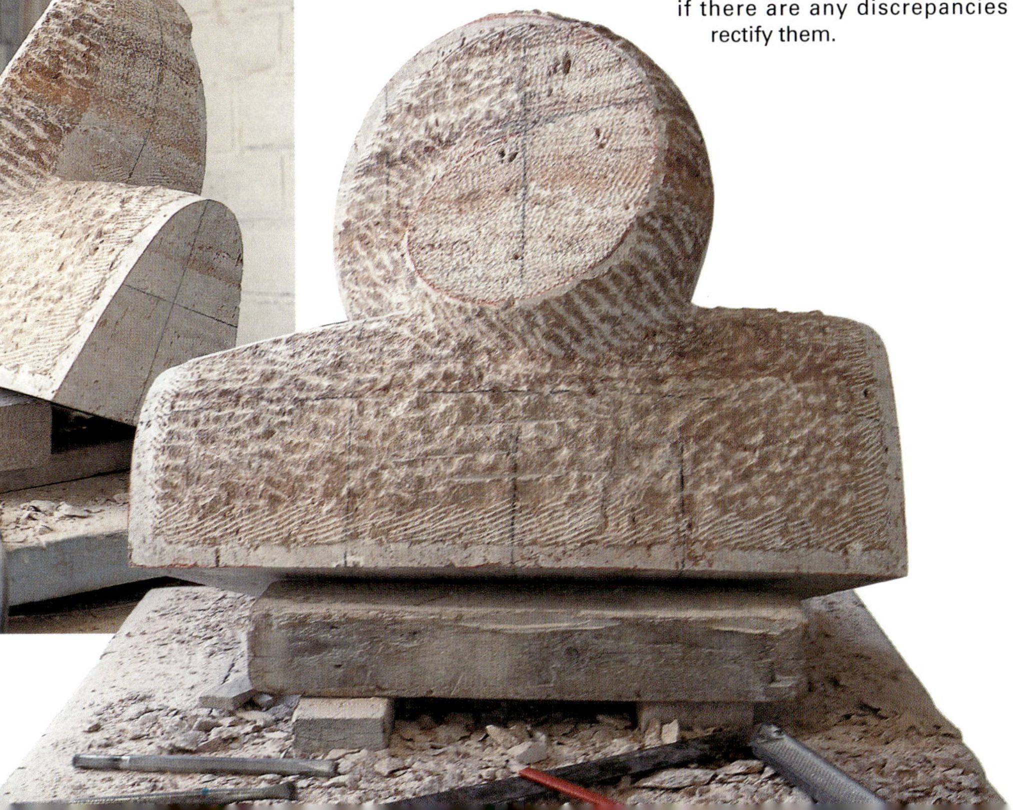

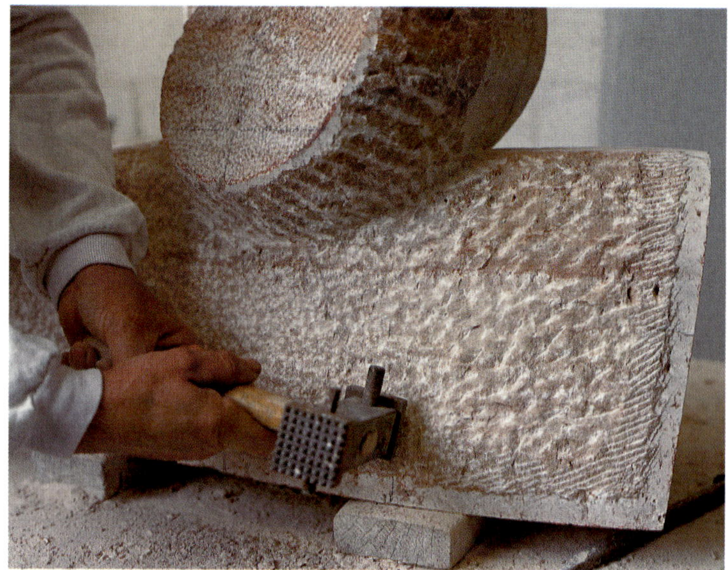

▲ **37.** With the bushhammer, we even out the different textures left by the point chisel and the grooves left by the tooth chisel. We are now only about a hundredth of an inch (a few mm) away from the finished surface.

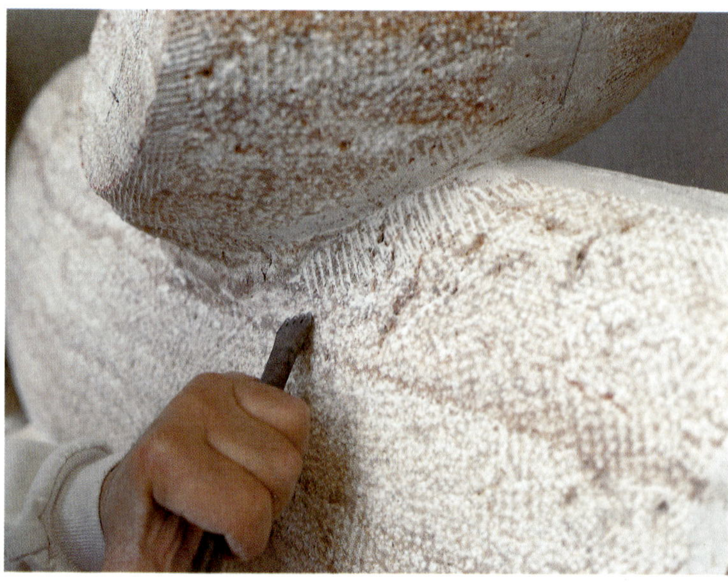

▲ **38.** The grid disappears as we make the entire surface uniform using the bushhammer; now we can start the details that need finishing. We use the tooth chisel to model a corner.

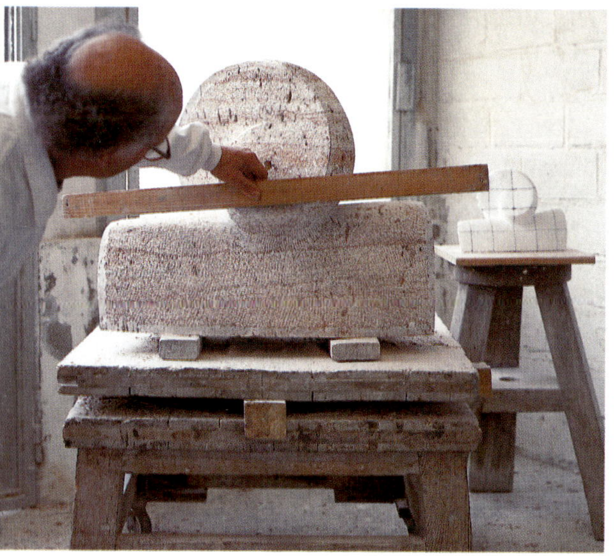

◀ **39.** Final checks: The incline tells us that the "shoulder" is appropriate. We can now put the maquette aside. The stone itself will let us know exactly what we need to do to finish the sculpture in a way that highlights its intrinsic nature.

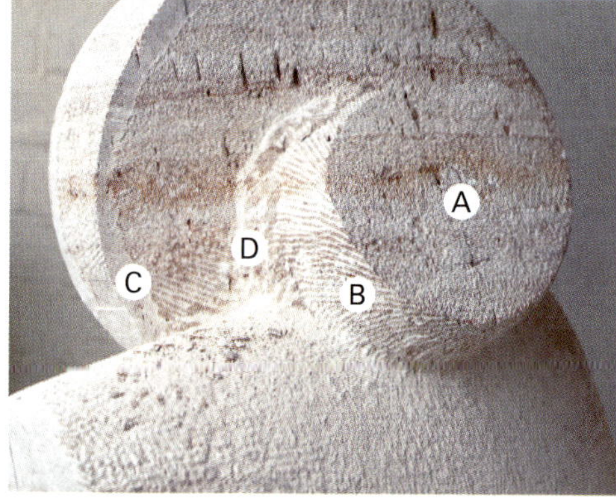

◀ **40.** We review the markings left behind by each tool: areas on which the bushhammer was used (A); grooves left behind by the tooth chisel (B); the master line etched by the chisel (C); several marks left by the point chisel (D).

▼ **41.** We use a tooth chisel to model one of the corners, eliminating traces left by the point chisel.

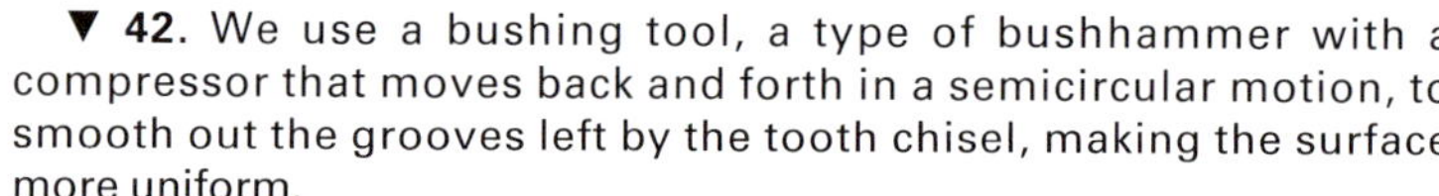

▼ **42.** We use a bushing tool, a type of bushhammer with a compressor that moves back and forth in a semicircular motion, to smooth out the grooves left by the tooth chisel, making the surface more uniform.

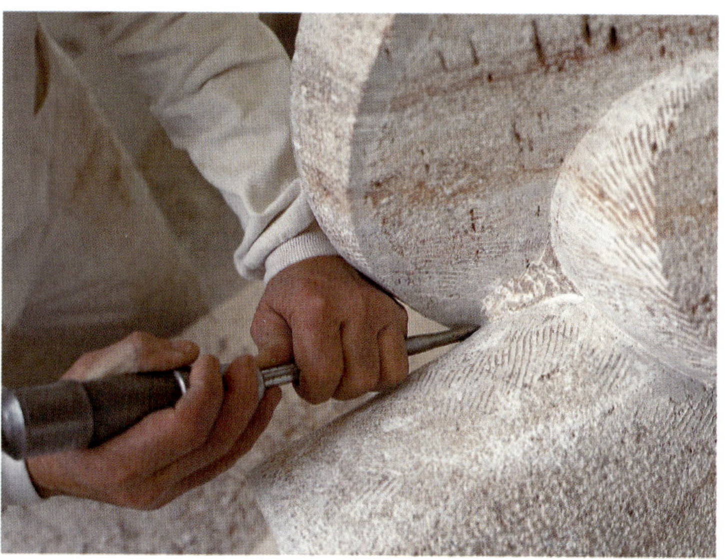

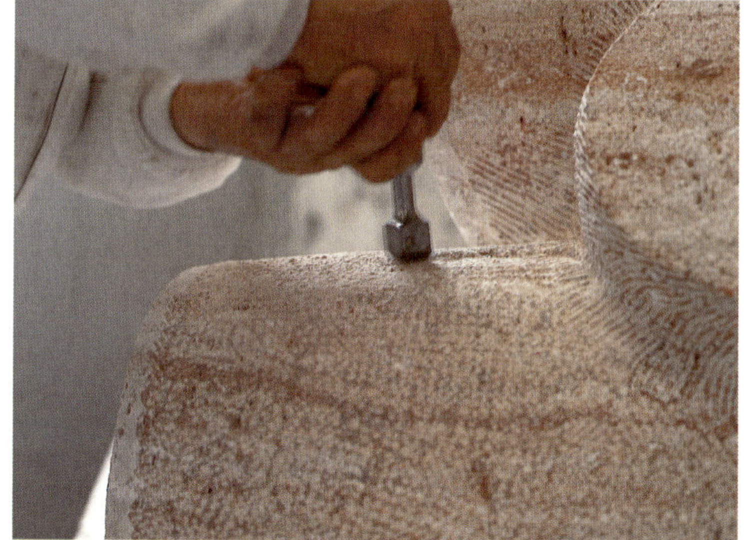

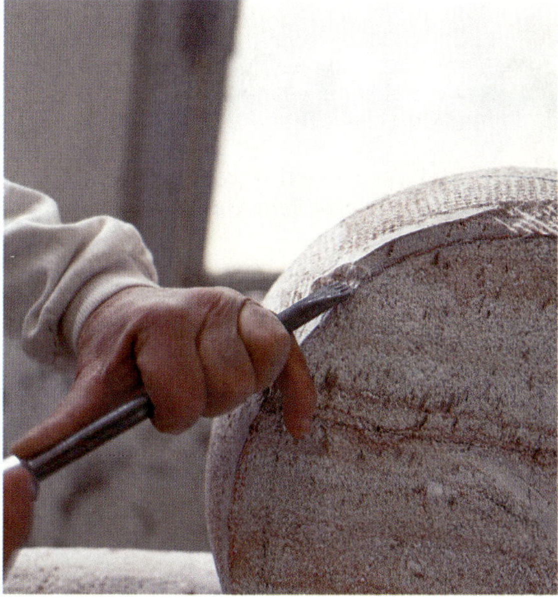

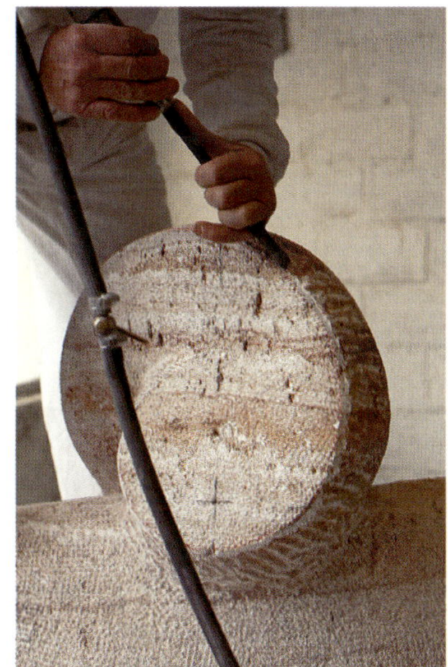

◄ **44.** We continue defining the outline. Here you can see the hose that transports the compressed air that moves the chisels and the shut-off valve that allows us to control it.

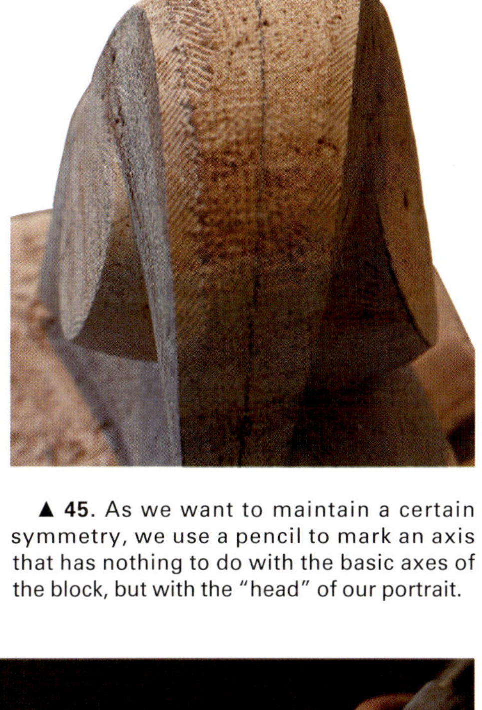

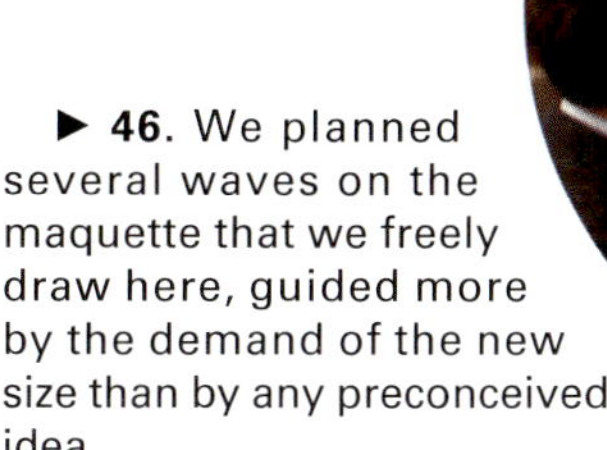

▲ **43.** After modeling the outside perimeter, we trim the broken edges. With a very steady hand (note the work of the little finger), Mariano begins a final master line.

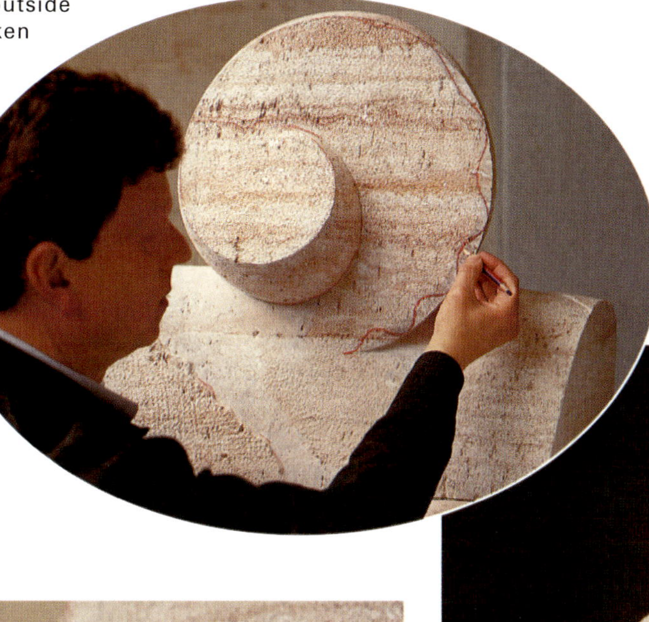

▲ **45.** As we want to maintain a certain symmetry, we use a pencil to mark an axis that has nothing to do with the basic axes of the block, but with the "head" of our portrait.

► **46.** We planned several waves on the maquette that we freely draw here, guided more by the demand of the new size than by any preconceived idea.

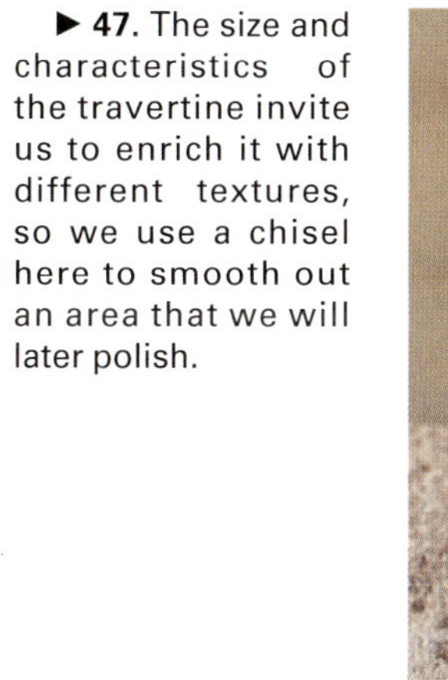

► **47.** The size and characteristics of the travertine invite us to enrich it with different textures, so we use a chisel here to smooth out an area that we will later polish.

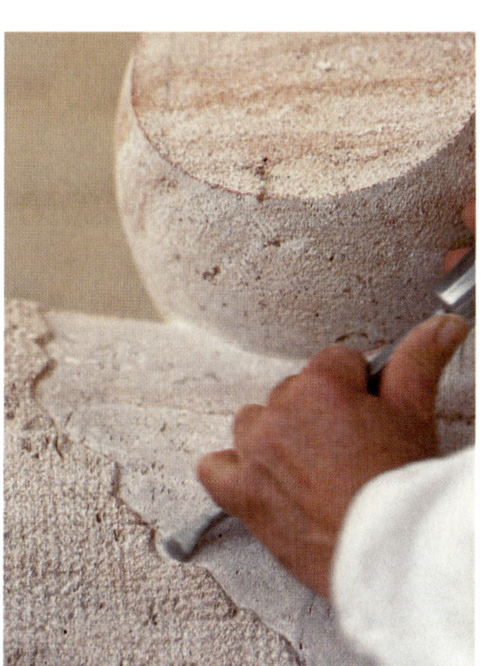

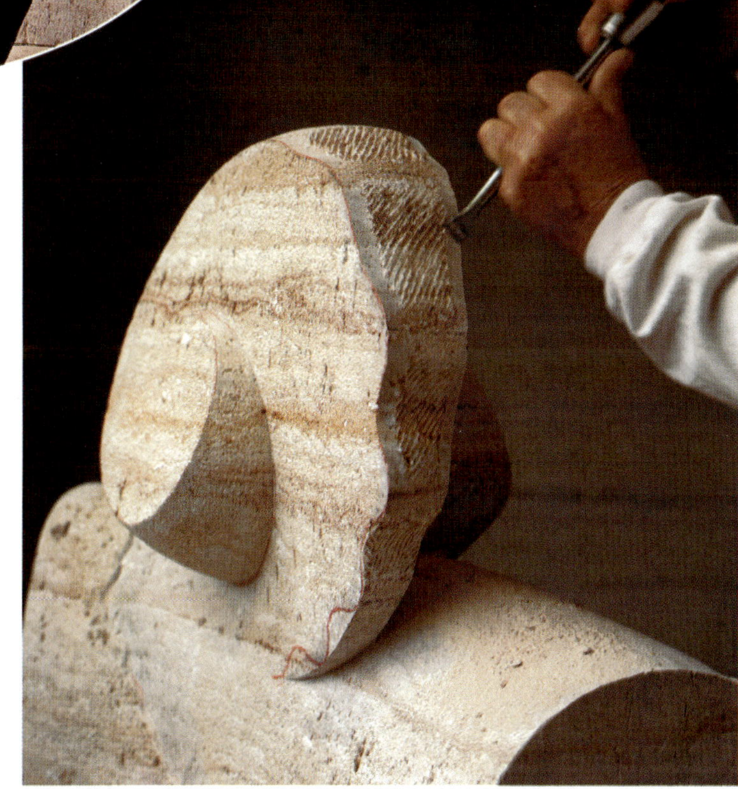

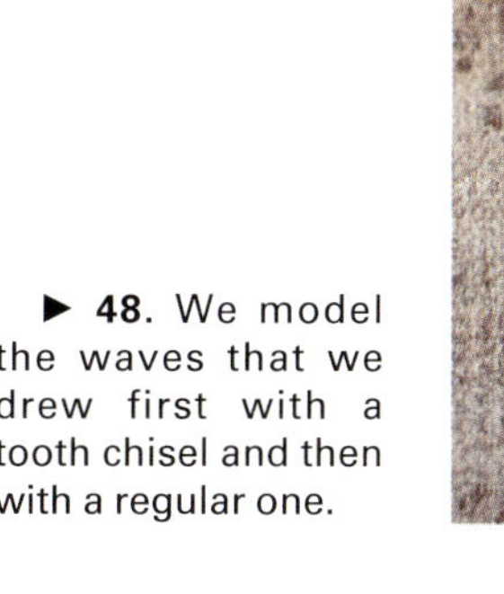

► **48.** We model the waves that we drew first with a tooth chisel and then with a regular one.

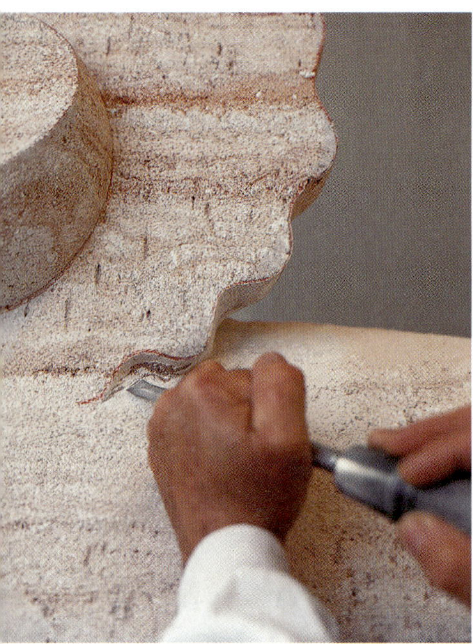

▲ **49.** With a tooth chisel, we clean a rather difficult corner where several volumes converge.

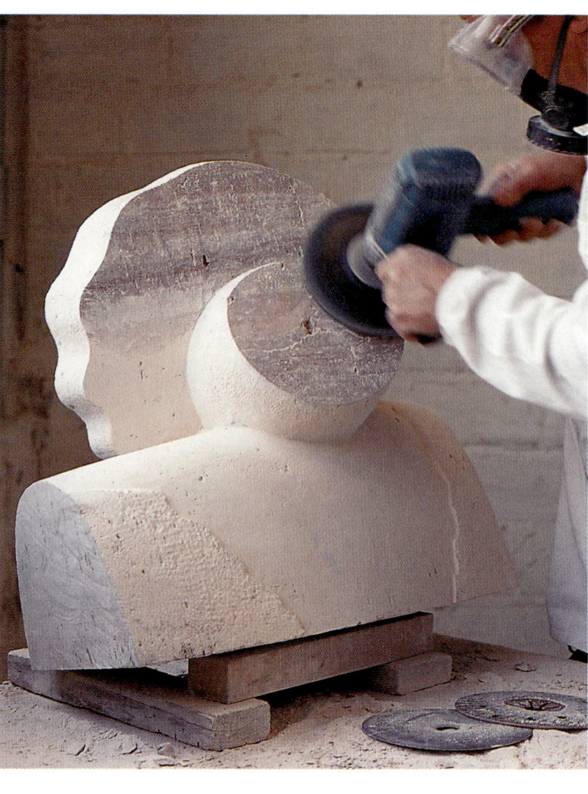

◀ **50.** Mariano passes a sandpaper disk attached to a polisher over several volumes. The tonal color of the veins emerge and in a short while we get a cleaning that would have taken hours to do by hand.

▼ **51.** We use three different tools to finish the sculpture: polisher (A); a bushhammer (B), and, finally, a chisel.

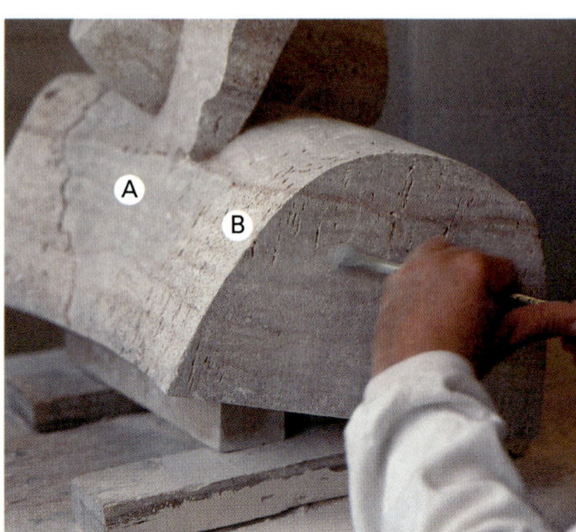

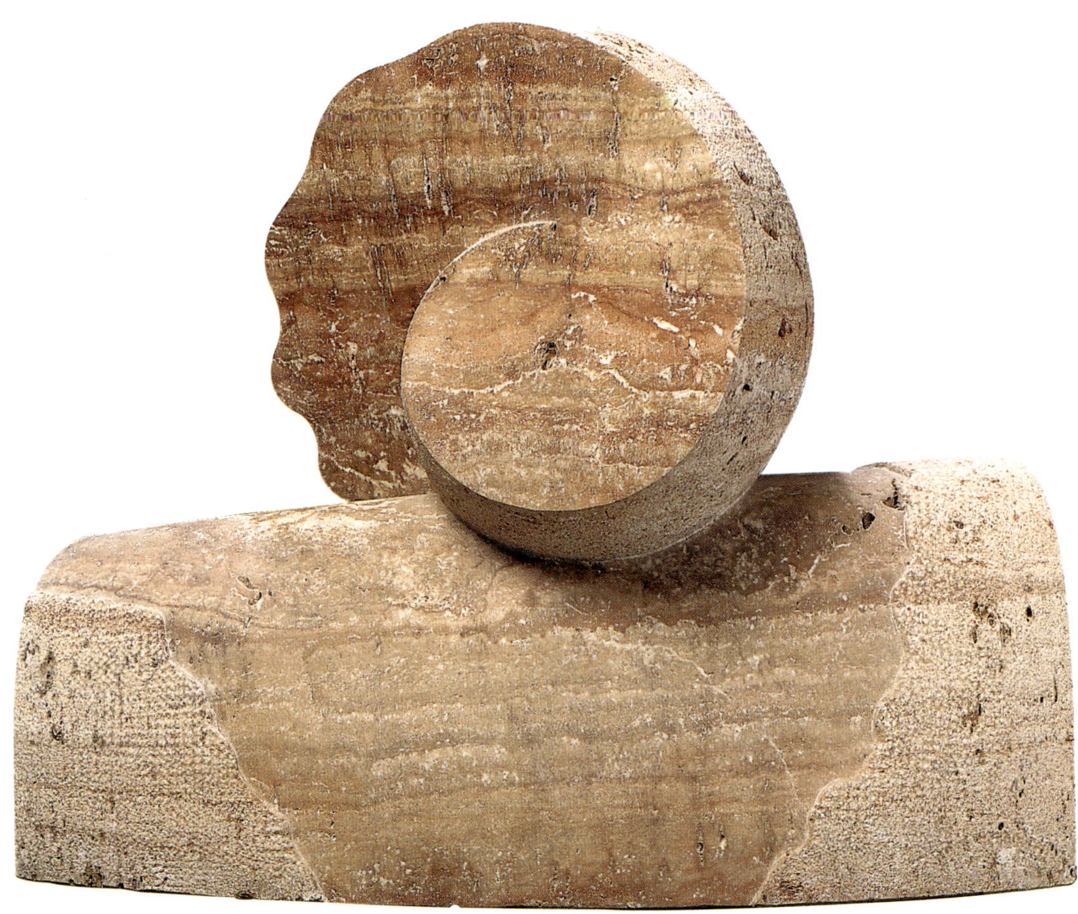

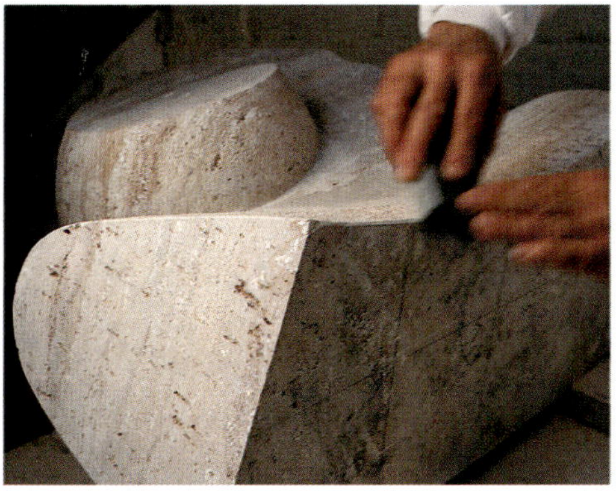

▲ **52.** We use a medium-grained carborundum stone to soften the edges.

► **53.** We adapt sandpaper to be used with water to a modeling palette to smooth out the corners and we buff them with a palm leaf fiber.

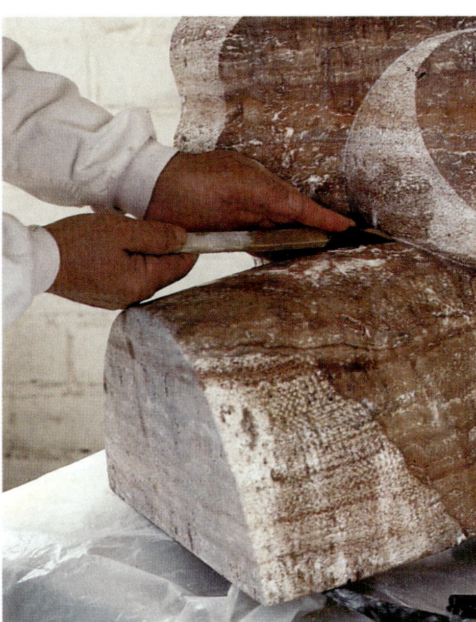

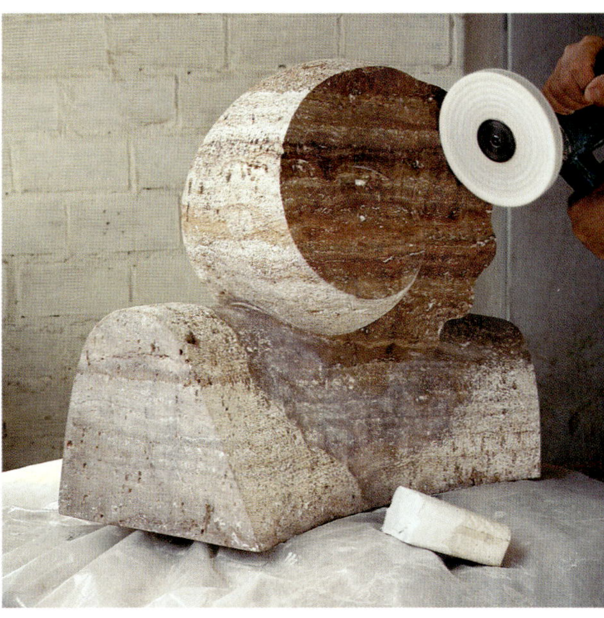

▲ **54.** We use a rotating disk to apply the polishing cream, putting pressure on the cartridge that is placed in the proper position so that the cream doesn't splatter. We highlight certain parts by using the same polish, only this time we apply with a fabric disk that has been soaked in the polishing cream.

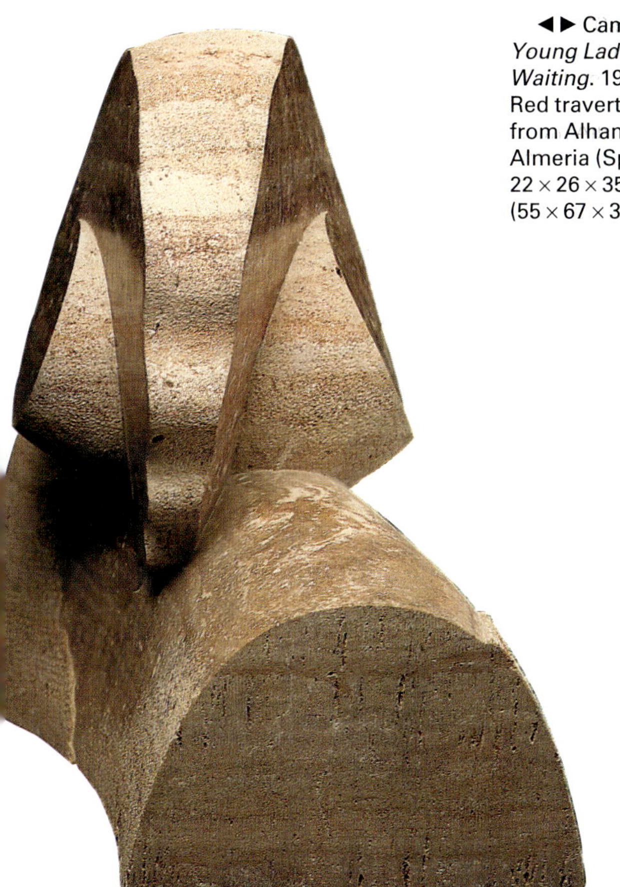

◄► Camí. *Young Lady in Waiting*. 1999. Red travertine from Alhama, Almeria (Spain). 22 × 26 × 35 inches (55 × 67 × 35 cm).

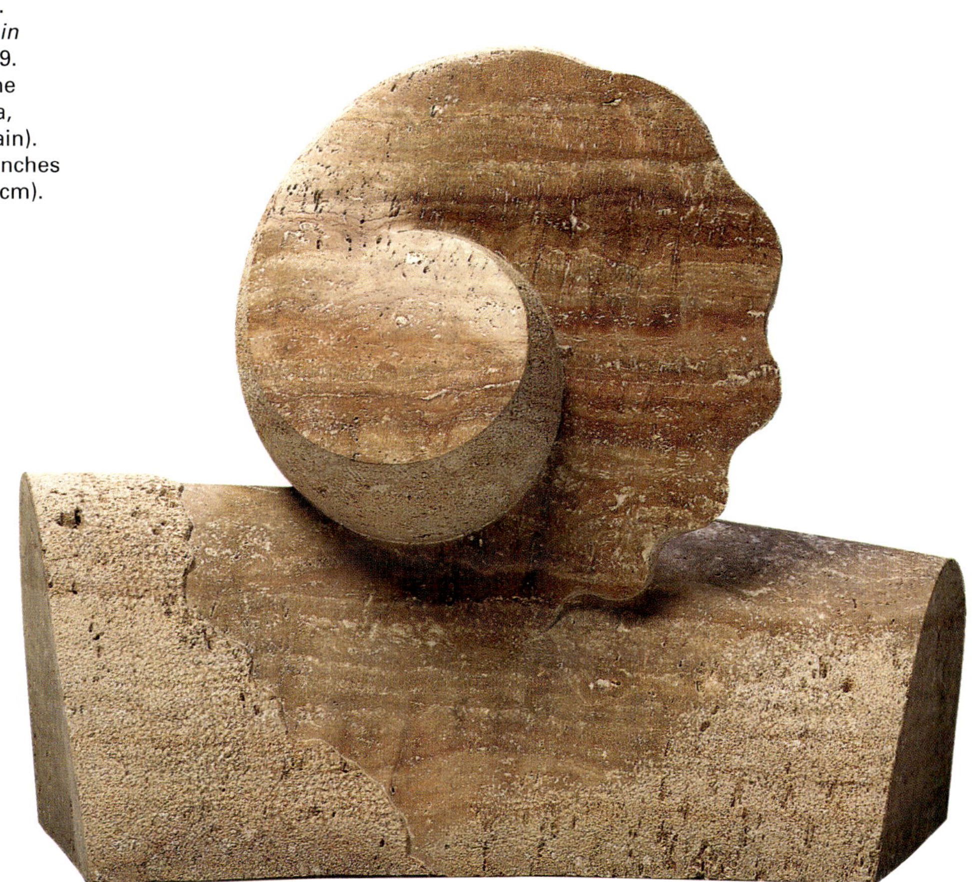

Copying by Points

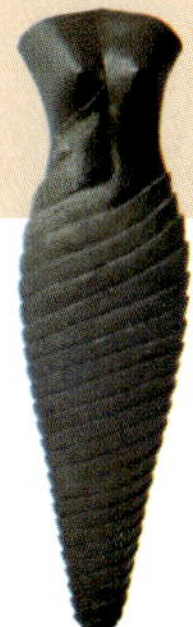

The most important part of this exercise is to understand that any point on a sculpture is located with three coordinates and that once they are "measured," they can be transcribed to a block of stone. In ancient times, this method required a complex set of tools, but today the pointing machine simplifies the task. We will see how easy it is to use this method and how even the most minute details can be reproduced. First Camí will model a figurative sculpture in clay, which is not typical of his current work. Then Mariano will reproduce it in the same size in black limestone.

Reproducing using the point system requires a model in a hard material such as plaster or terracotta. However, to avoid having to introduce techniques that are beyond the scope of this book, we will make a model in dry clay, though we are aware of the risk that the clay might deteriorate during the process.

In previous exercises we suggested making a maquette from compact material in order to help you become familiar with the subtraction process. However, most traditional sculptors prefer to use the addition process. By adding or subtracting, clay in our case, we can change the shape of the maquette as many times as we need to in order to arrive at the most satisfactory model.

This is a commissioned work and the individuals who commissioned it chose one sketch from among the several that we presented to them. And during the modeling process, they offered their opinions with respect to how the goddess—conch—amphora—lacrimarium should be shaped. This experience has made us reassess the role that patrons once played in the creative process.

The sculpture was conceived in black Belgium marble, but the sponsors chose a local stone: Calatorao limestone, Zaragoza (Spain), which grows between layers of clay.

Mariano will use the first pointing machine he acquired as a young man and that he proudly preserves. Unlike the pointing machines available today, this one requires the construction of a wooden cross arm.

For the carving, Mariano will use the tools he normally uses: a saw for the roughing out and a compressor with different types of chisels for modeling. He would get the same results if he used manual tools, but he would have to work a lot harder.

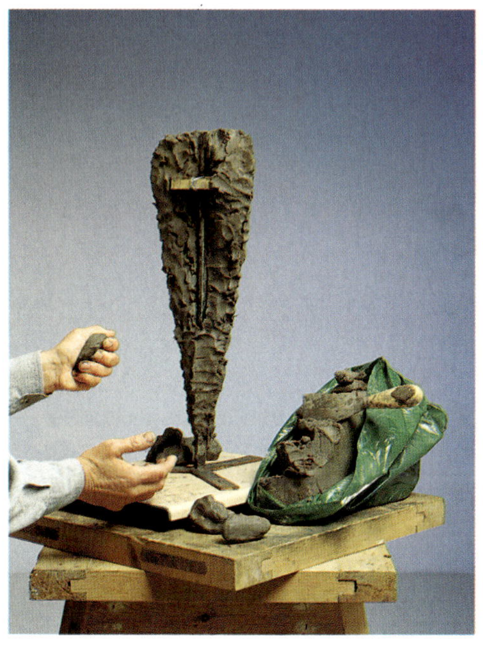

▲ **1.** We begin the model by screwing a T-shaped iron shaft wrapped in wire to a wooden platform to hold the clay. We add modeling clay to this structure, cutting with a palette knife and kneading.

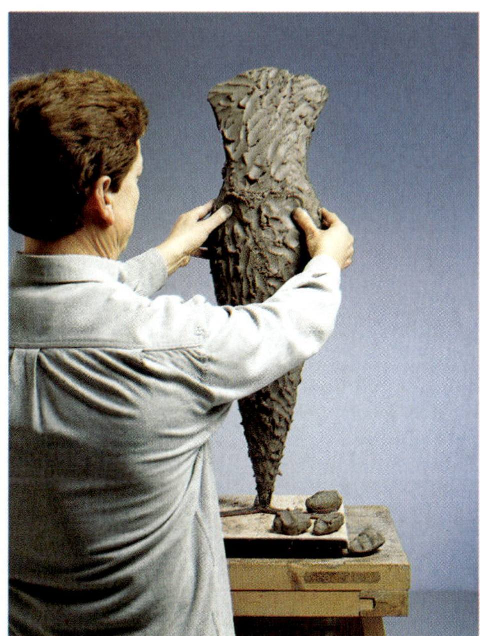

▲ **2.** Little by little, we continue covering the entire metal structure with the pieces of clay we have on the worktable until we get the shape we want.

▼ **3.** We use a square to check the symmetry and verticality of the piece; so as not to lose them, we mark the axes with the same metallic stick that we used for modeling.

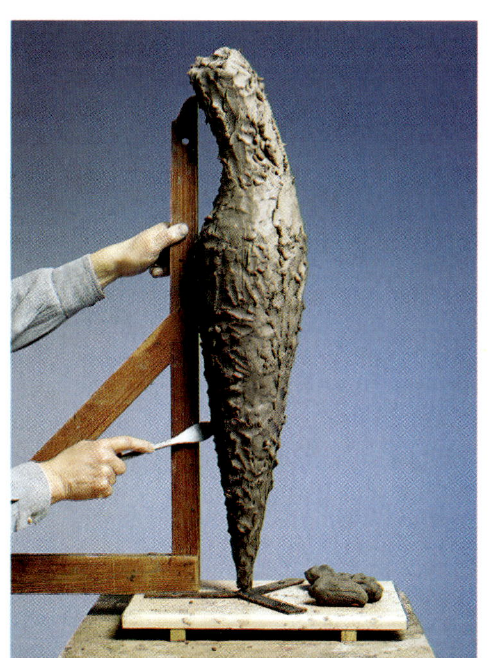

▼ **4.** We use a thumb to work the clay until it has been distributed to shape the necessary volumes.

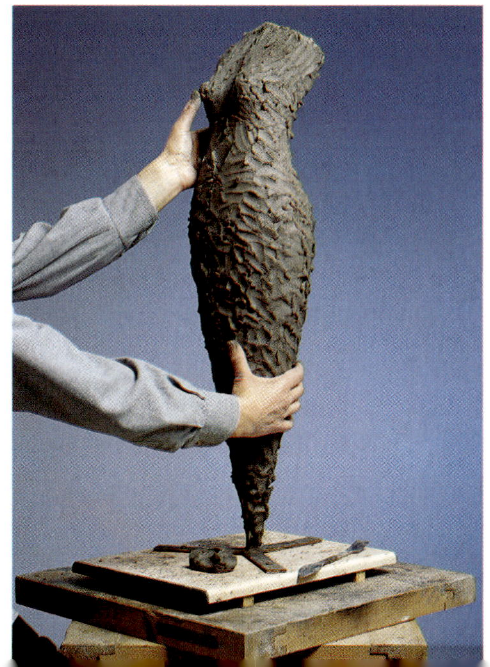

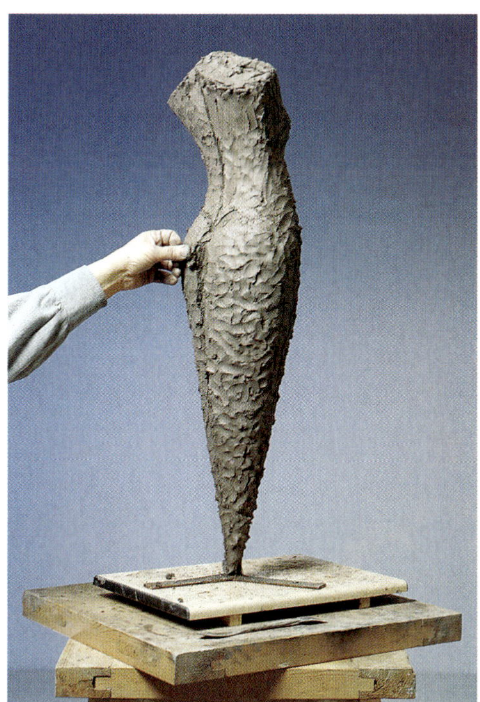

▲ **5.** We model the surface as we move around the figure, making sure that all of the outlines are correct and that they maintain a relationship with the axis symmetry.

▲ **6.** We use a slightly curved modeling stick to compress the clay and make it more compact, then we begin to define the shape.

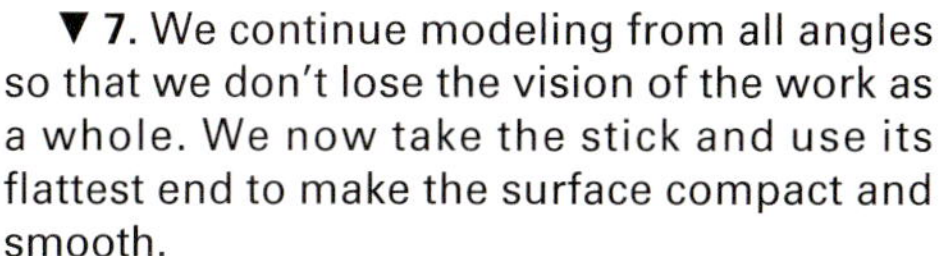

▼ **7.** We continue modeling from all angles so that we don't lose the vision of the work as a whole. We now take the stick and use its flattest end to make the surface compact and smooth.

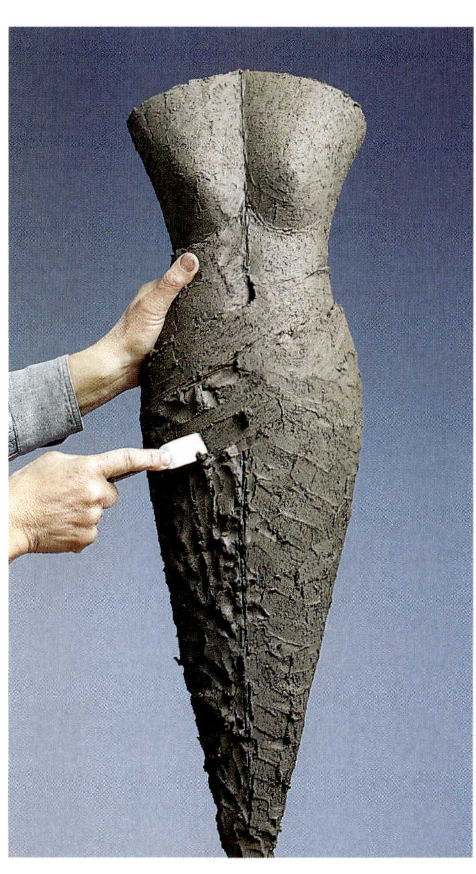

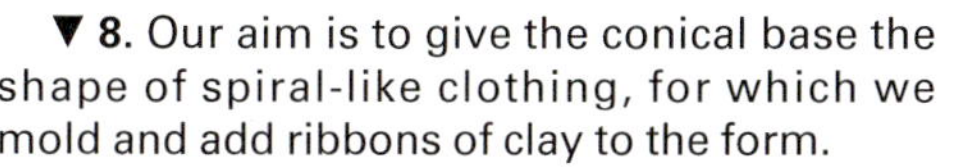

▼ **8.** Our aim is to give the conical base the shape of spiral-like clothing, for which we mold and add ribbons of clay to the form.

▼ **9.** A wet cloth helps keep the clay malleable and prevents it from cracking when we are not working it. Before letting it dry, we use a compass to check the symmetry and we add some final touches to the work.

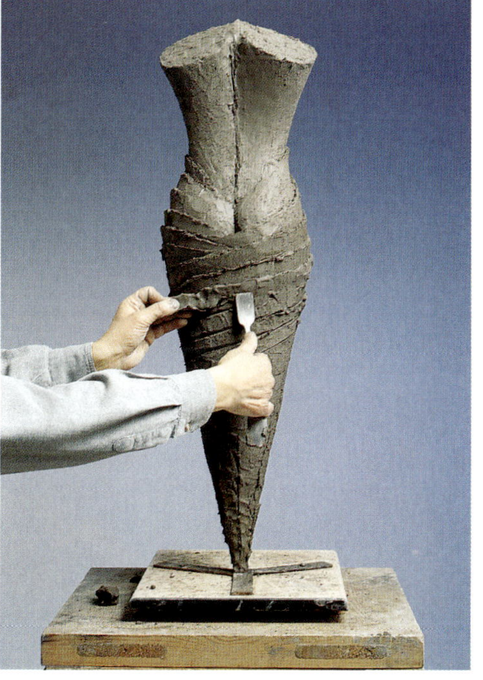

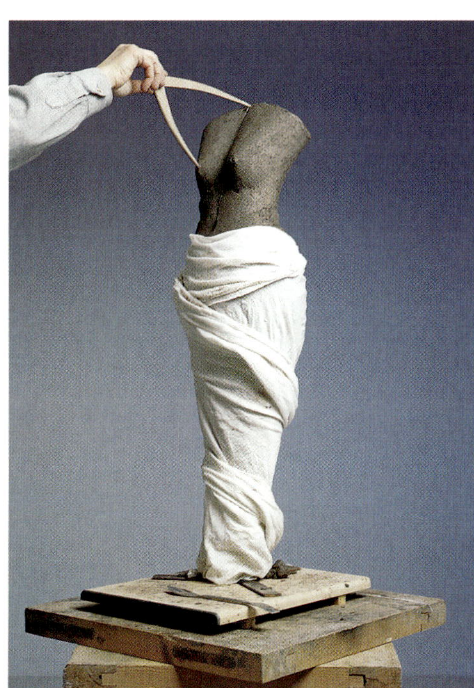

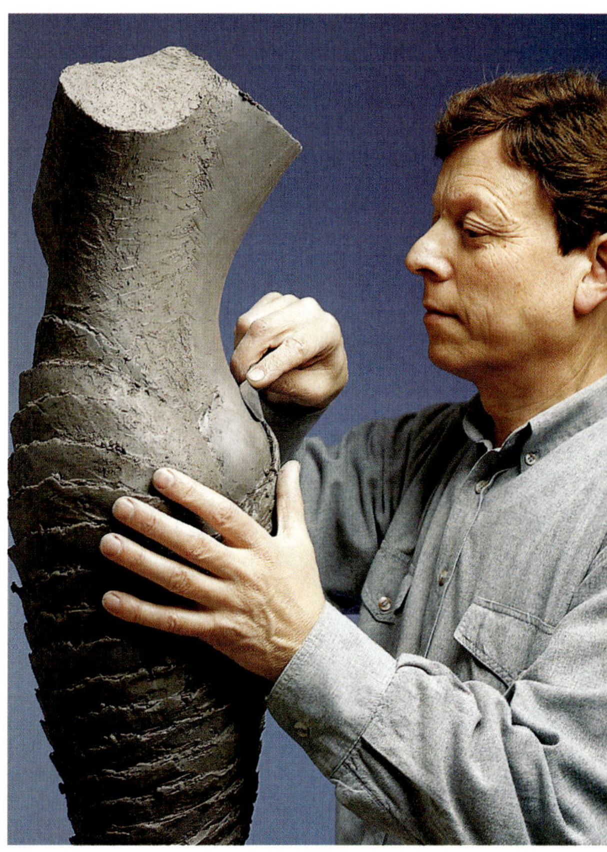

► **10.** When the clay is almost hard, we add some finishing touches. Here we use a curved stick to polish areas we want to give more light to. The only thing we have to do now is let the work dry slowly, avoiding abrupt changes in temperature that might crack the clay. It is not unusual to find that after several weeks our sculpture has shrunk by more than five percent.

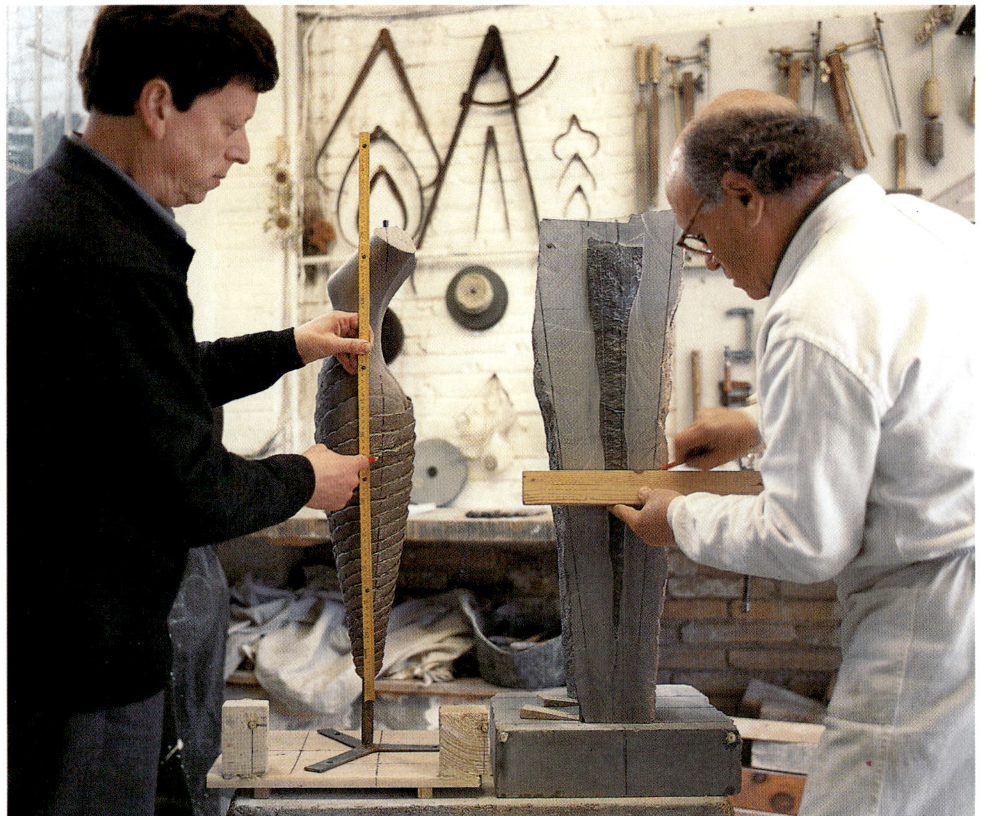

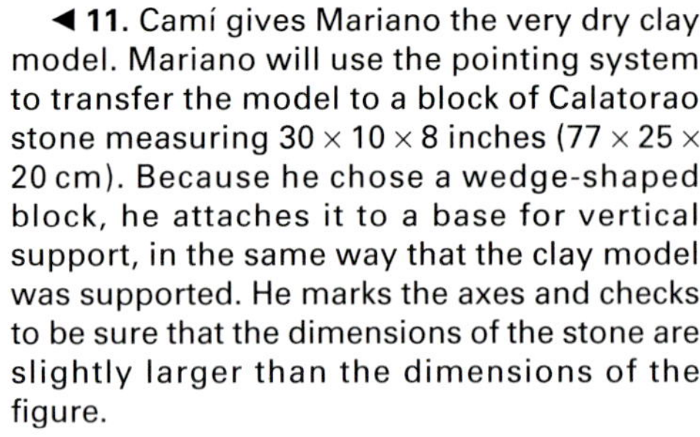

◄ **11.** Camí gives Mariano the very dry clay model. Mariano will use the pointing system to transfer the model to a block of Calatorao stone measuring 30 × 10 × 8 inches (77 × 25 × 20 cm). Because he chose a wedge-shaped block, he attaches it to a base for vertical support, in the same way that the clay model was supported. He marks the axes and checks to be sure that the dimensions of the stone are slightly larger than the dimensions of the figure.

▼ **12.** We make a hole at the top of the model to make a point of support for the cross arm. This is the perforation we will make on the model.

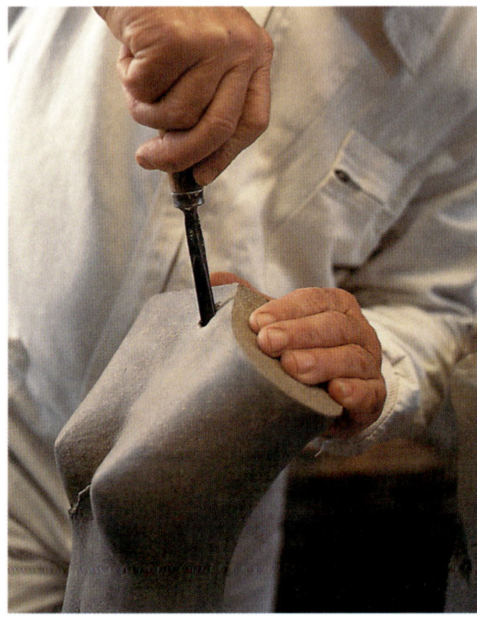

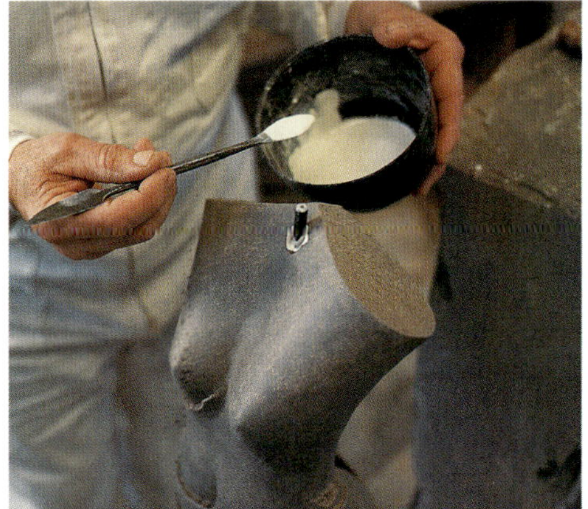

◄ **13.** We insert a metal rod into the hole, set it with plaster of Paris, and leave a small concave opening at the top where we will fit the cross arm. We use a metal rod to be sure that this important point of reference does not change during the process.

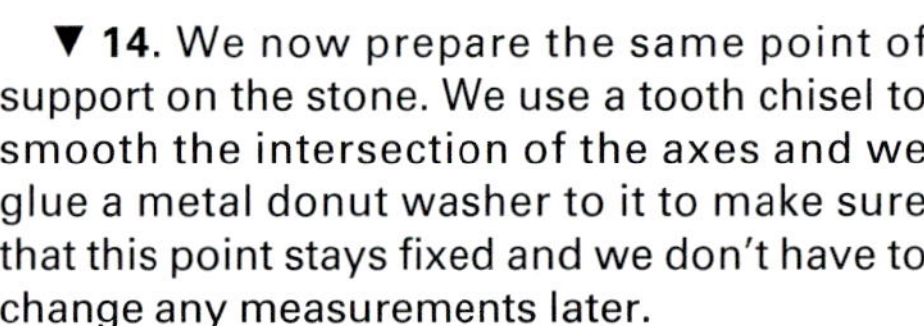

▼ **14.** We now prepare the same point of support on the stone. We use a tooth chisel to smooth the intersection of the axes and we glue a metal donut washer to it to make sure that this point stays fixed and we don't have to change any measurements later.

▼ **15.** Our pointing machine does not have a built-in cross arm. Therefore, we build one by gluing and nailing together two planks in the shape of a T, making it slightly larger than the width and height of the sculpture we want to copy.

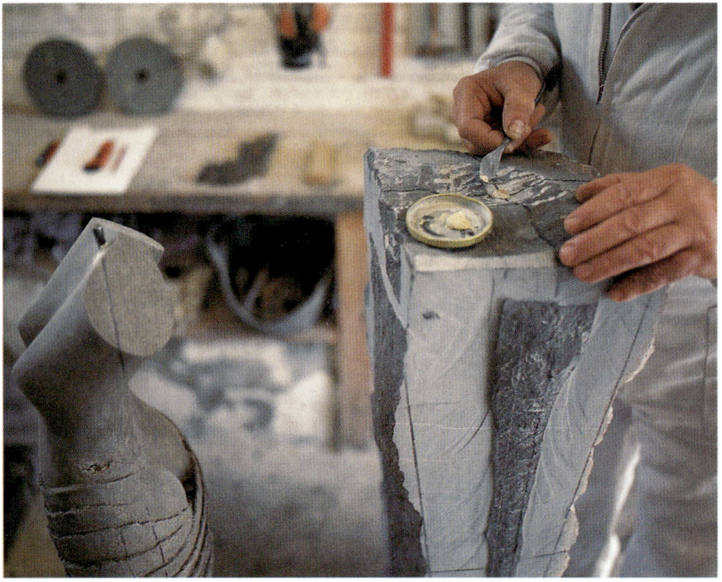

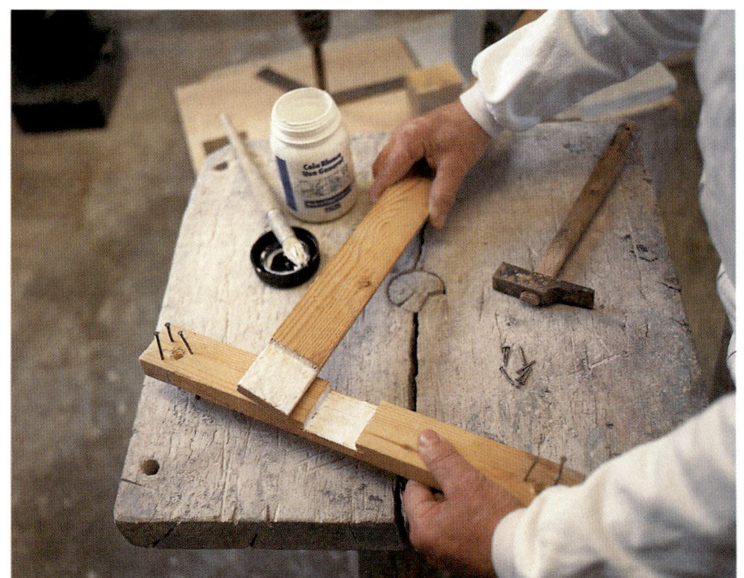

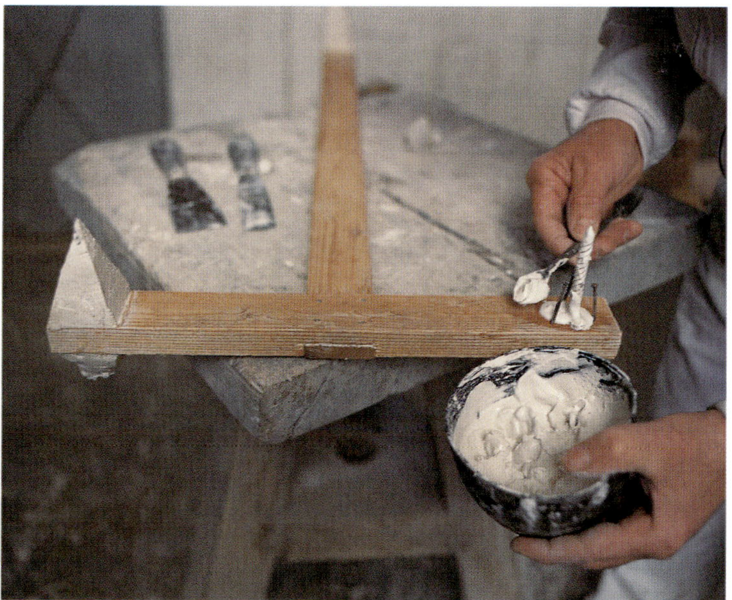

◀ **16.** A long nail should protrude from each end of the cross arm. The points of the nails will rest alternatively against the support points of the model and the block. We attach the nail with a pyramid of plaster supported by smaller nails.

▶ **17.** This is what the upper point of support looks like. Unlike the others, this one has to have a curved hook pointing downward.

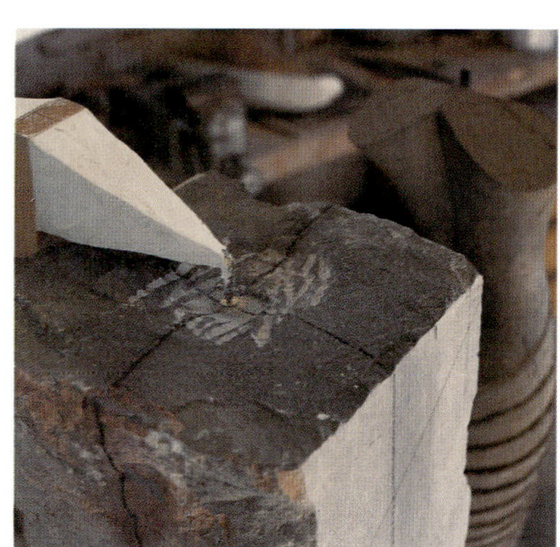

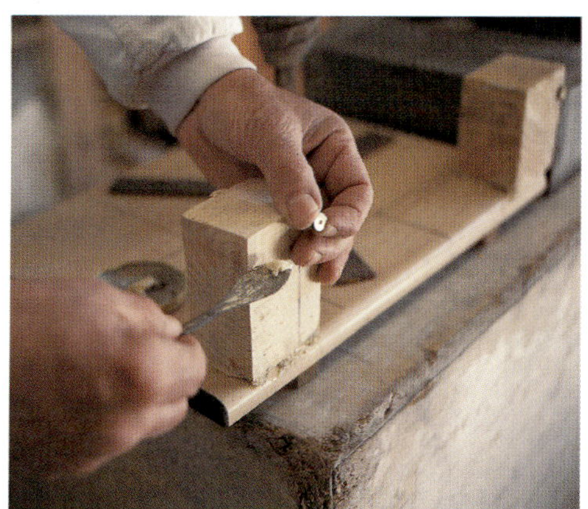

◀ **18.** We mark and fortify with metal washers the other two support points in the pedestal. As our sculpture does not have a base, Mariano had to glue these two wedges. The cross arm determines the distance between the three support points.

▶ **19.** We mark and reinforce the same lower points, but this time on the stone. Mariano complemented the plaster pyramids with other truncated ones that, though seeming unnecessary, serve as a counterweight and are also used as handles.

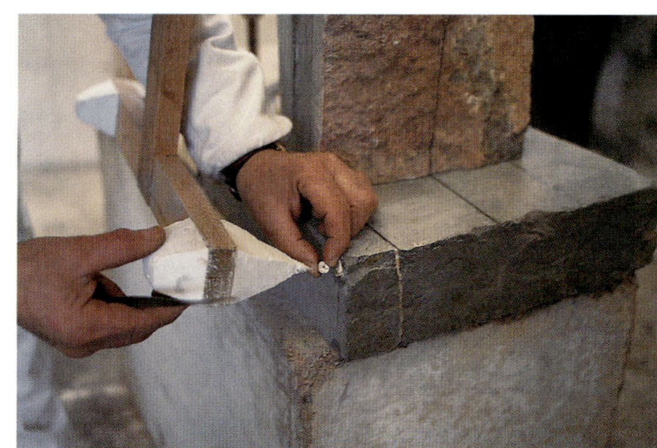

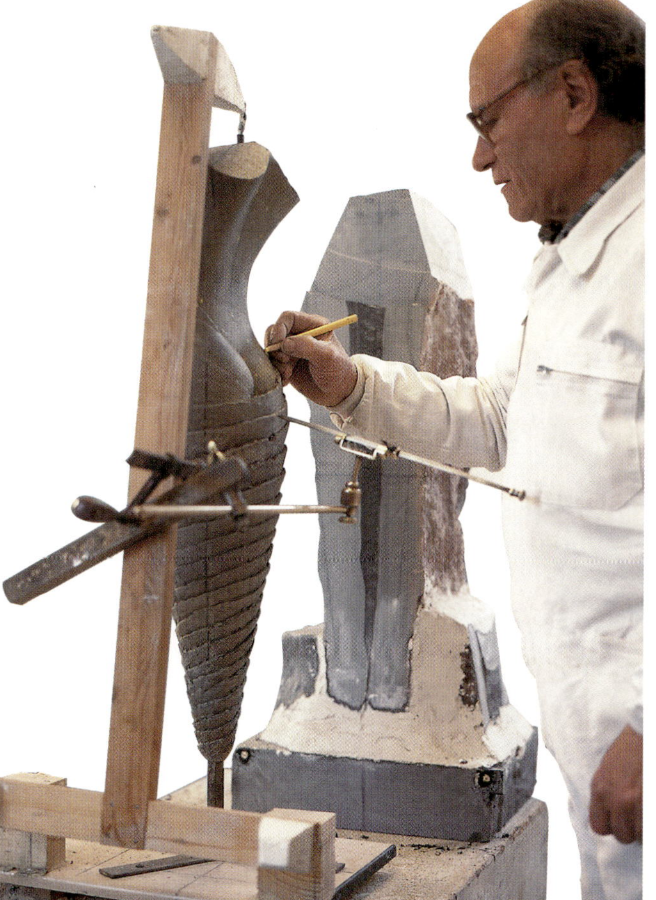

◀ **20.** Finally, we use a jack to adjust the articulated arm of the cross arm to any height, as long as there is no change in each measurement. The system is now ready to transcribe points from the model to the stone. We always place the pointing machine first on the model; we take a point . . .

▶ **21.** . . . then we transfer all of the equipment to the block, keeping the position of the arm the same; we hang it from the three supports and we transcribe the selected point to the stone. We will now see how to do this.

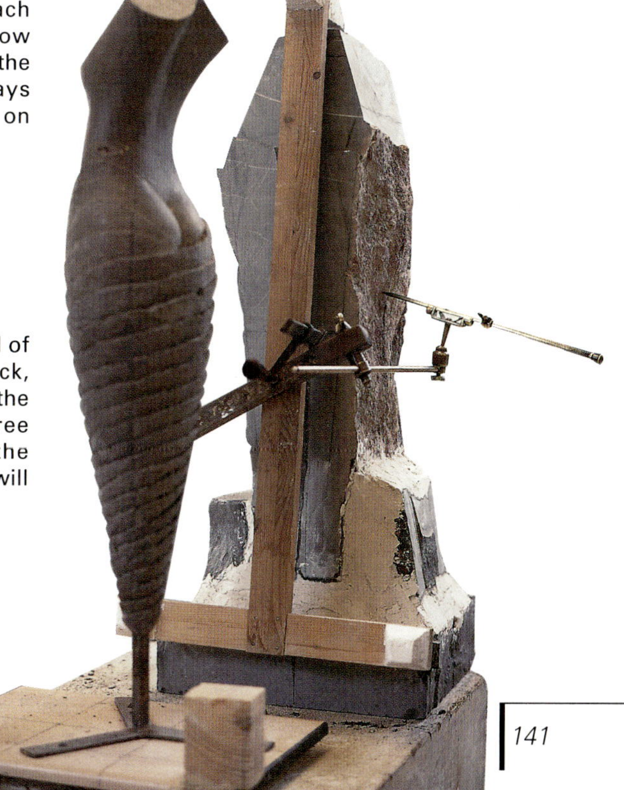

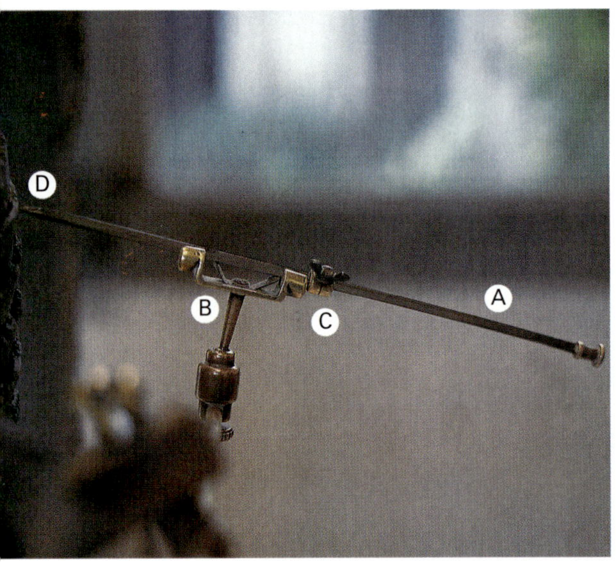

◀ **22.** The arm of the pointing machine, articulated by socket joints, serves as a support for a large needle (A) that can be slid over the support (B). A moveable screw (C) is then slid over the needle and once tightened, marks a benchmark. To point, we will rub the model with the end of the needle (D) and we tighten the screw next to the support. This is our benchmark.

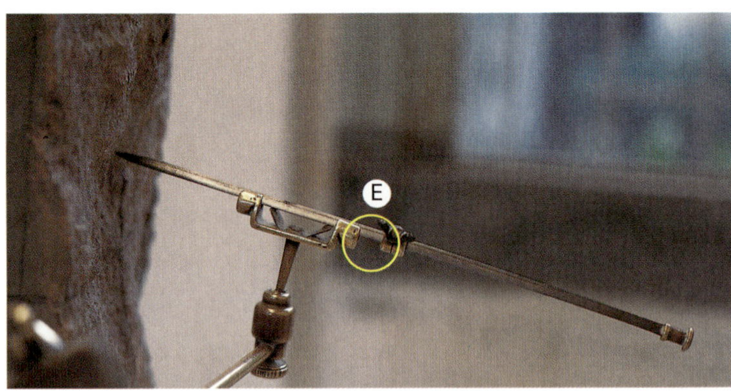

▲ **23.** When we transfer the cross arm to the block, keeping the articulation of the arm unchanged, we will see that the needle does not penetrate as deeply as it did on the model. The inches (E) that separate the screw from the benchmark indicate the quantity of stone that has to be removed. To insert the point, we will cut the stone back until the needle reaches the predetermined benchmark.

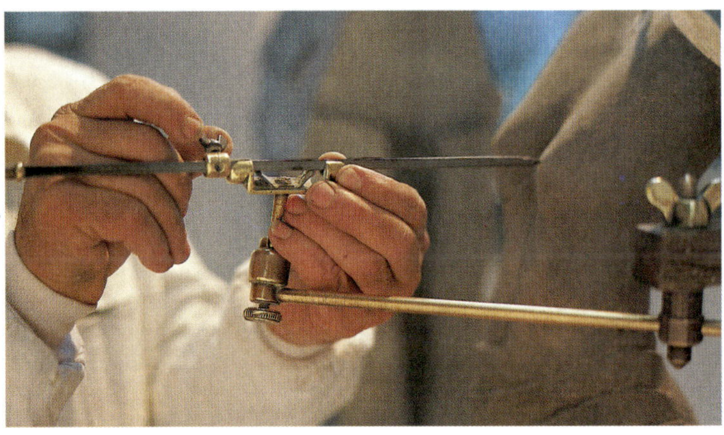

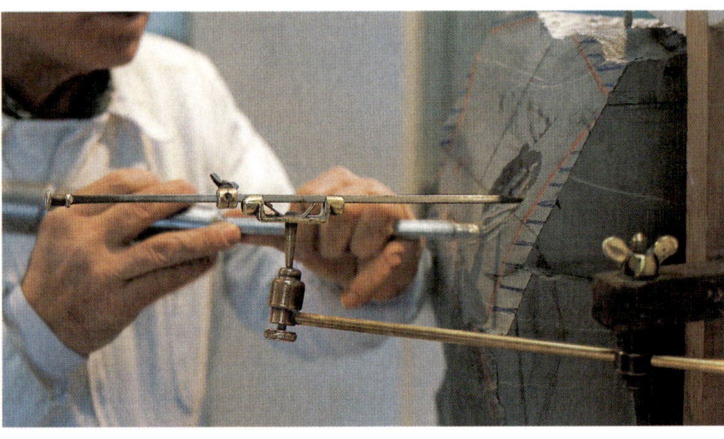

▲ **24.** To streamline the job, we will first look for the most prominent points and reduce them; we will insert the reeds again, continue to reduce the stone, and finally insert the deepest ones. We begin first by measuring the situation of the nipples on the model, then we mark the benchmark, and after marking the point taken from the model in yellow, we transfer the cross arm to the stone.

▲ **25.** Knowing that the position of the articulated arm indicates the height of the selected point, while the needle indicates the depth, our only concern will be to perforate the stone until the preestablished benchmark stops the needle. Here we use a point chisel to reduce the area around the point that we wish to insert.

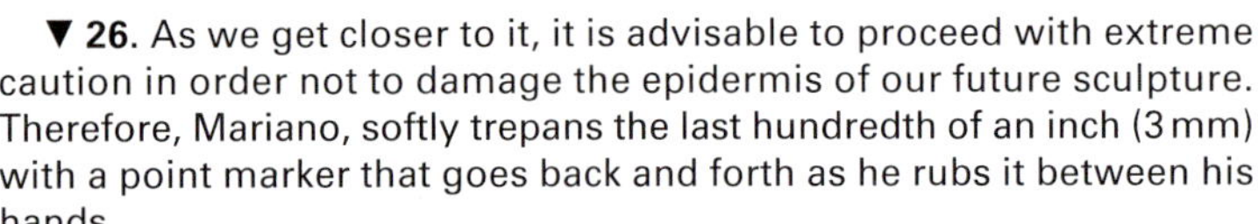

▼ **26.** As we get closer to it, it is advisable to proceed with extreme caution in order not to damage the epidermis of our future sculpture. Therefore, Mariano, softly trepans the last hundredth of an inch (3 mm) with a point marker that goes back and forth as he rubs it between his hands.

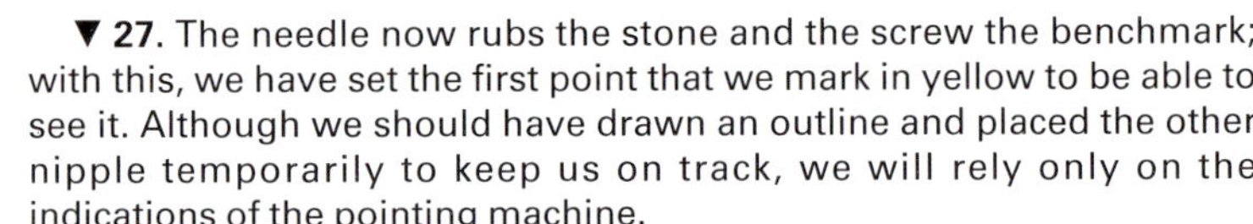

▼ **27.** The needle now rubs the stone and the screw the benchmark; with this, we have set the first point that we mark in yellow to be able to see it. Although we should have drawn an outline and placed the other nipple temporarily to keep us on track, we will rely only on the indications of the pointing machine.

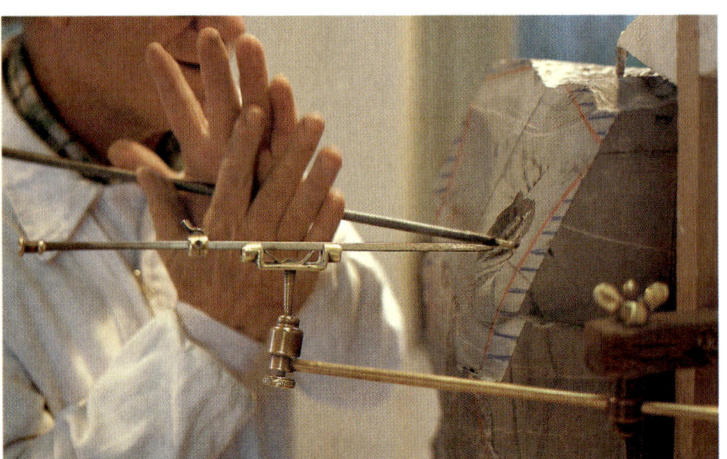

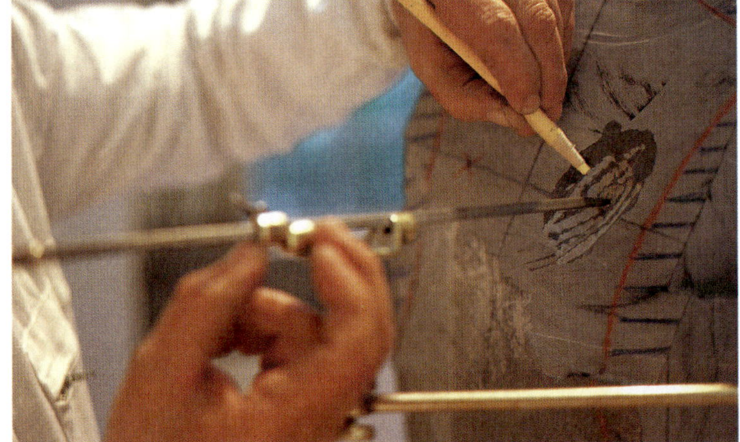

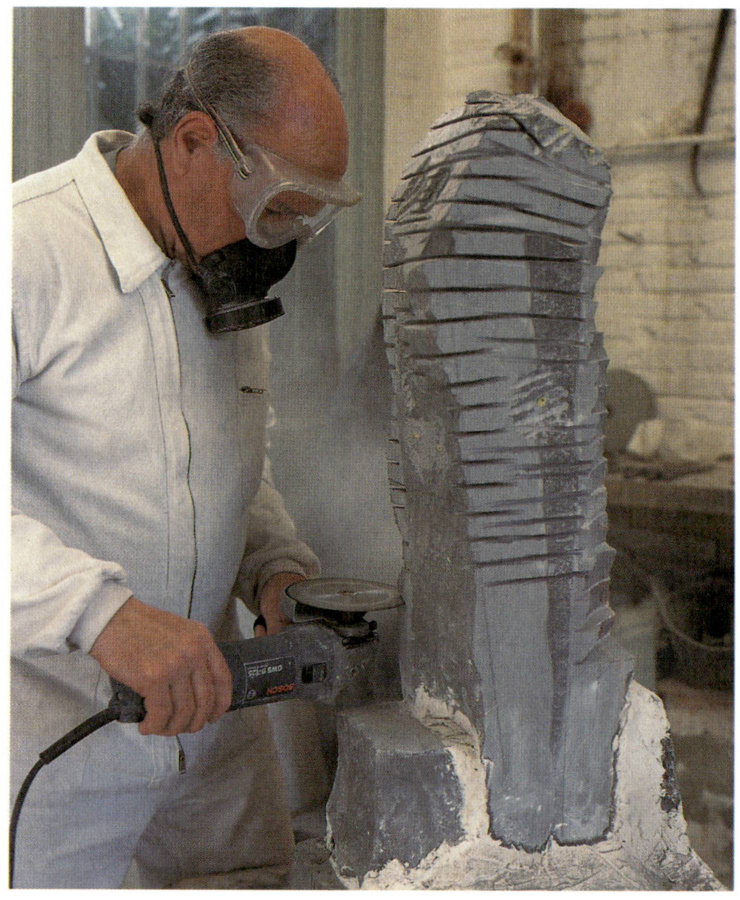

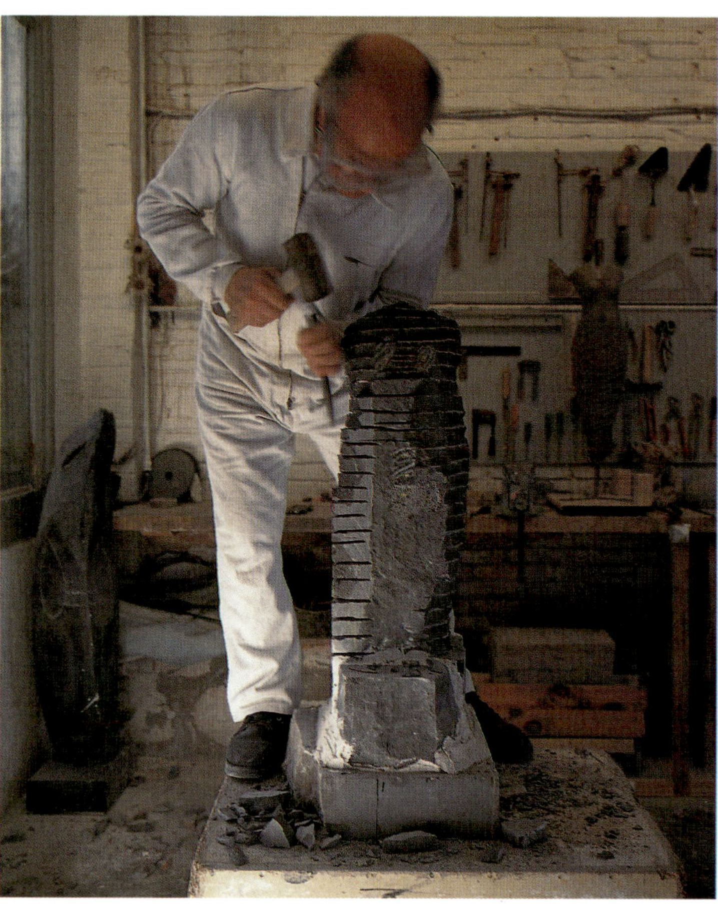

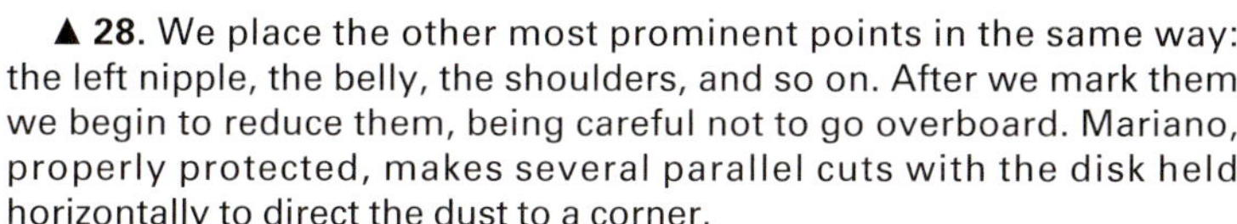

▲ **28.** We place the other most prominent points in the same way: the left nipple, the belly, the shoulders, and so on. After we mark them we begin to reduce them, being careful not to go overboard. Mariano, properly protected, makes several parallel cuts with the disk held horizontally to direct the dust to a corner.

▲ **29.** We smooth out the rough spots using a chisel to cut the layers marked with the circular saw. Mariano is not hesitant and he stands on top of the worktable to find the best angle.

▼ **30.** This is how the outline of the block remains after the first reduction. Because the circular saw is not very precise, we go closer to the yellow points with a broach chisel. The bottom hints at the next step—smoothing the surface by connecting the points.

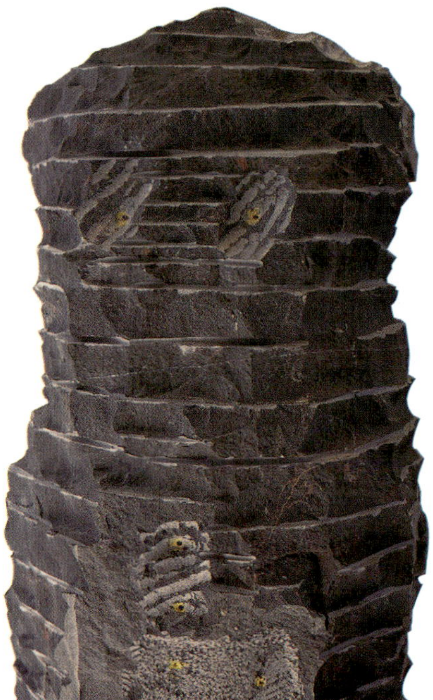

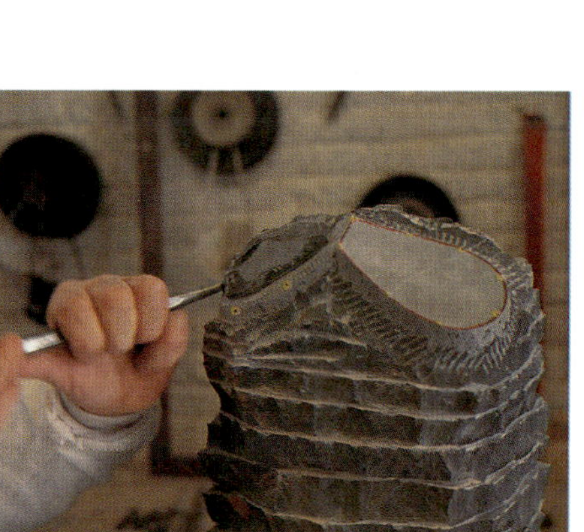

▼ **31.** This system of copying is so reliable that we are able to model several areas before reducing others. To define each shoulder, we have inserted eight points and by connecting them we have drawn their outline in red. After an initial reduction with a point chisel, we use a chisel to get closer to the limit and we define the first master line of the sculpture.

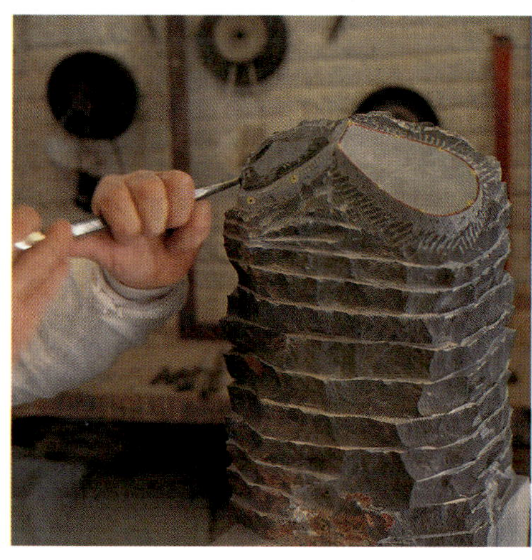

▼ **32.** Now that we have the limits marked, we can use the circular saw to smooth the shoulders. We do this without changing the support point of the cross arm, which is not visible because it emerges from the front face.

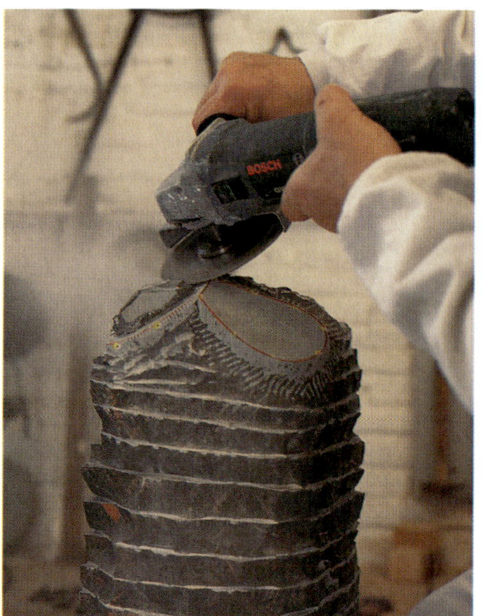

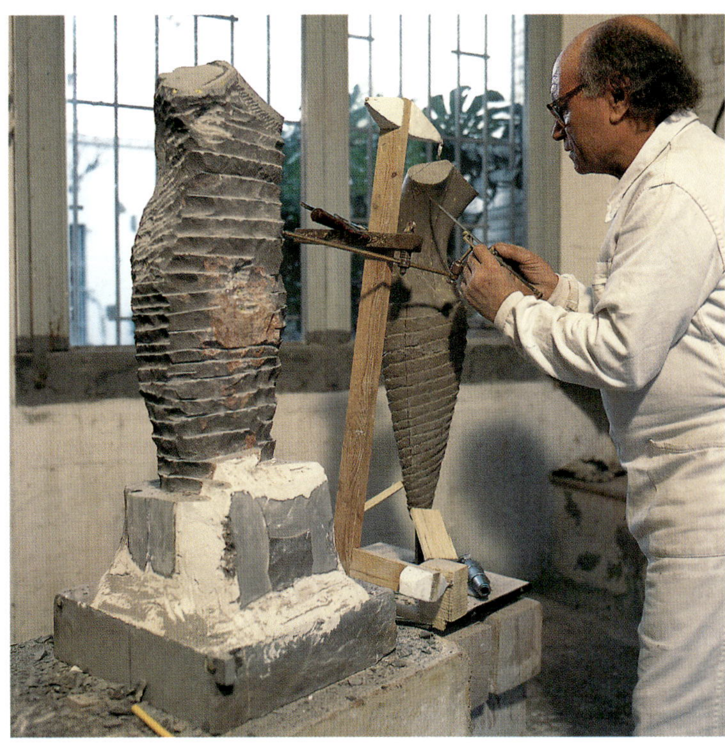

▲ **33.** Afterwards we continue removing the intermediate points of the back. The reddish mark of the stone reminds us of the layer of clay that covered the calatorao that we have barely reduced. With the cross arm over the model, Mariano removes a point of average depth.

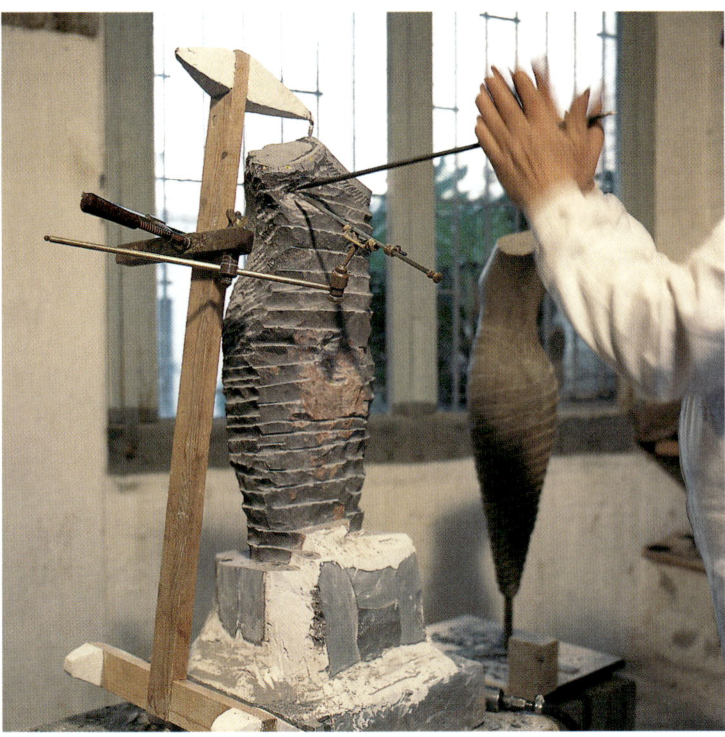

▲ **34.** We transfer the cross arm to the block and with a broach chisel we make a hole where the needle indicates, and there we again meticulously insert the point.

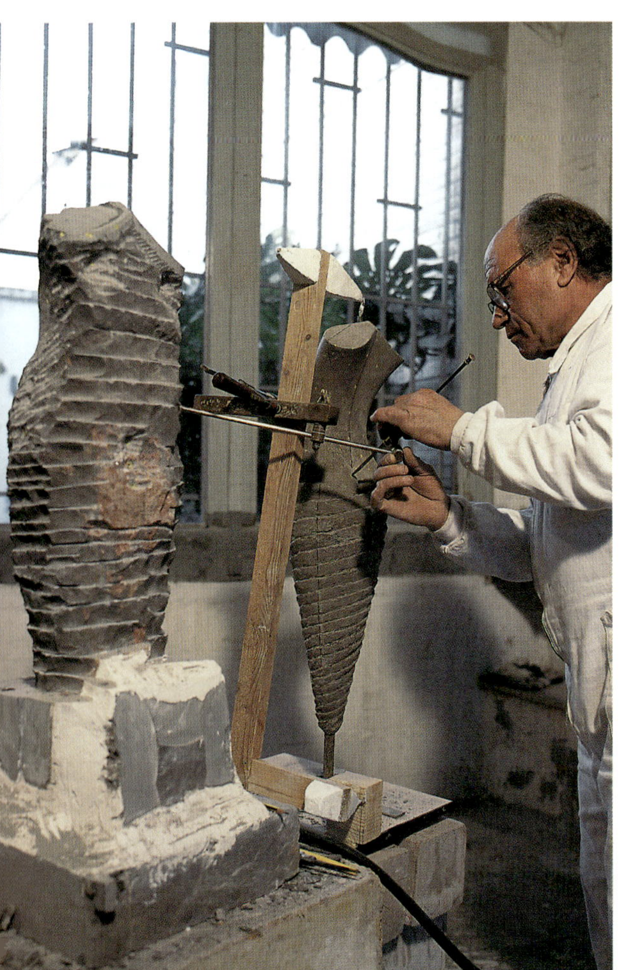

◀ **35.** We repeat the process this way as many times as we need to depending on the complexity of the shape and our insecurity. The time we invest results in precision. First, with the cross arm resting securely on the three support points, we place the articulated arm at the appropriate height, then we sink in the needle, we mark the point, we adjust the screw next to the benchmark . . .

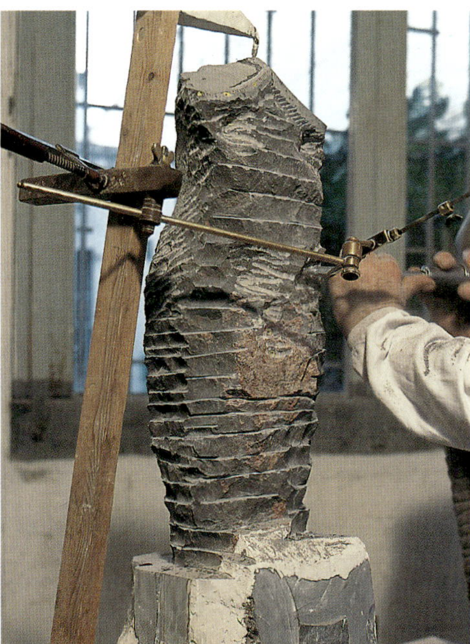

▲ **36.** . . . then we transfer the cross arm to the block and we drill it to the depth indicated by the needle . . .

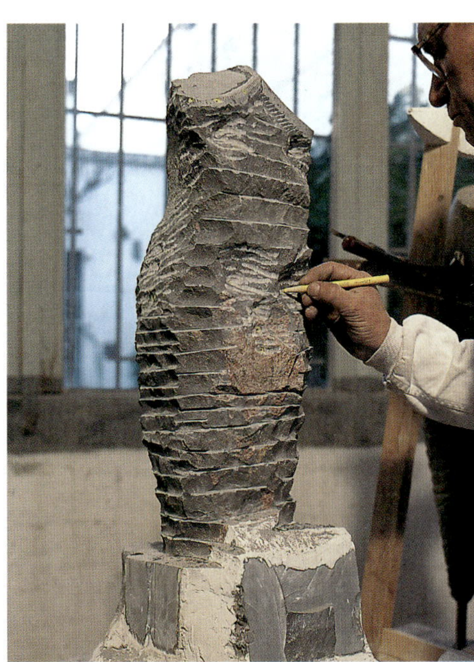

▲ **37.** . . . we mark the point, this time on the stone. We continue like this until we have transferred all of the points we think are important.

► **38.** When we have inserted enough points of average depth, we reduce the block by making cuts with the circular saw that are not as deep as the marked points. Here, between the horizontal and parallel cuts, Mariano has made a vertical one to better control the slices.

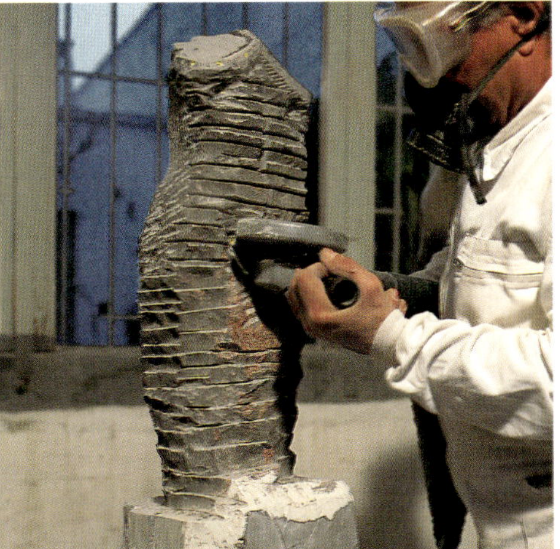

► **39.** As before, we use a chisel and a hammer to break the layers that the circular saw has left. If they are all appropriately deep, the sculpture will take on shape.

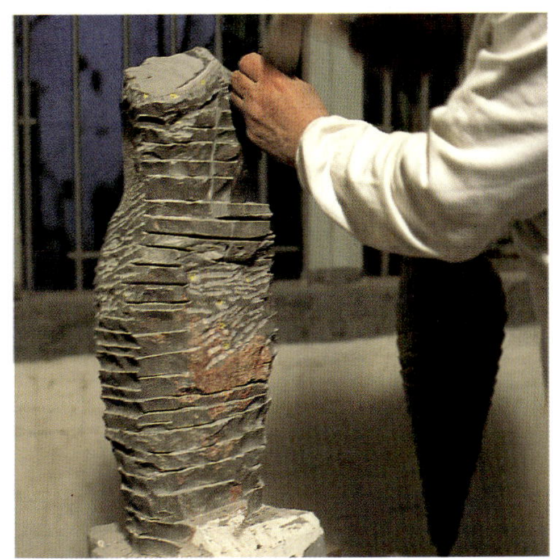

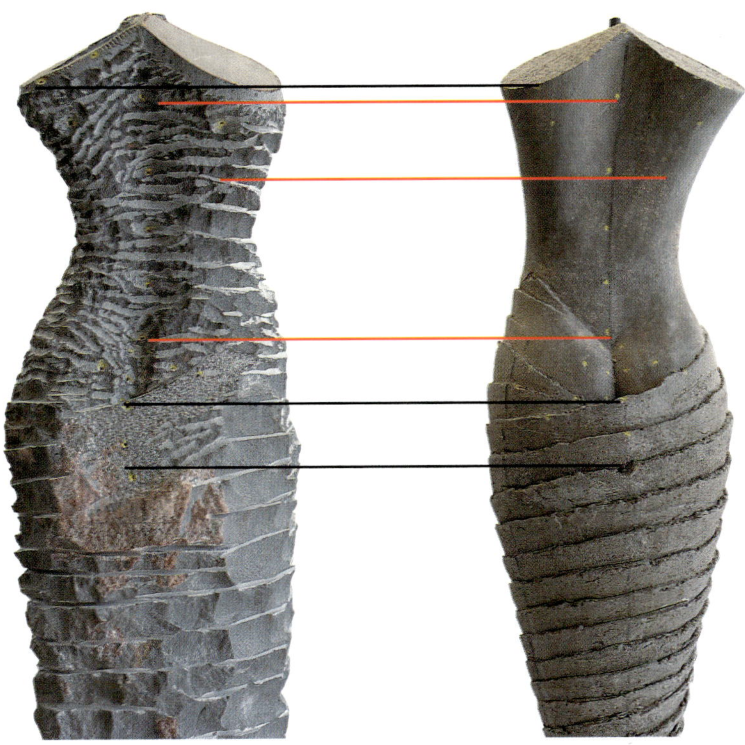

▲ **40.** In the third phase, we transfer the deepest points from the model to the stone, which here defines the spinal column. We reduce again, this time using a point chisel, which is more precise than the circular saw. Connecting the areas between the points gives continuity to the shape. We always try, and this is very important, to be sure that the points are deeper than what we reduce. We mark the superficial points black and the deeper ones red.

▼ **41.** After we have inserted all of the secondary points that we feel are necessary to work with certainty, we erase the traces of the point chisel with a bushing tool. We are only about one hundredth of an inch (a few mm) from the final surface, outlined in the shallow points.

▼ **42.** With a chisel we continue modeling the areas that the bushing tool cannot reach. The yellow spots let us know how many times we have placed the cross arm to copy this relatively simple shape. The calatorao had a surprise for us: A white vein girdles our lady. As we are not dealing with a hairline fracture, there is no danger. Our only consideration is whether we want to dye it or keep it as is.

▼ **43.** We now model the entire surface with the tooth chisel, and afterwards, with the chisel we erase the traces and also the point marks. Once the volume of the back is defined, the only thing left to do is to work the texture of the clothing.

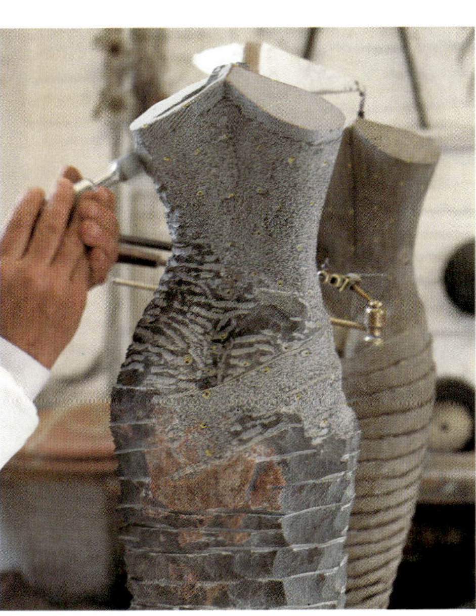

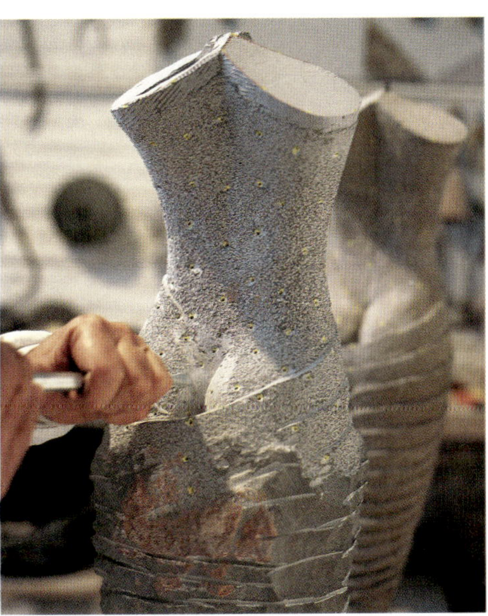

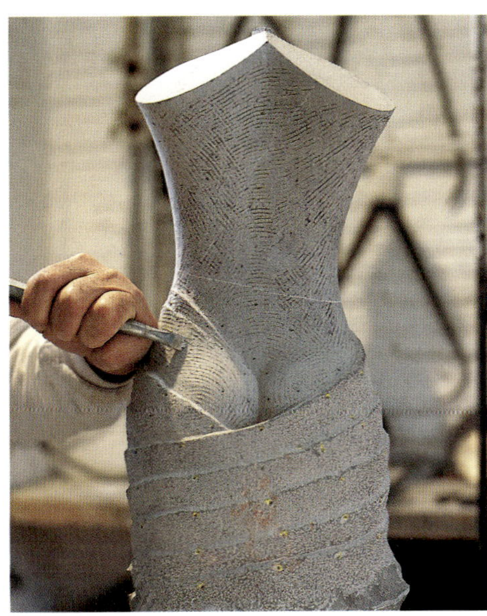

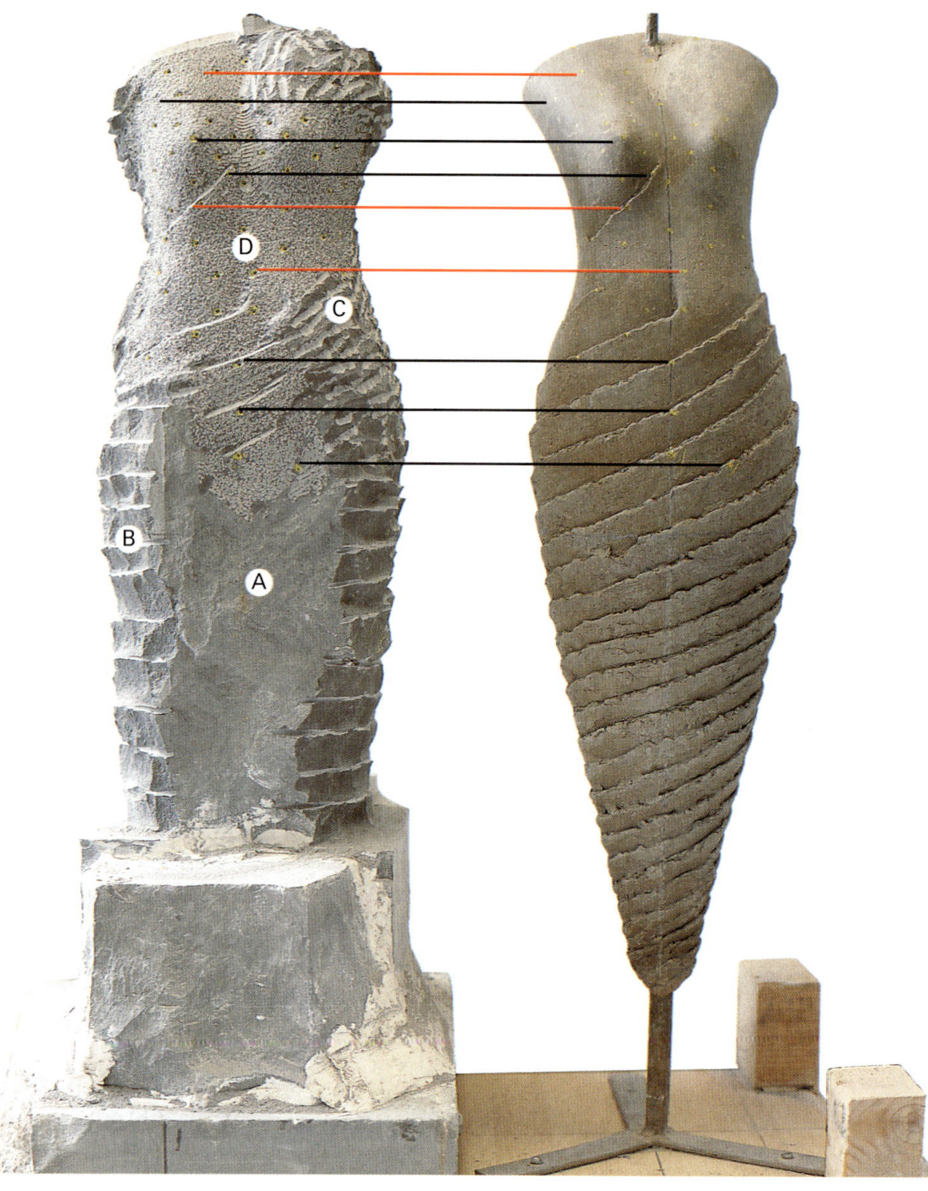

▼ ◀ **44.** While we modeled the back side of the sculpture, we also worked on the front face so that we would not lose sight of the work as a whole. Here we have the model and the sculpture with yellow specks, representing the numerous points that we inserted. We still conserve an original surface (A), grooves from the cutting disk (B), marks from the point chisel (C), and areas smoothed by the bushing tool (D).

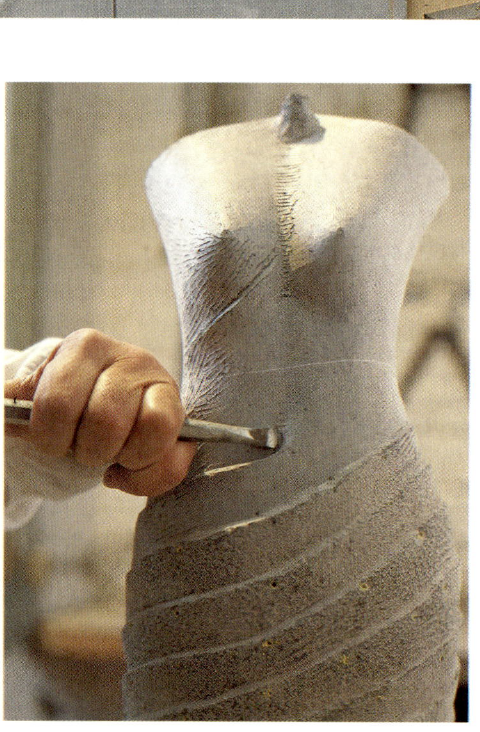

▶ **45.** Some areas require more meticulous work: We use a chisel to define the edges.

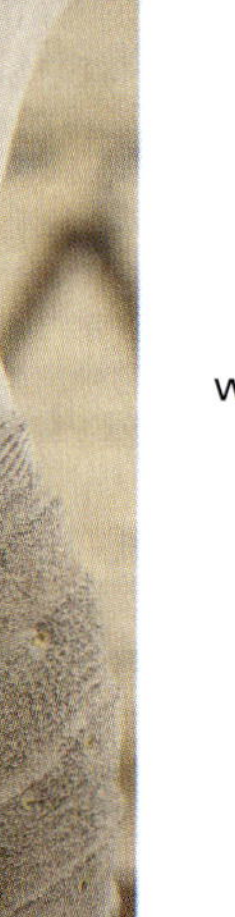

◀ **46.** We work the concave areas with a broach chisel.

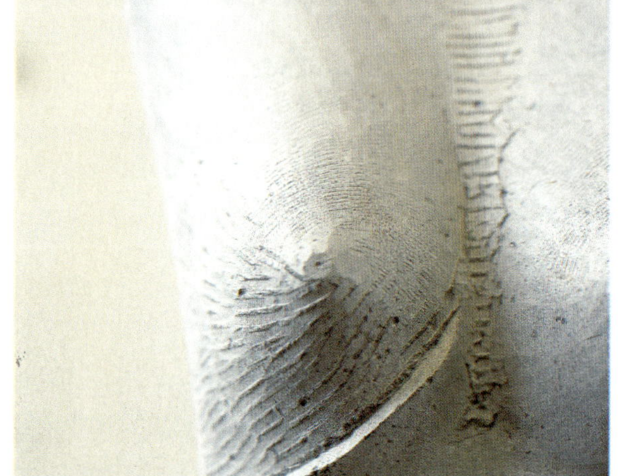

▶ **47.** We use the tooth chisel, first a thick one, then a thinner one to continue modeling.

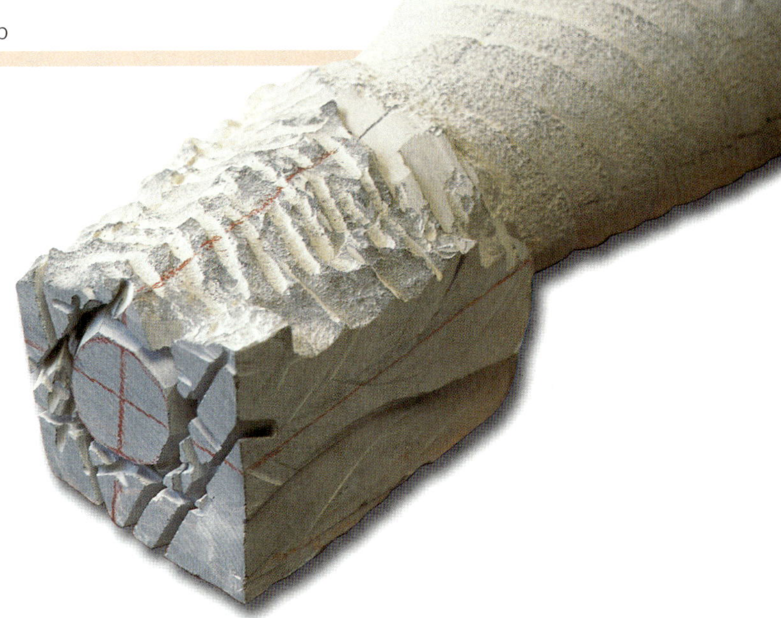

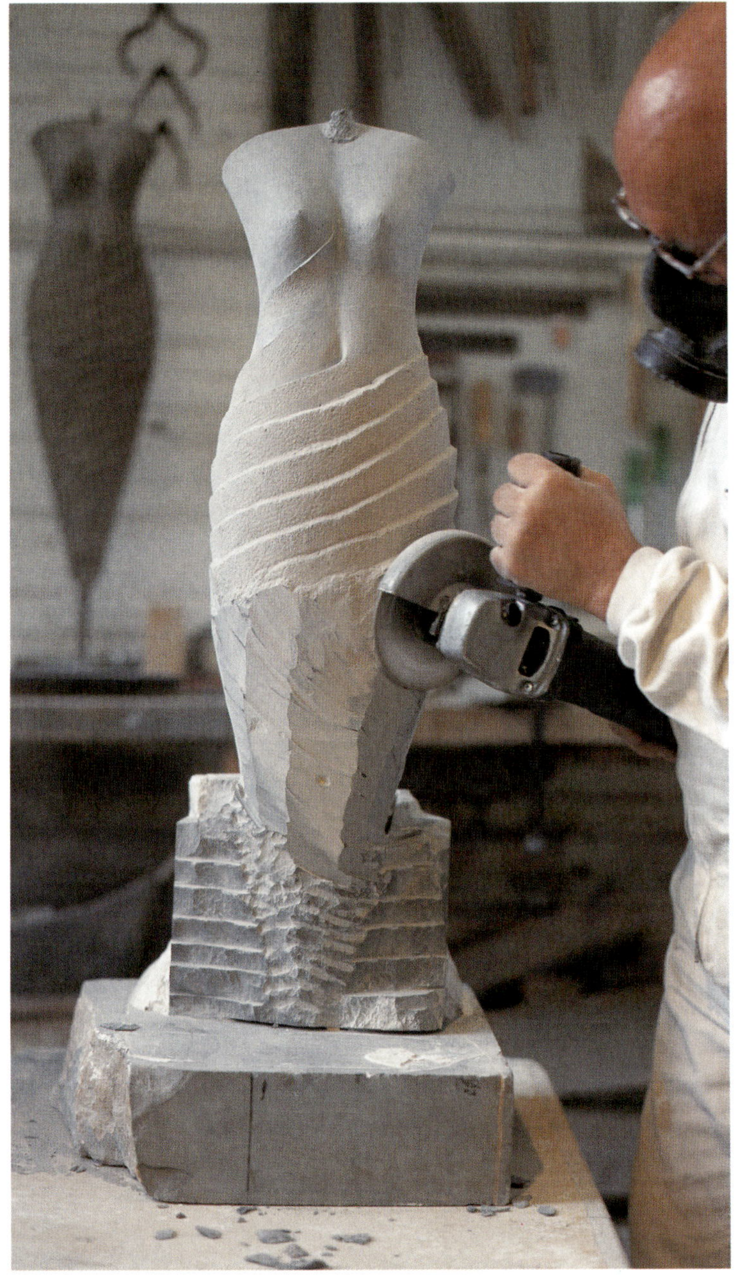

◄ **48.** After inserting new points that define the cone-shaped part of the sculpture, Mariano uses the circular saw to subtract large planes. He uses the point chisel, the tooth chisel, and the bushing tool in that order to complete the work.

► **49.** To furrow the inside of the border that encompasses the base, Mariano surprises us with a drill with a diamond disk, more commonly used by lapidaries.

▲ **50.** When the sculpture is modeled, heavy strikes are made to loosen the cast from the stones that help it to the base. We use the symmetrical axes as a guide for completing the removal.

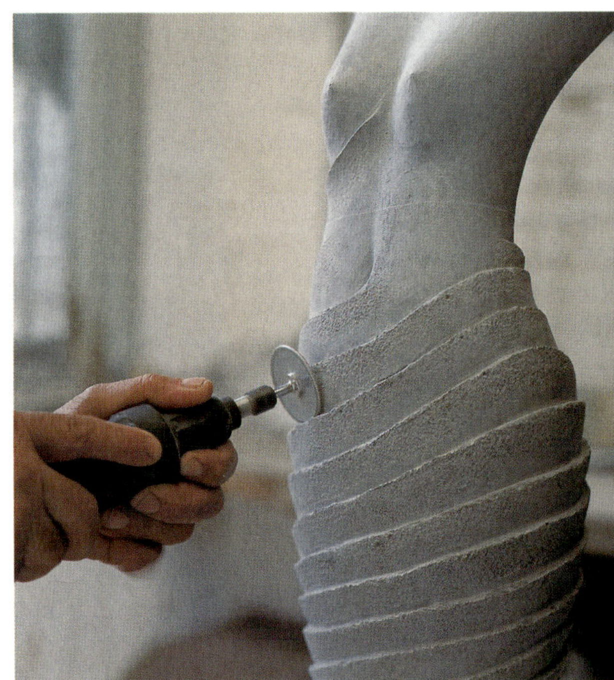

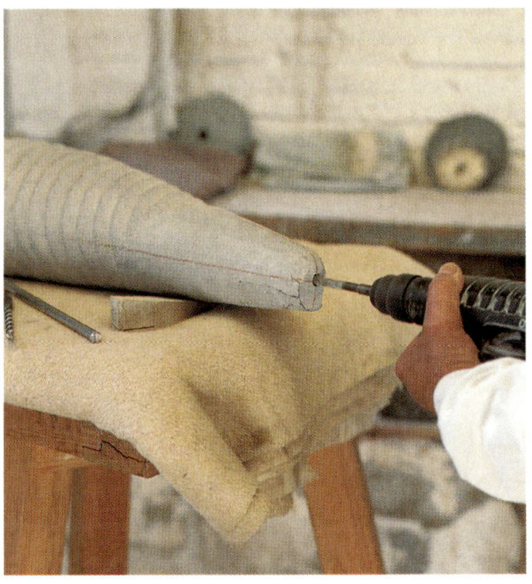

◄ **51.** With the sculpture lying securely on a blanket, and held tight by another person, a hole is drilled into it into which we will introduce a steel bar to fix the sculpture to a pedestal.

► **52.** Now that the sculpture is totally modeled, we can eliminate the support points of the cross arm. We chisel around the base to free it and then we even out the surface.

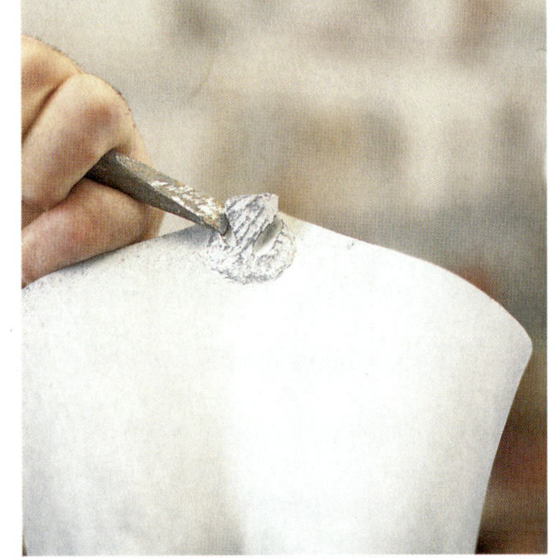

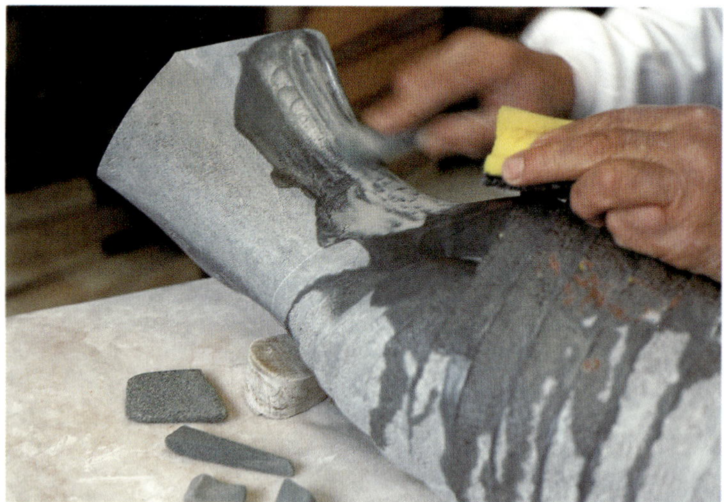

◀ **53.** To give more light to certain areas, we first smooth the surface with increasingly finer carborundum and use a wet sponge to clean the pores.

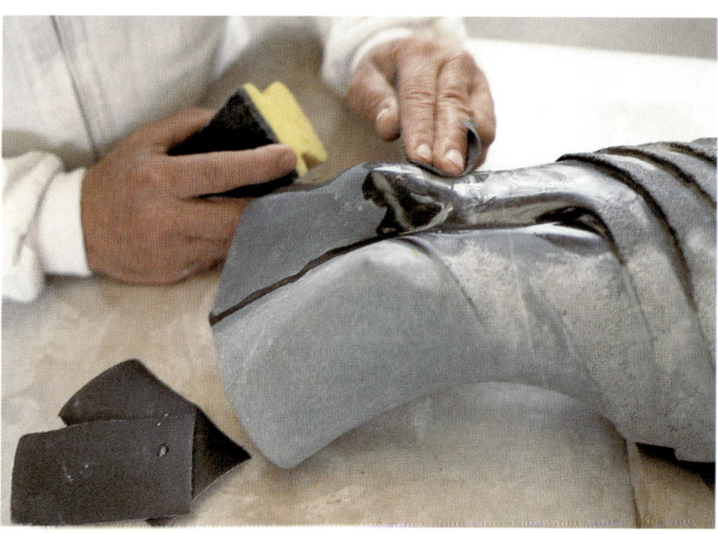

▲ **54.** The calatorao is very pleasing when it is cleaned. For this we use different wet sandpaper with increasingly finer grain.

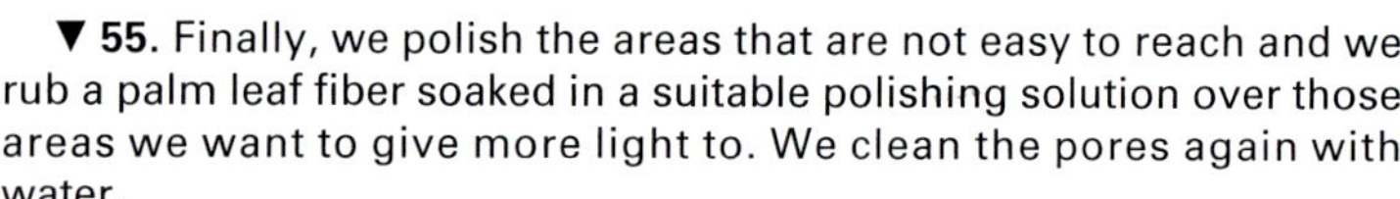

▼ **55.** Finally, we polish the areas that are not easy to reach and we rub a palm leaf fiber soaked in a suitable polishing solution over those areas we want to give more light to. We clean the pores again with water.

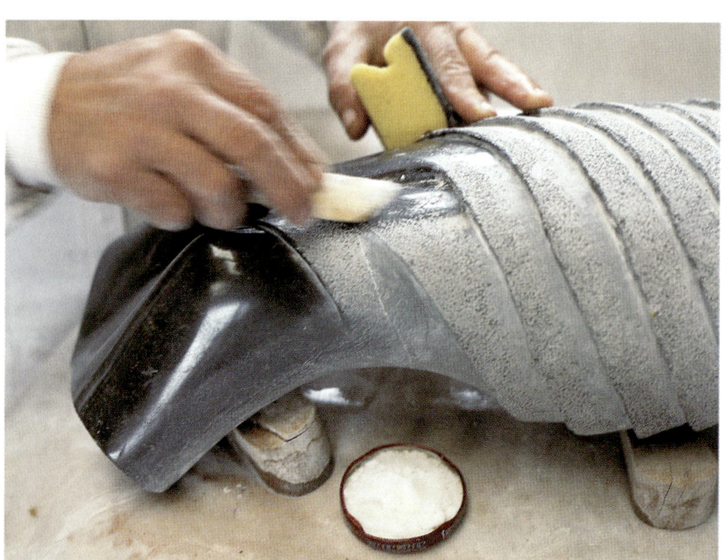

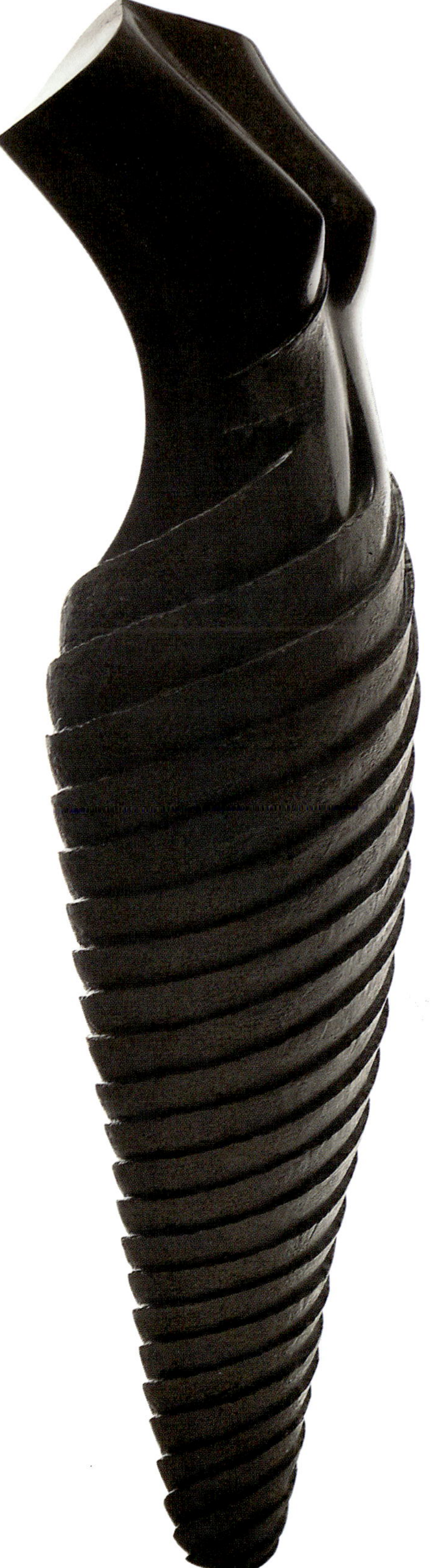

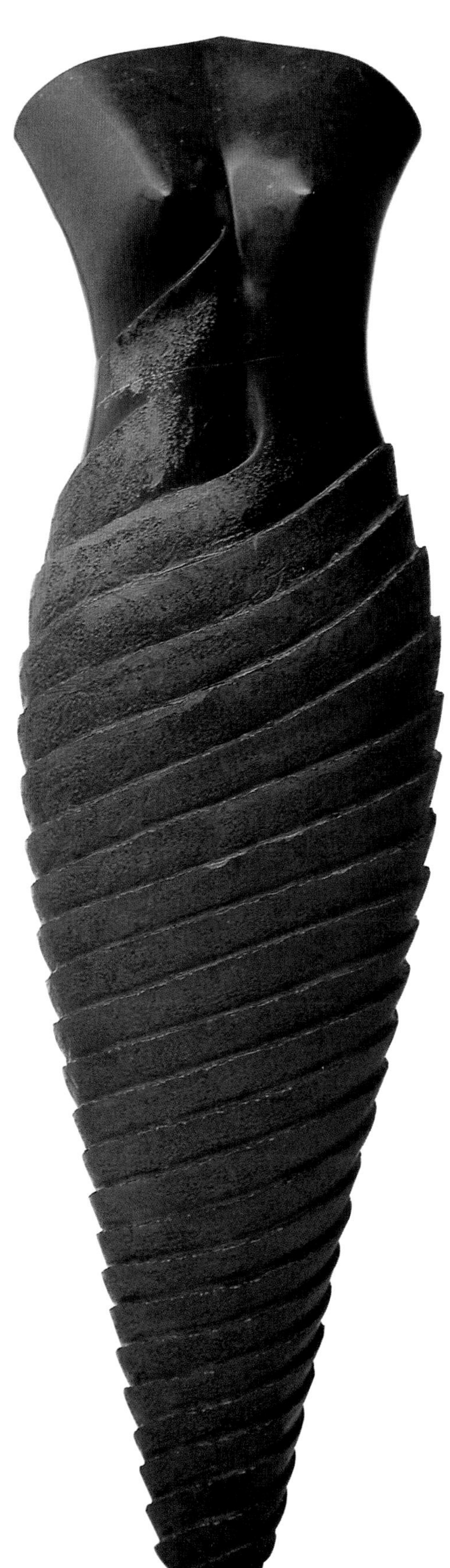

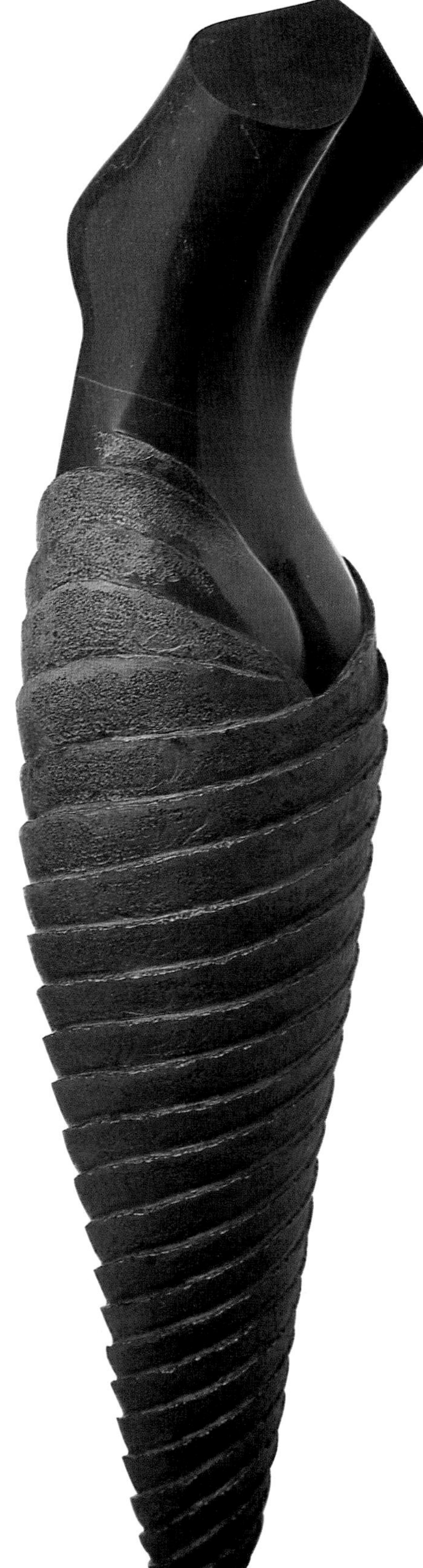

◄► **56.** At the suggestion of our clients, perfume artists who see in this sculpture, besides exuding an invitation to touch, a sublimation of terrestrial expression that becomes the essence of woman, we call this sculpture *Ambra*.

Camí.
Ambra. 1999.
Calatorao limestone.
29 × 7 × 5 inches (73 × 18 × 14 cm).

Enlarging by Compasses

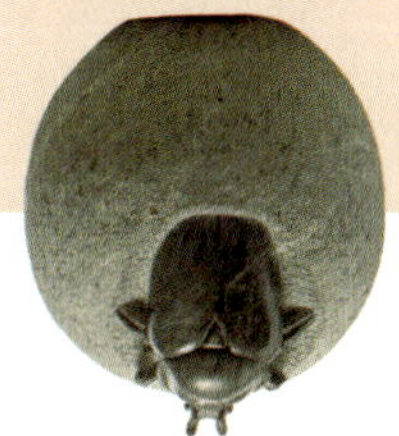

Again with the help of Mariano, we move on to another method, which like the pointing machine is also used to copy a model. It is especially used to enlarge the model, a process requiring greater precision than the grid.

In the same way that the pointing machine needed three constant support points, each one of the three compasses we will use in this exercise will also take measurements from a fixed point. But first we need to fix the three points, which we will call mother points, using a different system: the chassis system. Afterward, starting from the three mother points, we will determine the secondary points using three compasses.

We will see how both techniques, the chassis and the compasses, allow us to fix any point on a volume and to copy a model in a way that is similar to what we did with the pointing machine. The advantage of the former is that we can multiply or divide by a fixed number the opening of the compasses and thus be able to enlarge or reduce the dimensions of the maquette. Having located the points on a green Guatemala marble block imported from India and measuring 18 × 20 × 16 inches (45 × 50 × 40 cm), we will carve with tools and methods similar to those we used previously.

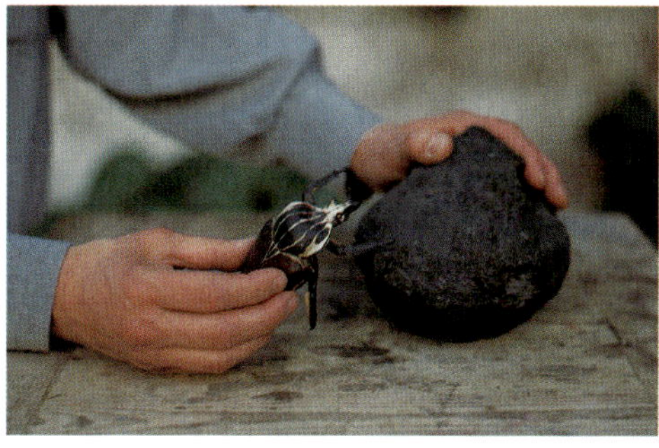

▲ **1.** To show how precise this method is, we are going to present this sculpture as a combination of two elements that already exist in nature: a volcanic rock and a large scarab, with their complex shapes.

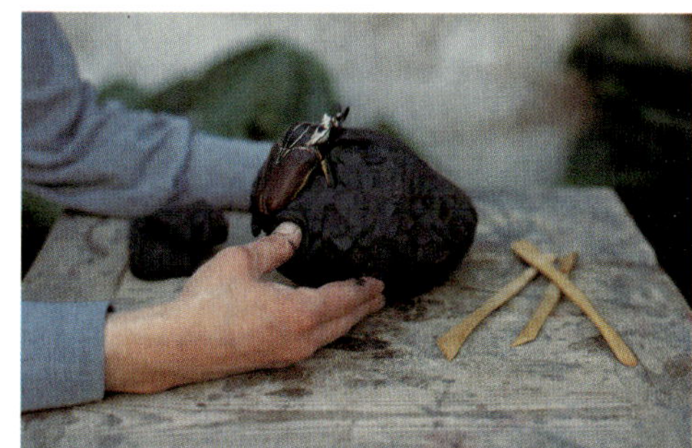

▲ **2.** We integrate the scarab into the stone using plaster of Paris until it gives a unified aspect to the composition.

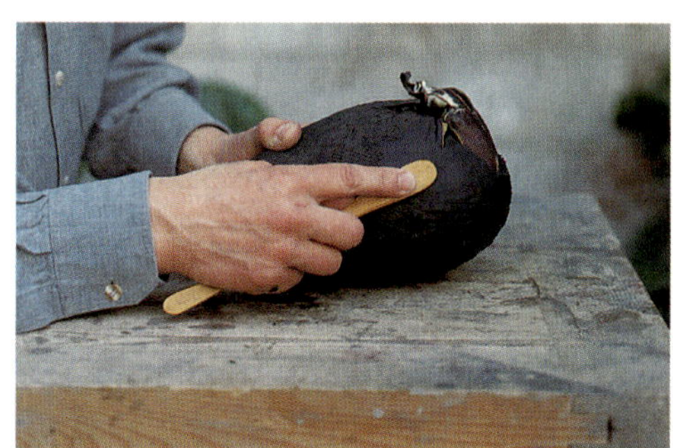

▲ **3.** Making the animal easily emerge in an ovoid shape is reminiscent of the arduous labor of the scarab, but at the same time suggesting the idea of regeneration, a theme with Egyptian connotations.

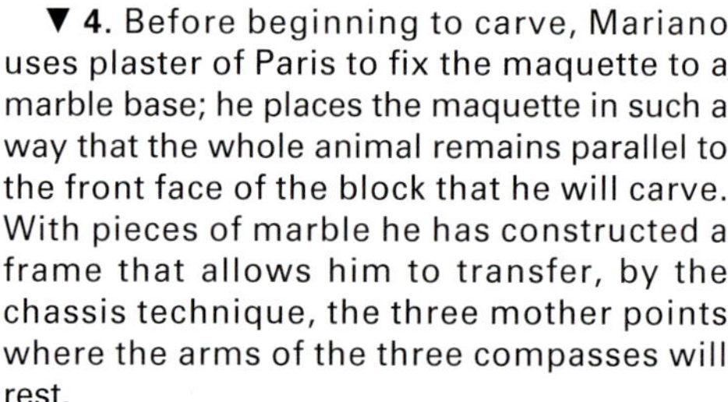

▼ **4.** Before beginning to carve, Mariano uses plaster of Paris to fix the maquette to a marble base; he places the maquette in such a way that the whole animal remains parallel to the front face of the block that he will carve. With pieces of marble he has constructed a frame that allows him to transfer, by the chassis technique, the three mother points where the arms of the three compasses will rest.

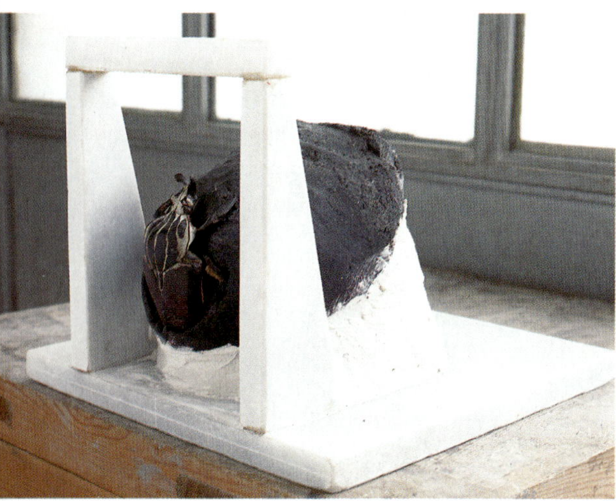

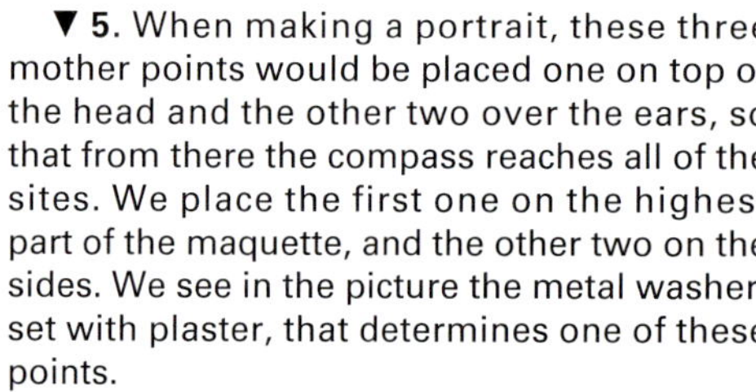

▼ **5.** When making a portrait, these three mother points would be placed one on top of the head and the other two over the ears, so that from there the compass reaches all of the sites. We place the first one on the highest part of the maquette, and the other two on the sides. We see in the picture the metal washer, set with plaster, that determines one of these points.

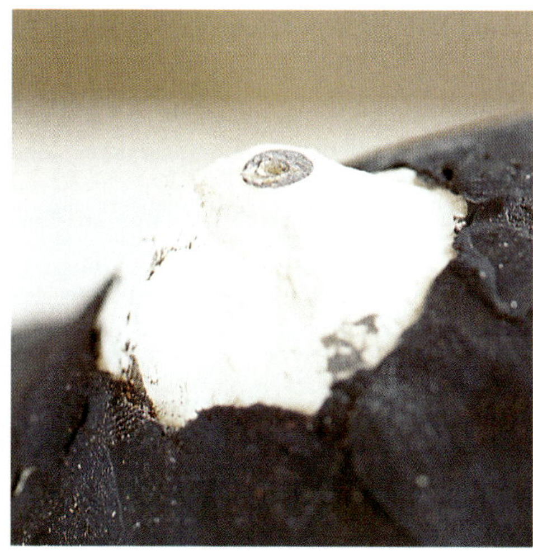

▼ **6.** The frames, with two coordinates (2 and 3, for example), allow us to place any point on a plane, while from the lead thread (1) we can measure the depth in order to place it on the volume. These three reference points will help us transcribe the location of the first mother point (A) onto the marble block.

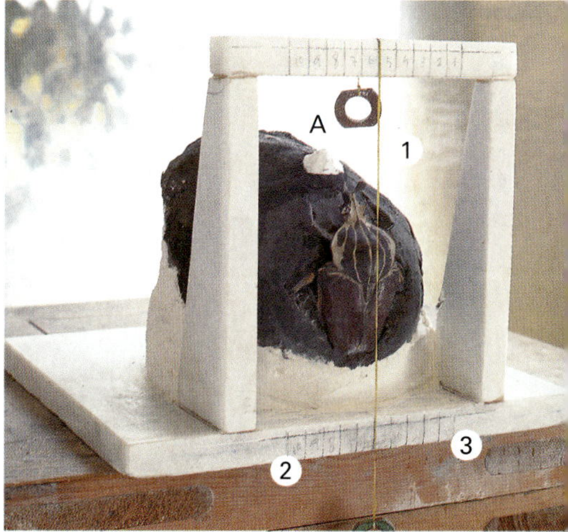

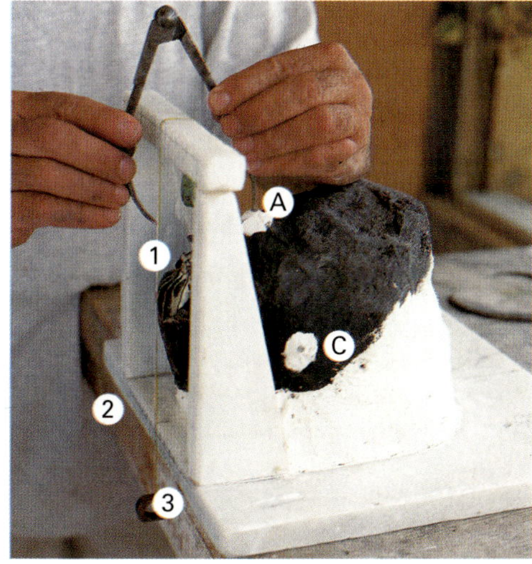

▲ **7.** Here we take the first of the three measurements with the compass, the one that goes from the plumb line (1) to the mother point (A); then we will take the measurements of points 2 and 3 to A. Turning the piece around allows us to see the two other mother points on the side (C) that we will transfer onto the block in the same way: from the plumb line to the two points on the base of the frame.

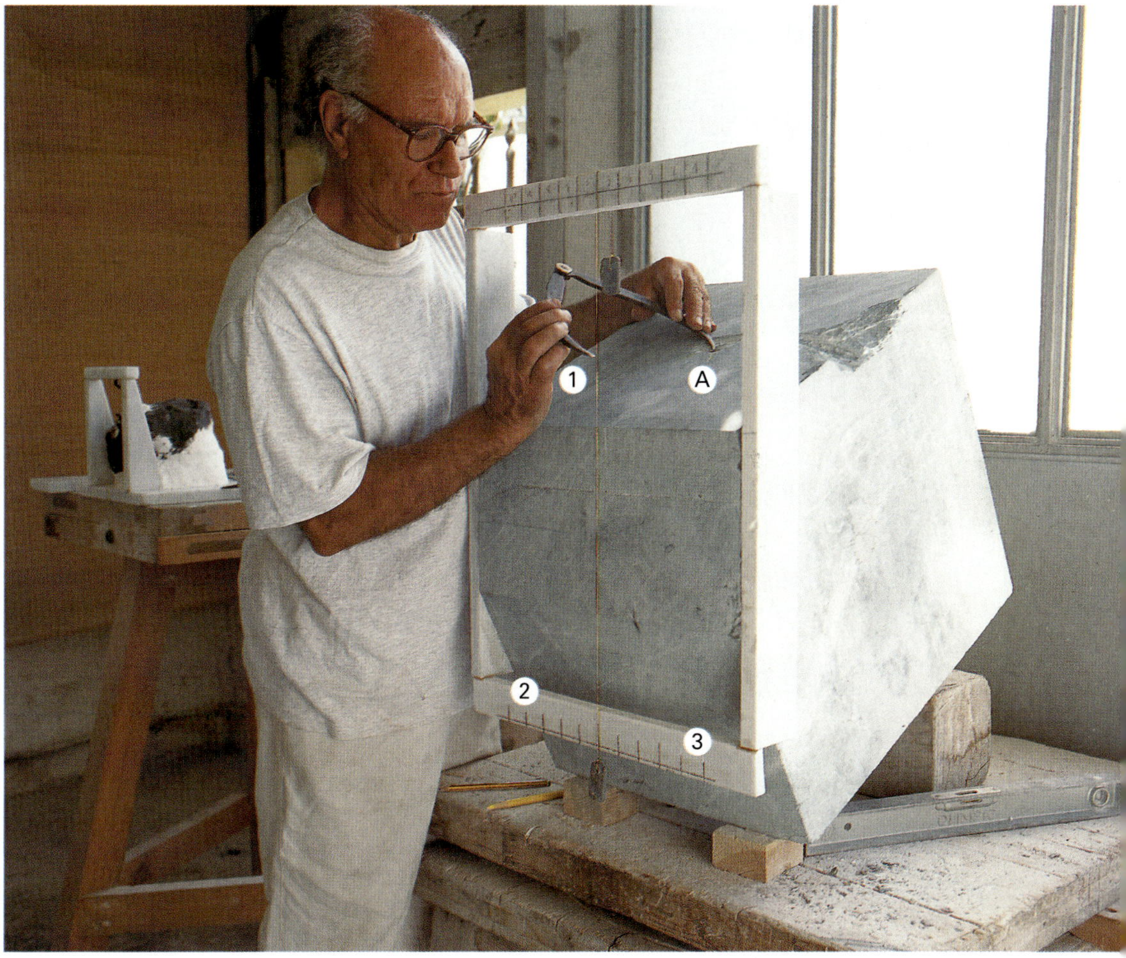

► **8.** The block's frame is three times longer than the maquette. We use it only to transfer the three support points for the three compasses. Here Mariano transfers the measurement he took before, after increasing it by three.

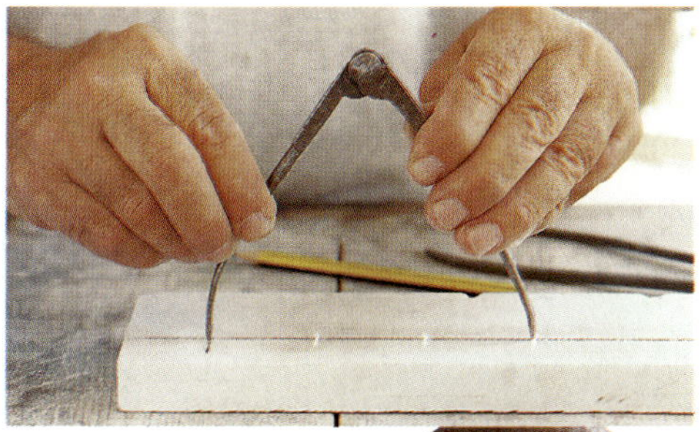

◄ **9.** To enlarge the scale we use a marble block, trace a straight line, and transfer the measurement taken from the maquette to the line as many times as needed for the enlargement. Here we show the three increments and now the arms of the compass are extended, spanning the enlarged measurement.

▼ **10.** Mariano transfers the mother point (B) in the same way. He will take the other two measurements from points 1 and 3.

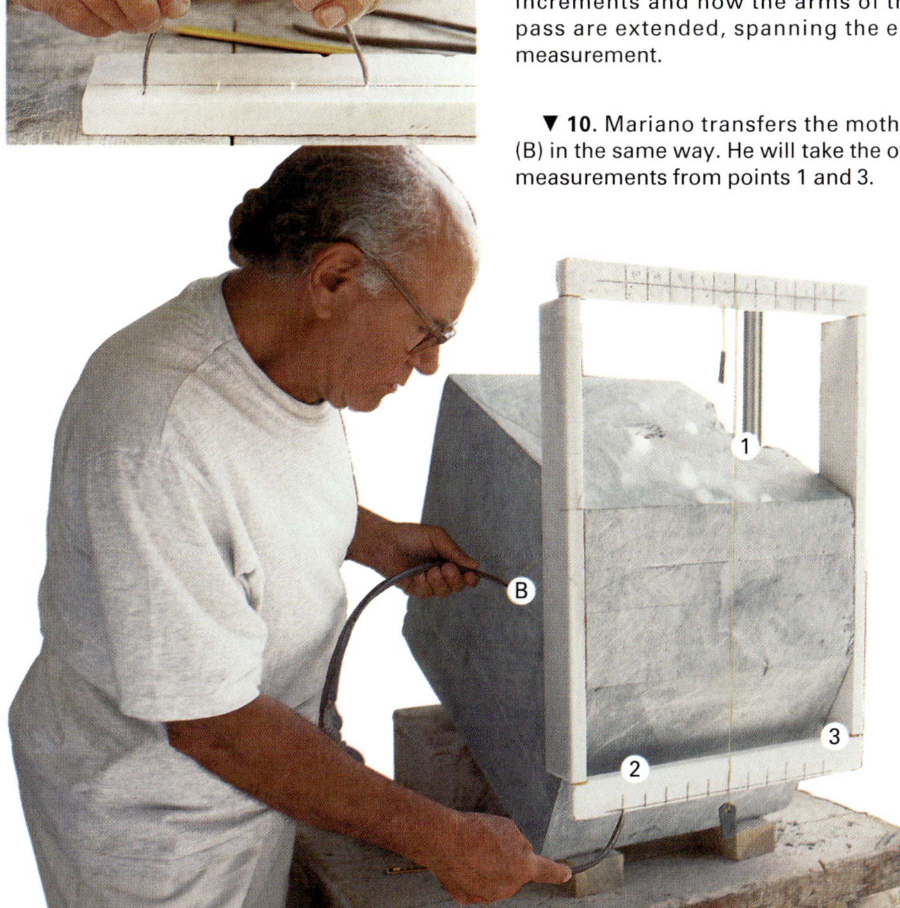

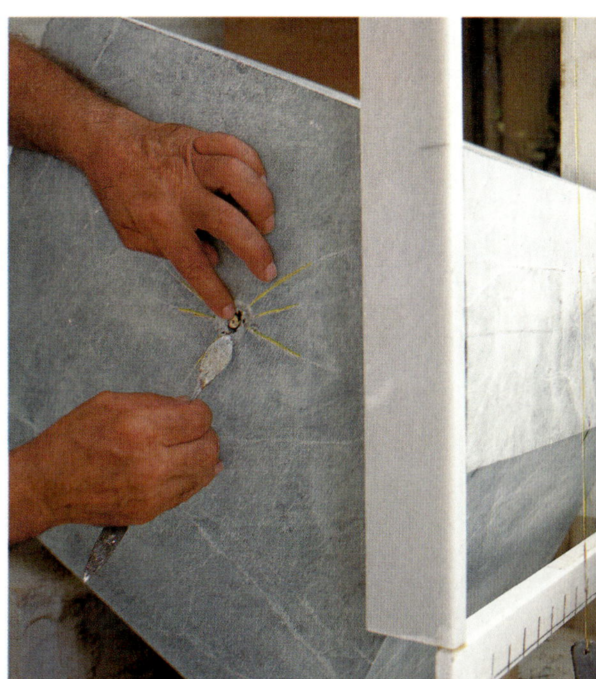

▲ **11.** The intersection of the three lines is our lateral mother, which we reinforce with a washer. The three points that we have located up to now, using the chassis technique, are equivalent to the three support points of the pointing machine from the previous step-by-step demonstration.

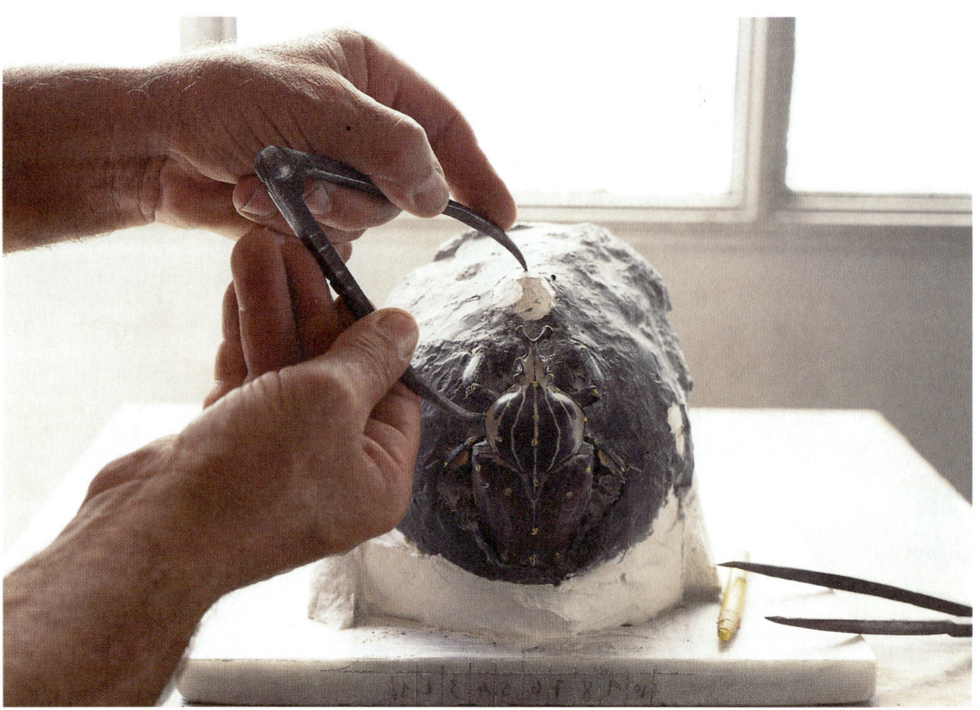

◀ **12.** Now that the mother points have been located, we no longer need the frame and we begin to apply the three-compasses technique. To transfer the reference points, we first locate the coordinates; we determine the height and width with the two lateral compasses, and we locate the depth using the compass that is supported on the highest mother point.

▼ **13.** After enlarging the span of the compass by three, we transfer onto the marble the most prominent point of the scarab shell, which is where the three arms of the compasses intersect. The arms of the compasses are curved to shun the edges, which being unnecessary here have been trimmed off. Mariano had the foresight, using a large circular saw, to cut one of the edges to make the trimming easier. The arms of the three compasses meet; this tells us that the intersecting point is close to the surface.

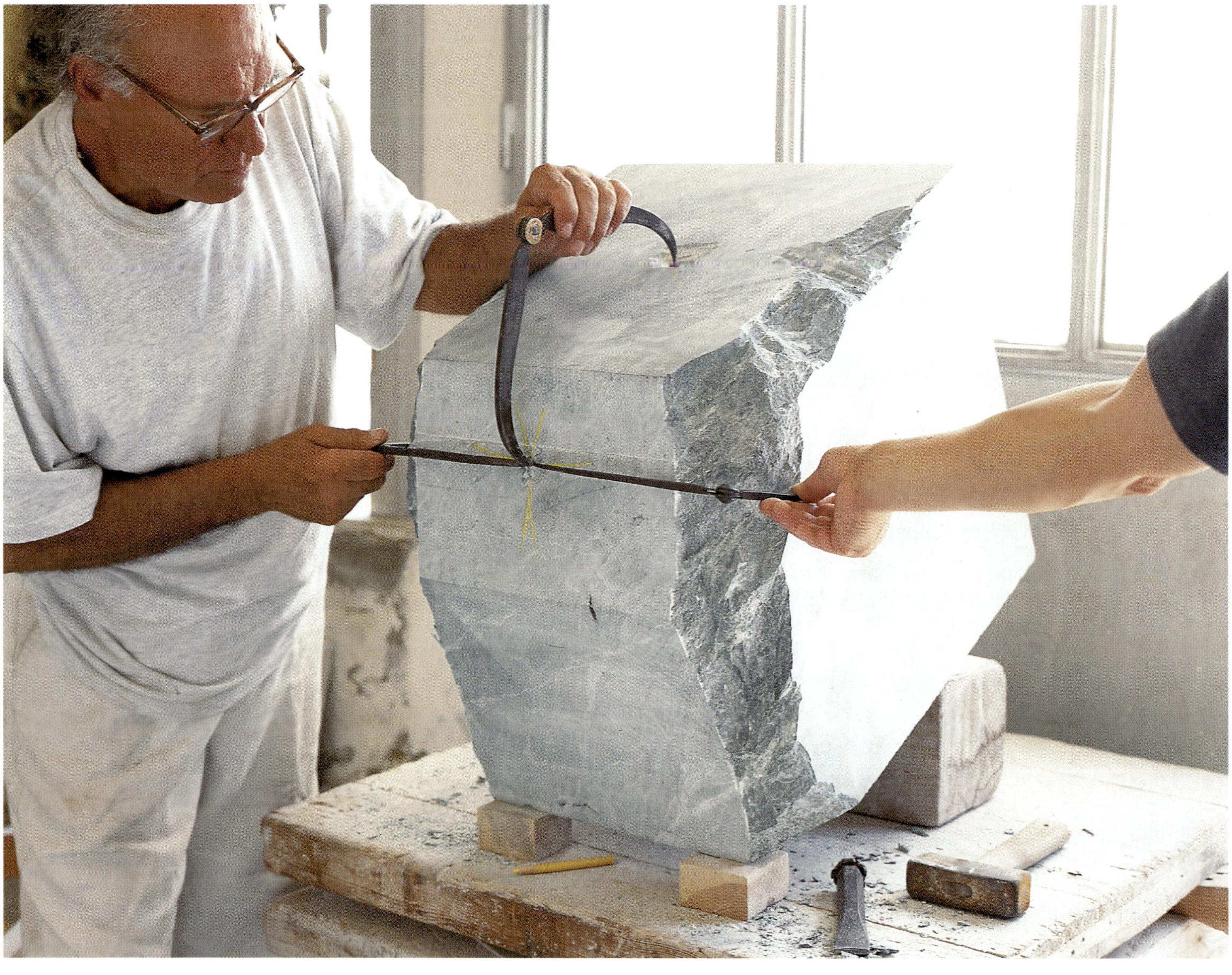

▼ **14.** As in the previous step-by-step demonstration, first we locate the most prominent points, and as we trim, we locate the middle points and the deeper ones.

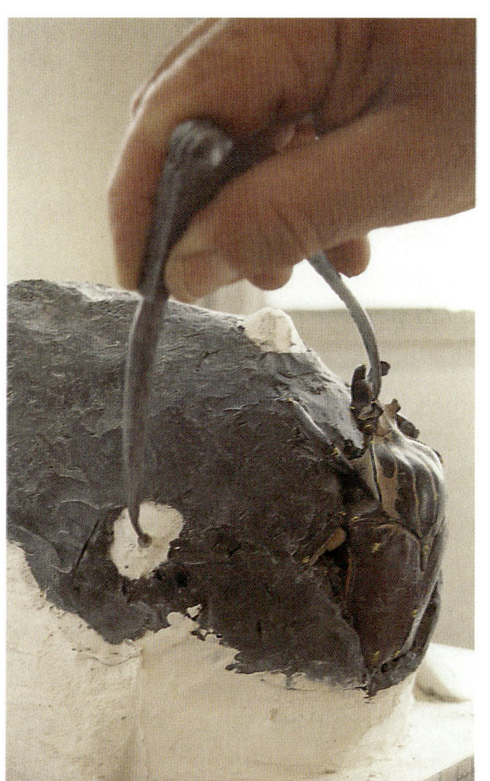

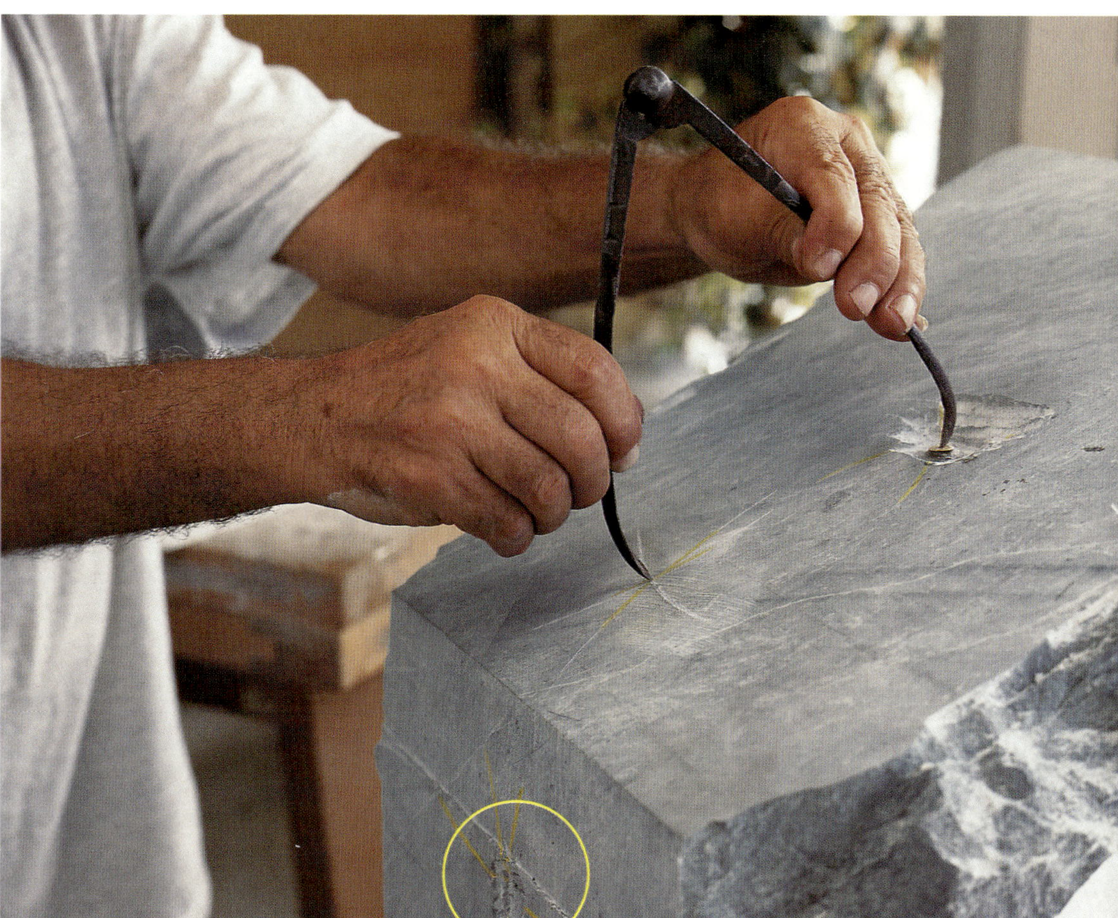

▲ **15.** We locate the side of one of the scarab's antennas; the intersection of the three compass marks also indicates to us that it lies on the surface. The point marked in the previous step can be seen at the bottom of the illustration.

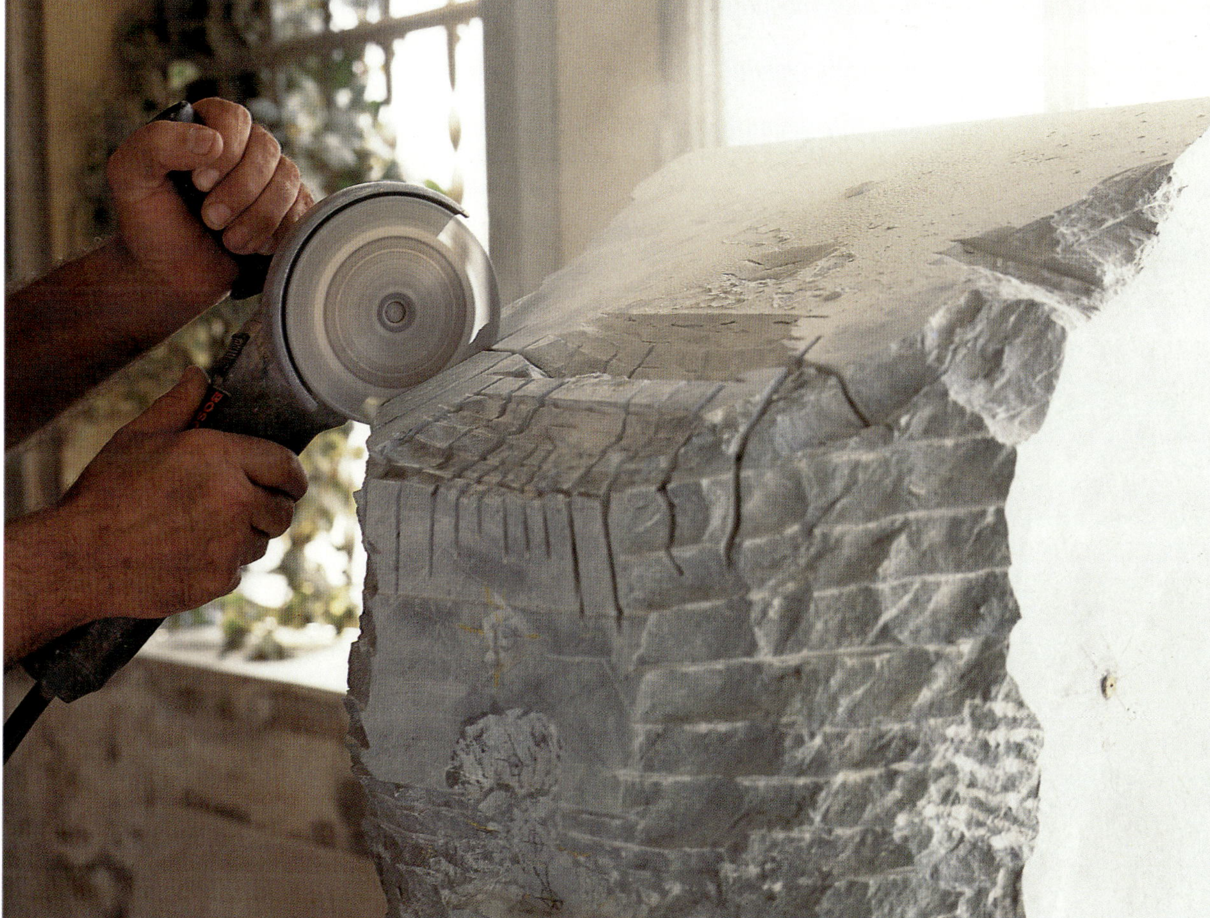

◄ **16.** Having located the two outermost points, we can now start to trim away the excess material between them by cutting with a circular saw and striking with a trimmer.

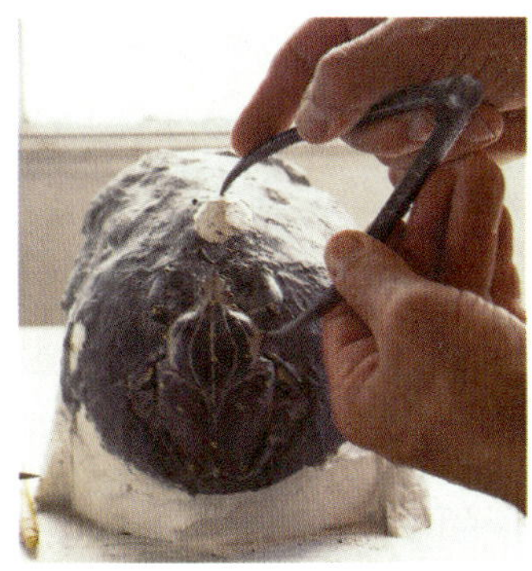

▲ **17.** We now locate the points of intermediate depth, in this case, the most prominent right side of the shell. We increase the three measurements by three and we transfer them to the block.

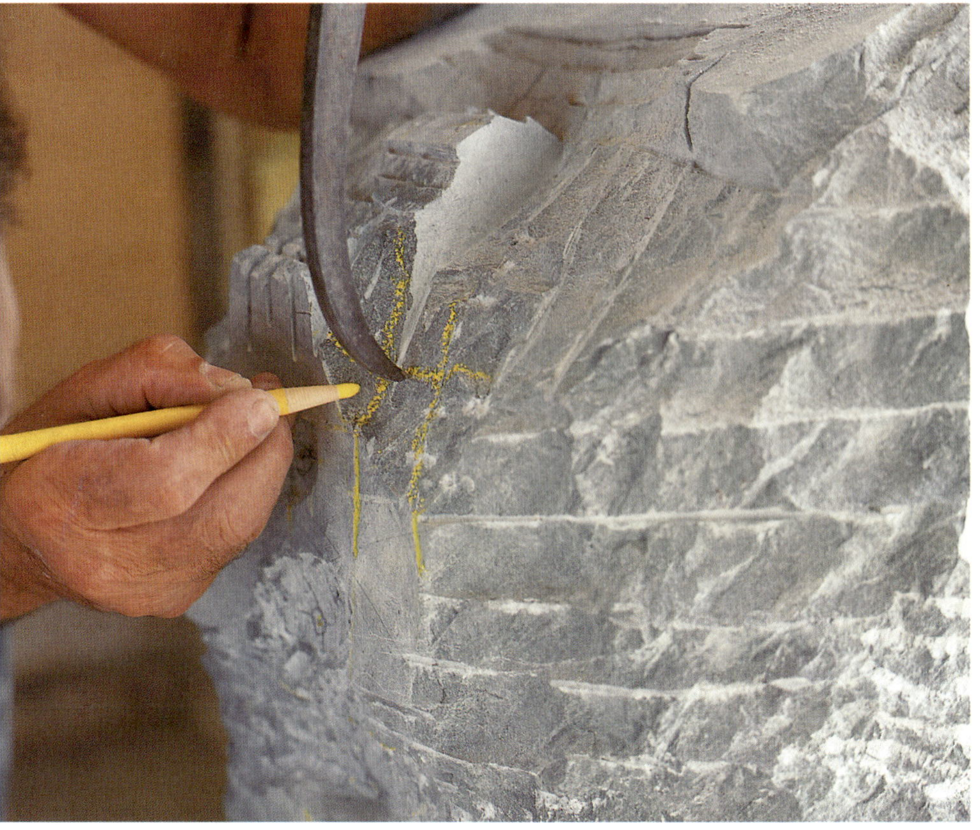

◄ **18.** But here the markings of the three compasses, highlighted in yellow, do not seem to converge at the same point. This is not an error; it is an indication that we need to continue trimming until the markings of the compasses coincide.

► **19.** We have trimmed the area where the three compasses converge and they almost coincide. If we carve a little more with a point marker, we will reach the exact convergent point whereby each compass has one of its arms resting on a mother point and the other on the point of convergence.

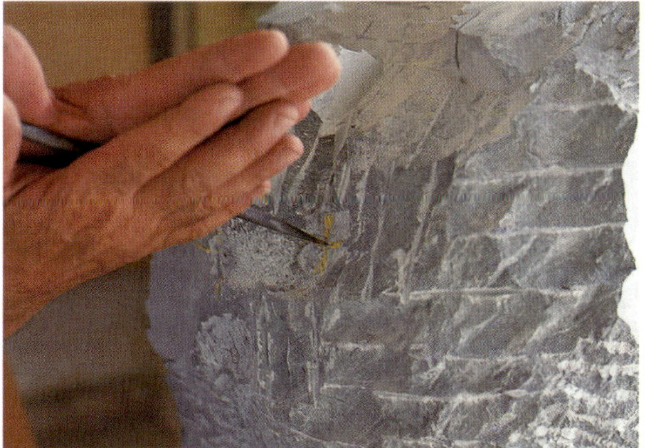

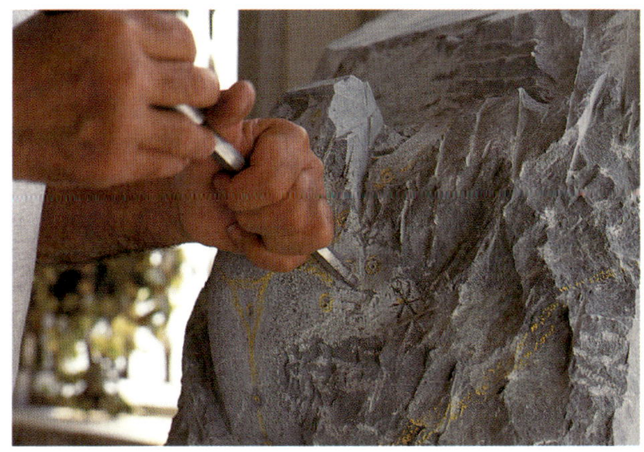

▲ **20.** In similar fashion, we have located other points that have allowed us to trim the stone until we have created the illusion that the scarab emerges from it. In the illustration, we can see one point under the little finger and another in front of the index finger, which indicates the position of the scarab's leg.

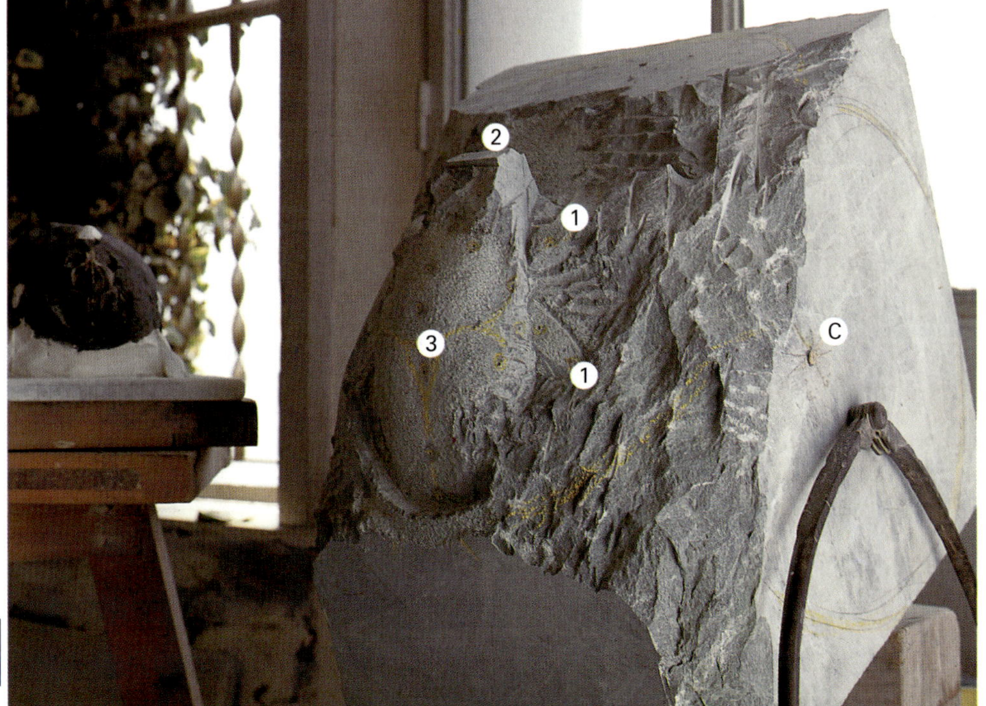

◄ **21.** From a lateral mother point (C), we have drawn a semicircle that indicates to us what we need to trim away to shape the ovoid form. We can also see three points that allow us to locate the feet (1); the four points for the antennae (2); and the six points of the central line (3). We have also seen and marked in yellow the uneven surfaces that we will smooth out to simulate the shape of the "egg."

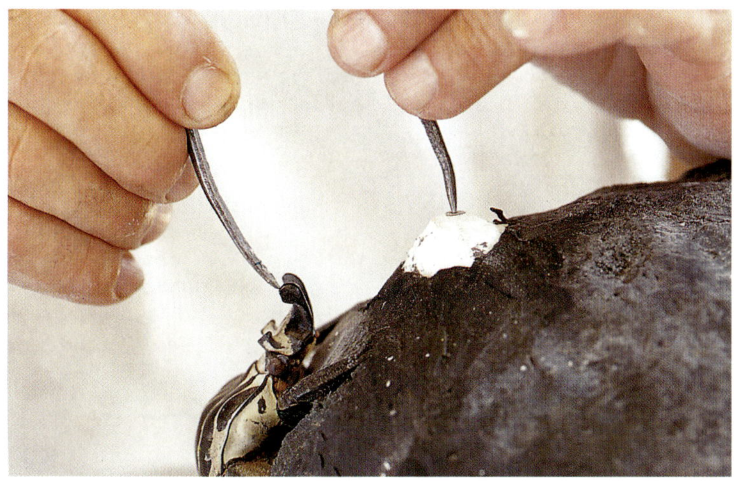

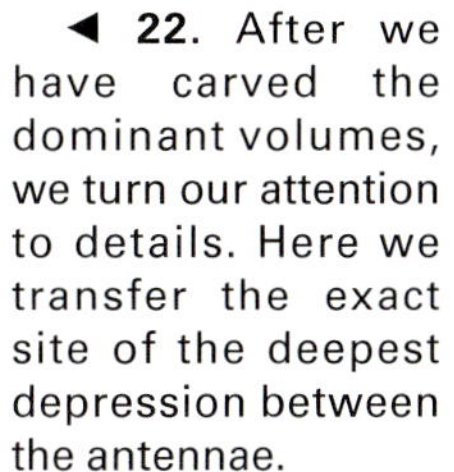

◄ **22.** After we have carved the dominant volumes, we turn our attention to details. Here we transfer the exact site of the deepest depression between the antennae.

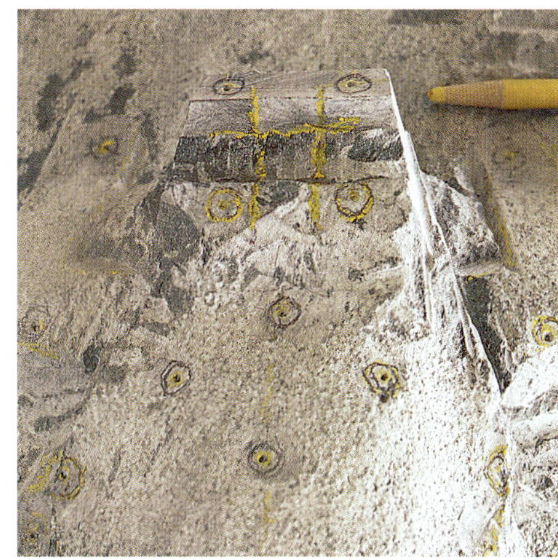

► **23.** The separation of the three compass marks tells us that we have to trim deeper.

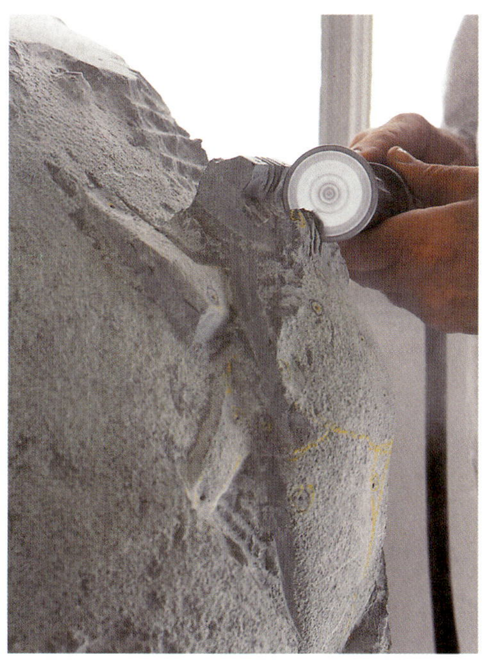

◄ **24.** Mariano reduces the area between the antennae with a diamond disk activated by a drill, making small parallel cuts that he will break afterwards until he finds the convergence point of the three compasses.

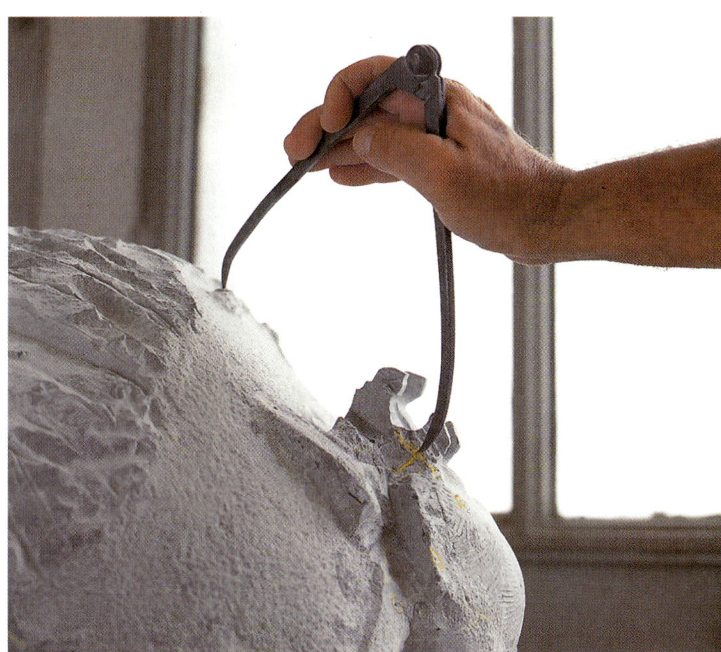

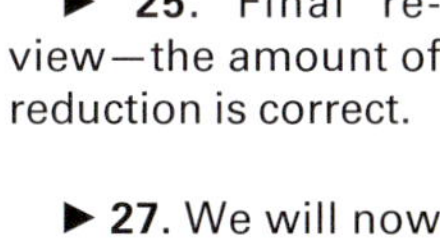

► **25.** Final review—the amount of reduction is correct.

▼ **26.** Here are the markings that have been left on our scarab. From each yellow point we took three measurements from mother points A, B, and C, which are seen on the plaster protuberances. The numbers indicate the order in which the material needs to be trimmed—from the outermost to the deepest.

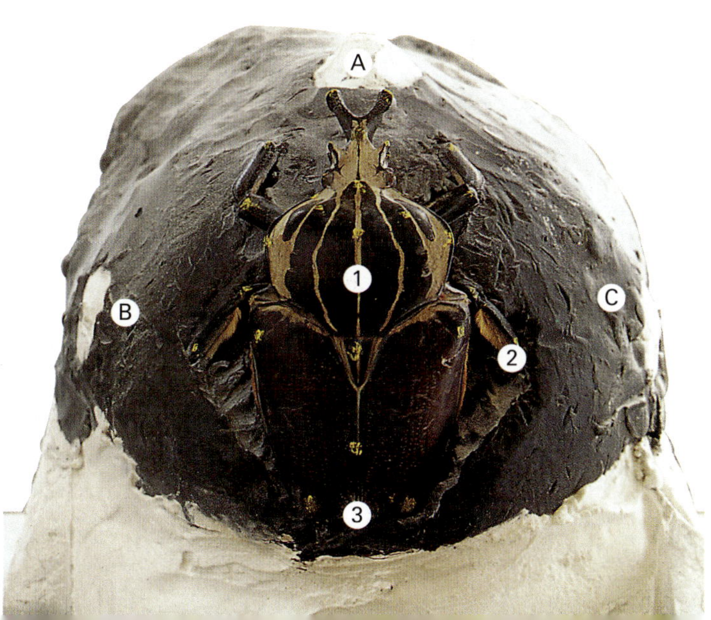

► **27.** We will now concentrate on the rest of the sculpture, using direct carving without worrying about reproducing details. The hardness of the marble wears the tools down.

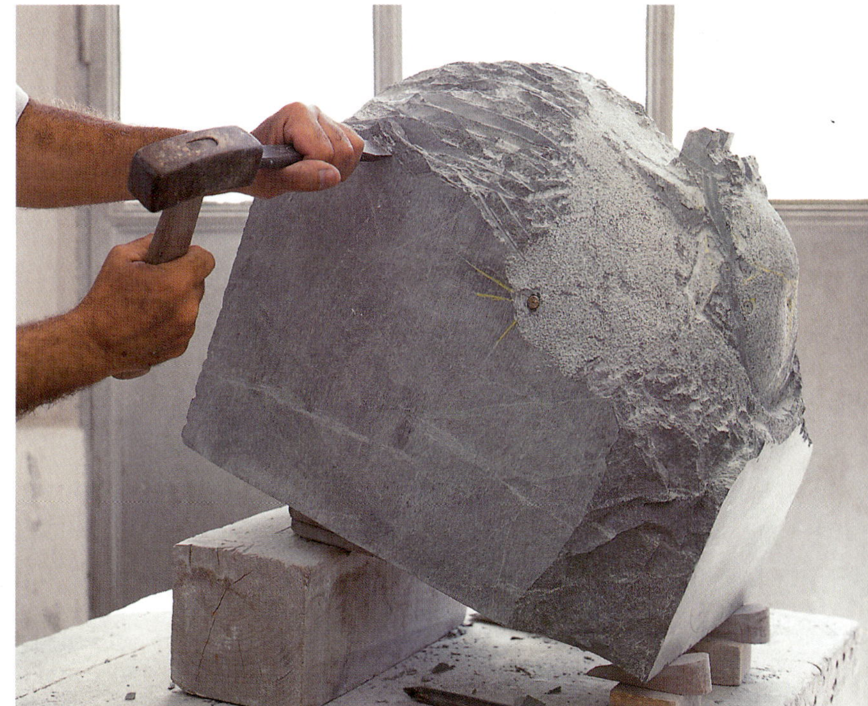

► **28.** Mariano uses the bushing tool to perfect a detail. The scarab is practically modeled, but still shows the markings of the different tools that appear on the worktable.

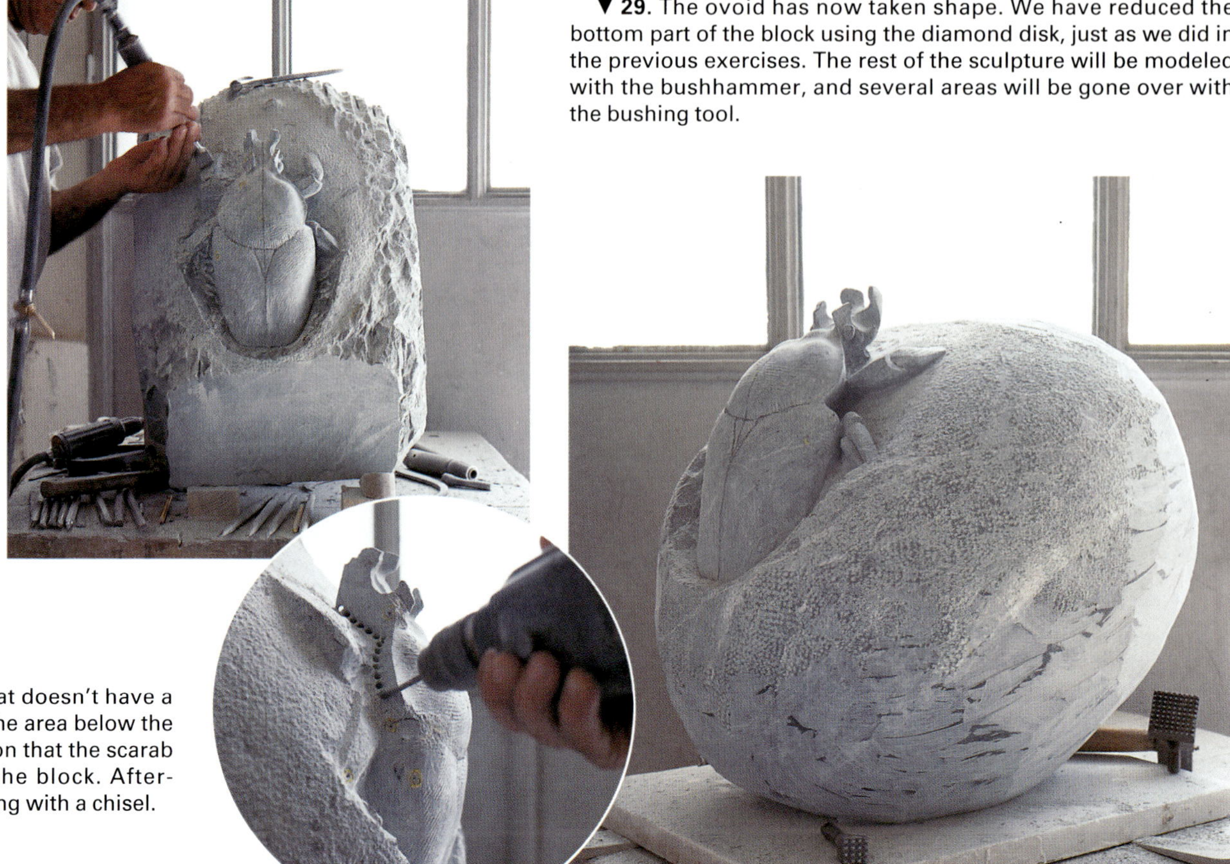

▼ **29.** The ovoid has now taken shape. We have reduced the bottom part of the block using the diamond disk, just as we did in the previous exercises. The rest of the sculpture will be modeled with the bushhammer, and several areas will be gone over with the bushing tool.

► **30.** Using a drill that doesn't have a striking pin, we trepan the area below the head to create the illusion that the scarab is freeing itself from the block. Afterwards, we finish modeling with a chisel.

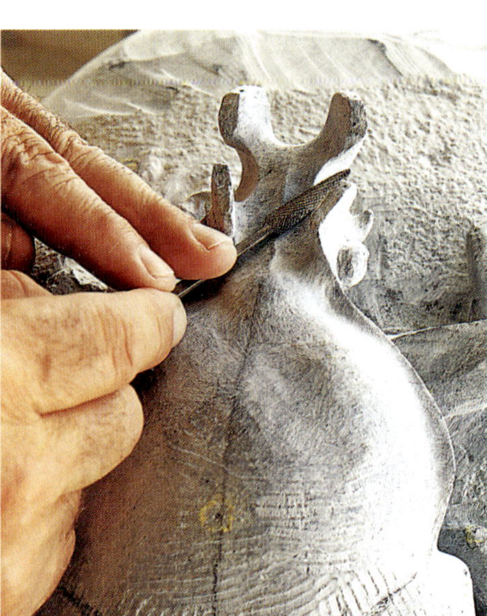

▲ **31.** When we have completed the modeling of the sculpture we begin the finishing process. Here we use a curved riffler to clean the areas that the bit doesn't enter, but this marble is quite hard and we need to persist patiently.

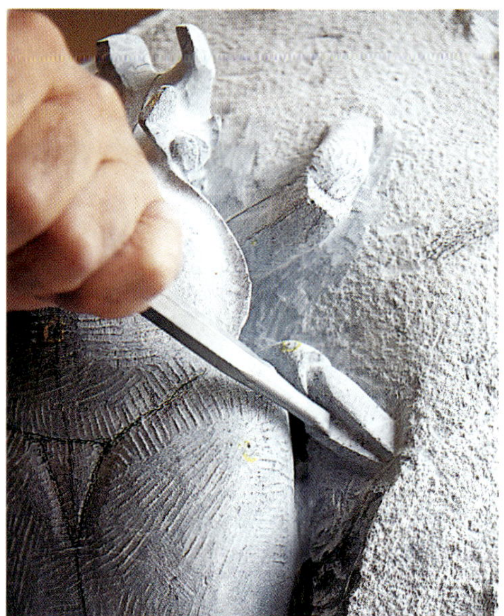

▲ **32.** We finish the texture of the feet. Our desire for realism brings up a question that Bernini already resolved: how to represent in marble the fuzz on the scarab's feet? We choose to consider it a volume, achieving in this way the greatest visual potential.

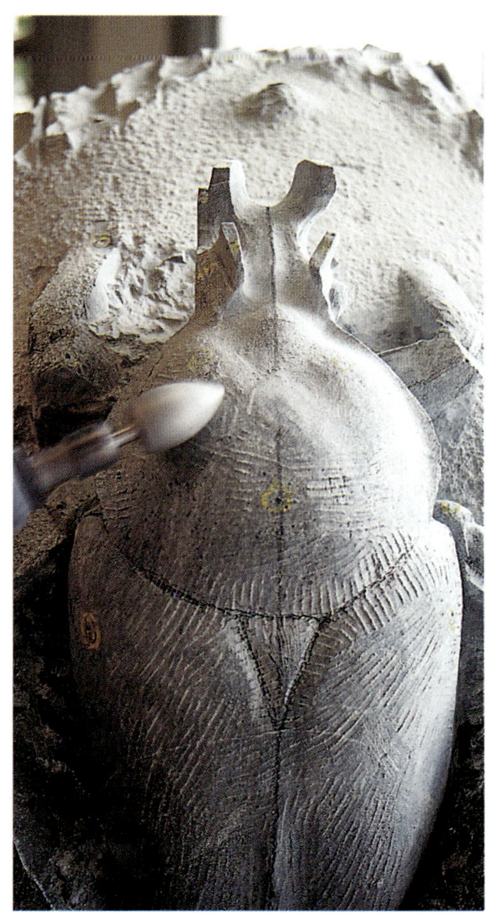

► **33.** With a diamond blade, harder than that of carborundum, we smooth the rough texture of the entire shell.

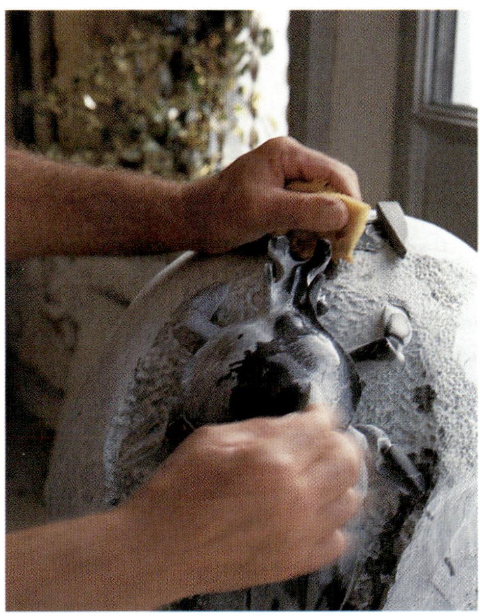

▲ **34**. We polish the entire scarab shell using carborundum stones of progressively finer grain, some small enough to fit corners into the corners.

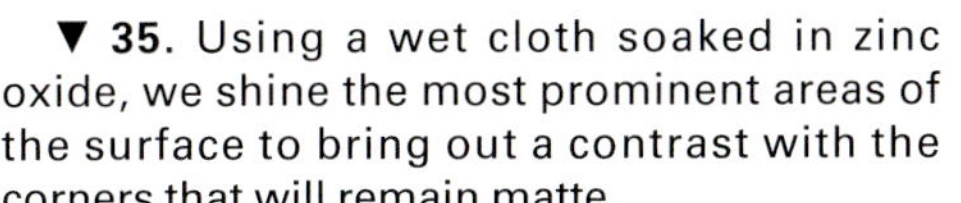

▼ **35**. Using a wet cloth soaked in zinc oxide, we shine the most prominent areas of the surface to bring out a contrast with the corners that will remain matte.

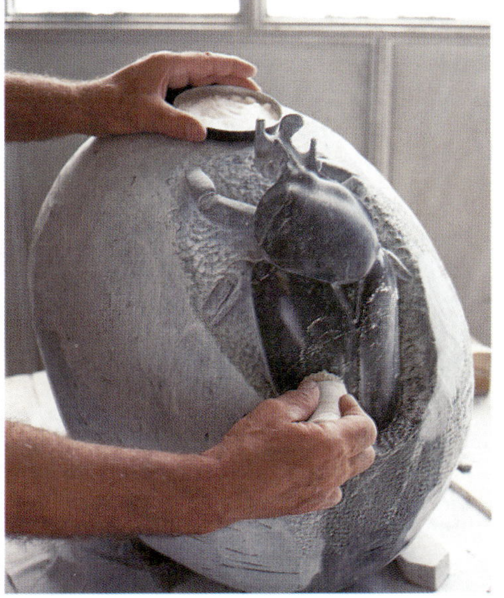

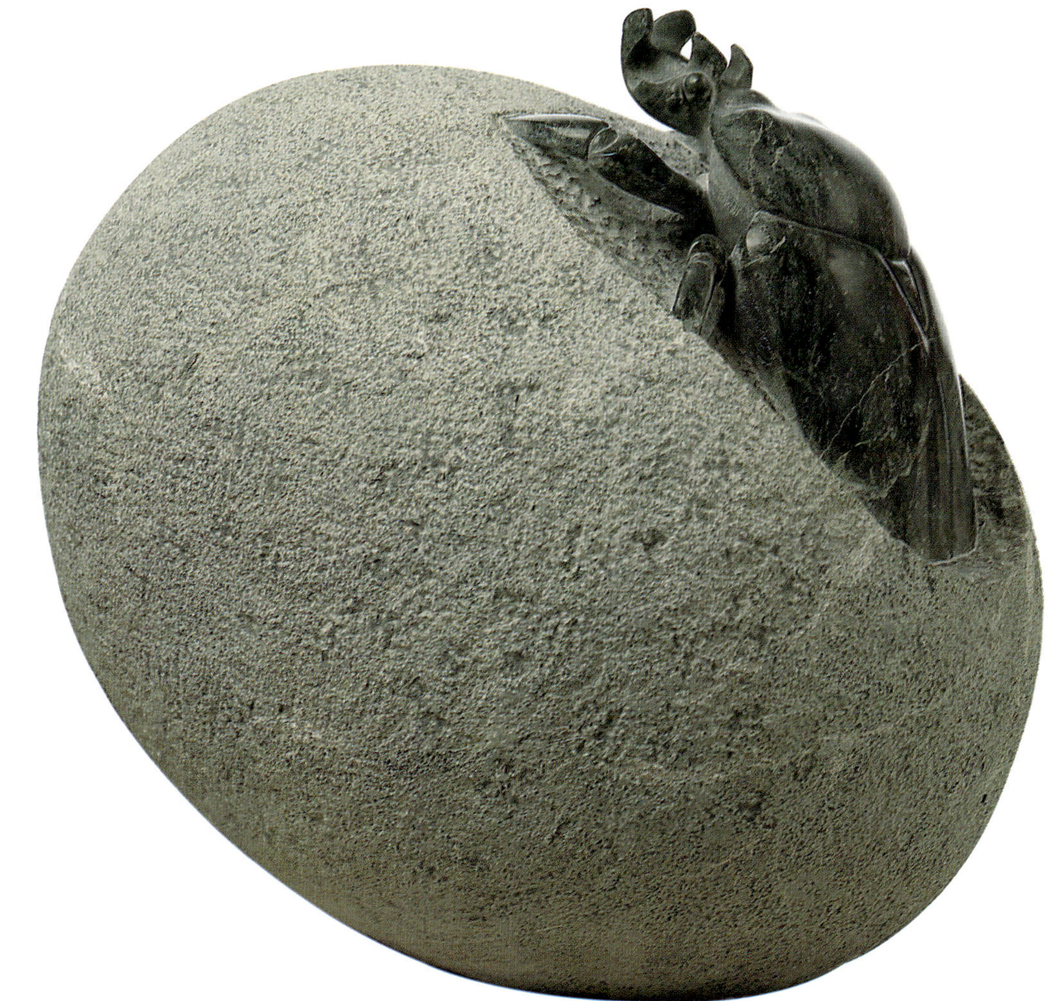

▶ **36**. Writings such as the following can be found on the Egyptian pyramids: *Hail to You, first born who begets himself. High one who stands over the stones, your name is Scarab Kepri!*

Camí.
Kepri. 1999.
Guatemala green marble,
From India.
18 × 20 × 15 inches (45 × 50 × 37 cm).

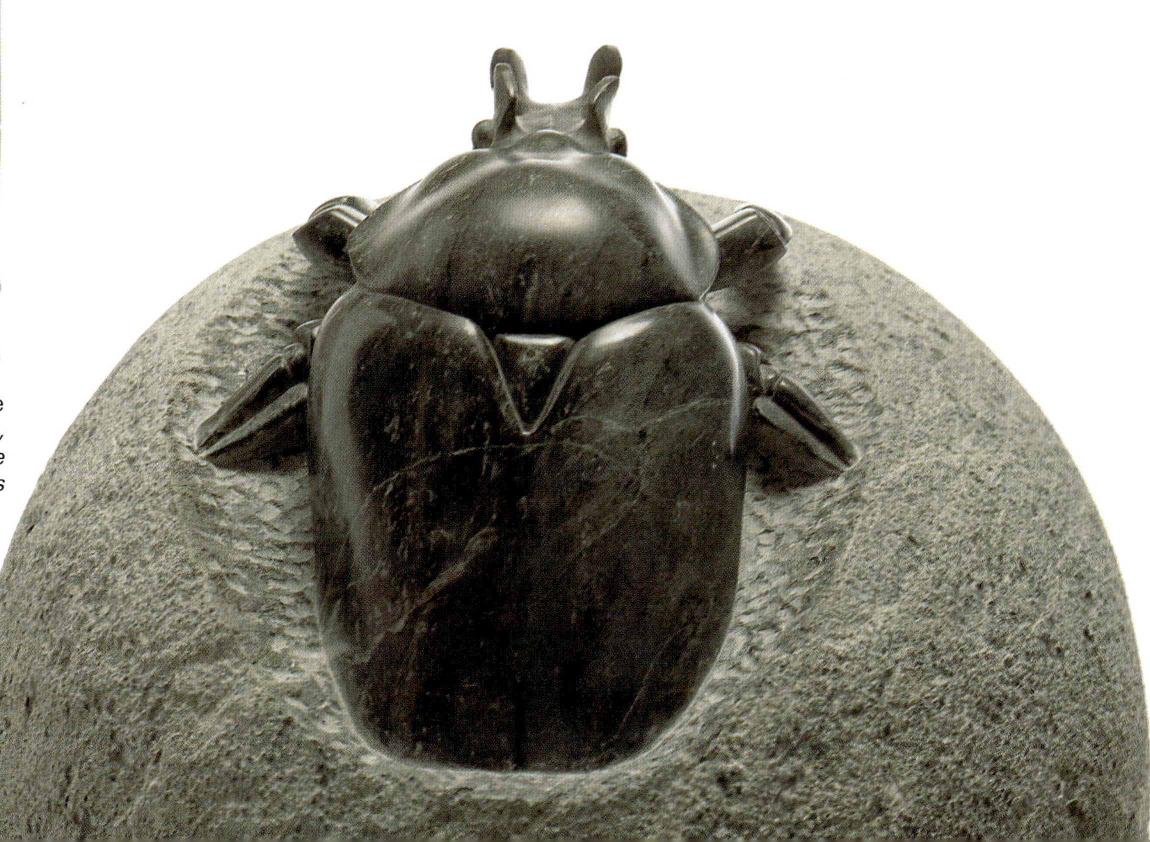

Large-Scale Sculptures, Enlarging by Templates

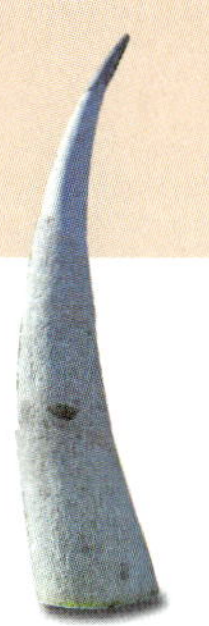

Again we will use patterns to enlarge our maquette; however, this project, which we undertook at the symposium in Santo Tirso (Portugal), presents added difficulty. Here we will see how a team is able to carve and mount a large-scale sculpture made out of four blocks. We have about 315 cubic feet (3 cu m) of granite from the regional quarry to work with and a limited amount of time. On the other hand, we have at our disposal the expertise of an industry that prides itself on a distinguished tradition in the country.

Public statues, whether in squares, parks, cemeteries, or temples, were part and parcel of the daily life of our ancestors; however, compared to the past, there are very few sculptures on display in our urban areas today.

Several public institutions have undertaken to remedy this situation by organizing public competitions. These sponsors, who combine needs with possibilities, select sites, materials, and local industries. In this way, public funds get reinvested in salaried jobs and the urban patrimony becomes richer. Generally, it is left to a commissioner—an art historian or critic—to select the sculptors, who then submit their proposals based on the request. In international competitions, restrictions are placed on the amount of time and size of a project in order to reduce costs.

The sculptor who takes on the challenge of leading the construction or producing a monument must abide by the terms of the contract and, at the same time, try to remain faithful to his own aesthetic criteria.

These last two step-by-step exercises demonstrate the process by which Camí, selected by commissioner Gerard Xuriguera to participate in symposia held in Portugal and South Korea, produced two sculptures.

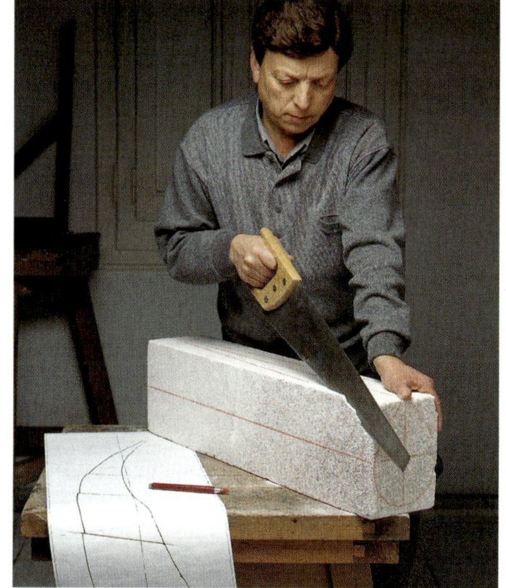

◄ **1.** The site we were assigned to in Santo Tirso, a crossroads at the entrance of the town, suggested the theme: a signpost. The rectilinear penchant in already existing sculptures motivates us to find the counterpoint, and the abundant vegetation determines the form: something organic, a bud, perhaps of a century plant, strikes our imagination, as in the case already shown on page 68.

In response to the invitation, plans and a maquette consisting of several sections were sent. The creation of the maquette was described on page 71. It would have been better to carve the sculpture from a single block; however, because of time constraints, we will carve four blocks and assemble them together later. Therefore, four teams will be working at the same time. The following pages show the simultaneous evolution of each block.

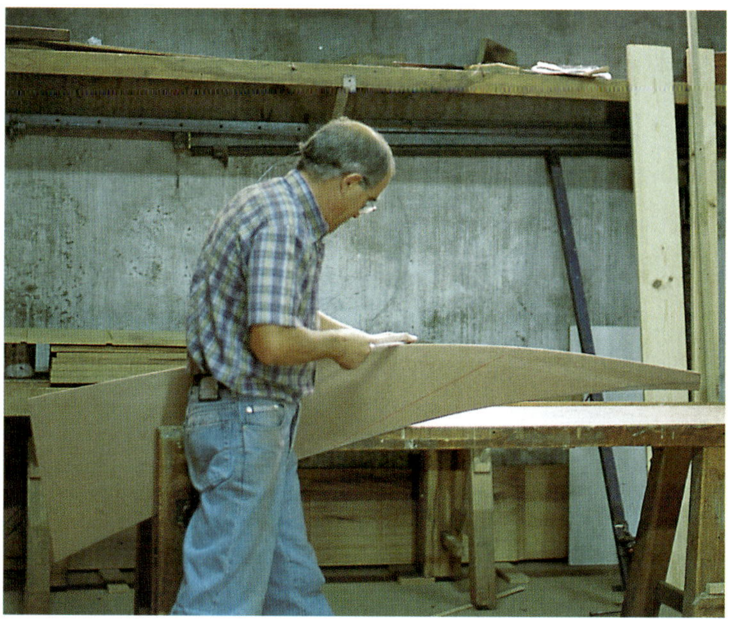

◄ ▼ **2.** We will enlarge the maquette using patterns. We are already in Santo Tirso where a carpenter, using the plans drawn up for the sculpture, saws several pieces of wood that we will use as patterns. These pieces will make it easier to control measurements for each block.

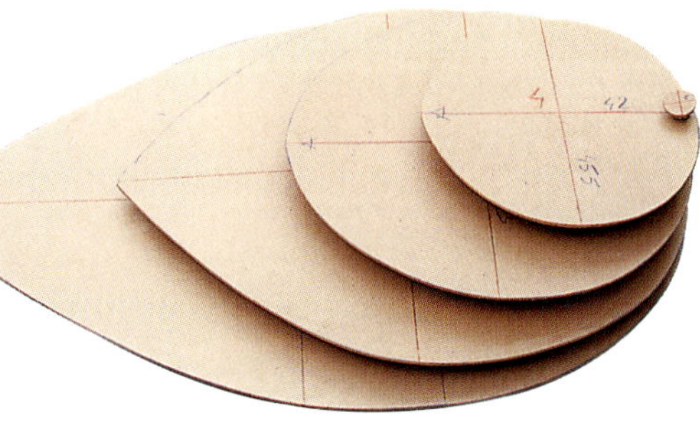

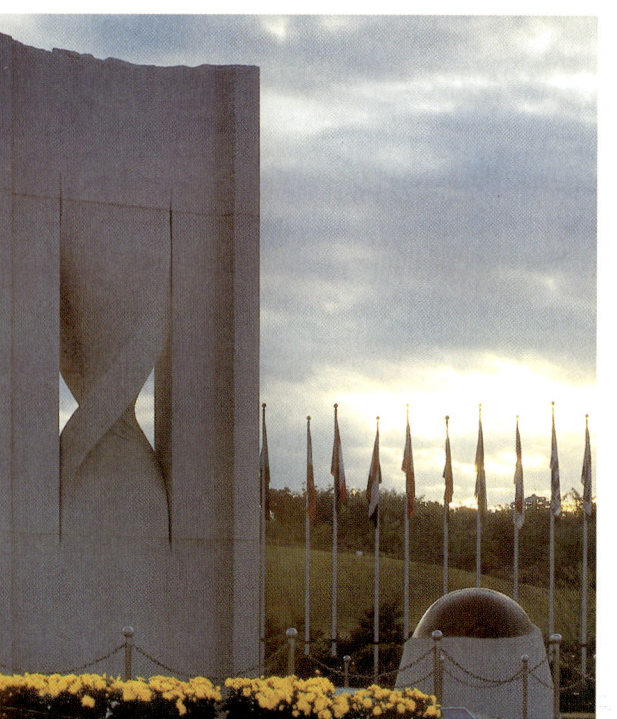

◄ Subirachs. *Olympic Movement Monument—Meeting in Seoul. Granite.* Entrance to the sculpture park. Seoul (South Korea).

Coinciding with the Olympic Games in 1988, one of the largest symposia for large-scale sculptures was held in this city. French commissioners George Restani and Gerard Xuriguera brought together more than 200 sculptors from different countries.

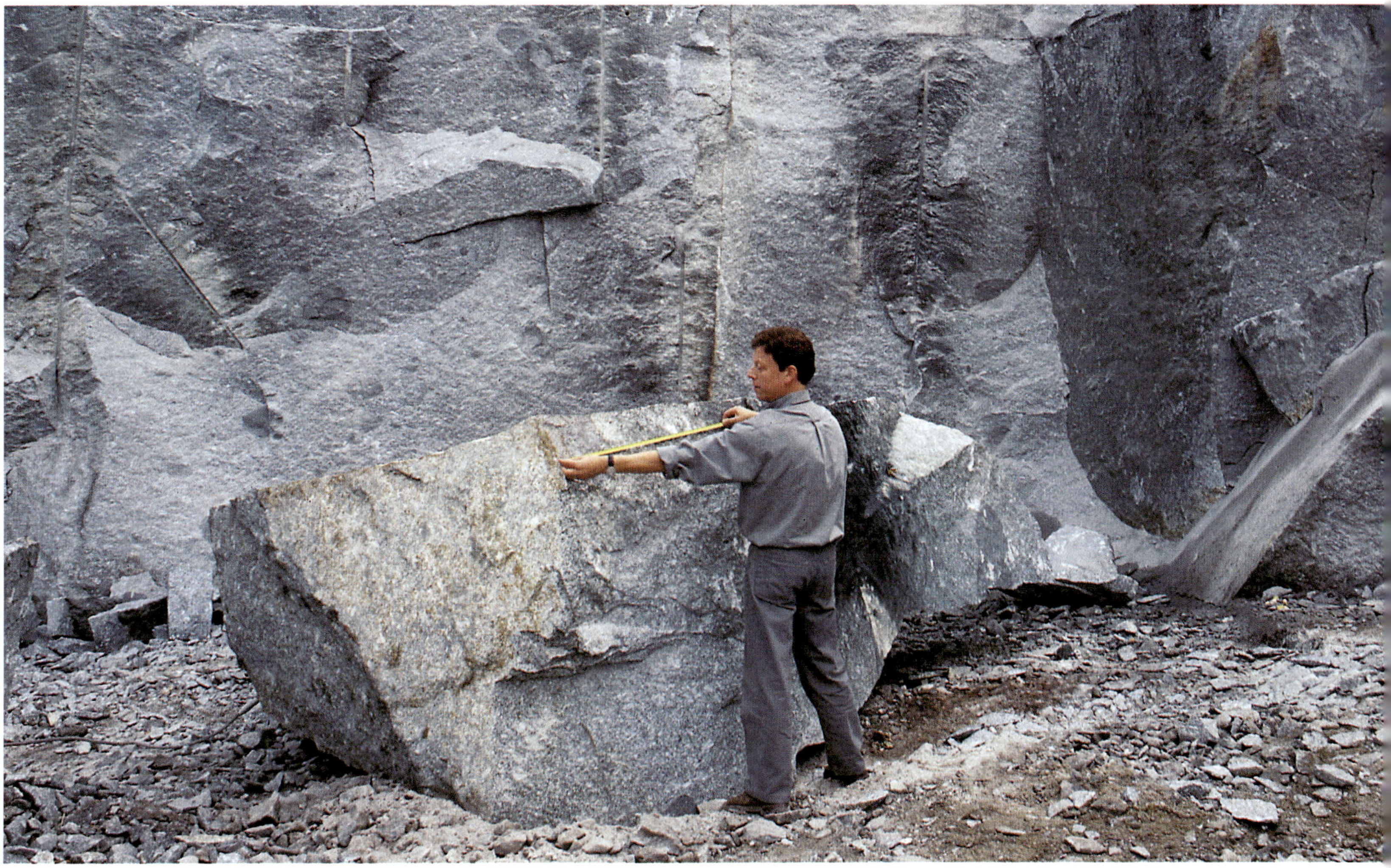

▲ **3.** We chose blocks from a quarry outside the city limits of Santo Tirso and based our selection on the external appearance of the blocks, our own intuition, and the advice of quarry workers. However, we had no guarantee that the blocks were devoid of internal fissures.

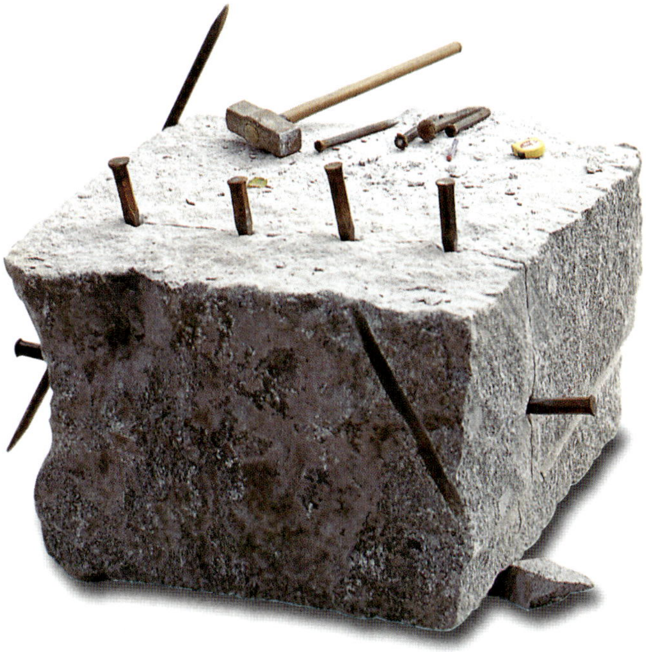

◄ ▼ **4.** It is important that the stone not be too small; on the other hand, it would be absurd to carry an excessively large block to the studios. Thus, a quarry worker reduces the size of the block through traditional wedging.

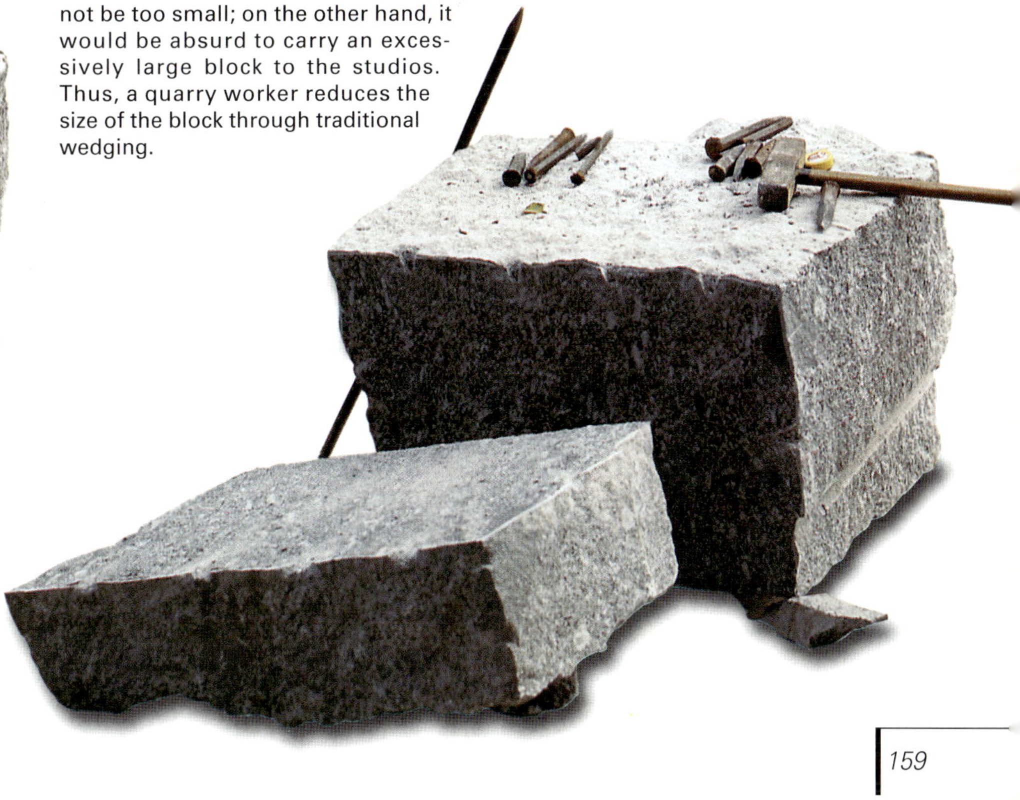

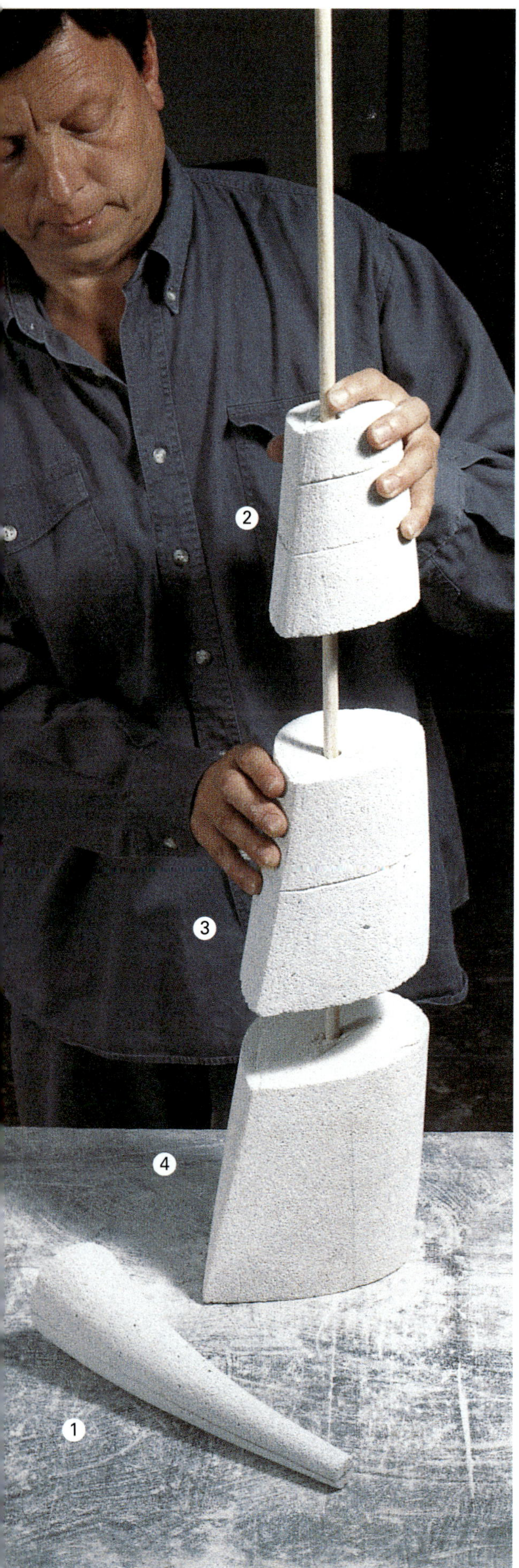

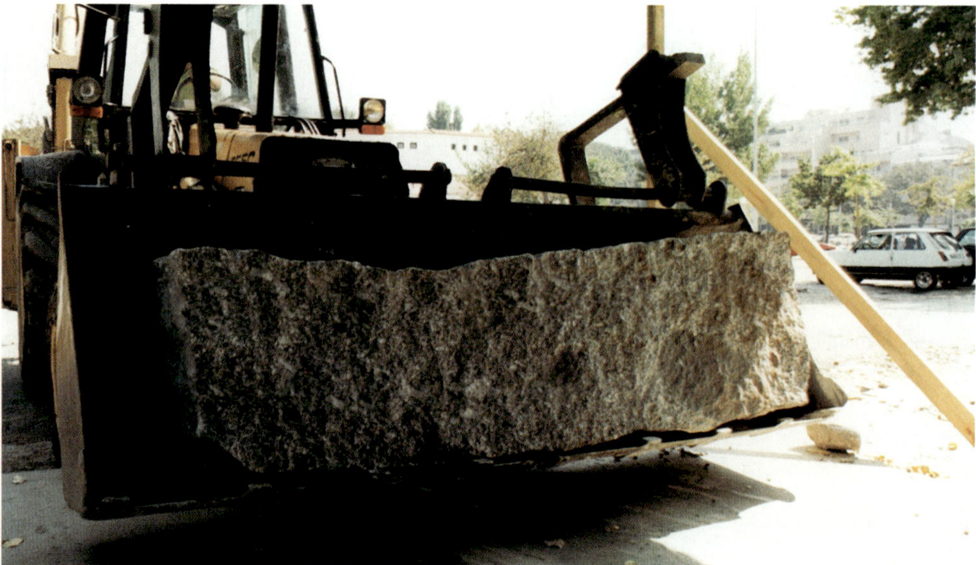

◄ 5. Conforming always to the four sections of the maquette, four teams of workers shape each block according to specifications.

▲ 6. The first block arrives from the quarry and is carried to the workshop by a forklift.

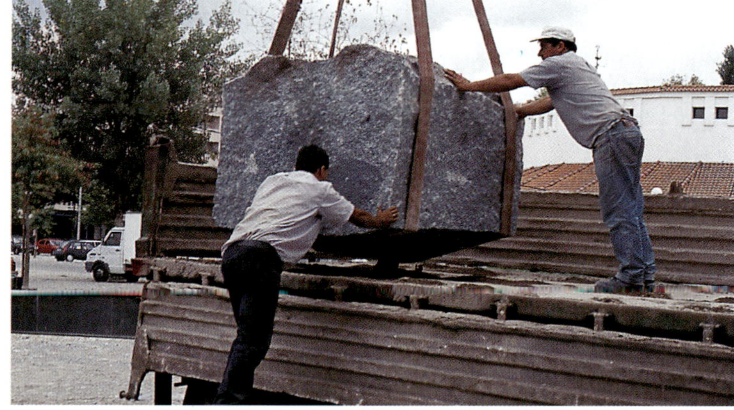

► 7. The second block also arrives.

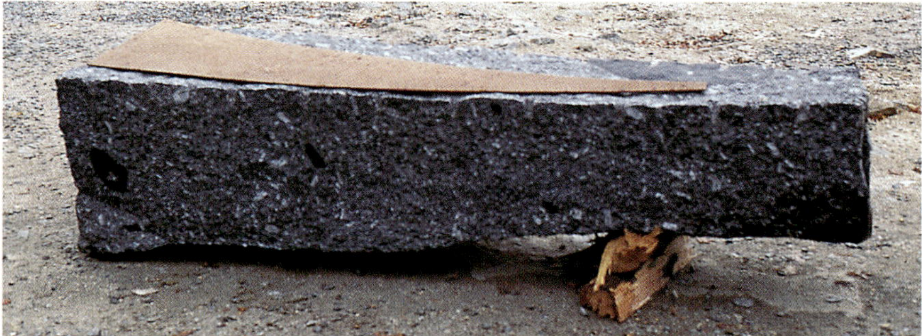

▲► 8. Though the first block is larger than the pattern called for, we decide to take advantage of its size and use the whole piece. We make the outline larger than we had originally planned, using the maquette as a reference and trying to get it as close as possible to the shape.

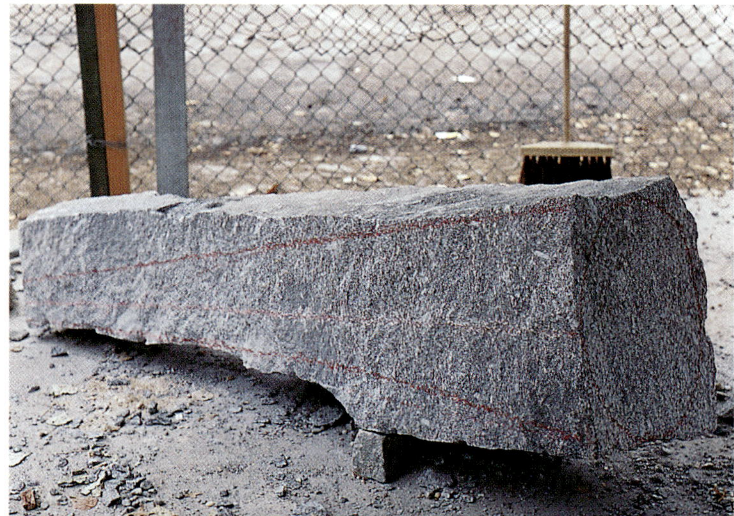

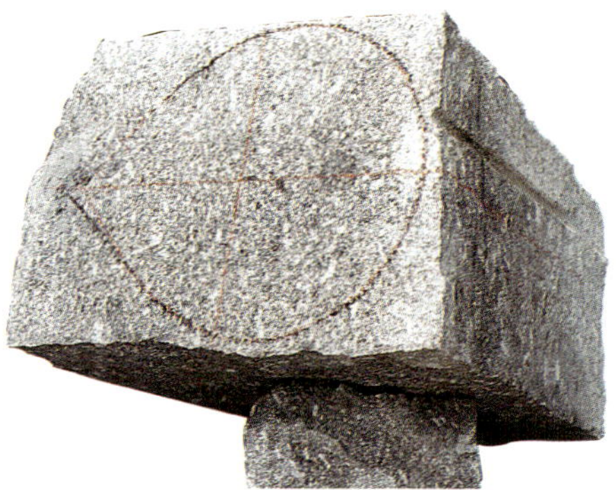

▲ **9.** We trace the outline of the pattern on block 2.

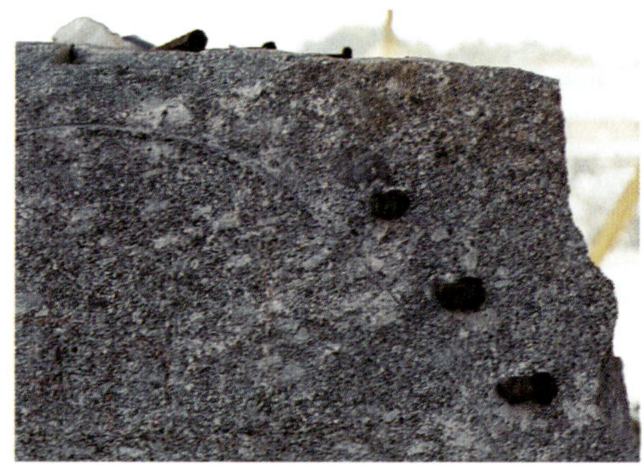

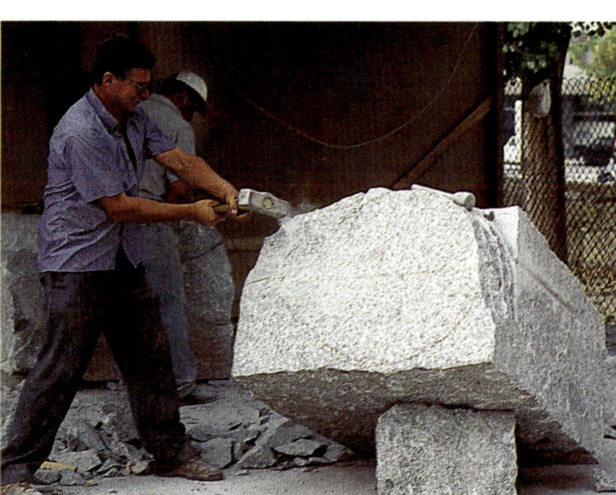

▲ ► **10.** A worker marks the outline using wedges. He then continues the process with a mallet and will finish it off with a circular saw.

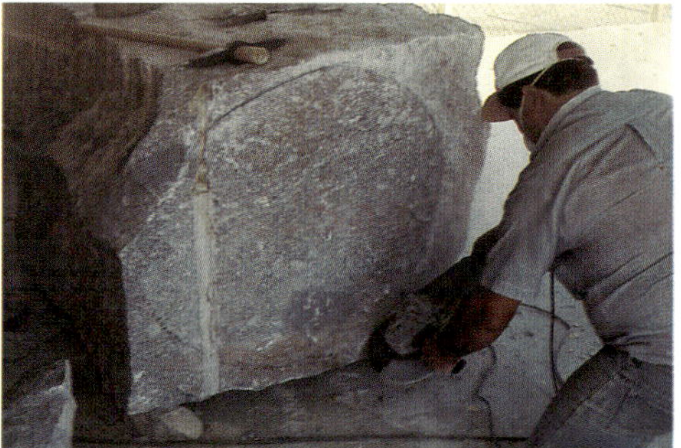

▲ **11.** The outline of block 3 is cut using a circular saw.

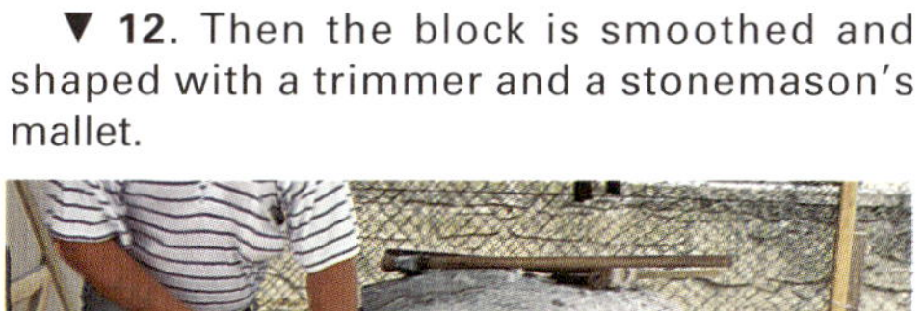

▼ **12.** Then the block is smoothed and shaped with a trimmer and a stonemason's mallet.

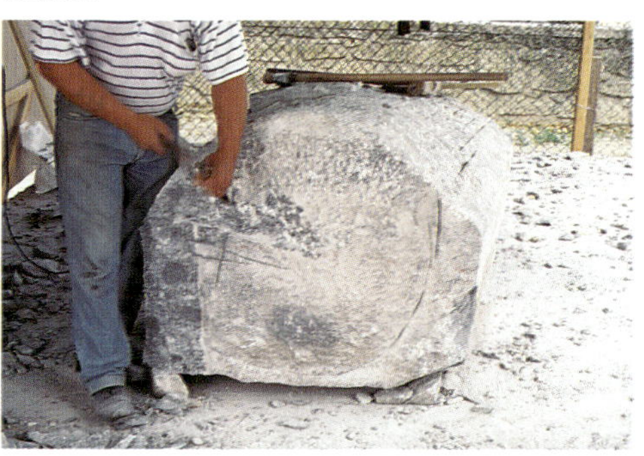

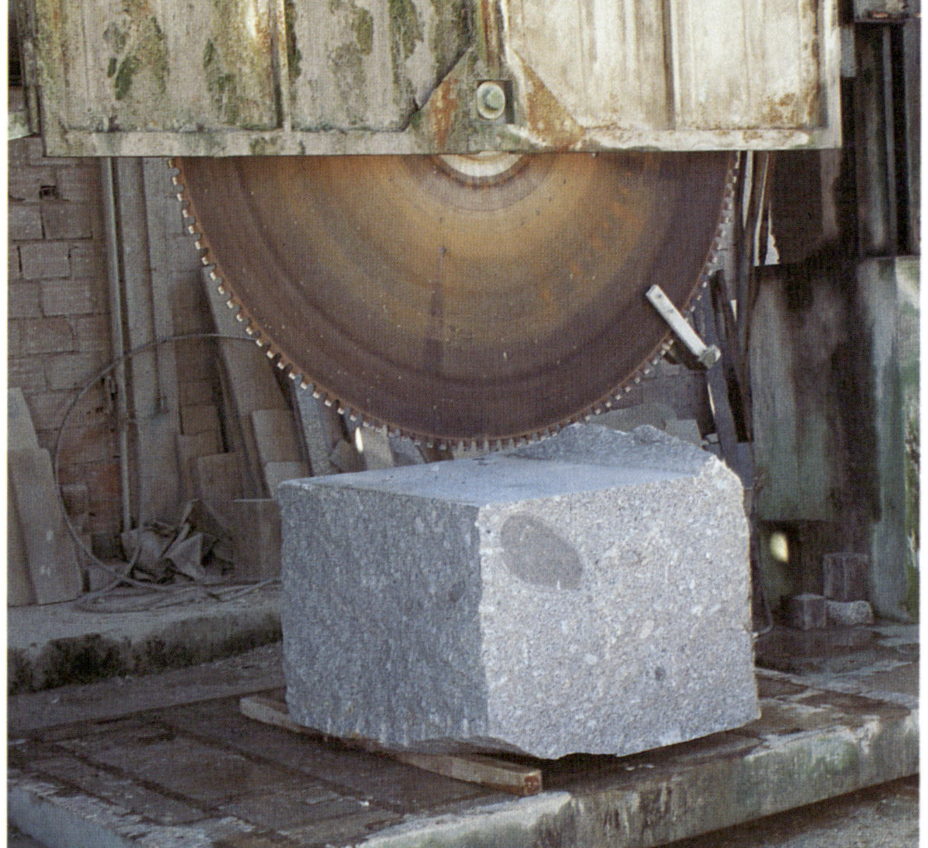

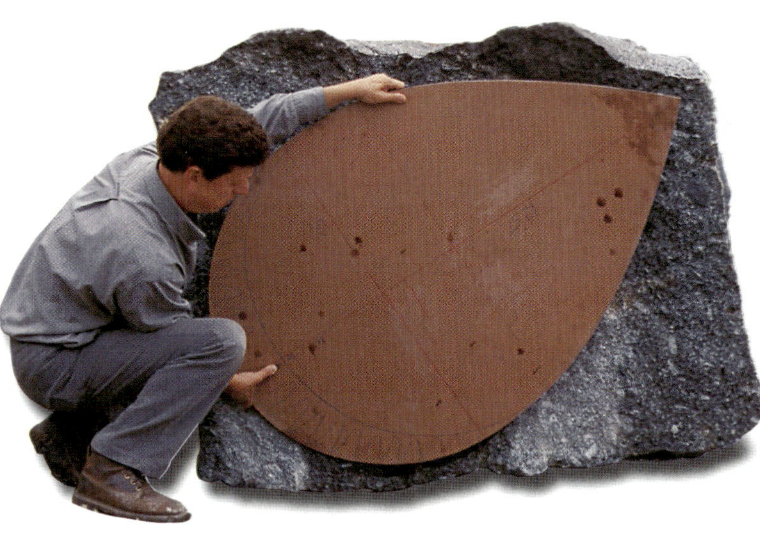

▲ ◄ **13.** Block 4, which weighs more than four tons, requires the use of a machine. After checking against the pattern to ensure that the specified measurements are adhered to, the outline is cut out by a large machine with a large cutting disk cooled by water.

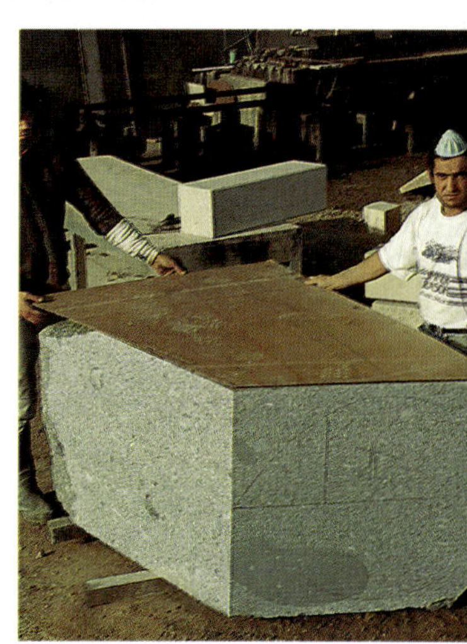

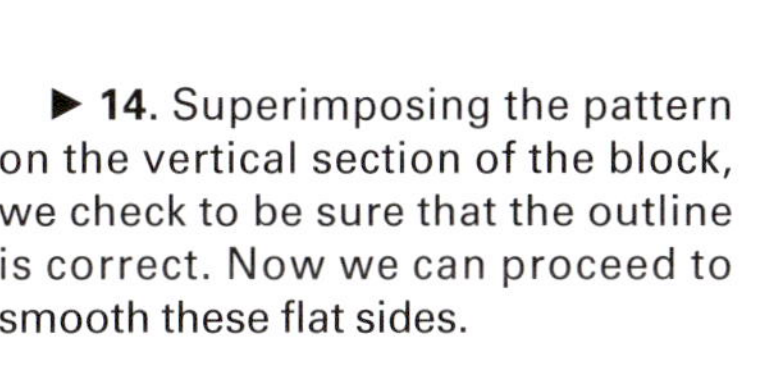

► **14.** Superimposing the pattern on the vertical section of the block, we check to be sure that the outline is correct. Now we can proceed to smooth these flat sides.

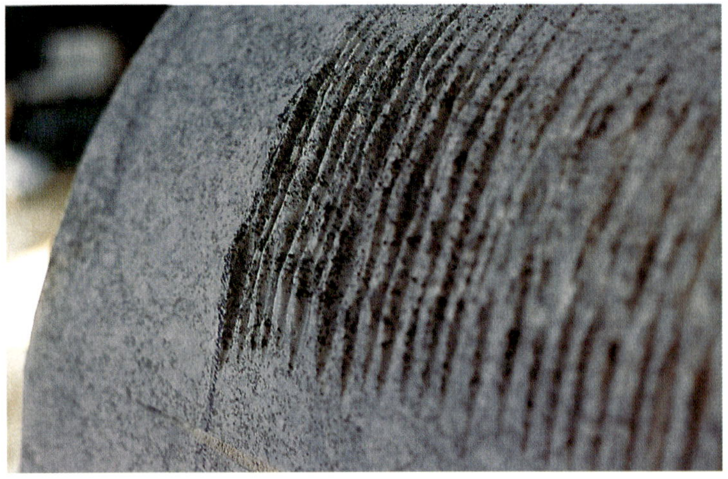

▲ **15.** Shaping block 1, which forms the pointed top, is especially difficult. Thus, the process is started by carving a conical contour that is shaped with a circular saw whose cutting blade leaves deep grooves in the granite.

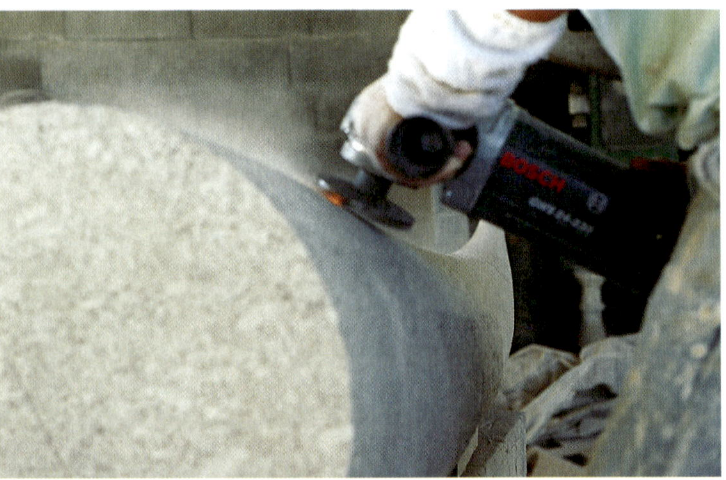

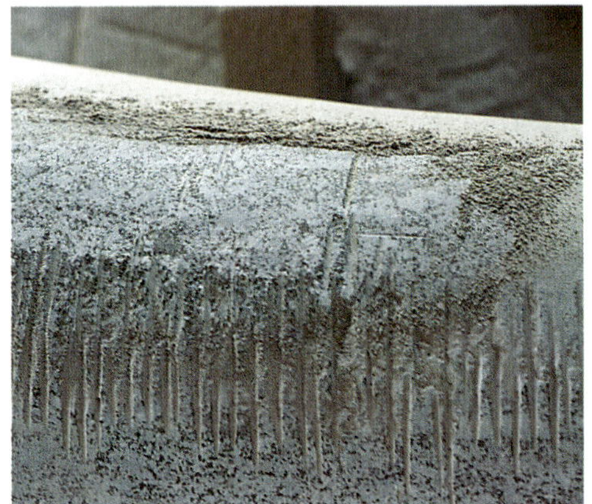

◄ ▲ **16.** Then a polisher is used to smooth out the rough edges and to accentuate the curved ones. It is important to keep the blade sliding continuously to avoid minor flattening of the edges.

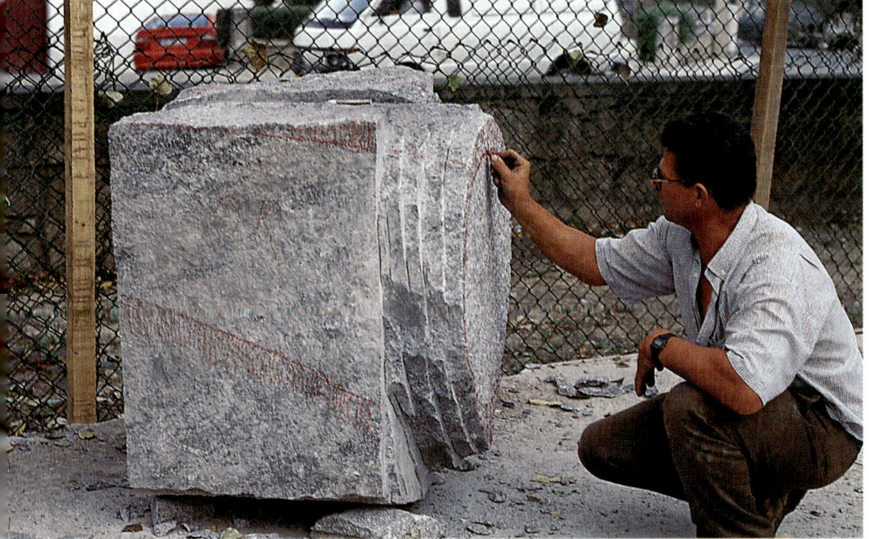

◄ ▼ **17.** Meanwhile, another worker has begun to smooth block 2 with determined cuts of the circular saw, using as reference the axes and outline tracings marked in red, which he now goes over.

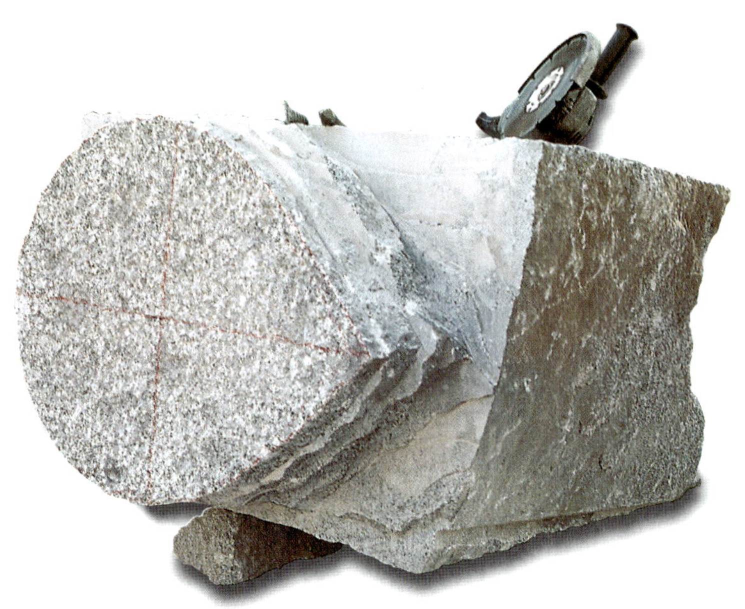

▼ **18.** Precision in measurements is crucial since blocks have to fit smoothly on top of each other.

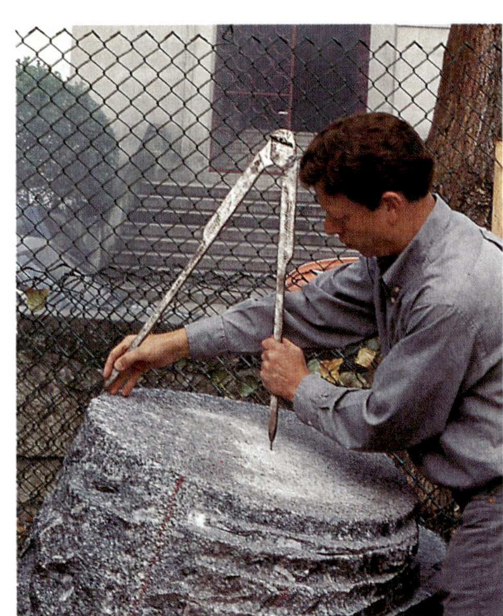

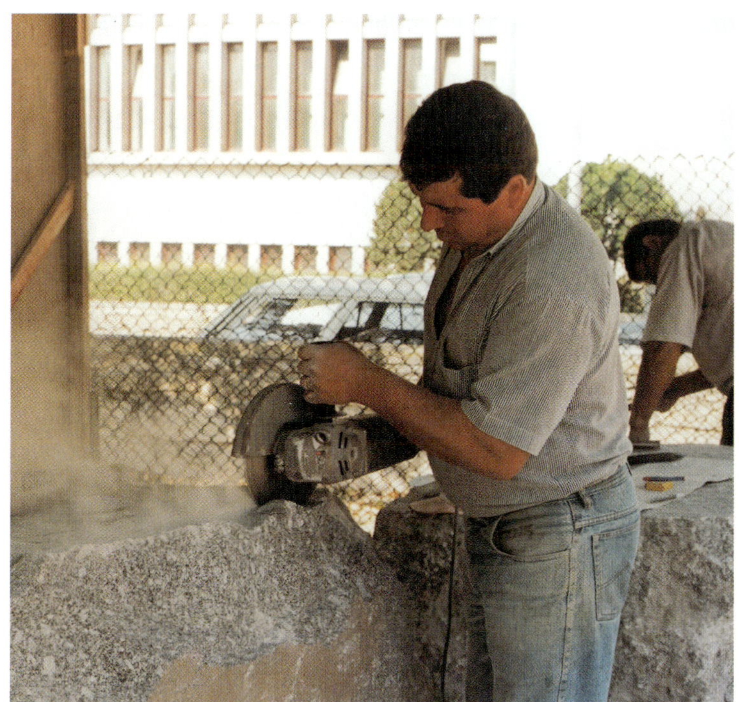

◄▼ **19.** As with the other two blocks, the smoothing process of block 3 is slow and a repeat: The granite is furrowed with a circular blade, making parallel cuts that afterwards are broken off with a heavy hammer.

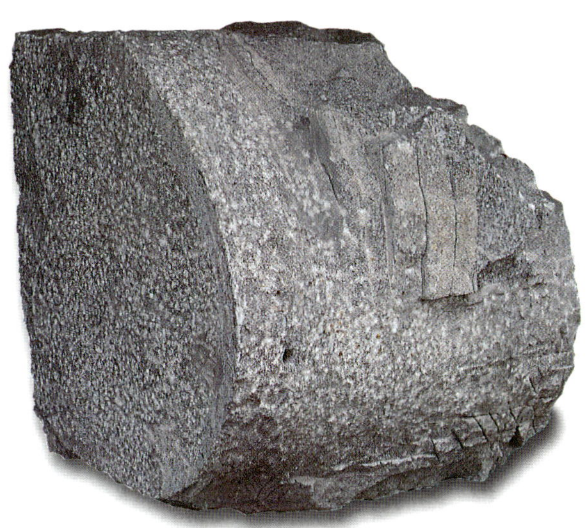

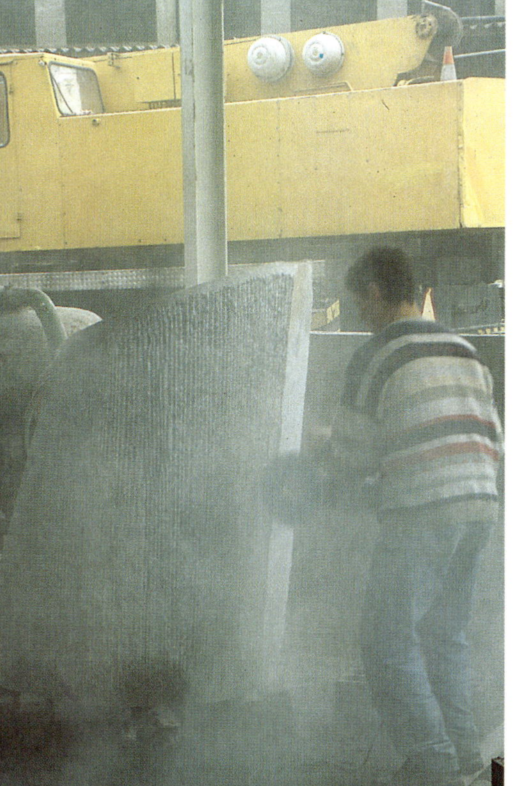

◄ **20.** Block 4, the base block, undergoes a similar process; in a cloud of dust holding the circular blade perpendicular to the granite, parallel furrows are made that, in this case, are lopped off at a slant.

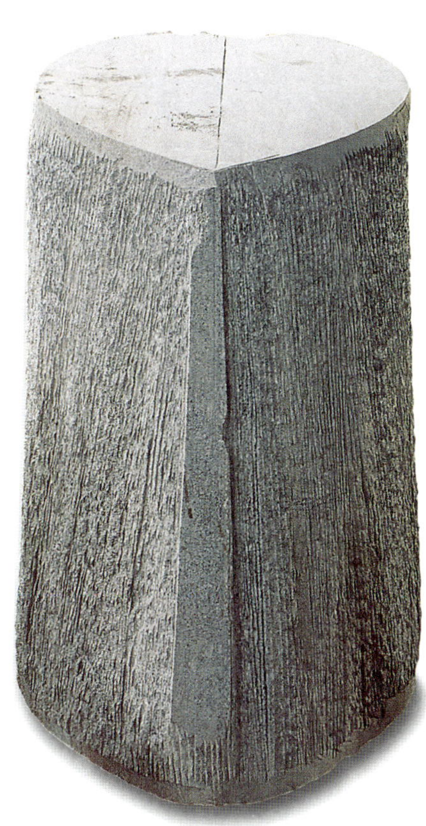

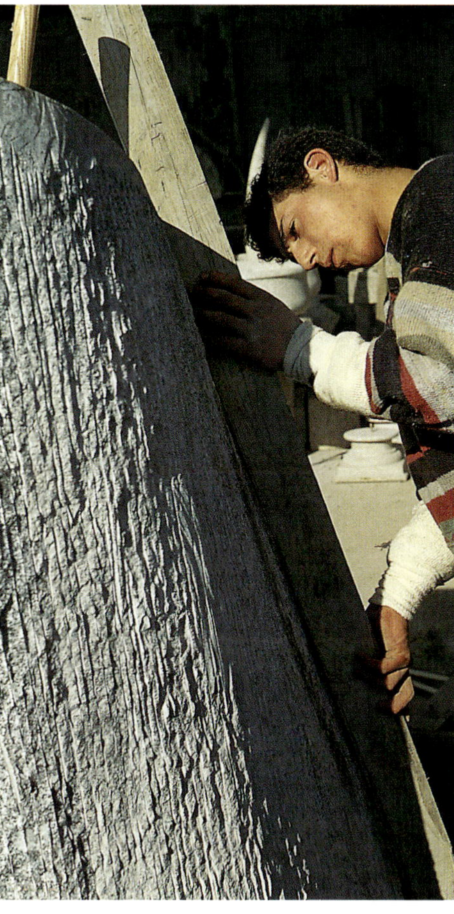

◄▲ **21.** The smoothing continues and the base begins to take shape; besides marking new axes on the block and comparing them with the maquette and the pattern, it is important to smooth out any unwanted irregularities that are detected.

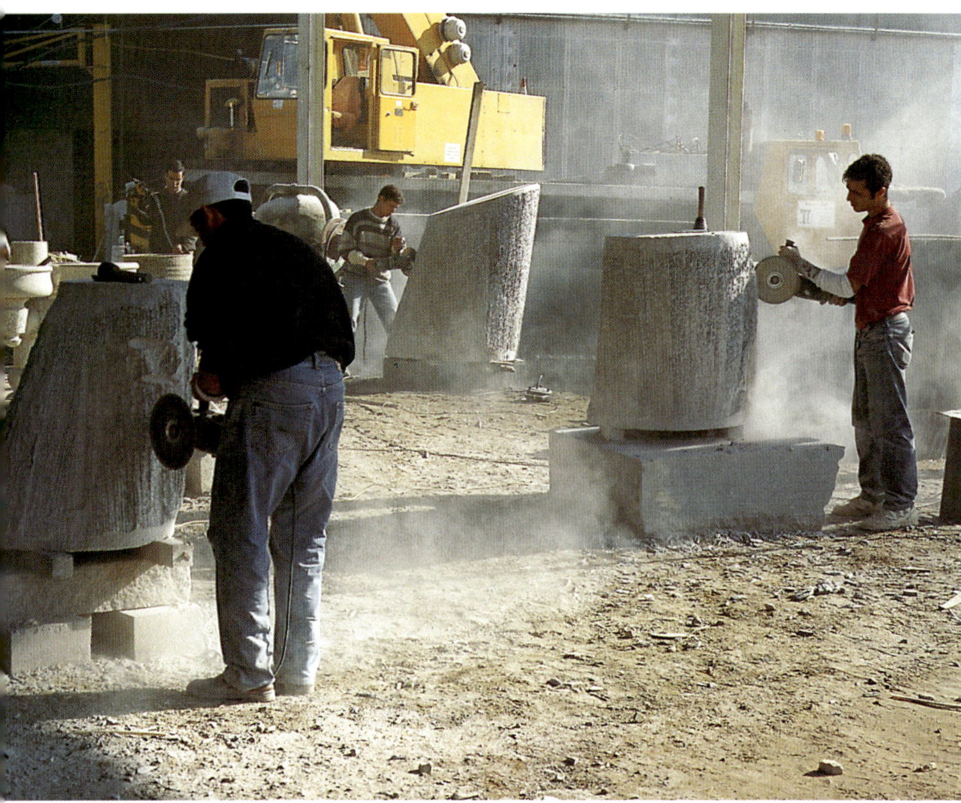

◀ **22.** During the shaping process of the block, workers will use tools dictated by the job at hand: hammer, trimmer, or industrial circular saw. Every worker uses a circular saw to trim the block but the choice of tools differs when smoothing edges. However, when the trimming process reduces the block near its final shape, everyone works together using a single technique.

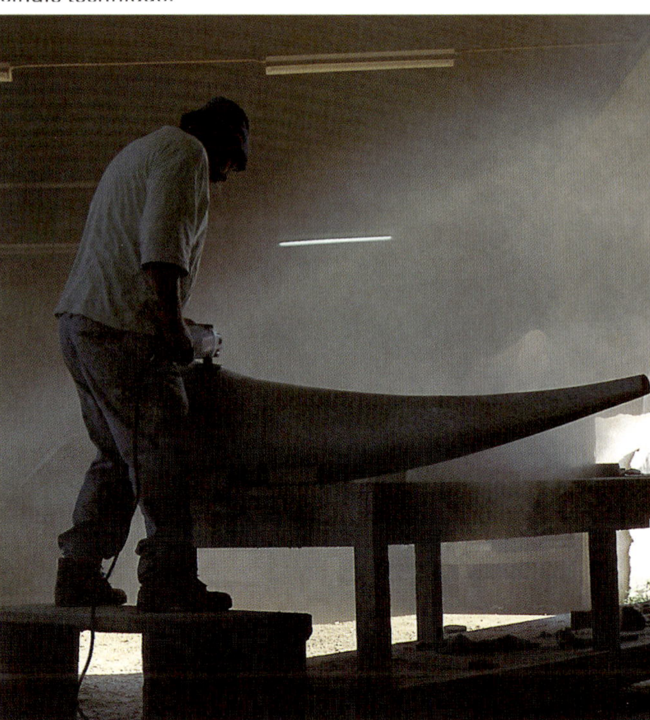

► **23.** except Jose, who continues smoothing out the surface of the conical stone with an abrasive circular tool.

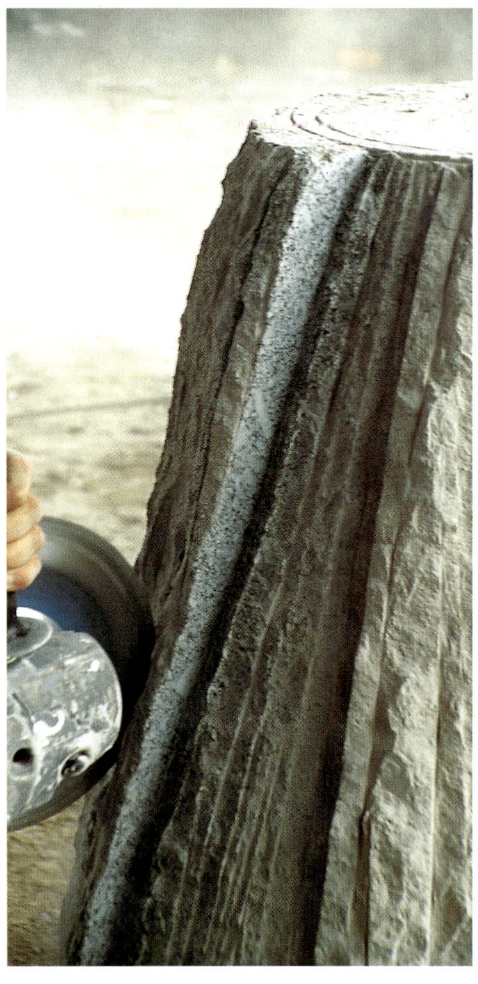

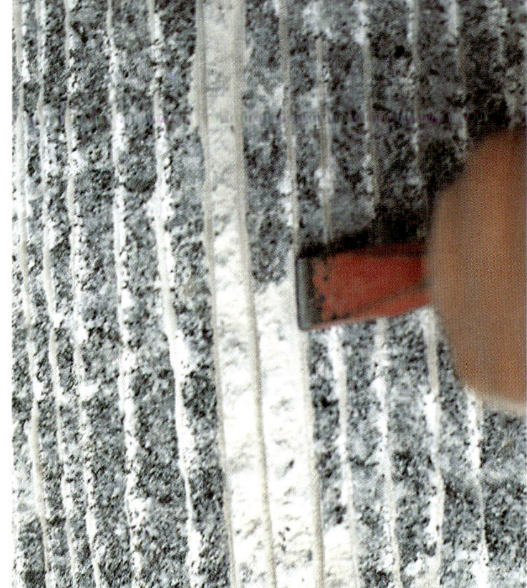

◀ ▲ **24.** The shaping technique for hard granite is the same that we have used on other occasions for trimming surfaces: We furrow with the circular saw the stone's surface with parallel shallow cuts and then we use a mallet to remove the excess stone within the furrows. The process is simple, but it requires a high degree of consistency and strength.

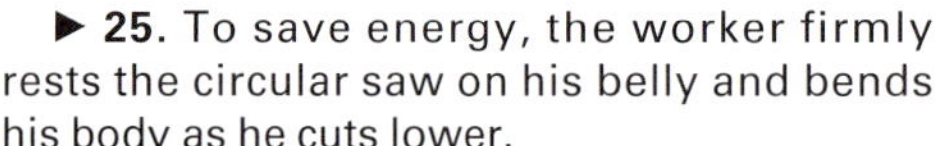

► **25.** To save energy, the worker firmly rests the circular saw on his belly and bends his body as he cuts lower.

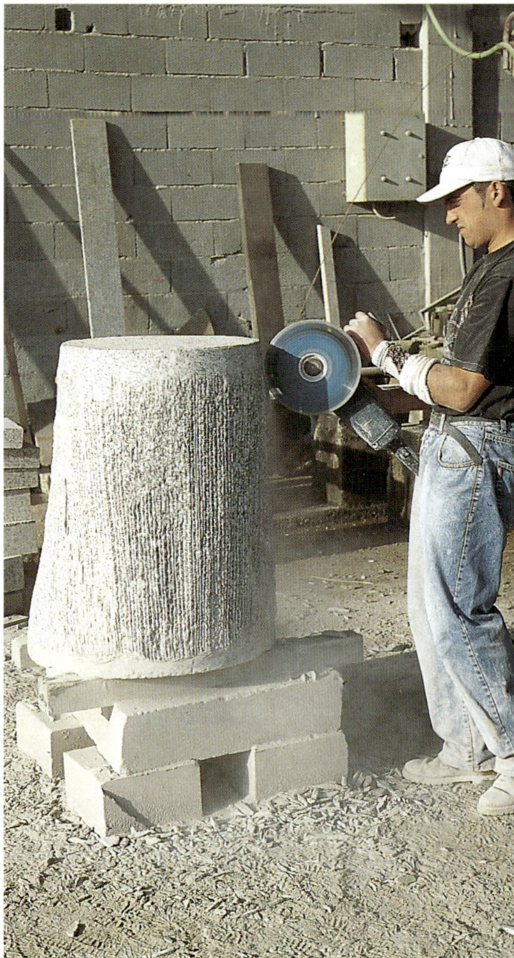

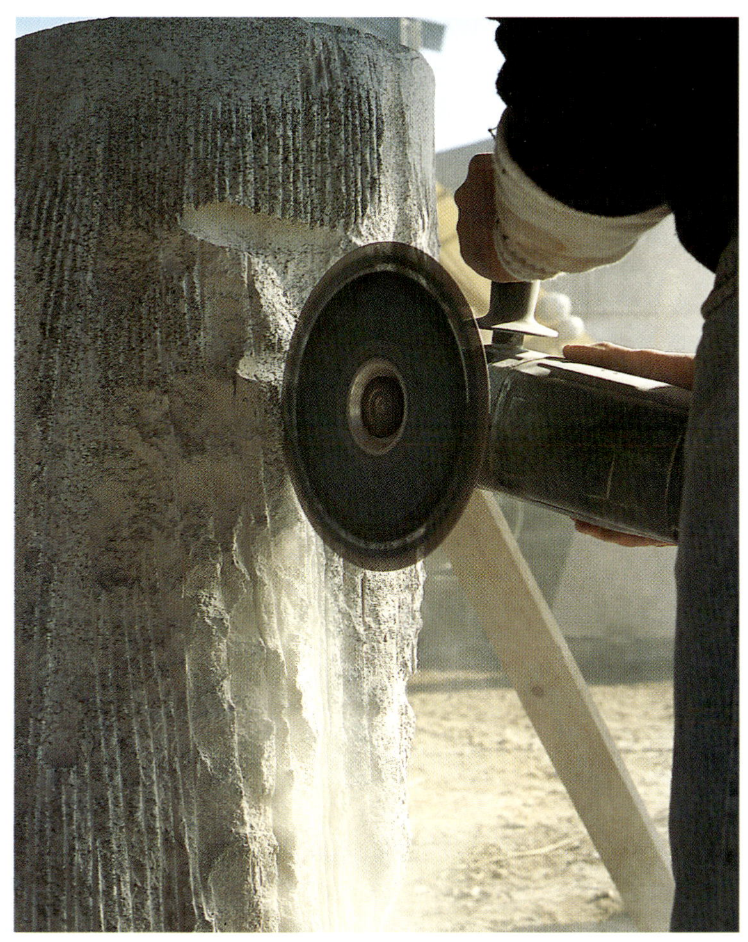

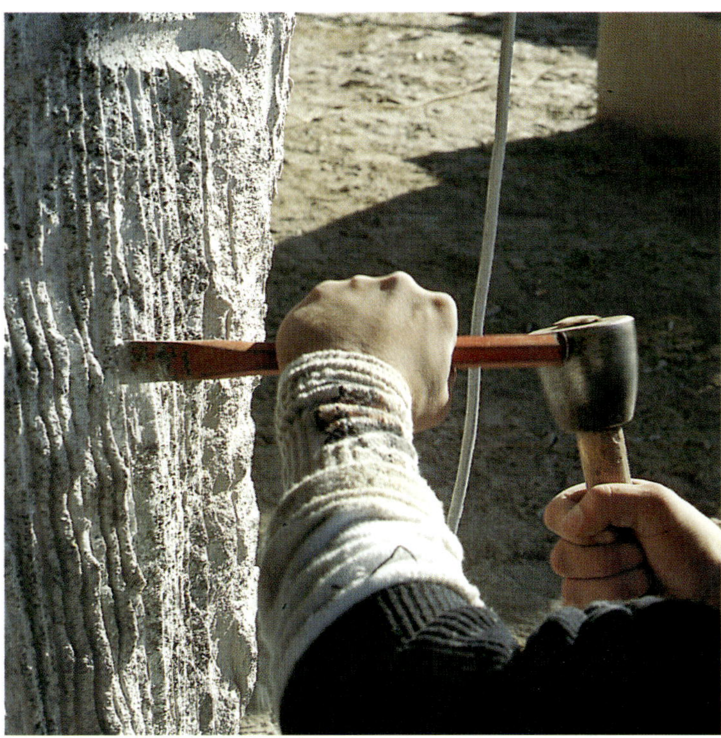

◀ ▲ **26**. The shaping of block 3 is done in the same way. To break away the hard edges within the furrows, the mallet is more effective than the chisel and the Portuguese mallet is easier to handle than other mallets.

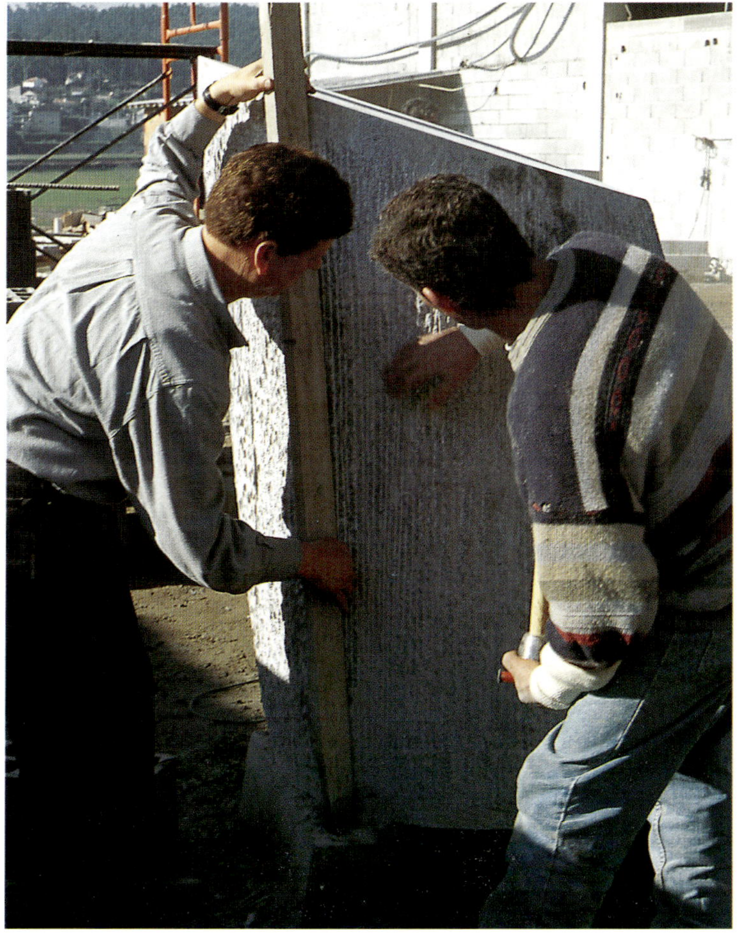

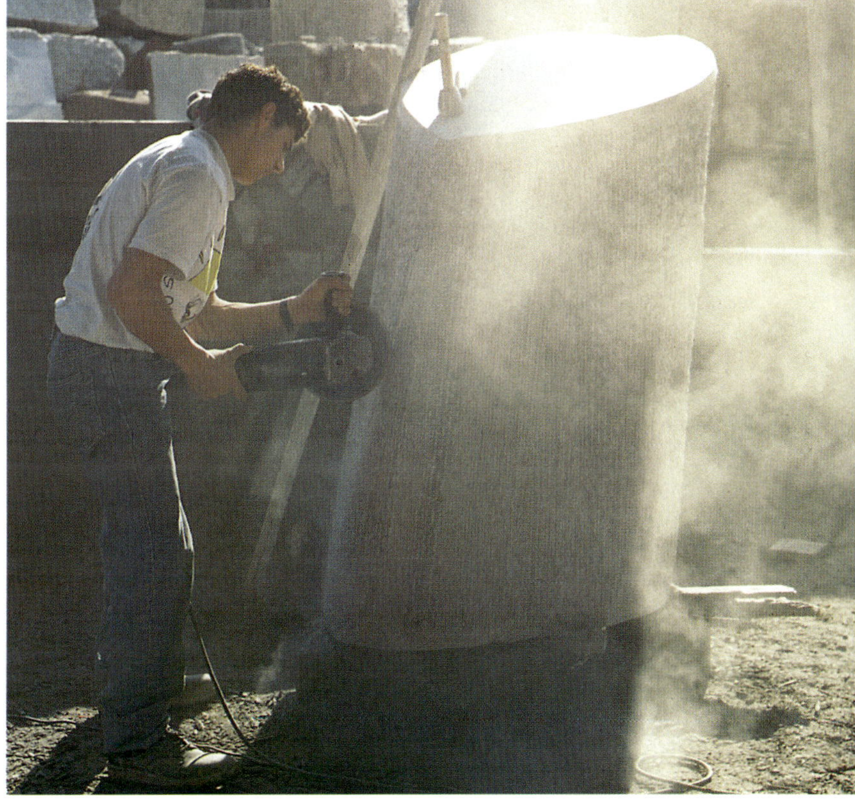

◀ ▲ **27**. We smooth the block again looking for possible shape irregularities and we apply the last touches. We will preserve the grooved markings left by the circular saw, as this texture accentuates the vertical nature of the block.

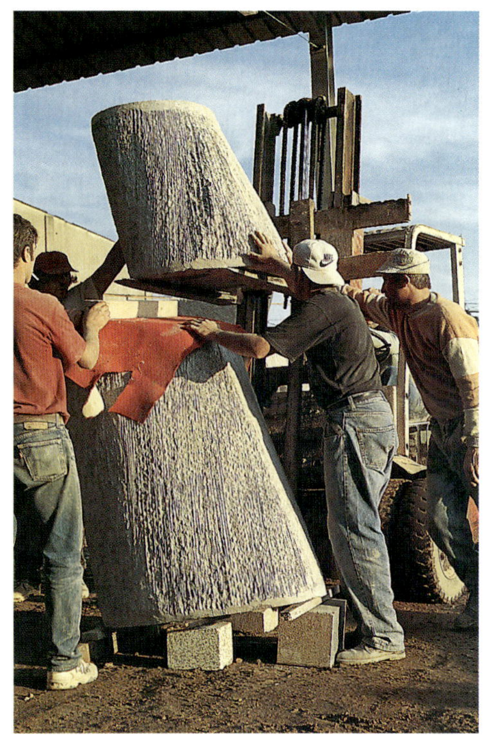

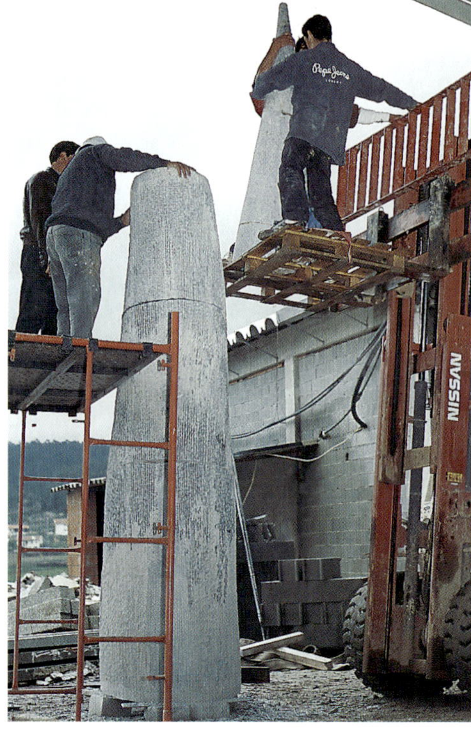

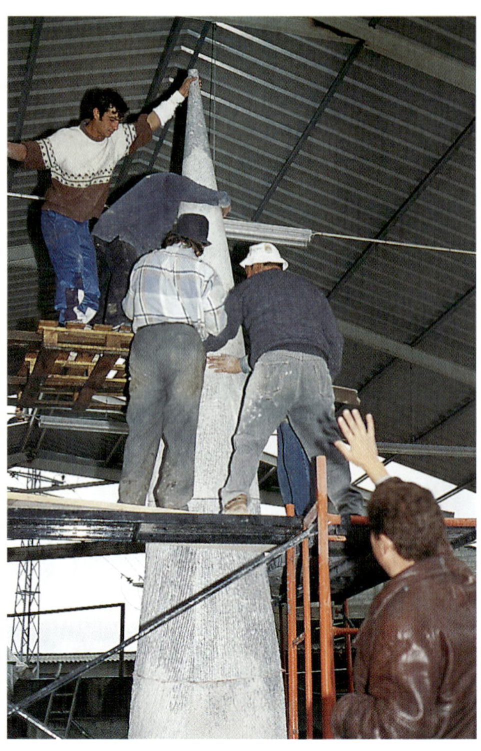

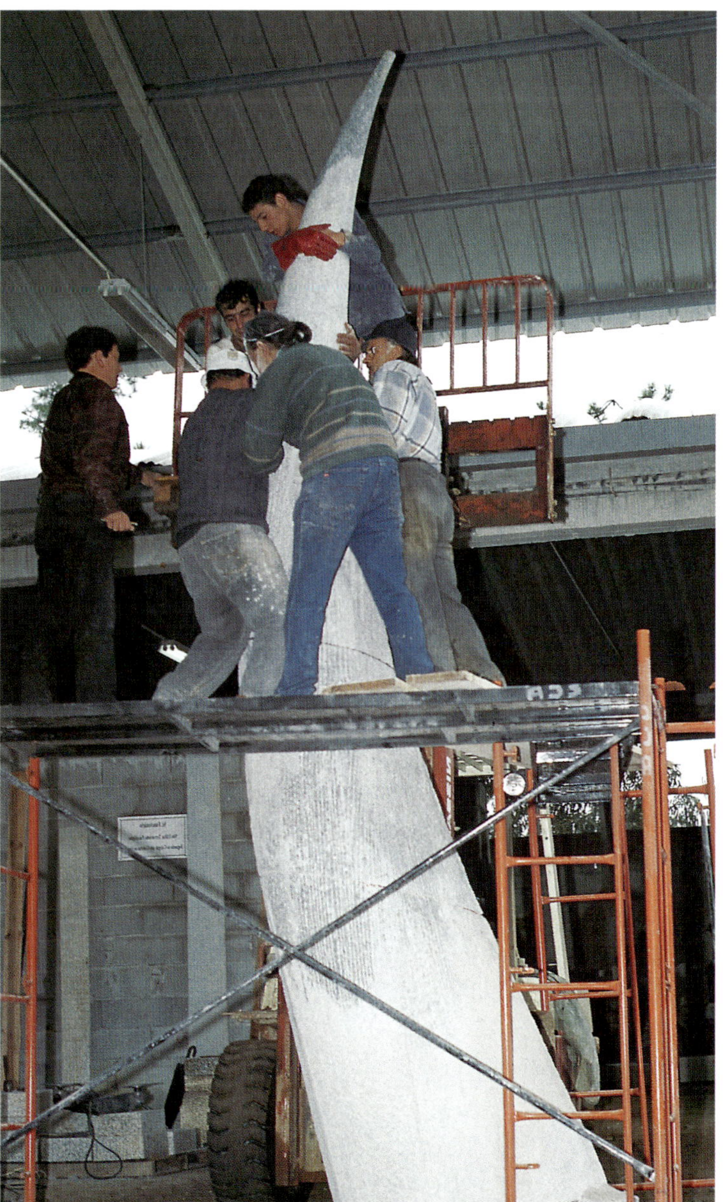

▲ ▲ ▲ ◄ **28.** Finally, after hours and hours of intense work, we have managed to tame the granite despite its resistance. The four blocks are put together and thanks to the sideview patterns we have ensured that adjoining surfaces are smooth and have the same dimensions. With a mechanical elevator, we provisionally mount the sculpture together. Because the sculpture is arched, we are careful to keep in balance and its base level. To prevent the blocks from slipping, we insert pieces of old carpet between them.

▼ **29.** We were afraid of this and expected it; although the bases of each block seemed to perfectly fit the modeling pattern, a tiny error in one of them calls for adjustments and for additional adjustments in another. The curvature in the sculpture's outline must be continuous as viewed from all angles. The four blocks have to appear as though they were one. We will not back down from the task until we dominate the hard granite.

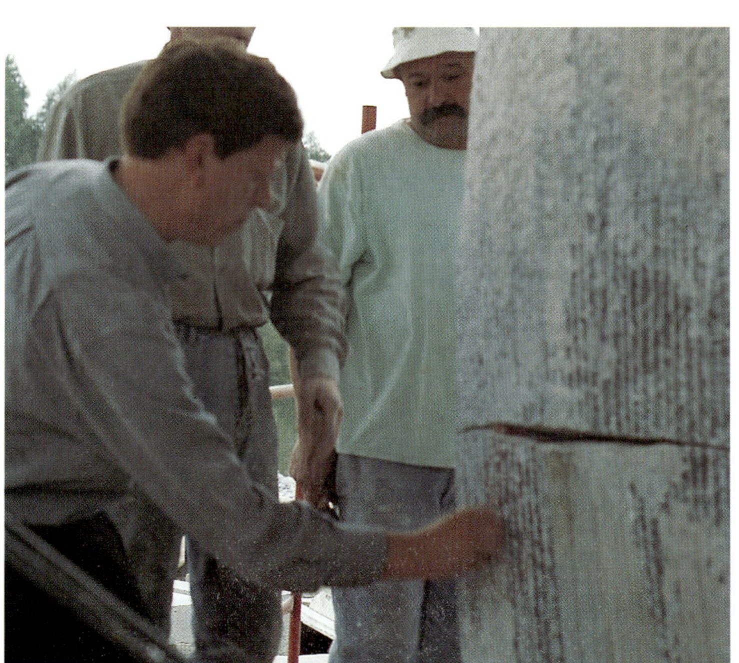

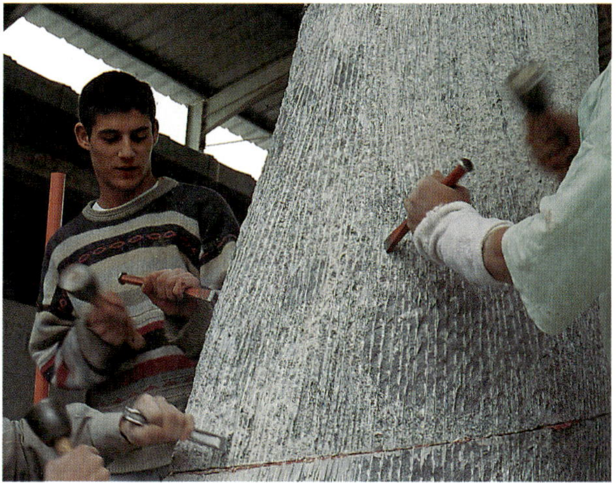

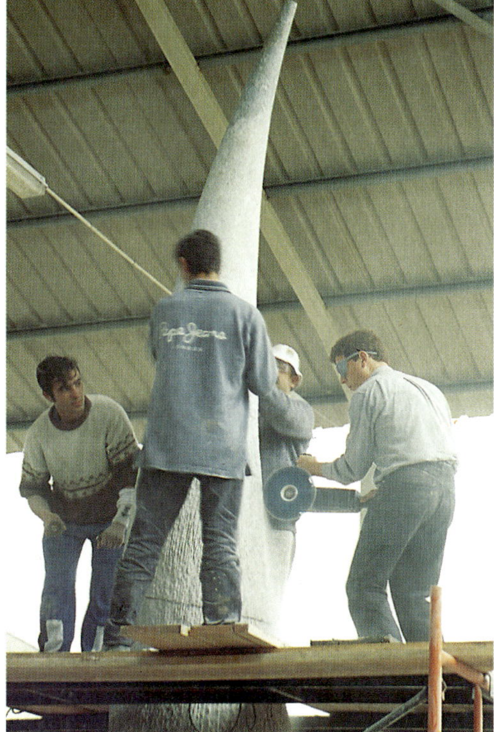

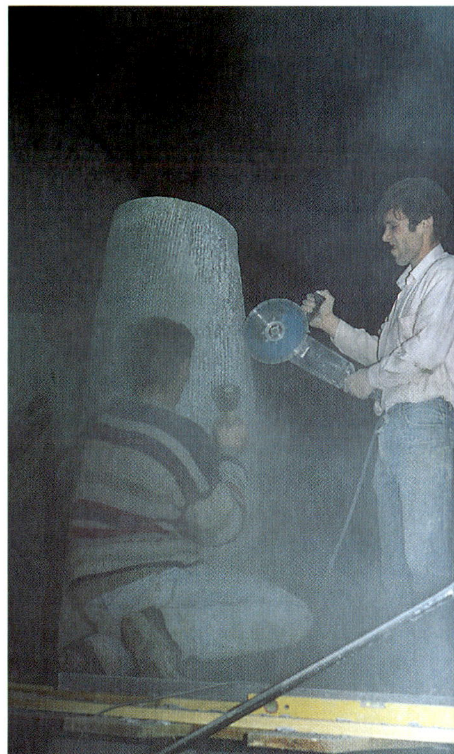

▲ ▶ ▶ **30.** Circular saws, scarps, arms—all work together in a cloud of dust and noise. A touch here and there. Always the same technique—cutting increasingly shallow furrows, discarding the cutouts, standing back so as not to lose sight of the whole, and modeling again. The night and day of the inauguration is closing in on us.

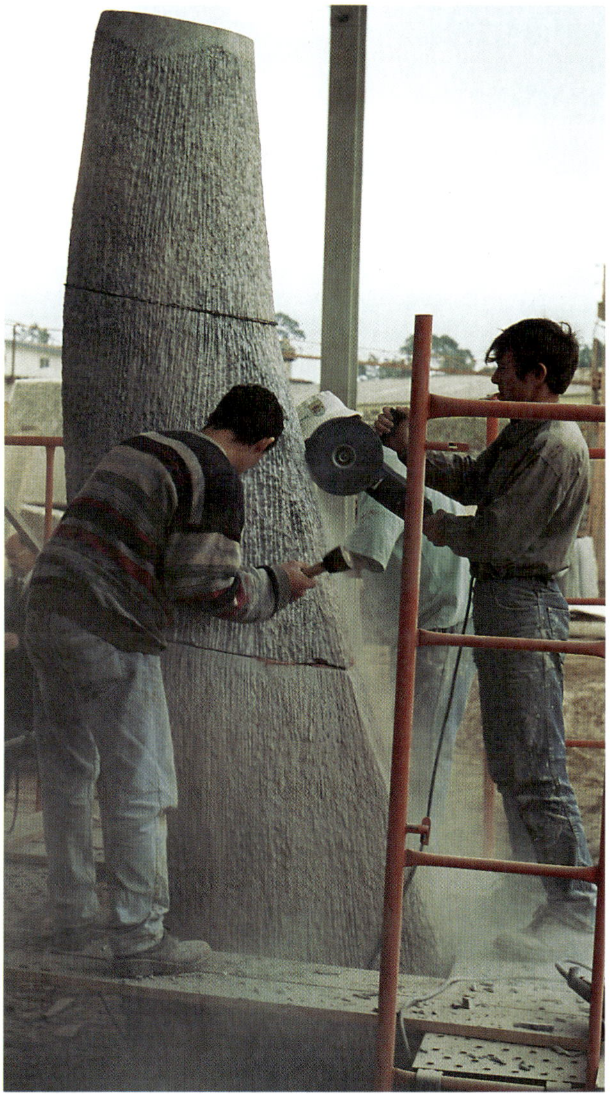

▶ ▶ **31.** We are careful with the incisions; the furrows by the circular saw in the upper blocks have to be parallel and continuous.

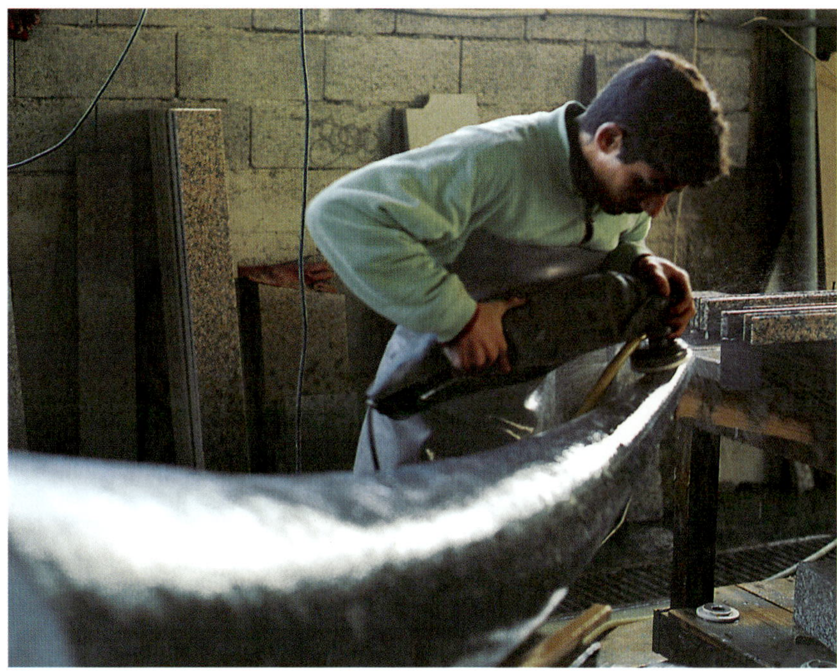

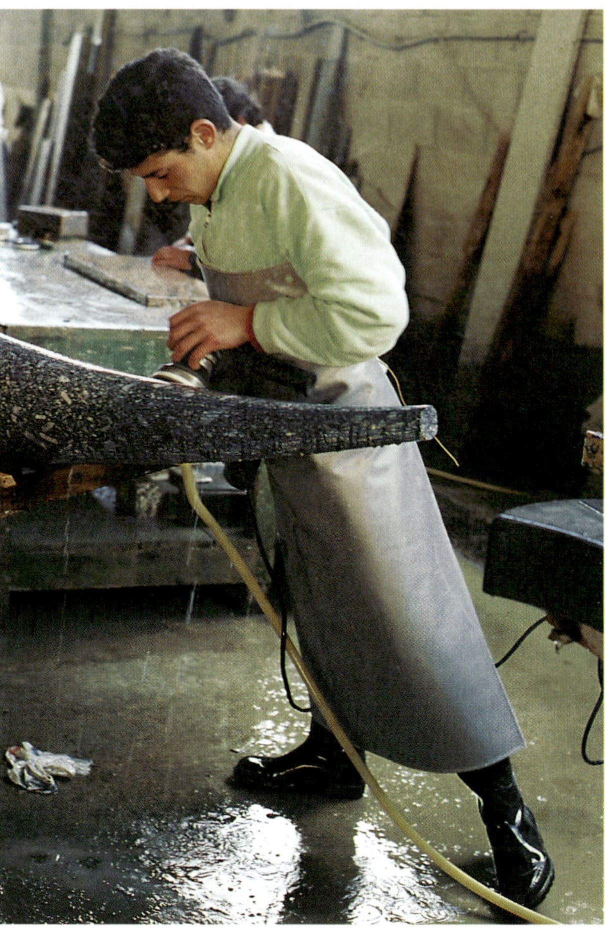

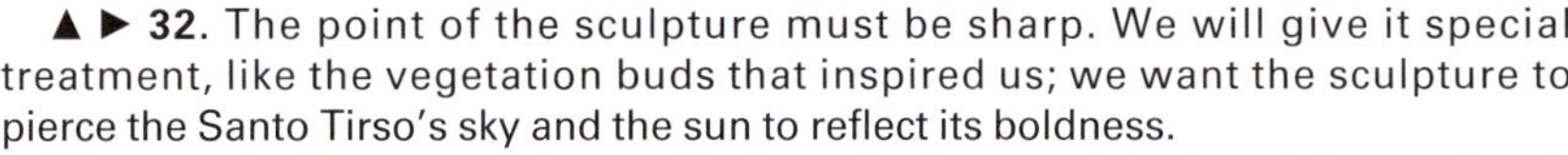

▲ ► **32.** The point of the sculpture must be sharp. We will give it special treatment, like the vegetation buds that inspired us; we want the sculpture to pierce the Santo Tirso's sky and the sun to reflect its boldness.

We want the furrows of the top block to give it a rough look and thus endow it with a shine. To achieve this effect, circular polishing tools with increasingly finer abrasive grains are passed repeatedly over the block. A steady stream of water helps these tools along. Here the strength of bodies combines with that of arms.

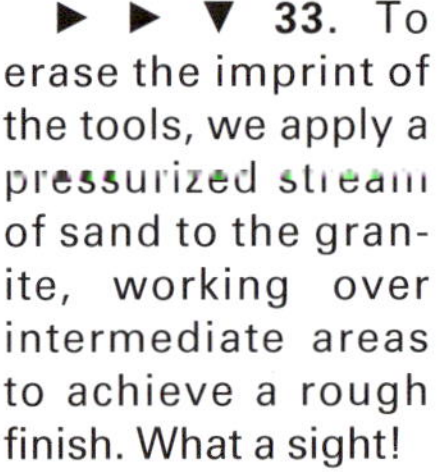

► ► ▼ **33.** To erase the imprint of the tools, we apply a pressurized stream of sand to the granite, working over intermediate areas to achieve a rough finish. What a sight!

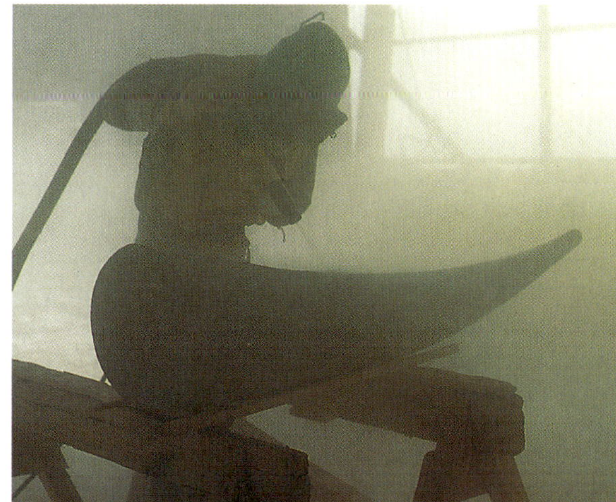

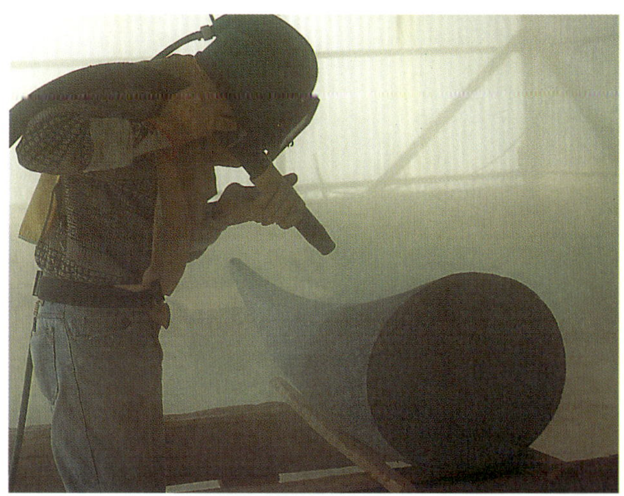

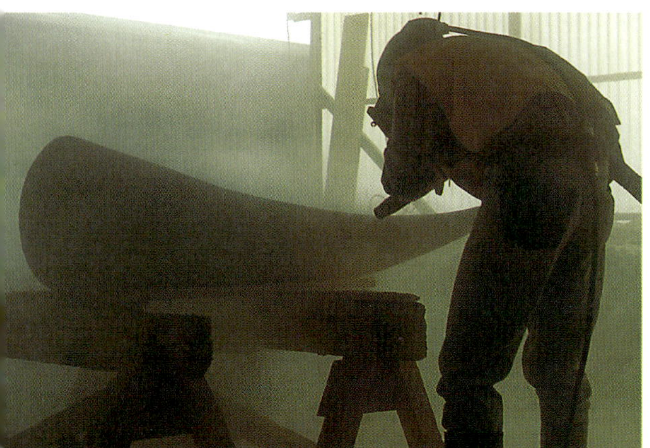

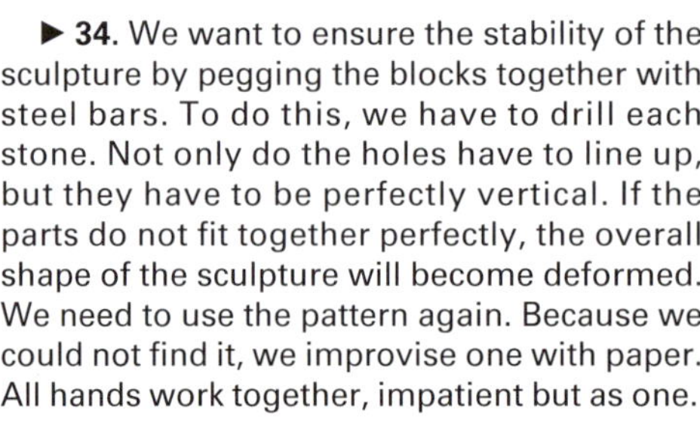

► **34.** We want to ensure the stability of the sculpture by pegging the blocks together with steel bars. To do this, we have to drill each stone. Not only do the holes have to line up, but they have to be perfectly vertical. If the parts do not fit together perfectly, the overall shape of the sculpture will become deformed. We need to use the pattern again. Because we could not find it, we improvise one with paper. All hands work together, impatient but as one.

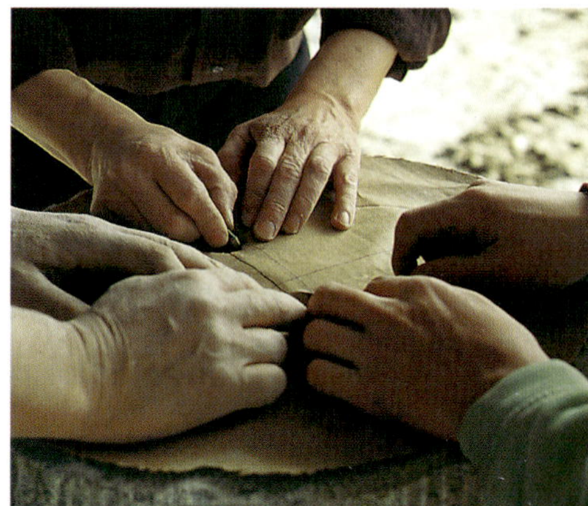

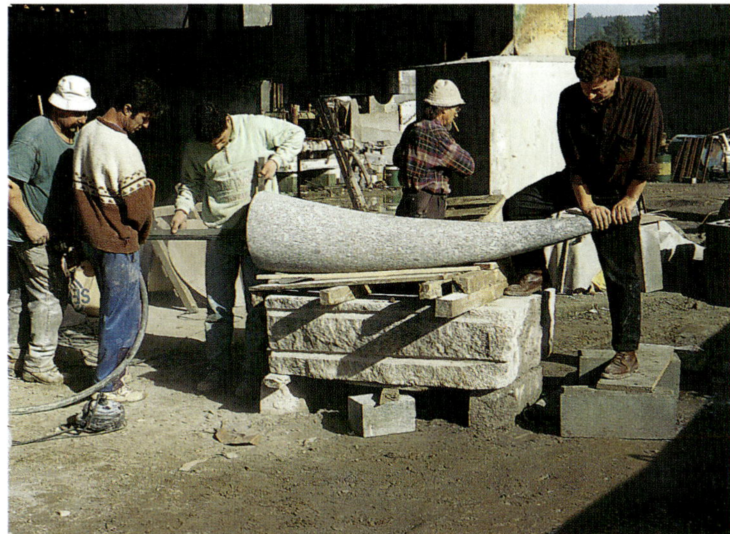

◄ ▼ **35.** With a large drill, guided more by hunch than by measurements, we carve the blocks. As if possessed by the spirit of intuition, or simply by tension, we associate the noise of the tool with Wagner's music of the Ride of the Valkyries.

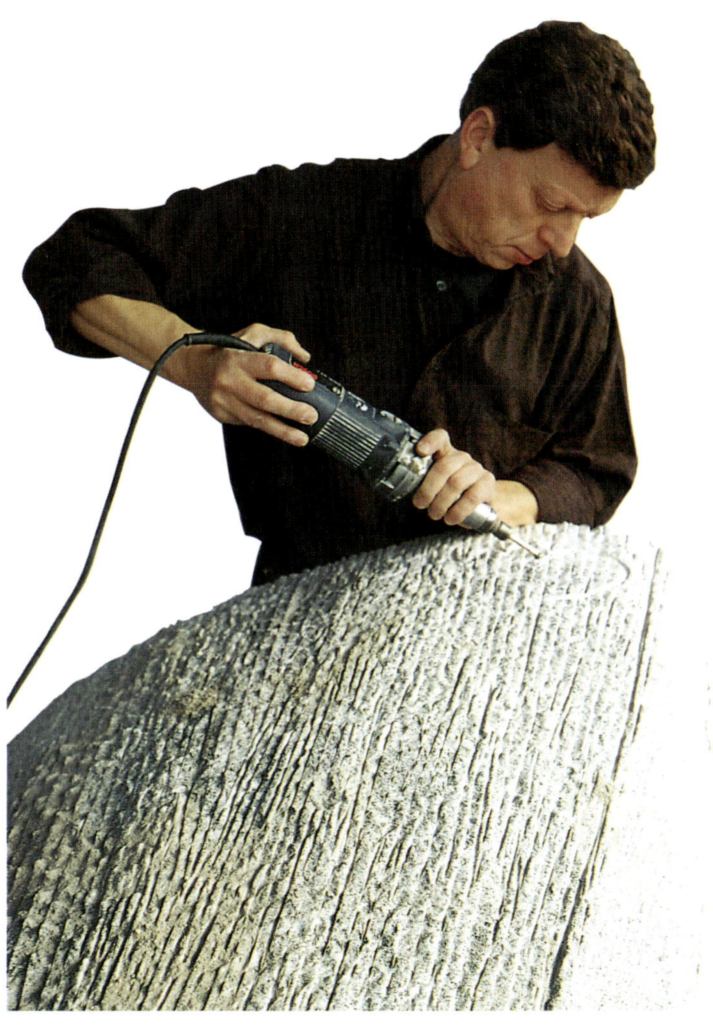

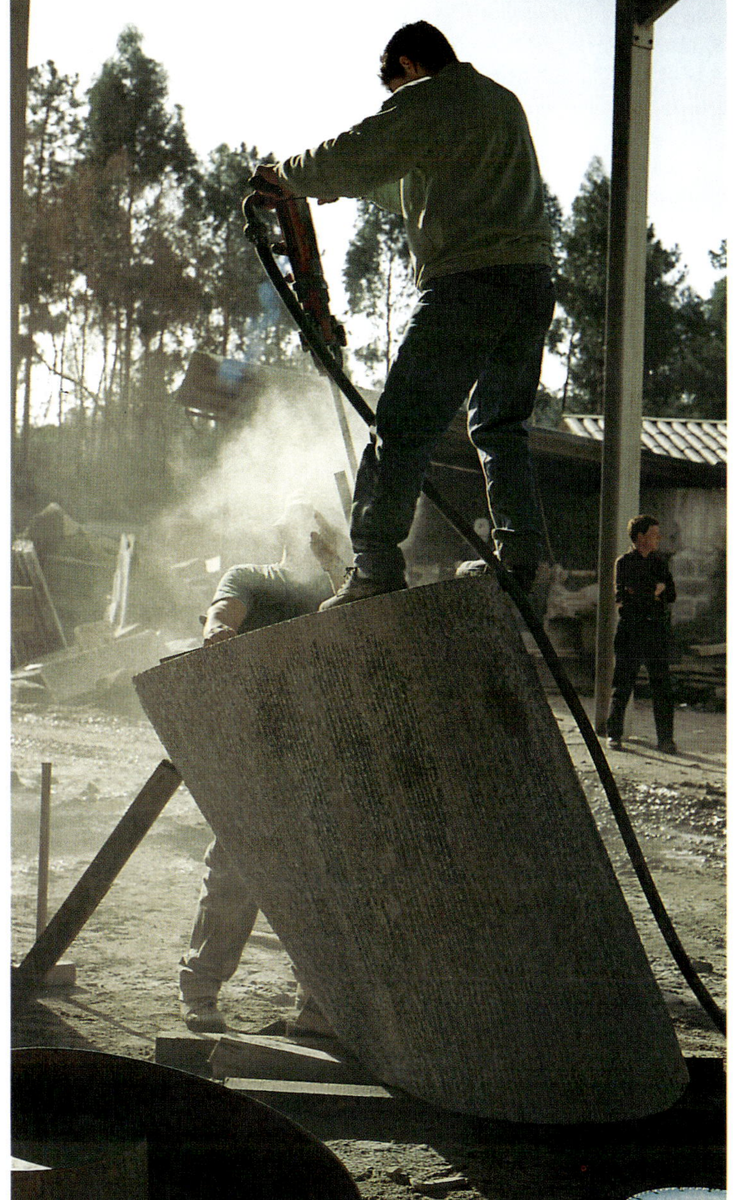

◄ **36.** Many people have worked together, but only the sculptor signs his name.

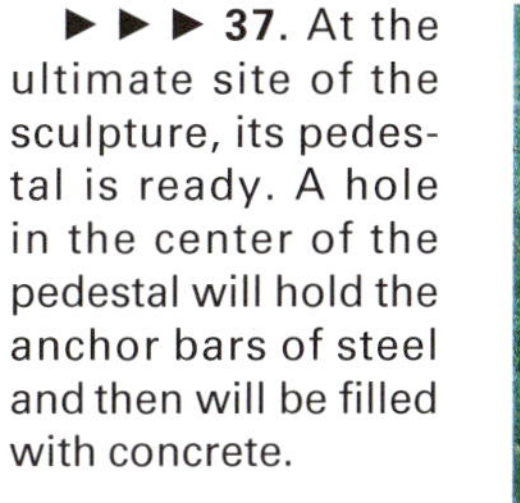

► ► ► **37.** At the ultimate site of the sculpture, its pedestal is ready. A hole in the center of the pedestal will hold the anchor bars of steel and then will be filled with concrete.

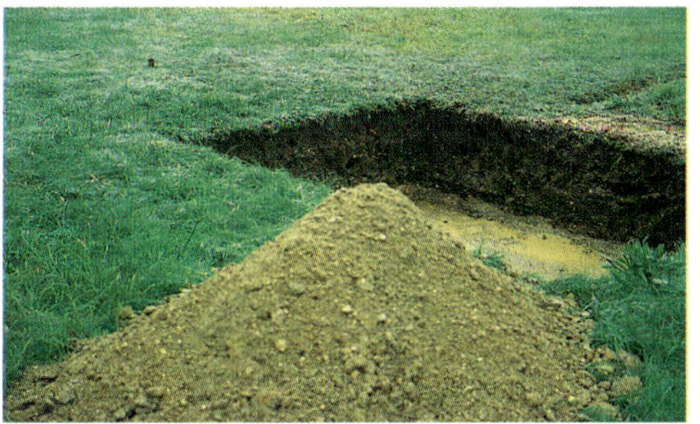

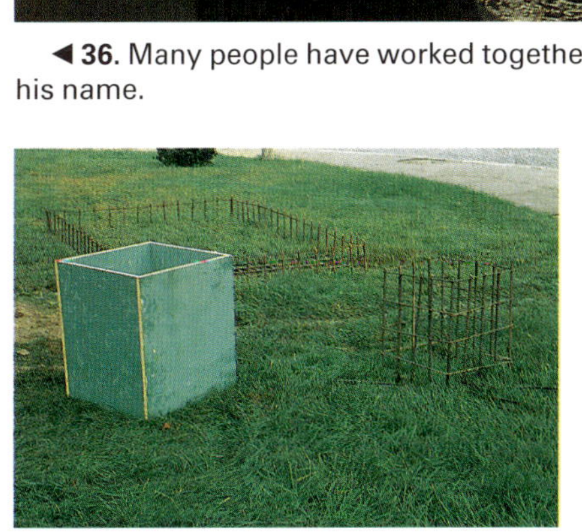

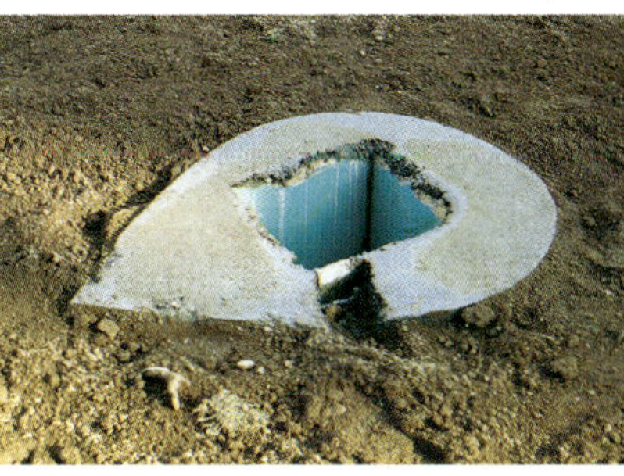

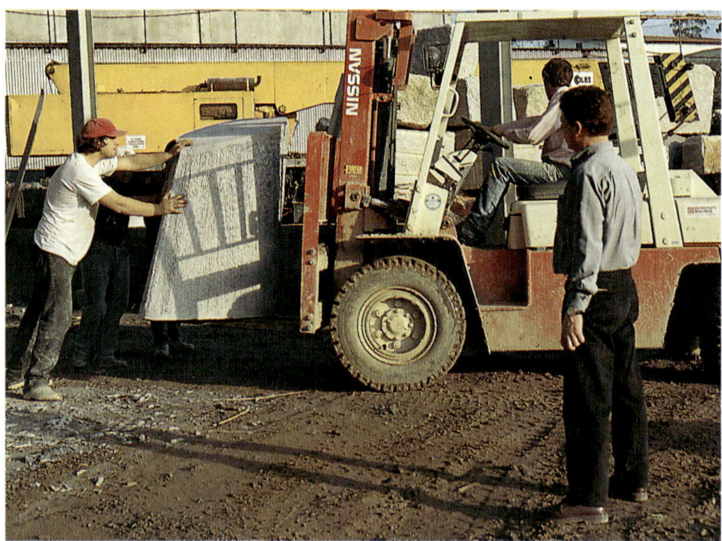

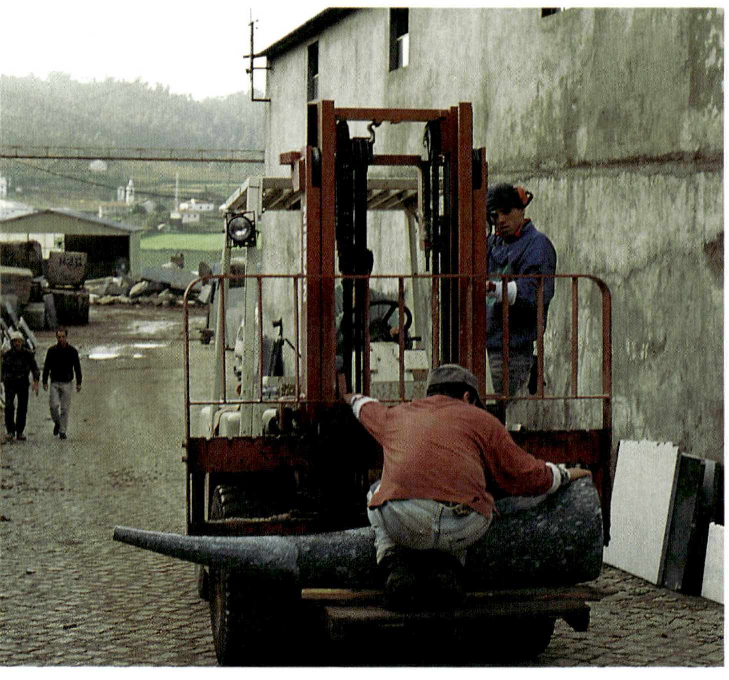

▲ ▶ **38.** The sculpture is now ready to leave the workshops. It is now time to rely on different types of equipment and to coordinate the scheduling of the truck, the crane, and the crews.

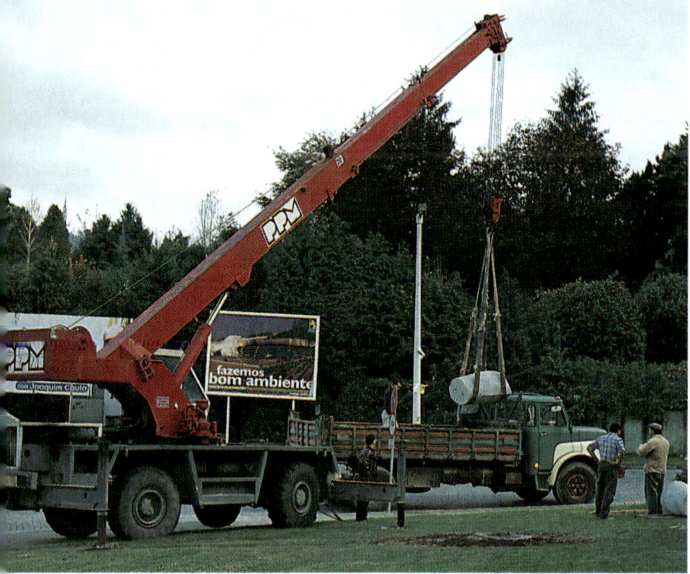

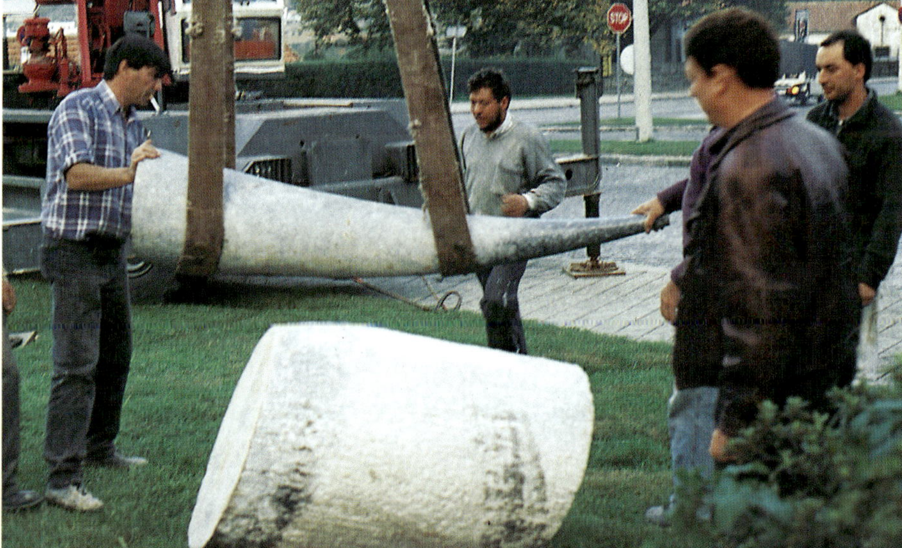

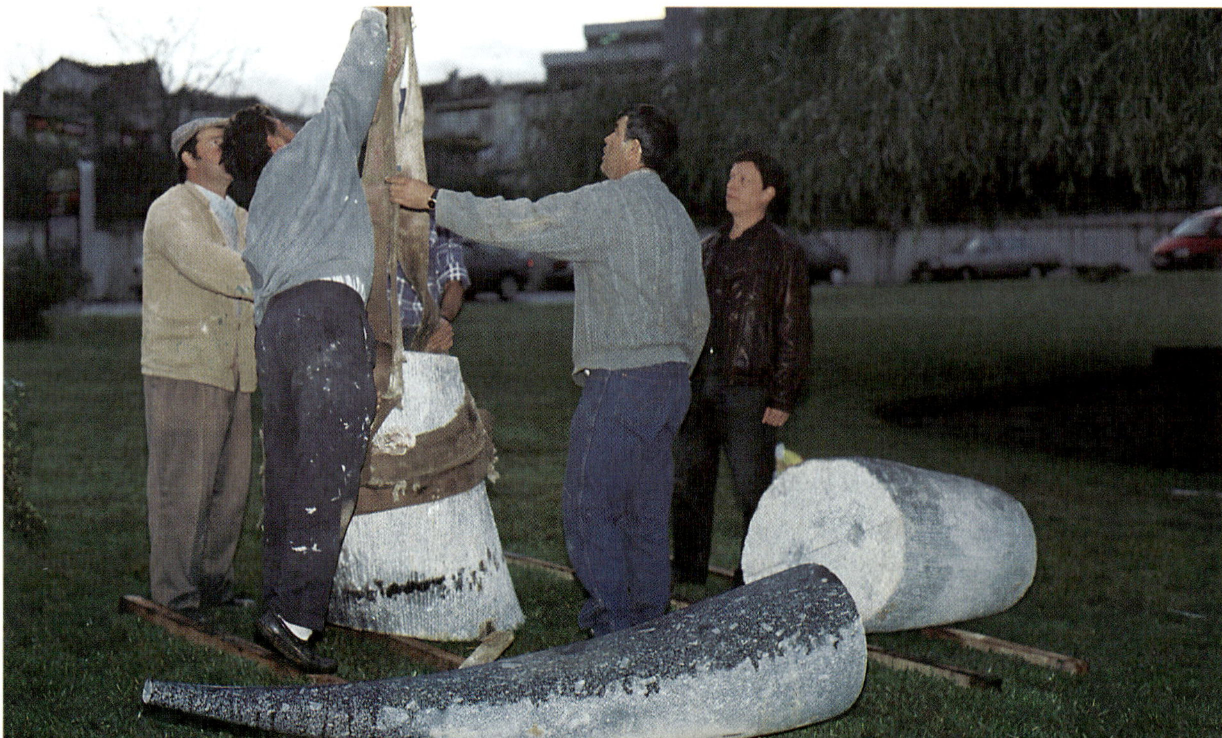

▲ ▲ ◀ **39.** It is threatening to rain when the sections of the sculpture arrive, on their way to their final destination.

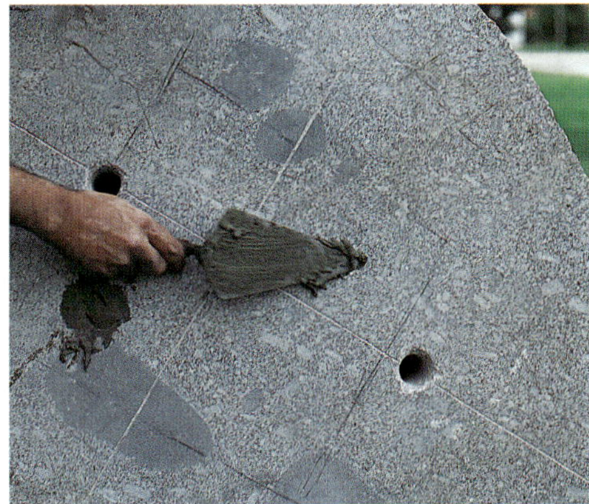

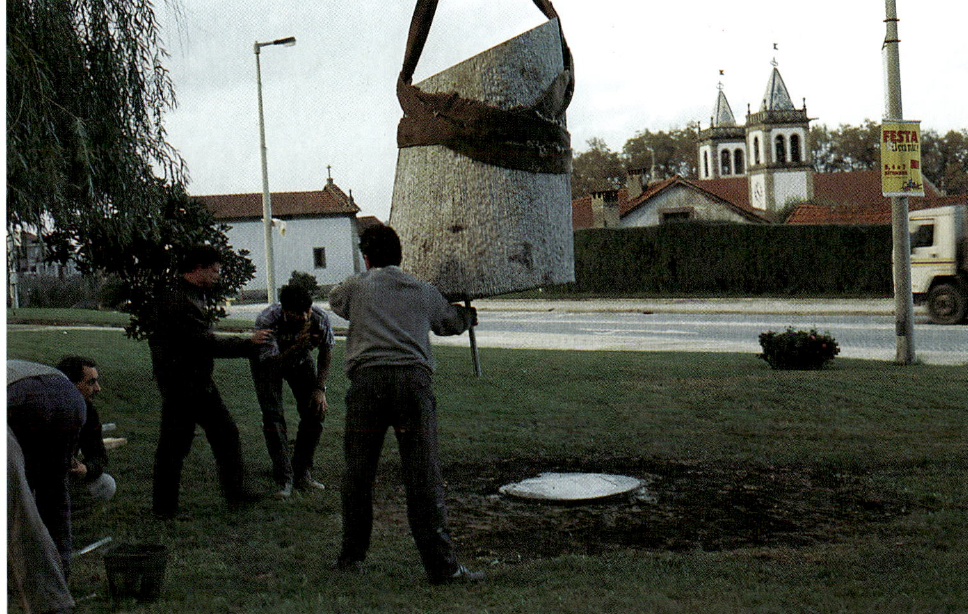

▲ ► ▼ **40.** We fix the bars of steel into the holes with cement that will set in a few hours, then we fit one block on top of the other.

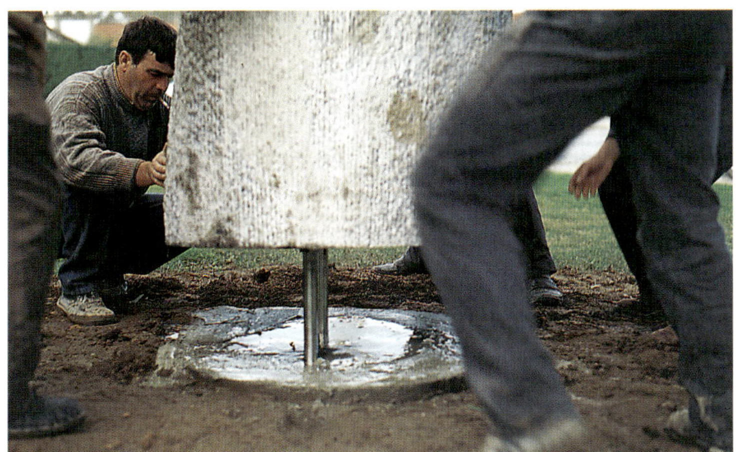

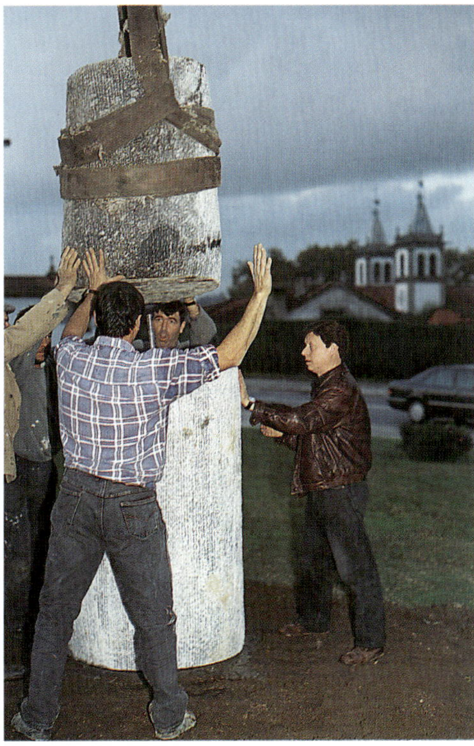

◄ **41.** This is the moment we have waited for and dreaded: If the anchoring is not perfect or if the bars loosen, the sculpture's outline will become distorted.

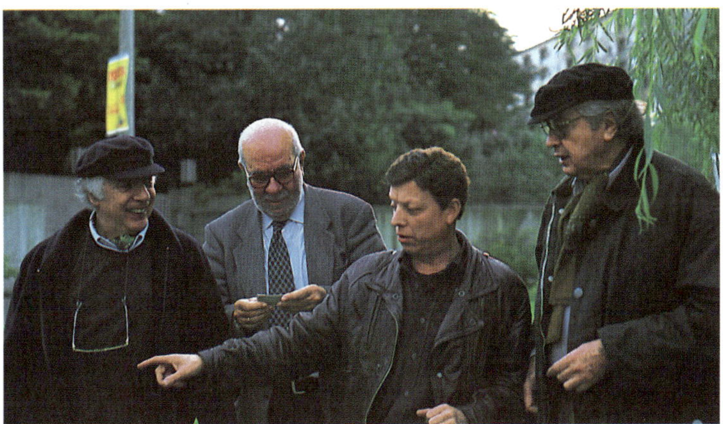

▲ **42.** In the meantime, the city is in the middle of an electoral campaign. Mr. Calem, organizer of the art competition, shares with us the views of his fellow citizens. As they look at the sculpture, several elderly gentlemen recall the time when oxen plowed the land; others find humor in the sculpture; many people, as if spellbound, are drawn to touch it. Everyone has his own interpretation. The work, in this case, is born an adult, and the author soon loses a monopoly on its interpretation.

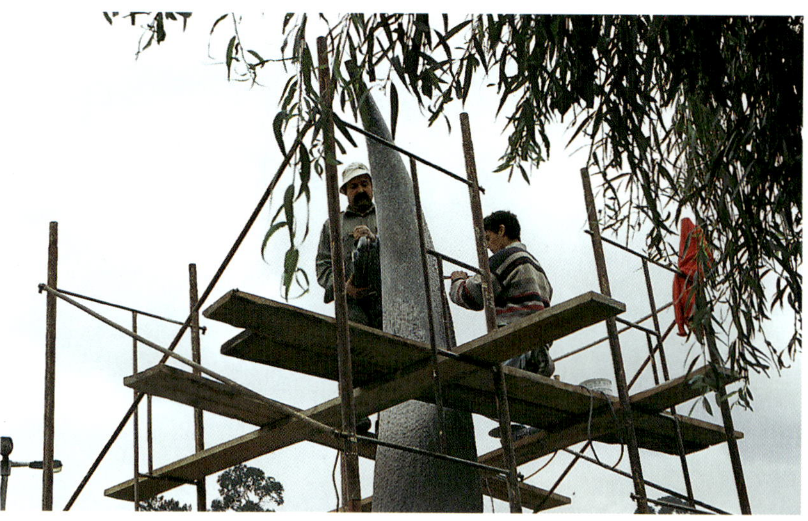

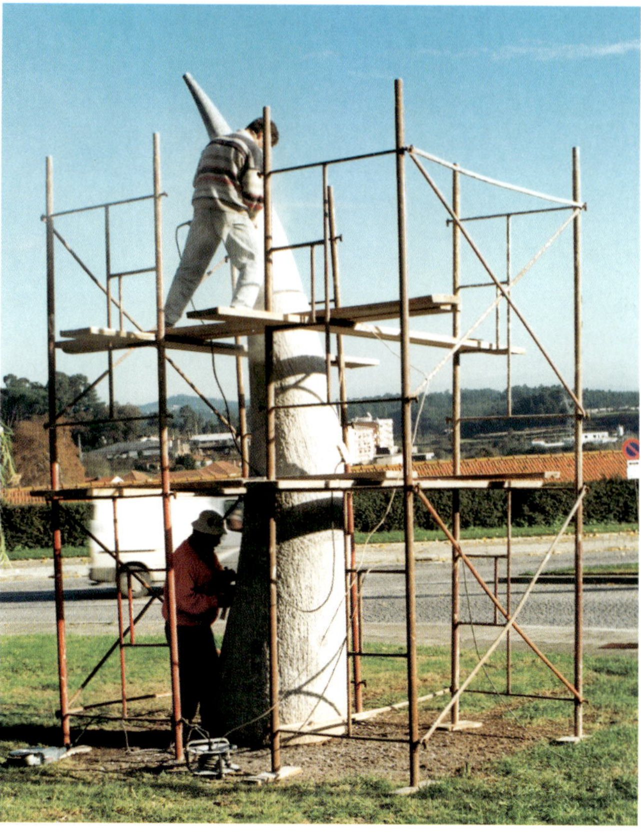

▲ ► **43.** Final touches still have to be applied on site. To do them, we need to set up a scaffold and find a generator to plug in electrical tools. We finish the work. Erosion will complete our work and will ultimately integrate the sculpture into the landscape of Santo Tirso.

▼ **44.** Camí is congratulated by another competition participant, Paul van Hoeydonck, the only artist to have a sculpture on the moon.

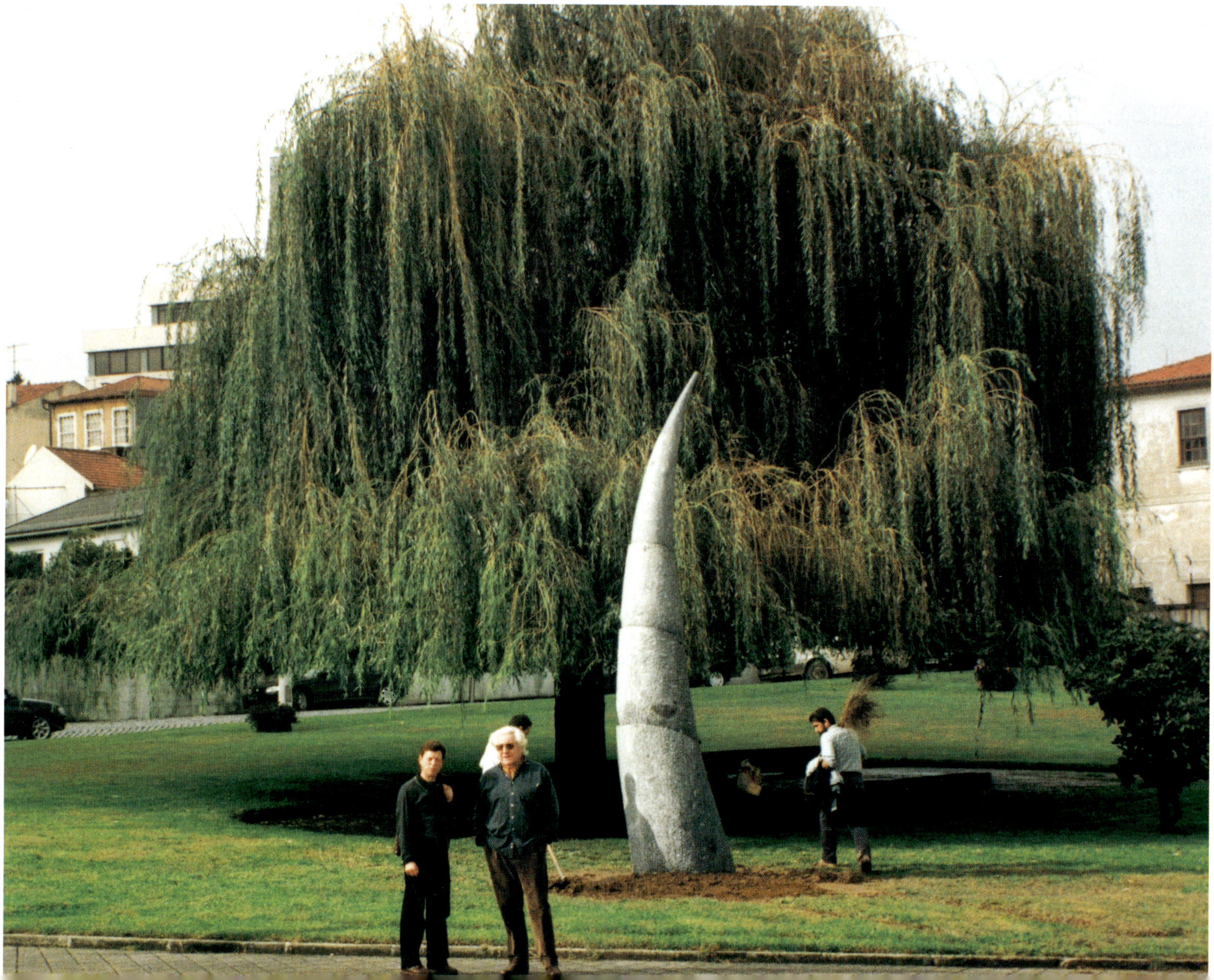

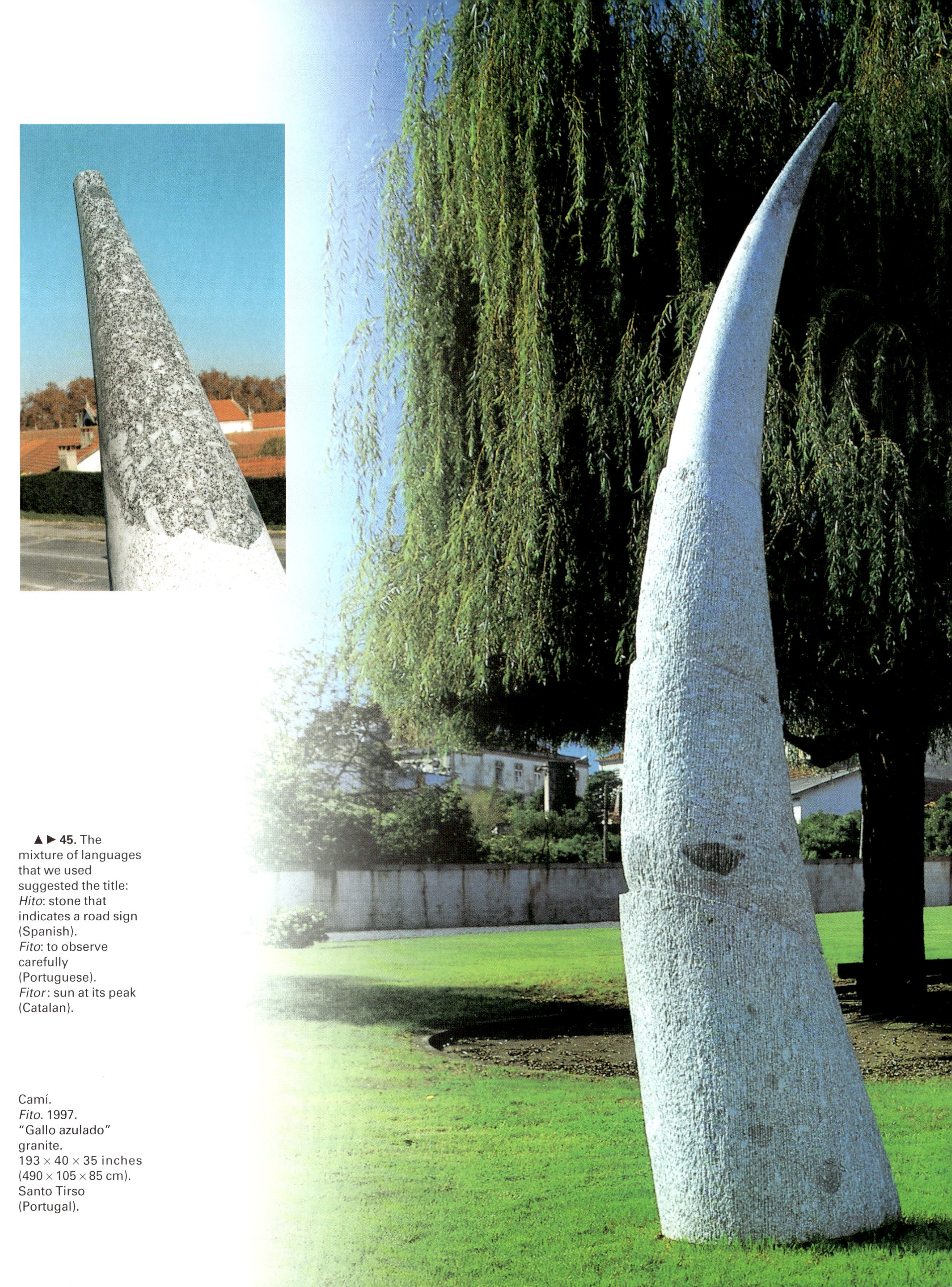

▲► **45.** The mixture of languages that we used suggested the title: *Hito*: stone that indicates a road sign (Spanish). *Fito*: to observe carefully (Portuguese). *Fitor*: sun at its peak (Catalan).

Camí.
Fito. 1997.
"Gallo azulado" granite.
193 × 40 × 35 inches (490 × 105 × 85 cm).
Santo Tirso (Portugal).

Large-Scale Sculptures, Enlarging by Squares

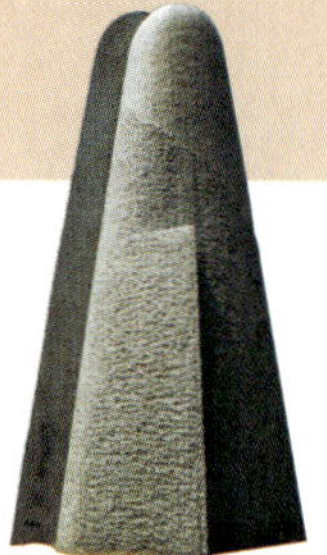

We will conclude this chapter by demonstrating another procedure for carving large-scale sculptures. For these types of sculpture we will follow a grid method. This step-by-step process has several aspects in common with the previous one. Here we repeat the same stonework process that recalls, regarding size and materials, the Portuguese sculpture. However, in this case the cultural and technical environments differ.

As in the previous competition and at the request of the same commissioner, the mayor of Puyo, an historical city in South Korea, has invited us to participate and has set the following conditions: The sculpture must be of granite and about 10 feet (3 m) in size. It must be carried out within one month and be based on the theme: "Unity, love, and eternity, a prayer for the union of the two Koreas." The sculpture will be placed in a park of symbolic sculptures in Seoul. Thirty sculptors from different countries participate in the competition.

The symposium also aims to promote Korea's artistic culture. For this reason a competition was held to select the 30 best sculptors. A public relations team and a group of volunteers were selected, and visits were arranged to promote the event.

The goal of our project, which is illustrated on page 73, is to express through volume the proposed theme: Two blocks of granite that symbolize two Koreas, which are divided by a crack that has no reason for being. The two Koreas, however, are united by a single foundation, the Taoist tradition. It is from its center that the sculpture will raise. Maquette, plans, and memos are sent in advance. The organizers of the event accept the project and order the block of granite from the quarry.

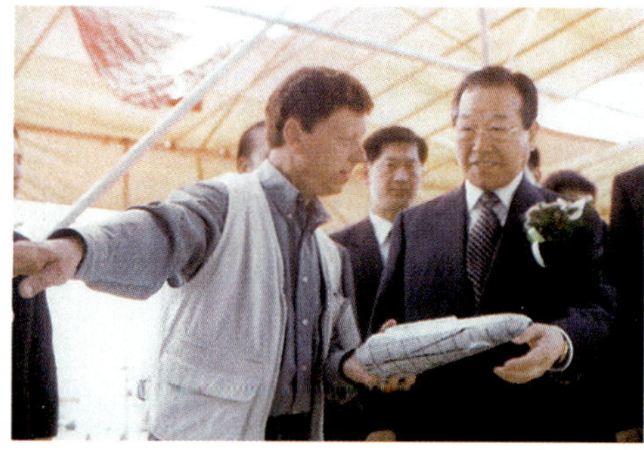

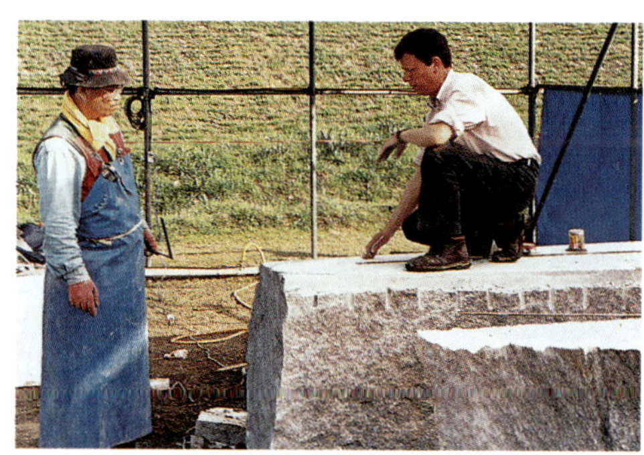

◀ The symposium is organized by the City Hall of Puyo, but draws national attention. Here Camí presents the maquette to Jong-Pil Kim, the Prime Minister of Korea.

◀ Lee Hyun-Chan of Seoul will carry out this work; in addition to having been selected to participate in this competition, we know that he has collaborated with well-known Korean sculptors.

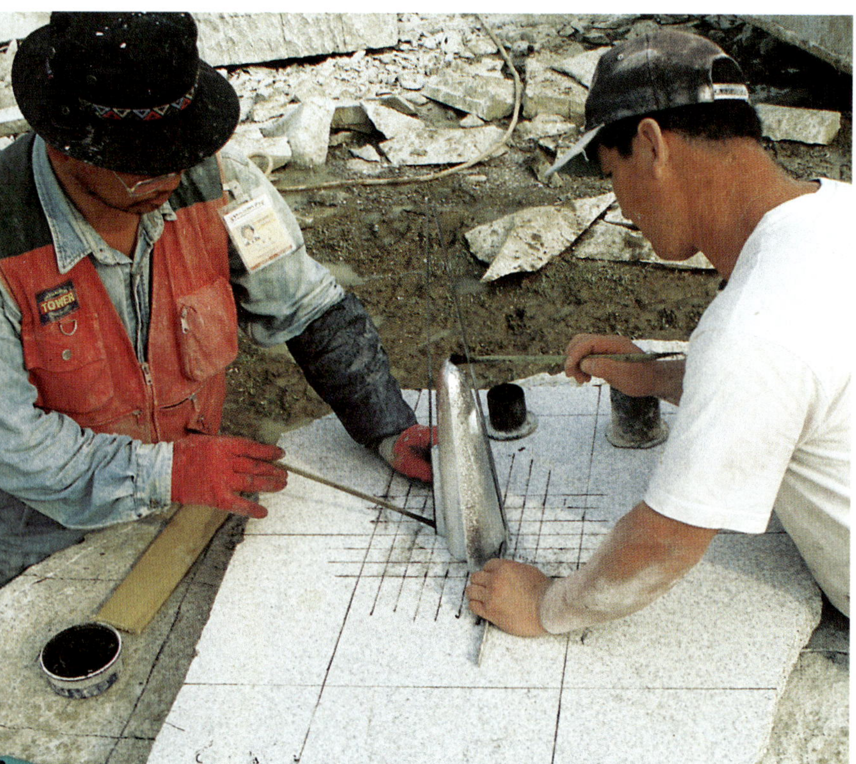

◀ **1.** Though we have submitted the maquette in fiber cement, Lee paints it over in silver paint to make the lines he is tracing more visible. Here he is helped by another worker with a piece of bamboo whose outer fibers have been almost completely peeled off in order to dip it in paint. He projects vertically to the maquette grid lines drawn on a flat surface. Then he draws equidistant horizontal parallel lines to complete the grid on the maquette. The resulting framework will serve as a reference for transferral to the granite form.

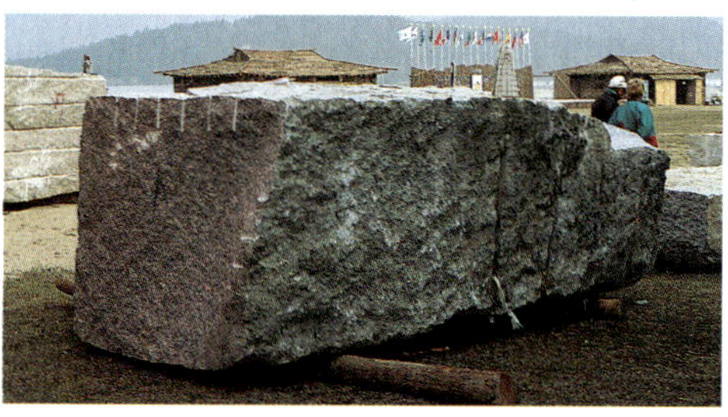

◀ **2.** Though we have ordered two small blocks, we were given this massive block of approximately 11 × 5 × 5 feet (3.4 × 1.6 × 1.5 m), weighing more than 20 tons. In splitting the block according to the project's design, we have unwittingly expressed the absurd division of Korea.

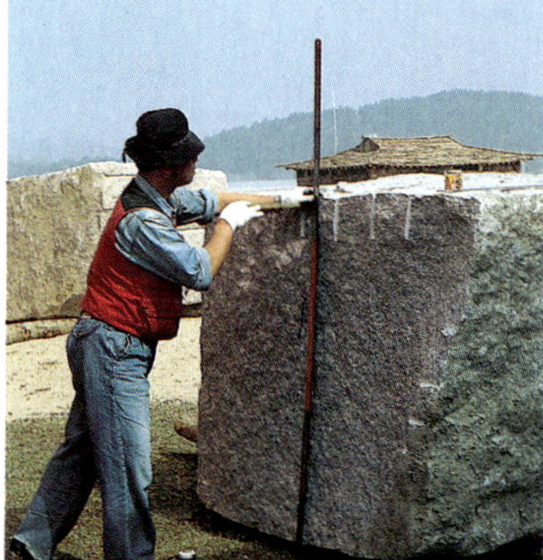

◀ **3.** Lee, who is familiar with granite works, chooses the right side of the block to split it in a controlled manner. Here he draws the dividing line.

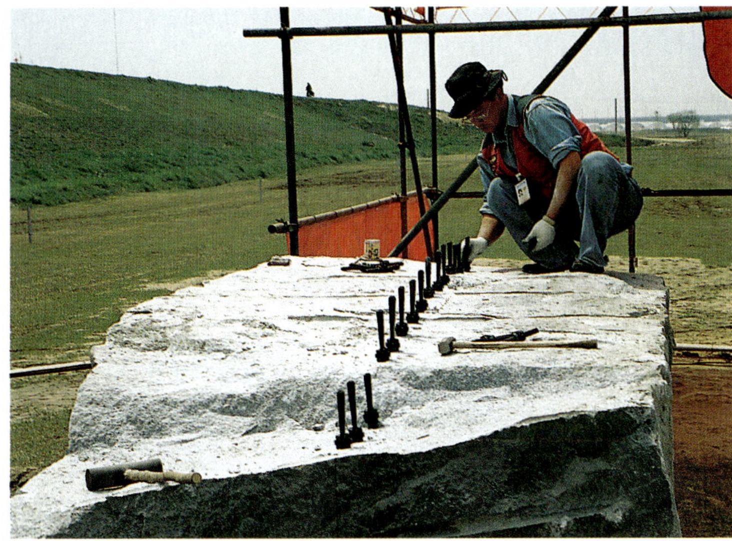

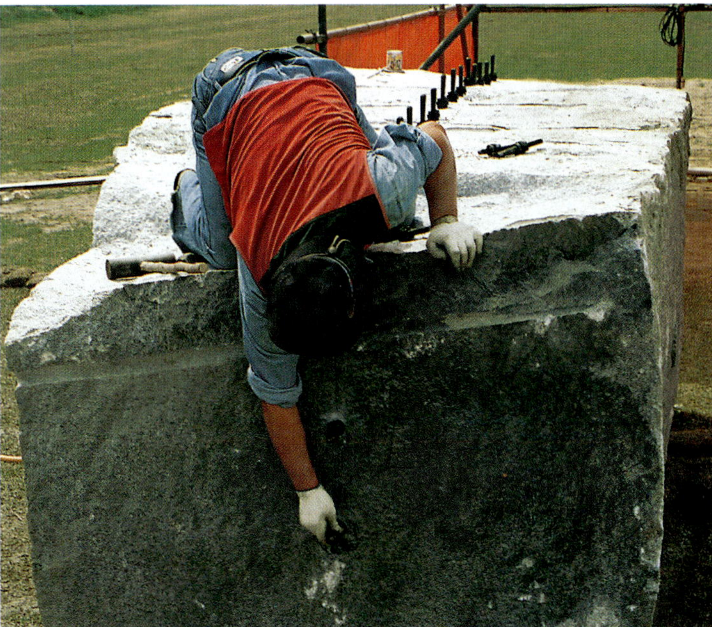

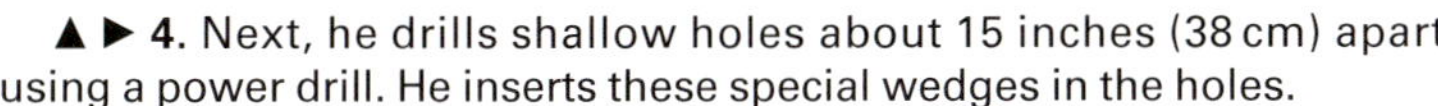

▲▶ **4.** Next, he drills shallow holes about 15 inches (38 cm) apart using a power drill. He inserts these special wedges in the holes.

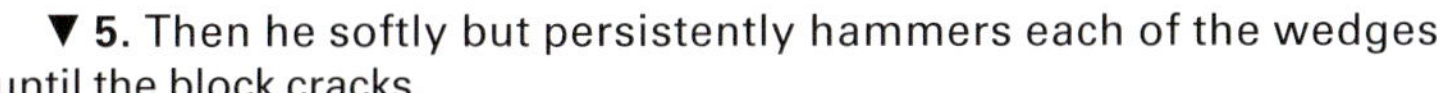

▼ **5.** Then he softly but persistently hammers each of the wedges until the block cracks.

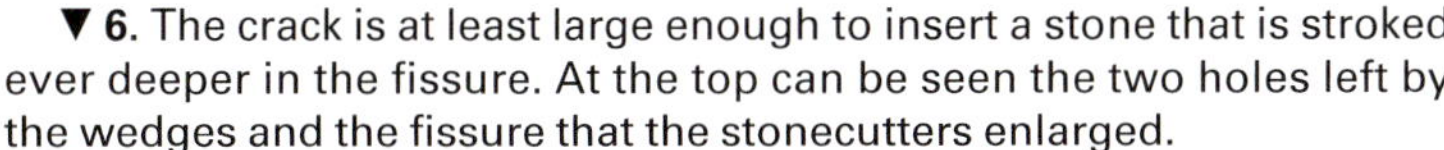

▼ **6.** The crack is at least large enough to insert a stone that is stroked ever deeper in the fissure. At the top can be seen the two holes left by the wedges and the fissure that the stonecutters enlarged.

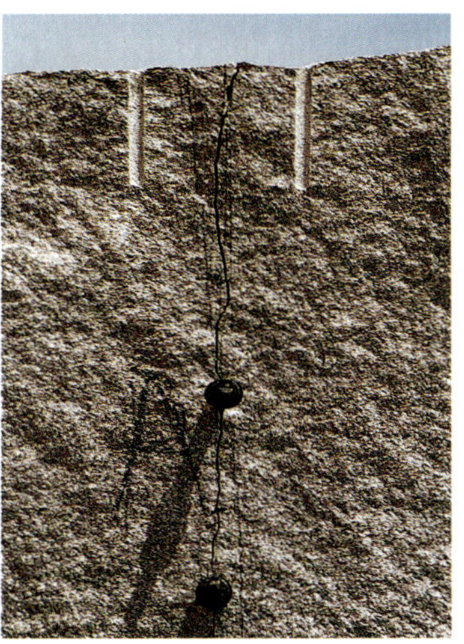

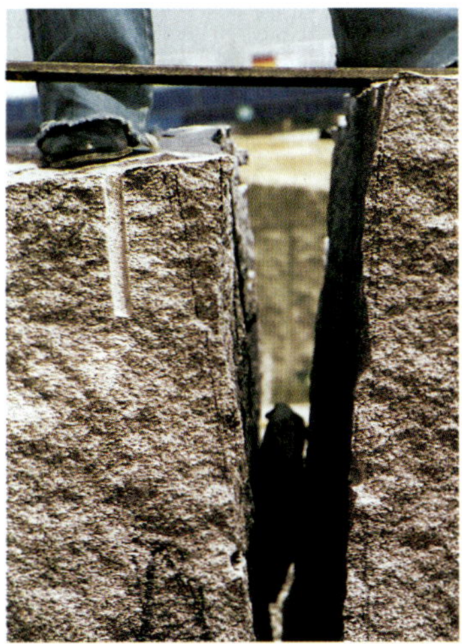

▶ **7.** The two tree trunks on which the granite rests prevent it from sinking into the ground. When the granite cracks, the trunks help Lee separate the two fractured blocks, despite their enormous weight, by simply using a crowbar as a lever.

▼ **8.** Then, with help, one of the blocks is flipped over and separated from the other so as to work on it separately.

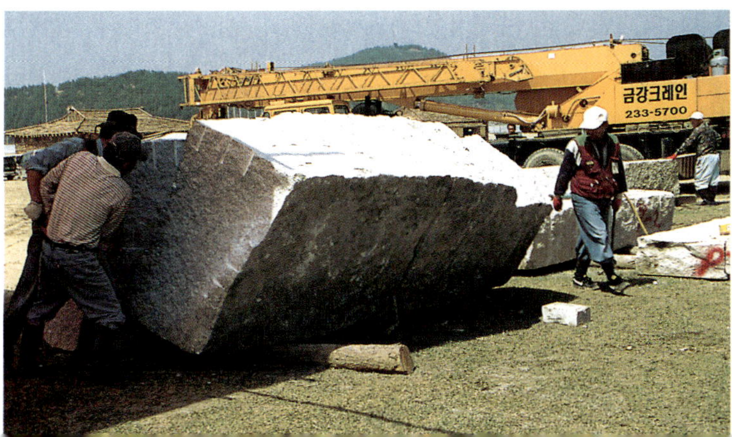

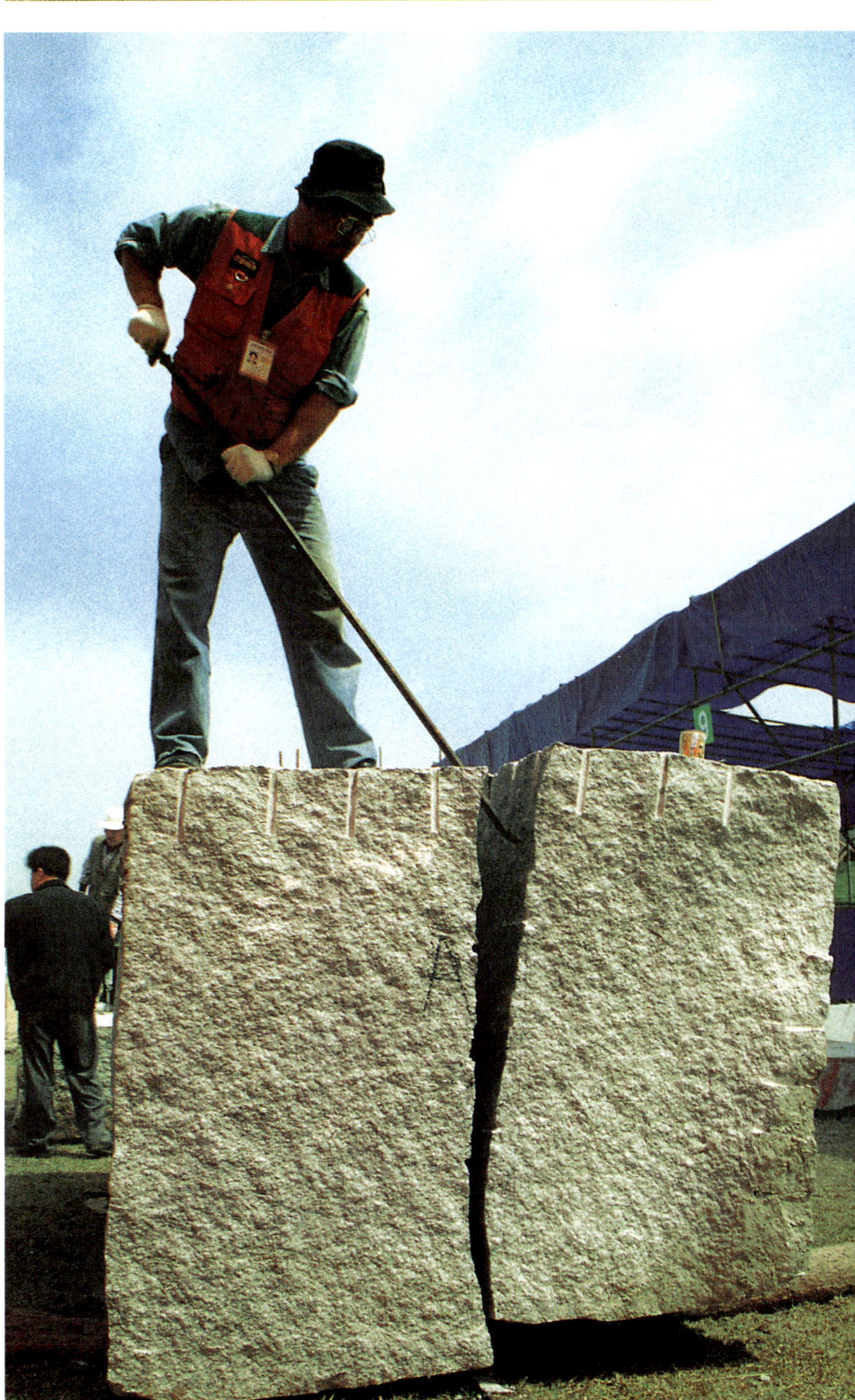

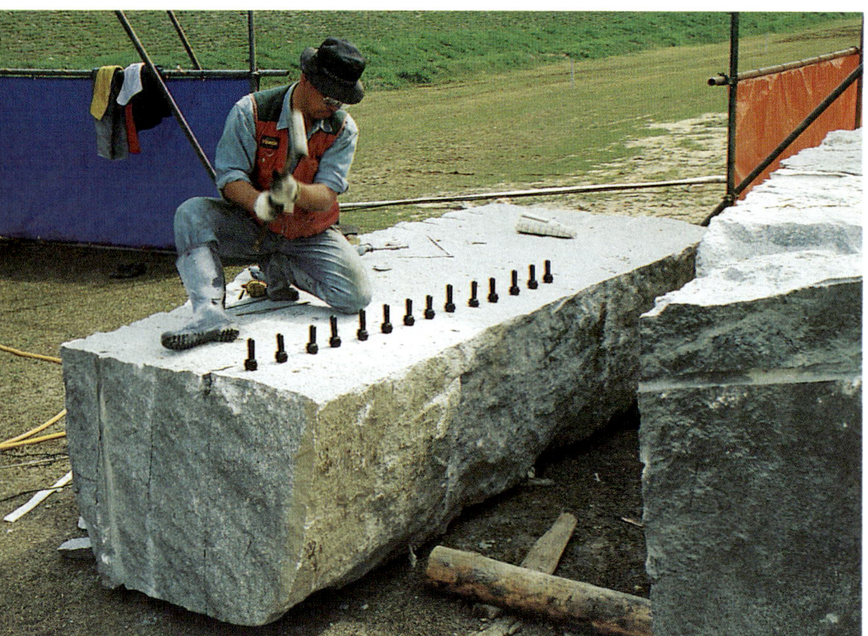

◀ **9.** We draw a grid on the block, scaling it up proportionately to the maquette. Using the maquette and the grid as a guide, we mark the outline of the sculpture. Now Lee goes over the outline hammering in the wedges. In this way, he starts shaping block 1, causing the large piece of excess stone to separate. We will convert this granite later into stones for the pavement.

▼ **10.** With a large circular saw with a diamond blade that has a water hose attached to prevent dust and overheating of the tool, Lee levels the inside surface of the block that will rest against the other one.

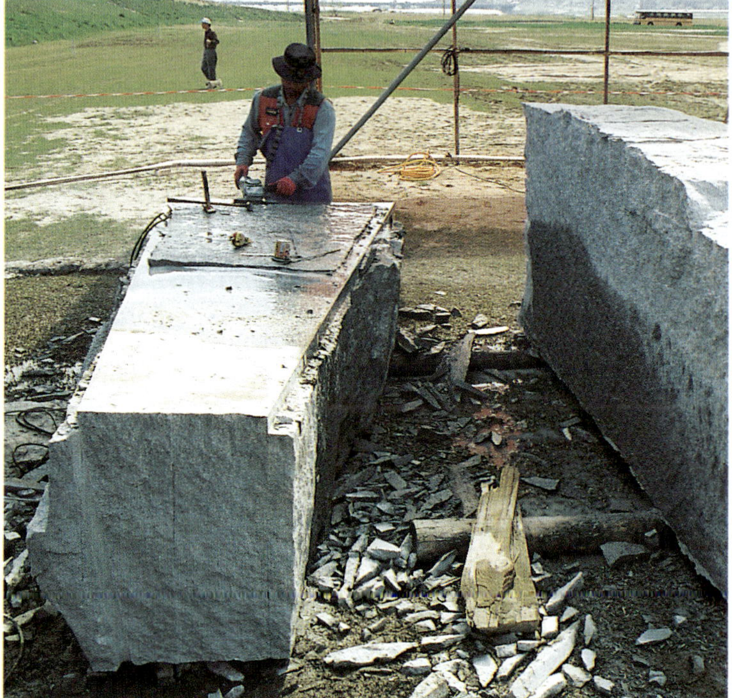

▼ **11.** With the maquette always in front of him, more out of habit than need, and using the block itself as a worktable, Lee uses the same circular saw to make vertical incisions and trace a reference line for later smoothing the base.

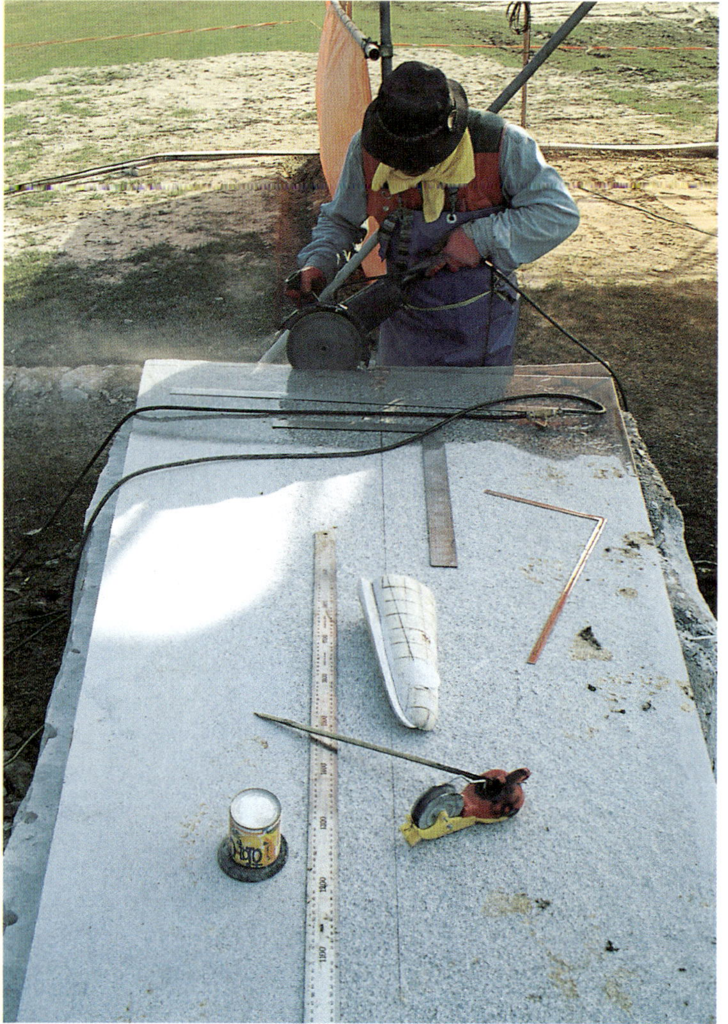

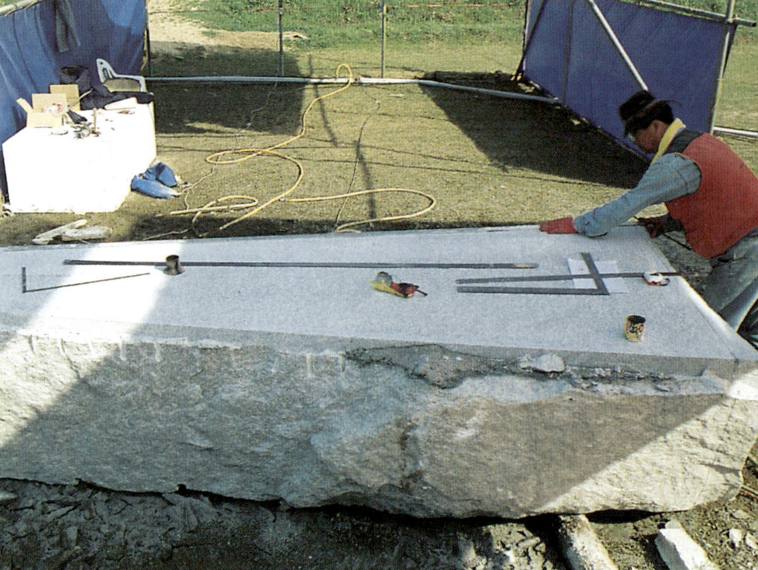

▲ **12.** During this outline tracing process, a trapezoidal stone shape emerges, which Lee perfects, drawing its edges with a metal ruler.

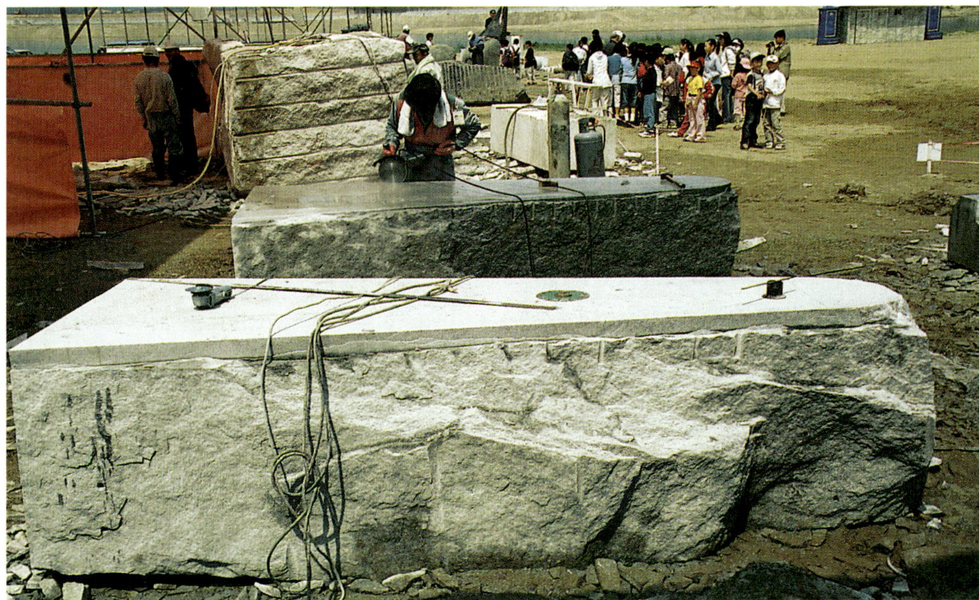

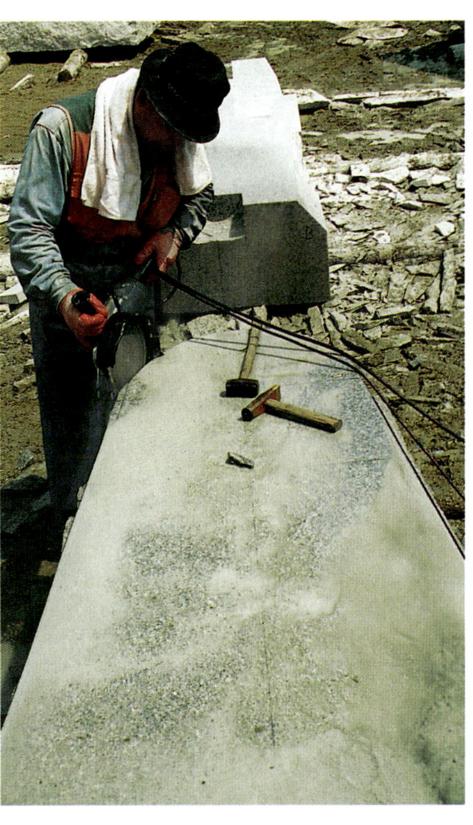

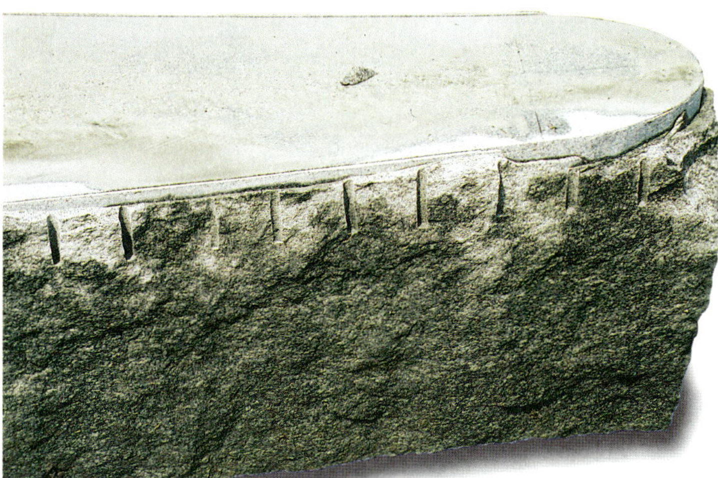

▲ **13.** The same process is repeated to outline block 2. We try to advance the shaping of both blocks alternately.

▲ **14.** After tracing the upper curve with a paper pattern, Lee, with firm pulse, continues to outline the curved edges of block 2 with the circular saw.

◀ **15.** This is how the tracing that marks the outline of the block looks. It is about 1 inch (2.5 cm) from the wedge holes that caused the stone fragmentation.

▼ **16.** The two blocks are now shaped and smoothed. The sculpture's interior surfaces that will rest on each other are now done. We maintain that the carving process was also a source of inspiration and the two "stone caskets" shown here confirm it.

▼ **17.** Lee has displayed a high level of professionalism; not only was he able to master the granite but he also knew how to identify with the sculptor's conception.

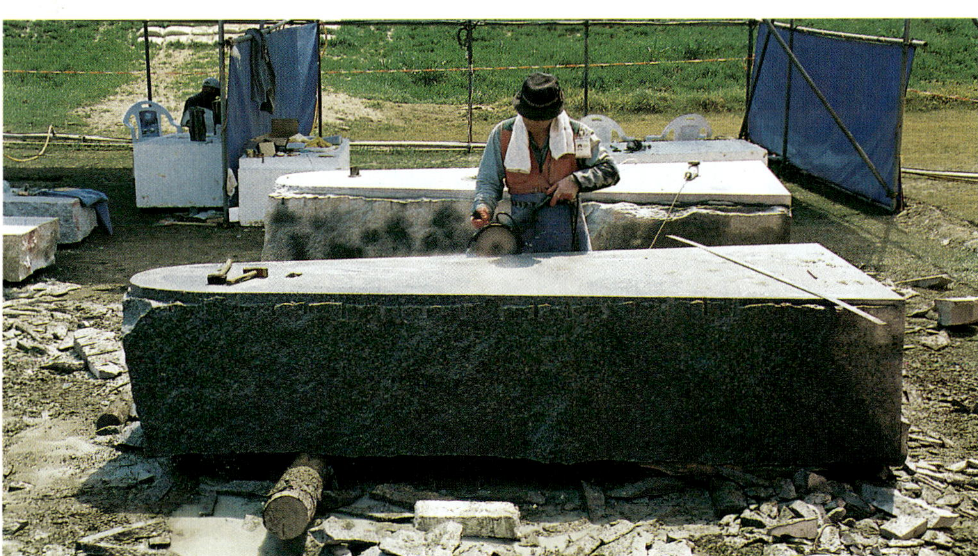

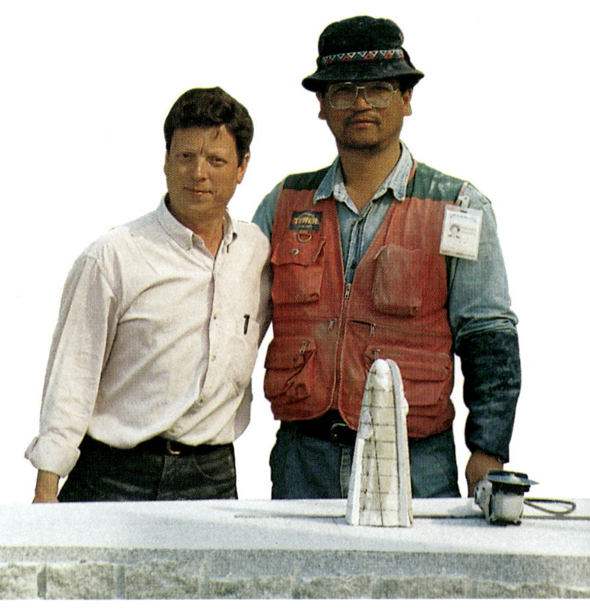

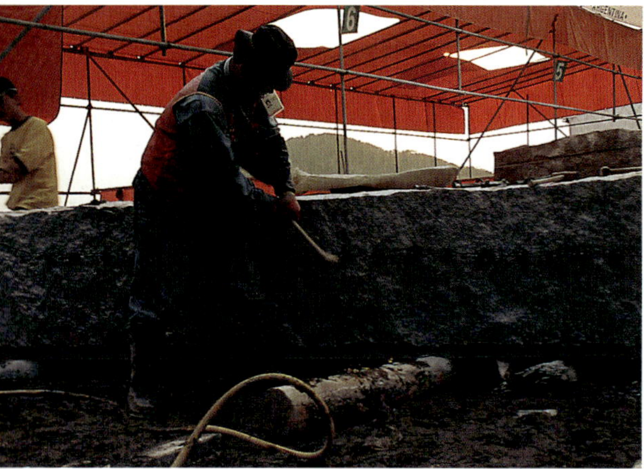

▲ **18.** After rotating the block we continue with the surface smoothing process. Lee again uses wedges to split off a large pyramid-shaped piece. The granite breaks up where it should, under his controlled mallet blows. It is risky to attempt one of these cuts without prior experience.

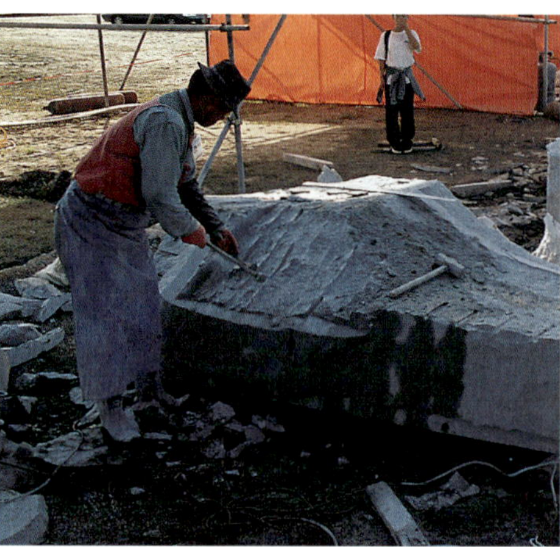

▲ **19.** The surface smoothing process advances simultaneously for both blocks. When he has to flake off small chips of stone, he relies on parallel incisions of the circular saw, then chips off the excess stone using his special trimmer with a handle.

▲ **20.** Little by little, the blocks take on a semiconical shape embodying a gap that hints at a partially open door. Notice how Lee, who now uses a mallet with a long handle, always works with control. He works some distance from the block, always composed.

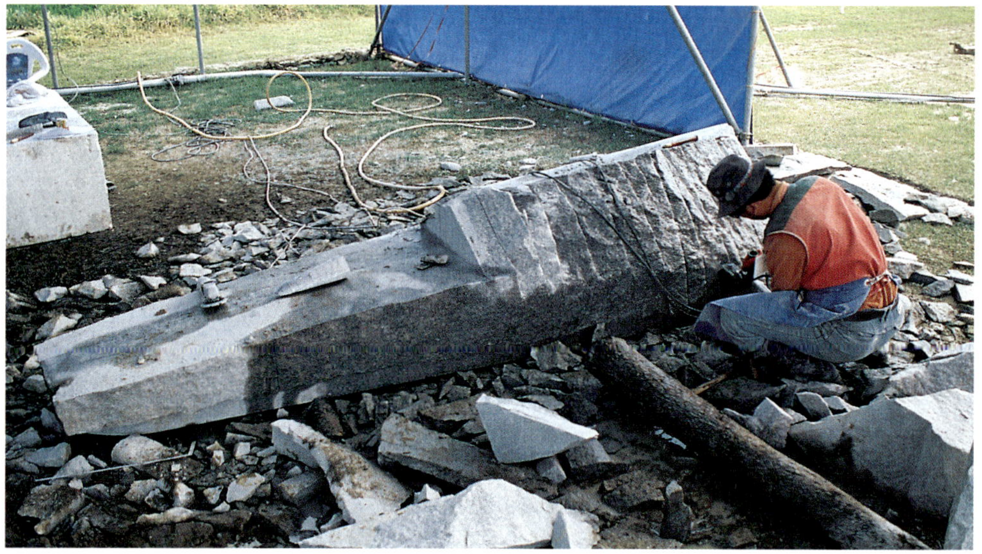

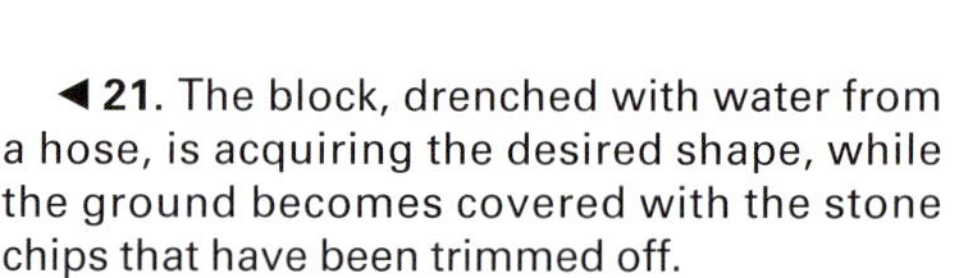

◀ **21.** The block, drenched with water from a hose, is acquiring the desired shape, while the ground becomes covered with the stone chips that have been trimmed off.

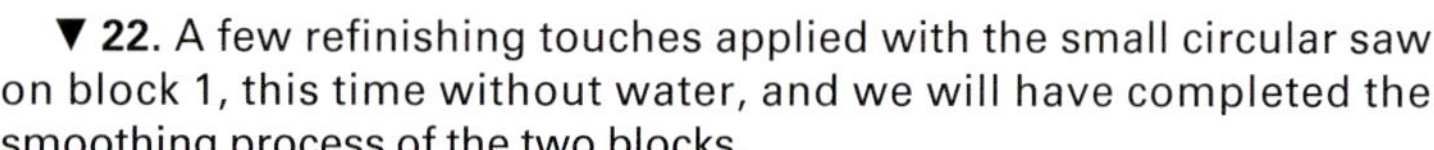

▼ **22.** A few refinishing touches applied with the small circular saw on block 1, this time without water, and we will have completed the smoothing process of the two blocks.

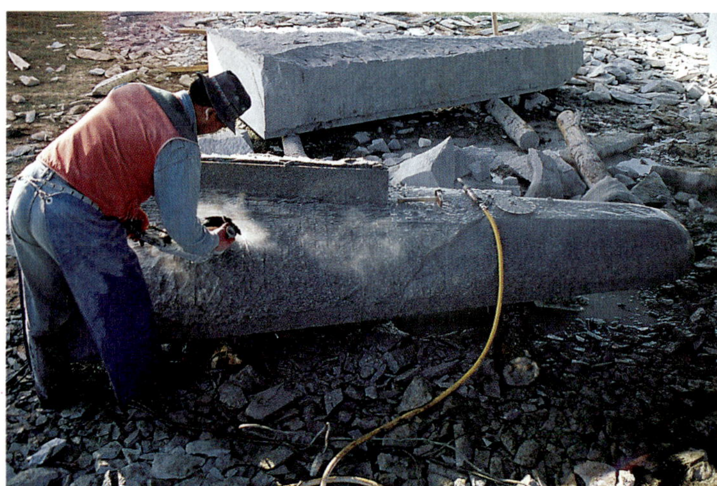

▼ **23.** After several trials, we decide on the definitive stone texture. The sculpture will display two very contrasting areas—one furrowed and rough and the other smooth.

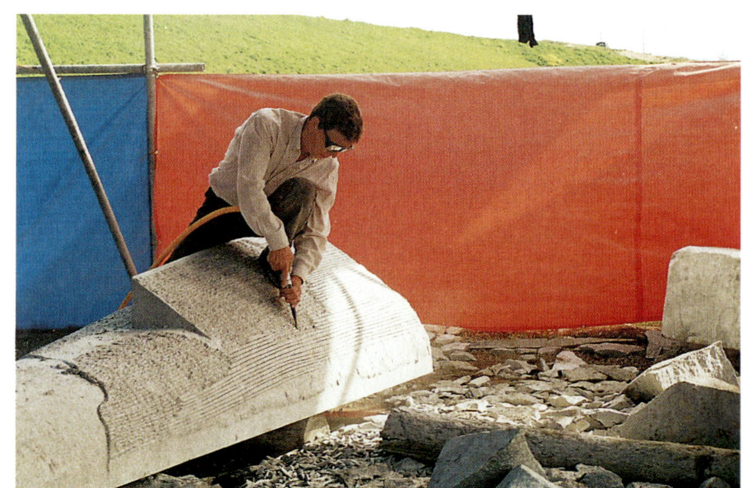

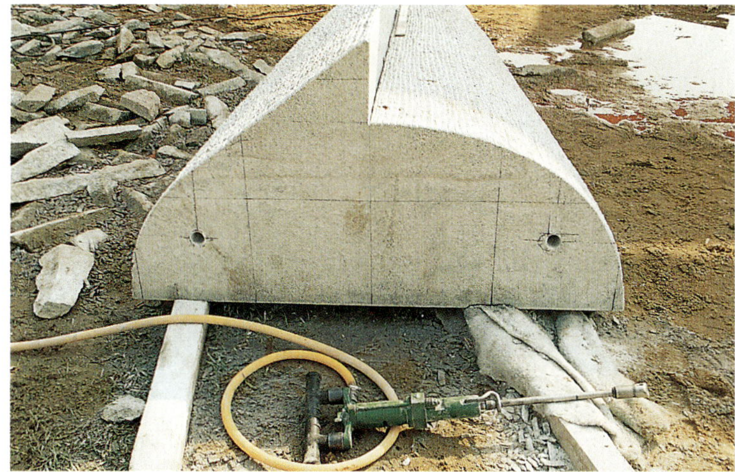

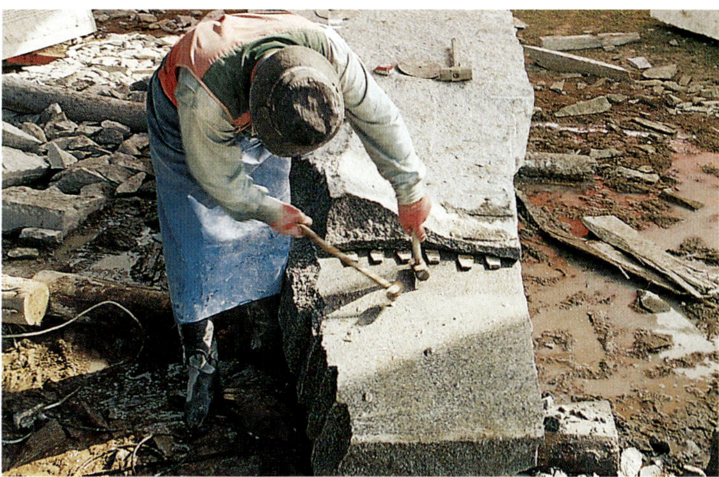

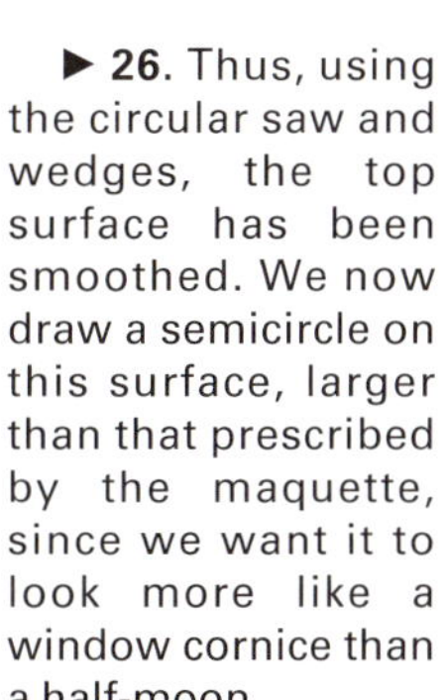

▲ **24.** On the base, which still displays the grid, we drill two holes to introduce pins of steel that will anchor the sections of the sculpture to the base of concrete.

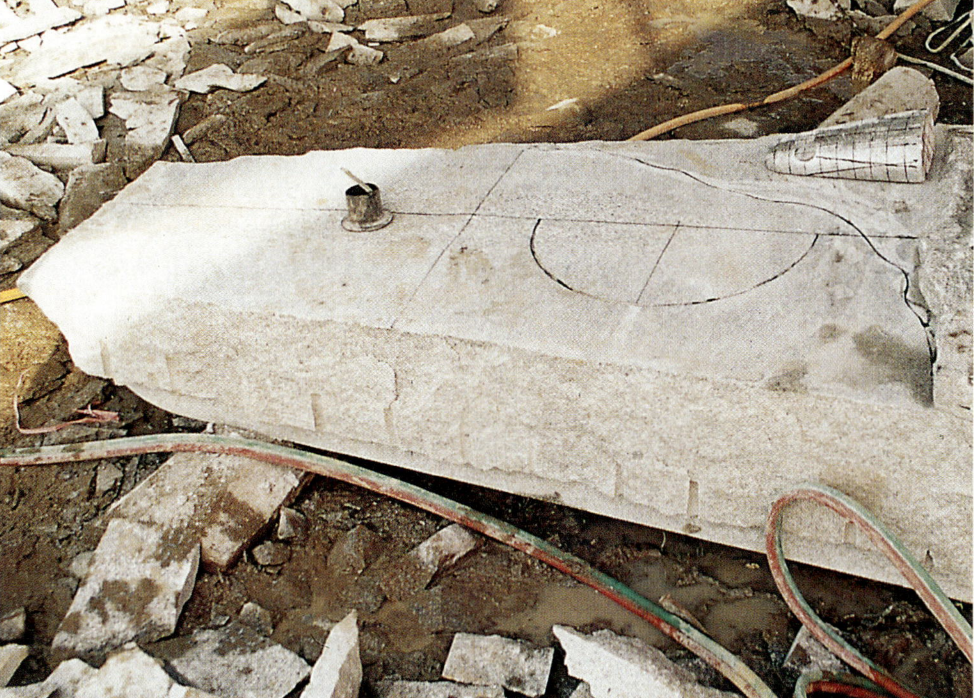

► **26.** Thus, using the circular saw and wedges, the top surface has been smoothed. We now draw a semicircle on this surface, larger than that prescribed by the maquette, since we want it to look more like a window cornice than a half-moon.

▲ **25.** We repeat the same smoothing process on block 2. Here, however, we see another way to do the trimming by using flat wedges. Lee places them perpendicular to the very narrow furrows left by the circular saw and, accurately, with his mallet and hafted chisel, he knocks them into the furrows left by the saw until a large thin slice of granite chips off.

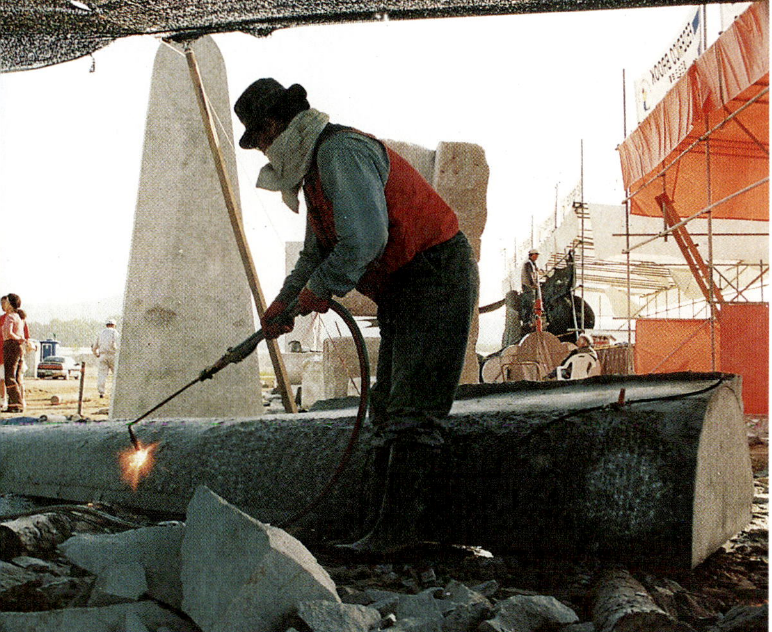

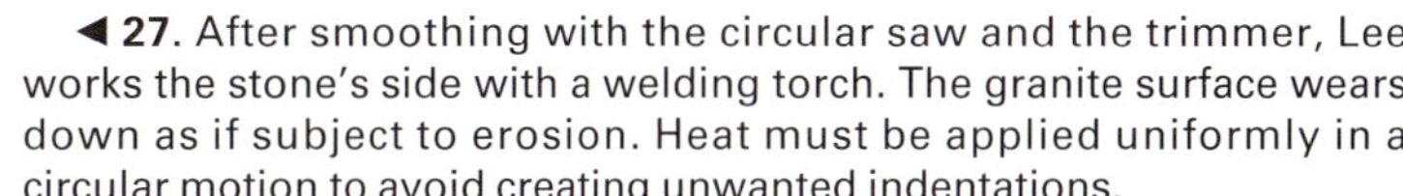

◄ **27.** After smoothing with the circular saw and the trimmer, Lee works the stone's side with a welding torch. The granite surface wears down as if subject to erosion. Heat must be applied uniformly in a circular motion to avoid creating unwanted indentations.

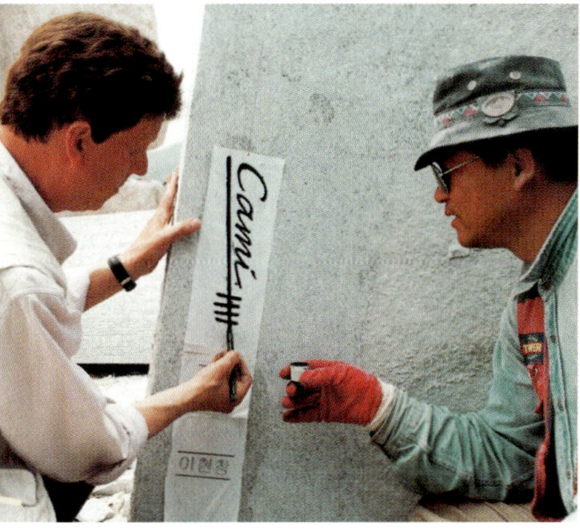

◄ **28.** When the task is finished, sculptor and carver sign the work. Using an overlay pattern, they carve the granite, then they apply paint and remove the overlay.

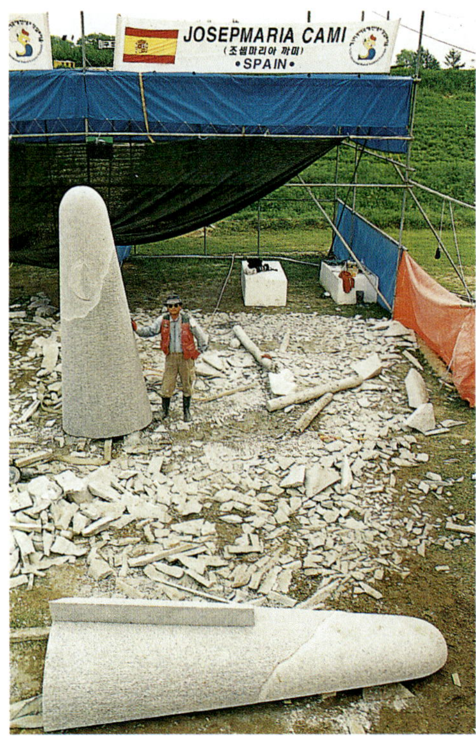

▲ **29.** Landscape after the battle: Lee has mastered the granite and poses satisfied between the two sections of the sculpture.

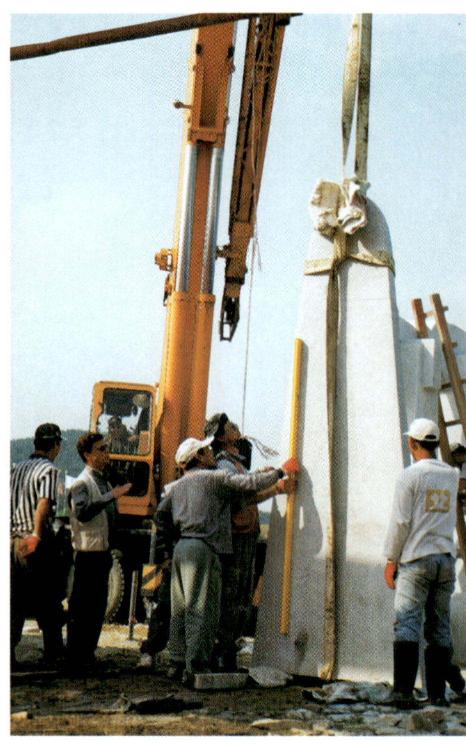

▲ **30.** Before moving the sculpture to its destination, we test the verticality of each block separately,

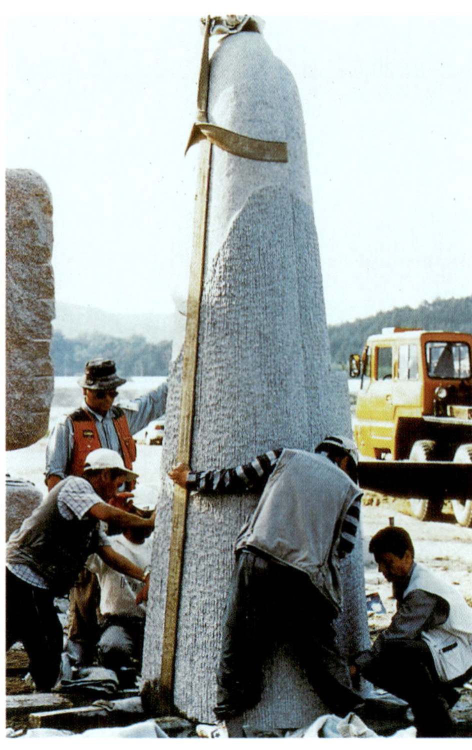

▲ **31.** and the relative positioning between the blocks that will be separated slightly by only $^1/_2$ inch (1 cm) and shifted by about $8^1/_2$ inches (22 cm) among themselves.

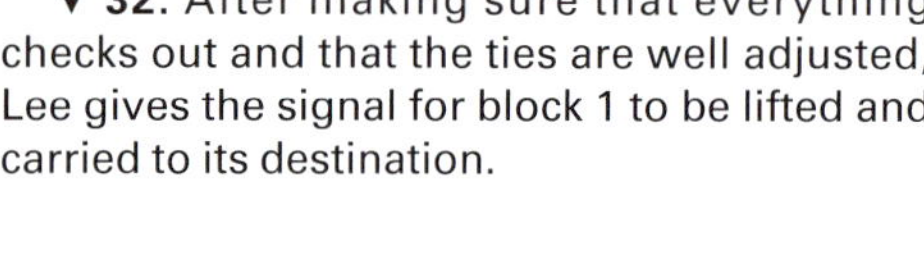

▼ **32.** After making sure that everything checks out and that the ties are well adjusted, Lee gives the signal for block 1 to be lifted and carried to its destination.

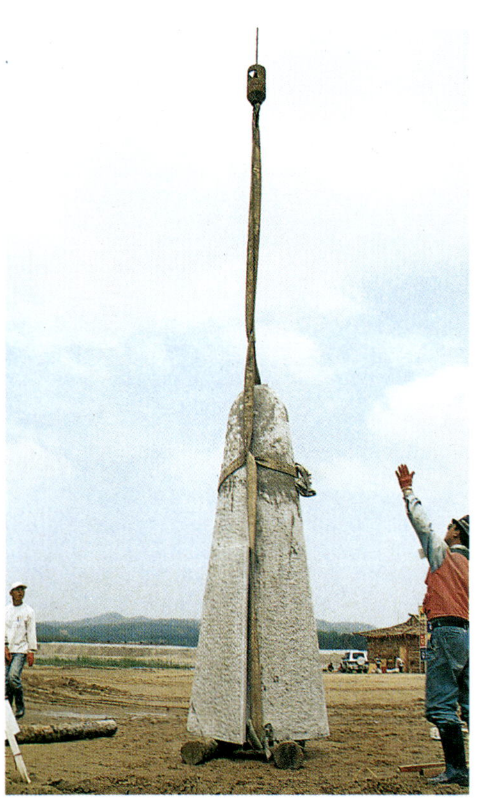

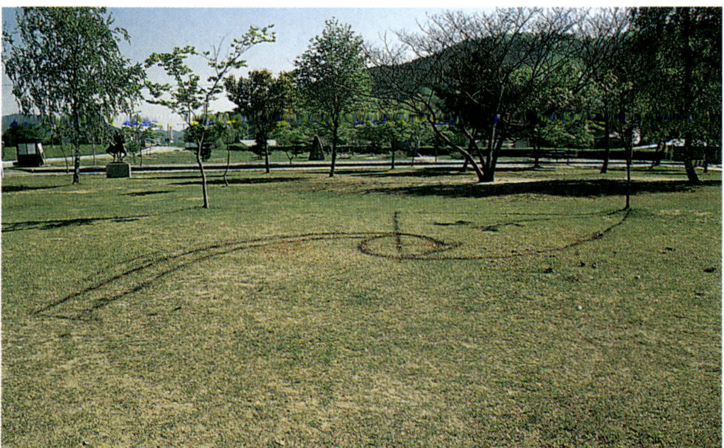

◀ **33.** This is where the sculpture will come to rest. It will be enclosed and projected on the ground by two parabolic lines that will link the sculptures with three young trees that surround it.

▶ **34.** With the leftover stone chips of the trimming, and following a modeling pattern, we make paving stones for the surface around the sculpture. In doing this we wish to leave a record of the carving process, give unity to the whole work, and create an encircling area that dignifies the sculpture.

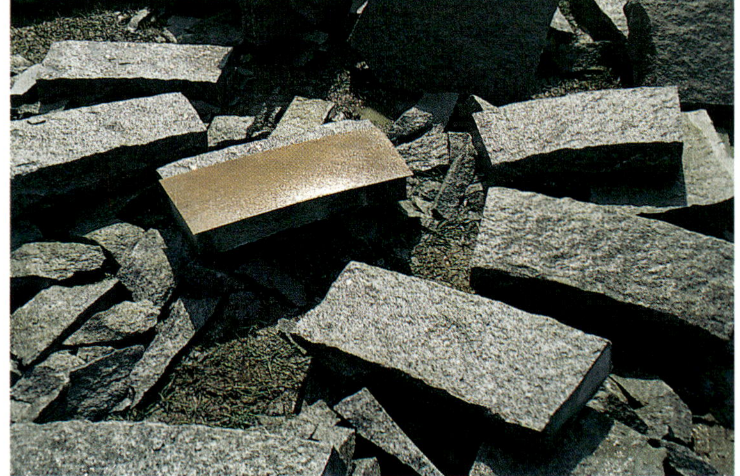

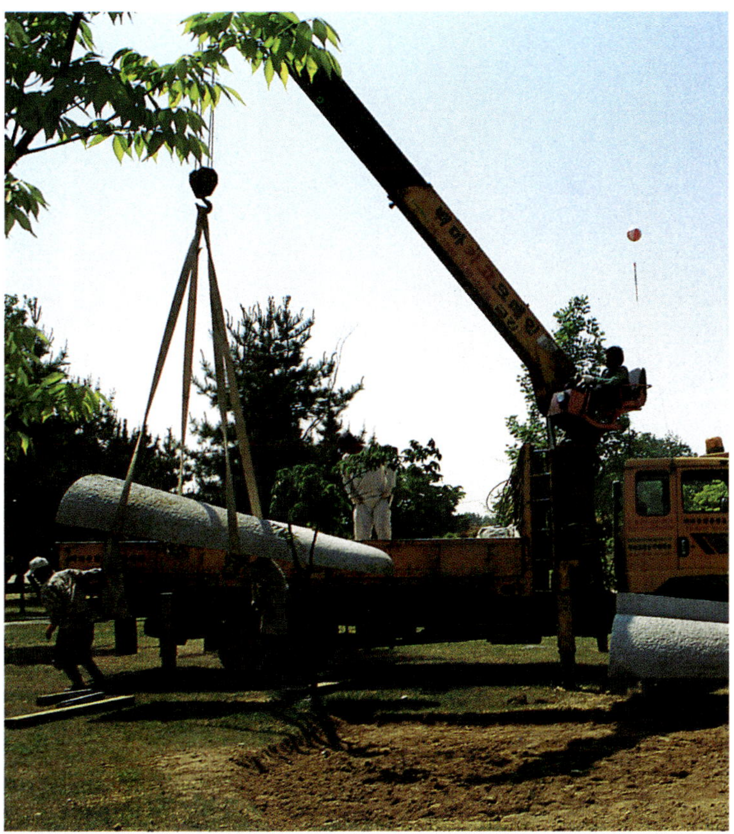

▲ **35.** An enormous crane transports both blocks to their destination and carefully unloads them.

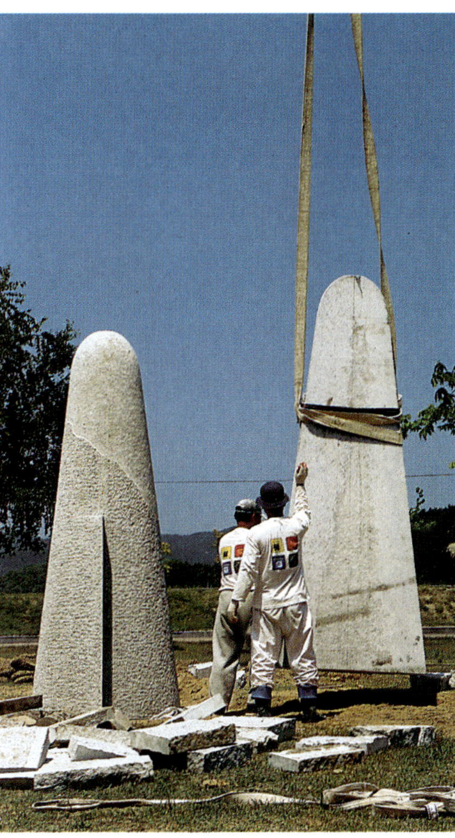

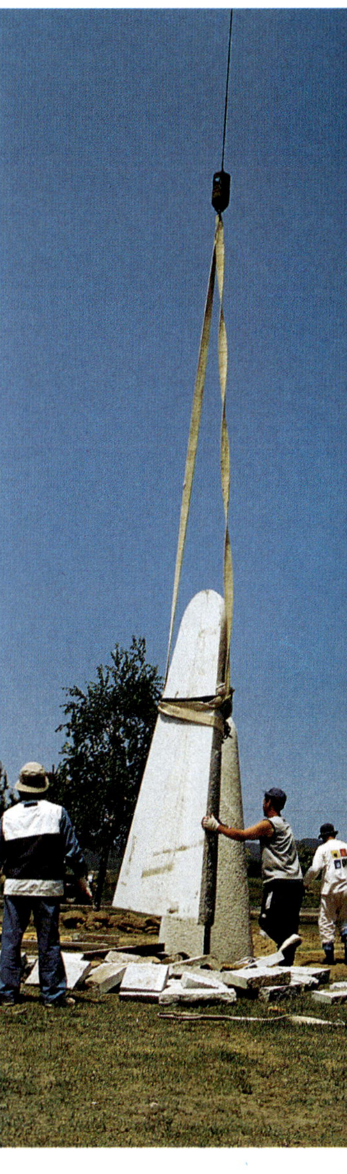

▲ ▶ **36.** The blocks are anchored in concrete at the designated site. Block 1 is positioned with the door pointing north, where the park faces the city; block 2 faces south, toward the river and the mountains.

▼ **37.** The light is filtered through the gap between the two blocks as anticipated, which also enables us to remove the flanges that were used during the transport.

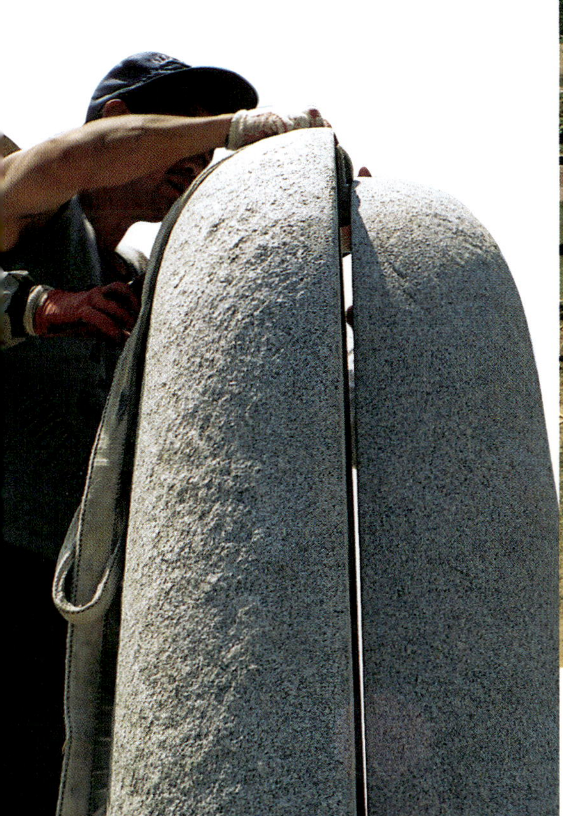

▼ **38.** The sculpture is in place and now all we have to do is pave and landscape the area.

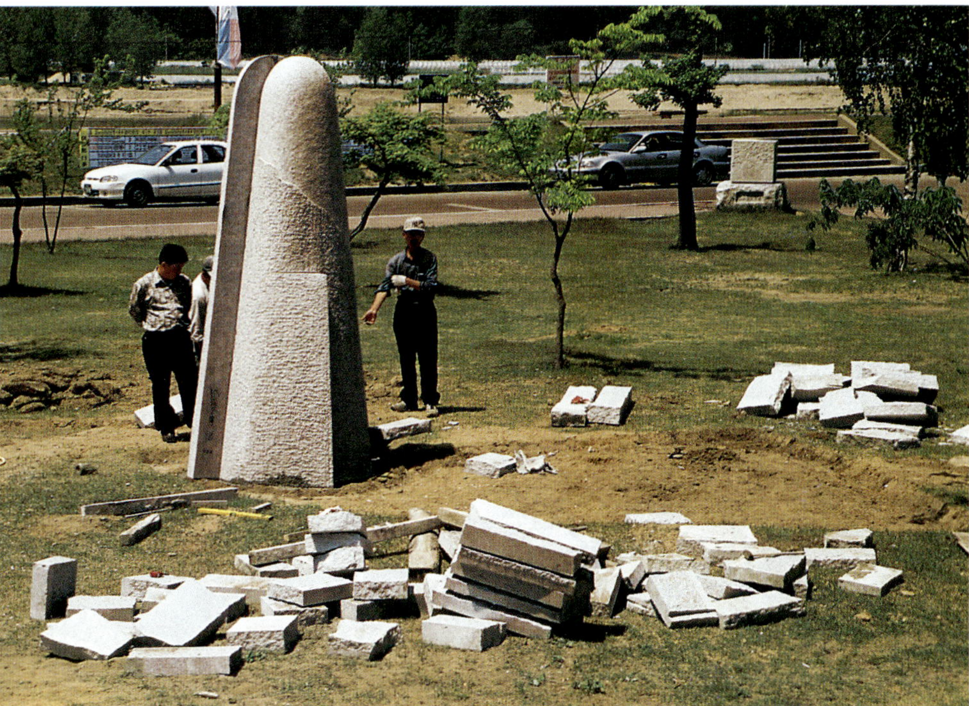

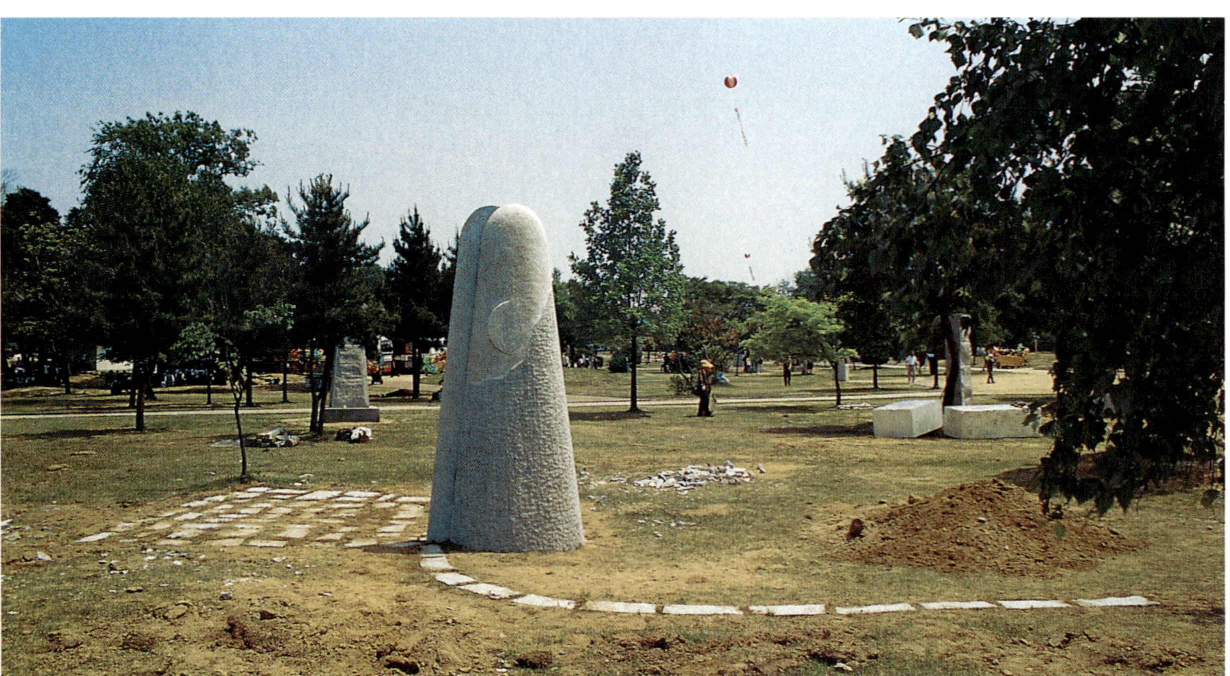

◀ **39.** The whole idea, simple in its conception, suggests to the viewer diverse interpretations related to the motto of the symposium: Unity, Love, and Eternity. *(Prayer for the Unification of Korea).*

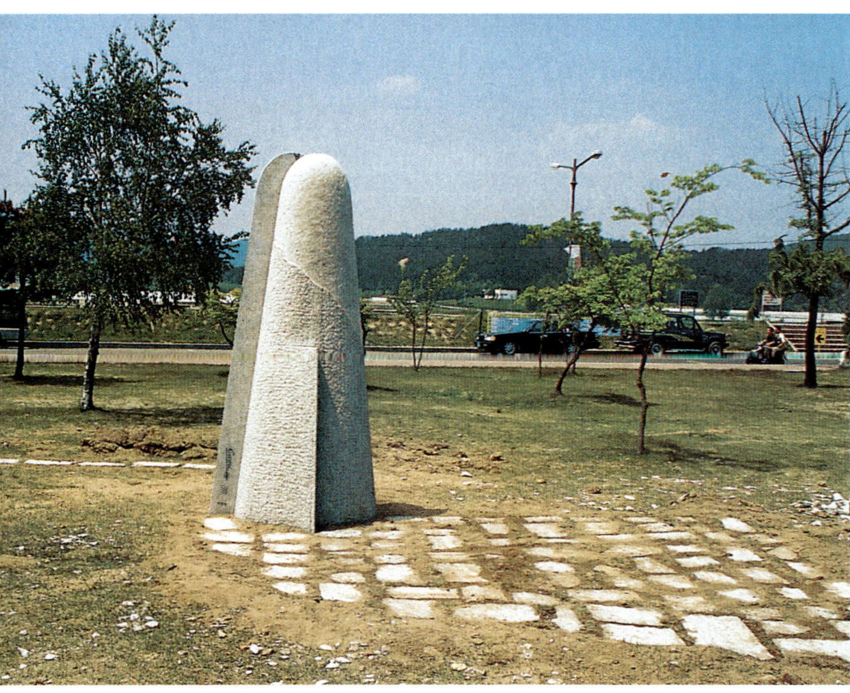

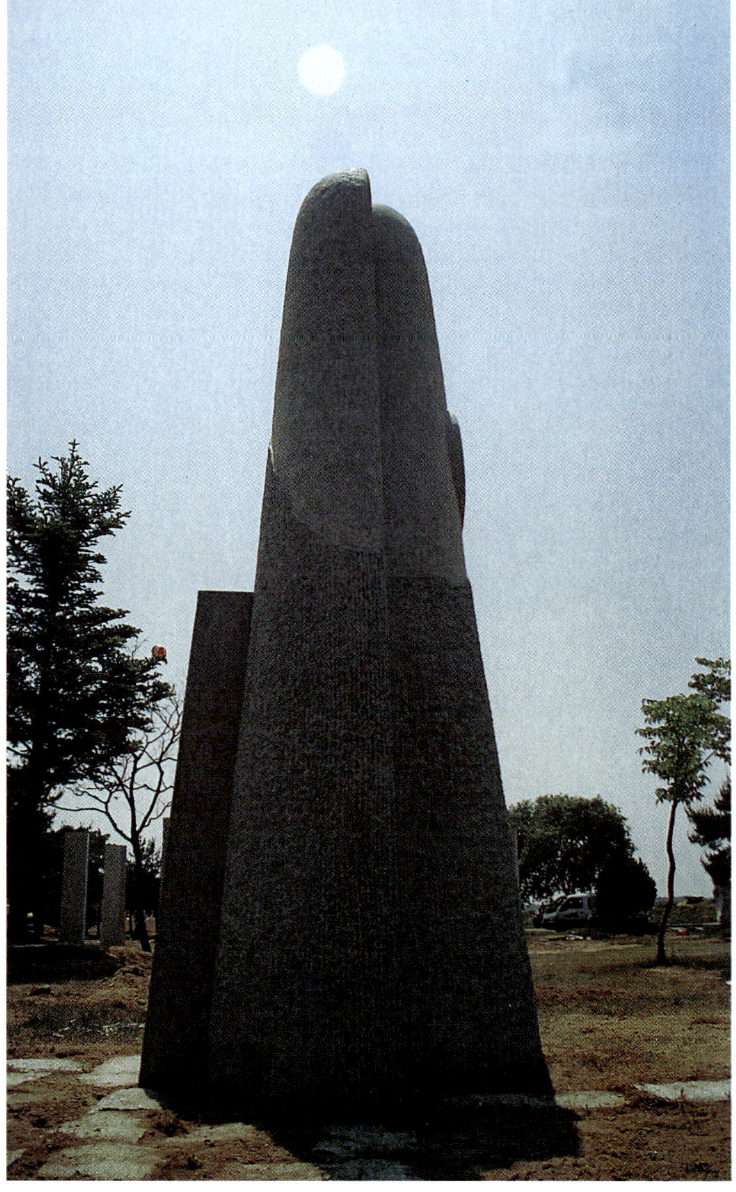

▲ ▶ **40.** *Unity*: two complementary volumes that tend to become one; two open spaces inspired by the yin and yang which fuse together. The book of Tao expresses it this way:
"A great kingdom is a place to which everything leads,
it is the mother figure of the world."

Love: two open spaces facing opposite directions, East and West; a home sanctuary in the shape of a cone: a magnet for desires; a hint of a partially opened door and window: an invitation to enter an intimate and familiar space: the father's house. Lao-Tse continues:
"The wise man who travels all day,
never forgets where his caravan is."

Eternity: the sculpture's granite material will be everlasting, as everlasting and universal are the teachings of Tao-te-King which inspired this work:
"That which in the past led to Unity . . ."

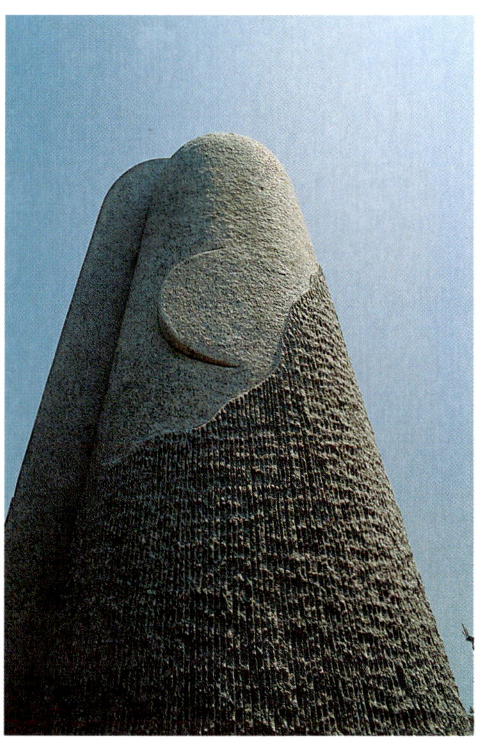

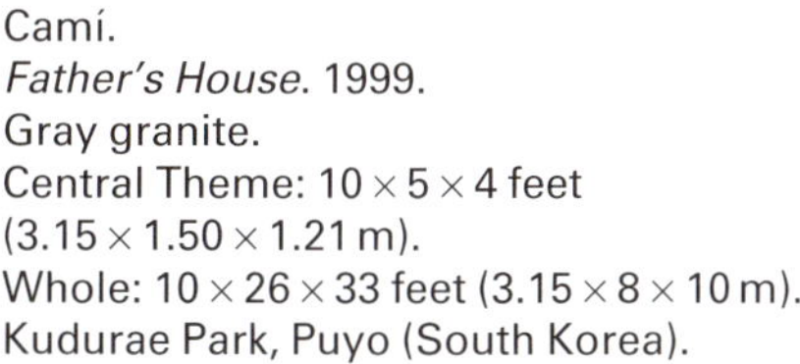

Camí.
Father's House. 1999.
Gray granite.
Central Theme: 10 × 5 × 4 feet
(3.15 × 1.50 × 1.21 m).
Whole: 10 × 26 × 33 feet (3.15 × 8 × 10 m).
Kudurae Park, Puyo (South Korea).

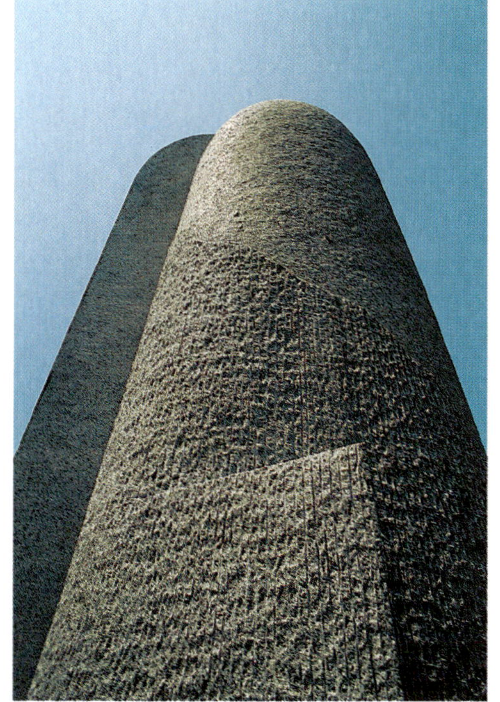

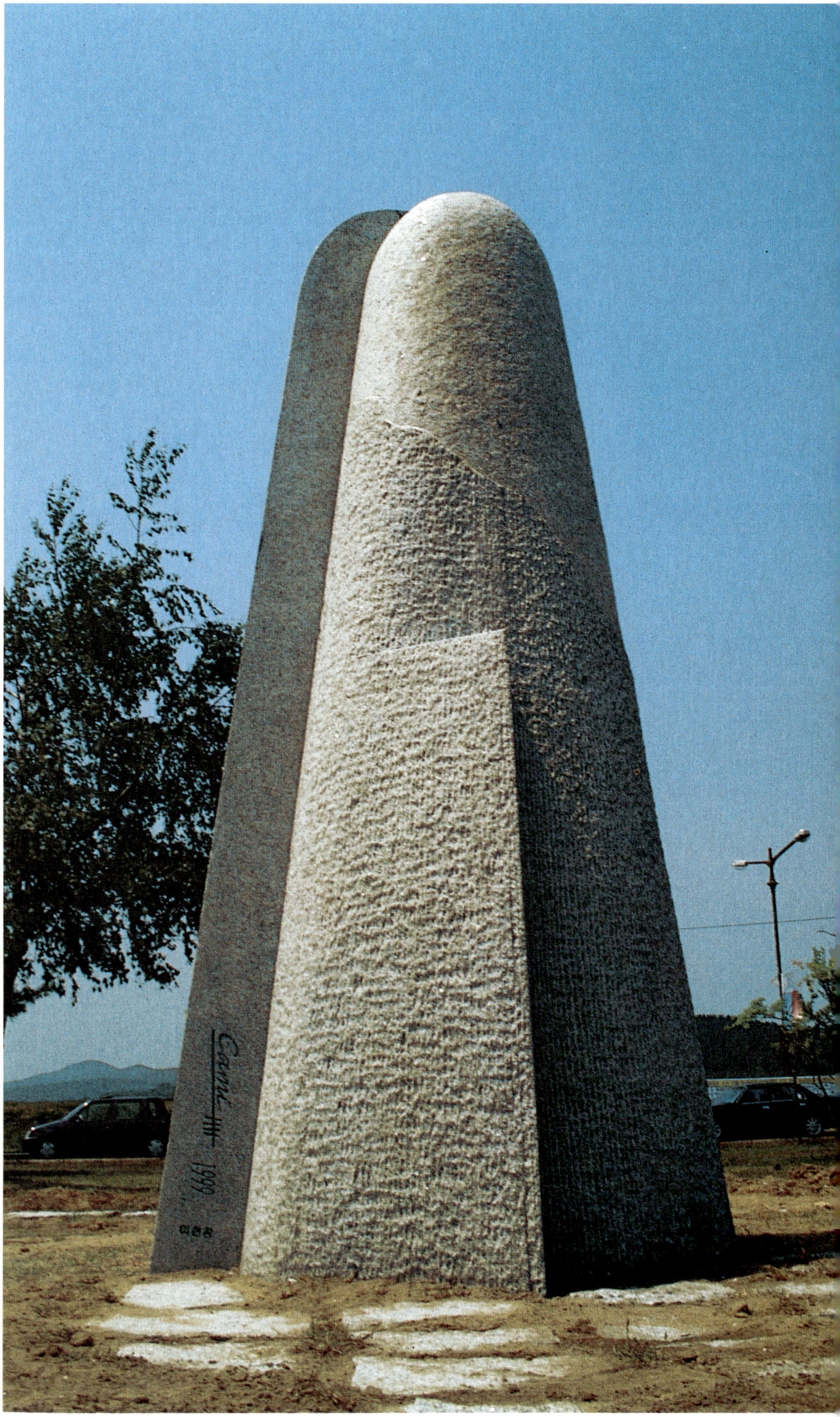

Concept Map

TOPICS
FUNERAL
Figurative
Portraits
Sarcophagi
Reclining Figures
Abstracts
Stelae
Menhirs
RELIGIOUS
Figurative
Reliefs
• in caves
• in architecture
Freestanding
• in architecture
• images
Abstracts
Talismans, lingams
POLITICAL
Figurative, that express:
Power: great empires
Publicity: Rome
Prestige: Renaissance
Abstracts
Obelisks, columns
FREE/ABSTRACTS
Natural: landscapes
Poetics: oriental gardens
Prestige: step monuments (New Hebrides)
Renewal of language: "ismos"
Monumentals: end of twentieth century
ROCKS
Composition
Formation
Examples
SILICATES
CARBONATES
IGNEOUS
SEDIMENTARY
SEDIMENTARY
METAMORPHIC
Granite
Sandstone
Alabaster
Marble

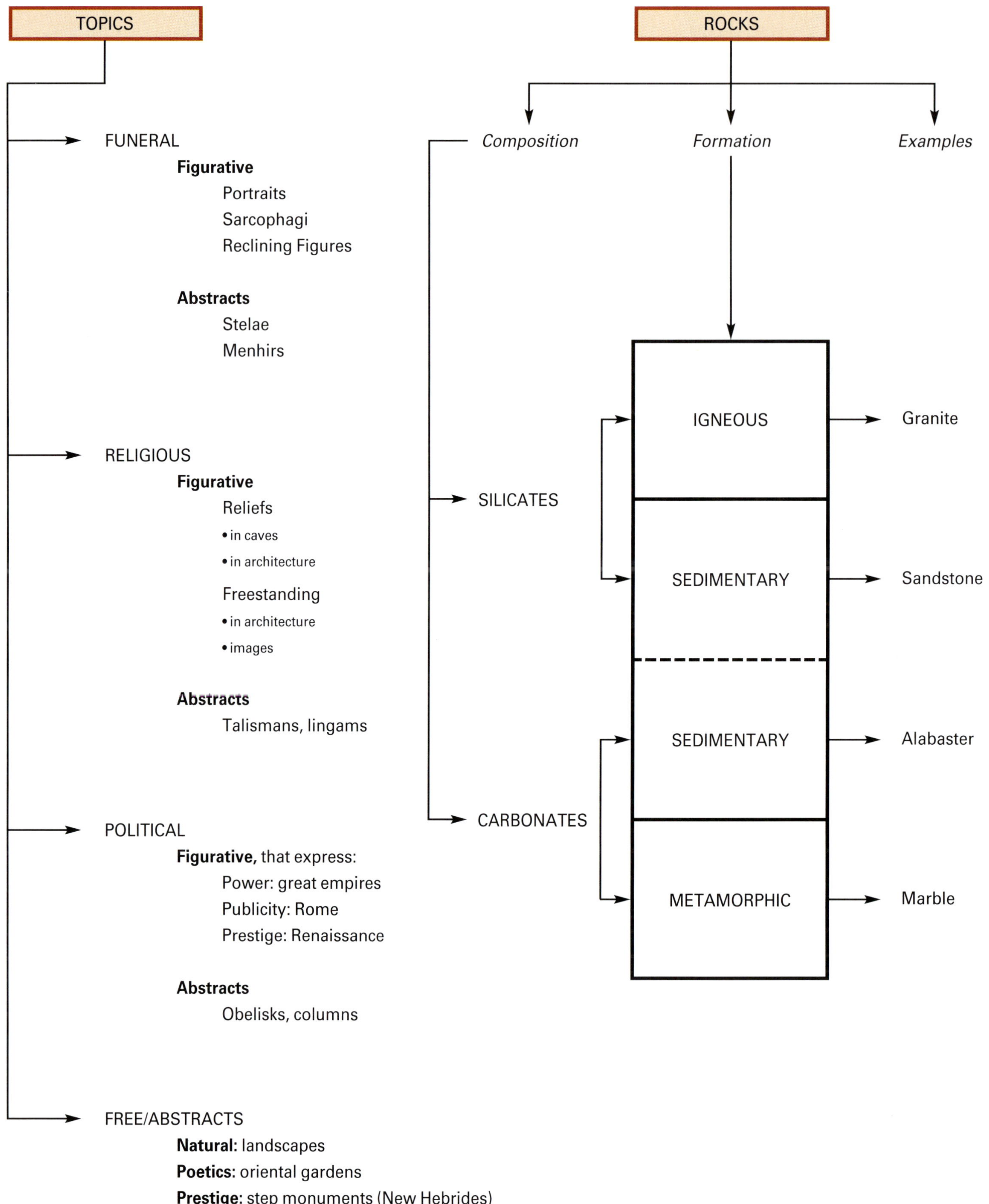

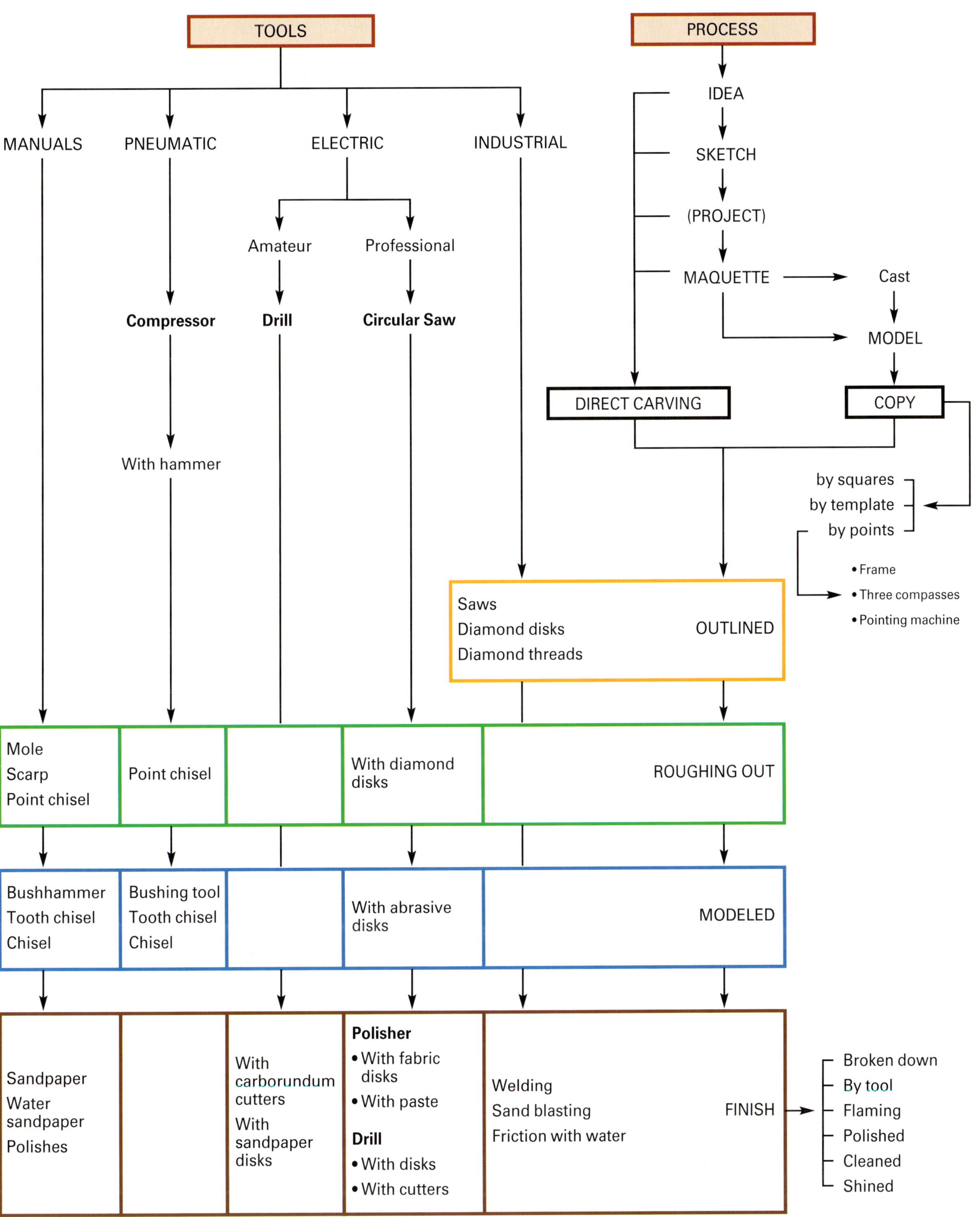
TOOLS
MANUALS
PNEUMATIC
ELECTRIC
INDUSTRIAL
Amateur
Professional
Compressor
Drill
Circular Saw
With hammer
PROCESS
IDEA
SKETCH
(PROJECT)
MAQUETTE
Cast
MODEL
DIRECT CARVING
COPY
by squares
by template
by points
• Frame
• Three compasses
• Pointing machine
Saws
Diamond disks
Diamond threads
OUTLINED
Mole
Scarp
Point chisel
Point chisel
With diamond disks
ROUGHING OUT
Bushhammer
Tooth chisel
Chisel
Bushing tool
Tooth chisel
Chisel
With abrasive disks
MODELED
Sandpaper
Water sandpaper
Polishes
With carborundum cutters
With sandpaper disks
Polisher
• With fabric disks
• With paste
Drill
• With disks
• With cutters
Welding
Sand blasting
Friction with water
FINISH
Broken down
By tool
Flaming
Polished
Cleaned
Shined

Glossary

a

Abrasive. Material that is worn down by rubbing.

Abstract. The opposite of figurative. We distinguish between *free forms* (obelisque) and *abstract forms* (Brancusi's Muses), thus reviving the philosophical notion of abstraction that implies a search for essential volumes free of anecdotal details.

Academy. An institution that establishes art precepts and that regulates and controls art. *Academic* is an antonym of modern.

Acrolith. A sculpture figure whose head and extremities are made of marble or stone while the rest is made of another material.

Addition. The process of creating volume by adding malleable materials such as clay.

Amulet. See **Talisman**.

Anaglyph. A stone that is roughly worked or inscribed.

Arabesque. A patterned design that is made by the cracks in some stones.

Armature. A supporting framework upon which a work in clay, wax, or plaster of Paris may be fashioned.

Atlas. A supporting column in the form of a male figure.

Attribute. To conjecture the authorship of a work without being able to prove it. We indicate this with a question mark (?).

Aureat. Known as the golden proportion, or ideal balance between the representation of strength and volume.

Authentic. A sculpture whose paternity is authenticated.

b

Baroque. A term applied to art of the seventeenth century.

Base. Volume that elevates a statue. Depending on its shape, it has several names, such as pedestal, plinth, footing, and so on.

Bas-relief. Relief sculpture in which the figures project slightly from the background; also called *low relief.*

Block. Stone prepared for sculpting.

Body. The main part of a flat chisel, pointed chisel, tooth chisel, and so on.

Bottega. A Renaissance house, workshop, and store where the master sculptor lived with his disciples.

Boucharde. See **Bushhammer**.

Bushhammer. A metal hammer with two striking ends divided into rows of pyramidal points or teeth; also known as a *boucharde*.

Bushing tool. A tool that when connected to a pneumatic hammer adds to the impact of the bushhammer, moving it in half circles and back-and-forth movements.

Bust. Representation of a human head.

c

Calvary. A sculptural complex that narrates the passion of Christ, which proliferated during the Middle Ages when the great plagues decimated the European population.

Canon. An idealized mathematical system for depicting the ideal proportions of the human body.

Carving. The art of cutting or subtracting material to shape a sculpture, generally done with tools such as chisels.

Caryatid. A supporting column in the form of a female figure.

Cast. A sculpture that has been produced by means of a mold.

Casting. The process involved in making a mold and reproducing a sculpture.

Chailyas. Temples carved into the rock by Buddhists in India in the second century before Christ.

Chassis. A calibrated framework used in making an enlarged or reduced replica of a model.

Chip. A flat fragment of stone that flies off when a stone is being worked.

Chisel. A metallic instrument, generally made of steel, one end of which serves as a cutting end while the other receives the motivating pressure or blow; the act of carving with or using a chisel.

Colossal. Larger than life-size, as in the Colossal Olmec heads.

Commissioned work. A sculpture that has been conceived to please an art sponsor, committent, or possible client and that does not necessarily reflect the concerns of the author at the time he carries it out.

Copy by points. Any copying system in which measurements are taken at the most important places on a sculpture. *Support point*: place where the cross arm of the pointing machine rests; *Mother points*: the principal markings determined by the intersection of the three compasses from which set measurements are taken. *Reference points*: other points that need to be located.

Coré. A Greek female figure.

Crystallization. The act or process of crystallizing.

d

Dead stone. A stone that is not well preserved or fresh. When struck with the sculptor's stone-carving hammer, a dead stone gives off a dull sound.

Direct Carving. The method of working straight into the stone without recourse to preliminary three-dimensional models such as maquettes; also known as *taille directe*.

Dolman. A structure usually regarded as a tomb, consisting of two or more large upright stones, set with a space between and capped by a horizontal stone.

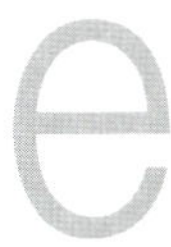

Escutcheon. Relief that depicts a shield or shieldlike surface. It is determined by a code of symbols established by the *heraldry*.

Exenta. See **Sculpture in the round.**

Expressionism. Style of art that is based on expressing the artists' emotions.

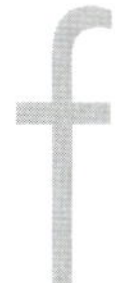

Fake. A fraudulent copy of a sculpture that is presented as authentic.

Figurative form. The faithful representation of a person, animal, or thing, both in reliefs and freestanding works.

File. An abrasive metal tool used to smooth stone.

Finish. A term that does not refer to those works rejected by their author during the execution phase (*non finito*), but rather to the multiple possibilities for working the textures of a sculpture, including sculptures that are made to look unfinished.

Flaming. A technique that simulates erosion by subjecting the surface of a stone to high temperatures using the flame of a welding tool.

Foreshortening. A sculpture that represents a figure from an unusual perspective that requires optical corrections.

Framework. See **Chassis**.

g

Gargoyle. A grotesquely carved figure of a human or animal projecting from the gutter of a building.

Glyptics. The art of engraving ornaments and seals. If the drawing is sunken it is known as *diaglyptic*; if it is in relief, it is known as *anaglyptic*.

Grade. The technique of smoothing a surface.

Griffin. The representation of a fantastic animal with the head and wings of an eagle and the body and ears of a lion.

h

Hair fissure. A barely perceptible crack in a stone that tells that it is damaged and warns of the possibility of a fracture when working it. Also called a hairline fracture.

Hieratic. A Greek statue that follows the sacred canon (*hieros* in Greek) established by the priests. Sculptures in this tradition are affectedly solemn or pompous.

High-relief. Relief sculpture in which the figures are strongly projected from the background.

i

Imago. Effigy of a Roman ancestor obtained from a death mask.

Imprint. The impression or expression of quality in a work.

Incrustation. The inlaying or addition of one material over another, frequently used to make the eyes prominent.

Indirect carving. A method of carving in which the approach is indirect and involves the use of a previously prepared three-dimensional model such as a maquette.

Installation. The ultimate placement of a sculpture outdoors.

Isms. Referring to the multiple artistic currents in the twentieth century that have renewed the conception of art: Primitivism, Cubism, Fauvism, Expressionism, Futurism, Constructivism or Neoplasticism, Dadaism, Surrealism, Informalism or Abstract Expressionism, Pop Art, Hyperrealism, Conceptual Art, Povera, Land Art, and so on.

k

Kouro, plural **Kouroi.** A sculptured representation of a Greek athlete prior to the fifth century B.C.E. Some are represented with a funeral character.

l

Lapidary. A person who cuts, engraves, and polishes precious stones.

Law. The growth pattern of a stone, which is detected through the direction of its veins.

Law of Frontality. Particular Egyptian form used to represent a person in relief.

Lithic. Pertaining to stones.

Live stone. A stone that is well preserved or fresh from the quarry. When struck with the sculptor's stone-carving hammer, it gives off a clear ringing sound.

Low relief. See **bas-relief**.

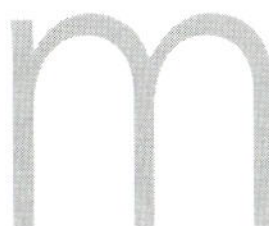

Mallet. A tool used to hit chisels when carving.

Maquette. A small model or three-dimensional sketch for a larger sculpture.

Markings. Traces left by a mold. If they represent a pattern made by tools, we refer to them as *calligraphy*.

Master Line. A slab that is cut first to define outlines and that serves as a guide for reducing the rest of the surface.

Medallion. Relief in circular or elliptical form.

Megalith. Stone of great size especially in ancient construction work, as in Cyclopean masonry, or in primitive monumental remains such as *menhirs* and *dolmens*.

Menhir. An upright monumental stone, either standing alone or with others.

Moai. Statues carved in volcanic rock that are typically found on Easter Island in the Pacific Ocean.

Model. A person or object that is used as a reference; a maquette in final scale that is used to be copied.

Modeling. Making forms with soft materials such as clay or wet plaster.

Mouth. The cutting edge of a tool.

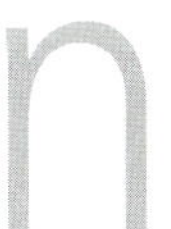

Naturalism. Art that adheres closely to reality.

Neoclassicism. Eighteenth- or nineteenth-century art using classical sculpture and themes.

O

Obelisk. A tapering four-sided shaft of stone, usually monolithic and having a pyramidal apex.

Obsidian. A very hard stone used as a chisel in some cultures.

Orant. Representation of a person in a praying position; can have a funeral character or represent the donor of a religious sculptural group.

Original. Sculpture from which copies have been made.

P

Patron. A person who finances the costs of a sculptor: A *committent* contracts for an original work; a *client* buys a work that already exists; an *agent* promotes the works of an artist in the market.

Pedestal. Base on which a sculpture is mounted.

Petroglyph. Drawings or carvings made on rock by prehistoric people; also known as *petrograph*.

Philosopher's stone. In alchemy, an imaginary substance or preparation believed capable of transmuting baser metals into gold or silver, or of prolonging life.

Pneumatic hammer. An element to which tungsten carbide tools are attached and that transforms the pressure of compressed air in rhythmic movements.

Pointing. A mechanical means of copying from a three-dimensional model.

Polish. To smooth the stone until it shines.

Polychromy. The art of using many colors.

Portrait. Sculpture that reflects the personality of the model; considered *idealized* when traits are perfected, *naturalistic* when defects are not hidden, and *caricature* when they are exaggerated.

Practitioner. An expert in the field of carving who produces or copies sculptures designed by someone else. He can also be a *collaborator* if he plays a minor role in the project or *assistant* if his role is major.

Proportion. The harmonious relationship between the parts of a sculpture and the relationship of the sculpture with its surroundings.

Pumice. A stone used to smooth a surface until it becomes matte.

Putti. In art, the figure of Cupid, small angels, or children.

R

Rasp. A metallic abrasive tool with sharp pyramidal teeth.

Realism. The representation of reality that does not exclude a certain idealization, as in Classical Greek art. When the less attractive traits are highlighted it is called *naturalism*.

Reclining figure. Sculpture that represents the dead person lying on his tomb.

Relief. A form of sculpture in which figures project from a flat background to which they adhere. See also **bas-relief** and **high-relief**.

Retouching. Changes that an author makes to a work after it is finished.

Riffler. A small file that comes in a variety of shapes and is used to reach difficult corners in stone.

S

School. A group of norms, artists, or works that share several common traits that distinguish them from the style to which they belong.

Sculptor. A person who conceives a work and to whom paternity is attributed whether he or she does the actual carving or commissions others to do it.

Sculpture in the round. Unlike reliefs, a freestanding piece that has been worked on all sides; also known as *exenta*.

Shrine. A small temple usually with a funeral character.

Sketch. The first plan for a sculpture that can be drawn on paper or made from a provisional material.

Stambha. A memorial pillar.

Statue. Realistic or traditional freestanding figure.

Stela. A small commemorative monolith usually with a funeral character. It can be in the form of a column (*cipo*), tablet, or pedestal.

Stonecutter. A sculptor who works mainly in construction.

Strata. The layers that form a stone as a result of the sedimentation process.

Subtraction. Sculptural process that consists of removing material. Although sculpting and cutting are synonymous, carving is generally used when referring to wood and precious stones.

Symposium. A meeting of sculptors generally organized by a commission, for the purpose of carrying out several sculptures at the same time.

Symbolism. Representation by means of symbols.

t

Talisman. A charm worn to ward off evil; also known as an *amulet*.

Temper. To apply a cold treatment to a metal tool to make it harder.

Template. A cutout pattern following the perimeter of a surface to be transferred to the block.

Torso. Sculpture that represents only the trunk of a human body.

Transit. A funerary image that shows the body in the state of decomposition.

Trepan. An instrument used to make perforations in a sculpture, either for the effect of high relief or to cause shadows.

Trophy. A monument that displays arms, shields, and other military trappings.

u

Urn. A small stone or metal vase used to hold the ashes of the dead.

v

Vaulted niche. An opening made in a wall to accommodate a statue.

Bibliography
and acknowledgments

HISTORY

Curtis, Penelope. *Sculpture 1900–1945.* New York: Oxford University Press, 1999.

Kenaan-Kedar, Nurith. *Marginal Sculpture in Medieval France.* Cambridge: Scolar University Press, 1983.

Pischel, Gina. *Historia universal de la escultura.* Bilbao: Asuri D.L., 1983.

Read, Herbert. *A Concise History of Modern Sculpture.* New York: Thames and Hudson, 1983.

Wittkower, Rudolf. *La escultura, procesos y principios.* Madrid: Alianza Editorial, 1977.

Varios autores. *Historia de la escultura.* Barcelona: Skira, 1996.

TECHNIQUE

Baudry, M. Therese and others. *La Sculpture, méthode et vocabulaire.* Paris: Imprimerie Nationale Éditions, 1978.

Padovano, Anthony. *The Process of Sculpture.* New York: A Da Capo Paperback, 1981.

Penny, Nicholas. *The Materials of Sculpture.* London: Yale University Press, 1993.

Various authors. *Guía práctica de la cantería.* León: Escuela Taller de Restauración, 1993.

Liebson, Milt. *Direct Stone Sculpture.* Schiffer Publishing Ltd., Pennsylvania, 1991.

PAPERS

Opie, Mary-Jane. *Escultura.* Barcelona: Blume, 1995.

Romei, Francesca. *La escultura, desde la antigüedad hasta hoy.* Barcelona: Serres, 1992.

AESTHETICS

Rawson, Philip. *Sculpture.* Philadelphia, Pennsylvania: University of Pennsylvania Press, 1997.

STONE

AA.VV. *Il Marmo nel Mondo.* Carrara: Società Editrice Apuana, 1986.

AA.VV. *Granito Español.* Madrid: ANGE, Asociación Nacional de Graniteros Españoles, 1996.

Bradley, Frederick. *Guida alle Cave di Marmo de Carrara.* Carrara: Internationale marmi e macchine Carrara, 1991.

García de los Ríos Cobo y Báez Mezquital. *La piedra en Castilla y León.* Valladolid: Dirección General de Industria, Energía y Minda, 1994.

Like any complex sculpture, this book is the result of the collaboration of several people. The authors wish to express their sincerest gratitude to:

Escavazione Marmi Lochi di Colonnata, the Rigoli Studio, and others in Carrara. We only wanted to visit their quarries and studios, but were met by the hospitality, with a capital H, and generosity of their establishments expressed in specific books.

It would not have been possible for us to organize our virtual studio without the collaboration of several friends. Thank you Ricard Mateu, for your contribution, and thanks, too, Pilar Miquela, for your perseverance.

During the "trimming" of this book several chips did bounce to our work colleagues from Massana, on one hand, and especially to the librarians Lluisa, Quim, and Fran, and on the other hand, to the librarians of the Bastida: Ana—What patience!—Montse, and Nuria in particular.

Part of the "modeling" of this book is due to the doctoral thesis of Jaume Ros i Vallverdu, various documents from the Galeria Greca de Barcelona, different sculptors, and also to the tools and machinery loaned to us by the companies of Moval of Barcelona and Fluvia S.L. of Vall de Bas, Girona.

The good image, the "polishing," and the "finishing" of this book have been the result of a well-organized team whose names, because they deserve their own credit, appear next to the Table of Contents. Thanks to all.

Camí and Santamera